Critical Legal Perspectives on Contemporary Slavery

Ius Comparatum

VOLUME 7

The titles published in this series are listed at *brill.com/iacl*

Critical Legal Perspectives on Contemporary Slavery

On the Presence of the Past

Edited By

Adelle Blackett
Laura Dehaibi
M. Adedayo Odusanya
Edward van Daalen

BRILL | NIJHOFF

LEIDEN | BOSTON

Library of Congress Cataloging-in-Publication Data

Names: Blackett, Adelle, 1967- editor. | Dehaibi, Laura, editor. | Odusanya, M. Adedayo, editor. | Daalen, Edward van, editor.
Title: Critical legal perspectives on contemporary slavery : on the presence of the past / edited by Adelle Blackett, Laura Dehaibi, M. Adedayo Odusanya, Edward van Daalen.
Description: Leiden ; Boston : Brill/Nijhoff, 2025. | Series: Ius comparatum, 2214-6881 ; volume 7 | Includes index.
Identifiers: LCCN 2024052441 (print) | LCCN 2024052442 (ebook) | ISBN 9789004723818 (hardback) | ISBN 9789004723801 (ebook)
Subjects: LCSH: Slavery–Law and legislation–History. | Race discrimination–Law and legislation–History. | Slave trade–History.
Classification: LCC K3267 .C75 2025 (print) | LCC K3267 (ebook) | DDC 342.08/7–dc23/eng/20241105
LC record available at https://lccn.loc.gov/2024052441
LC ebook record available at https://lccn.loc.gov/2024052442

Typeface for the Latin, Greek, and Cyrillic scripts: "Brill". See and download: brill.com/brill-typeface.

ISSN 2214-6881
ISBN 978-90-04-72381-8 (hardback)
ISBN 978-90-04-72380-1 (e-book)
DOI 10.1163/9789004723801

This book is printed on acid-free paper and produced in a sustainable manner.

Contents

Preface and Acknowledgements

For the 21st General Congress of the International Academy of Comparative Law (IACL), I proposed 'contemporary forms of slavery including causes and consequences' as a topic, out of a sense of urgency. There is no denying the depth of human suffering faced by workers in the contemporary global economy, along global value chains and global care chains. Decades of experimentation have been in place to rethink the regulation of trade, foster corporate social responsibility and due diligence frameworks, and thicken the normative bases for a truly transnational labour law. But increasingly, the language of 'modern slavery' has been invoked. Slavery is a particularly weighty invocation, and immediately conjures the horrors of the centuries-long history of the Black Atlantic. But it became rather readily apparent that the usage was in many senses metaphorical. Distance was being taken not only from the notion of 'chattel' slavery, but also from any suggestion that the racial stratification of the contemporary world that has ensued from slavery as a global institution played a role. As a person of African descent, I found this jarring, at best. Could it be that the concept of 'modern slavery' was being drawn upon primarily as a rhetorical device? I also found it deeply concerning. What were we missing about the legacies of enslavement on the lives of those who continue to embody its racial subordination? In the 2020 summer of racial reckoning following George Floyd's videotaped murder, our global community shut down by the Covid-19 pandemic was forced to witness and account for this persisting reality.

My own research has led me down the path of exploring the historical archives to understand better the early 20th century, ultimately colonial, bifurcation between slavery and forced labour. It also kindled my interest to understand better how slavery discourse is being deployed around the world. For the IACL this was a rare occasion where the person who proposed the topic was ultimately also selected for the general rapporteurship. I took this responsibility most seriously and built a questionnaire, included as an appendix to this volume, that sought explicitly to bring the law as it has related to Atlantic slavery in dialogue with invocations of the law of slavery in contemporary form. From the start, I sought to build a community of special national rapporteurs, and held a virtual meeting to discuss core themes and objectives. Once first drafts had been submitted and extensive comments were provided, I welcomed special national rapporteurs to participate in two instrumental scholarly gatherings.

The first generative event was a presentation that the Labour Law and Development Research Laboratory (LLDRL) curated at the Law and Society

Association's Annual Meeting in May 2022 in Lisbon. I was pleased to moderate a panel comprising the rapporteur on Barbados and St Vincent and the Grenadines, Professor Jason Hayes, who visited McGill as an O'Brien Fellow to the Centre for Human Rights and Legal Pluralism and the LLDRL in summer 2022, the rapporteur on Peru, Professor Laura Dehaibi, who was then the LLDRL Postdoctoral Fellow, the rapporteur on Ghana, Professor and Dean Julia Selman-Ayetey, who is also a doctoral candidate at McGill Faculty of Law, the rapporteur on Canada, Professor Yves Goguen, the rapporteur on Germany, Dr. Heiner Fechner, and one of the two rapporteurs on Sweden, Professor Niklas Selberg. We are grateful for the many thoughtful questions and comments from the audience, which enriched the final book.

The second gathering took place during the 21st General Congress of the IACL, held in Asunción in October 2022. In my capacity as general rapporteur, I was pleased to present the report to an engaged audience, with special presentations integrated throughout and offered by the four special national rapporteurs who were in attendance, on Canada, Ghana, Peru, and on the United Kingdom, Professor Shahrzad Fouladvand. We are all grateful to the IACL-appointed session chair, Professor Timothy Webster, who offered insightful comments and appreciated enthusiasm for our work.

It was meaningful to present our work on both sides of the Atlantic. Both in Portugal and in Paraguay, reckoning with the history and legacies of slavery remains nascent but inescapable. Participants in both events showed an appreciation for why it is necessary to be able to address slavery and the law both in international and comparative perspective, if we are to challenge an all too ready elision between historical and contemporary forms that leaves the legacies of slavery behind. We trust our work has helped to foster deepened understanding.

Throughout this process, I have been fortunate to have a superb team of researchers associated with the LLDRL at McGill University. This has been collective work, and the team has committed to carrying this project with great skill, professionalism and dedication. Professor Laura Dehaibi, was brought on board during her postdoctoral research fellow at the LLDRL early in the process as a co-editor of the volume. She provided stellar contributions to the co-authored general report. A team of dedicated research assistants were actively involved in keeping the numerous contributions organized, providing bibliographical support and in some cases providing editorial comments. I am pleased to acknowledge Navya Baradi (JD & BCL candidate), Anne-Raphaëlle Bolya (JD & BCL 2022), M. Adedayo Odusanya (JD & BCL 2024), Audrey Parent (JD & BCL 2023), Marc-Elder Piard (JD & BCL candidate) & Joscelyne Smith (LLM 2023). M. Adedayo Odusanya, then an LLDRL research assistant and currently a law clerk at the Ontario Superior Court of Justice, provided support throughout most of the project and was so engaged that his contributions are recognized as a co-editor of the volume. In the home stretch, Dr. Edward van Daalen, LLDRL postdoctoral research fellow 2023–2024, ably shouldered the lion's share of the responsibility for finalizing the revised contributions for publication.

Finally, I acknowledge with gratitude the Insight Grant from the Social Sciences and Humanities Research Council of Canada, entitled "Slavery is not a Metaphor", awarded under the October 2020 competition.

This work is the beginning of a much-needed conversation on the depths of human suffering in the world of work. This challenged world moment is a reminder that the ILO's founding principle, that universal and lasting peace can only be achieved through social justice, is as urgently relevant now as it was in 1919.

Adelle Blackett
New York, August 2024

Préface et remerciements

Pour le 21e congrès général de l'Académie internationale de droit comparé (AIDC), j'ai proposé comme thème « les formes contemporaines d'esclavage, y compris les causes et les conséquences », en raison d'un sentiment d'urgence. On ne peut nier l'ampleur de la souffrance humaine à laquelle sont confrontés les travailleurs dans l'économie mondiale contemporaine, le long des chaînes d'approvisionnement mondiales et des chaînes mondiales de soins. Des décennies d'expérimentation ont été mises en place pour repenser la régulation effective du commerce, favoriser la responsabilité sociale des entreprises et des devoirs de vigilance, et étoffer les cadres normatifs d'un droit du travail véritablement transnational. Mais de plus en plus, le langage de « l'esclavage moderne » s'est imposé. L'esclavage invoque des souvenirs et une histoire particulièrement lourde, en rappelant immédiatement les horreurs de l'histoire multi-centenaires de l'Atlantique noir.

Mais il est apparu assez rapidement que cet usage était à bien des égards métaphoriques. On prenait ses distances non seulement par rapport à la notion d'esclavage et de propriété privée de personnes, mais aussi par rapport à toute suggestion que la stratification raciale du monde contemporain, qui a découlé de l'esclavage en tant qu'institution mondiale, jouait un rôle. En tant que personne d'origine africaine, j'ai trouvé cela pour le moins déconcertant. Se pourrait-il que le concept d'« esclavage moderne » soit utilisé principalement comme un outil rhétorique ? J'ai également trouvé cela assez inquiétant. Qu'avons-nous manqué au sujet de l'héritage de l'esclavage sur la vie de ceux et celles qui continuent d'incarner sa subordination raciale ? Au cours de l'été 2020, lors duquel nous avons à nouveau fait face à la profondeur des préjudices raciales à la suite du meurtre filmé de George Floyd, notre communauté mondiale confinée par la pandémie de Covid-19 a été forcée de témoigner de cette réalité persistante et d'en rendre compte.

Mes propres recherches m'ont mené à explorer les archives historiques pour mieux comprendre la bifurcation entre esclavage et travail forcé qui s'est opérée au début du 20e siècle, en fin de compte, de manière coloniale. Cela a également éveillé mon intérêt pour approfondir notre compréhension du déploiement des discours sur l'esclavage à travers le monde. Pour l'AIDC, il s'agissait d'une occasion rare où la personne qui a proposé le sujet a ultimement également été sélectionnée pour le poste de rapporteur général. J'ai pris cette responsabilité très au sérieux et j'ai élaboré un questionnaire, inclus en annexe de ce volume, qui visait explicitement à mettre en dialogue le droit relatif à l'esclavage atlantique et les différentes facettes du droit de l'esclavage sous sa forme contemporaine. Dès le départ, j'ai cherché à créer une communauté de rapporteurs spéciaux au niveau national et j'ai organisé une réunion virtuelle pour discuter des principaux thèmes et objectifs. Dès que les ébauches de projets ont été soumises et qu'une première série de commentaires détaillés ont été formulés sur chaque contribution, j'ai invité les rapporteurs nationaux à participer à deux réunions scientifiques d'importance dans la genèse de cet ouvrage.

La première rencontre a été une présentation organisée par le Laboratoire de recherche sur le droit du travail et le développement (LLDRL) lors de la réunion annuelle de la « Law and Society Association » en mai 2022 à Lisbonne. J'ai eu le plaisir d'animer un panel composé du rapporteur sur la Barbade et Saint-Vincent-et-les-Grenadines, le professeur Jason Hayes, qui était en été 2022 un visiteur « O'Brien Fellow » au Centre pour les droits de l'homme et le pluralisme juridique et au Laboratoire de recherche sur le droit du travail et au LLDRL, le rapporteur sur le Pérou, la professeure Laura Dehaibi, qui était à ce moment boursière postdoctorale du LLDRL, le rapporteur sur le Ghana, la professeure et doyenne Julia Selman-Ayetey, qui est également candidate au doctorat à la faculté de droit de McGill, le rapporteur sur le Canada, le professeur Yves Goguen, le rapporteur sur l'Allemagne, Dr. Heiner Fechner, et l'un des deux rapporteurs pour la Suède, le professeur Niklas Selberg. Nous sommes infiniment reconnaissants pour les nombreuses questions et commentaires réfléchis de l'auditoire, qui ont enrichi le processus de rédaction et d'édition de ce livre.

Une deuxième rencontre a ensuite eu lieu lors du 21e Congrès général de l'AIDC, qui s'est tenu à Asunción en octobre 2022. En tant que rapporteuse générale, j'ai eu le plaisir de présenter le rapport à un public engagé, avec des présentations spéciales intégrées tout au long et offertes par les quatre rapporteurs spéciaux nationaux qui étaient présents pour le Canada, le Ghana, le Pérou, et le Royaume-Uni, la professeure Shahrzad Fouladvand. Nous sommes tous reconnaissants au président de séance désigné par l'AIDC, le professeur Timothy Webster, pour ses commentaires perspicaces et son enthousiasme pour notre travail.

Il était important de présenter notre travail des deux côtés de l'Atlantique. Tant au Portugal qu'au Paraguay, la reconnaissance et la prise en compte de l'histoire et de l'héritage de l'esclavage reste naissante mais inéluctable, comme c'est le cas dans le monde entier. Les participants aux deux événements ont montré qu'ils comprenaient pourquoi il est nécessaire de pouvoir aborder l'esclavage et le droit dans une perspec-tive internationale et comparative afin de remettre en question l'élision trop faciles des héritages de l'esclavage dans les formes historiques et contemporaines. Nous espérons que notre travail a contribué à une meilleure compréhension de ces dynamiques complexes.

Tout au long de ce processus, j'ai eu la chance de pouvoir compter sur une excellente équipe de chercheurs associés au Laboratoire de recherche sur le droit du travail et le développement (LLDRL) de l'Université McGill. Il s'agit d'un travail collectif, et l'équipe s'est engagée à mener à bien ce projet avec compétence, professionnalisme et dévouement. Laura Dehaibi, alors chercheuse postdoctorale au LLDRL de 2021 à 2022, et actuellement professeure adjointe en relations industrielles à l'Université Laval, a été recrutée dès le début du processus en tant que corédactrice de l'ouvrage. Elle a apporté d'excellentes contributions au rapport général coécrit. Une équipe d'assistants de recherche dévoués a participé activement à l'organisation des nombreuses contributions, en fournissant un soutien bibliographique et, dans certains cas, des commentaires éditoriaux. J'ai le plaisir de remercier Navya Baradi (candidate JD & BCL), Anne-Raphaëlle Bolya (JD & BCL 2022), M. Adedayo Odusanya (JD & BCL 2024), Audrey Parent (JD & BCL 2023), Marc-Elder Piard (candidat JD & BCL) et Joscelyne Smith (LLM 2023). M. Adedayo Odusanya, alors assistant de recherche au LLDRL et présentement auxiliaire juridique à la cour supérieure de justice de l'Ontario, a apporté son soutien pendant la majeure partie du projet et s'est tellement impliqué que ses contributions sont reconnues en tant que co-éditeur du volume. Pour la dernière ligne droite, Edward van Daalen, chercheur postdoctoral LLDRL 2023–2024, a assumé avec compétence la plus grande partie de la responsabilité de la finalisation des contributions révisées en vue de leur publication.

Enfin, je tiens à exprimer ma gratitude à l'égard de la Subventions Savoir du Conseil de recherches en sciences humaines du Canada, intitulée « L'esclavage n'est pas une métaphore », attribuée dans le cadre du concours d'octobre 2020.

Ce travail est le début d'une conversation nécessaire sur les abysses de la souffrance humaine dans le monde du travail. Ce moment de défi mondial nous rappelle que le principe fondateur de l'OIT, selon lequel une paix universelle et durable ne peut être obtenue que par la justice sociale, est aussi urgent aujourd'hui qu'il l'était en 1919.

Adelle Blackett
New York, Août 2024

Contributors

Editors

Professor Adelle Blackett
McGill University, Faculty of Law,
adelle.blackett@mcgill.ca

Professor Laura Dehaibi
Université Laval, Department of Industrial Relations,
laura.dehaibi@rlt.ulaval.ca

M. Adedayo Odusanya
Independent Scholar,
mohammed.odusanya@mail.mcgill.ca

Dr. Edward van Daalen
McGill University, Faculty of Law,
edward.vandaalen@mail.mcgill.ca

Rapporteure Générale

Professor Adelle Blackett
McGill University, Faculty of Law,
adelle.blackett@mcgill.ca

Rapporteurs

Dr. Béatrice Boissard
Université de Versailles Saint-Quentin-en-Yvelines,
Faculty of Law and Political Science,
beatrice.boissard@uvsq.fr

Professor Lolita Buckner Inniss
University of Colorado, Law School,
linniss@colorado.edu

Professor Laura Dehaibi
Université Laval, Department of Industrial Relations,
laura.dehaibi@rlt.ulaval.ca

Professor Filip Dorssemont
Université catholique de Louvain, Faculty of Law and Criminology,
filip.dorssemont@uclouvain.be

Dr. Heiner Fechner
University of Bremen, Institute Labour and Economy (IAW),
hfechner@uni-bremen.de

Professor Shahrzad Fouladvand
University of Sussex, School of Law, Politics and Sociology,
s.fouladvand@sussex.ac.uk

Professor Yves Goguen
Independent Scholar,
yves.goguen@gmail.com

Anthony Hallal
Monash University, Faculty of Law,
anthony.hallal@monash.edu

Professor Jason Haynes
University of Birmingham, Birmingham Law School,
j.k.haynes@bham.ac.uk

Karla Kotulovski
University of Rijeka, Faculty of Law,
kkotulovs@pravri.uniri.hr

Professor Sandra Laleta
University of Rijeka, Faculty of Law,
sandra.laleta@pravri.uniri.hr

Dr. Amin Parsa
Halmstad University, School of Education, Humanities and Social Sciences,
amin.parsa@hh.se

Professor Marilyn J. Pittard
Monash University, Faculty of Law,
marilyn.pittard@monash.edu

Professor Łukasz Pisarczyk
University of Silesia in Katowice, Faculty of Law and Administration,
lukasz.pisarczyk@us.edu.pl

Dr. Olivier Pluen
Université de Versailles Saint-Quentin-en-Yvelines,
Faculty of Law and Political Science,
olivier.pluen@uvsq.fr

Professor Bas Rombouts
Tilburg University, Tilburg Law School,
s.j.rombouts@tilburguniversity.edu

Professor Niklas Selberg
Lund University, Faculty of Law,
niklas.selberg@jur.lu.se

Professor Julia Selman Ayetey
University of Cape Coast, Faculty of Law,
jselman-ayetey@ucc.edu.gh

Professor Darja Senčur Peček
University of Maribor, Faculty of Law,
darja.sencur-pecek@um.si

Professor Marissabell Škorić
International University of Rijeka, Faculty of Law,
marissabell.skoric@pravri.uniri.hr

Professor Dagmara Skupień
University of Lodz, Faculty of Law and Administration,
dskupien@wpia.uni.lodz.pl

IACL General Report: Contemporary Forms of Slavery, including Causes and Consequences

Adelle Blackett and Laura Dehaibi

1 Introduction

It should be the source of grave concern that fundamental principles and rights at work – on the freedom of association, forced labour, child labour, equality law and occupational safety and health – are consistently and systemically breached across the global economy. The 2013 Rana Plaza factory fire that killed 1,134 workers barely weeks after corporate auditors had declared the enterprise safe should have been a global wakeup call about the risks of leaving the foxes to guard the chicken coup. But more than a decade on since that tragedy, despite a flurry of mixed public-private, international-local experimentalist engagements, there have been many more tragedies and growing confirmation that labour law across the globe is observed in the breach. The norm in the global economy may well be non-compliance.

The sense of urgency has led to a seemingly powerful conclusion: modern slavery must be condemned and criminalized. The conclusion seems incontrovertible – who could possibly be against condemning and criminalizing modern slavery? The moral presence of the past, in the unspoken memory of transatlantic slavery, hangs over the label. The world agreed in the 1926 Slavery Convention to abolish slavery, but the history of that instrument's drafting reminds us that in the colonial era, both imperial designs over the territory referred to as Abyssinia,[1] and a carve out to permit some forms of forced labour for public purposes,[2] reflect the inescapable politicization of the law of slavery. The division of labour between the ILO, which adopted the Forced Labour Convention, 1930 (No. 29), and the League of Nations at the time, reflected this division. The fractures – and politicization – in the definitions remain with us to this day.

1 See A. Getachew, *Worldmaking after Empire: The Rise and Fall of Self-Determination*, Princeton University Press, Princeton 2019.

2 *Convention to Suppress the Slave Trade and Slavery*, 25 September 1926, 60 L.N.T.S. 253 No. 1414, art. 5. For the equivalent of the 'public purposes' exception in the ILO Forced Labour Convention, see A. Blackett and A. Duquesnoy, 'Slavery Is Not a Metaphor: U.S. Prison Labor and Racial Subordination through the Lens of the ILO's Abolition of Forced Labor Convention' (2021) 67(6) *UCLA Law Review* 1504, pp. 1511–1513.

 | DOI:10.1163/9789004723801_002

Perhaps more powerful is the knowledge that today, the language of 'modern slavery' is far from politically neutral. The moral indignation has not led to decisive action that has actually abolished modern slavery in its contemporary forms. Instead, it has led to a sidestepping of the legacies of slavery, most notably witnessed in the prevalence of prison labour disproportionately undertaken by the descendants of Atlantic slavery in the Americas.[3] As concerns global value chains, through which the production of most consumer goods across geographies and multiple links to suppliers of varying size and formality, and often multinational, global behemoths of retailers, there is a troubling trend. A proliferation of studies over the past two decades increasingly attests that the language of 'modern slavery' has largely been marshalled through corporate social responsibility (CSR) mechanisms and at best due diligence reporting on those mechanisms that focus on singling out 'bad actors' in the wake of systemic problems. The disregard of labour laws and traditional labour enforcement is prevalent. Widespread labour exploitation is perceived to be unavoidable. The CSR-based auditing industry is a multi-billion-dollar industry, but the results are acknowledged – even by brand leaders – to be middling at best. It is crucial to analyse the implications for those concerned with the future of labour law, transnationally.

The following observation was made in 2001:

> Corporate self-regulatory initiatives change the delivery of … labor regulatory principles. They are typically characterized as securing the former purpose, worker protection. They do so by articulating protective standards that MNEs should ensure are implemented by enterprises directly or indirectly involved in the production process, anywhere on the globe. However, they do so while increasing the scope of management power, over-reaching or supplanting state protective action required to mediate the effects of disproportionate bargaining power (even in collective relations), and to prevent unacceptable bargains that might be arrived at through 'voluntary' collective bargaining. Furthermore, their ability to protect workers' rights through independent monitoring is severely contested.
>
> As to the latter democratic participation role, there is a certain irony in the fact that the move to view labor standards as human rights through universally-applied codes of corporate conduct has turned attention

3 M. Goodwin, 'The Thirteenth Amendment: Modern Slavery, Capitalism and Mass Incarceration' (2019) 104 *Cornell Law Review* 899; A. Blackett and A. Duquesnoy, above n. 2.

> away from some of the key insights of industrial relations that underpin the pluralism in regulatory and enforcement powers. By diverting attention to management monitoring systems, and away from classic voice mechanisms through labor-management dispute settlement machinery, self-regulatory initiatives run the risk of supplanting rather than buttressing democratic participation in the workplace.[4]

Does it remain true today?

This IACL general report proposes to take a step back, and contextualize. It is deliberate in its reliance on the notion of contemporary forms of slavery, including causes and consequences, the language adopted by the United Nations and that characterizes the mandate of the Special Rapporteur. It offers a close analysis of the regulatory framework, which interrogates the relationship between the centuries-long Atlantic slave trade, and slavery in its contemporary forms. It focuses on continuity and disjuncture in the analysis. In other words, it seeks to learn from the past in the contemporary framing of the field.

This general report builds on the learned contributions of special national reports submitted in respect of the following twenty countries: Australia,[5] Barbados and St. Vincent & The Grenadines,[6] Belgium,[7] Canada,[8] Croatia,[9] France,[10] Germany,[11] Ghana,[12] Hungary,[13] Japan,[14] the Netherlands,[15] Peru,[16] Poland,[17]

4 A. Blackett, 'Global Governance, Legal Pluralism and the Decentered State: A Labor Law Critique of Codes of Corporate Conduct' (2001) 8:2 *Indiana Journal of Global Legal Studies* 401, pp. 419–420.
5 Professor Marilyn J. Pittard and Anthony Hallal.
6 Professor Jason Haynes.
7 Professor Filip Dorssemont.
8 Professor Yves Goguen.
9 Professor Sandra Laleta, Professor Marissabell Škorić, and Karla Kotulovski.
10 Dr. Beatrice Boissard, Lecturer and Dr. Olivier Pluen, Lecturer.
11 Dr. Heiner Fechner, Research Fellow.
12 Professor Julia Selman Ayetey.
13 Professor Sára Hungler and Dr. Márton Leó Zaccaria, Lecturer.
14 Professor Chizuko Hayakawa.
15 Professor Bas Rombouts.
16 Professor Laura Dehaibi.
17 Professor Dagmara Skupień, and Professor Łukasz Pisarczyk.

Romania,[18] Slovenia,[19] Sweden,[20] Turkey,[21] the United Kingdom,[22] and the United States of America.[23] It does not seek to replicate them, but rather to bring them into dialogue with each other and with the themes. The deliberate focus of this IACL labour law theme is to put the institution and legacies of slavery as a global institution into meaningful dialogue with contemporary forms of slavery, including causes and consequences. Its core argument is that a failure to learn from the past and its persisting legacies will doom attempts to redress labour exploitation in the present to failure.

2 The Presence of the Past: Slavery as a Global Institution and Its Legacies

Both when the 1926 Slavery Convention was being drafted, and soon after its adoption, the League of Nations sent letters to members to ask about whether slavery existed on their territory. Most responses were consistently of the following variety: we have nothing to send, as under no form does slavery exist in our country. Even the United States, which never joined the League, responded to an inquiry through the Secretary of State, confirming that "he is pleased to inform the Secretary General that slavery and the slave trade are prohibited under the fundamental laws of the United States and by the laws and statutes in force in its several possessions." He added that the United States was "deeply interested in any movement which looks towards the abolishment of all forms of involuntary servitude."[24] That did not stop the United States from subsequently playing a significant role in the carve out of forced labour from Article 5 of the 1926 Convention.[25] Similarly, the High Commissioner for the Union of South Africa denied that the provisions of the draft Convention would affect existing conditions or customs in its territory. However, arguing that "forced or compulsory labour is either slavery or it is not," the High Commissioner wondered whether the "slave-owner proper, in regard to his real or proprietary slave, will be able to shield himself."[26] The Portuguese Delegation in Switzerland in

18 Professor Monica Gheorghe and Lucian Blaga.
19 Professor Darja Senčur Peček.
20 Professor Niklas Selberg, and Dr. Amin Parsa, Affiliated Researcher.
21 Professor Tankut Centel.
22 Dr. Shahrzad Fouladvand, Senior Lecturer.
23 Professor Lolita Buckner Inniss.
24 League of Nations Archives, Letter dated 17 May 1926.
25 League of Nations Archives.
26 League of Nations Archives, Letter dated 2 July 1926.

contrast offered detailed comments steeped in the racist assumptions of colonial administration. They addressed the perceived challenges faced by colonial administrations responsible for 'developing' the 'backward' natives through the use of forced labour, agreed to inviting the ILO to study the question of forced labour, and took particular exception to any proposal that would confide oversight responsibility for slavery (defined as 'theories' on systems of 'administration') to the Permanent Court of Justice.

The international legal framework on slavery that has ensued is devoid of direct enforcement mechanisms. There is no treaty body charged with monitoring the implementation of the 1926 Slavery Convention or the 1956 Supplementary Convention, only a special procedures mandate holder under the UN Human Rights Council serving without pay in their personal capacity. The ILO's conventions on forced labour are subject to the same supervisory system in place to monitor compliance with the entire corpus of international labour standards.[27]

Nearly a century later, most of the states covered by national reports have ratified the relevant instruments on slavery and forced labour, including the 1926 Slavery Convention.[28] In our IACL study, several reports, notably from the Netherlands, Sweden, France, the UK and Germany, explore the fraught relationship between slavery and forced labour, unflinchingly explaining the legacy of colonialism within their jurisdictions. The German report also undertakes a critical act of memory in the discussion of forced labour in the Holocaust.

Not surprisingly, then, IACL national reports tend also to declare that 'traditional' slavery does not, and in some cases never,[29] existed on their territory. Slavery is legally prohibited in all jurisdictions covered in the national reports, in many cases enshrined in the constitution. While the legacies of slavery and the slave trade constitute an important part of the self-identification of several of the jurisdictions,[30] for others the question itself may have seemed to be little known and even of little relevance.[31]

---

27 The Committee of Experts on the Application of Conventions and Recommendations, whose work can be found at, <https://www.ilo.org/global/standards/applying-and-promoting-international-labour-standards/committee-of-experts-on-the-application-of-conventions-and-recommendations/lang--en/index.htm>.

28 The U.S. national report recalls that the U.S. is one of the few states worldwide that has not ratified ILO *Convention concerning Forced or Compulsory Labour, 1930 (No. 29)*. It has ratified ILO *Convention concerning the abolition of Forced Labour, 1957 (No. 105)*.

29 Senčur Peček, Slovenia national report.

30 Buckner Inniss, United States national report; Fouladvand, United Kingdom national report; Haynes, Barbados and St. Vincent & The Grenadines; Selman Ayetey, Ghana national report; Fechner, Germany national report; Selberg and Parsa, Sweden national report; Rombouts, Netherlands national report.

31 Senčur Peček, Slovenia national report.

Yet the legacy of slavery is profound. After all, slavery was a global institution supported by a law of slavery.[32] It resulted in the forceable dispossession and trafficking of 12.8 million enslaved Africans for over 400 years. It entailed trade in people for goods, the dispossession of Indigenous peoples of their lands and their attempted enslavement, the production and refinement of crops not only like tobacco, cotton and sugar, but also the production of salted cod and corned beef along the coast of the Americas from Nova Scotia, Canada to Mendoza, Argentina to feed the enslaved cheaply. It enabled port cities and manufacturing towns to thrive economically and provided the capital and move away from the household economy,[33] necessary to fuel the Industrial Revolution. As Greg Grandin underscores, each generation seems condemned to relearn what Eric Williams theorized in his pathbreaking 1944 book, *Capitalism and Slavery*,[34] slavery made the modern world.[35]

The legacies, therefore, can be quite direct, as in the case of mass incarceration and the 13th Amendment to the U.S. constitution as interpreted to permit prison labour in the United States.[36] But they can also manifest themselves in persisting forms of disadvantage, experienced across the globe, and play a particular role in rendering workers susceptible to the kind of precarity that allows extreme forms of exploitation to emerge.

It should still be added that the line between slavery, forced labour and anti-discrimination provisions in constitutional and broader human rights-based equality law is not so readily visible. While the emergence of an international human rights corpus in the post-World War II period and in the aftermath of the atrocity of the Holocaust is largely understood to be an important genesis for this development,[37] the relationship between slavery

---

32 S. Beckert, *Empire of Cotton: A Global History*, Vintage, New York 2014.

33 J.P. Melish, *Disowning Slavery: Gradual Emancipation and "Race" in New England, 1780–1860*, Cornell University Press, Ithaca 2016.

34 E. Williams, *Capitalism and Slavery*, Capricorn Books, New York 1994.

35 G. Grandin, 'How Slavery Made the Modern World,' *The Nation*, (24.02.2014), <https://www.thenation.com/article/archive/how-slavery-made-modern-world/>.

36 Buckner Inniss, United States national report. This vision of the 13th Amendment has been roundly criticized, including by scholars who argue for a positive labour vision of the 13th Amendment that would instead provide a basis for labour protections. See J.G. Pope, 'Labor's Constitution of Freedom' (1997) 106:4 *Yale Law Journal* 941; and R.E. Zeitlow, *The Forgotten Emancipator: James Mitchell Ashley and the Ideological Origins of Reconstruction*, Cambridge University Press, Cambridge 2017.

37 Justice Abella puts it particularly poignantly in the Canadian *Nevsun* case, calling modern international human rights law "the phoenix that rose from the ashes of World War II and declared global war on human rights abuses," in *Nevsun Resources Ltd. v. Araya*, 2020 SCC 5 at para 1.

and conquest (including the doctrine of discovery) and the construction of race as inherent to particular blood lines is largely lost. That the descendants of the enslaved and the colonized are overrepresented amongst the most marginalized can similarly easily get lost or considered too remote for contemporary anti-discrimination law. Yet "the legal conflation of race with status under slavery remained embodied, and Black, after abolition."[38] Looking at histories of unfreedom provides a reminder, and a corrective.

From a legal history perspective, a legacy of slavery lies in understanding that slavery is foundational to core notions of private property, contract law, and individual liberties.[39] The emerging scholarship encompasses a challenge to the received narrative of labour law.[40] An emancipation-centred vision focuses labour law's founding rationale not only in protection but also in resistance and agency. It is a resolute call to pay attention to historically marginalized workers as pivotal to safeguarding labour standards for all. It challenges both the boundary between productive and so-called non-productive work that is market sustaining – notably care work – and the boundary between the individual state and the transnational. It refuses dichotomizations, because it recalls that slavery and various other forms of relative freedom in the labour market coexisted in the same space and at times in the same person.[41] A careful study of each of the reports submitted for this general report underscores the prevalence of contemporary forms of slavery as a transnational phenomenon affecting the most marginalized workers. The reports reaffirm the need to look carefully at root causes and the founding idea of labour law to redress the underlying causes of widescale labour exploitation in the global economy.

A focus on emancipation offers other lessons for thinking through the presence of the past. As will be discussed in the next section, much of the engagement with slavery in its contemporary forms has emphasized – often in heavily mediatized ways – forms of saviourism, in which valiant human

38 A. Blackett, *Everyday Transgressions: Domestic Workers' Transnational Challenge to International Labor Law*, Cornell University Press, Ithaca 2019, p. 54.

39 See e.g. K.S. Park, 'The History Wars and Property Law: Conquest and Slavery as Foundational to the Field' (2021–2022) 131:4 *Yale Law Journal* 1062. The challenge of cases emerging out of slavery cited as precedent without sufficient regard to the context is only recently obtaining careful scholarly attention. See also J. Simard, 'Citing Slavery' (2020) 72 *Stanford Law Review* 79.

40 A. Blackett, 'Emancipation in the Idea of Labour Law' in G. Davidov and B. Langille (eds), *The Idea of Labour Law*, Oxford University Press, Oxford 2011.

41 S. Rockman, *Scraping By: Wage Labor, Slavery, and Survival in Early Baltimore*, John Hopkins University Press, Baltimore 2009; D. Hay and P. Craven, 'Introduction' in D. Hay and P. Craven (eds), *Masters, Servants, and Magistrates in Britain and the Empire, 1562–1955*, University of North Carolina Press, Chapel Hill 2004.

rights actors rescue hapless victims from the grips of ruthless recruiters and other traffickers. The parallel is Wilberforce and the manner in which this framing enabled key participants in Atlantic slavery such as the UK to reclaim an alternative image as the state that worked to abolish the slave trade.[42] Its economic reasons for doing so are similarly swept away.[43] Yet this vision is not only simplistic. It takes the emphasis away from the ways in which workers resist oppression, often by acting collectively. The freedom of association – a fundamental principle and right at work – is conspicuously absent from much of the engagement with contemporary forms of slavery, despite its centrality to worker resistance historically. Looking closely at the history of slavery and emancipation enables alternative stories to be centered in how the law of slavery is understood.

Finally, the unavoidable historical insight lies in how enslavement itself is understood – not as an aberration, or an individualized circumstance, but a systemic, structural institution. If there is a parallel in the contemporary economy, the magnitude of the problem suggests that we are not looking at individual bad apples, but a much broader problem linked to the existing lack of a viable, transnational approach to labour law to redress systems of economic production and exchange that build labour exploitation resolutely into their business models.

3 Understanding the Causes and Consequences of Contemporary Slavery

3.1 *Recognition of the Problem of Slavery*

The discourse on slavery must be distinguished from the law on slavery. While all countries report that their legal corpus contains various laws applying to slavery, slave-like practice, and contemporary forms of human suffering, this does not amount necessarily to a recognition of the problem of slavery as a whole, that is, as including the legacies of the global institution of slavery.

42 Jenny S. Martinez offers a thorough account of this period in British history, going so far as to refer to this period as the first human rights period in J.S. Martinez, *The Slave Trade and the Origins of International Human Rights Law*, Oxford University Press, Oxford 2012. See also P. Alston, 'Does the Past Matter? On the Origins of Human Rights' (2013) 126 *Harvard Law Review* 2043; and A.C. Martineau, 'Contested Histories: Revisiting the Relationship Between International Law and Slavery' in S. Chalmers and S. Pahuja (eds), *Routledge Handbook of International Law and Humanities*, Routledge, London 2021.

43 See E. Williams, above n. 34.

Domestic legislative activity seems to follow the elaboration of international instruments on the matter. Most reporting countries have ratified the two UN conventions on slavery and the two ILO conventions on forced labour and this is reflected domestically in constitutional prohibitions of slavery and forced labour. Similarly, overwhelming support for the 2000 Palermo Protocol has led to modifications of domestic criminal codes to join the transnational fight against trafficking in human beings. This being said, the connections between slavery and contemporary forms of human suffering are not self-evident in the law on slavery. It is as if signing the international treaties constituted a sufficient break with the past.[44] Because of this, the way that legislation approaches the problem of slavery, including the legacy of the global institution of the transatlantic slave trade, appears at times to be superficial, barely scratching the surface of the root causes of exploitation.

Moreover, several reports show that states attempt to distance themselves from the global institution of slavery. States may argue that they did not participate in the transatlantic slave trade and therefore 'geographically' separate themselves from it.[45] Or, they may suggest that slavery is a thing of the past that has or is being dealt with, at least on their own territory.[46] Former metropolitan powers further emphasize their role in abolishing the slave trade and slavery in the 19th century as well as active involvement in drafting key international instruments prohibiting slavery and slave-like practices as a way of evidencing their redemption.[47] This reinforces the tendency to externalize the problem of exploitation, as something that happens elsewhere, usually in former colonies which have not reached the same 'level of enlightened humanity'

---

44 With the exception of Japan and Peru for the 1926 *Slavery Convention* and 1956 *Supplementary Convention on the Abolition of Slavery, the Slave Trade, and Institutions and Practices Similar to Slavery*. In the case of Peru, the country did sign onto the 1956 Supplementary Convention but did not ratify it. See, Dehaibi, Peru National Report. Japan also did not ratify the *Convention concerning the abolition of Forced Labour, 1957 (No. 105)*. Furthermore, the United States has not ratified the *Convention concerning Forced or Compulsory Labour, 1930 (No. 29)*.

45 See e.g. Selberg and Parsa, Sweden national report; Fechner, Germany national report; Skupień and Pisarcyk, Poland national report. The case of Sweden is particularly interesting since the distancing operated with colonial European countries contradicts history, given that Sweden was a slave-holding nation for almost a century in St-Barthélémy Island.

46 See e.g. Boissard and Pluen, France national report.

47 See e.g. Boissard and Pluen, France national report; and Fouladvand, United Kingdom national report.

as the West.[48] The process of 'othering' obviously ignores the (historical) connections between the highly racialized nature of migrant work in high-income countries and the well-documented labour exploitation of these workers.[49]

Recognition of the legacy of slavery in a jurisdiction is also affected by geopolitics, more specifically the geography of Westphalian borders. The creation of new national boundaries suffices to erase the heritage of former empires engaged in severe forms of exploitative labour. The Ottoman Empire, for instance, which reached deep into Europe, and ended in 1922, was actively engaged in slavery and the slave trade,[50] yet its dismantling was claimed to rid the future states left in its ashes from any responsibility or involvement in the continuation of these practices. In this sense, contemporaneous borders do not only establish new jurisdictions, but they also perform a break with the past, where new governments are detached from historic patterns of marginalization on their territory. But viewing the institution of slavery as a global institution allows us to better grasp its continued legacy across time and borders. The German and Romanian reports illustrate these continuities despite successive shifts in the political structure of their respective territory in the past centuries.

Why might contemporary discourse on slavery so carefully avoid linkage with the centuries long institution of Atlantic slavery from which it draws so much of its moral power? The French report argues that this omission may reflect the fear that such engagement would revive historical debates and calls for reparation of descendants of slavery's victims, an argument that resonates with the upsurge of contemporary international advocacy for reparations.[51] It is striking that some of the most proactive countries on contemporary slavery have sought to address trafficking of persons for the purpose of exploitation, forced labour, and child labour, while resolutely declining calls to apologize for their involvement in the transatlantic slave trade, and provide reparative justice.

Careful attention must be paid to the ways in which definitions of slavery and slave-like practices may reinforce the 'othering' of historical patterns of

---

48 For an illustration of this 'othering' process, see Fechner, Germany national report.

49 A. Blackett, 'Situated Reflections on International Labour Law, Capabilities, and Decent Work: The Case of *Centre Maraîcher Eugène Guinois*' (2007) *Quebec Journal of International Law* 223. See notes below on migration as a risk factor of contemporary forms of slavery.

50 Centel, Turkey national report; See also E.R. Toledano, 'Enslavement in the Ottoman Empire in the Early Modern Period' in D. Eltis and S.L. Engerman (eds), *The Cambridge World History of Slavery*, Cambridge University Press, Cambridge 2011, (evaluating that, annually, between 16,000 and 18,000 Africans were forcibly transported and enslaved in the empire throughout the nineteenth century, at p. 27).

51 See Boissard and Pluen, France national report.

human suffering.[52] The question that surrounds this study is whether to apprehend this truth of the persistence of profound human suffering: we must rely upon the "derivatively [acquired] symbolic association with the past."[53] This general report calls for a refocusing, on the gap in governance that allows labour exploitation to proliferate and reinforce historical patterns of marginalization on the basis of race.[54] Efforts to disentangle a highly criminal law focused approach to 'modern slavery' from a systemic approach to labour exploitation runs the risk not only of failing to redress, but actually legitimizing the exploitation.

3.2 *Definition of Slavery*

Understanding the causes and consequences of contemporary forms of slavery requires an essential first step, which is understanding the meaning of 'contemporary slavery' itself. Despite the prevalence of their use, it is striking that the legal conceptualization of words like 'slavery,' 'modern slavery,' 'contemporary (forms of) slavery' lacks clarity and uniformity across jurisdictions.[55] 'Slavery,' while broadly prohibited, does not seem to carry much legal consequence given that it is considered a thing of the past, and formal legislation will usually refer to the definition in the 1926 Slavery Convention (3.2.1). Concretely, its application is unclear, leading one country to simply not include the prohibition in its constitution.[56]

Where greater textual clarity exists is in the definition and action in relation to practices 'analogous' to slavery which together form what is now referred to as 'contemporary forms of slavery.' Drawing heavily on international treaties,

52 See F. Kurasawa, 'Show and Tell: Contemporary Anti-Slavery Advocacy as Symbolic Work' in A. Bunting and J. Quirk (eds), *Contemporary Slavery: The Rhetoric of Global Human Rights Campaign*, Cornell University Press, Ithaca 2018.

53 A. Blackett, 'Slavery Is Not a Metaphor: Contemporary Slavery: Popular Rhetoric and Political Practice' (2018) 66 *American Journal of Comparative Law* 927, 929, citing F. Kurasawa, above n. 52, p. 174.

54 A. Blackett, 'Racial Capitalism and the Contemporary International Law on Slavery: (Re) membering *Hacienda Brasil Verde*' (2022) 25 *Journal of International Economic Law* 334; P. Viseur Sellers, 'Sexualized Practices and Institutions of the Slave Trade and Slavery' in J.N. Stefanelli and E. Lovall (eds), *Reparations Under International Law for Enslavement of African Persons in the Americas and the Caribbean*, ASIL & University of the West Indies, Washington, DC 2021.

55 Confusion and disagreement regarding the reach of these different concepts is also present in scholarship on slavery, see K. Bales, *Disposable People: New Slavery in the Global Economy*, University of California Press, Berkeley 2000; J. Allain, *Slavery in International Law: Of Human Exploitation and Trafficking*, Martinus Nijhoff, Leiden 2012.

56 Selberg and Parsa, Sweden national report.

states have developed intricate legal frameworks for human trafficking, child labour, and forced labour, which, not coincidentally, are also the forms of 'contemporary' slavery which have been most discussed in international legal forums (3.2.2). Despite the similarity in vocabulary, the contemporary law on slavery generally remains silent on the historical continuities in the racialized economic processes of marginalization. In fact, it is unclear what ties classic and contemporary slavery together, and because of this, the question of reparation for past injustices and injuries related to slavery is not necessarily perceived as connected with current efforts in preventing severe forms of labour exploitation.

3.2.1 Classical Slavery: Property and Control

Without defining the terms, it is commonplace for many jurisdictions to distinguish between 'classical' and 'contemporary' or 'modern' slavery. One assumption is clear: 'classical' slavery is mostly considered to be a relic of the past. Are the contemporary prohibitions of slavery more than rhetorical?

International law offers a definition of 'classical' slavery in the 1926 Slavery Convention, which is generally accepted by States with little or no effort to adapt the definition to national realities.[57] Absent from this 'ownership' focused definition that evokes chattel slavery is the recognition of slavery's racialization.[58] It should be noted that the legal language of ownership came to be systematically employed by liberal European jurists both to justify the colonization of Indigenous lands in the Americas and the enslavement of African populations for commercial exploitation of new-found resources.[59] There is important analysis of the extent to which transatlantic slavery – the dominant global institution for centuries, foundational to the emergence of liberal legal frameworks[60] – can be considered 'legal' for the purposes of establishing it as

57 See e.g. division 270 of the Australian Criminal Code, referenced in Pittard and Hallal, Australia national report, reproducing the text of article 1 of the UN Slavery Convention. See similar framings in Boissard and Pluen, France national report; Fechner, Germany national report.

58 A. Blackett, above n. 53.

59 B. Arneil, 'Trade, Plantations, and Property: John Locke and the Economic Defense of Colonialism' (1994) 55:4 *Journal of the History of Ideas* 591; and O. Patterson, *Slavery and Social Death: A Comparative Study*, Harvard University Press, Cambridge 1982.

60 A. Blackett, 'Follow the Drinking Gourd: Our Road to Teaching Critical Race Theory and Slavery and the Law, Contemplatively, at McGill' (2017) 62:4 *McGill Law Journal* 1251; K.S. Park, above n. 39.

a crime against humanity in international law.[61] The 1926 Slavery Convention was seen to complete internationally a series of conventions that progressively prohibited slavery and the slave trade.[62]

Of course, slavery was not 'legal' merely because of the application of property law rules to human beings, but through a progressive process of institutional legitimization of white supremacy.[63] Orlando Patterson notes that the concept of *dominium*, of power over a thing, central to civil law property, but also influential in common law theory through Blackstone's famous quote,[64] derives in fact from the latin word used for slavemaster (*dominus*), suggesting that it is slavery that created rules of property, not the other way around: "it becomes impossible to comprehend why [the Romans] should want inner psychic power over [a thing] unless we understand that, for most purposes, the 'thing' on their minds was a slave."[65] In the process, property law offers a useful language to explain control over persons, that is, historical forms of subordination.[66]

These historical intricacies, in the modern definition of classical slavery, are absent. 'Classical' slavery is strictly defined as legal ownership over a person, and legal ownership over a person is considered – largely based on constitutional prohibitions – no longer to be authorized. 'Classical' slavery is therefore

61 See N. Wittman, 'Global Assessment of the Legality of Transatlantic Chattel Slavery' in J.N. Stefanelli and E. Lovall, *Reparations Under International Law for Enslavement of African Persons in the Americas and the Caribbean*, ASIL & University of the West Indies, Washington, DC 2021; M. Hébié, 'Transatlantic Chattel Slavery 1450–1550,' in J.N. Stefanelli and E. Lovall, *Reparations Under International Law for Enslavement of African Persons in the Americas and the Caribbean*, ASIL & University of the West Indies, Washington, DC 2021.

62 International Agreement for the Suppression of the White Slave Traffic (1904); Convention for the Prevention of Traffic in White Women (1910); Treaty of Saint-Germain-en -Laye (1919); International Convention for the Suppression of the Traffic in Women and Children (1921).

63 See e.g. the 1688 *Slave Code*, cited in Haynes, Barbados and St. Vincent & The Grenadines national report.

64 W. Blackstone, *Commentaries on the Laws of England*, J.B. Lippincott Co., Philadelphia 1893: "There is nothing which so generally strikes the imagination, and engages the affections of mankind, as the right of property; or that sole and despotic dominion which one man claims and exercises over the external things of the world, in total exclusion of the right of any other individual in the universe."

65 O. Patterson, above n. 59, pp. 31–32.

66 See L. Vandervelde, 'The Labor Vision of the Thirteenth Amendment' (1989) 138 *University of Pennsylvania Law Review* 437.

largely deemed to be a thing of the past. The opinion of the European Court of Human Rights (ECtHR) in *Siliadin v. France* reinforces this reasoning:

> [The Court] notes that this definition [in the 1926 Slavery Convention] corresponds to the "classic" meaning of slavery as it was practised for centuries. Although the applicant was, in the instant case, clearly deprived of her personal autonomy, the evidence does not suggest that she was held in slavery in the proper sense, in other words that Mr and Mrs B. exercised a genuine right of legal ownership over her, thus reducing her to the status of an 'object.'[67]

It is important to acknowledge the circularity of the reasoning, and to recognize that despite accepting broadened definitions, regional human rights tribunals have been able to accept the de facto existence of conditions that meet the classic test for slavery.[68] Moreover, while the ECtHR applied in *Siliadin* a narrow definition of slavery, there seems to be a growing acceptance of a slightly modified definition of (modern) slavery, where international and regional courts no longer merely rely on a criterion of 'legal ownership' but on the observation, through facts, of a broader standard of 'control,' as suggested by the ICTY case in *Prosecutor v Kunarac et al.*[69] The idea of *dominium*, or power, over a person appears more explicit in a definition of slavery based on control, and the position adopted by the ICTY seems to have found some echo at the domestic level, where the specific exploitation of factors of vulnerability (migratory status, poverty, lack of education) has weighed in the balance in courts' conclusion of modern slavery.[70] Close attention to the history of slavery yields the following observation: neither legal definition takes into account the enslaved persons' resistances.[71]

---

67 *Siliadin v. France*, no. 73316/01, ECHR 2005 at para. 122.

68 *Hacienda Brasil Verde Workers v. Brazil*, Preliminary Objections, Merits, Reparations and Costs, Judgment, Inter-Am.Ct.H.R. (ser. C) No. 318 (20 October 2016).

69 Defined enslavement as: "the restriction or control of an individual's autonomy, freedom of choice or freedom of movement; and, often, the accruing of some gain to the perpetrator." (*Prosecutor v. Dragoljub Kunarac, Radomir Kovac and Zoran Vukovic* (*Trial Judgment*), IT-96–23-T & IT-96–23/1-T, ICTY, 22 February 2001, para. 542). Kevin Bales also made the idea of control central to his definition of 'new' slavery, given that legal ownership of persons is no longer existent (see K. Bales, above n. 55). See also, on the shift to the idea of control or power over a person, J. Allain, above n. 55.

70 See e.g. court cases mentioned in Pittard and Hallal, Australia national report; and Laleta, Škorić and Kotulovski, Croatia national report.

71 Adelle Blackett, above n. 54.

3.2.2 Practices 'Analogous' to Slavery: Strong Influence of International Instruments

The creation in 2007 of the mandate of the Special Rapporteur on contemporary forms of slavery, including its causes and consequences, set a standard in the language used to describe a range of practices of severe exploitation of human beings.[72] The Rapporteur's mandate is understood to "include[e] but is not limited to issues such as: traditional slavery, debt bondage, serfdom, forced labour, children in slavery and slavery-like conditions, sexual slavery, forced and early marriages and servile forms of marriage."[73] It is also accepted that the Special Rapporteur will examine issues of human trafficking, which has come to overwhelm the discussion in the law on slavery. The ECtHR has interpreted art. 4 of the European Convention on Human Rights (ECHR) on the prohibition of slavery and forced labour as encompassing human trafficking, considering that the latter "by its very nature and aim of exploitation, is based on the exercise of powers attaching to the right of ownership."[74] Specifically, the Court considered that trafficking treated human beings as commodities.

---

72 See UNHRC Res 6/14 'Contemporary Forms of Slavery Including its Causes and Consequences' (28 September 2007) UN Doc A/HRC/RES/6/14, which was adopted without a vote:

> Bearing in mind that 2007 marks the two hundredth anniversary of the beginning of the abolition of the transatlantic slave trade,
>
> Convinced that the mandates of existing Special Rapporteurs do not adequately cover all slavery practices, and that the issue of contemporary forms of slavery needs to be given greater prominence and priority within the United Nations system if these practices are to be eradicated once and for all
>
> ... Decides that the Special Rapporteur shall examine and report on all contemporary forms of slavery and slavery-like practices, but in particular those defined in the Slavery Convention of 1926, and the Supplementary Convention on the Abolition of Slavery, the Slave Trade and Institutions and Practices Similar to Slavery of 1956, as well as all other issues covered by the Working Group on Contemporary Forms of Slavery including forced prostitution and its human rights dimensions; in the discharge of his/her mandate, the Special Rapporteur will:
>
> a. Focus principally on aspects of contemporary forms of slavery which are not covered by existing mandates of the Human Rights Council;
> b. Promote the effective application of relevant international norms and standards on slavery [...].

73 United Nations, 'Office of the High Commissioner for Human Rights, Overview of the mandate: Special Rapporteur on contemporary forms of slavery,' <https://www.ohchr.org/en/special-procedures/sr-slavery/overview-mandate>.

74 *Rantsev v. Cyprus and Russia*, no. 25965/04, ECHR 2010, para. 280.

Just like for classic slavery, domestic definitions of human trafficking stay close to the one provided in the Palermo Protocol at art. 3(a),[75] and within the realm of criminal law. The data provided by our rapporteurs show that many jurisdictions brought modifications to their criminal codes regarding the offence of trafficking in persons following the adoption of the 2000 Palermo Protocol.[76] In fact, the Protocol explicitly provides at article 5 that states must integrate human trafficking in their criminal laws, a call which was clearly widely answered.

The imprint of international instruments is also felt on constitutional provisions related to forced labour, many countries reporting lists of exceptions that mirror those provided for at article 2(2) of the ILO Forced Labour Convention (No. 29). Forced labour is usually linked with trafficking as one of its recurring outcomes, along sexual exploitation. Hence, institutional responses to forced labour have focused more on punitive measures against employers than on correcting the underlying causes that favour exploitation, even if provisions against forced labour, according to the reports that follow, are not only found in criminal laws, but also in constitutional provisions and even labour laws.

The fight against forced labour seems to have received renewed attention since the adoption of the 2014 ILO Protocol to the Forced Labour Convention, 1930 (No. 29) which emphasizes victim protection and prevention. One way this has concretized is through legislation on due diligence in global supply chains. This type of legislation offers a broader range of interventions since it is not, by its very nature, punitive, although, as we outline later, the way it has been framed also has the perverse effect of externalizing the problem of exploitation.

Both for human trafficking and forced labour, various aggravating factors are considered, usually based on characteristics of the victim. Age is obviously a dominant factor, and any of these offenses involving children are severely

75 See e.g. Article 175 of the Hungarian Criminal Code cited in Laleta, Škorić and Kotulovski, Croatia national report; Section 4 (c) of the Modern Slavery Act cited in Pittard and Hallal, Australia national report; Fechner Section 232 of the German Criminal Code cited in Fechner, Germany national report and Section 3 of the Trafficking in Persons Act (Barbados) and Section of the Trafficking in Persons Act (St. Vincent and the Grenadines) cited in Haynes, Barbados and St. Vincent and the Grenadines.

76 E.g. Canada did so in 2005; Croatia, 2004; France, 2003; Germany, 2005, then 2016; and Slovenia, 2004. See respective reports.

condemned.[77] Migratory status may also be considered, as well as social circumstances like poverty.[78] Actual *characterization* by the victim is not however considered relevant. Presenting the victim of slavery as helpless and backwards was key in creating a particular image of the enslaved person that explained their subjugation.[79] This personification of the victim as helpless is still present nowadays, with legal indicators of crimes of forced labour and human trafficking focusing on personal characteristics of the victim to determine their 'vulnerability' while undermining their expressed consent[80] and ignoring the complex, racialized, dynamics of power at play in labour exploitation.

From the data that were made available to us by the national rapporteurs, while trafficking in persons, sexual exploitation, and forced labour have received legislative attention in the past years, older concepts present in international instruments, like debt bondage, serfdom, or servitude are less defined in criminal codes or other domestic legislation. This seems to support the idea that recent international law-making is particularly influential at the national level.

While many national rapporteurs mentioned that their legislation conforms to international standards on various forms of severe exploitation, very few have addressed the influence of international bodies' monitoring of their respective performances. The exceptions are Peru and the Netherlands.[81] The fact that very few court cases have been heard on the issues may explain this in part, but it ultimately leads to overlooking some key insights from relevant observations. The special procedures mandate holders – notably the Special Rapporteur on contemporary forms of racism, racial discrimination,

77 See e.g. Haynes, Barbados and St. Vincent and the Grenadines national report; Laleta, Škorić and Kotulovski, Croatia national report; Goguen, Canada national report and Selman Ayetey, Ghana national report.

78 See e.g. Dorssemont, Belgium national report; Pittard and Hallal, Australia national report, Haynes, Barbados and St. Vincent and the Grenadines.

79 See for instance 1688 Barbados *Slave Code*, partially cited in Haynes, Barbados and St. Vincent & The Grenadines: "And forasmuch as the said [...] Slaves brought unto the People of this Island for that purpose, are of Barbarous, Wild, and Savage Natures, and such as renders them wholly unqualified to be governed by the Laws, Customs, and Practices of Our Nations."

80 See commentaries below regarding gender as a risk factor. See also case law cited in Pittard and Hallal, Australia national report.

81 In Rombouts, Netherlands national report, reports from the UN Committee on the Elimination of Racial Discrimination; in Dehaibi, Peru national report, reports of the Special Rapporteur on Contemporary Forms of Slavery and the ILO Committee of Experts on the Application of Conventions and Recommendations.

xenophobia and related intolerance – as well as treaty bodies monitoring compliance such as the UN Committee on the Elimination of Racial Discrimination, and the ILO Committee of Experts on the Application of Conventions and Recommendations – have on various occasions and to varying degrees acknowledged the link between current racialized labour exploitation and colonialism/the global institution of slavery.[82]

4 Contemporary Forms of Slavery: Causes

The national reports that follow identify a series of causal factors – or at least circumstances of heightened risk – in which extreme forms of exploitation are particularly observed. What we want to emphasize in this general report is that the causes are not dependent on inherent vulnerabilities of the persons being exploited. Rather, the causes reflect institutionalized and systemic practices that perpetuate exploitation and reduce the scope for workers' autonomy and exercise of agency.

Migration, for instance, is often cited as a leading risk factor in human trafficking or forced labour, but it is not merely movement or the lack of social and cultural familiarity with the destination country that makes a person vulnerable. A long history of colonial domination has brought states in the Global North to retain strict control over their borders. This has yielded largely racialized and gendered 'othering,' distinguishing between those who are enabled to travel legally, and those who are rendered 'illegal.'[83]

Causes of extreme forms of exploitation are not the same everywhere, but there are significant transnational patterns. While the majority of national reports emerge out of the reality of high-income countries, the reports from the Global South show that informality and weak institutional structures can play a significant role in the maintenance of human suffering through deprivation

82 See e.g., United Nations High Commissioner for Human Rights, *Promotion and protection of the human rights and fundamental freedoms of Africans and people of African descent against excessive use of force and other human rights violations by law enforcement officers*, 47th Sess, UN Doc A/HRC/47/53 (2021) at para 9; Special Rapporteur on Contemporary Forms of Racism, Racial Discrimination, Xenophobia and Racial Intolerance, 74th Sess, UN Doc A/74/321 (2019).

83 M. Khan, 'Imperial Anti-Trafficking in India' in K. Kempadoo and E. Shih (eds), *White Supremacy, Racism and the Coloniality of Anti-Trafficking*, Routledge, New York 2022. See also C. Dauvergne, *Making People Illegal: What Globalization Means for Migration and Law*, Cambridge University Press, Cambridge 2009.

of liberty and labour exploitation.[84] The commonality between reports is that the causes are linked through the global economy and global value and care chains.[85] Control over migration processes in the UK is in continuation of the control of the trade routes that they maintained for centuries,[86] whereas marked social inequalities in Peru follow the colonial divisions between European elites – masters – and Indigenous and African populations – servant/slave.[87] Similarly, we find commonalities in the integrated economic sectors associated with slavery across the globe as well as, once more, historical continuities, notably when it comes to domestic work, agriculture, and mining.

4.1 *Slavery, Colonialism, and Migration: the Role of Racial Capitalism*

Victims of contemporary forms of exploitation are often migrants and racialized persons.[88] Many countries, particularly in Eastern Europe, have noted that their territory constitutes at once a point of origin, a transit space, and a destination for trafficked persons, exposing the transnational nature of severe forms of exploitation.[89] Increased economic integration in Europe has indeed been accompanied by increased movement of people, both voluntary and forced, although, as Cedric Robinson establishes, racialized migration was long an integral part of Europe's economic development, first within that continent, and then through the transatlantic slave trade.[90]

Migration is not only a problem in the context of illegally trafficked persons who are coerced or lured into crossing borders to then be exploited. Rapporteurs explain that government migration programs can create conditions that favour exploitation, by institutionalizing the social isolation of migrant

84 See Selman Ayetey, Ghana national report; Dehaibi, Peru national report and Haynes, Barbados and St. Vincent and the Grenadines national report.

85 For example, Rhacel Salazar Parreñas refers to 'care work extraction' to address the relationship between structural adjustment policies and remittance-based labour migration that leads often well-educated Filipina women to migrate as domestic workers under schemes structured to enable abuse (in R.S. Parreñas, *Children of Global Migration: Transnational Families and Gendered Woes*, Stanford University Press, Stanford 2005).

86 See e.g., E. Williams, above n. 34; M. Khan, above n. 83.

87 C. Aguirre, *Breve historia de la esclavitud en el Perú*, Fondo editorial del Congreso del Perú, Lima 2005, cited in Dehaibi, Peru national report.

88 See e.g. Goguen, Canada national report; Laleta, Škorić and Kotulovski, Croatia national report; Fechner, Germany national report; Rombouts, Netherlands national report; and Senčur Peček, Slovenia national report.

89 See e.g. Fechner, Germany national report; Skupień and Pisarcyk, Poland national report; and Senčur Peček, Slovenia national report.

90 C. Robinson, *Black Marxism*, University of North Carolina Press, Chapel Hill 2000.

workers, who are often racialized.[91] Internal migration must be considered too: the Peruvian report outlines that work in mines heavily relies on internal migration,[92] and the first Inter-American case on slavery describes in detail how Afro-Brazilian workers were trafficked within Brazil to get to their hostile place of enslavement.[93] In the latter case, the historical continuity in the country that imported the greatest number of enslaved Africans was quite remarkably negated.[94] Much work remains to address the relationship between racialization, slavery, and persisting postcolonial patterns of labour exploitation.

It is critical to recall that it is less that these migrant and racialized 'others' are considered 'foreign,' but rather it is Indigenous people experiencing ongoing settler colonialism or the descendants of the enslaved and other racialized communities who bear the legacies of systems of white supremacy. By recalling how colonial policies divided society artificially along racial and ethnic lines,[95] it is also possible to contextualize what several European rapporteurs have observed: the Romani are overrepresented amongst the victims of contemporary forms of human exploitation.[96] Moreover, the U.S. Department of

91 One example of this is to attach migratory status to a single employer. See e.g., Pittard and Hallal, Australia national report; and Goguen, Canada national report. See also A. Blackett, above n. 49.

92 See Dehaibi, Peru national report.

93 See *Hacienda Brasil Verde Workers v. Brazil*, Preliminary Objections, Merits, Reparations and Costs, Judgment, Inter-Am.Ct.H.R. (ser. C) No. 318 (20 October 2016).

94 A. Blackett, above n. 54.

95 S. Hall, *The Fateful Triangle: Race, Ethnicity, Nation*, Harvard University Press, Cambridge 2017.

96 See e.g. Hungler and Zaccaria, Hungary national report; Gheorghe and Blaga, Romania national report; and Senčur Pešek, Slovenia national report. Indeed, the lack of cultural nuance in response to forced marriage in minors within Romani communities seems to mirror the racist strategy of pitting Western European values against 'backward' traditions, which in turn has the effect of "silenc[ing] critiques of certain practices from within oppressed communities and [...] deflect[ing] attention from institutionalized marginalization in Romania." A. Oprea, 'The Arranged Marriage of Ana Maria Cioaba, Intra-Community Oppression and Romani Feminist Ideals: Transcending the "Primitive Culture" Argument' (2005) 12(2) *European Journal of Women's Studies* 133, 136. According to the author, the media coverage of the wedding displayed blatant racism against Roma, and an effort to select specific aspects of Roma culture that confirm a narrative of homogeneous backwardness. It is worth mentioning that controlling Roma women's bodies is not new, women having been subjected to forced sterilization campaigns across Europe far within the 20th century. Control of racialized women's reproductive capacity, whether by encouraging it or impeding it, is an integral part of the history of slavery, colonialism, and capitalism. See J.L. Morgan, *Reckoning with Slavery: Gender, Kinship, and Capitalism in the Early Black Atlantic*, Duke University Press, Durham 2021.

State has had to acknowledge the "historical and ongoing harm" of systemic racism in the context of human trafficking.[97]

In many ways, the United States and other governments face human trafficking challenges and trends today that reflect the living legacy of the systemic racism and colonization globalized during the transatlantic slave trade through chattel slavery and regional practices of Indigenous dispossession. U.S. and global data show human traffickers disproportionately target those in positions of socioeconomic or political vulnerability due to discriminatory policies, notably people of colour or racial minorities. While U.S. efforts to combat human trafficking have grown in magnitude and sophistication over the years, the U.S. still struggles with how to address the disparate effects of human trafficking on racial minority communities.

Years of studies, data, and the direct knowledge of those with lived experience of human trafficking demonstrate that systemic racism undercuts the intended goals of prosecuting traffickers, protecting those victimized, and preventing human trafficking in significant ways. This body of information provides a strong foundation from which to learn. For instance, advocates, survivors, and other experts have found that ingrained racial biases and stereotypes, which were created to dehumanize certain racial communities to justify their exploitation and exclusion, hinder progress in anti-trafficking efforts. This is in no small measure because they lead to racially disparate assumptions about who is a trafficker and who should have access to victim protection and services. These stereotypes may affect, for example, which communities law enforcement target for anti-trafficking operations, which witnesses the criminal justice system deems credible, and which individuals process their experiences as exploitation and seek help. Traffickers, in turn, factor these racial biases and stereotypes into schemes and strategies aimed at reducing their own risk of getting caught while increasing the risk of law enforcement improperly penalizing victims.[98]

It has, moreover, been admitted that discriminatory government policies themselves "create disparities in access to economic means of opportunities, which traffickers exploit to compel victims in sex trafficking or forced labor."[99] While the U.S. report calls for an approach that addresses underlying causes of

97 U.S. Department of State, Office to Monitor and Combat Trafficking in Persons, 'Acknowledging Historical and Ongoing Harm: The Connections Between Systemic Racism and Human Trafficking' (01.07.2021), <https://www.state.gov/acknowledging-historical-and-ongoing-harm-the-connections-between-systemic-racism-and-human-trafficking/>.

98 *Ibid.*

99 *Ibid.*

inequality, the approach does not call into question the anti-trafficking work itself. Instead, it is to be rooted in "racial equity" and draw from communities themselves.

4.2 *Gender*

Women are overrepresented among the accounted-for cases of contemporary forms of exploitation. Many jurisdictions note that the majority of cases of trafficking relate to sexual exploitation.[100] There is a tendency to distinguish this from labour exploitation. Sex work, significantly performed by migrant and racialized women, is with very few exceptions criminalized.

The contemporary approach to coerced sex work needs to be evaluated against the troubled history behind the regulation of trafficking in human beings. Referred to in the past as 'white slavery', its protective approach was inherently built on racialized assumptions and specifically targeted white women working in prostitution. The assumption was that sex work was necessarily performed against a person's will; it infantilized women and undermined their consent.

The criminalization of human trafficking in the contemporary context has yielded concern that the international approach constitutes yet another form of control over women's bodies.[101] The Palermo Protocol specifically mentions that "the consent of a victim of trafficking in persons to the intended exploitation [...] shall be irrelevant" if it is considered that threat or use of force, coercion, abduction, fraud, deception, or abuse of power or a position of vulnerability.[102] Protective in tone, it risks circumscribing the extent to which a person's lived experience can inform institutional response to their situation. Since both human trafficking and sex work are treated under criminal law, if a person does not identify as a victim based on the standards set for them in abstract legal instruments, they automatically become a perpetrator.[103] While some immigration schemes provide for provisional visas to enable victims of

100 See, e.g., Haynes, Barbados and St. Vincent and the Grenadines national report; and Senčur Peček, Slovenia national report.

101 R. Andrijasevic and N. Mai, 'Editorial: Trafficking (in) Representations: Understanding the Recurring Appeal of Victimhood and Slavery in Neoliberal Times' (2016) 7 *Anti-Trafficking Review* 1; P. Kotiswaran, 'The Sexual Politics of Anti-Trafficking Discourse' (2021) 29 *Feminist Legal Studies* 43.

102 *Protocol to Prevent, Suppress and Punish Trafficking in Persons, Especially Women and Children, Supplementing the United Nations Convention Against Transnational Organized Crime* (Palermo Protocol), 15 November 2000, U.N.T.S. A-39574, art. 3(b).

103 I.K. Thiemann, 'Beyond Victimhood *and* Beyond Employment? Exploring Avenues for Labour Law to Empower Women Trafficked into the Sex Industry' (2019) 48:2 *Industrial Law Journal* 199.

abuse to bring complaints and see them through,[104] the focus remains on the punishment of the crime's perpetrator. Moreover, the interplay of race and gender are seldom addressed in the context of human trafficking, despite the well-documented policing of racialized women bodies.[105] Being treated as commodities, in the ECtHR's word, trafficking victims are effectively silenced, both by offenders and by the judicial process.[106]

4.3 *Property, Poverty, and Informality*

Enslaved Africans were treated as property. It is often suggested that property law has little role to play in contemporary forms of slavery. This, however, only addresses one way in which the legal institution of property enabled slavery. It is now well documented that the massive use of enslaved labour from the 16th century onward was made necessary by settler colonialism, involving the dispossession of Indigenous populations of their lands and its commercial exploitation throughout the Americas and beyond.[107] The primitive accumulation of capital required strong, recognizable and accountable entitlements to land, facilitating the management of resources and market exchanges. Liberal property law offered just that.[108]

The prohibition of the slave trade and of slavery did not end the accumulation of property and capital, nor did it end the quest for maximized resource exploitation, which both continue to this day to justify unfree labour. The creation of legal structures to force formerly enslaved Africans to continue working for a certain period of time after emancipation or the exploitation of 'coolies' from the Indian sub-continent on plantations right after the abolition of slavery by means of indentured servitude illustrates this point.[109] It is therefore not a surprise, as we will see later, that many of the sectors that are associated with contemporary forms of human exploitation, are associated with resource exploitation (e.g. agriculture and mining).

104 See e.g. Goguen, Canada national report; Pittard and Hallal, Australia national report; Senčur Peček, Slovenia national report; Dorssemont, Belgium national report; and Haynes, Barbados and St, Vincent and the Grenadines national report.

105 R. Andrijasevic and N. Mai, above n. 101.

106 *Rantsev v. Cyprus and Russia*, no. 25965/04, ECHR 2010.

107 See e.g. E. Williams, above n. 34; C. Robinson, above at n. 90; and C.L.R. James, *The Black Jacobins: Toussaint L'Ouverture and the San Domingo Revolution*, Random House, New York 1963/1989.

108 On Locke's justification of property, see e.g., B. Arneil, above n. 59.

109 See e.g. Goguen, Canada national report; Boissard and Pluen, France national report; Dehaibi, Peru national report.

Accumulation of property is also associated with increased social inequalities, and poverty is widely cited as a risk factor for contemporary forms of slavery.[110] Poverty can lead to social isolation, especially for migrant workers, workers in rural settings, and homeless people. As the Romanian report explains in the context of the Roma minority, poverty is also often exacerbated by systemic racial discrimination. The COVID-19 pandemic further isolated marginalized workers: on the one hand, it has led to higher rates of unemployment, reducing people's financial flexibility, on the other it has affected the work of organizations involved in the identification and protection of victims of human trafficking and forced labour.[111]

Informal or undeclared work adds a layer of invisibility that favours exploitation. While informality is often perceived as a problem in low income or emerging countries where weak institutions and endemic poverty converge,[112] it is also increasingly observed in European or North American markets, which tend to use instead the language of 'precarious' work.[113] The problem is that labour legislation tends only to recognize traditional employer-employee relationships, which offer far from a complete depiction of contemporary labour markets.[114] Contemporary labour markets are organized across global supply chains that include as part of the very business model temporary workers, sub-contracted workers, informal economy workers,[115] and a wide gamut of recruitment-based practices.[116] Recourse to this broad range of precarious work relationships cannot be disentangled from a management approach designed to circumvent the traditional employer-employee relationships that

110 See e.g. Selman Ayetey, Ghana national report; Hungler and Zaccaria, Hungary national report; Dehaibi, Peru national report; Skupień and Pisarcyk, Poland national report; and Gheorghe and Blaga, Romania national report.

111 See e.g. Dorssemont, Belgium national report; and Senčur Peček, Slovenia national report.

112 See e.g. Dehaibi, Peru national report; and Centel, Turkey national report.

113 See Gheorghe and Blaga, Romania national report; and Laleta, Škorić and Kotulovski, Croatia national report. See also A. Blackett, above n. 38.

114 Characterized, among other, by informality, sub-contracting, global supply chains, and the gig economy.

115 See S.A. Khan, 'Struggles and Actions for Legal Space in the Urban World: The Case of Informal Economy E-waste Workers' (2018) 33:2 *Canadian Journal of Law and Society* 115.

116 See recently G. LeBaron, *Combatting Modern Slavery: Why Labour Governance is Failing and What We Can Do About It*, Polity Press, Cambridge 2020. See also S.J. Rombouts, 'The International Diffusion of Fundamental Labor Standards: Contemporary Content, Scope, Supervision, and Proliferation of Core Workers' Rights under Public, Private, Binding, and Voluntary Regulatory Regimes' (2019) 50:3 *Columbia Human Rights Law Review* 78.

are the focus of labour law.[117] The absence of an enforceable employment contract means that workers are left on their own to defend their rights, and legislative inertia in that regard contributes to the problem, in particular when it fails to uphold a variety of lived employment relationships.

4.4 *Deficient Institutions*

Many reporting countries have developed elaborate legal frameworks to prevent and combat contemporary forms of slavery, from the ratification of key international instruments to the adoption of laws to prevent, limit and prosecute contemporary forms of slavery. These may even be accompanied by detailed action plans,[118] as well as more permanent infrastructures meant to address problems on a sustained basis.[119] Countries have also reported a discrepancy between the existence of these frameworks and their practical application and enforcement.[120] Enforcement can be affected by limited attribution of financial and human resources to address these issues, but also by practical obstacles in accessing the justice system, especially for migrant workers.[121]

While weak institutions, underdeveloped infrastructure, and lack of funding have been portrayed as problems of the Global South, a look at the data provided by national rapporteurs reveals that institutional problems in the fight against contemporary forms of extreme exploitation run at a deeper level, and are transnational.[122] At minimum, an effective strategy to fight contemporary forms of slavery would require a shared and intricate understanding of the problem and the concept it involves. The lack of legal clarity – both in terms of substantial definitions and of understanding the root causes – is far from

117 *Ibid.* For an early labour law critique of corporate governance mechanisms, see A. Blackett, above n. 4.

118 See e.g., Hayakawa, Japan national report; Dehaibi, Peru national report; Skupień and Pisarcyk, Poland national report; and Senčur Peček, Slovenia national report.

119 See e.g., Poland's Human Trafficking Research Center in Skupień and Pisarcyk, Poland national report; the Netherlands' National Rapporteur on Human Trafficking in Rombouts, Netherlands national report; and Slovenia's Inter-ministerial Working Group on trafficking in human beings in Senčur Peček, Slovenia national report.

120 See e.g., Selman Ayetey, Ghana national report; Dehaibi, Peru national report; and Gheorghe and Blaga, Romania national report. See also commentaries in Dorssemont, Belgium national report, on challenges of the pandemic on enforcement.

121 See e.g., Skupień and Pisarcyk, Poland national report.

122 The absence of a clear statistical portrait does not help. See e.g., Pittard and Hallal, Australia national report; Dorssemont, Belgium national report; Boissard and Pluen, France national report; Selman Ayetey, Ghana national report; Dehaibi, Peru national report; Senčur Peček, Slovenia national report; and Centel, Turkey national report.

neutral; despite the flurry of activity, it may actually divert attention from systemic problems and contribute to the maintenance of severe forms of human exploitation.[123]

Institutional response to the complexity of human exploitation cannot rely on a one-size-fits-all solution. Currently, most efforts have focused on criminalization, which concentrate on individual perpetrators and victims, and do not allow for more in-depth engagement with the social, cultural, geographic context within which exploitation occurs. As authors Andrikavesic and Mai explain:

> Humanitarian representations tend to frame victims as 'exceptions' rather than 'products' of the globalisation of neoliberal politics and to locate these victims outside of a supposedly shared humanity that actually expresses the privileges and moralities of the global North.[124]

In addition, actors beyond the criminal justice system are less involved than they should be in institutional responses. For instance, reports that were made available to us did not account for a significant involvement of trade unions in combatting severe forms of labour exploitation, apart from participation in broader initiatives targeting corporate social responsibility and human rights for businesses,[125] or indirectly through work with migrant workers.[126] Yet, trade unions have an important part to play in fighting human exploitation, whether by advocating for safer and more inclusive work places or through their capacity to disseminate knowledge on available resources to a greater number of workers.

4.5 *Sectors Associated with Slavery*

The most cited sectors associated with practices of slavery, forced labour, child labour and human trafficking are sex work, agriculture and the agribusiness (including transformation, like meat processing and packing, and the fishing industry), the mining industry or mineral extraction, domestic care work,

---

123 At least two reporting countries noted that law enforcement officers were not well equipped in identifying instances of forced labour or trafficking (Hungler and Zaccaria, Hungary national report; and Dehaibi, Peru national report). Cultural training is also essential, as noted in Selman Ayetey, Ghana national report. This conclusion is repeatedly underscored in the scholarly literature. See e.g. G. LeBaron, above n. 116.

124 R. Andrijasevic and N. Mai, above n. 101.

125 See e.g., Senčur Peček, Slovenia national report; and Rombouts, Netherlands national report.

126 See e.g., Fechner, Germany national report; and Goguen, Canada national report.

construction, the hospitality industry and the garment industry. In numerical terms, most cases denounced related to sexual exploitation, although labour exploitation cases are on the rise.[127] Low-skilled, low-pay jobs (hospitality, garment, agriculture) are often singled out as susceptible of leading to exploitation. Such employment is often occupied by migrants, women, and racialized persons.

Many of the identified sectors are historically associated with slavery, in particular agriculture, the mining industry, and domestic care work. The transatlantic slave trade particularly sought to provide a workforce in export-oriented plantations, and compensation to slave-owners after the abolition of slavery was in part justified by the need to compensate the financial losses of farm owners and ensure continuity in agricultural production.[128] Back then and now, fear of food shortages have been used to justify exploitation of – foreign – workers,[129] to the point where the original version of ILO Convention No. 29

127 See e.g., data from Fechner, Germany national report; Hungler and Zaccaria, Hungary national report; Rombouts, Netherlands national report; and Senčur Peček, Slovenia national report. We are applying the distinction between sexual exploitation and labour exploitation as used in special reports. However, it should be noted that distancing 'sex' from 'work' has the adverse effect of denying labour rights protection for consensual sex workers, hence the call of many organizations to decriminalize sex work as a way both to provide labour protections to the workers and prevent human trafficking.

128 See e.g., K. Manjapra, 'Plantation Dispossessions: The Global Travel of Agricultural Racial Capitalism' in S. Beckert and C. Desan (eds), *American Capitalism: New Histories*, Columbia University Press, New York 2018.

129 For the use of the discourse of agricultural exceptionalism in the context of deficient labour protection of migrant workers, see L. Dehaibi, 'Idéal champêtre ou enfer ouvrier? Démystifier la terre pour renforcer les droits des travailleurs agricoles' (2022) 90 *Labour/Le Travail* 11; A.M. Weiler, J. McLaughlin et D.C. Cole, 'Food Security at Whose Expense? A Critique of the Canadian Temporary Farm Labour Migration Regime and Proposals for Change' (2017) 55:4 *International Migration* 48; E. Reid-Musson, 'Grown Close to Home™: Migrant Farmworker (Im)mobilities and Unfreedom on Canadian Family Farms' (2017) 107:3 *Annals of the American Association of Geographers* 716; and A.A. Smith, 'Bunk House Rules: Housing Migrant Labour in Ontario' (2015) Osgoode Legal Studies Research Paper Series 98, at <https://digitalcommons.osgoode.yorku.ca/cgi/viewcontent.cgi?article=1096&context=olsrps>. For similar literature on reporting countries other than Canada, see e.g. I. García-Colón, *Colonial Migrants at the Heart of Empire: Puerto Rican Workers on U.S. Farms*, University of California Press, Oakland 2020; M. Nishitani and H. Lee, 'Becoming "Overstayers": The Coloniality and the Resilience of Pacific Farm Workers' in V. Stead and J. Altman (eds), *Labour Lines and Colonial Power: Indigenous and Pacific Islander Labour Mobility in Australia*, Australian National University Press, Canberra 2019, pp. 159–184 ("These poor conditions, including the exploitation and ill-treatment of [Seasonal Worker Programme] employees, have now been well documented and have received considerable media and scholarly attention. There is some recognition by the Australian Government of these problems, as indicated by the inclusion of testimony on the SWP within the

authorized "compulsory cultivation as a method of precaution against famine or a deficiency of food supplies."[130] Enslaved Africans were also massively employed in domestic work, and to this day, workers in this sector remain overwhelmingly racialized.[131] As for the mining industry, it has been particularly involved in practices of forced labour.[132] These historical continuities of exploitation within industries that are essential for human survival and social reproduction and hire a great number of marginalized people militate against the discourse of exceptionality of human suffering within the world's economy, but rather speaks to the continued relationship between capitalism and marginalization.

5 Usefulness of the Appellation of Contemporary Forms of Slavery: Erasing the Past and Overlooking Context

The appellation 'contemporary forms of slavery' does not bear any distinct legal consequences. It is part of a narrative used to describe severe forms of exploitation, formally defined through various legal concepts such as slavery, trafficking, forced labour, child labour. The use of the word 'slavery' is no accident: it is powerful and elicits the need to condemn the contemporary forms of human exploitation that it decries.[133] But the state dissociation from the legacies of the global institution of slavery should tell us something. The associative use of the moral indignation against slavery seems not to lead to the obvious parallel – that is the systemic character of the labour exploitation – but rather to the aberrations. It leaves the structures in place. This, then, is not abolition.

As some rapporteurs have noted, uprooted from its institutional framing, the word 'slavery' can easily be trivialized.[134] Blending all forms of severe

---

inquiry into establishing a Modern Slavery Act in Australia, conducted in 2017 by the Joint Standing Committee of the Department for Foreign Affairs, Defence and Trade. Yet, the government's focus remains mainly on the illegal status of those who breach their contracts" at p. 169).

130 Art. 19, deleted pursuant to Article 7 of the Protocol of 2014 to the Forced Labour Convention, 1930; see also Dorssemont, Belgium national report.

131 A. Blackett, above n. 38.

132 See e.g. Goguen, Canada national report; and Dehaibi, Peru national report.

133 A. Blackett, 'On the Presence of the Past in the Future of International Labour Law' (2020) 43:2 *Dalhousie Law Journal* 947, p. 958.

134 See Haynes, Barbados and St. Vincent & The Grenadines national report; and Selman Ayetey, Ghana national report.

exploitation together under the general umbrella of 'slavery' also has the effect of evading the necessary exercise of recognizing the historical continuities between the global institution of slavery and current inequities in contemporary legal institutions, like labour law or migration law, through racial capitalism.

The lack of contextualization not only trivializes the horrors of the transatlantic slave trade, but it may also affect the response to specific forms of exploitation grouped under the appellation 'contemporary' slavery. The case of child labour in the traditional fishing industry mentioned in the Ghana report offers an illustrative example of this, since the abstract criminalization of child labour automatically blocks engagement with cultural history, leading to potential backlash and rejection of the legal framework against contemporary forms of slavery. The criminalization relies on the core idea that they impede human dignity and therefore must be forcefully prohibited. In fact, many countries have started using more systematically the language of human dignity as a common denominator between past and current forms of severe human exploitation and suffering, thus moving away from the property-personal liberty nexus.[135] But the language of 'human dignity' is unhelpful if it does not engage with localized lived experiences, which include complex networks of social and cultural relationships.[136]

Combining all forms of exploitation under a vaguely defined concept with limited legal applicability is at best unhelpful, and at worst, turns attention away from addressing systemic causes. If slavery in global value chains is not exceptional and extreme, but rather part of the structural organization, then a punitive, criminal law lens that seeks to separate out and punish only the most extreme, individualized examples will fail to redress exploitation.[137]

In other words, to treat these instances as exceptional is also part of the process of 'othering' the problem, which affects the response to victims. Domestic

135 See e.g., France's inclusion of 'violation of dignity' in Loi n° 2013-711 du 5 août 2013 portant diverses dispositions d'adaptation dans le domaine de la justice an application du droit de l'Union européenne et des engagements internationaux de la France (documented in Boissard and Pluen, France national report); and Peru's inclusion of 'crimes against human dignity' in its Penal Code (documented in Dehaibi, Peru national report).

136 See M. Mutua, 'Human Rights in Africa: The Limited Promise of Liberalism' (2008) 51:1 *African Studies Review* 17; M. Mutua, 'The Complexity of Universalism in Human Rights' in A. Sajó, (ed), *Human Rights with Modesty: The Problem of Universalism*, Springer, Berlin 2004; and S.E. Merry and P. Levitt. 'The Vernacularization of Women's Human Rights' in S. Hopgood, J. Snyder and L. Vinjamuri (eds), *Human Rights Futures*, Cambridge University Press, Cambridge 2017.

137 A. Blackett, above n. 133, p. 958.

systems may develop protective and reparative schemes for victims of human trafficking, granting for instance temporary residence for migrants if they collaborate in the criminal proceedings,[138] but means of prevention are lacking. Notably, many rapporteurs mentioned how migrant workers are marginalized by the structural constraints imposed on their freedom of movement and of choice by immigration laws,[139] yet none have reported legislative action to correct that. In fact, it has been argued that state action related to human trafficking is not incompatible with attempts to assert control over national borders in a context of globalization. In other words, anti-trafficking rules may serve to appease "anxieties over state authority" rather than concretely end human exploitation.[140]

After more than twenty years of the Palermo Protocol, successful prosecution of cases of human trafficking or forced labour in the reporting countries are episodic, not because actual cases are few (many countries rather report increasing numbers),[141] but because legal operators often struggle to meet the stringent burden of proof for these crimes.[142] The fact that trafficking has been equated with slavery is not foreign to that, since it puts a higher evidentiary threshold where the type of exploitation evaluated must show a level of control so high that it equates to the exercise of attributes of ownership.[143] A recent civil case in Canada, *Attorney General of Canada v. Manoukian*,[144] offers an example of this, when the Québec Court of Appeal confirmed the Superior Court's decision that the employment circumstances of a domestic worker, while highly exploitative and in violation of the province's labour and employment laws, did not equate to trafficking.[145]

---

138 See e.g. Dorssemont, Belgium national report; Skupień and Pisarcyk, Poland national report; and Senčur Peček, Slovenia national report.

139 See e.g. Goguen, Canada national report; and Laleta, Škorić and Kotulovski, Croatia national report.

140 See M. Khan, above n. 83.

141 See e.g., Hungler and Zaccaria, Hungary national report; Hayakawa, Japan national report; and Rombouts, Netherlands national report. Processes of globalization are said to contribute to the increase in cases, see A. Crane, G. LeBaron, J. Allain and L. Behbahani, 'Governance gaps in eradicating forced labor: From global to domestic supply chains' (2019) 13:1 *Regulation & Governance* 86, p. 87.

142 See e.g., Rombouts, Netherlands national report.

143 See *Rantsev v. Cyprus and Russia*, no. 25965/04, ECHR 2010; See e.g., Laleta, Škorić and Kotulovski, Croatia national report; Hungler and Zaccaria, Hungary national report; and Dehaibi, Peru national report.

144 *Attorney General of Canada v. Manoukian*, 2020 QCCA 1486.

145 Troublingly, this enabled an action in defamation to be pursued. See also *P.T. v. Mohammed Naqeeeb*, 2021 QCCS 1378 (finding a violation of labour laws by the employers

Decisions of this nature give pause from a labour law perspective, particularly when the national reports suggest a diversion away from robust redress of labour exploitation through labour law. This is something that has been particularly criticized in sex work advocacy, given that most sex work performed is reported not to be coerced, yet the only mechanisms that exist to protect sex workers is through anti-trafficking legislation.[146] But has the anti-trafficking movement failed to significantly reduce the frequency of sex trafficking?[147] Does it actually protect the 'victim'? As workers in an industry that is often illegal, sex workers are less likely to denounce violence and criminal acts, increasing their marginalization. Rather than embalming the issue in an anti-trafficking frame, should labour lawyers not be looking more closely at whether decriminalization of sex work can offer more effective tools to protect sex workers' rights, including by reducing the incidence of coercion and exploitation?[148] Without purporting to answer this weighty question, it should be noted that a consequence of decriminalization would be that labour laws and other social protections – including occupational safety and health laws – would apply to sex workers.

It is not surprising that the national rapporteurs underscore the importance of redressing labour exploitation through robust labour administrations sufficiently well-funded and staffed to be able to carry out comprehensive, proactive labour inspections.[149] These rooted labour law responses take us back to the pivotal role of the state in redressing labour exploitation, systemically and contextually. That contextual approach will be incomplete unless it

---

of a domestic worker, accepting the expert testimony on the meaning of forced labour in international law, but finding that no forced labour had occurred).

146 R. Andrijasevic and N. Mai, above n. 101.

147 Interviews conducted by the organization Decriminalize Sex Work reported that trafficking victims in the U.S. sex industry had been arrested an average of seven times during the course of their exploitation, showing the failures to combat sex trafficking through criminalization. Decriminalize Sex Work, 'Human Trafficking and Sex Work,' <https://decriminalizesex.work/why-decriminalization/briefing-papers/human-trafficking-and-sex-work/>.

148 I.K. Thiemann, above n. 103. See the work of NGO Decriminalize Sex Work at <https://decriminalizesex.work/>. The World Health Organization also refers to studies indicating that decriminalization would have a positive influence on reducing HIV infections in sex workers (see *Consolidated guidelines on HIV, viral hepatitis and STI prevention, diagnosis, treatment and care for key populations*, World Health Organization, Geneva 2022, <https://www.who.int/publications/i/item/9789240052390>).

149 See e.g., Pittard and Hallal, Australia national report; Goguen, Canada national report; Laleta, Škorić and Kotulovski, Croatia national report; Hungler and Zaccaria, Hungary national report; Rombouts, Netherlands national report; and Skupień and Pisarcyk, Poland national report.

engages with continuing, intersecting patterns of subordination on the basis of historically-constructed difference.

6 Redressing and Recalibrating Contemporary Slavery

6.1 *Redressing Contemporary Slavery*

Legislative initiatives have been multiplying to redress contemporary slavery, many of which concern intervention in the global supply chains. The sectors named above are integrated in one way or another to global supply chains which complexify employment and service relationships and therefore favour exploitation.[150] This situation has prompted the adoption of the UN Guiding Principles on Business and Human Rights (2011).[151] That same year, the OECD revised its *Guidelines for Multinational Enterprises* to incorporate a human rights chapter and "a new and comprehensive approach to due diligence and responsible supply chain management."[152] Most legal innovations in the Global North in the past few years targeting forced labour and child labour in global supply chains have entailed legislation imposing an obligation of due diligence to certain businesses.[153]

There are two emerging approaches highlighted by several of the national rapporteurs, reflecting distinct conceptualizations of 'modern slavery.' The first is epitomized by the UK Modern Slavery Act 2015,[154] and has been a source of

150 J. Fudge, 'Regulating for Decent Work in a Global Economy' (2018) 43:2 *New Zealand Journal of Employment Relations* 10.

151 The influence of Alliance 8.7 is less clear. Many rapporteurs indicated their country's participation to it, but very little substantiated on the impact it has had. For contextual information on the adoption of the UN Guiding Principles, see one of its authors' reflective recounting of the process in J.G. Ruggie, 'The Social Construction of the UN Guiding Principles on Business and Human Rights' in S. Deva and D. Birchall (eds), *Research Handbook on Human Rights and Business*, Edward Elgar Publishing, Cheltenham 2020.

152 See Foreword notes of *OECD Guidelines for Multinational Enterprises* (2011), <http://dx.doi.org/10.1787/9789264115415-en>. The OECD has since adopted various due diligence guides, including one specifically for mineral supply chains. For a detailed account on the OECD Guidelines, see Rombouts, Netherlands national report.

153 See e.g., Pittard and Hallal, Australia national report; Fouladvand, United Kingdom national report; Fechner, Germany national report; and Boissard and Pluen, France national report. Similar legislation have been reported to be in the works in Goguen, Canada national report, and Rombouts, Netherlands national report. Skupień and Pisarcyk, Poland national report, and Senčur Peček, Slovenia national report, have both reported the adoption of action plans to encourage businesses to adopt principles of due diligence.

154 *Modern Slavery Act* 2015 (2015 c. 30), <https://www.legislation.gov.uk/ukpga/2015/30/contents/enacted>. The British Report focuses on historical slavery, but key scholarship

inspiration for draft legislation emerging from other jurisdictions.[155] A model based on criminal enforcement with a significant immigration law thrust creating a "hostile environment for illegal migrants,"[156] it includes corporate transparency features rather than more robust due diligence mechanisms.[157]

Another model, reflective of the French Law of 27 March 2017 on the 'Duty of Vigilance' focuses more rigorously on due diligence reporting for large enterprises.[158] It includes a deliberately broad framing of the notion of the enterprise, built on "established commercial relationships," but would exclude "indirect" subcontractors, and as a National Assembly review underscores, would lead it to miss subcontractors such as those implicated in the Rana Plaza tragedy.[159] It is worth pointing out that even the most robust legislation on due diligence,

---

abounds on the Modern Slavery legislation, see e.g. V. Mantouvalou, 'The UK Modern Slavery Act 2015 Three Years On' (2018) 81:6 *The Modern Law Review* 1017; J. Haynes, 'The Modern Slavery Act (2015): A Legislative Commentary' (2016) 37:1 *Statute Law Review* 33; and O. Martin-Ortega, 'Due Diligence, Reporting and Transparency in Supply Chains: The United Kingdom Modern Slavery Act' in A. Bonfanti (ed), *Business and Human Rights in Europe: International Law Challenges*, Rutledge, New York 2018, pp. 110–121.

155 See e.g. Goguen, Canada national report, on *An Act to enact the Modern Slavery Act and to amend the Customs Tariff* S-216 2020; and Pittard and Hallal, Australia national report, on the *Modern Slavery Act* 2018 (No. 153).

156 J. Fudge, 'Why Labour Lawyers Should Care About the Modern Slavery Act 2015' (2018) 29(3) *King's Law Journal* 377, 378.

157 For a thorough discussion of the UK Modern Slavery Act 2015 and its difficult relationship to labour law enforcement, see J. Fudge, above n. 156. Most notably, the UK Modern Slavery Act, just like its Australian equivalent, imposes a reporting obligation on the steps taken to prevent slavery and human trafficking in the supply chains, but does not impose any obligation to take such steps, see *Modern Slavery Act* 2015 (2015 c. 30), above n. 154. This is made clear in Section 54(4)b): "[or] a statement that the organisation has taken no such steps." On the limits of this due diligence reporting mechanism, see J. Ford and J. Nolan, 'Regulating Transparency on Human Rights and Modern Slavery in Corporate Supply Chains: The Discrepancy Between Human Rights Due Diligence and the Social Audit' (2020) 26:1 *Australian Journal of Human Rights* 27.

158 See *Loi n° 2017-399 du 27 mars 2017 relative au devoir de vigilance des sociétés mères et des entreprises donneuses d'ordre*.

159 Assemblée nationale, *Rapport d'information déposé en application de l'article 145-7 du Règlement par la Commission des lois constitutionnelles, de la législation et de l'administration générale de la République sur l'évaluation de la loi du 27 mars 2017 relative au devoir de vigilance des sociétés mères et des entreprises donneuses d'ordre* (24 février 2022), N° 5124, <https://www.assemblee-nationale.fr/dyn/15/rapports/cion_lois/l15b5124_rapport-information>. For a consolidated evaluation of the French model, see E. Savourey and S. Brabant, 'The French Law on the Duty of Vigilance: Theoretical and Practical Challenges Since its Adoption' (2021) 6:1 *Business and Human Rights Journal* 141. For a review of the challenges and opportunities of human rights due diligence mechanisms in the garment industry, see J. Nolan 'Chasing the Next Shiny Thing: Can Human Rights Due Diligence Effectively Address Labour Exploitation in Global Fashion Supply Chains?' (2022) 11:2 *International Journal for Crime, Justice and Social Democracy* 1.

like the French model, usually only covers particularly large corporations (evaluated either based on the number of employees or on annual income).[160] Consequently, some applicability issues may arise in light of the very nature of global supply chains and transnational labour markets. Evaluating the number of employees, for instance, may be difficult based on the presence of informal labour relationships, subcontracting and the use of temporary workers in the global supply chains.[161]

Despite these limitations, the French model has understandably gained significant traction for its ability to move around the strictures of private international law.[162] It has also been closely reviewed, including through a 2022 French National Assembly review, pointing out the challenges with many of the reporting requirements.[163] Ultimately, though, it draws litigation towards the home state of the corporation itself.[164]

The French model has served as inspiration for the development of due diligence reporting guidelines at EU level, which has been favourably commented upon by national rapporteurs.[165] In February 2022, the European Commission agreed on a proposal for EU Directives on Corporate Sustainability Due Diligence,[166] which was approved by the Council of the European Union in May

160 See e.g., the Modern Slavery Act as documented in Pittard and Hallal, Australia national report; bill S-216 as documented in Goguen, Canada national report; the Companies Act, which implements Directive 2014/95/EU, as documented in Senčur Peček, Slovenia national report; the Law on Corporate Due Diligence in Supply Chains as documented in Fechner, Germany national report; and the recent proposal for a Due Diligence direction by the European Commission as documented in Rombouts, Netherlands national report.

161 See e.g., in the mining industry, discussed in Dehaibi, Peru national report, or in the agricultural industry, in L. Dehaibi, above n. 129; A.M. Weiler, J. McLaughlin and D.C. Cole, above n. 129 ; and E. Reid-Musson, above n. 129.

162 See É. Pataut, 'Le devoir de vigilance : Aspects de droit international privé' (2017) 10 *Droit Social 833*, <https://halshs.archives-ouvertes.fr/halshs-02200261/document>. ("La herse de fer qui sépare les ordres juridiques les uns des autres reste baissée et la règle de conflit de lois reste encore la technique principale de rattachement, avec ses qualités mais aussi ses défauts, dont le principal – ne permettre le rattachement qu'à un seul ordre juridique – reste indépassable.")

163 Assemblée nationale, above n. 159. See also assessment in E. Savourey and S. Brabant, above n. 159.

164 It should be noted that several of the recommendations pertain to rendering the civil responsibility regime more amenable to victims of labour abuse. Recommendation No. 2 speaks to reversing the burden of proof; Recommendation No. 3 calls for specific tribunals to be rendered specially competent in this matter.

165 See e.g. Rombouts, Netherlands national report and Goguen, Canada national report.

166 Proposal for a Directive of the European Parliament and of the Council on Corporate Sustainability Due Diligence and amending Directive (EU) 2019/1937 [2022] COM(2022) 71 final 2022/0051 (COD), <https://eur-lex.europa.eu/legal-content/EN/TXT/?uri=CELEX%3A52022PC0071>.

2024. The purpose of these Directives is to offer a common standard for all EU members in a context of proliferation of national initiatives regarding due diligence in the global supply chains. An innovation of the EU directives is that they would apply to companies with lower turnover and less employees, but which are considered to be part of high impact sectors (e.g., garment, agriculture, mineral extraction) and also to third-country companies involved in the EU market.[167] The EU's recognition of the need to respond globally and horizontally to problems that are global in nature is an encouraging step forward.[168]

It is worth mentioning that legislation on global supply chains, just like earlier prohibitions of slavery or anti-trafficking legislation, runs the risk of displacing the problem, if their premise is that problems of forced labour happen elsewhere than on the territory of countries that have adopted such legislation.[169] The legislation extends the jurisdictional reach of human rights through multinational enterprises headquartered in the Global North, into countries of the Global South where the protections are presumed to be lacking due to lower levels of development. Consider that the MNEs in question have higher annual earnings than the GDP of many of the countries in which they carry out their work. Their power is disproportionate. But that power is also disproportionate vis-à-vis the subcontractors and other local service providers with whom they interact. The requirements at best set in place a pattern of reporting. However, the challenge remains that they might similarly fail to yield responsibility for the perpetuation of these practices, and worse, might create legitimacy around corporate actors for their due diligence efforts. Why, if the matter is as serious as slavery, child labour, and grave occupational safety and health violations including building collapse leading to mass death, is the responsibility to respect fundamental labour rights not one of means, but of results?

Surrounding modern slavery legislation are broader initiatives to redress corporate action through concerted action or home-jurisdiction initiatives. While the UN Guiding Principles on Business and Human Rights were referenced by some rapporteurs for their framework of responsibility through the 'protect, respect and remedy' framework, alongside classic mechanisms like the OECD Guidelines and the initiatives in Alliance 8.7 to which some states

167 *Ibid.*

168 See e.g., *ibid*:

> [...] Member States' legislation alone in the area is unlikely to be sufficient and efficient. As regards specific transboundary problems, such as pollution, climate change, biodiversity etc. individual action is hampered in case of inaction by other Member States [...] Furthermore, risks resulting from adverse human rights and environment impacts present in companies' value chains have often cross-border effects (e.g. pollution, transnational supply and value chains).

169 See on this A. Crane, G. LeBaron, J. Allain and L. Behbahani, above n. 141.

had joined but for which there was little concrete awareness of actions, attention was turned instead to mechanisms emerging through national legislation to put in place the UN Guiding Principles and focus national efforts on redressing labour exploitation. Notably, the Canadian rapporteur identified the Canadian Ombudsperson for Responsible Enterprise as one legislatively created example, which includes significant investigative powers. A host of alternative dispute resolution mechanisms in a complaints-based structure are also gaining prominence and attention, but Professor Surya Deva, Vice-Chairperson of the UN Working Group on Business and Human Rights, has called for it to meet the effectiveness criteria in Principle 31 of the UN Guiding Principles on Business and Human Rights, to have the full power to "investigate, compel documents and testimony, and enforce its recommendations against companies."[170] The goal, according to the UN Working Group, is not only to remediate but to prevent overseas human rights abuses.

It is important also to acknowledge movement in trade agreements, such as the Canada-U.S.-Mexico Agreement underscored by the Canadian rapporteur for the specific prohibition on the importation of slave labour and the innovative compliance and enforcement mechanisms put in place to ensure respect of Chapter 23 on Labour.[171] The European Commission is also working on a proposal to prohibit importation of products made by forced labour.[172]

It is the link to litigation that is finding important entry points in other jurisdictions, directly through transnational litigation. In Canada, the *Nevsun* decision is pathbreaking: Justice Abella's 5–4 majority decision accepts the possibility of jurisdiction on customary international law – notably *jus cogens* norms. The majority explicitly considered international law "partly *our* law,"[173]

---

170 United Nations Human Rights Procedures, Statement by Mr. Surya Deva, Vice Chairperson, Working Group on the issue of human rights and transnational corporations and other business enterprises at the Canadian House of Commons (23.03.2021), <https://www.ohchr.org/sites/default/files/Statement-re-CORE-2021.pdf>.

171 Goguen, Canada national report. See also Haynes, Barbados and St. Vincent & The Grenadines national report (CARICOM draft Investment Code, which, although not currently incorporated, "seeks to impose certain minimum human rights and labour standards" for foreign investors").

172 Communication from the Commission to the European Parliament, the Council and the European Economic and Social Committee on decent work worldwide for a global just transition and a sustainable recovery, COM/2022/66 final, <https://eur-lex.europa.eu/legal-content/EN/TXT/PDF/?uri=CELEX:52022DC0066&from=EN>. Note however that these initiatives tend to underplay the presence of forced labour in domestic supply chains, including in high income countries who profit the most from forced labour, see generally A. Crane, G. LeBaron, J. Allain and L. Behbahani, above n. 141.

173 *Nevsun Resources Ltd. v. Araya*, 2020 SCC 5 at para 94, citing S.J. Toope, 'Inside and Out: The Stories of International Law and Domestic Law' (2001) 50 *University of New Brunswick Law Journal* 23.

thus joining the "choir" of domestic court judgments around the world shaping the "substance of international law."[174] In *Nevsun*, three Eritrean workers and refugees to Canada, Gize Yeboyo Araya, Kesete Tekle Fshazion and Mihretab Yemane Tekle, brought charges in British Columbia for breaches of domestic tort law and breaches of customary international law against forced labour, slavery, cruel, inhuman or degrading treatment, and crimes against humanity, conditions they and over 1,000 other workers allegedly faced through a national service program compelling them to work in Bisha gold, copper and zinc mine between 2008 and 2012.[175] Nevsun, the Vancouver-headquartered mining company operating in Eritrea through subsidiaries and holding 60% shares in Bisha mine, brought a motion to strike on the basis of the "act of state doctrine" arguing that Canadian courts were precluded from assessing the sovereign acts of foreign governments. They also argued that the claims based on customary international law had no reasonable prospect of success so should be struck.[176]

The majority acknowledged that the act of state doctrine is "a known (and heavily criticized) doctrine in England and Australia" adding that it has, "by contrast, played no role in Canadian law."[177] Rather, Canadian law has relied on the twin principles of conflicts of laws and judicial restraint.[178] Customary international law, unlike conflict of laws jurisprudence, is not a matter of foreign law – formal proof by evidence was therefore not required. Justice Abella accepted that crimes against humanity generally and slavery specifically are violations of *jus cogens* norms, adding that forced labour is at least a rule of customary international law while citing the ILO's Commission of Inquiry Report on Myanmar for the principle that it is indeed a *jus cogens* norm.[179]

Nevsun's contention that as a corporation, it is immune to liability was rejected under an evolutive understanding of international law.[180] No Canadian

174 *Nevsun Resources Ltd. v. Araya*, 2020 SCC 5 at para 72, citing O. Grady Shwartz, 'International Law and National Courts: Between Mutual Empowerment and Mutual Weakening' (2015) 23 *Cardozo Journal of International and Comparative Law* 587, p. 616.

175 *Nevsun Resources Ltd. v. Araya*, 2020 SCC 5 at paras 2–7.

176 *Ibid.*, at paras 5–7.

177 *Ibid.*, at para 28.

178 *Ibid.*, at para 44. The majority affirmed the importance of considering human rights of foreign states in a number of contexts, including extradition and deportation cases (at paras 47–59).

179 *Ibid.*, at paras 100–102. The prohibition against cruel, inhuman and degrading treatment was referred to as an "absolute right" (at para 103).

180 *Ibid.*, at para 113 (with the caveat that for norms that are of a strictly interstate character, a trial judge would need to make specific determinations on the norms and whether the common law should evolve to extend their scope to bind corporations). For Jason Haynes, this was a "seemingly cowardly approach" (J. Haynes, 'The Shifting Pendulum: Foreign

laws were considered to conflict with the adoption of the breaches of customary international law, or *jus cogens* norms, as part of the common law.[181]

The watershed character of the *Nevsun* decision has been widely acknowledged by learned commentators,[182] recognizing that customary international law can inform the evolving nature and content of the common law of torts. As Walton argues:

> By reinvigorating the function of the common law in customary international law claims, the Nevsun majority offers a rebuttal to the argument that international law is as of yet underspecified in relation to corporations, significantly disarming the dissent. Far from stretching international law, as the dissent contends, the majority's approach can instead be read as relatively modest in relation to it. Each of the claims at issue – the direct customary claims and the torts – in reality entails a combination of domestic and international law.[183]

Several commentators have underscored the decision's importance for other common law jurisdictions worldwide,[184] while engaging closely with potential break given the strength of the dissenting reasoning.[185]

It is broadly agreed that whatever promise lies in the *Nevsun* model will ultimately depend on the nature of that very particular kind of case that is

---

Investors' Liability Under Canada's Common Law for Breaches of Customary International Law' (2021) 36 *Canadian Journal of Law and Society* 447, p. 458).

181 *Nevsun Resources Ltd. v. Araya*, 2020 SCC 5 at para 114 (note that at para 115, the Supreme Court majority referenced the creation of the Canadian Ombudsperson for Responsible Enterprise). The partial dissent by Justices Brown and Rowe vigorously critiqued this reasoning, including its reliance on law review articles to establish the claim.

182 See e.g., B.A. Walton, 'Nevsun Resources Ltd. v. Araya' (2021) 115:1 *American Journal of International Law* 107, p. 112 (acknowledging that "*Nevsun* also charts a novel course for transnational human rights litigation. While the Nevsun majority and dissent debate whether the plaintiffs' international law claims are better conceived of as claims under customary international law directly or as new domestic torts inspired by it, both approaches stand in contrast to recent routes taken in other courts.").

183 *Ibid.*, p. 113.

184 See A. Aseeva, 'UK and Canada Domestic Courts' Game-changing Rulings and International Custom: A Dress Rehearsal for Global Sustainability Law?' [2020] *Harvard International Law Journal*, at <https://journals.law.harvard.edu/ilj/2020/06/uk-and-canada-domestic-courts-game-changing-rulings-and-international-custom/>; and J. Haynes, above n. 180 (arguing that the decision is of "fundamental importance to the international investment community because … it arguably has the effect of rebalancing the traditionally uneven relationship between foreign investor and host states" at pp. 447–448).

185 J. Haynes, above n. 180, pp. 460–464.

ultimately brought forward for decision on the substance. The mining company involved in *Nevsun*, not surprisingly, settled this matter out of court.[186]

Crucial recent developments, beyond regional decisions mentioned above, such as the July 2022 UK Supreme Court decision of *Basfar* v. *Wong*,[187] attest to a growing recognition of the need to address hard cases through a principled approach to the law that allows it to evolve. In *Basfar*, the majority found that the exception to diplomatic immunity for "commercial activity" could apply to domestic workers subject to trafficking, forced labour or domestic servitude in the course of employment.[188]

6.2 *Recalibrating the Contemporary Law of Slavery*

These foregrounded initiatives suggest the extent to which the contemporary law of slavery needs not only to be redressing slavery, but also recalibrating the law. The deeply unequal architecture in the governance of labour in the contemporary economy is at the core of this reflection. Capital through investment rules enjoys strong international treaty-based protections.[189] The world trading system enshrines the trade in goods and most services in a multilateral framework, however significant the current institutional challenges to multilateralism may be.[190] But labour mobility through a regime of reasonable labour market access is at best aspirational. The regulation of labour remains resolutely tied to the local, and that regulation has been allowed to lag. Initiatives to regulate slavery in its contemporary form are, or should be, initiatives to rethink transnational labour regulation. They are, in other words, at the core of labour law as understood transnationally including the movement of persons.[191]

---

186 Y. Brend, 'Landmark settlement is a message to Canadian companies extracting resources overseas: Amnesty International' (23.10.2020) CBC *News*, <https://www.cbc.ca/news/canada/british-columbia/settlement-amnesty-scc-africa-mine-nevsun-1.5774910>.

187 *Basfar v. Wong* [2022] UKSC 20, 6 July 2022.

188 For a particularly prescient comment, see J. Haynes, 'Revisiting the relationship between human trafficking and diplomatic immunity' (2023) 139:1 Law Quarterly Review 204.

189 The terms of the unequal exchange are increasingly contested. For an initial challenge to the asymmetry, see G. Abi-Saab, 'The Newly Independent States and the Rules of International Law: An Outline' (1962) 8 *Howard Law Journal* 95. South Africa has been one of the leaders in revisiting the framework. The Canada-U.S.-Mexico Agreement revisits investor-state dispute resolution but retains it vis-à-vis Mexico.

190 See e.g. A. Blackett, *Trade Liberalization, Labour Law, and Development: A Contextualization*, ILO (International Institute for Labour Studies), Geneva 2007, <https://labordoc.ilo.org/discovery/fulldisplay/alma994022153402676/41ILO_INST:41ILO_V2>.

191 A. Blackett, 'Theorizing Emancipatory Futures of International Labor Law' (2019) 113 *AJIL Unbound* 391; A. Blackett, above n. 133; and A. Blackett, 'On Social Regionalism in Transnational Labour Law' (2020) 159:4 International Labour Review 591.

The most significant feature, therefore, is the capacity to underscore, through the national studies, how limited and experimental the existing legal tools appear to be in actually redressing slavery in its contemporary forms. They call for a recalibration.

Perhaps as argued throughout this general report, the most challenging, yet urgent, dimension of the recalibration emerges out of the history of transatlantic slavery. The criminalization model that assumes that slavery is an aberration takes us away from seeing the extent to which, like the institution of slavery, labour exploitation has become part and parcel of the transnational business model, one that is constituted and sustained through law. The recalibration is a structural one.

A related recalibration flows out of the focus on who is particularly susceptible to enslavement. The histories of subjugation have been lost, and their legacies in the systemic patterns that lead to overrepresentation of black and brown bodies in labour exploitation warrants close attention and some rethinking of the very definitions – not to increase the burden of establishing slavery but rather to see the patterns that need to be redressed.[192] In this regard, Professor Fudge presciently cautions that "law is constitutive of 'free' wage labour" and that the labour contract in particular in Steinberg's terms, that "is an institutional process through which domination is realized."[193] She expresses a wariness of the search for the right legal definition, if one is not alive to the ways in which the process itself can serve to enhance state coercive power over workers' bodies,[194] rather than redressing labour exploitation. While some turn to analysing the relationship between slavery and free labour on a continuum, even that runs the risk of flattening out, in Catherine Costello's terms, the "different forms of work relations that are legal institutions, not only distinguished by their degree of freedom or voluntariness, but also institutionalized and underpinned by different regulatory forms" such as a "distinctive law of slavery" alongside the range of legal fields including criminal law and property law.[195] The constitutive role of law in and beyond slavery requires more attention than might traditionally be acknowledged.

---

192 A. Blackett, above n. 54.

193 See J. Fudge, 'Modern Slavery, Unfree Labour and the Labour Market: The Social Dynamics of Legal Characterization' (2018) 27 *Social & Legal Studies* 414, p. 419, citing M. Steinberg, *England's Great Transformation: Law, Labor and the Industrial Revolution* University of Chicago Press, Chicago 2016, p. 32.

194 J. Fudge, above n. 193, p. 424.

195 See C. Costello, 'Migrants and Forced Labour: A Labour Law Response' in A. Bogg, A. Davies and J. Prassl (eds), *The Autonomy of Labour Law*, Hart, Oxford 2015, p. 200. See also J. Fudge, above n. 193, p. 421.

The next set of recalibrations emerges quite directly from taking labour law seriously, resolutely returning to it as a basis for redressing widescale labour exploitation. That might seem counterintuitive given the challenges of holding multinational enterprises accountable across global value chains. However, Jennifer Gordon's research on joint liability in recruitment chains offers promising responses;[196] it is framed as an 'opportunity for intervention' in the face of the barriers to direct regulation of recruiters. Reinforced labour inspections are a hallmark and an area in which commitment of resources has lagged.[197] What corporate social responsibility initiatives have come to supplant may be precisely what labour lawyers should seek to revitalize.

Academic References

A. Aseeva, 'UK and Canada Domestic Courts' Game-changing Rulings and International Custom: A Dress Rehearsal for Global Sustainability Law?' (2020) *Harvard International Law Journal.*

A.A. Smith, 'Bunk House Rules: Housing Migrant Labour in Ontario' (2015) *Osgoode Legal Studies Research Paper Series* 98.

A. Blackett, 'Emancipation in the Idea of Labour Law' in G. Davidov and B. Langille (eds), *The Idea of Labour Law,* Oxford University Press, Oxford 2011, pp. 420–436.

A. Blackett, *Everyday Transgressions: Domestic Workers' Transnational Challenge to International Labor Law*, Cornell University Press, Ithaca 2019.

A. Blackett, 'Follow the Drinking Gourd: Our Road to Teaching Critical Race Theory and Slavery and the Law, Contemplatively, at McGill' (2017) 62:4 *McGill Law Journal* 1251.

196 See notably J. Gordon, *Global Labour Recruitment in a Supply Chain Context* (2015) International Labour Organization (Fundamentals Working Papers), Geneva 2015, <https://www.ilo.org/wcmsp5/groups/public/---dgreports/---dcomm/documents/publication/wcms_377805.pdf>. Gordon's focus is on reshaping recruitment services by focusing on "employers in destination countries at the top of the labour supply chain" and builds on regulatory initiatives in the Philippines, the Netherlands, the United Kingdom, as well as select Canadian provinces, alongside agreements between U.S. employers and agricultural workers (at p. 3).

197 See M.J. Piore, 'Enforcement of Labour Standards in Developing Countries: Challenges and Solutions' in M. Chen and F. Carré (eds), *The Informal Economy Revisited: Examining the Past, Envisioning the Future*, Routledge, London 2021; and S. Mustchin and M. Martínez Lucio, 'The Fragmenting Occupation of Labour Inspection and the Degradation of Regulatory and Enforcement Work Inside the British State' (2023) 44:2 *Economic and Industrial Democracy Economic and Industrial Democracy*, 526.

A. Blackett, 'Global Governance, Legal Pluralism and the Decentered State: A Labor Law Critique of Codes of Corporate Conduct' (2001) 8:2 *Indiana Journal of Global Legal Studies* 401.

A. Blackett, 'On Social Regionalism in Transnational Labour Law' (2020) 159:4 *International Labour Review* 591.

A. Blackett, 'On the Presence of the Past in the Future of International Labour Law' (2020) 43:2 *Dalhousie Law Journal* 947.

A. Blackett, 'Racial Capitalism and the Contemporary International Law on Slavery: (Re)membering Hacienda Brasil Verde' (2022) 25 *Journal of International Economic Law* 334.

A. Blackett, 'Situated Reflections on International Labour Law, Capabilities, and Decent Work: The Case of Centre Maraîcher Eugène Guinois' (2007) *Quebec Journal of International Law* 223.

A. Blackett, 'Slavery Is Not a Metaphor: Contemporary Slavery: Popular Rhetoric and Political Practice' (2018) 66 *American Journal of Comparative Law* 927.

A. Blackett, 'Theorizing Emancipatory Futures of International Labor Law' (2019) 113 *AJIL Unbound* 391.

A. Blackett, *Trade Liberalization, Labour Law, and Development: A Contextualization*, ILO (International Institute for Labour Studies), Geneva 2007.

A. Blackett and A. Duquesnoy, 'Slavery Is Not a Metaphor: U.S. Prison Labor and Racial Subordination through the Lens of the ILO's Abolition of Forced Labor Convention' (2021) 67:6 *UCLA Law Review* 1504.

A.C. Martineau, 'Contested Histories: Revisiting the Relationship Between International Law and Slavery' in S. Chalmers and S. Pahuja (eds), *Routledge Handbook of International Law and Humanities,* Routledge, London 2021, pp. 279–289.

A. Crane, G. Lebaron, J. Allain and L. Behbahani, 'Governance gaps in eradicating forced labor: From global to domestic supply chains' (2019) 13:1 *Regulation & Governance* 86.

A. Getachew, *Worldmaking after Empire: The Rise and Fall of Self-Determination*, Princeton University Press, Princeton 2019.

A.M. Weiler, J. McLaughlin and D.C. Cole, 'Food Security at Whose Expense? A Critique of the Canadian Temporary Farm Labour Migration Regime and Proposals for Change' (2017) 55:4 *International Migration* 48.

A. Oprea, 'The Arranged Marriage of Ana Maria Cioaba, Intra-Community Oppression and Romani Feminist Ideals: Transcending the "Primitive Culture" Argument' (2005) 12:2 *European Journal of Women's Studies* 133.

B. Arneil, 'Trade, Plantations, and Property: John Locke and the Economic Defense of Colonialism' (1994) 55 *Journal of the History of Ideas* 591.

B.A. Walton, 'Nevsun Resources Ltd. v. Araya' (2021) 115:1 *American Journal of International Law* 107.

C. Aguirre, *Breve historia de la esclavitud en el Perú*, Fondo editorial del Congreso del Perú, Lima 2005.

C. Costello, 'Migrants and Forced Labour: A Labour Law Response' in A. Bogg, A. Davies and J. Prassl (eds), *The Autonomy of Labour Law*, Hart, Oxford 2015, pp. 189–227.

C. Dauvergne, *Making People Illegal: What Globalization Means for Migration and Law*, Cambridge University Press, Cambridge 2009.

C.L.R. James, *The Black Jacobins: Toussaint L'Ouverture and the San Domingo Revolution*, Random House, New York 1963/1989.

C. Robinson, *Black Marxism*, University of North Carolina Press, Chapel Hill 2000.

D. Hay and P. Craven, 'Introduction' in D. Hay and P. Craven (eds), *Masters, Servants, and Magistrates in Britain and the Empire, 1562–1955*, University of North Carolina Press, Chapel Hill 2004, pp. 1–58.

É. Pataut, 'Le devoir de vigilance: Aspects de droit international privé' (2017) 10 *Droit Social* 833.

E. Reid-Musson, 'Grown Close to Home™: Migrant Farmworker (Im)mobilities and Unfreedom on Canadian Family Farms' (2017) 107:3 *Annals of the American Association of Geographers* 716.

E.R. Toledano, 'Enslavement in the Ottoman Empire in the Early Modern Period' in D. Eltis and S.L. Engerman (eds), *The Cambridge World History of Slavery*, Cambridge University Press, Cambridge 2011, pp. 25–46.

E. Savourey and S. Brabant, 'The French Law on the Duty of Vigilance: Theoretical and Practical Challenges Since its Adoption' (2021) 6:1 *Business and Human Rights Journal* 141.

E. Williams, *Capitalism and Slavery*, Capricorn Books, New York 1994.

F. Kurasawa, 'Show and Tell: Contemporary Anti-Slavery Advocacy as Symbolic Work' in A. Bunting and J. Quirk (eds), *Contemporary Slavery: The Rhetoric of Global Human Rights Campaign*, Cornell University Press, Ithaca 2018, pp. 158–178.

G. Abi-Saab, 'The Newly Independent States and the Rules of International Law: An Outline' (1962) 8 *Howard Law Journal* 95.

G. Lebaron, *Combatting Modern Slavery: Why Labour Governance is Failing and What We Can Do About It*, Polity Press, Cambridge 2020.

I. García-Colón, *Colonial Migrants at the Heart of Empire: Puerto Rican Workers on U.S. Farms*, University of California Press, Oakland 2020.

I.K. Thiemann, 'Beyond Victimhood and Beyond Employment? Exploring Avenues for Labour Law to Empower Women Trafficked into the Sex Industry' (2019) 48:2 *Industrial Law Journal* 199.

J. Allain, *Slavery in International Law: Of Human Exploitation and Trafficking*, Martinus Nijhoff, Leiden 2012.

J. Ford and J. Nolan, 'Regulating Transparency on Human Rights and Modern Slavery in Corporate Supply Chains: The Discrepancy Between Human Rights Due Diligence and the Social Audit' (2020) 26:1 *Australian Journal of Human Rights* 27.

J. Fudge, 'Modern Slavery, Unfree Labour and the Labour Market: The Social Dynamics of Legal Characterization' (2018) 27 *Social & Legal Studies* 414.

J. Fudge, 'Regulating for Decent Work in a Global Economy' (2018) 43:2 *New Zealand Journal of Employment Relations* 10.

J. Fudge, 'Why Labour Lawyers Should Care About the Modern Slavery Act 2015' (2018) 29:3 *King's Law Journal* 377.

J. Haynes, 'Human Trafficking, Diplomatic Immunity, and the Use of Distancing Devices in Hard Cases: The Promise of Basfar v Wong' (2023) 139:1 Law Quarterly Review 204.

J. Haynes, 'The Modern Slavery Act (2015): A Legislative Commentary' (2016) 37:1 *Statute Law Review* 33.

J. Haynes, 'The Shifting Pendulum: Foreign Investors' Liability Under Canada's Common Law for Breaches of Customary International Law' (2021) 36 *Canadian Journal of Law and Society* 447.

J. Nolan, 'Chasing the Next Shiny Thing: Can Human Rights Due Diligence Effectively Address Labour Exploitation in Global Fashion Supply Chains?' (2022) 11:2 *International Journal for Crime, Justice and Social Democracy* 1.

J. Simard, 'Citing Slavery' (2020) 72 *Stanford Law Review* 79.

J.G. Pope, 'Labor's Constitution of Freedom' (1997) 106:4 *Yale Law Journal* 941.

J.G. Ruggie, 'The Social Construction of the UN Guiding Principles on Business and Human Rights' in S. Deva and D. Birchall (eds), *Research Handbook on Human Rights and Business*, Edward Elgar Publishing, Cheltenham 2020, pp. 63–86.

J.L. Morgan, *Reckoning with Slavery: Gender, Kinship, and Capitalism in the Early Black Atlantic*, Duke University Press, Durham 2021.

J.P. Melish, *Disowning Slavery: Gradual Emancipation and "Race" in New England, 1780–1860*, Cornell University Press, Ithaca 2016.

J.S. Martinez, *The Slave Trade and the Origins of International Human Rights Law*, Oxford University Press, Oxford 2012.

K. Bales, *Disposable People: New Slavery in the Global Economy*, University of California Press, Berkeley 2012.

K. Manjapra, 'Plantation Dispossessions: The Global Travel of Agricultural Racial Capitalism' in S. Beckert and C. Desan (eds), *American Capitalism: New Histories*, Columbia University Press, New York 2018, pp. 361–388.

K.S. Park, 'The History Wars and Property Law: Conquest and Slavery as Foundational to the Field' (2021–2022) 131:4 *Yale Law Journal* 1062.

L. Dehaibi, 'Idéal champêtre ou enfer ouvrier? Démystifier la terre pour renforcer les droits des travailleurs agricoles' (2022) 90 *Labour/Le Travail* 111.

L. Vandervelde, 'The Labor Vision of the Thirteenth Amendment' (1989) 138 *University of Pennsylvania Law Review* 437.

M. Goodwin, 'The Thirteenth Amendment: Modern Slavery, Capitalism and Mass Incarceration' (2019) 104 *Cornell Law Review* 899.

M. Hébié, 'Transatlantic Chattel Slavery 1450–1550,' in J.N. Stefanelli and E. Lovall (eds), *Reparations Under International Law for Enslavement of African Persons in the Americas and the Caribbean*, ASIL & University of the West Indies, Washington, DC 2021.

M.J. Piore, 'Enforcement of Labour Standards in Developing Countries: Challenges and Solutions' in M. Chen and F. Carré (eds), *The Informal Economy Revisited: Examining the Past, Envisioning the Future*, Routledge, London 2021, pp. 116–119.

M. Khan, 'Imperial Anti-Trafficking in India' in K. Kempadoo and E. Shih (eds), *White Supremacy, Racism and the Coloniality of Anti-Trafficking*, Routledge, New York 2022, pp. 195–201.

M. Mutua, 'Human Rights in Africa: The Limited Promise of Liberalism' (2008) 51:1 *African Studies Review* 17.

M. Mutua, 'The Complexity of Universalism in Human Rights' in A. Sajó, (ed), *Human Rights with Modesty: The Problem of Universalism*, Springer, Berlin 2004, pp. 51–64.

M. Nishitani and H. Lee, 'Becoming "Overstayers": The Coloniality and the Resilience of Pacific Farm Workers' in V. Stead and J. Altman (eds), *Labour Lines and Colonial Power: Indigenous and Pacific Islander Labour Mobility in Australia*, Australian National University Press, Canberra 2019.

M. Steinberg, *England's Great Transformation: Law, Labor and the Industrial Revolution*, University of Chicago Press, Chicago 2016.

N. Wittman, 'Global Assessment of the Legality of Transatlantic Chattel Slavery' in J.N. Stefanelli and E. Lovall, *Reparations Under International Law for Enslavement of African Persons in the Americas and the Caribbean*, ASIL & University of the West Indies, Washington, DC 2021.

O. Grady Schwartz, 'International Law and National Courts: Between Mutual Empowerment and Mutual Weakening' (2015) 23 *Cardozo Journal of International and Comparative Law* 587.

O. Martin-Ortega, 'Due Diligence, Reporting and Transparency in Supply Chains: The United Kingdom Modern Slavery Act' in A. Bonfanti (ed), *Business and Human Rights in Europe: International Law Challenges*, Rutledge, New York 2018, pp. 110–121.

O. Patterson, *Slavery and Social Death: A Comparative Study*, Harvard University Press, Cambridge 1982.

P. Alston, 'Does the Past Matter? On the Origins of Human Rights' (2013) 126 *Harvard Law Review* 2043.

P. Kotiswaran, 'The Sexual Politics of Anti-Trafficking Discourse' (2021) 29 *Feminist Legal Studies* 43.

P. Viseur Sellers, 'Sexualized Practices and Institutions of the Slave Trade and Slavery' in J.N. Stefanelli and E. Lovall (eds), *Reparations Under International Law for Enslavement of African Persons in the Americas and the Caribbean*, ASIL & University of the West Indies, Washington, DC 2021.

R. Andrijasevic and N. Mai, 'Editorial: Trafficking (in) Representations: Understanding the Recurring Appeal of Victimhood and Slavery in Neoliberal Times' (2016) 7 *Anti-Trafficking Review* 1.

R.E. Zeitlow, *The Forgotten Emancipator: James Mitchell Ashley and the Ideological Origins of Reconstruction*, Cambridge University Press, Cambridge 2017.

R.S. Parreñas, *Children of Global Migration: Transnational Families and Gendered Woes*, Stanford University Press, Stanford 2005.

S.A. Khan, 'Struggles and Actions for Legal Space in the Urban World: The Case of Informal Economy E-waste Workers' (2018) 33:2 *Canadian Journal of Law and Society* 115.

S. Beckert, *Empire of Cotton: A Global History*, Vintage, New York 2014.

S.E. Merry and P. Levitt. 'The Vernacularization of Women's Human Rights' in S. Hopgood, J. Snyder and L. Vinjamuri (eds), *Human Rights Futures*, Cambridge University Press, Cambridge 2017, pp. 213–236.

S. Hall, *The Fateful Triangle: Race, Ethnicity, Nation*, Harvard University Press, Cambridge 2017.

S.J. Rombouts, 'The International Diffusion of Fundamental Labor Standards: Contemporary Content, Scope, Supervision, and Proliferation of Core Workers' Rights under Public, Private, Binding, and Voluntary Regulatory Regimes' (2019) 50:3 *Columbia Human Rights Law Review* 78.

S.J. Toope, 'Inside and Out: The Stories of International Law and Domestic Law' (2001) 50 *University of New Brunswick Law Journal* 23.

S. Mustchin and M. Martínez Lucio, 'The Fragmenting Occupation of Labour Inspection and the Degradation of Regulatory and Enforcement Work Inside the British. State' (2023) 44:2 *Economic and Industrial Democracy Economic and Industrial Democracy*, 526.

S. Rockman, *Scraping By: Wage Labor, Slavery, and Survival in Early Baltimore*, John Hopkins University Press, Baltimore 2009.

V. Mantouvalou, 'The UK Modern Slavery Act 2015 Three Years On' (2018) 81:6 *The Modern Law Review* 1017.

W. Blackstone, *Commentaries on the Laws of England*, J.B. Lippincott Co., Philadelphia 1893.

Anti-Slavery Law and Practice in Contemporary Australia

Marilyn J. Pittard and Anthony Hallal

"[*T*]*here can be no slavery in a free land, and consequently no slaves*," declared Captain Arthur Phillip, the first governor of the New South Wales penal colony, when envisaging a future colonial society.[1] These valiant words, sadly, were not prophetic in Australia. Although slavery was not legalised in Australia as it was elsewhere,[2] it remains a feature of Australia's past and present.

1 Slavery as a Feature of Australia's Past and Present

Convict labour played a significant role in Australia's development. The question of whether prisoners transported from Britain were truly slaves was debated at the time and has been interrogated more recently in scholarship.[3] Prisoners provided labour as part of 'chain gangs' to the newly developing colony, and some were also assigned to others as private labour.[4] Generally, their labour was compulsory, and they were subject to physical punishment.

Australia also felt the influence of the transatlantic slave trade. Some who had profited in the slave trade and who were compensated for slavery's abolition in Britain were influential figures in Australia's history.[5] Emma Christopher's research suggests that although slavery was not legalised in Australia, those with experience managing enslaved people in America were sought to

1 G.B. Barton, *History of New South Wales from the Records, Volume 1 – Governor Phillip*, Charles Potter, Sydney 1892, p. 53.

2 See e.g. *R v Tang* (2008) 237 CLR 1, paragraphs 33, 140.

3 See e.g. J. Jeppesen, '"Within the protection of law": Debating the Australian convict-as-slave narrative' (2019) 16:3 *History Australia* 534; H. Maxwell-Stewart, '"Like poor galley slaves …": Slavery and convict transportation' in M. Fernandes Dias (ed), *Legacies of Slavery: Comparative Perspectives*, Cambridge Scholars Publishing, Newcastle 2007, pp. 48–61.

4 *Ibid.*

5 See e.g. G. Arnott, 'Lachlan Macquarie was a slave owner and he wasn't the only one. It's time to update the history books,' *ABC News*, (05.12.2021), <https://www.abc.net.au/news/2021-12-15/lachlan-macquarie-was-slave-owner-time-to-update-history-books/100573218>.

 | DOI:10.1163/9789004723801_003

oversee workers in Australia.[6] The result was the continuation of Caribbean slave practices in Australia. As Christopher explains: "Caribbean planters and their children did not only bring money to Australia, but also ideas of how sugar could best be grown. They were experts in what labourers should look like: dark-skinned, cheap, and easy to control by restricting options for escape."[7]

The practice of 'blackbirding' brought Pacific Islanders to Australia during the 19th century, often through deception or kidnapping, as indentured labour to work on plantations in Queensland.[8] From the 1860s, there were approximately 62,000 South Sea Islanders working on plantations in Australia.[9] Many worked in slavery-like conditions, the effects of which still "[live] on in the hearts and minds of descendants of the trade."[10] After they had provided labour in these conditions, grossly discriminatory legislation was passed in 1901 to deport them.[11] Some Papuan and New Guinean people too were brought to Australia as domestic workers in the 20th century.[12] Stead and Davies cogently argue this is "one more piece in the fractured pattern of racialised labour exploitation and slavery-like conditions extending unevenly across the history of [Australia]."[13]

First Nations Australians, who are Aboriginal and Torres Strait Islander peoples,[14] were also engaged by pastoralists under conditions in which they

6 E. Christopher, 'From the Caribbean to Queensland: Re-examining Australia's "blackbirding" past and its roots in the global slave trade,' *The Conversation*, (04.06.2021), <https://theconversation.com/from-the-caribbean-to-queensland-re-examining-australias-blackbirding-past-and-its-roots-in-the-global-slave-trade-158530>. See also E. Christopher, 'An illegitimate offspring: South Sea Islanders, Queensland sugar, and the heirs of the British Atlantic slave complex' (2020) 90 *History Workshop Journal* 233.

7 E. Christopher, above n. 6. See also J. Lydon, Anti-Slavery in Australia: No Slavery in a Free Land?, Routledge, New York 2022, pp. 64–84.

8 W. Higginbotham, 'Blackbirding: Australia's history of luring, tricking and kidnapping Pacific Islanders,' *ABC News*, (17.09.2017), <https://www.abc.net.au/news/2017-09-17/blackbirding-australias-history-of-kidnapping-pacific-islanders/8860754>.

9 E. Christopher, 'The saviour and the revolutionary: Afro-Caribbean responses in a Queensland/New Guinea kidnapping case' (2019) 40:2 *Slavery and Abolition* 321, p. 322.

10 Submission 185 by the National Australia South Sea Islanders Association to the Joint Standing Committee on Foreign Affairs, Defence and Trade, inquiring into establishing a Modern Slavery Act in Australia, <https://www.aph.gov.au/Parliamentary_Business/Committees/Joint/Foreign_Affairs_Defence_and_Trade/ModernSlavery/Submissions>; V. Stead and L. Davies, 'Unfree labour and Australia's obscured Pacific histories: Towards a new genealogy of modern slavery' (2021) 45:3 *Journal of Australian Studies* 400.

11 *Pacific Island Labourers Act 1901* (Cth).

12 V. Stead and L. Davies, above n. 10.

13 *Ibid.*, p. 412.

14 This chapter refers to Aboriginal and Torres Strait Islander peoples collectively as 'First Nations Australians.' However, it is acknowledged that there is great diversity, including in language and culture, amongst First Nations Australians, and that one collective term

were not free, were exploited by underpayment or non-payment of wages, and were regarded as slaves.[15] Legislation enabled such practices.[16] It was only in 1966, for example, that some First Nations stockmen, previously excluded from enforceable minimum wage determinations and paid five times less than others, were granted equal pay.[17] Reprehensibly, First Nations children were forcibly removed from their families (known as the Stolen Generation). Many were compelled into indentured labour, for example, as domestic servants.[18] In recent times, claims for the stolen wages of First Nations Australians have been initiated in attempts at recompense.[19] There has also been an official apology for their mistreatment.[20] The use of Pacific Islander labour, which started with blackbirding practices, continues in today's Pacific Australia Labour Mobility program for seasonal workers.[21] Generally, migrant workers under visa arrangements, including these workers, are vulnerable to exploitation.

Slavery and slavery-like practices continue to exist in contemporary Australia. These practices are broadly known as *modern slavery*, and are now encompassed within the legal definition of the term in Australia's *Modern Slavery Act 2018*

---

does not capture that diversity: L. Pearson, 'Why we will never find the 'most appropriate' term to refer to all Indigenous Australians,' *IndigenousX*, (10.11.2015), <https://indigenousx.com.au/why-we-will-never-find-the-most-appropriate-term-to-refer-to-all-indigenous-australians>.

15 R. Kidd, *Hard Labour, Stolen Wages: National Report On Stolen Wages*, Australians for Native Title and Reconciliation (2007); S. Gray, 'The elephant in the drawing room: Slavery and the stolen wages debate' (2007) 11:1 *Australian Indigenous Law Review* 30; S. Gray, 'Holding the government to account: The 'stolen wages' issue, fiduciary duty and trust law' (2008) 32:1 *Melbourne University Law Review* 115; B.A. Hocking and Y. Methu, 'Australasian reflections on modern slavery' (2012) 5:4 *Journal of Politics and Law* 69, p. 80.

16 *Ibid.* See e.g. *Aboriginals Ordinance 1918* (Cth); *Aboriginals Protection and Restriction of the Sale of Opium Act 1897*.

17 *Cattle Station Industry (Northern Territory) Award Case* (1966) 113 CAR 651.

18 See e.g. I. Walden, '"That was slavery days": Aboriginal domestic servants in New South Wales in the twentieth century' (1995) 69 *Labour History* 196; E. Archibald-Binge, ''They ruled our lives': What impact has slavery had in Australia?,' *Sydney Morning Herald*, (10.01.2021), <https://www.smh.com.au/national/they-ruled-our-lives-what-impact-has-slavery-had-in-australia-20200630-p557ht.html>.

19 See e.g. T. Anthony, 'Stolen wages: Northern Territory class action will hold the Commonwealth to account,' *The Conversation*, (18.06.2021), <https://theconversation.com/stolen-wages-northern-territory-class-action-will-hold-the-commonwealth-to-account-149155>.

20 Apology Speech of Prime Minister of Australia, (13.02.2008), <https://parlinfo.aph.gov.au/parlInfo/search/display/display.w3p;query=Id%3A%22chamber%2Fhansardr%2F2008-02-13%2F0003%22>. For a discussion of developments post-apology, including in relation to remedy schemes, see F. Dominello, State Apologies to Indigenous Peoples: Law, Politics, Ethics, Routledge, London 2024, pp. 163–197.

21 Australian Government, Pacific Australia Labour Mobility, <https://www.palmscheme.gov.au/>.

(Cth) ('MSA').[22] It is difficult to measure modern slavery due to its hidden nature, but estimates of its prevalence in Australia are typically in the thousands, with some estimating 41,000 victims.[23] Whilst workers in some industries (e.g. agriculture, cleaning, and fishing) are particularly vulnerable to modern slavery,[24] modern slavery risks can exist in all industries, and in their supply chains.

This chapter considers Australia's legal interventions against modern slavery. Two key elements of the Australian anti-slavery landscape are discussed in detail: the utilisation of the criminal law, particularly the *Criminal Code Act 1995* (Cth) ('Criminal Code'); and the mobilisation of businesses through the MSA.

2 Combating Modern Slavery through Legal Interventions

Australia's legal response to modern slavery is unique. Australia has no national Bill of Rights, and Australia's Constitution is silent about slavery.[25] Nevertheless, Australia's legal interventions against modern slavery are broad, and exist at both the international and domestic levels.

At the international level, Australia has ratified the *International Covenant on Civil and Political Rights*,[26] containing Article 8 on the right to freedom from slavery, servitude, and forced or compulsory labour. Australia has also ratified several International Labour Organization ('ILO') Conventions dealing with forced labour and child labour,[27] including *ILO Convention No. 182 concerning the Prohibition and Immediate Action for the Elimination of the Worst Forms of*

22 References to 'modern slavery' in this chapter are references to the term as it is defined in the MSA, discussed further in section 5.1.

23 Walk Free, *Global Slavery Index 2023: Australia*, at <https://www.walkfree.org/global-slavery-index/country-studies/australia/>. For consistency with the literature and law, this chapter uses the terms 'victim' and 'survivor' to describe a person who has experienced modern slavery. However, it is acknowledged that not all individuals who have experienced modern slavery identify with these terms.

24 *Ibid.*

25 C.f. *R v Director-General of Social Welfare (Vic); Ex parte Henry* (1975) CLR 369 at 388 (Murphy J). See also M. Pittard and S. Butterworth, 'The rich panoply of sources of labor law: National, regional and international' in M. Finkin and G. Mundlak (eds), *Comparative Labor Law*, Elgar Publishing, Cheltenham 2015, pp. 22–29.

26 Adopted 16.12.1966, entered into force 23.3.1976, 999 UNTS 171, ratified 13.08.1980.

27 ILO Convention concerning Forced or Compulsory Labour, adopted 28.06.1930, entered into force 1.05.1932, No. 29, ratified 02.01.1932; ILO Convention concerning the Abolition of Forced Labour, adopted 25.06.1957, entered into force 17.01.1959, No 105, ratified 07.06.1960.

Child Labour ('ILO Convention 182').[28] Other ratified treaties addressing slavery and like practices include the *Slavery Convention*,[29] the *Supplementary Convention on the Abolition of Slavery, the Slave Trade, and Institutions and Practices Similar to Slavery*,[30] and the *Protocol to Prevent, Suppress and Punish Trafficking in Persons, Especially Women and Children* ('Palermo Protocol').[31] Australia is also a party to the *Convention against Transnational Organized Crime*,[32] and the *Optional Protocol to the Convention on the Rights of the Child on the sale of children, child prostitution and child pornography*.[33] Australia's ratification of these international instruments signified early anti-slavery support. However, to become legally binding at the domestic level, the substance of a treaty must be incorporated into Australian law through an Act of Parliament (or in some cases, through the Executive).[34] Consequently, Australia's anti-slavery sentiments at the international level did not immediately trigger a change in Australian law.

While slavery has been unlawful in Australia since the early 19th Century through the operation of British law,[35] it was not until 1999 that the Australian Parliament enacted legislation amending the Criminal Code to criminalise slavery.[36] That legislation was based on recommendations by the Australian Law Reform Commission,[37] and was introduced to "ensure that Australia's international obligations are fulfilled, and that the elements of the offences and the penalties that apply are clear."[38] Today, Australia discharges its anti-slavery obligations under international law through a mix of legislative measures at the domestic level. The Criminal Code, and more recently the MSA, are at the centre of these legislative efforts, and are discussed later in this chapter. However, other complementary legal innovations militating against slavery exist in Australia.

---

28 Adopted 17.06.1999, entered into force 19.11.2000, No. 182, ratified 19.12.2006.

29 Adopted 25.09.1926, entered into force 09.03.1927, 60 LNTS 254, ratified 18.06.1927.

30 Adopted 07.09.1956, entered into force 30.04.1957, 266 UNTS 3, ratified 06.01.1958.

31 Adopted 15.11.2000, entered into force 25.12.2003, 2237 UNTS 319, ratified 14.09.2005.

32 Adopted 15.11.2000, entered into force 29.09.2003, 2225 UNTS 209, ratified 27.05.2004.

33 Adopted 25.05.2000, entered into force 18.01.2002, 2171 UNTS 227, ratified 08.01.2007.

34 See e.g. *Dietrich v The Queen* (1992) 177 CLR 292, 305; G. Triggs, *International Law: Contemporary Principles and Practices*, LexisNexis Butterworths, Sydney 2010, pp. 178–179.

35 *Act for the Abolition of the Slave Trade 1807*; *Slave Trade Act 1824*; *Slavery Abolition Act 1833*; *Slave Trade Act 1843*; *Slave Trade Act 1873*.

36 *Criminal Code Amendment (Slavery and Sexual Servitude) Act 1999* (Cth).

37 Australian Law Reform Commission, *Criminal Admiralty Jurisdiction and Prize* (Report No 48, 1990); Parliament of the Commonwealth of Australia, *Explanatory Memorandum to the Criminal Code Amendment (Slavery and Sexual Servitude) Bill 1999*, paragraph 2.

38 Commonwealth, *Parliamentary Debates*, Senate, Second Reading Speech, Criminal Code Amendment (Slavery and Sexual Servitude) Bill 1999, 24.03.1999, 3075 (Ian Macdonald).

Australia has a strong legal framework for the enforcement of labour standards,[39] and workplace health and safety (WHS), for example.[40] At a normative level, the expectations set by employment and WHS laws highlight the chasm between modern slavery practices and acceptable standards of work. The scheme of compliance and enforcement for basic labour and WHS standards under Australian law is vital in the armoury against exploitation for those at risk of modern slavery.[41] Contraventions of minimum employment and WHS standards may escalate to *become* modern slavery over time.[42] Accordingly, early interventions by industrial and WHS regulators can derail some of the precursors of modern slavery. Furthermore, where modern slavery prosecutions under the Criminal Code have failed or are not pursued by prosecutors, penalties under Australian employment and WHS laws may be used to punish and deter some wrongdoers, including accessories to the wrongdoing.[43] In certain circumstances, Australian employment law may also provide survivors of modern slavery with an avenue for obtaining redress, for example, through the back-payment of wages.[44] Since 2020, a grave form of labour exploitation, dishonestly withholding employee entitlements, has also been criminalised in some Australian jurisdictions through the offence of 'wage theft.'[45] Australia also recently passed Magnitsky-style amendments to its *Autonomous Sanctions Act 2011* (Cth) and *Autonomous Sanctions Regulations 2011* (Cth). These

---

39 *Fair Work Act 2009* (Cth). The Fair Work Ombudsman enforces compliance with this Act including enforcing minimum labour standards. See M. Pittard, 'Protecting vulnerable workers, fairness and state intervention' in A. Bogg and others (eds), *The Constitution of Social Democracy*, Hart, New York 2020, chapter 13.

40 Each Australian State and Territory has workplace health and safety laws and regulators to enforce them.

41 M. Pittard and B. Moore, *Australian Labour and Employment Law*, LexisNexis, 2nd ed., Australia 2024, chapter 11.

42 See e.g. M. Boersma and J. Nolan, 'Modern slavery and the employment relationship: Exploring the continuum of exploitation' (2022) 64:2 *Journal of Industrial Relations* 165.

43 See e.g. *Fryer v Yoga Tandoori House Pty Ltd* [2008] FMCA 288; *DPP v Shaik* [2020] VCC 909; *Fair Work Ombudsman v Shaik* [2016] FCCA 2345; *Ram v D&D Indian Fine Food Pty Ltd & Anor* [2015] FCCA 389. See F. Simmons, J. Burn and F. Mcleod, 'Modern slavery and material justice: The case for remedy and reparation' (2022) 45:1 *University of New South Wales Law Journal* 148, pp. 170–173.

44 *Ibid.* For example, during the 2021–22 financial year, the Fair Work Ombudsman recovered $532 million in workers' wages: S. Parker, 'Looking back, looking forwards: Reflections on the role of the Fair Work Ombudsman and a new era for enforcement – Fair Work Ombudsman's speech to the Australian Labour Law Association' (2023) 28:7 *Employment Law Bulletin* 74.

45 *Wage Theft Act 2020* (Vic); *Criminal Code and Other Legislation (Wage Theft) Amendment Act 2020* (Qld); *Fair Work Legislation Amendment (Closing Loopholes) Act 2023* (Cth).

enable the imposition of financial sanctions and travel bans on certain entities involved in serious abuses or violations of human rights, including those relating to slavery.[46] The *Proceeds of Crime Act 2002* (Cth) (POCA) provides a framework for tracing, restraining and confiscating the proceeds of modern slavery offences. Section 298 enables confiscated proceeds to be used to fund crime prevention and law enforcement measures, and certain initiatives relating to the treatment of drug addiction and illegal drug use. In limited certain circumstances, the POCA can also be used to obtain compensation for the survivors of modern slavery offences via a ministerial direction made under section 100(2).

Furthermore, some Australian States and Territories have enacted specific human rights legislation.[47] Among other things, these laws require public entities, and some private entities performing public functions, to act in a way that is compatible with human rights relating to slavery, and to properly consider those rights when making decisions. Australia's whistleblower protection laws further support the identification and remediation of corporate involvement in modern slavery.[48] That regime operates in certain circumstances to protect eligible whistleblowers who disclose (among other things) information that they reasonably suspect indicates a company's criminal involvement in modern slavery.[49] Additionally, Australian tort law can be used by those impacted by modern slavery to obtain a remedy in certain circumstances.[50] Although plaintiffs must overcome significant obstacles before a remedy can be obtained, modern slavery practices will often involve tortious wrongdoing, such as assault, battery, false imprisonment and deceit.[51] Australia's migration legislation contains additional offences relevant to modern slavery.[52] It also facilitates the Australian Government's Human Trafficking Visa Framework, which enables suspected victims of modern slavery who are not Australian citizens to remain lawfully in Australia and to access the Government's Support

46 *Autonomous Sanctions Amendment (Magnitsky-style and Other Thematic Sanctions) Act 2021* (Cth); *Autonomous Sanctions Amendments (Magnitsky-style and Other Thematic Sanctions) Regulations 2021* (Cth).

47 *Human Rights Act 2004* (ACT); *Human Rights Act 2019* (Qld); *Charter of Human Rights and Responsibilities Act 2006* (Vic).

48 *Corporations Act 2001* (Cth), part 9.4AAA. Separate legislation applies to the public sector.

49 See *Corporations Act 2001* (Cth), S1317AA(5)(d).

50 See e.g. P. Stewart, 'Tortious remedies for deliberate wrongdoing to victims of human trafficking and slavery in Australia' (2011) 34:3 *University of New South Wales Law Journal* 898.

51 *Ibid.*

52 *Migration Act 1958* (Cth), part 2, division 12.

for Trafficked People Program.[53] While their scope and accessibility have attracted some criticism,[54] these initiatives remain important aspects of Australia's response to modern slavery. They exist alongside Australia's general labour and WHS laws (discussed above), which also protect migrant workers.[55]

Although Australia's anti-slavery landscape is broad, there remain some gaps. Most notably, despite international pressure and forceful arguments calling for a national compensation scheme for survivors of modern slavery in Australia, none currently exists.[56] There have been some patchy, largely inadequate reparations paid to First Nations Australians,[57] and there are general schemes to compensate victims of crimes, to compensate workplace injuries, and to recover underpayments of wages. However, without a specific modern slavery compensation scheme, survivors are unlikely to have access to an effective remedy that is commensurate with the serious abuse of their human rights. Furthermore, in 2021 the Australian Senate voted in favour of a Bill to prohibit the importation into Australia of goods produced or manufactured by forced labour.[58] While the Government agreed with the Bill in principle, the import ban was not ultimately enacted due partly to the practical challenges of effectively implementing such a ban.[59] Noting these gaps in Australia's anti-slavery framework, we turn now to two key features of Australian anti-slavery law: first, the criminalisation of slavery and similar wrongdoing in the Criminal Code; and second, the mobilisation of businesses through the MSA.

---

53 See Australian Government, *Support for Trafficked People Program*, <https://www.dss.gov.au/women/programs-services/reducing-violence/anti-people-trafficking-strategy/support-for-trafficked-people-program>.

54 See e.g. Joint Standing Committee on Foreign Affairs, Defence and Trade, *Hidden in Plain Sight: An inquiry into establishing a Modern Slavery Act in Australia* (2017), paragraphs 6.28–6.65.

55 See e.g. *Australasian Meat Industry Employees Union v Dick Stoner Pty Ltd (No 2)* [2022] FCA 1263.

56 See e.g. UN Committee against Torture, *Concluding observations on the sixth periodic report of Australia*, CAT/C/AUS/CO/6 (05.12.2022); P. Stewart, above n. 50, 904–907; F. Simmons, 'Making possibilities realities: Compensation for trafficked people' (2012) 34:3 *Sydney Law Review* 511; F. Simmons, J. Burn and F. Mcleod, above n. 43; R. Dominguez, 'Australia urgently needs a compensation scheme for victims of slavery: Without it there can be no justice,' *The Guardian*, (06.08.2021), <https://www.theguardian.com/commentisfree/2021/aug/06/australia-urgently-needs-a-compensation-scheme-for-victims-of-slavery-without-it-there-can-be-no-justice>.

57 See e.g. T. Anthony, above n. 19; F. Dominello, above n. 20, pp. 163–197.

58 *Customs Amendment (Banning Goods Produced By Forced Labour) Bill 2021* (Cth).

59 Australian Government, *Australian Government Response to the Senate Foreign Affairs, Defence and Trade Legislation Committee report: Customs Amendment (Banning Goods Produced By Uyghur Forced Labour) Bill 2020* (2022).

3 Slavery in Contemporary Australian Criminal Law

The Criminal Code is at the centre of Australia's statutory response to the bundle of crimes that are now commonly referred to as *modern slavery* – a term defined in the MSA by reference to the Criminal Code.

Division 270 of the Criminal Code defines and criminalises slavery. *Slavery* is defined in section 270.1 as "the condition of a person over whom any or all of the powers attaching to the right of ownership are exercised, including where such a condition results from a debt or contract made by the person." Consideration of that definition by Australia's judiciary has both influenced,[60] and been influenced by,[61] foreign and international understandings of slavery. The offences relating to *slavery* have universal jurisdiction.[62] That jurisdictional position "accords with the prohibition of slavery as a *jus cogens* (peremptory) norm of customary international law," slavery's "[express prohibition] by a number of treaties to which Australia is a party," and "Australia's recognition of universal jurisdiction as a well-established principle of international law, and one which extends to a range of crimes."[63] Section 268.10 separately criminalises e*nslavement* in similar terms to the *slavery* provisions in Division 270, but with the additional requirement that the perpetrator's conduct is committed "intentionally or knowingly as part of a widespread or systematic attack directed against a civilian population."[64] Division 270 also defines and criminalises slavery-like offences, including servitude, forced labour, deceptive recruiting for labour or services, forced marriage and debt bondage. Division 271 then defines and criminalises trafficking in persons.[65] Notably, corporations can contravene the modern slavery offences in Divisions 270 and 271.[66] A victim's consent or acquiescence is not a defence in proceedings under Division 270

60 See e.g. *R v Matamata* [2020] NZHC 877 (NZ), paragraphs 13–18; S. Tully, 'Sex, slavery and the High Court of Australia: The contribution of R v Tang to international jurisprudence' (2010) 10:3 *International Criminal Law Review* 403.

61 See e.g. *R v Tang* (2008) 237 CLR 1, paragraphs 26, 149–155.

62 Criminal Code, ss15.4, 270.3A.

63 Parliament of the Commonwealth of Australia, *Revised Explanatory Memorandum to the Crimes Legislation Amendment (Psychoactive Substances and Other Measures) Bill 2014*, 83; *R v Tang* (2008) 237 CLR 1, paragraph 111.

64 See S. Bronnitt and B. McSherry, *Principles of Criminal Law*, 4th ed., Thomson Reuters, Sydney 2017, p. 1056.

65 For a concise summary of the Division 270 and 271 offences, see Australian Government, *National Action Plan to Combat Modern Slavery 2020–25* (2020), 42–43.

66 Criminal Code, ss12.1–12.6.

or 271.[67] However, it remains important to recognise the lived experiences and individual circumstances of those impacted by modern slavery. These criminal provisions have been used to prosecute cases that demonstrate many of the unfortunate realities of modern slavery: that often it hides in plain sight, takes place close to home yet may transcend national borders, impacts the vulnerable, involves the exploitation of significant power imbalances, and can easily enter the operations or supply chains of businesses.

The first Australian conviction for the crime of slavery was in the landmark case of *R v Tang*, where Ms Tang was convicted for possessing and using five migrant workers in conditions of slavery (contrary to section 270.3(1) of the Criminal Code) within her public-facing business.[68] Tang owned a licensed brothel in Victoria and engaged five Thai nationals as sex workers. The arrangement involved Tang's syndicate paying $20,000 to 'recruiters' in Thailand to 'purchase' four of the five woman, the creation of a $42,000–$45,000 debt which each worker was required to 'work off' at a rate of $50 per customer, and the workers were "effectively restricted to the premises."[69] *Tang* was significant for several reasons. It demonstrated that slavery continues to exist in modern Australia, and that even public-facing businesses can be closely connected to slavery. The High Court's decision in *Tang* also clarified the definition of *slavery* under the *Slavery Convention* from which the Criminal Code's definition of *slavery* is derived.[70] The High Court recognised, contrary to the European Court of Human Rights in *Siliadin v France*,[71] that the *Slavery Convention*'s definition of *slavery* captures circumstances where the individual is subject to the condition of being a slave without being legally recognised as such (*de facto* slavery).[72] Given that the legal status of being owned by another person "has been legislated out of existence,"[73] the High Court's broader understanding of

67 Criminal Code, ss270.11, 271.11B. See also Parliament of the Commonwealth of Australia, *Explanatory Memorandum to the Crimes Legislation Amendment (Slavery, Slavery-Like Conditions and People Trafficking) Bill 2012*, 31; A. Schloenhardt and H. Bowcock, '"Sex slaves" and shrewd business women: The role of victim consent in trafficking in persons in Australia' (2015) 39:2 *Melbourne University Law Review* 592.

68 (2008) 237 CLR 1.

69 *Ibid.*, paragraphs 6–18.

70 *R v Tang* (2008) 237 CLR 1, paragraphs 21, 110, 136. See J. Allain, 'R v Tang: Clarifying the definition of 'slavery' in international law' (2009) 10:1 *Melbourne Journal of International Law* 246.

71 No. 73316/01, ECHR 2005, paragraph 122.

72 *R v Tang* (2008) 237 CLR 1, paragraphs 19–35, 136–165.

73 J. Allain, 'Contemporary slavery and its definition in law' in A. Bunting and J. Quirk (eds), *Contemporary Slavery: The Rhetoric of Global Human Rights Campaigns*, Cornell University Press, Ithaca 2017, p. 36.

slavery under the *Slavery Convention* gives contemporary relevance to the concept of slavery, and recognises the enduring existence of slavery in the modern world.

More recently, in 2020 a married couple pleaded guilty to forced labour offences under section 270.6A of the Criminal Code (among other things).[74] The couple reportedly kept a woman from the Philippines in forced labour for over three years, during which she performed household and nanny duties at the couple's home, and further duties in their grocery store and café, working long hours for minimal pay.[75] We note that any business that catered its corporate events using food from the couple's grocery store or café during that period may have *contributed to*, or otherwise been *directly linked to*, modern slavery in its supply chain, as contemplated in the UN Guiding Principles on Business and Human Rights (UNGPs). Another recent example is *DPP (Cth) v Kannan & Anor* where another married couple was found guilty of intentionally possessing and using a slave, contrary to the Criminal Code, section 270.3(1).[76] The judge stated that the couple had "grossly exploited a vulnerable person."[77] The victim was a 67-year-old woman, who had lived in southern India before arriving in Australia. The Supreme Court of Victoria described the victim's life as characterised by "an exceedingly low level of education, illiteracy in language and numeracy," noting that "[h]er life in India has been dominated by financial struggle and deprived circumstances."[78] The Kannans brought the woman to Australia on

74 See Australian Federal Police, 'Sydney couple sentenced for forced labour,' (25.06.2021), <https://www.afp.gov.au/news-media/media-releases/sydney-couple-sentenced-forced-labour>; L. Chung, 'Sydney couple who kept woman like 'slave' will repay $70,000 and face jail time,' *Sydney Morning Herald*, (27.06.2021), <https://www.smh.com.au/national/nsw/sydney-couple-who-kept-woman-like-slave-will-repay-70-000-and-face-jail-time-20210625-p5846q.html>. No official judgment was reported for this case.

75 *Ibid.*

76 [2021] VSC 439. The offences prosecuted were determined by the DPP. The Kannans' house in which these slavery offences took place was seized and then sold under the POCA, and for the first time, a ministerial direction was made by the Commonwealth Attorney-General under section 100(2) of the POCA which required the sum of $485,411.12 to be paid to the victim in recognition of the unpaid wages and other entitlements she did not receive. Following the initial conviction, Mrs Kannan was convicted of the further offence of attempting to pervert the course of justice by attempting to deter the victim from giving evidence: [2023] VCC 1165. See also Office of the Commonwealth Director of Public Prosecutions, Woman sentenced for perverting the course of justice after landmark slavery case (2023), <https://www.cdpp.gov.au/case-reports/woman-sentenced-perverting-course-justice-after-landmark-slavery-case>; A. Hudson and J. Layman, 'Parliament confirms: Visa conditions no bar to workplace protections' (2024) 29:1 *Employment Law Bulletin* 7.

77 [2021] VSC 439, paragraph 223.

78 *Ibid.*, paragraph 6.

a visa, which lapsed. They kept her in their suburban home from 2007 until 2015, when she was "found [by paramedics] lying on a bathroom floor, barely conscious and in a pool of urine."[79] Upon hospitalisation, she was 'emaciated,' weighing only approximately 40 kilograms: she had extreme hypothermia, septicemia, uncontrolled diabetes, and no teeth.[80] During her eight years of slavery, the woman performed domestic and childcare duties for the Kannans for 'meagre' pay.[81] In these three cases, custodial sentences were imposed. These examples illustrate that the Criminal Code offences are capable of capturing at least some of the modern slavery that arises in contemporary Australia.

However, in practice, as with proceedings to enforce labour laws, there remain evidentiary challenges that create barriers to prosecuting even the worst forms of wrongdoing. This is reflected in the fact that few (approximately 30) people have been convicted of offences under Divisions 270 and 271 in the last two decades.[82] The practical scope of Divisions 270 and 271 is effectively limited by issues relating to the admissibility and reliability of evidence, the credibility of witnesses, and the reality that successful prosecution is unlikely where the victim is unwilling or unable to cooperate with Australian authorities.[83] Evidentiary challenges were observed in the Findings Report of the Australian Government's 2023 *Targeted Review of Modern Slavery Offences in Divisions 270 and 271 of the Criminal Code Act 1995* (*Cth*).[84] These limitations of the criminal process highlight the important role of businesses in combatting modern slavery risks.

4 Using Businesses to Address Modern Slavery

A distinctive feature of Australia's response to modern slavery is the significant role of the business community.[85] The MSA is Australia's flagship legal

79 *Ibid.*, paragraphs 16–25.

80 *Ibid.*, paragraphs 7, 79.

81 *Ibid.*, paragraphs 55, 223.

82 Attorney-General's Department, *Targeted Review of Divisions 270 and 271 of the Criminal Code Act 1995* (*Cth*): *Discussion Paper* (2022), pp. 18, 61; Attorney-General's Department, Targeted Review of Divisions 270 and 271 of the Criminal Code Act 1995 (Cth): Findings Report (2023).

83 See e.g. Judicial College of Victoria, *Modern Slavery: Guidance for Australian Courts* (15.12.2021), <https://www.judicialcollege.vic.edu.au/bench-books/modern-slavery-guidance-australian-courts>.

84 This Report can be accessed at: <https://consultations.ag.gov.au/crime/modern-slavery-offences/>.

85 See e.g. Australian Government, *National Action Plan to Combat Modern Slavery 2020–25* (2020).

innovation for mobilising businesses in the fight against modern slavery. Enacted in 2018 following substantial consultation, its main provisions commenced on 1 January 2019. It was introduced with the "primary objective to assist the business community in Australia to take proactive and effective actions to address modern slavery."[86]

Modelled on part of the United Kingdom's *Modern Slavery Act 2015* (UK), the MSA is one of Australia's key contributions to the growing body of legislation intended to prompt businesses to take steps towards respecting human rights. In summary, it requires certain entities (called *reporting entities*) to disclose the modern slavery risks in their operations and supply chains,[87] and the actions they have taken to respond to those risks during their previous financial year or other annual accounting period (being the entity's *reporting period*).[88] Reporting entities must make such disclosures annually by preparing a *modern slavery statement* that satisfies a set of prescribed mandatory criteria with respect to their reporting period,[89] and is published in a public register. The Attorney-General is currently responsible for the MSA's administration.

Which businesses are mobilised under the MSA? The most significant type of *reporting entity* is an entity which has consolidated revenue of at least $100 million for the reporting period ('Revenue Threshold'), and which is also either an Australian entity or an entity that carries on business in Australia during the reporting period.[90] Entities below the Revenue Threshold can still become a *reporting entity* by volunteering to comply with the MSA.[91] The Commonwealth of Australia,[92] as well as corporate Commonwealth entities and Commonwealth companies meeting the Revenue Threshold, are also *reporting entities*.[93] The Commonwealth's modern slavery statements report on the modern slavery risks in the operations and supply chains of the Australian public sector.

The Revenue Threshold was controversial during the consultation process preceding the MSA's enactment, with arguments made for and against

86 Parliament of the Commonwealth of Australia, *Explanatory Memorandum to the Modern Slavery Bill 2018*, paragraph 2.

87 MSA, S5. For analysis of the types of reporting entities, see A. Hallal and M. Pittard, 'Considering the scope of Australia's Modern Slavery Act: Who should report on their modern slavery risks?' (2022) 27:7–8 *Employment Law Bulletin* 90.

88 MSA, Part 2.

89 MSA, ss12–16.

90 MSA, S5(1)(a).

91 MSA, ss5(1)(d), 6.

92 MSA, ss5(1)(b).

93 MSA, S5(1)(c).

alternatives.[94] Some supported the current $100 million threshold on the basis that lowering it would create too heavy a regulatory burden by capturing some smaller businesses that lack sufficient resources and leverage to engage meaningfully with the reporting requirement.[95] Others supported lower thresholds to ensure consistency with other Australian laws or equivalent modern slavery legislation in other jurisdictions.[96] A parliamentary committee recommended a Revenue Threshold of $50 million to align with the UK's modern slavery reporting regime.[97] Some also suggested supplementing or replacing the Revenue Threshold with a risk-based approach, whereby entities in high-risk industries would be required to report based on those risks, rather than solely their revenue.[98] Support for a $100 million threshold ultimately prevailed on the basis that it would ensure that the MSA's reporting obligation covers entities that have "the capacity to meaningfully comply' and 'the market influence to effect change in their supply chains."[99] As the definition of *reporting entity* is crucial to the legislation's scope and efficacy, this issue continues to attract attention. For example, in 2022–2023 the MSA underwent a statutory review of its first three years of operation,[100] and the report of that review again recommended a $50 million threshold following substantial consultation with various stakeholders.[101]

Future consideration of Revenue Thresholds no doubt will be pragmatic. Currently there are approximately 20,000 reporting entities:[102] expanding this number would further increase the workloads of public servants who

94 E.g. Senate Legal and Constitutional Affairs Legislation Committee, *Modern Slavery Bill 2018 [Provisions]* (24.08.2018), paragraphs 3.35–3.50; Joint Standing Committee on Foreign Affairs, Defence and Trade, *Hidden in Plain Sight: An Inquiry into Establishing a Modern Slavery Act in Australia* (2017), paragraphs 5.40–5.50. See also S. Rao, *Modern Slavery Legislation: Drafting History and Comparisons between Australia, UK and the USA*, Routledge, New York 2020, pp. 75–76.

95 *Ibid.*

96 *Ibid.* E.g. the *Corporations Act 2001* (Cth) defines a 'large proprietary company' as one with, inter alia, consolidated revenue of $25 million.

97 Joint Standing Committee on Foreign Affairs, Defence and Trade, *Hidden in Plain Sight: An Inquiry into Establishing a Modern Slavery Act in Australia* (2017), paragraphs 5.48–5.49.

98 See e.g. Senate Legal and Constitutional Affairs Legislation Committee, *Modern Slavery Bill 2018 [Provisions]* (24.08.2018), paragraphs 3.46–3.50.

99 Parliament of the Commonwealth of Australia, *Explanatory Memorandum to the Modern Slavery Bill 2018*, paragraphs 34–39, 78.

100 The review was mandated under S24.

101 J. McMillan, *Report of the Statutory Review of the Modern Slavery Act 2018 (Cth): The First Three Years*, Australian Government (2023) 50–55.

102 See <https://modernslaveryregister.gov.au/>.

must review their statements, engage with them during the reporting cycle, and enforce compliance. Additional government investment would likely be required to avoid the regime becoming unwieldly. Pragmatism, however, must be weighed against risks of modern slavery escaping the reporting net. Furthermore, businesses in *every* sector are likely to have some modern slavery risks in their operations or supply chains. Defining *reporting entities* through a risk-based approach would need to account for this reality to avoid ignoring modern slavery practices that do occur in otherwise low-risk locations or sectors based on general risk data, which may not reflect the lived experiences of some survivors. The quality of modern slavery statements published to date has been diverse.[103] Some have demonstrated entities' proactivity and maturity in identifying, assessing, and addressing their modern slavery risks, and in their broader approach to respecting human rights. Others have been rudimentary. Nonetheless, for many businesses the MSA has served as an entry point to the idea that they may be connected to modern slavery practices, and broader adverse human rights impacts, through their operations or business relationships.

The Australian State of New South Wales (NSW) enacted its own *Modern Slavery Act 2018* (NSW) alongside the Federal one. The NSW law establishes a unique Anti-Slavery Commissioner, and requires corporations owned by the State of NSW to comply with the Federal MSA on the basis that "the scale of the [NSW] Government's procurement ... places it in a unique position."[104]

The Federal MSA has triggered a significant shift in businesses by bringing concerns about modern slavery squarely into Australia's most influential boardrooms. Some key features of the MSA are discussed in the next section.

5 Features of Australia's Modern Slavery Act: Strengths and Areas for Improvement

This section addresses (1) the MSA's definition of *modern slavery*; (2) the mandatory criteria that must be covered in every modern slavery statement and their relationship with human rights due diligence; and (3) compliance, the

103 See e.g. N. Pham, B. Cui and U. Ruthbah, *Modern Slavery Statement Disclosure Quality: ASX100 Companies*, Monash Centre for Financial Studies (2021); A. Coward, *Moving from Paper to Practice: ASX200 Reporting under Australia's Modern Slavery Act*, Australian Council of Superannuation Investors (2021).

104 New South Wales, *Parliamentary Debates*, Legislative Assembly, Second Reading Speech, Modern Slavery Bill 2018, 06.06.2018, 81 (Paul Lynch).

expectation of continuous improvement, and enforcement. While the enactment of the MSA itself is a major step forward, there are some challenges that must be overcome in the future.

5.1 *Australia's Definition of 'Modern Slavery'*

The MSA uses the term *modern slavery* to describe the bundle of crimes that are the subject of the reporting requirement. However, other appellations were also available. For example, *contemporary slavery*, *contemporary forms of slavery*, and *new slavery* have all been used to describe the same or similar practices.[105] Notwithstanding its shortcomings,[106] the term *modern slavery* has gained significant traction in Australia and abroad,[107] and has proven to be a powerful tool to concisely convey the enduring existence of slavery and similar practices to lay audiences, including businesses. The definition of *modern slavery* is a key feature of the MSA. That definition makes Australia the first jurisdiction globally to define *modern slavery* through national legislation.[108] It determines the type of conduct that reporting entities must consider when preparing their modern slavery statements. The definition in section 4 provides:

> **modern slavery** means conduct which would constitute:
> a. an offence under Division 270 or 271 of the Criminal Code [being slavery, servitude, forced marriage, forced labour, debt bondage, deceptive recruiting for labour services, and trafficking in persons]; or
> b. an offence under either of those Divisions if the conduct took place in Australia; or
> c. trafficking in persons, as defined in Article 3 of the [Palermo Protocol]; or
> d. the worst forms of child labour, as defined in Article 3 of [ILO Convention 182].

Evidently, 'modern slavery' is defined broadly under the MSA, by reference to the Criminal Code (discussed above) and to international instruments, with

105 See e.g. J. Allain, above n. 73, pp. 36-62; K. Bales, *Disposable People: New Slavery in the Global Economy*, University of California Press, California 2012.

106 See e.g. R. Vijeyarasa, 'Women, work and global supply chains: The gender-blind nature of Australia's modern slavery regulatory regime' (2020) 26:1 *Australian Journal of Human Rights* 74, 77.

107 See e.g. Submission 91 to the Joint Standing Committee on Foreign Affairs, Defence and Trade, *Inquiry into establishing a Modern Slavery Act in Australia* (28.4.2017), paragraph 2.1.4.

108 See Attorney-General's Department, *Commonwealth Modern Slavery Act 2018: Guidance for Reporting Entities* (2023) 8.

guidance notes providing some indicators and examples of modern slavery risks.[109] Sensibly, the definition does not capture all types of sub-standard working conditions, such as underpayments, WHS issues and wage theft.[110] At a normative level, confining the definition in this way allows the term *modern slavery* to retain the stigma and weight associated with the worst forms of wrongdoing.[111] At a practical level, doing so limits the regulatory burden imposed by the MSA by narrowing the reporting requirement to egregious matters. Interestingly, the definition of *modern slavery* under the MSA includes, but is not limited to, the crime of slavery under the Criminal Code. Whilst the concept of ownership is an element of *slavery* under the Criminal Code, it is not an element of all other crimes in Divisions 270 and 271 which are captured by the definition of *modern slavery*. Accordingly, the notion of ownership is central to the definition of *slavery* under Australian criminal law,[112] but it is not an essential element of *modern slavery*, thereby properly extending the reach of the MSA.

5.2 *Approaching Human Rights Due Diligence: What Must Modern Slavery Statements Contain?*

The mandatory criteria that modern slavery statements must address are detailed in the MSA. Modern slavery statements must: (1) identify the reporting entity; (2) describe the entity's structure, operations and supply chains; (3) describe the risks of modern slavery practices in the operations and supply chains of the reporting entity (and any entities that the reporting entity owns or controls); (4) describe the actions taken by the reporting entity (and any owned or controlled entities) to assess and address those risks, 'including due diligence and remediation processes'; (5) describe how the reporting entity assesses the effectiveness of such actions; (6) describe the process of consultation with any owned or controlled entities (and certain other entities where relevant); and (7) include any other relevant information.[113]

The MSA's focus is narrower than that of the UNGPs. For example, the UNGPs set out the expectation that *all* businesses (not just reporting entities) respect *all* human rights (not just those relating to modern slavery) across their *full* value chains (not just their upstream supply chains).[114] However, the

109 *Ibid.*, 8, 75–79.

110 These are regulated by other laws. However, many instances of 'modern slavery' could also involve sub-standard working conditions: see section 2 above.

111 See *R v Tang* (2008) 237 CLR 1, paragraph 32.

112 *R v Tang* (2008) 237 CLR 1, paragraphs 20–49; J. Allain, above n. 73, pp. 36-62.

113 MSA, S16(1).

114 UNGPs, Principles 11–24.

mandatory criteria under the MSA are also closely aligned in some respects with the elements of human rights due diligence articulated in the UNGPs.[115] The UNGPs introduced the concept of human rights due diligence as a key process that businesses should carry out to discharge their responsibility to respect human rights. In particular, human rights due diligence enables businesses to "identify, prevent, mitigate and account for how they address their adverse human rights impacts."[116] That process has some similarities to the reporting requirement of the MSA. In effect, both the UNGPs and the MSA set out an expectation that businesses will identify and assess their actual and potential risks of modern slavery or broader adverse human rights impacts.[117] Both also require businesses to consider risks to people rather than only risks to the business,[118] and they both require businesses to communicate publicly how they are addressing those risks.[119] The MSA's aim to prompt reporting entities to carry out a process resembling human rights due diligence is strengthened by the explicit reference to 'due diligence' in the fourth mandatory criterion, the legislation's Explanatory Memorandum, and the Australian Government's published guidance.[120] As Nolan and Frishling observe, "meaningful compliance with the [MSA] can only be achieved when businesses commit to implementing a comprehensive human rights due diligence program" that is consistent with the UNGPs.[121]

Although the MSA, in effect, prompts a process resembling human rights due diligence, a reporting entity can technically comply with the Act's requirements *without* engaging in such a process, or only doing so superficially. For example, if a reporting entity does nothing to assess and address their modern slavery risks, a modern slavery statement describing that inaction would technically

115 J. Nolan and N. Frishling, 'Australia's Modern Slavery Act: Towards meaningful compliance' (2019) 37:2 *Company and Securities Law Journal* 104, p. 114.

116 UNGPs, Principle 17.

117 MSA, S16(1)(c)-(d); UNGPs, Principles 17–18.

118 Attorney-General's Department, *Commonwealth Modern Slavery Act 2018: Guidance for Reporting Entities* (2023) 40; UNGPs, Commentary to Principle 17. C.f. Principle 7 and Recommendation 7.4 of the *ASX Corporate Governance Council Principles and Recommendations* (2019), which set out recommended corporate governance practices relating to 'social risks' (including modern slavery risks) for ASX-listed entities, focusing on risks to the business.

119 MSA, S16(1)(d); UNGPs, Principles 17, 21.

120 Parliament of the Commonwealth of Australia, *Explanatory Memorandum to the Modern Slavery Bill 2018*, paragraphs 2, 127–133; Attorney-General's Department, *Commonwealth Modern Slavery Act 2018: Guidance for Reporting Entities* (2023) 10, 29–30, 46–49, 87, 93. See also J. Nolan and N. Frishling, above n. 115, pp. 115–126.

121 J. Nolan and N. Frishling, above n. 115.

comply with the MSA. Indeed, it is already evident that some reporting entities have taken a 'box-ticking' approach to complying with the mandatory criteria.[122] However, increasing human rights awareness and sophistication amongst stakeholders (including consumers, regulators and civil society) gives rise to potential reputational risks for businesses that report too little in their modern slavery statements by taking a superficial approach to reporting. Interestingly, that same growth in stakeholder awareness and sophistication simultaneously creates litigation risks for businesses that report too much in their statements by embellishing their modern slavery efforts though misleading or deceptive representations (a practice known as *bluewashing*).

While it is arguable that the MSA already presupposes that reporting entities will carry out modern slavery (or broader human rights) due diligence, it is likely that the expectation of due diligence will be mandated more explicitly in the future by legislation as businesses become more accustomed to assessing and addressing their risks, and as the expectation that they respect human rights gains mainstream traction. Indeed, the introduction of mandatory due diligence was recommended by the report of the MSA's statutory review following extensive stakeholder consultation.[123] However, even if mandated, regrettably, some reporting entities may continue adopting cosmetic approaches to due diligence,[124] thereby threatening the efficacy of anti-slavery legislation.

5.3 *Compliance, Continuous Improvement and Market-Based Enforcement*

The MSA does not currently impose monetary penalties (fines) on reporting entities that fail to comply with the reporting requirement. Rather, non-compliant entities may be asked to provide an explanation for the non-compliance and/ or undertake remedial action to rectify it.[125] If that request is ignored, the relevant Minister (currently the Attorney-General) may publicly identify the

122 See e.g. A. Sinclair and F. Dinshaw, *Paper Promises? Evaluating the Early Impact of Australia's Modern Slavery Act*, Human Rights Law Centre and others (2022), <https://www.hrlc.org.au/reports-news-commentary/2022/2/3/paper-promises-evaluating-the-early-impact-of-australias-modern-slavery-act>, pp. 54–60; F. Dinshaw, J. Nolan and others, *Broken Promises: Two Years of Corporate Reporting under Australia's Modern Slavery Act*, Human Rights Law Centre and others (2022), <https://www.hrlc.org.au/reports-news-commentary/broken-promises>, pp. 3, 17–18.

123 J. McMillan, *Report of the Statutory Review of the Modern Slavery Act 2018 (Cth): The First Three Years*, Australian Government (2023) 67–72.

124 I. Landau, 'Human rights due diligence and the risk of cosmetic compliance' (2019) 20:1 *Melbourne Journal of International Law* 221.

125 MSA, S16A(1).

entity and the details of their non-compliance.[126] Accordingly, only flagrant non-compliance can be published.

The approach to enforcing the MSA during its first few years of operation has been deliberately non-punitive to provide businesses with a productive and engaging introduction to modern slavery reporting.[127] This approach is consistent with the Government's expectation that "most cases of non-compliance [during the first three years] will be due to lack of awareness about the Modern Slavery Reporting Requirement or a lack of understanding about how to comply."[128] The Government's stated position is that "in these instances, the strongest driver of compliance will be through dialogue and support for entities, rather than imposing punitive penalties."[129] In practical terms, the current response to non-compliance under the MSA uses *naming and shaming* as its ultimate escalation point. In doing so, it utilises the market as an enforcement mechanism.[130] It assumes that entities have a sufficiently strong preference against being publicly identified as non-compliant, so as to drive satisfactory reporting and continuous improvement. That assumption relies on consumers, investors, and others using modern slavery statements to inform their decisions.

No reporting entity's non-compliance has been published to date, and so the regime's key enforcement mechanism has not yet been tested. In some cases, this is because detected non-compliance has been remedied or explained by the impugned reporting entity once they are notified of their failure to comply – the Act's *naming and shaming* powers cannot be used if an explanation is given or remedial action is undertaken.[131] In other cases, discretion not to name and shame non-compliant entities may have been exercised. Some non-compliance may also be undetected. It is particularly challenging to identify non-compliance involving a failure to submit a modern slavery statement altogether. In practice, revenues, business structures, and the locations at which entities carry on business, are fluid. Identifying reporting entities that have failed to submit a statement is therefore an ongoing process that can be onerous and resource-intensive for the Government and other stakeholders. Nevertheless, a more stringent response to non-compliance should emerge as Australian businesses' experience and maturity in modern slavery reporting

126 MSA, ss16A(4)–16A(5).

127 Parliament of the Commonwealth of Australia, *Supplementary Explanatory Memorandum to the Modern Slavery Bill 2018*, paragraphs 9–10.

128 *Ibid.*

129 *Ibid.*

130 See H. Harris and J. Nolan, 'Outsourcing the enforcement of modern slavery: Overcoming the limitations of a market-based disclosure model' (2021) 64:2 *Journal of Industrial Relations* 223.

131 MSA, S16A(5).

develop. Indeed, the Australian Government in a welcome move allocated in its 2023–24 Federal Budget $8 million over four years to establish a federal Anti-Slavery Commissioner to support compliance with the MSA and "help fight modern slavery in Australia and abroad."[132]

Although the MSA itself creates no cause of action, improper or inaccurate reporting can expose reporting entities to regulatory action or litigation initiated by consumers, shareholders or other stakeholders.[133] In circumstances where an entity claims without basis that there are no modern slavery risks in its operations or supply chains, or makes a commitment to implement anti-slavery controls without reasonable grounds for that representation, the entity may be exposed to liability for misleading or deceptive conduct, or similar causes of action. Furthermore, contractual obligations requiring compliance with modern slavery laws may expose non-compliant entities to liability for breach of contract.[134]

While there can be consequences for non-compliance with the MSA, it is arguable that, beyond promoting transparency and prompting businesses to turn their attention to modern slavery, the MSA's impact has been limited. Evidence has emerged that many entities' initial modern slavery statements amount to mere 'paper promises,' with limited effective action to improve conditions for those at risk of modern slavery.[135] Disappointingly, an analysis of 102 modern slavery statements from the first reporting cycle revealed that 77% of those statements failed to comply with the basic legislative requirement of addressing all mandatory criteria; while conspicuous modern slavery risks were not identified in 52% of statements; and only 27% indicated that effective actions to address their modern slavery risks were being taken.[136] Notwithstanding the expectation that reporting entities will continuously improve their modern

132 Commonwealth of Australia, *Budget Paper No. 2: Budget Measures 2023–24* (2023) 60; *Modern Slavery Amendment (Australian Anti-Slavery Commissioner) Act 2024* (Cth).

133 See e.g. M. Cusenza and V. Brand, '"A tiger without teeth"? The forthcoming review of the Modern Slavery Act 2018 (Cth) and the place of "traditional" penalties' (2021) 38:3 *Company and Securities Law Journal* 152, pp. 167–170; P. Redmond, 'Regulating through reporting: An anticipatory assessment of the Australian Modern Slavery Acts' (2020) 26:1 *Australian Journal of Human Rights* 5, pp. 20–21.

134 See e.g. A. Hallal and M. Pittard, above n. 87, pp. 93–94.

135 A. Sinclair and F. Dinshaw, above n. 122. See also K. Christ and R. Burritt, 'Exploring effectiveness of entity actions to eliminate modern slavery risk: Early Australian evidence' (2021) 55:1 *British Accounting Review* 1; S. Pryde, J. Nolan and others, 'Understanding remedy under the Australian Modern Slavery Act: From conceptualisation to provision of remedy' (2024) 9:1 Journal of Modern Slavery 70; S. Kotoky and C. Di Lernia, 'Selective disclosures with minimal impact: Information disclosed under Australia's Modern Slavery Act' (2023) 40:1 *Company and Securities Law Journal* 4.

136 *Ibid.*

slavery programs and reporting over time,[137] a sequel to that analysis which reviewed the same entities' statements from the second reporting cycle (where available) found only limited improvement.[138] Augmenting the MSA's initial approach to enforcement by introducing a penalty regime is often suggested as a solution to that problem, so as to strengthen inroads into modern slavery practices.[139] A difficult question arises as to precisely what should be penalised. A sensible starting point would be to penalise recalcitrant reporting entities that repeatedly fail to submit a modern slavery statement altogether or submit statements that entirely ignore some of the mandatory criteria. However, an overly broad penalty regime should be avoided as it may operate to disincentivise transparency and encourage a 'box-ticking' approach to compliance.

Currently, the MSA's market-based enforcement model and lack of penal provisions are at odds with the effective compliance mechanisms of other Australian laws that impose obligations (including reporting obligations) on businesses.[140] This cries out for attention – and indeed reform is likely as the 2023 report of the MSA's statutory review recommended the introduction of a carefully balanced penalty regime,[141] and the Government, sensibly, has indicated that a penalty regime may be forthcoming.[142]

6 Future Directions

Slavery is a feature of Australia's past and present. Although a suite of legal innovations endeavour to ensure that it is not a part of Australia's future, modern slavery remains an insidious problem. Australia's anti-slavery framework does not currently feature a dedicated compensation scheme for survivors

---

137 Attorney-General's Department, *Commonwealth Modern Slavery Act 2018: Guidance for Reporting Entities* (2023), 15, 26, 30–31, 96.

138 F. Dinshaw, J. Nolan and others, above n. 122. Cf N. Pham, B. Cui and U. Ruthbah, *Modern Slavery Statement Disclosure Quality: ASX100 Companies Update 2022*. See also S. Marshall, V. Bhakoo and others, Australia's Modern Slavery Act: Is it Fit for Purpose?, Business and Human Rights Centre and others (2023), <https://www.humanrights.unsw.edu.au/research/testing-effectiveness-Australia-modern-slavery-act>.

139 *Ibid.* See also M. Cusenza and V. Brand, above n. 133; A. Sinclair and F. Dinshaw, above n. 122; F. McGaughey, R. Rowe and C. Lappel, 'Strengthening Australia's response to modern slavery: Lessons from comparative human rights due diligence laws' (2023) 51:1 *University of Western Australia Law Review* 62.

140 See e.g. consequences of non-compliance with the *Corporations Act 2001* (Cth), *Competition and Consumer Act 2010* (Cth) and *Fair Work Act 2009* (Cth).

141 J. McMillan, *Report of the Statutory Review of the Modern Slavery Act 2018 (Cth): The First Three Years*, Australian Government (2023) 87–90.

142 See e.g. The Hon Justine Elliot MP, Speech at National Modern Slavery Conference, (27.06.2023), <https://ministers.dss.gov.au/speeches/11556>.

of modern slavery. As a result, effective remedies, including reparations, for survivors are lacking and should be provided to address human rights abuses appropriately. The criminal justice response to slavery is an important part of Australia's anti-slavery landscape, and so too is the role of the business community, as discussed. The MSA and the modern slavery offences in the Criminal Code have had beneficial impacts. The MSA has prompted thousands of businesses and their leaders to consider their potential connection to modern slavery, and to human rights impacts more broadly. The Criminal Code has also been used (albeit rarely) to successfully prosecute deplorable modern slavery crimes. There are weaknesses, however, that need rectification. Both the MSA and the Criminal Code's modern slavery offences were under review by the Australian Government in 2022 and 2023. The Australian Parliament now has an opportunity to reconsider the MSA's Revenue Threshold, its approach to mandating modern slavery (and broader human rights) due diligence, and its approach to enforcement and non-compliance. It also has an opportunity to consider the contemporary relevance and practical utility of the offences in Divisions 270–271 of the Criminal Code. It is anticipated that aspects of Australia's anti-slavery landscape will be updated and strengthened following these reviews. Australia is now poised to enhance its anti-slavery efforts.

Academic References

A. Coward, 'Moving from Paper to Practice: ASX200 Reporting under Australia's Modern Slavery Act,' (2021) *Australian Council of Superannuation Investors.*

A. Hallal and M. Pittard, 'Considering the scope of Australia's Modern Slavery Act: Who should report on their modern slavery risks?' (2022) 27:7–8 *Employment Law Bulletin* 90.

A. Hudson and J. Layman, 'Parliament confirms: Visa conditions no bar to workplace protections' (2024) 29:1 *Employment Law Bulletin* 7.

A. Schloenhardt and H. Bowcock, '"Sex slaves" and shrewd business women: The role of victim consent in trafficking in persons in Australia' (2015) 39:2 *Melbourne University Law Review* 592.

B.A. Hocking and Y. Methu, 'Australasian reflections on modern slavery' (2012) 5:4 *Journal of Politics and Law* 69.

E. Christopher, 'An illegitimate offspring: South Sea Islanders, Queensland sugar, and the heirs of the British Atlantic slave complex' (2020) 90 *History Workshop Journal* 233.

E. Christopher, 'The saviour and the revolutionary: Afro-Caribbean responses in a Queensland/New Guinea kidnapping case' (2019) 40:2 *Slavery and Abolition* 321.

F. Dominello, *State Apologies to Indigenous Peoples: Law, Politics, Ethics*, Routledge, London 2024.

F. McGaughey, R. Rowe and C. Lappel, 'Strengthening Australia's response to modern slavery: Lessons from comparative human rights due diligence laws' (2023) 51:1 *University of Western Australia Law Review* 62.

F. Simmons, 'Making possibilities realities: Compensation for trafficked people' (2012) 34:3 *Sydney Law Review* 511.

F. Simmons, J. Burn and F. McLeod, 'Modern slavery and material justice: The case for remedy and reparation' (2022) 45:1 *University of New South Wales Law Journal* 148.

G.B. Barton, *History of New South Wales from the Records, Volume 1 – Governor Phillip*, Charles Potter, Sydney 1892.

G. Triggs, *International Law: Contemporary Principles and Practices*, LexisNexis Butterworths, Sydney 2010.

H. Harris and J. Nolan, 'Outsourcing the enforcement of modern slavery: Overcoming the limitations of a market-based disclosure model' (2021) 64:2 *Journal of Industrial Relations* 22.

H. Maxwell-Stewart, '"Like poor galley slaves ... ": Slavery and convict transportation' in M. Fernandes Dias (ed), *Legacies of Slavery: Comparative Perspectives*, Cambridge Scholars Publishing, Newcastle 2007.

I. Landau, 'Human rights due diligence and the risk of cosmetic compliance' (2019) 20:1 *Melbourne Journal of International Law* 221.

I. Walden, '"That was slavery days": Aboriginal domestic servants in New South Wales in the twentieth century' (1995) 69 *Labour History* 196.

J. Allain, 'R v Tang: Clarifying the definition of 'slavery' in international law' (2009) 10:1 *Melbourne Journal of International Law* 246.

J. Allain, 'Contemporary slavery and its definition in law' in A. Bunting and J. Quirk (eds), *Contemporary Slavery: The Rhetoric of Global Human Rights Campaigns*, Cornell University Press 2017, pp. 36–62.

J. Jeppesen, '"Within the protection of law": Debating the Australian convict-as-slave narrative' (2019) 16:3 *History Australia* 534.

J. Lydon, *Anti-Slavery in Australia: No Slavery in a Free Land?*, Routledge, New York 2022.

J. Nolan and N. Frishling, 'Australia's Modern Slavery Act: Towards meaningful compliance' (2019) 37:2 *Company and Securities Law Journal* 104.

K. Bales, *Disposable People: New Slavery in the Global Economy*, University of California Press, California 2012.

K. Christ and R. Burritt, 'Exploring effectiveness of entity actions to eliminate modern slavery risk: Early Australian evidence' (2021) 55:1 *British Accounting Review* 1.

M. Boersma and J. Nolan, 'Modern slavery and the employment relationship: exploring the continuum of exploitation' (2022) 64:2 *Journal of Industrial Relations* 165.

M. Cusenza and V. Brand, '"A tiger without teeth"? The forthcoming review of the Modern Slavery Act 2018 (Cth) and the place of "traditional" penalties' (2021) 38:3 *Company and Securities Law Journal* 152.

M. Pittard, 'Protecting vulnerable workers, fairness and state intervention' in A. Bogg and others (eds), *The Constitution of Social Democracy*, Hart, New York 2020, pp. 237–260.

M. Pittard and B. Moore, *Australian Labour and Employment Law*, LexisNexis, 2nd ed., Australia 2024.

M. Pittard and S. Butterworth, 'The rich panoply of sources of labor law: National, regional and international' in M. Finkin and G. Mundlak (eds), *Comparative Labor Law*, Elgar Publishing, Cheltenham 2015, pp. 22–29.

N. Pham, B. Cui and U. Ruthbah, *Modern Slavery Statement Disclosure Quality: ASX100 Companies* (2021) *Monash Centre for Financial Studies.*

P. Redmond, 'Regulating through reporting: An anticipatory assessment of the Australian Modern Slavery Acts' (2020) 26:1 *Australian Journal of Human Rights* 5.

P. Stewart, 'Tortious remedies for deliberate wrongdoing to victims of human trafficking and slavery in Australia' (2011) 34:3 *University of New South Wales Law Journal* 898.

R. Kidd, *Hard Labour, Stolen Wages: National Report On Stolen Wages* (2007) *Australians for Native Title and Reconciliation.*

R. Vijeyarasa, 'Women, work and global supply chains: The gender-blind nature of Australia's modern slavery regulatory regime' (2020) 26:1 *Australian Journal of Human Rights* 74.

S. Bronnitt and B. McSherry, *Principles of Criminal Law*, 4th ed., Thomson Reuters, Sydney, 2017.

S. Gray, 'The elephant in the drawing room: Slavery and the stolen wages debate' (2007) 11:1 *Australian Indigenous Law Review* 30.

S. Gray, 'Holding the government to account: The 'stolen wages' issue, fiduciary duty and trust law' (2008) 32:1 *Melbourne University Law Review* 115.

S. Kotoky and C. Di Lernia, 'Selective disclosures with minimal impact: Information disclosed under Australia's Modern Slavery Act' (2023) 40:1 *Company and Securities Law Journal* 4.

S. Parker, 'Looking back, looking forwards: Reflections on the role of the Fair Work Ombudsman and a new era for enforcement – Fair Work Ombudsman's speech to the Australian Labour Law Association' (2023) 28:7 *Employment Law Bulletin* 74.

S. Pryde, J. Nolan and others, 'Understanding remedy under the Australian Modern Slavery Act: From conceptualisation to provision of remedy' (2024) 9:1 *Journal of Modern Slavery* 70.

S. Rao, *Modern Slavery Legislation: Drafting History and Comparisons between Australia, UK and the USA*, Routledge, New York 2020.

S. Tully, 'Sex, slavery and the High Court of Australia: The contribution of R v Tang to international jurisprudence' (2010) 10:3 *International Criminal Law Review* 40.

V. Stead and L. Davies, 'Unfree labour and Australia's obscured Pacific histories: Towards a new genealogy of modern slavery' (2021) 45:3 *Journal of Australian Studies* 400.

A Critical Assessment of Contemporary Slavery in Select Commonwealth Caribbean Jurisdictions: Barbados and St Vincent and the Grenadines

Jason Haynes

1 Introduction

The peoples of the Commonwealth Caribbean are no stranger to exploitation. In fact, for over two hundred years, Caribbean peoples endured arguably one of the greatest forms of exploitation known to mankind – the transatlantic slave trade, the genocide of native peoples and chattel slavery. Although slavery in the Caribbean was abolished in 1834, the legacies of slavery largely remain, notwithstanding ongoing debates about reparatory justice. In addition to having to contend with the lasting legacies of slavery, Caribbean peoples have also had to contend with modern manifestations of exploitation, such as trafficking in persons, forced labour and domestic servitude. Although the law has, in some respects, caught up to these forms of exploitation, significant regulatory and policy gaps remain.

This chapter has three main aims: first, to examine slavery as a global institution and its legacies in Barbados and St Vincent and the Grenadines; second, to assess the causes and consequences of contemporary slavery; and third, to evaluate ongoing efforts to redress and recalibrate contemporary slavery. Although the paper focuses primarily on Barbados and St Vincent and the Grenadines, the findings and analyses contained herein have broader relevance for the rest of the Commonwealth Caribbean.

2 The Presence of the Past: Slavery as a Global Institution and Its Legacies

2.1 *Overview*

Both Barbados and St Vincent and the Grenadines share an intimate relationship to the centuries-long, largely legal, and global institution of slavery, including the transatlantic slave trade.

 | DOI:10.1163/9789004723801_004

Barbados, the easternmost Caribbean Island, was claimed by the British in 1625.[1] In the ensuing years, Barbados quickly became one of the largest importers of African slaves. In fact, over 40,000 were reported to have been working on sugar plantations by 1655,[2] which enabled Barbados to become the main producer of sugar in the Caribbean, thanks largely to a socio-economic and political system, backed by the Slave Codes of 1661, 1676, 1682, and 1688, that legitimized slavery and the slave trade.[3] Historians estimate that, by the early 18th century, Barbados' value as a colony was somewhere in the range of £5,500,000, largely due to its mass production of sugar, its main export.[4] Although the slave trade was abolished in 1807, slavery continued for nearly three decades thereafter.[5] The continued existence of slavery during this period, as legitimized by the 1688 Slave Code, supported Britain's economic imperatives by conceptualizing African slaves as property, in keeping with *lex mercatoria*. African slaves were effectively owned by their white slave masters and mistresses; they were prevented from assembling, playing instruments, and exercising any other indicia of freedom.[6] The penalties prescribed by the Codes, including mutilation, flogging and executions, kept slaves, who were frequently replenished by new slaves imported from West Africa, in an endless cycle of exploitation that served the economic interests of Britain and its trading partners.[7] The Codes stifled rebellions by prescribing stringent penalties, including the death sentence, without appropriate due process guarantees. In fact, 'Bussa's rebellion' of 1816, which arose because of widespread dissatisfaction with the socio-economic conditions at the time and the lack of reform of the antiquated and brutish Slave Code, was quickly quelled by the British militia, resulting in the capture, mutilation, and execution of several thousands of so-called 'rebels'.[8] Slavery was eventually abolished in the British Empire in 1834, albeit that Barbados and the rest of the British West Indian colonies did not achieve full emancipation from slavery until 1838. The period 1834–1838

1 V.T. Harlow, *A History of Barbados, 1625–1685*, Clarendon Press, Oxford 1926, pp. XVIII, 347.

2 M.E. Gettleman, 'Entrepreneurship in Barbados, 1625-1660' (1959) 21:1 *The Historian* 200.

3 J.S. Handler, 'Custom and law: The status of enslaved Africans in seventeenth-century Barbados' (2016) 37:2 *Slavery & Abolition* 233.

4 D. Elitis, 'The total product of Barbados, 1664–1701' (1995) 55:2 *The Journal of Economic History* 321.

5 M. Sherwood, *After Abolition*, I.B. Tauris, London 2007.

6 E.B. Rugemer, 'The development of mastery and race in the comprehensive slave codes of the greater Caribbean during the seventeenth century' (2013) 70:3 *William & Mary Quarterly* 429.

7 D.V. Armstrong, 'Capitalism and the Shift to Sugar and Slavery in Mid-Seventeenth-Century Barbados' (2019) 53:3 *Historical Archaeology* 468.

8 C.M. Scott, 'Bussa's Rebellion (1816)' (2007) *Encyclopedia of Slave Resistance and Rebellion* 90.

was characterized by a so called 'apprenticeship period', wherein enslaved persons had to work, without pay and without the possibility of refusing to do so, on plantations as a form of reparation to the plantation owners who claimed to have suffered loss as a result of the abolition of slavery.

Meanwhile, just 80 miles west of Barbados, the slave trade in St Vincent and the Grenadines began with the French importing African slaves into the islands in 1719 to cultivate sugar.[9] However, St. Vincent and the Grenadines was soon thereafter ceded to Britain by the Treaty of Paris in 1763.[10] From then on, despite resistance from the native Caribs, the British succeeded in importing thousands of slaves on a consistent basis to replenish the African population that was being quickly depleted by overwork and diseases. The Treaty of Versailles (1783), which later gave the British complete control over the islands after a short period of French control, further entrenched British brutality and ruthlessness.[11] Although St Vincent and the Grenadines did not produce nearly as much sugar as Barbados, its sugar cultivation, coupled with its cultivation of coffee, indigo, tobacco, cotton, and cocoa nonetheless contributed significantly to the rapid expansion of Britain's economy.[12] After many decades, the slave trade in St Vincent and the Grenadines was eventually abolished in 1807, like Barbados. The abolition of slavery later followed in 1834, although most historians now agree that real emancipation only occurred in 1938.[13]

2.2 *The Legality of Slavery*

As intimated above, the enslavement of Africans was rendered legal by the Slave Codes, which characterized African slaves as "negroes" who were "barbarous, wild and savage".[14] The 1688 Slave Code, in particular, provided that African slaves were unqualified to be governed by "the laws, customs and practices" of England because they were apparently "naturally prone and inclined"

---

9 H. Rubenstein, 'Economic history and population movements in an eastern Caribbean Valley' (1977) 24:1 *Ethnohistory* 19.

10 B. Marshall, 'The Black Caribs-Native Resistance to British Penetration into the Windward Side of St. Vincent 1763–1773' (1973) 19:4 *Caribbean Quarterly* 4.

11 A. DeGraff and K. Baldwin, *Participatory Mapping of Heritage Sites in the Grenadine Islands*, CERMES Technical Report (No. 65), The University of the West Indies, Cave Hill Campus, 2013, p. 51.

12 M. Quintanilla, 'Mercantile Communities in the Ceded Islands: The Alexander Bartlet & George Campbell Company' (2004) 79:1/2 *International Social Science Review* 14.

13 C.H. Wesley, 'The Negro in the West Indies, slavery and freedom' (1932) 17:1 *The Journal of Negro History* 51.

14 W.M. Wiecek, 'The statutory law of slavery and race in the thirteen mainland colonies of British America' (1977) 34:2 *The William and Mary Quarterly: A Magazine of Early American History* 258.

toward "cruelties and insolences". The Code prescribed that the enslaved peoples were to work every day on the plantation, except "on Sabbath-days, Holy days, or any other time". It strictly curtailed assembling by enslaved persons, especially on Saturday nights, Sundays and other Holy days. It also prevented enslaved persons from carrying clubs, wooden swords or "other mischievous and dangerous weapons". More than this, it prohibited the keeping and playing of drums, horns and other loud instruments, which may "call together, or given sign or notice to one another of their wicked designs and purposes". Enslaved Africans who were found outside of their designated plantation without a letter from their masters or a ticket, and not in the company of a white man, were "corrected by a moderate whipping". Meanwhile, any instruments found in their possession were confiscated and burned.

Separately, under the Codes, if an enslaved African inflicted any violence on a "Christian, by striking or the like", the enslaved person was "fervently whipped". If the act was repeated a second time, the person was "fervently whipped", their nose was "slit", and they were "burned in some part of his face with a hot iron". On a further infraction, the enslaved would receive such greater punishment as the Governor and Council saw fit. In cases where the enslaved African committed or attempted to commit murder, burglary, robbery, rape or arson, or murder, or maimed or destroyed an animal belonging to their master, the person was sentenced to death. Similarly, if an enslaved African was found with any instrument that may be used in a rebellion, that person was subject to "death or other pains". Meanwhile, petty larceny attracted a penalty of up to 40 lashes. African slaves, as "property" of their White elite, were given a change of clothes once every year. Men were given "drawers and caps", while women were given "petticoats and caps".

Professor Elsa Goveia, critically reflecting on the Slave Codes, has noted that the West Indian slave laws of the 18th century justified the system of slavery.[15] These laws were the original basis of slavery in the West Indian colonies and were "essential for the continued existence of slavery as an institution".[16] In her learned view, "slavery [was] undoubtedly accepted as legal."[17] Professor Goveia considered that the laws defined the position of the enslaved and slavery; enslaved Africans were deemed as subordinates to whites. In this connection, she posited that in the British system of slavery, African slaves were deemed to be property, such that they could be bought and sold. By contrast, she noted

15 E.V. Goveia, 'The West Indian Slave Laws of the Eighteenth Century' (1960) 1 *Revista de ciencias sociales* 75.

16 *Ibid.*, p. 75.

17 *Ibid.*, p. 77.

that the Spanish 'Partidas' treated the slave as a person and not mere property. In short, according to Professor Goveia, the English Slave laws in the West Indies worked against the slave because it reduced their status to mere property".[18] Similarly, historian Richard Dunn has argued that "the slave laws enacted by the islands legislatures in the 17th century tell us a good deal about the treatment of Negroes, and the character of slavery".[19]

2.3 *Abolition of the Slave Trade and Slavery*

Several historians argue that British Abolitionists lobbied the British Parliament to abolish the slave trade.[20] The Abolitionists contended that the slave trade was no longer economically, politically, or socially viable.[21] Meanwhile, leading Caribbean scholars Sir Hilary Beckles and Professor Verene Shepherd proffer that the slave trade was abolished because, in addition to abolitionist voices and public pressures, "blacks pursued their freedom by all means possible", having "declared war on the system and fought bloody battles in the process".[22]

The first attempt at abolishing the slave trade was instigated in 1790 when a Bill calling for the abolition of the slave trade was unsuccessfully presented to the British Parliament.[23] Then, again, in 1792, a second attempt at abolishing the slave trade failed.[24] It was only in 1807 that the Bill – an *Act for the Abolition of the Slave Trade* – was finally successfully passed. This Act of parliament abolished the slave trade in the British Empire, including Barbados and St Vincent and the Grenadines.[25] Meanwhile, slavery in the West Indies was abolished by the *Slavery Abolition Act, 1833*. The Act, which became effective

18 *Ibid.*, p. 82.

19 R.S. Dunn, *Sugar and slaves: The rise of the planter class in the English West Indies, 1624–1713*, UNC Press Books, Chapel Hill 2012, p. 238.

20 S. Drescher, 'Whose abolition? Popular pressure and the ending of the British slave trade' (1994) 143 *Past & Present* 136.

21 E. Williams, *From Columbus to Castro: The History of the Caribbean 1492–1969*. Harper & Row, New York 1970, p. 576.

22 V. Shepherd and H.M. Beckles, *Caribbean Slavery in The Atlantic World: A Student Reader*, Ian Randle Publishers, Kingston 2000.

23 H.A. Ohline, 'Slavery, Economics, and Congressional Politics, 1790' (1980) 46:3 *The Journal of Southern History* 335.

24 G. Taylor, 'Anti-Slave Trade Drama in England: 1786–1808' (1999) 13:1 *South African Theatre Journal* 8.

25 K. Paugh, 'The politics of childbearing in the British Caribbean and the Atlantic world during the age of abolition, 1776–1838' (2013) 221:1 *Past & Present* 119.

in 1834, did not, however, completely emancipate the African slaves.[26] In fact, they were obliged to work for another four years on plantations.[27] Meanwhile, their white masters, including several British families who had either moved back to England or had been living in England at the time, were collectively paid £20 million in compensation.[28]

2.4 *Legacies of Slavery*

Leading Caribbean historians, Sir Hilary Beckles[29] and Professor Verene Shepherd,[30] have written extensively about the legacies of slavery in Barbados, St Vincent and the Grenadines, and the wider Caribbean. Among other things, they highlight high levels of illiteracy due to the non-inclusion of enslaved Africans in educational programmes; social and cultural alienation due to the systematic curtailing of languages, customs and religion and their substitution with British ethos; racism; discrimination; identity crises; health problems; and widespread indebtedness. Beckles' and Shepherd's analyses drew on the Moyne Commission's report,[31] which, among other things, noted that the descendents of Africans in the Caribbean have the highest incidence in the world of chronic diseases in the forms of hypertension and type two diabetes. This health pandemic is the direct result of the nutritional experience, physical and emotional brutality, and overall stress profiles associated with slavery. They also explain that the high levels of indebtedness are largely because Caribbean governments that emerged from slavery and colonialism inherited a crisis of community poverty and institutional unpreparedness for development. These governments still engage in the business of cleaning up the economic colonial mess daily to prepare, but with little success.

Regrettably, post-emancipation, the former enslaved did not receive lands or money. Instead, various laws were systematically implemented to force

26 M. Taylor, *The Interest: How the British establishment resisted the abolition of slavery*, Random House, New York 2020.

27 A.D.V. Phillips, 'Emancipation Betrayed: Social Control Legislation in the British Caribbean (with Special reference to Barbados), 1834–1876'. (1994) 70 *Chi.-Kent L. Rev.* 1349.

28 C. Hall, 'The slavery business and the making of "race" in Britain and the Caribbean' (2020) 61:22 *Current Anthropology* 172.

29 H. Beckles, *Britain's Black Debt: Reparations for Caribbean Slavery and Native Genocide*, University of the West Indies Press, Saint Andrew Parish 2013.

30 V.A. Shepherd, 'Slavery, Shame and Pride: Debates Over the Marking of the Bicentennial of the Abolition of the British Trans-Atlantic Trade in Africans in 2007' (2010) 56:1–2 *Caribbean Quarterly* 1.

31 M. Chamberlain, 'Elsa Goveia: History and Nation' (2004) 58:1 *History Workshop Journal* 167.

them to stay on the plantations, such as Squatting and Vagrancy Acts.[32] As Walter Rodney has noted, slavery and the slave trade depressed and destabilized Africa,[33] while simultaneously, as Eric Williams[34] and C.L.R. James[35] have noted, slavery was central to the growth of industry in Western Europe. Indeed, in the eighteenth century, the ownership of sugar estates in the West Indies was the main foundation of the fortunes of many wealthy British families.

2.5 *Reparation*

Since the abolition of the slave trade and slavery in Barbados and St Vincent and the Grenadines, and indeed the wider Caribbean, Britain has not paid reparation to the descendants of former African slaves.[36] In fact, the British government has never formally apologized for its role in the perpetuation of slavery; it has only ever 'regretted' slavery and the slave trade.[37] Nor has any systematic restorative justice process or truth and reconciliation mechanisms materialized over the years, despite best efforts by the Caribbean Community (CARICOM) Reparation Commission, individual countries' Reparation Commissions, and the University of the West Indies (UWI) Center for Reparation.[38] Interestingly, on the abolition of slavery, while the descendants of African slaves have to date received no reparation, the former slave owners were compensated £20 million, and the apprenticeship system (1834–1838) was part of the compensation package, where Africans had to work for 40.5 hours per week to compensate slave owners for the loss of their 'property'.[39]

2.6 *The Relationship of Barbados and St Vincent and the Grenadines to International Instruments*

Conscious of the gravity of slavery and the slave trade and in an effort to prevent their recurrence in the future, both Barbados and St Vincent and

32 A.D.V. Phillips, 'Emancipation Betrayed: Social Control Legislation in the British Caribbean (with Special reference to Barbados), 1834–1876'. (1994) 70 *Chi.-Kent L. Rev.* 1349.

33 W. Rodney, *How Europe Underdeveloped Africa*, Verso Books, London 2018.

34 E. Williams, *Capitalism and Slavery*, University of North Carolina Press, Chapel Hill 1944.

35 C.L.R. James, *The Black Jacobins: Toussaint L'ouverture and the San Domingo revolution*, Penguin UK, London 2001.

36 H.M. Beckles, 'The Reparation Movement: Greatest Political Tide of the Twenty-first Century' (2019) 68:1/2 *Social and Economic Studies* 11.

37 P. Clegg, 'The Caribbean Reparations Claim: What Chance of Success?' 103:4 *The Round Table* 435, pp. 435–437.

38 C.R. Eugene, 'Towards a Framework for Caribbean Reparations' (2019) 44:3 *Journal of Eastern Caribbean Studies* (*Special Issue Demystifying Caribbean Civil Society*) 54.

39 P.X. Scanlan, 'Emancipation and captivity in the British Empire' (2019) 30:5 *History and Anthropology* 503.

the Grenadines have ratified several international conventions that prohibit slavery and the slave trade, as indicated in the table below. Regrettably, regional courts have not yet had occasion to interpret the provisions of these instruments.

Convention	Date of ratification by Barbados	Date of ratification by St Vincent and the Grenadines
Slavery Convention, 1926 adopted by the League of Nations, as amended by the Protocol of 1953	22 July 1976	9 November 1981
Supplementary Convention on the Abolition of Slavery, the Slave Trade, and Institutions and Practices Similar to Slavery, 1956	9 August 1972	9 November 1981
ILO Forced Labour Convention, 1930 (No. 29)	8 May 1967	12 October 1998
Abolition of Forced Labour Convention, 1957 (No. 105)	8 May 1967	21 October 1998

In light of Barbados' and St Vincent and the Grenadines' historical relationship to slavery, the constitutions of the respective jurisdictions expressly prohibit the commission of slavery or servitude, as discussed in Part II below. No derogation is permissible from these norms, although exceptions are permitted in respect of forced labour. For example, section 4 of the St Vincent and the Grenadines constitution provides:

1. No person shall be required to perform forced labour.
2. For the purposes of this section, the expression "forced labour" does not include—

a. any labour required in consequence of the sentence or order of a court;
b. labour required of any person while he is lawfully detained that, though not required in consequence of the sentence or order of a court, is reasonably necessary in the interests of hygiene or for the maintenance of the place at which he is detained;
c. any labour required of a member of a disciplined force in pursuance of his duties as such or, in the case of a person who has conscientious objections to service as a member of a naval, military or air force, any labour that that person is required by law to perform in place of such service;

d. any labour required during any period of public emergency or in the event of any other emergency or calamity that threatens the life and well-being of the community, to the extent that the requiring of such labour is reasonably justifiable in the circumstances of any situation arising or existing during that period or as a result of that other emergency or calamity, for the purpose of dealing with that situation.

3 Understanding the Causes and Consequences of Contemporary Slavery

This section aims to critically assess the causes and consequences of contemporary slavery in select Caribbean jurisdictions. It draws on doctrinal analyses of applicable legislative provisions and case law, as well as empirical insights drawn from focus group discussions with stakeholders actively working in the anti-slavery field across the Caribbean, to argue that contemporary slavery is an evolving issue in the Caribbean, in relation to which there are significant policy and legal developments, but also significant regulatory gaps.

3.1 *Contemporary Slavery in Select Jurisdictions*

While there is no evidence that slavery, serfdom and forced marriage are present in Barbados and St Vincent and the Grenadines today, interviews with stakeholders in both jurisdictions, as well as various reports, suggest that child labour, debt bondage, compulsory/forced labour and human trafficking exist in these jurisdictions, although their scale is undetermined.

The United States Department of Labour, in its most recent report on the worst forms of child labour, has indicated that over 1300 children under the age of 14 years in Barbados work in illicit activities, including drug trafficking and commercial sexual exploitation.[40] While precise figures are not available for St Vincent and the Grenadines, the United States Department of Labour has reported that many children in that jurisdiction regularly engage in street vending, including selling fruits and vegetables at local farmers markets, drug trafficking and commercial sexual exploitation, including by their relatives, in exchange for money or goods.[41]

40 "Child Labor and Forced Labor Reports – Barbados" (US Department of Labour, 2014), <https://www.dol.gov/agencies/ilab/resources/reports/child-labor/barbados>.

41 "Child Labor and Forced Labor Reports – St Vincent and the Grenadines" (US Department of Labour, 2020), <https://www.dol.gov/agencies/ilab/resources/reports/child-labor/st-vincent-and-grenadines>.

In so far as human trafficking is concerned, in respect of Barbados, it appears that, given its relative economic prosperity, the jurisdiction has quickly become a destination country for persons trafficked for sex and, to a lesser extent, labour exploitation. These victims have reportedly originated from as far as Ukraine and India and as near as Guyana and the Dominican Republic. The first case of human trafficking in Barbados was reportedly investigated in 2004, when authorities identified two adult Guyanese women as having been trafficked for sexual exploitation.[42] A year later, one female minor was found to have been a victim of sexual exploitation.[43] This was followed by a number of Indian nationals who were identified as having been trafficked for the purposes of forced labour, having worked for a construction company in Barbados for wages of about US $1 per week.[44] It was not until 2013 that another case of human trafficking was recorded in Barbados, this time involving five Guyanese girls who were reportedly rescued by police from a bar in Nelson Street, Bridgetown.[45] Reports are that these girls were forced into prostitution by their traffickers, who demanded that they offer their sexual services for as little as BBD $10, which was immediately taken away from them by a 76-year-old woman, who sources say posed as a grandmother of young recruits from Guyana. Of the amounts made weekly by the girls, $150 was then deducted by the alleged traffickers to cover rent, albeit the girls reportedly shared makeshift rooms. The girls were purportedly not allowed to have friends; their conversations in the bar with prospective clients were frequently interrupted; and their shopping expeditions into Bridgetown for clothes were only allowed if they were accompanied by the accused or her associates.[46] Although the full scale of human trafficking in Barbados remains unclear, it has been suggested that traffickers in that country typically have a particular preference for young, vulnerable Guyanese and Jamaican girls, who are reportedly easily forced into prostitution due to their poor education and job prospects and unfavourable living conditions at home. Many of these victims never escape the psychological and physical constraints imposed by their traffickers, partly because they

42 T. Durbin and J. St George, 'Human Trafficking in Barbados: Achievements and Continuing Hurdles' (2013) 38:1–2 *Journal of Eastern Caribbean Studies* 126.

43 *Ibid.*

44 'Internationally Recognised Core Labour Standards in Barbados Report for The WTO General Council Review of the Trade Policies of Barbados' (International Trade Union Confederation, Geneva, 17 and 19 September 2008).

45 'Barbados duo charged with trafficking in five Guyanese women' *Stabroek News* (23.04.2013).

46 'Done in by $10 … The Guyana – Barbados human trafficking case' *Kaieteur News* (07.05.2013).

themselves believe that living in Barbados affords them a better quality of life than remaining in Guyana or Jamaica, but also because human trafficking does not appear to be high on the national agenda in Barbados.[47]

Meanwhile, St Vincent and the Grenadines have also had to confront the phenomenon of human trafficking in recent years, particularly in the realm of sexual exploitation and forced labour. Indeed, while there has been no successful conviction for human trafficking in that country to date,[48] over 20 suspected cases of human trafficking have reportedly been investigated by the country's Anti-Trafficking Unit since it became fully operationalised.[49] At the time of writing, the latest of these investigations involved allegations that a number of Asian employees at a certain factory in St Vincent had been stripped of their passports, made to be completely dependent on their alleged trafficker for food and lodging and forced to work for said person, without commensurate remuneration.[50] Despite repeated high-level statements from policymakers in St Vincent and the Grenadines which suggest that the country does not have a human trafficking problem,[51] it is nonetheless widely accepted that the multifarious nature of the islands and cays that comprise this jurisdiction, their porous borders and a lack of adequate surveillance, especially of uninhabited internal areas and hard to reach coastal regions, render the country at risk of becoming a source, transit and destination country for human trafficking, particularly the trafficking of women from Venezuela, Guyana and the Dominican Republic for sexual exploitation.[52] In early 2022, the government reported that there was evidence that vulnerable Vincentian women were being trafficked for the purpose of domestic servitude in the United Kingdom.[53] According to reports, these women, who are often uneducated and desperately in search

---

47 George Alleyne, 'Barbados Branded Negligent on Human Trafficking' *Caribbean News Life* (10.07.2018).

48 'Case collapses, but investigators lauded' *The Vincentian* (15.04.2016). The Prosecution, in this case, withdrew its case for a want of evidence in an alleged labour trafficking case involving three Jamaican nationals.

49 '2018 Trafficking in Persons Report' (Office to Monitor and Combat Trafficking in Persons, US Department of State, 2018).

50 'Police free human trafficking victims across the Caribbean' *WLNS* (30.04.2018); 'St Vincent: Victims of Human Trafficking Rescued By INTERPOL' (*NEWS784*, 30.04.2018).

51 'Interpol "overextended" facts about SVG's human trafficking raid' *IWitness News* (03.05.2018).

52 'Vincentian PM: Men complained after suspected sex workers deported' *Loop News* (04.05.2018).

53 'Woman admits she underpaid Vincy babysitter 'Stacy' in England', *IWitness News*, (11.02.2022), <https://www.iwnsvg.com/2022/02/11/woman-admits-she-underpaid-vincy-babysitter-stacy-in-england/>.

of economic opportunities abroad, are recruited by a 'nanny' firm in the UK, and subsequently required to work for more than 14 hours a day below the minimum wage. Although Barbados and St Vincent and the Grenadines are significant tourist destinations, and there have long been suspicions that there might be a link between the tourism industry and contemporary slavery, there are no documented cases of exploitation occurring in this industry.

3.2 *Definition of Slavery*

The constitutions of Barbados and St Vincent and the Grenadines respectively prohibit, *inter alia*, slavery. Section 14 of Barbados' constitution reads: "14. (1) No person shall be held in slavery or servitude". St Vincent and the Grenadines' Constitution, in section 4, reads similarly.

No definition of slavery is, however, included in the respective Constitutions. That said, because of the customary international law status of the prohibition of slavery, as well as the fact that both Barbados and St Vincent and the Grenadines are parties to various international conventions, itemised above, which define slavery, it is arguable that municipal courts will countenance the internationally recognised definition of slavery, namely the status or condition of a person over whom any or all the powers attaching to the right of ownership are exercised. Although, because of the dualist nature of Barbados and St Vincent and the Grenadines under international law, international law is not directly effective domestically in these jurisdictions, courts have adopted an approach of conform interpretation over the years to international law.[54] In this context, to the extent that there is no conflict with domestic law, courts will give effect to the international definition and, indeed, prohibition of slavery.

Interestingly, although Caribbean constitutions do not contain a definition of slavery, the Trafficking in Persons legislation in both Barbados and St Vincent and the Grenadines define slavery as the status or condition of a person over whom any or all the powers attaching to the right of ownership are exercised. It is not uncommon for courts in the region to draw inspiration from definitions contained in municipal statutes and, indeed, from the European Court on Human Rights (ECtHR) in the context of its interpretation of the European Convention on Human Rights.[55] Although Caribbean courts have not treated with the issue of slavery in the context of the prohibition of slavery, according to the Eastern Caribbean Supreme Court case of *Jermaine Browne v The Attorney General of Saint Christopher and Nevis et al*,[56] slavery-like treatment may

54 D.S. Berry, *Caribbean Integration Law*, Oxford University Press, Oxford 2014.

55 Minister of Home Affairs v. Fisher [1980] A.C. 319.

56 Claim No. SKBHCV2016/0074.

fall under the prohibition of inhuman and degrading treatment. More pointedly, the court in that case explained that:

> It is no surprise that such a constitutional prohibition [against inhuman and degrading treatment] found its way in Commonwealth Caribbean constitutions given our history with the barbarism associated with centuries of the slave trade and slavery. No doubt the drafters of section 7 of the Constitution had in mind the types of punishments meted out to slaves for over 300 years.[57]

That said, while it is certainly commendable that Barbados and St Vincent and the Grenadines' Constitutions contain specific prohibitions of slavery and, indeed, the prohibition of inhuman and degrading treatment or punishment, it must be recalled that these rights apply vertically, and not horizontally. More pointedly, the provision on slavery clearly covers circumstances in which the State and its agencies exercise any or all of the powers attaching to the right of ownership over a private citizen. In such circumstances, the person so adversely affected has *locus standi* to seek redress before the High Court. However, unlike the Jamaica Charter of Fundamental Rights and Freedoms, which allows for the horizontal application of human rights,[58] the constitutions of Barbados and St Vincent and the Grenadines would not allow a constitutional claim to be brought by a private person alleging that another person has committed the act of slavery against him or her. The absence of horizontal application of the prohibition of slavery does not, however, mean that a prosecution cannot be brought in respect of the commission of slavery by one person against another, at least in Barbados. This is because, under section 33 of Barbados' Offenses Against the Persons Act (1994), the offense of 'buying or disposing of a person as a slave' is prohibited. It reads:

> Any person who imports, exports, removes, buys, sells or disposes of any person as a slave, or accepts, receives or detains against his will any person as a slave is guilty of an offence and is liable on conviction on indictment to imprisonment for life.

Regrettably, St Vincent and the Grenadines' Criminal Code (CAP 171) does not contain a similar provision. In this context, the horizontal application of the

57 *Ibid.*, [63].

58 T.S. Robinson, A. Bulkan, and A. Saunders, *Fundamentals of Caribbean Constitutional Law*, Sweet & Maxwell, Mytholmroyd 2015.

prohibition of slavery would only arise where a person has been trafficked for the purpose of slavery, pursuant to the Trafficking in Persons Act. By contrast, in Barbados, where slavery is committed in the trafficking context, it would be covered by the Trafficking in Persons Act, and where it is committed outside of that context, it will be covered by the Offenses Against the Persons Act.

3.3 *The Persuasive Influence of International Case Law*

Municipal courts in the Caribbean, in their assessment of the prohibition of slavery, may be persuasively guided by the case, *Prosecutor v Kunarac*,[59] which made it clear that the *actus reus* of slavery involves the exercise of any or all of the powers attaching to the right of ownership over a person, while the *mens rea* involves the intentional exercise of such powers. They will also likely be guided by the indicia of enslavement as outlined in *Kunarac* case, namely:

> the restriction or control of an individual's autonomy, freedom of choice or freedom of movement; and, often, the accruing of some gain to the perpetrator. The consent or free will of the victim is absent. It is often rendered impossible or irrelevant by, for example, the threat or use of force or other forms of coercion; the fear of violence, deception or false promises; the abuse of power; the victim's position of vulnerability; detention or captivity, psychological oppression or socio-economic conditions. Further indications of enslavement include exploitation; the exaction of forced or compulsory labour or service, often without remuneration and often, though not necessarily, involving physical hardship; sex; prostitution; and human trafficking.[60]

Interestingly, the Tribunal in the *Kunarac* case further considered that:

> the "acquisition" or "disposal" of someone for monetary or other compensation, is not a requirement for enslavement. Doing so, however, is a prime example of the exercise of the right of ownership over someone. The duration of the suspected exercise of powers attaching to the right of ownership is another factor that may be considered when determining whether someone was enslaved; however, its importance in any given case will depend on the existence of other indications of enslavement.

59 Case No.: IT-96-23-T & IT-96-23/1-T.
60 *Ibid.*, 542.

> Detaining or keeping someone in captivity, without more, would, depending on the circumstances of a case, usually not constitute enslavement.[61]

The Tribunal then outlined the factors that will be taken into consideration in determining whether enslavement was committed:

> These are the control of someone's movement, control of physical environment, psychological control, measures taken to prevent or deter escape, force, threat of force or coercion, duration, assertion of exclusivity, subjection to cruel treatment and abuse, control of sexuality and forced labour.[62]

3.4 *References to Slavery in Private Law*

Although no courts in the region have grappled with the question of 'ownership' in the context of slavery, it is likely that if a case of slavery were to come before the Courts of Barbados or St Vincent and the Grenadines, said courts would consider whether the accused person has exercised the incidents of ownership, which have been described by the Jamaican Court of Appeal case of *Da Costa v Warburton et al*,[63] albeit in a private law context, as "complete freedom of action with regard to the enjoyment, disposition, and management of the property".[64] Even further, because the definition of slavery speaks to 'status or condition', the court may not take a rigid approach of requiring evidence of 'genuine legal ownership'; a circumstance in which a person exercises on a *de facto* (as opposed to *de jure*) basis the incidents of ownership over another person will constitute slavery.

In private law, the implications of making an award of specific performance in the context of employment relationships which may amount to slavery have been recognised by municipal courts. In fact, in the Barbadian case of *Emtage v Queen Elizabeth Hospital Board*,[65] the court made it clear that:

> Courts have refused to grant injunctions which, in effect, would, require specific performance of a contract of employment. The reason is to be found in the clarification by the judge of the employment relationship

61 *Ibid.*

62 *Ibid.*, 543.

63 (1971) 17 WIR 334.

64 *Ibid.*, 338.

65 BB 2014 HC 36.

> as being between two equal contracting parties. Since, it is said, it would "turn contracts of service into contracts of slavery" if employers could compel their employees to continue in service, therefore, on the principle of reciprocity between contracting parties, and the need to maintain mutual confidence, the employee should not be able to compel the employer to keep him in service.[66]

3.5 *The Concept of "Exploitation" in Domestic Law*

Apart from the Trafficking in Persons Acts of the respective jurisdictions, no other domestic law expressly addresses the question of 'exploitation'. Under section 2 of St Vincent and the Grenadines' Trafficking in Persons Act, which mirrors section 3 of the Barbados Trafficking in Persons Act, trafficking in persons is prohibited:

> "trafficking in persons" means the recruitment, transportation, transfer, harbouring or receipt of persons by means of the threat or use of force or other means of coercion, of abduction, of fraud, of deception, of the abuse of power or of a position of vulnerability, or of giving or receiving of payment or benefits to achieve the consent of a person having control over another person, for the purpose of exploitation.

The provision then defines the purpose element – 'exploitation' – broadly to include:

a. keeping a person in a state of slavery;
b. subjecting a person to practices similar to slavery;
c. compelling or causing a person to provide forced labour or services;
d. keeping a person in a state of servitude, including domestic and sexual servitude;
e. child pornography; the exploitation of the prostitution of another;
f. engaging in any form of commercial sexual exploitation, including but not limited to pimping, pandering, procuring, profiting from prostitution, maintaining a brothel;
g. engaging in sexual exploitation;
h. the illicit removal of human organs;
i. causing a person to transport illegal items within or across borders; and
j. deriving a benefit through the abuse of another person.

66 *Ibid.*, 123.

Meanwhile, 'practices similar to slavery' have been defined to include debt bondage, serfdom, forced or servile marriages, and delivery or receipt of children for exploitation. Courts in the Caribbean have not had occasion to pronounce upon the definition of 'exploitation', but it is very likely that if the question were to arise in future, they will take a broad view of exploitation, particularly since the provision is drafted in non-exhaustive language, namely "exploitation includes", instead of "exploitation means". Courts are likely also adopt the approach that exploitation need not be actually committed for the offense of trafficking in persons to be made out, in a similar vein to the Ontario Supreme Court case of *R v D'Souza*,[67] which ruled that trafficking in persons is a crime of specific intent; the presence of 'acts' coupled with 'means' for the 'purpose of exploitation' is sufficient, at least in respect of the trafficking of adults.

The Trafficking in Persons Acts of Barbados and St Vincent and the Grenadines treat slavery and practices similar to slavery as manifestations of the offense of trafficking in person, rather than being synonymous with trafficking in persons. In fact, when one looks at the definition of exploitation contained in the respective Acts, it is clear that it is intended to capture circumstances, for example, where an 'act' (e.g. recruitment) is present alongside certain 'means' (e.g. coercion) for the 'purpose of exploitation' (e.g. slavery). A similar approach applies in respect of debt bondage, servitude, forced labour, serfdom, forced marriage and practices similar to slavery; they will only be deemed manifestations of trafficking in persons if they are the end result of the 'acts' when combined with the 'means' elements.

Presumably, however, outside of the trafficking context, courts tasked with determining the definition of slavery and practices similar to slavery contained in other legislation, like the Offenses Against the Persons Act, may, in addition to countenancing applicable principles of international law, also consider the definitions contained in Trafficking in Persons Acts as persuasive, namely:

> "debt bondage" means the status or condition of a debtor arising from a pledge by the debtor of his personal services or those of the persons under his control as a security for debt, if the value of those services as reasonably assessed is not applied toward the liquidation of the debt or the length and nature of those services are not respectively limited and defined;
>
> "forced labour" means labour or services obtained or maintained through force, threat of force, or other means of coercion or physical restraint;

---

67 *R v D'Souza* 2016 ONSC 2749.

> "servitude" means a condition of dependency in which the labour or services of a person are provided or obtained by threats of serious harm to that person or another person, or through any scheme, plan or pattern intended to cause the person to believe that, if the person did not perform such labour or services, that person or another person will suffer serious harm;
>
> "slavery" means the status or condition of a person over whom any or all the powers attaching to the right of ownership are exercised.

It means, therefore, that when interpretating a provision like section 207 of St Vincent and the Grenadines Criminal Code, courts may take judicial notice, even if persuasively, of the definition of forced labour contained in the TIP Acts. Section 207 of the Constitution reads:

> Any person who unlawfully compels any other person to labour against the will of that person is guilty of an offence and liable to imprisonment for two years.

3.6 *Indicators of Contemporary Forms of Slavery*

The Labour Departments of Barbados and St Vincent and the Grenadines, respectively, use, as a matter of practice, the ILO's Indicators of Forced Labour in order to determine whether there are reasonable bases for concluding that a person has been subject to forced labour.[68] These indicators are non-exhaustive. Meanwhile, the Anti-Trafficking Units of Barbados and St Vincent and the Grenadines, respectively, rely heavily upon the UN Office on Drugs and Crime's (UNODC) list of indicators to determine whether a trafficking situation is in issue.[69] These factors are, of course, non-exhaustive.

3.7 *The Influence of the Reports of Treaty Bodies*

Because of the dualist nature of Barbados and St Vincent and the Grenadines under international law,[70] courts in the region are not obliged to take judicial notice of the reports of the supervisory bodies of international organisations when they render decisions on the issue of contemporary slavery. There is

68 "ILO Indicators of Forced Labour" (ILO), <https://www.ilo.org/wcmsp5/groups/public/---ed_norm/---declaration/documents/publication/wcms_203832.pdf>.

69 "Human Trafficking Indicators" (United Nations Office on Drugs and Crime) <https://www.unodc.org/pdf/HT_indicators_E_LOWRES.pdf>.

70 D.E. Pollard, 'Juridical and constitutional implications of CARICOM treaty practice' (2009) 35:1 *Commonwealth Law Bulletin* 7.

nothing, however, that prevents these courts from treating these reports as persuasive only, to the extent that they assist judges to understand the historical, international, or contemporary contexts of the norms in issue.

There is one, albeit highly contentious and truly exceptional, case to date in which a regional court has treated the report of a treaty as indispensable to a decision – the Barbadian case of *Boyce and Joseph v AG of Barbados*.[71] In that case, two men, having been convicted of murder and sentenced to death by municipal courts, argued that although Barbados had not incorporated the American Convention on Human Rights' provisions into domestic law, as is constitutionally required for dualist countries wishing to give domestic effect to international obligations, given the serious nature of the charge as well as the fact that the men's representations before the Inter-American Human Rights Commission (IAHRC) was their last opportunity to argue in favour of the commutation of their life sentence, Barbados' conduct in ratifying the Convention gave rise to a legitimate expectation that the Governor General would receive and consider the report of the IAHRC before arriving at a decision as to whether or not to commute their execution. In this context, the Caribbean Court of Justice (CCJ) found that, having not waited to receive the report from the IAHRC, the Barbados Privy Council (BPC) and the state by parity of reasoning had acted in breach of the appellants' legitimate expectations. Although this case, at least for Barbados, whose apex court is the CCJ, is binding authority, one must be careful not to exaggerate its wider implications. Indeed, their Lordships in *Boyce and Joseph v AG* itself cautioned that this case should not be taken as laying down a *per se* rule that domestic bodies must wait for the report of an international treaty body before deciding upon the outcome of a particular case. In the court's view, this was a truly exceptional case involving the right to life, and particularly, the irrevocable nature of the death sentence. It was the last opportunity for the mitigating circumstances of the men, as indicated in the treaty body's report, to be considered by the Governor General.

Returning to the discussion around the influence of the reports of treaty bodies on slavery and cotemporary forms of slavery, it is submitted that courts will likely treat the reports of bodies, such as the Human Rights or the ILO's Committee of Experts, as persuasive. Indeed, given the exacting nature of dualism in the Caribbean, the *sui generis* nature of the *Joseph and Boyce* case, and regional courts' general treatment of foreign sources only as persuasive authority,[72] it seems very likely that the reports of international treaty bodies

71 [2006] CCJ 1 (AJ).

72 J. Haynes, 'The Transplantation of the European Principle of 'State Liability' in Caribbean Community (Caricom) Law: A Normative Assessment' (2014) 14:1 *Oxford University Commonwealth Law Journal* 73.

on questions of contemporary slavery, like the reports of the United Nations Special Rapporteur on contemporary forms of slavery, will be treated only as persuasive authority. Similarly, Caribbean courts are likely to treat the decisions on slavery and contemporary slavery emanating from foreign jurisdictions as persuasive authority only. In fact, as far back as 1978, the Privy Council in *Minister of Home Affairs v Fisher*[73] had held that, because of the historical antecedents of Caribbean constitutions reflecting the provisions of the European Convention on Human Rights, municipal courts in the Caribbean *may* countenance decisions of foreign tribunals, including the ECtHR. In this regard, leading ECtHR cases on slavery and contemporary slavery, like *Siliadin v France*[74] and *Rantsev v Russia and Cyprus*[75] may be countenanced, albeit as persuasive authority, by municipal courts in the region.

3.8 *The Appellation 'Contemporary Slavery' or 'Modern Slavery'*

Stakeholders actively working in the anti-slavery field in the Caribbean do not generally use the term 'contemporary slavery' or 'modern slavery' to describe serfdom, debt bondage, forced marriage, child labour, forced/compulsory labour and human trafficking. In fact, stakeholders typically make a deliberate decision, as a matter of policy, legislation and everyday vernacular, to distinguish slavery from practices that are similar to slavery.[76]

The first objection shared by Caribbean anti-slavery stakeholders against the use of 'contemporary slavery' or 'modern slavery' is the fact that these terminologies incorrectly assume that all practices similar to slavery are subsumed into the concept of slavery and are therefore synonymous with slavery. In their view, this false equivalence is not correct as a matter of international law nor domestic law. Indeed, international law treats slavery as a peremptory norm from which no derogation is permitted and defines it as the *de jure* or *de facto* exercise of the powers attaching to the right of ownership. By contrast, certain practices similar to slavery, namely forced or compulsory nature, countenance exceptions and are therefore not peremptory norms of international law and, in any event, are not even defined in terms relative to ownership. For example, Article 2(2) of the ILO Forced Labour Convention outlines certain exceptions to the prohibition of forced labour, which clearly intimates that it is not a peremptory norm of international law.

---

73 [1980] A.C. 319.

74 ECHR Application no. 73316/01.

75 ECHR Application no. 25965/04.

76 J. Haynes, 'Paradoxes and Anomalies in Caribbean Anti-Trafficking Law and Practice' (2023) 40:1 *Journal of Global South Studies* 145.

More than this, stakeholders in the anti-slavery field in the Caribbean are concerned that the use of 'contemporary slavery' or 'modern slavery' mischaracterizes the true gravity of slavery by implicitly assuming continuities between slavery and practices similar to slavery. Indeed, although there can conceivably be cases in which a person may, for example, be trafficked for the purpose of slavery, these represent only a handful of cases. In the vast majority of cases, the rights attached to ownership are not exercised in the course of a trafficking enterprise. In this regard, in terms of gravity, to implicitly suggest that practices similar to slavery are contemporary manifestations of slavery is, as a matter of simple logic, indefensible. Of course, all forms of exploitation are harmful, including practices that are similar to slavery, but the use of slavery to describe a phenomenon should only be legitimately done in the clearest and gravest of cases.

Given the Caribbean's experience of slavery, stakeholders in the anti-slavery field in the Caribbean do not lightly reference slavery in their work or conversations. They object to the flippant use of the term 'slavery' as a political tool to shore up support against modern forms of exploitation. In their view, the use of the terms 'contemporary slavery' or 'modern slavery' as synonyms for 'slavery' trivializes the gravity of slavery experienced by Caribbean peoples in the context of the Transatlantic Slave Trade in that it treats the legacies of slavery, including inter-generational trauma, in a dismissive way. For them, describing forms of contemporary exploitation as slavery is historically, legally and politically incorrect. In view of the foregoing, stakeholders in the Caribbean would much prefer the use of the term 'practices similar to slavery' or 'contemporary forms of exploitation' to describe what we now call 'contemporary slavery'. In this way, the term slavery is reserved only for the most egregious forms of exploitation involving the exercise of powers attaching to the right of ownership.

4 Redressing and Recalibrating Contemporary Slavery

4.1 *The Enactment of Trafficking in Persons Legislation*

Both Barbados and St Vincent and the Grenadines enacted Trafficking in Persons legislation in 2011 and 2016, respectively. The respective legislation countenance the four 'Ps' approach to combating trafficking in persons, namely: prevention, prosecution, protection and partnership.[77]

77 J. Haynes, *Caribbean Anti-Trafficking Law and Practice*, Bloomsbury Publishing, London 2019.

The legislation criminalises trafficking in persons in accordance with the Palermo Protocol by prescribing penalties of up to life imprisonment. Whereas the 'acts' (e.g. recruitment or transportation), 'means' (e.g. deception or coercion) and 'purpose' (e.g. sexual exploitation or forced labour) elements must be satisfied to establish the trafficking of an adult, the 'means' element need not be present for there to be a case of child trafficking. Meanwhile, the alleged consent of victims of trafficking to their exploitation cannot be used as a defence by a trafficker. Nor can the victim's sexual history be used in evidence as indicative of his/her sexual predisposition.[78]

The legislation, apart from prescribing periods of imprisonment, also prescribe forfeiture of the instrumentalities used in the commission of a trafficking offense, as well as confiscation of the assets resulting from the commission of the offense. The legislation contemplates that where the trafficker has been convicted, the court will grant an award of restitution, which is intended to cover the costs of medical and psychological treatment; physical and occupational therapy and rehabilitation; necessary transportation, temporary housing and childcare; lost income; attorney's fees and other legal costs; and any other related losses.

Separately, in the realm of protection, the legislation, first, mandates competent authorities to correctly identify victims of trafficking and refer them to appropriate support and assistance mechanisms. They also stipulate that victims must be provided with a range of support measures, including medical and psychological assistance; legal, documentary and interpretation services; and accommodation. The legislation also provides for the discretionary grant of leave to remain in the respective jurisdictions and the non-punishment of trafficked victims for offenses that they have committed as a direct result of having been trafficked.

As a matter of practice, legislation in both Barbados and St Vincent and the Grenadines strike a good balance between criminalization and the protection of trafficked victims. That said, Barbados' legislation introduces a greater burden on trafficked persons to benefit from the non-punishment provision, compared to St Vincent and the Grenadines' TIP Act. Section 14 of Barbados' Act provides:

> Where a victim has been compelled to engage in unlawful activities as a direct result of being trafficked, and the victim has committed any immigration-related offence or any other criminal offence for which he

78 *Ibid.*

> is being prosecuted, the victim may offer as a defence, evidence of having been compelled as a victim of trafficking to engage in such unlawful activities.

This provision, in addition to requiring evidence of a sufficient nexus between the trafficking experience and offense committed by the victim, also requires the provision of evidence of compulsion before they could benefit from the non-punishment provision. Courts in various cases have indicated that compulsion requires evidence that the culpability of the victim in question was extinguished by the trafficking experience, and that, to impose this threshold on child victims of trafficking, in particular, is highly problematic.[79]

In the area of partnership, the legislation mandates competent national authorities to form partnerships with both local and international organisations and countries aimed at combatting trafficking in persons. Meanwhile, in the realm of prevention, the respective TIP Acts require that competent national authorities raise awareness about the nature of and impact of human trafficking; train and sensitise stakeholders actively working in the anti-trafficking field; collaborate with domestic, regional and international bodies, including civil society organisations; and address the structural conditions and risk factors that fuel trafficking in persons, including poverty, discrimination, unemployment and the lack of educational opportunities. At the institutional level, the respective Counter-Trafficking Units are tasked with undertaking the foregoing activities and, more generally, monitoring the implementation of anti-trafficking norms in the respective jurisdictions. Outside of the trafficking in persons context, the Ministries of Labour and Registration Departments monitor and investigate instances of forced labour and forced marriages, respectively, in Barbados and St Vincent and the Grenadines.

4.2 *Transnational Initiatives on Contemporary Slavery*

Neither Barbados nor St Vincent and the Grenadines are a part of transnational initiatives on contemporary slavery. Indeed, although the governments of both of these jurisdictions refer to Sustainable Development Goal 8.7 in international meetings, policy briefings and press releases,[80] very little is tangibly done to join international initiatives like Alliance 8.7 formally. Instead, governments of the region are principally concerned with their rankings in the context of the annual US Trafficking in Persons (TIP) Reports. These reports,

79 *R v Sermanfure Joseph* [2017] EWCA Crim 36.

80 See for example: 'Barbados' (UN Sustainable Development Goals Knowledge Platform), <https://sustainabledevelopment.un.org/memberstates/barbados>.

which seek to rank countries according to their compliance with minimum standards under the US Trafficking Victims Protection Act, have seemingly become the gold standard for Barbados and St Vincent and the Grenadines.[81] To the extent that they take sufficient efforts not to be ranked on the tier two watch list or the tier three list, they are content and do not consider other strategic alliances that could redound to the benefit of exploited persons.

Meanwhile, although Labour Departments and TIP Units in Barbados and St Vincent and the Grenadines investigate the commission of contemporary slavery by transnational businesses, neither jurisdiction has formally incorporated the United Nations Guiding Principles on Business and Human Rights into domestic legislation or policy or administrative frameworks. In fact, a review of the International Investment Agreements entered into by these States illustrates that the protection of human rights and respect for labour standards do not form part of these agreements.[82] Meanwhile, although CARICOM has long drafted an Investment Code, which seeks to impose certain minimum human rights and labour standards of foreign investors, these countries have not incorporated these standards into their existing or new international investment agreements. As such, it can be argued that the United Nations Guiding Principles on Business and Human Rights remain primarily at the international plane, having not been incorporated into domestic law, and somewhat esoteric in their orientation as neither domestic courts nor tribunals typically refer to them in their adjudication.

5 Conclusion

This paper has argued that the existing national legal architecture on slavery and contemporary slavery in Barbados and St Vincent and the Grenadines, and the Caribbean more generally, is reasonably strong but that there are significant policy and legislative gaps that need to be addressed. It contends that, for a people who have endured many years of slavery, it is disappointing that, with the exception of Jamaica, the constitutional prohibition of slavery does not contemplate its horizontal application. It also expresses disappointment that Caribbean courts have not had occasion to provide a definition of slavery, although it is likely that developments in international law on this question

81 J. Haynes, 'The Constitutional Limits of Anti-Trafficking Norms in the Commonwealth Caribbean' (2022) 18 *Anti-Trafficking Review* 139.

82 J. Haynes, 'Reforming the Bilateral Investment Treaty Landscape in the Caribbean: A Clarion Call' (2022) 38:1 *ICSID Review – Foreign Investment Law Journal* 72.

will be countenanced in future by regional courts, given their outward-facing stance. The paper argues against the appellation 'contemporary slavery' or 'modern slavery', contending that a more apt description might be 'contemporary forms of exploitation'. It notes that although the region has come a long way in eradicating exploitation, there are still cases in which such exploitation occurs today, which are exacerbated by a lax political approach to redressing the issue, as well as various gaps in the regulatory frameworks of the jurisdictions in question. Nonetheless, it applauds the movement toward the enactment and implementation of anti-trafficking legislation in the region, which it considers will no doubt redound to the benefit of exploited peoples.

Academic References

A. Degraff, and K. Baldwin, *Participatory Mapping of Heritage Sites in the Grenadine Islands*, CERMES Technical Report (No. 65), The University of the West Indies, Cave Hill Campus, 2013.

A.D.V. Phillips, 'Emancipation Betrayed: Social Control Legislation in the British Caribbean (with Special reference to Barbados), 1834–1876'. (1994) 70 *Chi.-Kent L. Rev.* 1349.

B. Marshall, 'The Black Caribs—Native Resistance to British Penetration into the Windward Side of St. Vincent 1763–1773' (1973) 19:4 *Caribbean Quarterly* 4.

C. Hall, 'The slavery business and the making of "race" in Britain and the Caribbean' (2020) 61:22 *Current Anthropology* 172.

C.H. Wesley, 'The Negro in the West Indies, slavery and freedom' (1932) 17:1 *The Journal of Negro History* 51.

C.L.R. James, *The Black Jacobins: Toussaint L'ouverture and the San Domingo revolution*, Penguin UK, London 2001.

C.M. Scott, 'Bussa's Rebellion (1816)' (2007) *Encyclopedia of Slave Resistance and Rebellion* 90.

C.R. Eugene, 'Towards a Framework for Caribbean Reparations' (2019) 44:3 *Journal of Eastern Caribbean Studies (Special Issue Demystifying Caribbean Civil Society)* 54.

D. Elitis, 'The total product of Barbados, 1664–1701' (1995) 55:2 *The Journal of Economic History* 321.

D.E. Pollard, 'Juridical and constitutional implications of CARICOM treaty practice' (2009) 35:1 *Commonwealth Law Bulletin* 7.

D.S. Berry, *Caribbean Integration Law*, Oxford University Press, Oxford 2014.

D.V. Armstrong, 'Capitalism and the Shift to Sugar and Slavery in Mid-Seventeenth-Century Barbados' (2019) 53:3 *Historical Archaeology* 468.

E.B. Rugemer, 'The development of mastery and race in the comprehensive slave codes of the greater Caribbean during the seventeenth century' (2013) 70:3 *William & Mary Quarterly* 429.

E.V. Goveia, 'The West Indian Slave Laws of the Eighteenth Century' (1960) 1 *Revista de ciencias sociales* 75.

E. Williams, *Capitalism and Slavery*, University of North Carolina Press, Chapel Hill 1944.

E. Williams, *From Columbus to Castro: The History of the Caribbean 1492–1969*. Harper & Row, New York 1970.

G. Taylor, 'Anti-Slave Trade Drama in England: 1786–1808' (1999) 13:1 *South African Theatre Journal* 8.

G. Taylor, *The Interest: How the British establishment resisted the abolition of slavery*, Random House, New York 2020.

H.A. Ohline, 'Slavery, Economics, and Congressional Politics, 1790' (1980) 46:3 *The Journal of Southern History* 335.

H.M. Beckles, *Britain's Black Debt: Reparations for Caribbean Slavery and Native Genocide*, University of the West Indies Press, Saint Andrew Parish 2013.

H.M. Beckles, 'The Reparation Movement: Greatest Political Tide of the Twenty-first Century' (2019) 68:1/2 *Social and Economic Studies* 11.

H. Rubenstein, 'Economic history and population movements in an eastern Caribbean Valley' (1977) 24:1 *Ethnohistory* 19.

J. Haynes, 'The Transplantation of the European Principle of 'State Liability' in Caribbean Community (Caricom) Law: A Normative Assessment' (2014) 14:1 *Oxford University Commonwealth Law Journal* 73.

J. Haynes, *Caribbean Anti-Trafficking Law and Practice*, Bloomsbury Publishing, London 2019.

J. Haynes, 'Reforming the Bilateral Investment Treaty Landscape in the Caribbean: A Clarion Call' (2022) 38:1 *ICSID Review – Foreign Investment Law Journal* 72.

J. Haynes, 'The Constitutional Limits of Anti-Trafficking Norms in the Commonwealth Caribbean' (2022) 18 *Anti-Trafficking Review* 139.

J. Haynes, 'Paradoxes and Anomalies in Caribbean Anti Trafficking Law and Practice' (2023) 40:1 *Journal of Global South Studies* 145.

J.S. Handler, 'Custom and law: The status of enslaved Africans in seventeenth-century Barbados' (2016) 37:2 *Slavery & Abolition* 233.

K. Paugh, 'The politics of childbearing in the British Caribbean and the Atlantic world during the age of abolition, 1776–1838' (2013) 221:1 *Past & Present* 119.

M. Chamberlain, 'Elsa Goveia: History and Nation' (2004) 58:1 *History Workshop Journal* 167.

M.E. Gettleman, 'Entrepreneurship in Barbados, 1625-1660' (1959) 21:1 *The Historian* 200.

M. Quintanilla, 'Mercantile Communities in the Ceded Islands: The Alexander Bartlet & George Campbell Company' (2004) 79:1/2 *International Social Science Review* 14.

M. Sherwood, *After Abolition*, IB Tauris, London 2007.

P. Clegg, 'The Caribbean Reparations Claim: What Chance of Success?' (2014) 103:4 *The Round Table* 435.

P.X. Scanlan, 'Emancipation and captivity in the British Empire' (2019) 30:5 *History and Anthropology* 503.

R.S. Dunn, *Sugar and slaves: The rise of the planter class in the English West Indies, 1624–1713*, UNC Press Books, Chapel Hill 2012.

S. Drescher, 'Whose abolition? Popular pressure and the ending of the British slave trade' (1994) 143 *Past & Present* 136.

T. Durbin, and J. St George, 'Human Trafficking in Barbados: Achievements and Continuing Hurdles' (2013) 38:1–2 *Journal of Eastern Caribbean Studies* 126.

T.S. Robinson, A. Bulkan, and A. Saunders, *Fundamentals of Caribbean Constitutional Law*, Sweet & Maxwell, Mytholmroyd 2015.

V. Shepherd, and H.M. Beckles, *Caribbean Slavery in The Atlantic World: A Student Reader*, Ian Randle Publishers, Kingston 2000.

V.A. Shepherd, 'Slavery, Shame and Pride: Debates Over The Marking of The Bicentennial of The Abolition of The British Trans-Atlantic Trade in Africans in 2007' (2010) 56:1–2 *Caribbean Quarterly* 1.

V. T. Harlow, *A History of Barbados, 1625–1685*, Clarendon Press, Oxford 1926.

W. Rodney, *How Europe Underdeveloped Africa*, Verso Books, London 2018.

W.M. Wiecek, 'The statutory law of slavery and race in the thirteen mainland colonies of British America' (1977) 34:2 *The William and Mary Quarterly: A Magazine of Early American History* 258.

Les formes contemporaines d'esclavage, y compris les causes et les conséquences : Belgique

Filip Dorssemont

1 La présence du passé : l'esclavage en tant qu'institution mondiale et ses héritages

1.1 *La Belgique et l'institution juridique de l'esclavage : l'ombre du passé (pré) colonial*

La Belgique a obtenu son indépendance en 1830. Cette année-là, le Royaume-Uni des Pays-Bas (1815–1830) est alors scindé en deux États séparés : le Royaume des Pays-Bas et la Belgique, qui se transformera en monarchie constitutionnelle en 1831. Le passé de la Belgique pertinent pour l'histoire de l'esclavage se confond avec l'histoire politique de l'Espagne (1555–1705), de l'Autriche (1705–1794) et de la France (1794–1815). La pertinence de la Belgique pour l'histoire de l'esclavagisme pendant cette période dépend de son histoire portuaire. Or, le port le plus important, celui d'Anvers, ayant pu servir de carrefour, a été bloqué pour la plus grande partie de cette période (de la reconquête de cette ville par les forces armées espagnoles (1585) jusqu'au Traité du 12 mai 1863 pour le rachat du péage de l'Escaut[1]). Ce blocage n'a été suspendu que pendant des périodes relativement courtes de la période française et hollandaise. Le port secondaire d'Ostende n'a été développé que dans la période autrichienne. C'est ainsi que Everaert a pu affirmer que « dans le cercle international des trafiquants d'esclaves, les Pays-Bas méridionaux occupent sans doute une place assez médiocre, car ils n'ont déployé qu'une activité négrière (*sic*) restreinte aussi bien dans le temps que par son intensité »[2].

Si le cas de la Belgique présente un intérêt particulier, c'est dû avant tout à la mobilisation par Léopold II d'un argumentaire abolitionniste en vue de justifier la reconnaissance de l'État indépendant du Congo (1885–1908) dans

1 Voir R. Depoortere, *Le rachat du péage de l'Escaut,* Académie Royale de Belgique, Bruxelles 1991, p. 414.

2 J.G. Everaert, 'Commerce d'Afrique et traite négrière dans les Pays-Bas autrichiens' (1975) 62 *Revue Francaise d'Histoire d'Outre-Mer* 177, p. 177.

 | DOI:10.1163/9789004723801_005

le cadre du Traité de Berlin de 1885[3]. Dans un deuxième temps, la volonté alléguée de combattre des pratiques de travail forcé a été mobilisée pour justifier la reprise de l'État indépendant du Congo par l'État belge à titre de colonie belge (1908–1960)[4]. Ces deux argumentaires sont à la base de récits dont il faut aujourd'hui contester la crédibilité. Léopold II, le chef de l'État indépendant du Congo, s'est engagé comme celui qui allait libérer le Congo du joug de l'esclavagisme dit « arabe ». L'article 9 du Chapitre II du Traité de Berlin (1885) reconnaissant au plan international l'État indépendant du Congo contenait donc une Déclaration interdisant la traite des esclaves[5].

Ce récit est au cœur de nombreux monuments érigés par l'État belge à l'époque coloniale, commémorant les « bienfaits » de l'État indépendant du Congo. Les représentants du peuple congolais y sont sculptés de manière anonymes et nus dans le registre inférieur, rendant grâce aux libérateurs belges bien vêtus et identifiés. Le souverain blanc est représenté chevauchant, les mercenaires ou les missionnaires sont debout, tandis que les « noirs » sont agenouillés[6]. Dans la réalité, le régime de Léopold II a substitué le travail forcé à l'esclavagisme. Plusieurs formes de travail forcé seront institutionnalisées dans les rapports entre les peuples dits « indigènes » (lisez : la population autochtone) et l'État indépendant du Congo. Les soldats de la force publique ont été qualifiés de « volunteers in chains »[7] et des taxes sont levées *in natura*, forçant les populations autochtones à récolter du caoutchouc ou à apporter des quantités d'ivoire à titre de paiement de leur dette fiscale. Face à la critique émergente dans la presse et l'opinion publique internationale, l'État belge prétendra changer de cap. L'article 2 de la Charte coloniale disposait ainsi : « Nul ne peut

---

3 G. Deneckere, T. De Paepe, B. De Wever et G. Vanthemsche, *Een geschiedenis van België*, Academia Press, Gent 2017, pp. 159–161.

4 *Ibid.*, pp. 165–166.

5 « Conformément aux principes du droit des gens, tels qu'ils sont reconnus par les Puissances signataires, la traite des esclaves étant interdite, et les opérations qui, sur terre ou sur mer, fournissent des esclaves à la traite devant être également considérées comme interdites, les Puissances qui exercent ou qui exerceront des droits de souveraineté, ou une influence dans les territoires formant le bassin conventionnel du Congo, déclarent que ces territoires ne pourront servir ni de marché ni de voie de transit pour la traite des esclaves, de quelque race que ce soit. Chacune de ces Puissances s'y engage à employer tous les moyens en son pouvoir pour mettre fin à ce commerce et pour punir ceux qui s'en occupent. » *Acte général de la conférence de Berlin de 1885*.

6 Pour un aperçu : M.G. Stanard, *The Leopard, The Lion, and the cock. Colonial Memories and Monuments in Belgium*, Leuven University Press, Leuven 2019, p. 338.

7 A. Hochschild, *King Leopold's Ghost*, Pan Books, London 2006, p. 130.

être contraint de travailler pour le compte ou au profit de particuliers ou de sociétés »[8].

Cette charte est muette quant à l'interdiction dans le chef de l'État belge d'organiser lui-même le travail forcé. Le texte de l'article 2 était innovant en ce qu'il n'y avait alors aucune disposition légale applicable en zone métropolitaine interdisant explicitement le travail forcé. Pendant la période coloniale, l'État belge a continué à avoir recours au travail forcé dans le cadre des travaux publics (ferroviaires) et de la transformation de l'agriculture en faveur de *cash crops* au détriment de la souveraineté alimentaire du Congo. Les taxes *in natura* furent formellement abolies, mais le refus de les payer était sanctionné par du travail forcé. Malgré la disposition explicite de la Charte coloniale, l'État belge n'a pas protégé les indigènes des pratiques de travail forcé des sociétés privées. Le cas de l'extraction de l'huile de palmier par la firme de Monsieur Lever, ayant recours à du travail forcé, est bien documenté[9]. Même si les indigènes entrent également dans un contrat de travail, l'utilisation d'un droit disciplinaire sanctionné par des peines corporelles crée un flou entre le contrat de travail librement consenti et le travail exercé sous la menace d'une peine. Cette pratique fait preuve d'un pluralisme juridique de mauvais aloi, sachant que le pouvoir disciplinaire issu du contrat de travail ne permettait pas du tout aux employeurs en Belgique d'infliger des coups et des blessures, ce qui était contraire au droit pénal[10].

1.2 *Le travail forcé (pré)colonial face aux instruments internationaux et européens*

Sur un plan purement juridique, la question se pose de savoir comment l'État belge a pu marier ces pratiques organisées ou tolérées avec les traités interdisant le travail forcé et la traite qui émergent progressivement pendant la période coloniale. Il convient tout d'abord de constater que l'État belge a été très réticent à ratifier ces traités. Cette réticence a disparu à partir de 1960, lorsque le Congo a obtenu son indépendance.

8 Voir L. Petillon, 'Des Habitants et de leurs droits', dans *Les Novelles, Droit colonial, Éditions E. Picard, Bruxelles 1931*. La Charte coloniale est la loi qui règle les modalités du transfert de l'Etat indépendant au Congo à titre de colonie de la Belgique, <https://www.droitcongolais.info/files/1.02.-Charte-coloniale-de-1908.pdf>.

9 B. Henriet, '"Elusive natives': Escaping colonial control in the Leverville oil palm concession, Belgian Congo, 1923–1941' (2015) 49 *Canadian Journal of African Studies* 339.

10 J. Seibert, *In die Globale Wirtschaft gezwungen. Arbeit und kolonialer Kapitalismus im Kongo (1885–1960)*, Campus Verlag, Frankfurt 2016, p. 247; R. Loffman et B. Henriet, 'We are left with barely anything: Colonial Rule, Dependency, and the Lever Brothers in the Belgian, Congo, 1911–1960' (2020) 48:1 *The Journal of Imperial and Commonwealth History* 71.

Pour retracer l'histoire de leur réception dans l'ordre juridique belge, il convient d'étudier ces instruments dans l'ordre chronologique de leur ratification. La première organisation internationale à adopter des instruments pour combattre le *travail forcé* a été l'Organisation internationale du travail. En 1930, la Conférence générale adopte la Convention (n°29) sur le travail forcé[11]. Cet instrument n'imposait pas une interdiction du travail forcé dans l'immédiat. Il y avait une période de transition permettant d'abolir progressivement le travail forcé. La Convention tendait donc aussi à réglementer le travail forcé pendant cette période transitoire. Il y avait toujours moyen de déroger à la convention au détriment des zones non-métropolitaines.[12] Malgré l'extrême maniabilité de cet instrument, il a tout de même fallu attendre les désastres de la Deuxième Guerre mondiale, confrontant les citoyens belges aux misères du travail forcé de Belges déportés en Allemagne, pour que le gouvernement belge en exil décide de ratifier cette convention. La procédure parlementaire de ratification prévue par la Constitution belge n'a pas été respectée. La décision de ratifier en 1943 sera communiquée en janvier 1944 au Bureau international du travail. La Belgique transmettra des rapports à la Commission pour l'application des conventions et recommandations (ci-après la CEACR) de 1946 à 1960 pour documenter le respect de cette convention, y compris dans les territoires non-métropolitains. L'analyse de ces rapports et des observations de la CEACR n'est pas dénuée d'intérêt. La version originale de la Convention n°29 énumérait une panoplie d'exemples de travail forcé devant être progressivement supprimés, qui se lisent quasiment comme une description de l'histoire congolaise précoloniale et coloniale. À ce titre, on pourrait signaler :

> imposer ou laisser imposer le travail forcé ou obligatoire au profit de particuliers, de compagnies ou de personnes morales privées (article 4);
>
> accorder des concessions à des compagnies ou à des personnes morales privées générant l'imposition d'une forme quelconque de travail forcé ou obligatoire en vue de produire ou de recueillir les produits que ces particuliers, compagnies ou personnes morales privées utilisent ou dont ils font le commerce (article 5);
>
> demander le travail forcé ou obligatoire à titre d'impôt et imposer le travail forcé ou obligatoire pour des travaux d'intérêt public par des chefs qui exercent des fonctions administratives (article 10);

11 C029 – Convention (n° 29) sur le travail forcé, 1930.

12 En 2014, la Conférence internationale du Travail a adopté le Protocole relatif à la Convention n° 29, qui a expressément prévu la suppression des dispositions transitoires.

> Imposer le travail forcé ou obligatoire pour le transport de personnes ou de marchandises, par exemple pour le portage et le pagayage (article 18).

Hormis ces obligations de supprimer le travail forcé, l'article 19 de la Convention n°29 prévoyait que « les autorités compétentes ne devraient autoriser le recours aux cultures obligatoires que dans le but de prévenir la famine ou une disette de produits alimentaires et toujours sous la réserve que les denrées ou les produits ainsi obtenus devront rester la propriété des individus ou de la collectivité qui les auront produits ».

Vers la fin de la période coloniale, la CEACR a exprimé des critiques[13]. On apprend que la justification du gouvernement belge pour imposer aux Congolais un travail forcé dans des plantations de *cash crops*, pour des raisons dites pédagogiques (*educational purposes*), était incompatible avec la logique de la Convention n°29. Le gouvernement a dû reconnaître que des taxes étaient payées indirectement à travers du travail forcé. Or, la Convention interdit cette pratique. La CEACR a également condamné les pratiques de travail forcé à titre de punition collective suite à des émeutes lorsqu'une communauté n'assurait pas des dommages-intérêts (1959). La CEACR a aussi constaté l'existence de travail forcé dans le secteur du transport. De manière générale, elle a critiqué les conditions de travail inacceptables dans lesquelles le travail forcé était exécuté. Par contre, il est étonnant que l'application de sanctions corporelles n'ait pas fait l'objet de critiques. Ces pratiques sont pourtant de nature à dénaturer un travail librement consenti.

La Belgique ne ratifiera la Convention de l'OIT (n°105) sur l'abolition du travail forcé (1957) qu'au lendemain de la décolonisation (23 janvier 1961)[14]. On peut supposer que certaines de ses dispositions interdisant le travail forcé comme méthode de mobilisation et d'utilisation de la main-d'œuvre à des fins de développement économique et comme mesure de discipline auraient pu poser des problèmes.

Quant aux instruments onusiens, il convient de mentionner la Convention relative à l'esclavage de 1926 qui a été ratifiée par la Belgique le 23 septembre 1927[15]. Le Protocole additionnel de 1953 n'a été ratifié qu'après la décolonisation, le 13 décembre 1962. La Convention relative à l'abolition de l'esclavage,

13 International Labour Conference, Report III (Part I), Geneva, 1959, 68–69 et International Labour Conference, Report III (Part I), Geneva, 1960, 60–61.

14 C105 – Convention (n° 105) sur l'abolition du travail forcé, 1957.

15 Protocole additionnel à la Convention des Nations Unies contre la criminalité transnationale organisée visant à prévenir, réprimer et punir la traite des personnes, en particulier des femmes et des enfants.

de la traite des esclaves et des institutions et pratiques analogues à l'esclavage (1956) a également été ratifiée le 13 décembre 1962[16]. Le Protocole dit « de Palerme », soit le Protocole additionnel à la Convention des Nations Unies contre la criminalité organisée visant à prévenir, réprimer et punir la traite des personnes, en particulier des femmes et des enfants[17], a été ratifié le 24 juin 2004.

Ces ratifications n'ont jamais conduit à des modifications constitutionnelles. La Constitution belge, dont le texte original remonte à 1831 et n'a jamais été remplacé intégralement par une constitution successive, ne contient aucune disposition interdisant formellement l'esclavage, la servitude ou le travail forcé. Même si l'article 12[18] de la Constitution se marie mal avec l'institution de l'esclavage et les pratiques de servitude et de travail forcé, cet article reflète avant tout l'idée du *Habeas Corpus* dans le sens du droit pénal. Cette disposition de la Constitution belge qui abolit la mort civile et interdit son rétablissement, reflète bien l'idée qu'un être humain dans le cadre d'une procédure pénale ne peut pas être privé de sa qualité de sujet de droit face à un ordre juridique.

La disposition la plus pertinente pour empêcher les pratiques de servitude et de travail forcé se situe dans le Code civil de 1804, qui est resté en vigueur après l'indépendance de la Belgique. L'article 1780 du Code civil belge, qui entame une section relative au louage des domestiques et ouvriers, dispose : « On ne peut engager ses services qu'à temps, ou pour une entreprise déterminée ». Bien qu'il soit très clair que cette disposition ne s'applique qu'au travailleur qui engage ses services et non pas l'employeur qui offre un emploi, la loi sur les contrats de travail du 3 juillet 1978 a opté pour une formule plus large *ratione personae*. L'article 7 de cette loi dispose que le contrat de travail ne peut jamais être conclu à vie.[19]

Les dispositions constitutionnelles ayant trait à l'égalité et à l'interdiction de la discrimination n'ont jamais été inspirées par une volonté de combattre

16 Convention supplémentaire relative à l'abolition de l'esclavage, de la traite des esclaves et des institutions et pratiques analogues à l'esclavage (Genève, 7 septembre 1956).

17 Protocole additionnel à la Convention des Nations Unies contre la criminalité transnationale organisée visant à prévenir, réprimer et punir la traite des personnes, en particulier des femmes et des enfants.

18 Art. 12 Constitution belge : « La liberté individuelle est garantie. Nul ne peut être poursuivi que dans les cas prévus par la loi, et dans la forme qu'elle prescrit. Hors le cas de flagrant délit, nul ne peut être arrêté qu'en vertu d'une ordonnance motivée du juge qui doit être signifiée au plus tard dans les quarante-huit heures de la privation de liberté et ne peut emporter qu'une mise en détention préventive. »

19 Cass. 31 octobre 1975, *Arr. Cass.* 1975, 287 et Cass. 30 septembre 1991, *Revue de droit social,* 1991, 343.

la discrimination raciale[20]. Une partie de ces dispositions remonte à 1831 et a été intégrée dans un titre intitulé « Des belges [sic] et de leurs droits ». Les dispositions plus récentes introduisant la notion de discrimination n'évoquent que la discrimination basée sur le sexe et n'évoquent que les minorités idéologiques et philosophiques. Les dispositions les plus originelles se réfèrent à l'idée de l'égalité devant la loi, et se concentrent sur les « ordres » sociaux. Ces ordres se réfèrent aux trois états (clergé, aristocratie et bourgeoisie). Le seul critère de discrimination qui a été intégré ultérieurement dans l'article 10 de la Constitution concerne la discrimination basée sur le sexe. Bref, l'histoire de la colonisation n'a eu aucun impact ni sur la formulation originelle de la Constitution, ni sur sa réforme ultérieure.

La première loi combattant le racisme de manière explicite remonte à 1981. La Loi tendant à réprimer certains actes inspirés par le racisme ou la xénophobie pénalise l'incitation à la haine raciale[21]. La transposition de la Directive 2000/43 a été l'occasion d'y ajouter des dispositions combattant la discrimination basée sur la race à travers des dispositions de droit civil[22]. Il nous semble donc peu probable d'expliquer historiquement l'introduction de ces dispositions pénales aux legs de l'esclavage ou du travail forcé précolonial. Il convient d'ailleurs de noter que peu de Congolais se sont effectivement installés en Belgique pendant la période coloniale et dans les premières décennies de l'indépendance du Congo[23]. Nous constatons d'ailleurs que les Congolais n'apparaissent quasiment jamais dans les données sur l'esclavage moderne repris dans les rapports de Myria, le Centre fédéral Migration[24]. Bref, il n'y pas une relation de causalité entre l'introduction de la Loi tendant à réprimer certains actes inspirés par le racisme ou la xénophobie et l'histoire du colonialisme belge et de ses pratiques de travail forcé. L'adoption de cette loi a été provoquée par la ratification par la Belgique de la Convention internationale sur l'élimination de toutes les formes de discrimination raciale, en 1975. Ce constat

20 Articles 10 et 11 de la Constitution belge.

21 La Loi tendant à réprimer certains actes inspirés par le racisme ou la xénophobie, *Moniteur belge*, 8 août 1981.

22 Directive 2000/43/CE du Conseil du 29 juin 2000 relative à la mise en œuvre du principe de l'égalité de traitement entre les personnes sans distinction de race ou d'origine ethnique, *Journal officiel n°* L 180 du 19/07/2000, 22–26.

23 M. Zana Etambala, 'De Congolese gemeenschap in België : een ongewild 'neveneffect' van de koloniale overheersing?' dans I. Goddeeris, A. Lauro & Guy Vanthemsche (dir.), *Koloniaal Congo. Een geschiedenis in vragen*, Polis, Kalmthout 2020. I. Goddeeris mentionne une évolution de 2.585 Congolais en 1961 à 40.301 en 2006; I. Goddeeris, 'Post-Colonial Belgium: The Memory of the Congo' (2015) 17:3 *International Journal of Postcolonial Studies* 444.

24 <https://www.myria.be/fr/publications>.

n'enlève rien au racisme endémique de l'histoire coloniale de la Belgique. Il n'y avait pas en 1981 une prise de conscience suffisante du caractère raciste de cette histoire coloniale, à défaut d'une diaspora congolaise suffisamment dense en Belgique. Pour cette raison, d'autres minorités ont été victimes de racisme à l'heure de l'adoption de cette loi. Par contre, dans son rapport (2021), « la commission spéciale chargée d'examiner l'État indépendant du Congo (1885–1908) et le passé colonial de la Belgique au Congo (1908–1960), au Rwanda et au Burundi (1919–1962), ses conséquences et les suites qu'il convient d'y réserver », a bien mis en exergue les liens entre le racisme dont sont victimes les africains subsahariens résidant en Belgique et l'histoire du colonialisme[25].

Il convient d'évoquer une réforme opérée par la Loi du 12 janvier 2005[26]. Cette loi abolit le régime du travail pénitentiaire imposé en vertu de l'article 30*ter* du Code pénal. Le service pénitentiaire obligatoire a donc été aboli. Notons que le statut du travail pénitentiaire est *sui generis* : il ne s'agit pas d'une relation de travail à laquelle la Loi du 3 juillet 1978 sur les contrats de travail s'applique[27].

En guise de conclusion, il convient donc de souligner qu'hormis l'article 2 de la Charte coloniale[28], il n'y a aucune disposition explicite qui peut être mise en relation avec le phénomène du travail forcé qui a caractérisé la période de l'État indépendant du Congo et qui a persisté tout au long de la période coloniale *sensu stricto*. En raison de l'indépendance du Congo, cette Charte est devenue sans objet. À l'heure actuelle, il n'y a aucune norme en Belgique qui consacre le principe de la liberté du travail. Une disposition du Code pénal qui pénalisait des entraves à la liberté du travail et de l'industrie dans le contexte tout à fait différent des conflits collectifs du travail a été abolie en 1921.

Il n'y a aucune norme belge qui interdit ou pénalise en tant que tel l'esclavage, la servitude ou le travail forcé. Vu le caractère moniste du rapport qu'entretient l'ordre juridique belge avec d'autres ordres juridiques internationaux, le justiciable belge peut invoquer les instruments internationaux interdisant l'esclavage, la servitude ou le travail forcé directement devant les juridictions belges. Ce constat paraît troublant dans un premier temps, en ce que la Cour

---

25 Doc 55 1462/ (2019/2020), pp. 599–611, <https://www.dekamer.be/FLWB/PDF/55/1462/55K1462002.pdf>.

26 Loi du 12 janvier 2005 de principes concernant l'administration pénitentiaire ainsi que le statut juridique des détenus, *Moniteur belge,* 1 févier, 2005.

27 Loi du 3 juillet 1978 relative aux contrats de travail, *Moniteur belge,* 22 août 1978. Cf. K. Nevens, 'Penitentiaire arbeid : dringt het arbeidsrecht de gevangenis binnen ?' (2007) 3 *Revue de droit social* 231.

28 Loi sur le gouvernement du Congo belge du 18 octobre 1908, *Bulletin Officiel du Congo Belge*, 1908, 65.

européenne des droits de l'homme (CEDH) semble avoir insisté dans l'arrêt *Siliadin contre France*[29] sur l'importance de l'existence de dispositions pénales offrant « une protection concrète et effective » contre le travail forcé et la servitude. La Cour a condamné la France en considérant qu'en droit français l'esclavage et la servitude ne sont pas en tant que tels réprimés par le droit pénal. La Cour européenne des droits de l'homme a noté que les dispositions invoquées par le gouvernement français (articles 225–13 et 225–14 du Code pénal) ne visaient pas spécifiquement les droits garantis par l'article 4 de la Convention, mais concernaient, de manière beaucoup plus restrictive, l'exploitation par le travail et la soumission à des conditions de travail ou d'hébergement incompatibles avec la dignité humaine.

Le simple fait qu'aucune disposition ne pénalisait l'esclavage ou la servitude n'a pas conduit la Cour à condamner la France. Il convenait plutôt d'examiner si les articles mis en place permettaient de sanctionner effectivement les agissements dont la requérante a été victime. Inéluctablement, la question se pose de savoir si la Belgique a des dispositions pénales réprimant de manière efficace les pratiques de travail forcé et de servitude.

1.3 *Les dispositions de droit pénal interdisant le trafic et la traite*

En Belgique, deux dispositifs de droit pénal ont été mis en place pour combattre des pratiques de travail forcé et de servitude. Ni les mots « travail forcé » ni le mot « servitude » n'y figurent. Quant à l'esclavage *sensu stricto* dans son acception historique issue de la Convention de l'OIT n°29, il convient de préciser que ce mutisme du législateur ne constitue pas un problème en soi. L'esclavage dans son acception historique ne doit pas être défini comme une pratique émanant d'employeurs, mais comme une institution juridique instituée par un ordre juridique. C'est ainsi que la Convention n°29 relative à l'esclavage du 25 septembre 1926 définit l'esclavage comme « l'état ou condition d'un individu sur lequel s'exercent les attributs du droit de propriété ou certains d'entre eux ».

Dans l'arrêt *Siliadin contre France*, la CEDH a fait sienne cette définition de l'esclavage[30]. Le refus du législateur belge d'instituer l'institution de l'esclavage n'a pas empêché des *tentatives* contractuelles de réduire des sujets de droits à l'état de simples objets de propriété. Dans un arrêt de la Cour de cassation du 29 septembre 2008, il est question d'une clause contractuelle dans laquelle un joueur reconnaît être la propriété exclusive d'un certain Monsieur G[31]. La

29 CEDH, 26 juillet 2005, nr. 73316/01 (*Siliadin contre France*).

30 CEDH, 26 juillet 2005, nr. 73316/01 (*Siliadin contre France*).

31 Cour de cassation, 29 septembre 2008, C.06.0443.F, <https://juricaf.org/arret/BELGIQUE-COURDECASSATION-20080929-C060443F>.

Cour a statué que la convention contenant cette clause était contraire à l'ordre public, en ce que « La liberte d'exercer une activite professionnelle rémunérée ne peut subir d'autres restrictions que celles qui sont prevues par la loi ».

Le premier dispositif de droit pénal est la Loi du 15 décembre 1980 sur l'accès au territoire, le séjour, l'établissement et l'éloignement des étrangers[32]. Les étrangers y sont définis comme des personnes non ressortissantes de l'UE. Le dispositif ne concerne donc pas le sort des personnes ressortissantes de l'UE qui feraient l'objet d'un trafic[33]. Son article 77 bis pénalise « l'infraction de trafic des êtres humains », qui est défini comme :

> ... le fait de contribuer, de quelque manière que ce soit, soit directement, soit par un intermédiaire, à permettre l'entrée, le transit ou le séjour d'une personne non ressortissante d'un Etat membre de l'Union européenne sur ou par le territoire d'un tel Etat ou d'un Etat partie à une convention internationale relative au franchissement des frontières extérieures et liant la Belgique, en violation de la législation de cet Etat, en vue d'obtenir, directement ou indirectement, un avantage patrimonial.

Le deuxième dispositif de droit pénal concerne la traite des êtres humains. La Belgique a voulu combattre l'esclavage contemporain essentiellement par le biais de l'introduction de dispositions réprimant « la traite » dans le Code pénal en 2005[34]. Cette réforme a introduit un nouveau « Chapitre III*ter*, De la traite des êtres humains ». Les dispositions concernées ont été adoptées en vue de la ratification du Protocole de Palerme. C'est ainsi que l'article 433*quinquies* du Code pénal interdit la traite à des fins d'exploitation de la prostitution ou d'autres formes d'exploitation sexuelle, d'exploitation de la mendicité, de travail ou de services dans des conditions contraires à la dignité humaine, et d'exploitation par le prélèvement d'organes ou de matériel corporel humain. Cette disposition interdit également la traite afin de faire commettre par une personne un crime ou un délit, contre son gré[35].

---

32 Loi du 15 décembre 1980 sur l'accès au territoire, le séjour, l'établissement et l'éloignement des étrangers *Moniteur belge*, 31 décembre 1980.

33 C.-É. Clesse, *La traite des êtres humains : droit belge éclairé des législations française, luxembourgeoise et suisse*, Larcier, Bruxelles 2013, pp. 165–190.

34 *Ibid.*, pp. 191–330.

35 Art 433*quinquies* du Code pénal **§ 1er.** Constitue l'infraction de traite des êtres humains le fait de recruter, de transporter, de transférer, d'héberger, d'accueillir une personne, de prendre ou de transférer le contrôle exercé sur elle :
1° à des fins d'exploitation de la prostitution ou d'autres formes d'exploitation sexuelle;
2° à des fins d'exploitation de la mendicité;

2 La compréhension des causes et des conséquences de l'esclavage contemporain

2.1 *À propos de la notion d'esclavage contemporain*

La notion d'esclavage *contemporain* nécessite une excursion sémantique. Comme il a été indiqué ci-dessus, l'esclavage en tant qu'institution juridique n'a jamais existé tout au long de l'histoire de l'État de la Belgique, fondé en 1830. Le problème majeur du passé est le phénomène du travail forcé qui a caractérisé la période de l'État indépendant du Congo et la période coloniale. La notion d'esclavage *contemporain* ne peut donc pas être appréhendée utilement sans altérer le sens classique de cette notion. La question de savoir si l'institution de l'esclavage dans le sens de la Convention n°29 précitée, telle que reçue par la CEDH dans l'affaire précitée *Siliadin contre France* persiste aujourd'hui ne peut qu'être répondue de façon négative. Cette définition de l'esclavage n'est pas formulée en fonction d'une époque. Dans des arrêts ultérieurs, la Cour européenne des droits de l'homme s'est servie de l'expression « esclavage moderne », sans se donner la peine de redéfinir la notion d'esclavage[36]. Dans le seul arrêt d'une Grande Chambre relative à l'article 4 de la Convention européenne des droits de l'homme, *S.M. c. Croatie,* qui concerne un cas de traite des êtres humains, la Grande Chambre a considéré :

> Dans l'arrêt *Rantsev*, la Cour a relevé que la traite des êtres humains était souvent qualifiée de forme moderne d'esclavage. Elle en a conclu que la traite portait en elle-même atteinte à la dignité humaine, qu'elle était incompatible avec une société démocratique ainsi qu'avec les valeurs consacrées par la Convention et qu'elle relevait donc du champ de l'interdiction posée par l'article 4 sans qu'il fût nécessaire de déterminer si elle devait être qualifiée d'« esclavage », de « servitude » ou de « travail forcé »[37].

À notre avis, le terme d'« esclavage contemporain » n'est pas d'une utilité inéluctable afin de traiter ses causes et ses conséquences. L'article 433*quinquies* du Code pénal permet d'attaquer des pratiques précises en indiquant des cas

3° à des fins de travail ou de services, dans des conditions contraires à la dignité humaine;
4° à des fins d›exploitation par le prélèvement d›organes ou de matériel corporel humain;
5° ou afin de faire commettre par cette personne un crime ou un délit, contre son gré.

36 CEDH, 7 janvier 2010, nr. 25965/04 (*Rantsev c Chypre et Russie*) et CEDH, 25 juin 2020, nr. 60561/14 (*S.M. contre Croatie*).

37 CEDH, 25 juin 2020, nr. 60561/14 (*S.M. contre Croatie*), § 56.

spécifiques tout en mobilisant la notion plus générique d'exploitation économique. Le caractère flou de la notion de dignité humaine n'a pas empêché les juges de condamner sévèrement des cas d'esclavage moderne qui peuvent s'opérer tant dans la sphère domestique que dans l'industrie du sexe ou sur les autres secteurs de l'économie.

Le droit pénal belge a investi la notion d'*exploitation*, qui pourrait être assimilée à de l'esclavage contemporain *sensu lato*[38]. Dans la majorité des cas, cette exploitation par des tiers à un but lucratif découle de la nature de « la prestation de travail » exigée (la prostitution, la mendicité, le prélèvement d'organes ou de matériel corporel humain, la commission de crimes ou de délits contre le gré de cette personne). Dans le cas de la disposition la plus générique, la traite à des fins de travail ou de services, le législateur ne mobilise pas la notion d'exploitation, mais insiste sur le dessein de faire travailler une personne « dans des conditions contraires à la dignité humaine ». Cette notion relativement floue n'est pas sans rappeler la critique de la CEDH exprimée dans l'arrêt *Siliadin contre France*[39] à l'égard des dispositions françaises qui font référence à des conditions de travail (et de vie) contraires à la dignité humaine. Le caractère relativement flou de ces notions (exploitation et dignité humaine) ne suffit pas selon nous pour apprécier la conformité du droit belge à l'aune de la Convention européenne des droits de l'homme. Un tel exercice requiert une analyse fine de la jurisprudence belge ayant concrétisé ces notions. Il faut d'ailleurs se demander si un législateur serait capable d'épuiser le potentiel de la notion de dignité humaine en dressant un faisceau de critères exhaustifs et non cumulatifs.

Il est important dans un premier temps d'examiner les causes et les conséquences de l'esclavage contemporain en Belgique. Pour reconstruire la traite en Belgique, nous nous appuierons sur les rapports annuels du Centre fédéral Migration Myria, qui depuis le 15 mars 2014 exerce en tant qu'organisme public indépendant trois missions complémentaires. Myria a été habilité à veiller au respect des droits fondamentaux des étrangers, à informer sur la nature et l'ampleur des flux migratoires et à stimuler la lutte contre la traite et le trafic des êtres humains[40].

Dans un deuxième temps, il convient d'examiner comment les cours et les tribunaux ont essayé de faire face à ces pratiques en mobilisant les dispositions les plus adéquates dont elle dispose.

38 Voir l'article Art. 433quinquies du Code pénal belge.

39 CEDH, 26 juillet 2005, nr. 73316/01 (*Siliadin contre France*).

40 'À propos de Myria', <https://www.myria.be/fr/propos-de-myria>.

2.2 *Esclavage contemporain en Belgique*

Les rapports annuels de Myria fournissent des données quantitatives et qualitatives sur les victimes de la traite des êtres humains[41]. Ces rapports sont publiés sur leur site depuis 2000. Leurs données sont articulées avec celles des années précédentes, ce qui permet d'étudier les évolutions.

En ce qui concerne les chiffres ayant trait à la première année de la pandémie (2020), il convient de noter que la crise sanitaire a fortement compliqué la capacité des acteurs habilités à identifier des victimes de la traite, à les assister et à les accompagner. Des chiffres relatifs à la deuxième année de la pandémie (2021) seront communiqués vers la fin de 2022. Pour cette raison, il nous semble adéquat de se focaliser sur les rapports de 2017 à 2020, relatifs à la période de 2016 à 2019.

Une autre source utile, non récurrente, constitue l'étude menée par Irène Wintermayr et Dr Amy Weatherburn à la demande du Bureau de l'OIT (Union européenne et Benelux) de 2021[42]. Cette étude porte sur la situation en Belgique et aux Pays-Bas. Au sein du Conseil de l'Europe, les rapports du Groupe d'experts sur la lutte contre la traite des êtres humains (GRETA) contiennent des recommandations adressées au Gouvernement belge dans le cadre d'un cycle de contrôle périodique relatif à la Convention du Conseil de l'Europe sur la lutte contre la traite des êtres humains. Deux rapports ont été rédigés en 2013 et 2017[43]. Ces rapports doivent être lus à la lumière des réponses du gouvernement belge à un questionnaire du GRETA. Ni le site du GRETA ni la base de données Hudoc ne donnent un accès public au questionnaire et aux réponses du Gouvernement, ce qui réduit sensiblement l'utilité de ce cycle de contrôle dans le cadre d'une analyse de la traite des êtres humains en Belgique. Dans le cadre de cette analyse nous avons parcouru les rapports de Myria de 2017 à 2021, qui couvrent la période de 2016 à 2020. Les chiffres de Myria doivent être interprétés avec précaution. Ils se réfèrent toujours à des cas de traite identifiés

41 'Myria, Publications', <https://www.myria.be/fr/publications>.

42 I. Wintermayr et A. Weatherburn, *Access to protection and remedy for victims of human trafficking for the purpose of labour exploitation in Belgium and the Netherlands*, ILO (2020), <https://www.ilo.org/wcmsp5/groups/public/---europe/---ro-geneva/---ilo-brussels/documents/publication/wcms_783811.pdf>.

43 GRETA, *Rapport concernant la mise en œuvre de la Convention du Conseil de l'Europe sur la lutte contre la traite des êtres humains par la Belgique – Premier cycle d'évaluation* (2013) <https://rm.coe.int/CoERMPublicCommonSearchServices/DisplayDCTMContent?documentId=0900001680630d10>; GRETA, *Rapport concernant la mise en œuvre de la Convention du Conseil de l'Europe sur la lutte contre la traite des êtres humains par la Belgique – Deuxième cycle d'évaluation* (2017) <https://rm.coe.int/2nd-rd-rpt-bel/1680766bdb>.

par des acteurs du terrain. Ces acteurs sont différents et opèrent dans des cadres juridiques distincts. Il s'agit :

de la Police belge;
des Service d'Inspection de l'Organisation nationale de la Sécurité Sociale (ONSS);
du Collège des Procureurs généraux (poursuites pénales);
de l'Office des Etrangers (OE);
des centres spécialisés dans l'accueil des victimes (PAG-ASA, Payoke et Sürya);
du Service de Politique criminelle du Service Publique Fédéral de Justice (pour les condamnations).

Les chiffres du Collège des Procureurs et de la Politique criminelle ne renseignent que sur le nombre d'affaires et non pas sur le nombre de victimes. C'est pourquoi nous les écartons de cette étude. Ils donnent une idée sur la part relative des cas liés aux objectifs d'exploitation distincts. Les chiffres de la Police sont les plus élevés. Ils différencient également les cas en fonction de l'objectif de l'exploitation. Ils ne concernent que le nombre d'infractions, et ne nous renseignent pas sur le nombre de victimes liées à ces infractions. Les chiffres du service d'Inspection de l'ONSS ont l'avantage d'identifier la nationalité des victimes et le secteur d'activité. Ils sont basés sur des procès-verbaux et nous renseignent sur le nombre de victimes.

De manière générale, les chiffres de l'Office des Étrangers (OE), des centres spécialisés dans l'accueil des victimes, du collège des Procureurs généraux et du Service de Politique criminelle sont nécessairement moins élevés. Les centres d'accueil spécialisés ne peuvent que comptabiliser les victimes qui veulent se faire accompagner. Les chiffres de l'OE ne concernent que les victimes qui veulent collaborer avec les autorités judiciaires. Ces derniers chiffres distinguent les cas en fonction de l'objectif de l'exploitation et indiquent la nationalité de ces victimes. Les chiffres de la police concernant le nombre des infractions pénales sur les années 2016 à 2019 sont les suivants : 2016 : 400; 2017 : 329; 2018 : 358; 2019 : 331; 2020 : 278.

Les chiffres de l'ONSS relatifs aux victimes sur les années 2016 à 2019 sont les suivants : 2016 : 52; 2017 : 48; 2018 : 65; 2019 : 82; 2020 : 156. Vu que le nombre des cas répertoriés par l'ONSS a augmenté en 2020, il convient de présumer que sa capacité d'investigation n'a pas été affectée par la crise COVID.

L'aperçu des rapports de Myria permet de présumer que le problème de la traite concerne essentiellement l'exploitation dite sexuelle et celle dite économique. Les chiffres de la Police sur les années 2016 au 2020 sont très indicatifs à cet égard. La traite des êtres humains pour des objectifs d'exploitation en vue d'une implication dans la criminalité organisée[44], en vue de la mendicité organisée[45], ou en vue du trafic d'organes[46] est nettement moindre. Ces catégories sont basées sur l'approche du législateur belge et méconnaissent que l'exploitation sexuelle revêt également une dimension économique. Contrairement à la notion d'exploitation sexuelle, la notion d'exploitation économique ne donne pas une idée assez nette des secteurs de l'économie dans lesquels elle se situe. Les chiffres de l'ONSS sur la période de 2016 à 2020 permettent d'identifier deux secteurs plus perméables à la traite : le secteur de la construction et le secteur de l'*Horeca* (le secteur d'activités de l'hôtellerie, de la restauration et des cafés).

On constate une judiciarisation beaucoup plus poussée de l'exploitation sexuelle que de l'exploitation économique, si on compare les chiffres du Collège des Procureurs généraux par rapport à cette répartition dans les chiffres de la police. L'accompagnement des victimes de la traite économique et de la traite sexuelle par des centres d'accueils spécialisés est par contre plus équilibré. En revanche, on constate que dans les données de l'Office des étrangers, les victimes de traite économique sont plus représentées que les victimes de l'exploitation sexuelle. On peut en déduire que ces dernières sont plus frileuses de collaborer avec les autorités judiciaires[47].

Les rapports de Myria ne permettent pas d'identifier les causes de la traite des êtres humains et ne nous renseignent pas sur le rôle des entreprises transnationales, des chaînes de valeur mondiales et des chaînes de soins mondiales dans la prolifération de l'esclavage contemporain. Ils permettent de dresser quelques traits caractéristiques de ces victimes. Les victimes de la traite en vue de l'exploitation sexuelle sont presqu'exclusivement des femmes. La nationalité nigérienne en particulier est surreprésentée. Quant aux victimes de la traite en vue de l'exploitation économique, il s'agit essentiellement d'hommes. Certaines nationalités sont beaucoup plus représentées que d'autres, telles que le Maroc, la Bulgarie, l'Inde, la Chine et l'Ukraine.

La question de savoir si l'histoire et les héritages de l'esclavage en tant qu'institution mondiale sont liés à l'esclavage contemporain ou s'ils sont distincts de celui-ci nous semble mériter une réponse négative pour ce qui concerne le

---

44 Voir le Rapport du Myria (2019), p. 13, <https://www.myria.be/files/Rapport_annuel_2019_Traite_et_trafic_des_%C3%AAtres_humain.pdf>.

45 *Ibid.*, p. 6.

46 *Ibid.*, p. 1.

47 OE : Rapport 2018 : 33 victimes de traite sexuelle et 75 victimes de traite économique. Rapport 2019 : 52 victimes de traite sexuelle et 88 victimes de traite économique. Rapport 2020 : 25 victimes de traite sexuelle et 48 victimes de traite économique.

passé colonial belge. Dans les statistiques de Myria, les citoyens de la République démocratique du Congo ne figurent pas parmi les victimes de la traite. Il n'est pas non plus toujours possible de trouver un lien avec des héritages de l'esclavage situés dans d'autres colonies. Hormis, le cas des victimes nigériennes, celles du Maroc, et de l'Inde, les nationalités les plus représentées n'ont pas eu une période coloniale proprement dite. Les rapports du Myria ne contiennent pas des développements sur les liens entre le phénomène du travail forcé et les héritages de l'esclavage.

2.3 *La construction juridique de la traite par le prisme de l'exploitation et de la dignité humaine*

Le législateur belge n'a pas forgé l'expression « esclavage contemporain », mais il a essayé de combattre ce phénomène par la notion juridique de la traite. La traite en droit belge a été définie par le biais d'un élément matériel (une action) et un élément moral (un objectif). La définition légale n'a pas incorporé les moyens qui sont mobilisés pour mettre en œuvre la traite, mais l'utilisation de certains moyens peut constituer une circonstance aggravante[48].

L'élément moral désigne le dol spécial qui est requis. Cet élément est généralement construit autour de la notion d'exploitation. Il suffit que l'action ait été menée en vue d'en tirer un profit pour qu'il y ait eu une intention d'exploitation. Pour le cas très fréquent de la traite dite économique, il suffit que l'action ait été menée « à des fins de travail ou de services, dans des conditions contraires à la dignité humaine »[49].

Il est donc essentiel d'analyser les critères qui ont été pris en compte par la jurisprudence belge pour conclure à l'existence des conditions contraires à la dignité humaine. Charles-Éric Clesse a déduit un faisceau de critères dans sa thèse de doctorat relative à la traite des êtres humains basée sur une analyse de la jurisprudence entre 2005 et 2013[50]. Ces critères restent d'une grande actualité. Une analyse de la jurisprudence belge ne permet pas de déduire une hiérarchie entre ces critères. Dans la pratique, plusieurs conditions diverses peuvent être contraires à la dignité humaine. Ces conditions doivent être appréhendées de manière large. Il s'agit d'un faisceau de critères, dénué d'une hiérarchie. Charles-Éric Clesse distingue ainsi : la rémunération; le temps de travail; la non-déclaration du travail; les conditions du travail en matière de santé et de sécurité; le harcèlement; l'absence de travail; et le travail des enfants. L'auteur souligne d'une part que la conception de la dignité humaine

48 C.-É. Clesse, *supra* n. 33, pp. 191–195.

49 Article 433 quinquies 3° Code pénal belge.

50 C.-É. Clesse, *supra* n. 33, 266–283.

doit être appréhendée d'après les standards du pays d'accueil, mais d'autre part que le simple fait de la violation des règles en matière de droit social n'est pas *in se et per se* suffisant pour constater l'existence de conditions de travail contraire à la dignité humaine[51]. Il doit s'agir de violations graves des normes de droit social. Il convient de ne pas confondre la traite et le travail non déclaré.

Il est d'ailleurs intéressant de constater que la violation du principe de discrimination, qui figure parmi les principes et droits fondamentaux de l'OIT, ainsi que le caractère forcé du travail n'ont pas été repris dans cet aperçu de l'état de la jurisprudence en 2013, ce qui reflète l'inadvertance de la jurisprudence à cette question.

Une analyse de la jurisprudence postérieure à la recherche doctorale de Charles-Éric Clesse confirme la pertinence des critères retenus pour les années successives[52]. La jurisprudence des Cours d'appel illustre une attention accrue sur la servitude des travailleurs. Ainsi, la détention arbitraire des travailleurs en les privant de leur liberté de se mouvoir en dehors des heures de travail a été retenue comme un indice important[53]. La pratique de la rétention par les employeurs des documents d'identité (passeports) de leurs travailleurs a également été condamnée[54].

Il convient d'ailleurs d'indiquer que certaines conditions « aggravantes » sont identifiées par le législateur comme des indications de conditions contraires à la dignité humaine. On pourrait mentionner « le fait d'abuser de la situation de vulnérabilité dans laquelle se trouve une personne en raison de sa situation administrative illégale ou précaire, de sa situation sociale précaire, de son âge, d'un état de grossesse, d'une maladie, d'une infirmité ou d'une déficience physique ou mentale, de manière telle que la personne n'a en fait pas d'autre choix véritable et acceptable que de se soumettre à cet abus » ; le fait d'user « de façon directe ou indirecte, de manœuvres frauduleuses, de violence, de menaces ou d'une forme quelconque de contrainte, ou en recourant

51 Dans le même sens, Cour d'appel de Gand, 19 janvier 2017.

52 'Myria, Jurisprudence', <https://www.myria.be/fr/traite/jurisprudence>.

53 Cour d'appel de Mons, 11 mars 2020.

54 Cour d'appel de Liège, 23 janvier 2020 (le fait de détenir les documents d'identité) ; Cour d'appel de Liège, 13 février 2020 (le passeport des victimes était dissimulé dans le conduit d'une cheminée) ; Cour d'appel de Bruxelles, 2 décembre 2019 (confiscation du passeport) ; Cour d'appel de Gand, 11 septembre 2019 (fait qu'elles avaient dû leur remettre leurs documents de séjour.) ; Cour d'appel de Gand, 24 avril 2019 (confiscation des papiers) ; Cour d'appel de Mons, 26 juin 2015 (retenir des documents de travail et de permis de séjour) ; Cour d'appel Anvers, 23 avril 2014 (le prévenu retenait par ailleurs son passeport et une partie de son salaire pour soi-disant effectuer les démarches nécessaires à sa « légalisation »).

à l'enlèvement, à l'abus d'autorité ou à la tromperie », le fait de mettre « en danger la vie de la victime délibérément ou par négligence grave », ou le fait de causer « une maladie paraissant incurable, une incapacité de travail personnel de plus de quatre mois la perte complète d'un organe ou de l'usage d'un organe, ou une mutilation grave »[55].

2.4 *Observations transversales*

Les tribunaux belges n'ont pas l'habitude de faire référence aux instruments internationaux ou européens dans leur interprétation de l'article 433*quinquies* du Code pénal. Ils ne font pas référence au travail du Rapporteur spécial des Nations Unies sur les formes contemporaines d'esclavage. L'article 4 de la Convention européenne des droits de l'homme a été invoqué (en vain) dans un certain nombre de procédures devant la Cour constitutionnelle, toujours pour attaquer des situations qui sont très éloignées des cas de travail forcé Ces procédures concernaient des législations relatives à des militaires ayant reçu une formation gratuite leur interdisant de terminer la relation de travail ou les obligeant à rembourser une partie des frais de cette formation[56], l'imposition aux établissements financiers de communiquer à l'administration fiscale des informations sans aucune rémunération[57], l'obligation pour des avocats de contribuer à l'organisation de l'aide juridique de deuxième ligne (*pro deo*)[58], ou encore l'extension de la charge enseignante par au travail collaboratif des membres du personnel de l'enseignement de la Communauté française[59].

Les effets de la pandémie mondiale liée au Covid sur le sort des victimes de la traite ont été analysés dans le Rapport de Myria de l'année 2020 à partir des contributions externes de quatre acteurs clés dans le combat contre la traite : l'Inspection de l'ONSS, l'auditorat du travail, les services de la Police ainsi que les centres d'accueil. Leurs conclusions convergent et soulignent des problèmes épineux inhérents à cette crise[60].

La pandémie a eu un impact négatif sur la capacité de détecter la traite et d'identifier leurs victimes. Même si le constat de la traite est basé sur un faisceau de critères, les services de contrôle prémentionnés ont été particulièrement vigilants à la question de la santé, de la sécurité et de l'hygiène au travail

55 Art. 433*septies* du Code pénal.

56 Cour constitutionnelle, 14 décembre 1995, n° 81/95.

57 Cour constitutionnelle, 14 février 2013, n° 6/2013.

58 Cour constitutionnelle, 29 mars 2018, n° 41/2018 ; Cour constitutionnelle, 21 juin 2018, n° 77/2018.

59 Cour constitutionnelle, 2 mars 2021, n° 35/2021.

60 Voir le Rapport du Myria (2020), <https://www.myria.be/files/MYRIA_Rapport_d%C3%A9valuation_2020_Traite_et_trafic_des_%C3%AAtres_humains.pdf>.

pendant la crise pandémique. Des secteurs qui ne se prêtaient pas au télétravail, tels que la construction ou l'industrie du sexe, ont posé des problèmes de protection de la santé et de sécurité. Le fait que des travailleurs ont continué à travailler dans des conditions mettant en péril leur propre santé est un indicateur potentiel d'exploitation. Les conditions d'accès à un marché de l'emploi affecté par le chômage accru ont rendu les travailleurs beaucoup plus vulnérables aux pratiques de traite. La pandémie a également été un défi pour les centres d'accueil qui voulaient garder un contact avec les victimes accueillies pendant le confinement. Le rapport d'Irène Wintermayr et Dr Amy Weatherburn confirme la difficulté de l'Inspection Sociale à surveiller des cas de traite alors que le contrôle des règles sanitaires absorbait beaucoup de ressources[61].

3 La remédiation et la redéfinition des formes de l'esclavage contemporain

La Belgique a adopté une approche pénaliste pour combattre l'esclavage contemporain, essentiellement par le biais de l'introduction en 2005 de dispositions réprimant la traite des êtres humains dans le Code pénal.

Cette approche pénaliste comporte trois volets essentiels : la détection des cas d'esclavage moderne, la sanction des auteurs de la traite et l'assistance aux victimes de la traite.

Une particularité de l'approche belge en comparaison avec l'approche suivie dans le Protocole de Palerme réside dans le refus d'intégrer des moyens permettant la traite à l'intérieur de la définition de la traite[62]. Ces moyens sont dissociés de la définition et figurent dans une disposition énumérant

61 I. Wintermayr et A. Weatherburn, *Access to protection and remedy for victims of human trafficking for the purpose of labour exploitation in Belgium and the Netherlands*, ILO (2020), <https://www.ilo.org/wcmsp5/groups/public/---europe/---ro-geneva/---ilo-brussels/documents/publication/wcms_783811.pdf>.

62 Art. 433*septies*. L'infraction prévue à l'article 433*quinquies*, § 1er, sera punie de la réclusion de dix ans à quinze ans et d'une amende de mille euros à cent mille euros dans les cas suivants :

2° lorsqu'elle a été commise en abusant de la [1 situation de vulnérabilité dans laquelle se trouve une personne en raison de sa situation administrative illégale ou précaire, de sa situation sociale précaire, de son âge, d'un état de grossesse, d'une maladie, d'une infirmité ou d'une déficience physique ou mentale de manière telle que la personne n'a en fait pas d'autre choix véritable et acceptable que de se soumettre à cet abus; 3° lorsqu'elle a été commise en faisant usage, de façon directe ou indirecte, de manœuvres frauduleuses, de violence, de menaces ou d'une forme quelconque de contrainte, ou en recourant à l'enlèvement, à l'abus d'autorité ou à la tromperie;

des circonstances aggravantes qui ont un impact sur la détermination de la peine[63]. Une deuxième distinction importante est le refus du législateur de ranger formellement le travail ou les services sous la catégorie d'exploitation. Le législateur a ainsi préféré forger une expression relativement floue de « travail ou de services, dans des conditions contraires à la dignité humaine ». Comme il a été expliqué auparavant, la jurisprudence belge a développé des critères permettant de constater une telle atteinte à la dignité humaine.

D'autres éléments, qui ne concernent pas les moyens, ont également été retenus comme des circonstances aggravantes, telles que la qualité de la victime[64] ou de l'auteur[65], ainsi que certains effets sur l'intégrité physique de la victime[66]. Plusieurs instances contribuent en Belgique à la détection des cas d'esclavage moderne et à l'identification des victimes. On peut citer les services de l'inspection de l'ONSS, les officiers de la Police et le Ministère Public. Les victimes de la traite n'ayant pas la nationalité belge et ne disposant pas d'un titre de séjour qui collaborent avec les autorités judiciaires et qui sont accompagnées par un centre spécialisé dans l'accueil des victimes peuvent obtenir un titre de séjour temporaire de 45 jours[67]. Ce titre doit leur donner la possibilité d'introduire une plainte ou de faire des déclarations concernant les personnes ou les réseaux qui se seraient rendus coupables de l'infraction reprochée. Cette période de réflexion de 45 jours permettra à la victime d'introduire une plainte

---

3*bis*° lorsqu'elle a été commise au moyen de l'offre ou de l'acceptation de paiements ou d'avantages quelconques pour obtenir le consentement d'une personne ayant autorité sur la victime ; 6° lorsque l'activité concernée constitue une activité habituelle;

7° lorsqu'elle constitue un acte de participation à l'activité principale ou accessoire d'une association, et ce, que le coupable ait ou non la qualité de dirigeant.

63 Art. 433*septies* du Code pénal.

64 Art. 433*septies*. L'infraction prévue à l'article 433*quinquies*, § 1er, sera punie de la réclusion de dix ans à quinze ans et d'une amende de mille euros à cent mille euros dans les cas suivants :1° lorsque l'infraction a été commise envers un mineur.

65 Art. 433*sexies*. L'infraction prévue à l'article 433*quinquies*, § 1er, sera punie de la réclusion de cinq ans à dix ans et d'une amende de sept cent cinquante euros à septante-cinq mille euros lorsque l'infraction aura été commise : 1° par une personne qui a autorité sur la victime, ou par une personne qui a abusé de l'autorité ou des facilités que lui confèrent ses fonctions ; 2° par un officier ou un fonctionnaire public, un dépositaire ou un agent de la force publique agissant à l'occasion de l'exercice de ses fonctions. L'amende sera appliquée autant de fois qu'il y a de victimes.

66 Art. 433*sexies*. 4° lorsque la vie de la victime a été mise en danger délibérément ou par négligence grave ; 5° lorsque l'infraction a causé une maladie paraissant incurable, une incapacité de travail personnel de plus de quatre mois la perte complète d'un organe ou de l'usage d'un organe, ou une mutilation grave.

67 Art. 61/2, § 2 de la loi du 15 décembre 1980 sur l'accès au territoire, le séjour, l'établissement et l'éloignement des étrangers.

ou une déclaration contre les auteurs allégués de la traite. Le dépôt d'une plainte ouvre un droit à un document de séjour pour une durée de validité de trois mois au maximum[68].

Les centres d'accueils reconnus par les autorités – les services d'aides spéciales – s'occupent de l'hébergement des victimes de la traite, de son encadrement social, linguistique, médical, psychologique et juridique. La Belgique permet aux victimes de la traite de profiter d'une aide juridique, sous certaines conditions. Si les victimes entament une poursuite civile, les tribunaux peuvent leur accorder des indemnités.

Une personne qui ne détient pas la nationalité belge et qui est impliquée dans une enquête peut également recevoir un permis de séjour d'une durée de six mois, sous certaines conditions[69]. Le titre de séjour peut être prorogé ou renouvelé. Le ministre, ou son délégué, peut mettre fin au séjour de l'étranger et peut lui donner l'ordre de quitter le territoire, s'il constate que :

> 1° l'étranger a activement, volontairement et de sa propre initiative, renoué un lien avec les auteurs présumés de l'infraction visée à l'article 433*quinquies* du Code pénal ou à l'article 77*bis*;
> 2° l'étranger a cessé de coopérer;
> 3° les autorités judiciaires ont décidé de mettre fin à la procédure.

L'alinéa 1er est également applicable lorsque le ministre ou son délégué considère l'étranger comme pouvant compromettre l'ordre public ou à la sécurité nationale ou estime, en coopération avec les autorités judiciaires, que la coopération de l'étranger est frauduleuse ou que sa plainte est frauduleuse ou non fondée[70]. L'article 61/5 de la loi de 1980 dispose que le ministre ou son délégué peut autoriser au séjour pour une durée illimitée l'étranger victime

68 Art. 61/3, § 1 de la loi du 15 décembre 1980 sur l'accès au territoire, le séjour, l'établissement et l'éloignement des étrangers.

69 Voir L'article 61/4 de la loi du 15 décembre 1980 : « lorsque le Procureur du Roi ou l'auditeur du travail lui a confirmé que l'enquête ou la procédure judiciaire est toujours en cours, que l'étranger manifeste une volonté claire de coopération et pour autant que celui-ci ait rompu tout lien avec les auteurs présumés de l'infraction visée à l'article 433*quinquies* du Code pénal ou à l'article 77*bis* de la loi du 15 décembre 1980, et n'est pas considéré comme pouvant compromettre l'ordre public ou à la sécurité nationale ».

70 Article 61/4, § 2 de la loi du 15 décembre 1980 sur l'accès au territoire, le séjour, l'établissement et l'éloignement des étrangers.

de l'infraction visée à l'article 433*quinquies* du Code pénal ou victime, dans certaines circonstances.[71]

La Belgique n'a pas (encore) adhéré à l'Alliance mondiale pour éradiquer le travail forcé, l'esclavage moderne, la traite des êtres humains et le travail des enfants (Alliance 8.7), y compris les initiatives de responsabilité sociale des entreprises. Un certain nombre d'entreprises multinationales ayant leur siège en Belgique ont conclu des accords d'entreprise transnationaux exprimant leur volonté de combattre le travail forcé[72].

4 Conclusion

La question de savoir si le cadre juridique national de la Belgique est approprié et suffisant afin de remédier à toutes les formes d'exploitation humaine tombant sous la dénomination « esclavage contemporain » ne peut pas être tranchée aisément. D'abord, la notion d'esclavage contemporain n'est pas consacrée par des instruments juridiques proposant une définition fine. Puis, il est inhérent à la nature illicite de la traite des êtres humains que l'étendue du phénomène reste inconnue. Par contre, il vaut la peine de répertorier les recommandations critiques adressées à l'État belge par les organes de contrôle des instruments internationaux interdisant le travail forcé.

Les conclusions du dernier rapport du Groupe d'experts sur la lutte contre la traite des êtres humains (GRETA 2022) proposent plusieurs mesures à prendre pour mieux combattre la traite des êtres humains.[73] Ces mesures se situent dans une panoplie de domaines, tels que celui de la prévention, de l'identification des victimes de la traite, de l'assistance aux victimes, de la traite des enfants, de l'accès à un permis de séjour.

La CEACR de l'OIT a demandé dans le cadre du cycle de contrôle de 2014 relatif à la Convention n°29 à l'État belge de lui fournir plus d'informations relatives aux mesures dans le domaine de la prévention de la traite. Elle a

---

71 Il s'agit des circonstances visées à l'article 77*quater*, 1°, en ce qui concerne uniquement les mineurs non accompagnés, à 5°, de l'infraction au sens de l'article 77*bis*, lorsque sa déclaration ou sa plainte a abouti à une condamnation ou si le Procureur du Roi ou l'auditeur du travail a retenu dans ses réquisitions la prévention de traite des êtres humains ou de trafic des êtres humains sous les circonstances aggravantes prévues à l'article 77*quater*.

72 Voir la base de données relative aux accords d'entreprise transnationaux, <https://ec.europa.eu/social/main.jsp?catId=978&langId=en>.

73 GRETA, *Rapport d'évaluation Belgique. L'accès à la justice et à des recours effectifs pour les victimes de la traite des êtres humains – Troisième cycle d'évaluation* (2022), pp. 58–60 <https://rm.coe.int/3eme-cycle-d-evaluation-du-greta-sur-la-belgique/1680a8940c>.

également demandé de recevoir des informations statistiques plus précises quant aux procédures judiciaires entamées et aux peines infligées[74]. Dans le cadre du contrôle de 2018, la CEACR a demandé à l'État belge de :

> … continuer de fournir des informations sur les mesures prises pour assurer une meilleure identification et protection des victimes ainsi qu'une assistance et une indemnisation, comme prévu par la législation, en indiquant le nombre de victimes qui ont bénéficié d'une aide, notamment le nombre de victimes qui ont été indemnisées pour le préjudice subi ou qui ont pu faire valoir leurs droits auprès des autorités compétentes et ont pu obtenir le paiement de leur salaire dû[75].

La CEACR conclut en demandant au gouvernement belge de « continuer de fournir des informations sur les poursuites engagées, les condamnations prononcées et les peines appliquées sur la base des dispositions du Code pénal criminalisant la traite des personnes à des fins d'exploitation au travail ou d'exploitation sexuelle, ainsi que sur les mesures visant à renforcer les capacités des organes chargés du contrôle de l'application de la loi »[76]. Dans ce rapport, le CEACR continue à demander plus d'informations[77].

Il est périlleux de déduire de ces observations une évaluation positive ou négative, vu que la CEACR se situe encore à une phase d'étude de la question de conformité et que les informations nécessaires ne lui sont pas parvenues. L'étude précitée de Wintermayr et Weatherburn a le mérite d'aborder la question de la protection et des remèdes pour les victimes de la traite indépendamment de la question technique de la conformité aux instruments internationaux et européens. Cette étude remet en question de manière radicale la conditionnalité belge de l'assistance aux victimes de la traite basée sur

74 'Demande directe' CEACR (2014), <https://www.ilo.org/dyn/normlex/fr/f?p=1000:13100:0::NO:13100:P13100_COMMENT_ID.3191533>.

75 'Demande directe' CEACR (2019) <https://www.ilo.org/dyn/normlex/fr/f?p=1000:13100:0::NO:13100:P13100_COMMENT_ID,P13100_COUNTRY_ID:3780408,102560>.

76 *Ibid.*

77 *Ibid.* Notamment sur les éléments suivants : « i) les mesures prises pour continuer à sensibiliser le public et les autorités compétentes à l'identification de la traite des personnes tant à des fins d'exploitation sexuelle que d'exploitation au travail; ii) la suite donnée aux recommandations du Myria en ce qui concerne l'amélioration du système d'aide juridique aux victimes et leur indemnisation; iii) l'évaluation de la mise en œuvre du nouveau plan d'action national réalisée par la Cellule interdépartementale de coordination de la lutte contre la traite et le trafic des êtres humains, ainsi que les propositions formulée par cette dernière; et iv) les procédures judiciaires engagées, les décisions de justices prononcées dans les affaires de traite et la réparation octroyée aux victimes. »

leur volonté de coopérer aux procédures judiciaires. Dans le même esprit, cette étude plaide en faveur de la dissociation de la période dite de réflexion et de la question de la poursuite pénale de la traite. Cette étude plaide également en faveur d'une avance de l'État quant à la compensation des victimes de la traite[78].

Remerciements

L'auteur de ce rapport tient à exprimer sa gratitude envers Julie Antoine, stagiaire-étudiante de recherche à l'Université catholique de Louvain qui lui a donné une aide précieuse dans la collection des données bibliographiques et qui a eu la gentillesse de retoucher linguistiquement une version précédente de ce rapport rédigé par un auteur dont la langue maternelle ne correspond pas à la langue utilisée dans ce rapport.

Références académiques

A. Hochschild, *King Leopold's Ghost,* Pan Books, London 2006.

B. Henriet, "Elusive natives': Escaping colonial control in the Leverville oil palm concession, Belgian Congo, 1923–1941' (2015) 49 *Canadian Journal of African Studies* 339.

C.-É. Clesse, *La traite des êtres humains : droit belge éclairé des législations française, luxembourgeoise et suisse*, Larcier, Bruxelles 2013.

G. Deneckere, T. De Paepe, B. De Wever et G. Vanthemsche., *Een geschiedenis van België,* Academia Press, Gent 2017.

I. Goddeeris, 'Post-Colonial Belgium: The Memory of the Congo' (2015) 17:3 *International Journal of Postcolonial Studies* 444.

J.G. Everaert, 'Commerce d'Afrique et traite négrière dans les Pays-Bas autrichiens', (1975) 62 *Revue Francaise d'Histoire d'Outre-Mer* 177.

J. Seibert, 'In die Globale Wirtschaft gezwungen. Arbeit und kolonialer Kapitalismus im Kongo (1885–1960)', Campus Verlag, Frankfurt 2016.

K. Nevens, 'Penitentiaire arbeid : dringt het arbeidsrecht de gevangenis binnen ?' (2007) 3 *Revue de droit social* 231.

78 I. Wintermayr et A. Weatherburn, *Access to protection and remedy for victims of human trafficking for the purpose of labour exploitation in Belgium and the Netherlands*, ILO (2020), <https://www.ilo.org/wcmsp5/groups/public/---europe/---ro-geneva/---ilo-brussels/documents/publication/wcms_783811.pdf>.

L. Petillon, 'Des Habitants et de leurs droits', dans *Les Novelles, Droit colonial,* Éditions E. Picard, Bruxelles 1931.

M.G. Stanard, *The Leopard, the Lion, and the Cock: Colonial Memories and Monuments in Belgium*, Leuven University Press, Leuven 2019.

M. Zana Etambala, 'De Congolese gemeenschap in België : een ongewild 'neveneffect' van de koloniale overheersing?', dans I. Goddeeris, A. Lauro & G. Vanthemsche (dir.) *Koloniaal Congo. Een geschiedenis in vragen*, Polis, Kalmthout 2020, pp. 197–206.

R. Depoortere, *Le rachat du péage de l'Escaut,* Académie Royale de Belgique, Bruxelles 1991.

R. Loffman et B. Henriet, 'We are left with barely anything: Colonial Rule, Dependency, and the Lever Brothers in the Belgian, Congo, 1911–1960' (2020) 48:1 *The Journal of Imperial and Commonwealth History* 71.

Les formes contemporaines d'esclavage, y compris les causes et les conséquences : Canada

Yves Goguen

1 Introduction

> Coincé entre un passé colonial qu'il veut oublier et un essor républicain sans cesse ajourné, [le Canada] n'excelle que dans la médiocrité de ses politiques d'extrême centre, mais il livre à la pensée politique un objet d'importance : la condition du colon, qui fut celle de la majorité de sa population et qui le reste de mille façons inavouées.
>
> […]
>
> La colonie n'est pas seulement dominée par les entreprises, mais elle se confond à elles ; elle est une entreprise[1].

L'histoire du Canada, c'est aussi celle de la cupidité, la force motrice des esclavagistes au prix de la dignité humaine. L'esclavage en tant qu'institution mondiale est profondément ancré dans l'héritage du projet politique canadien :

> L'enrichissement colossal des pays européens et des anciennes colonies britanniques telles que le Canada, grâce au commerce des esclaves et à la colonisation de l'Afrique, constitue une réalité historique bien établie. Le pays s'est bâti sur des terres volées aux Autochtones – et grâce aussi aux marchandises produites par les plantations esclavagistes cultivées sous d'autres latitudes ; du point de vue économique, le Canada dépendait ainsi du travail des esclaves noirs et des coolies venus de Chine, du Japon et d'autres pays sud-asiatiques. Au Canada, la subordination des populations africaines autrefois réduites en esclavage et colonisées ainsi que l'accaparement croissant des terres autochtones par les colons se sont déployés en parallèle[2].

---

1 A. Deneault, *Bande de colons, une mauvaise conscience de classe*, LUX, Montréal 2020, p. 35.

2 R. Maynard, *NoirEs sous surveillance: esclavage, répression, violence d'État au Canada*, Mémoire d'encrier, Montréal 2018, p. 82.

 | DOI:10.1163/9789004723801_006

Ce sont les grandes lignes du contexte historique qui éclairent nos interrogations sur les pratiques commerciales et les droits du travail à l'ère du néolibéralisme, car si l'on peut situer officiellement l'esclavage dans le passé, les dynamiques politiques, économiques et culturelles mises en place par la domination coloniale demeurent néanmoins, en dépit de quelques ajustements, fermement enracinées dans la vie contemporaine[3]. Après avoir facilité pendant plusieurs années la réorganisation du système économique ayant mené à l'expansion des chaînes d'approvisionnement à travers le monde, les pays occidentaux cherchent depuis peu à remédier, en prenant la voie législative, aux intenses souffrances humaines que peut recouvrir l'expression « formes contemporaines d'esclavage ». Dans ce cadre, les axes d'interrogation autour desquels s'articule notre recensement transversal des mesures juridiques ou réglementaires mises en œuvre au Canada depuis 2020 sont : la chaîne d'approvisionnement transfrontalière, la traite humaine et le travail forcé, ainsi que l'exploitation de la main d'œuvre migrante temporaire.

2 Exploitation de la main-d'œuvre à l'étranger

D'après l'Indice mondial de l'esclavage de 2023, des produits importés au Canada à hauteur de milliards de dollars, tels que des ordinateurs, des téléphones portables, des vêtements et des accessoires, des minéraux extraits, ainsi que des produits dérivés de la pêche et de la canne à sucre, porteraient des traces d'esclavage moderne dans leurs chaînes d'approvisionnement[4].

Le Canada ne s'intéresse depuis trop peu longtemps à la mise en place d'un cadre de lutte contre les violations des droits de la personne et du travail commises par les grandes entreprises, y compris les compagnies minières, pétrolières et gazières. Néanmoins, deux développements juridiques méritent l'attention. D'abord, en 2020, le plus haut tribunal du pays a rendu une décision autorisant un recours collectif contre une société minière canadienne opérant en Afrique pour violation du droit international coutumier, un arrêt clé sur la responsabilité délictuelle des entreprises à l'étranger. Plus récemment encore, en 2023, le Parlement canadien a adopté une loi qui

3 R.D.G. Kelley, 'Introduction: A Poetics of Anticolonialism', *Discourse on colonialism* (Aimé Césaire), Monthly Review Press, New York 2000, p. 27, tel que rapporté par R. Maynard, précité à la p. 82.

4 Global Slavery Index, 'Modern Slavery in Canada' (2023), <https://cdn.walkfree.org/content/uploads/2023/09/28133439/GSI-Snapshot-Canada.pdf>.

impose aux multinationales des exigences de déclaration et des contrôles à l'importation pour veiller à ce que les chaînes d'approvisionnement soient exemptes de travail forcé et de travail des enfants à n'importe quelle étape de la production.

2.1 *Recours civils issus des normes internationales impératives*

Dans l'affaire *Nevsun Resources Ltd. c. Araya*[5], un groupe de travailleurs érythréens ont témoigné avoir été contraints, entre 2008 et 2010, de travailler au moins douze heures par jour, six jours par semaine, à des températures de près de 50 degrés Celsius. Ces conditions difficiles ont été endurées par plus de mille travailleurs dans le cadre d'un programme de service national les obligeant à travailler aux mines de Bisha.

Trois de ces travailleurs, après avoir obtenu le statut de réfugié au Canada, ont intenté un recours collectif contre Nevsun Resources Ltd. pour des violations du droit national de la responsabilité délictuelle et des violations du droit international coutumier relatives au travail forcé, à l'esclavage et aux traitements cruels ou dégradants. Nevsun Resources Ltd., dont le siège social est à Vancouver, détenait 60 % des parts de ces mines en Érythrée où sont exploités de l'or, du cuivre et du zinc. La société minière a présenté une motion visant à invalider les réclamations des travailleurs, sur la base de la « doctrine de l'acte d'État », arguant que les tribunaux canadiens n'avaient pas la compétence d'évaluer les actes souverains des gouvernements étrangers.

Ce litige soulève des questions cruciales : une corporation peut-elle être tenue responsable, au Canada, des violations du droit de la personne et du travail encourues dans le cadre d'activités à l'étranger ? L'interdiction du travail forcé, de l'esclavage et des traitements cruels, inhumains ou dégradants, peut-elle servir de fondement à une action en dommages-intérêts contre une partie non étatique ?

Sous la plume de la juge Rosalie Abella, une majorité de juges de la Cour suprême du Canada – à 5 contre 4 – ont répondu par l'affirmative et ont accepté la possibilité d'une compétence fondée sur le droit international coutumier, notamment les normes de *jus cogens* ou « normes impératives », des règles qui sont si importantes que personne n'a le droit de les enfreindre.

L'interdiction de l'esclavage est considérée comme l'une de ces normes impératives. La Cour suprême du Canada souligne qu'en 2002, le Haut-Commissariat des Nations Unies aux droits de l'homme a confirmé que « l'interdiction de l'esclavage et des pratiques analogues est désormais un principe bien établi

5 *Nevsun Resources Ltd. c Araya*, 2020 CSC 5 (Cour suprême du Canada).

de droit international qui a rang de règle de droit international coutumière et de *jus cogens* »[6]. L'interdiction du travail forcé a aussi valeur de *jus cogens.* La majorité fait sienne les mots de l'Organisation internationale du travail (OIT), qui affirme « qu'il existe aujourd'hui en droit international une norme qui interdit de manière impérative tout recours au travail forcé, le droit de ne pas être astreint à accomplir un travail ou service comptant parmi les droits fondamentaux de la personne humaine »[7]. Toujours est-il, précise l'OIT, « dans la mesure où il pourrait y avoir débat quant à la question de savoir si l'interdiction du travail forcé constitue une norme impérative, il ne fait aucun doute qu'elle constitue à tout le moins une norme de droit international coutumier »[8]. Quant à l'interdiction relative aux traitements cruels, inhumains ou dégradants, la Cour suprême du Canada est catégorique et rappelle que cette interdiction a été qualifiée de « droit absolu qu'aucun objectif social ni aucune urgence ne saurait restreindre »[9].

À la lumière d'une compréhension évolutive du droit international, l'argument de Nevsun, qui soutenait qu'en tant que société commerciale elle était immunisée contre toute responsabilité, a été rejeté par la majorité. En examinant si le droit international coutumier devrait être considéré comme applicable à un acteur non étatique, la majorité a identifié un changement dans le droit international au cours des 70 dernières années, par lequel l'ordre mondial s'est éloigné de son approche historiquement centrée sur l'État pour adopter une perspective plus humaniste. Cette évolution a créé un grand intérêt international pour la protection des individus, de leur liberté, de leur santé et de leur éducation, qui peuvent être violés non seulement par des États, mais aussi par des sociétés commerciales, même au-delà des frontières nationales. Comme le remarque la juge Abella, dans d'autres domaines du droit international, comme en droit pénal international, des acteurs privés ou non étatiques ont été tenus responsables de leurs actes. Par l'effet du *Pacte international relatif aux droits civils et politiques* (1976), le Canada a l'obligation de garantir un recours utile aux victimes de violations de ces droits. Pour expliquer la nature de cette obligation, la majorité précise que, selon le Comité des droits de l'homme des Nations Unies, dans l'*Observation générale nº 31 : La nature de l'obligation juridique générale imposée aux États partis au Pacte*, les

6 *Ibid.*, au para. 101, citant D. Weissbrodt et la Société antiesclavagiste internationale, *Abolir l'esclavage et ses formes contemporaines*, Doc. N.U. HR/PUB/02/4, 2002, p. 3.

7 *Ibid.*, au para. 102, citant Organisation internationale du travail, « Travail forcé au Myanmar (Birmanie) », *Bulletin officiel du B.I.T. : supplément spécial*, vol. LXXXI, 1998.

8 *Ibid.*, para. 102.

9 *Ibid.*, para. 103.

États signataires doivent assurer une protection non seulement contre les violations de droits commises par les États, mais aussi contre celles commises par des personnes privées, physiques ou morales. Le Comité mentionne également que les États partis doivent accorder la jouissance des droits reconnus dans le Pacte à tous les individus, notamment les « demandeurs d'asile, réfugiés, travailleurs migrants et autres personnes qui se trouveraient sur le territoire de l'État parti ou relèveraient de sa compétence »[10]. Quant aux recours, le Comité a noté ce qui suit :

> [L]es tribunaux peuvent de diverses manières garantir effectivement l'exercice des droits reconnus par le Pacte, soit en statuant sur son applicabilité directe, soit en appliquant les règles constitutionnelles ou autres dispositions législatives comparables, soit en interprétant les implications qu'ont pour l'application du droit national les dispositions du Pacte[11].

Par conséquent, la majorité a conclu que chacune des revendications en cause – travail forcé, esclavage, traitement dégradant et inhumain – pouvait en effet relever à la fois du droit national de la responsabilité civile et du droit international coutumier. En somme, une majorité de juges de la Cour suprême du Canada ont signalé que les violations des normes impératives constituent de graves violations de droits qui doivent toujours et partout être fortement découragées. Ce faisant, les tribunaux peuvent entendre une cause portant sur la responsabilité d'une société canadienne qui contrevient à ces normes, même à l'extérieur des frontières nationales. Le tribunal d'appel de dernière instance du pays réfute l'argument selon lequel les sociétés commerciales devraient être épargnées de l'application du droit international, ce qui aura sans doute pour effet de revitaliser la fonction de la responsabilité civile délictuelle dans le cadre des réclamations en droit international coutumier.

Néanmoins, d'autres questions au cœur de ce litige demeurent sans réponse. Le bien-fondé de la cause des travailleurs érythréens devait être entendu une nouvelle fois par la cour de première instance de la Colombie-Britannique, avec l'avantage des jugements majoritaire et dissident de la Cour suprême du Canada. Bien que la majorité ait décidé que les revendications des travailleurs pouvaient aller de l'avant et être entendues, une décision sur le fond n'a jamais

---

10 *Pacte international relatif aux droits civils et politiques, Observation générale n° 31 : La nature de l'obligation juridique générale imposée aux États parties au Pacte*, Doc NU CCPR/C/21/Rev.1/Add.13 (26.05.2004), para. 10.

11 *Ibid.*, para. 15.

vu le jour puisque la société minière a réglé l'affaire à l'amiable, empêchant ainsi le tribunal de première instance d'évaluer les dommages associés aux multiples délits contrevenant au droit international coutumier, comme le travail forcé et d'autres crimes contre l'humanité[12].

Or, au Canada, les procès intentés pour violation des droits de la personne par des entreprises canadiennes opérant à l'étranger ont eu des résultats mitigés. Au moins neuf procès de ce type ont été portés devant les tribunaux canadiens, dont aucun n'a jusqu'à présent abouti sur le fond. Quatre de ces affaires ont été rejetées à un stade préliminaire de la procédure, tandis que deux autres se sont conclues par un règlement. En 2021, trois d'entre elles, toutes des affaires impliquant Hudbay Minerals, une compagnie minière canadienne avec des activités au Guatemala, étaient en cours devant les tribunaux[13], sans aucune certitude d'être éventuellement entendues sur le fond. C'est ce qui donne par ailleurs un sens particulier aux interventions législatives subséquentes qui visent, au moyen de la transparence accrue ou de la diligence raisonnable, à combler les lacunes constatées en matière de responsabilité pénale des entreprises.

2.2 *Légiférer les chaînes d'approvisionnement*

2.2.1 Ombudsman canadien de la responsabilité des entreprises

Le gouvernement canadien a annoncé en 2018 la création du Bureau de l'ombudsman canadien de la responsabilité des entreprises (OCRE), une entité qui devait avoir pour mandat de servir de chien de garde contre les violations en matière de droits de la personne commises à l'étranger. Cependant, il a fallu attendre jusqu'en 2021 pour que la personne nouvellement nommée par le gouvernement au poste d'ombud révèle les détails derrière l'annonce, dont les limites de son pouvoir réel. Le bureau de l'OCRE peut recevoir des plaintes concernant les activités à l'étranger des entreprises canadiennes extractives et textiles, déposées via un formulaire en ligne, mais sa capacité à résoudre les différends est restreinte à la médiation – qui peut seulement avoir lieu avec l'accord de toutes les parties – et à la publication des rapports publics sur les conclusions rendues[14]. En effet, l'OCRE peut assurer un suivi avec le plaignant

12 *Radio-Canada*, 'Entente à l'amiable entre trois réfugiés érythréens et une minière canadienne', (23.10.2020), <https://ici.radio-canada.ca/nouvelle/1743866/nevsun-resources-cour-supreme-droit-international>.

13 T. Meshel, 'From *Nevsun v Araya* to the Core: Taking Stock of State-Based Business and Human Rights Grievance Mechanisms in Canada' (2021) 54 *U.B.C. Law Review* 203.

14 Site web du Bureau de l'Ombudsman canadienne de la responsabilité des entreprises, <https://core-ombuds.canada.ca/index.aspx?lang=fra>.

pour mener à bien une série d'étapes d'enquête et ensuite formuler des recommandations correctives au ministre du Commerce international[15], sans toutefois être habileté à imposer des réparations juridiquement contraignantes.

D'après l'ombud, l'OCRE est « le premier du genre dans le monde » dont le mandat est axé sur la responsabilisation des entreprises pour leurs activités à l'étranger[16]. Bien que son institution constitue un développement non négligeable, la faiblesse de ses pouvoirs d'enquête et de sanction lui a fait mériter un nombre de critiques de la part de personnes expertes qui ne manquent pas de mettre en lumière que les compétences de l'OCRE s'en tiennent à « promouvoir, conseiller, examiner, recommander »[17]. Par exemple, l'OCRE peut mener des enquêtes sans pour autant pouvoir contraindre les entreprises de fournir les documents nécessaires ou de faire comparaître des témoins. À l'issue de son enquête, l'ombud ne dispose pas non plus du pouvoir d'obliger une corporation visée à réparer le préjudice. L'OCRE peut recommander l'adoption de certaines mesures, telles que le changement des pratiques et l'octroi d'une compensation financière, mais les entreprises sont libres d'appliquer ces recommandations ou non[18]. Le manque d'indépendance de l'OCRE, illustré par sa création par un arrêté ministériel plutôt que par une loi du Parlement, ainsi que le poste de lobbyiste pour le compte de l'Association canadienne des producteurs de pétrole précédemment occupé par l'ombud, ont aussi fait réagir[19].

2.2.2 Lois contre le travail forcé et le travail des enfants

Les nombreuses critiques formulées à l'encontre de l'OCRE et la pression exercée de toutes parts ont assurément influencé le gouvernement canadien qui, après plusieurs d'années de tergiversations, a décidé de faire avancer un projet de loi visant à interdire le travail forcé ou le travail des enfants dans les chaînes

15 L'Ombudsman canadien de la responsabilité des entreprises, 'L'Ombudsman canadien pour les droits de la personne lance un processus de plainte en ligne dans le cadre du mandat mondial de protection des droits' (15.03.2021), <https://core-ombuds.canada.ca/core_ombuds-ocre_ombuds/news-nouvelles/complaint_process-processus_de_plainte.aspx?lang=fra>.

16 L'Ombudsman canadienne de la responsabilité des entreprises, 'Promouvoir, Conseiller, Examiner, Recommander : Rapport annuel 2019–2021 (29.10.2021), p. 5, <https://publications.gc.ca/collections/collection_2022/amc-gac/FR81-1-2021-fra.pdf>.

17 *Ibid.*, p. 14.

18 L. Jolin-Dahel, 'Entreprises canadiennes: un ombudsman sans pouvoir à Ottawa', *Le Devoir* (26.07.2019), <https://www.ledevoir.com/politique/canada/559450/entreprises-canadiennes-l-ombudsman-doit-avoir-des-pouvoirs-d-enquetes-reitere-l-onu>. I. Tchotourian et A. Langenfeld, 'Le fédéral manque son coup avec un ombudsman sans pouvoirs' (19.04.2021).

19 D. Tougat, 'Un ombudsman sans mordant', *Revue Relations*, (septembre-octobre 2019), <https://cjf.qc.ca/revue-relations/publication/article/un-ombudsman-sans-mordant/>.

d'approvisionnement et créer une responsabilité pénale pour les entreprises contrevenantes et leurs dirigeants. Parrainée par la sénatrice québécoise Julie Miville-Dechêne, la *Loi sur la lutte contre le travail forcé et le travail des enfants dans les chaînes d'approvisionnement*[20] représente un premier pas vers le renforcement de la vigilance et de la transparence exigées des entreprises dans le cadre de leurs pratiques commerciales transfrontalières. Après l'approbation du Sénat et l'étude du Comité des affaires étrangères de la Chambre des communes, le cheminement législatif du projet de loi S-211 s'est achevé avec son adoption à la majorité, le 3 mai 2023, grâce au soutien de la députation des partis Libéral et Conservateur.

Ailleurs dans le monde, d'autres États avaient déjà adopté une telle législation, dont la France, le Royaume-Uni, la Suisse, les Pays-Bas, l'Allemagne, la Norvège et l'Australie[21]. Il fait nul doute que la nouvelle loi canadienne s'inspire surtout de la *Modern Slavery Act* du Royaume-Uni[22] car, à l'instar de la loi britannique, l'obligation imposée aux grandes entreprises de faire rapport sur les mesures identifiées pour prévenir et réduire les violations du droit du travail constitue l'enjeu central. La loi canadienne comporte également des éléments semblables à ce que l'on retrouve dans les lois de l'Australie[23] et de la Californie[24].

Plus précisément, la *Loi sur la lutte contre le travail forcé et le travail des enfants dans les chaînes d'approvisionnement* vient assujettir les grandes corporations qui produisent ou vendent des marchandises, au Canada ou ailleurs, ou qui importent au pays des produits à l'extérieur du Canada[25], ainsi qu'à certaines institutions fédérales[26], une obligation de déclaration, sous forme de rapports annuels détaillant les mesures prises pour prévenir et réduire le recours au travail forcé ou au travail des enfants à toute étape du processus de production, tant au Canada qu'à l'étranger[27].

---

20 *Loi sur la lutte contre le travail forcé et le travail des enfants dans les chaines d'approvisionnement*, LC 2023, c 9.

21 Emploi et développement social Canada, 'L'exploitation de la main-d'œuvre dans les chaînes d'approvisionnement mondiales : Rapport – Ce que nous avons entendu', (2022), <www.canada.ca/content/dam/esdc-edsc/documents/programs/international-affairs/reports/what-we-heard-forced-labour-global-supply-chain/Forced_Labour_WWHR(FR)-v2.pdf>.

22 *Modern Slavery Act 2015* (R-U), c 30.

23 *Modern Slavery Act* N° 153, 2018 (Cth) ; *Modern Slavery Act* 2018 N° 30 (NSW).

24 *California Transparency in Supply Chains Act*, California Civil Code.

25 *Loi sur la lutte contre le travail forcé et le travail des enfants dans les chaines d'approvisionnement, supra* n. 20, arts. 9–10.

26 *Ibid.*, art. 5.

27 *Ibid.*, arts. 6 et 11.

Rappelons que, depuis 2021, le Canada impose déjà une obligation de déclaration aux entreprises canadiennes qui s'approvisionnent directement ou indirectement au Xinjiang ou auprès d'entités recourant à la main-d'œuvre ouïghoure, qui y sont établies ou qui cherchent à s'engager sur son marché. Ces entités commerciales doivent signer une « déclaration d'intégrité », soit une affirmation faisant foi que : l'entreprise est consciente de la situation des droits de la personne au Xinjiang; qu'elle se conforme à toutes les lois canadiennes et internationales pertinentes; qu'elle respecte les droits de la personne et s'efforce de respecter les principes directeurs de l'Organisation de coopération et de développement économiques à l'intention des entreprises multinationales et les principes directeurs des Nations Unies relatifs aux entreprises et aux droits de la personne; et qu'elle ne s'est pas procurée sciemment des produits ou des services auprès d'un fournisseur impliqué dans le travail forcé ou d'autres violations des droits de la personne liées à la répression des Ouïghours[28].

La nouvelle loi canadienne prescrit une pénalité en cas de non-conformité aux exigences de déclaration obligatoires, notamment afin de décourager les entreprises qui ne voudraient soumettre aucune information. Les corporations qui ne déposeront pas un rapport annuel ou qui fourniront des informations fausses ou trompeuses s'exposent à des amendes pouvant atteindre 250 000 dollars[29]. Par ailleurs, la création d'un régime d'inspection donne au ministre de la Sécurité publique le pouvoir d'exiger des entreprises visées qu'elles fournissent certaines informations[30]. Si une infraction est commise, c'est-à-dire si l'obligation de déclaration n'est pas respectée, tout administrateur ou dirigeant de la société qui est autorisé ou qui a participé à l'infraction est aussi considéré comme coupable du délit et passible, en cas de condamnation, de la peine prévue[31].

En s'appuyant sur l'Accord Canada-États-Unis-Mexique (ACEUM), en vigueur depuis 2020[32] – selon lequel les pays signataires ont convenu de coopérer à l'identification et à la circulation des marchandises produites par le travail forcé par l'adoption et le maintien en vigueur d'une loi relative à l'élimination

28 Affaires mondiales Canada, 'Le Canada annonce de nouvelles mesures pour lutter contre les violations des droits de la personne au Xinjiang, en Chine', <www.canada.ca/fr/affaires-mondiales/nouvelles/2021/01/le-canada-annonce-de-nouvelles-mesures-pour-lutter-contre-les-violations-des-droits-de-la-personne-au-xinjiang-en-chine.html>.

29 *Loi sur la lutte contre le travail forcé et le travail des enfants dans les chaines d'approvisionnement, supra* n. 20, arts. 19–21.

30 *Ibid.*, art. 18.

31 *Ibid.*, arts. 20–21.

32 *Loi de mise en œuvre de l'Accord Canada – États-Unis – Mexique*, LC 2020, c 1.

de toutes les formes de travail forcé – la *Loi sur la lutte contre le travail forcé et le travail des enfants dans les chaînes d'approvisionnement* consolide l'interdiction de l'importation commerciale au Canada de marchandises extraites, fabriquées ou produites en tout ou en partie par le travail forcé ou le travail des enfants, sous peine de sanctions pécuniaires, peu importe l'origine particulière des produits importés[33].

Parmi les définitions provenant des conventions internationales auxquelles se réfère le législateur canadien dans le cadre de la nouvelle loi, il y a celle du « travail forcé » de l'OIT :

> un travail ou un service fourni ou offert par une personne dans des circonstances qui pourraient raisonnablement amener la personne à croire que sa sécurité ou celle d'une personne qu'elle connaît serait menacée si elle ne fournissait pas ou offrait de fournir le travail ou le service ; ou qui constituent un travail forcé ou obligatoire au sens de l'article 2 de la *Convention sur le travail forcé, 1930*[34].

Il va de même pour l'expression « travail des enfants », qui est définie comme le travail ou le service fourni par des personnes âgées de moins de 18 ans dans des circonstances dangereuses « qui constituent les pires formes de travail des enfants telles que définies à l'article 3 de la *Convention sur les pires formes de travail des enfants, 1999* »[35].

Contrairement à la loi britannique sur laquelle elle s'inspire, la version législative canadienne ne fournit toutefois pas de définition du terme « esclavage moderne » ; la servitude pour dettes ou la traite des êtres humains ne sont également pas visées.

Quant au champ d'application de la loi canadienne, dans sa mouture actuelle, seules sont assujetties les grandes entreprises qui répondent à deux des trois critères suivants : avoir des actifs d'au moins 20 millions de dollars ; avoir des ventes d'au moins 40 millions de dollars ; et employer en moyenne au moins 250 personnes[36]. Elle s'applique aussi aux entités contrôlées par une entreprise qui répond à cette définition[37]. Les entreprises couvertes par la législation naissante reflètent d'ailleurs celles qui sont visées par la *Loi sur les*

33 *Loi sur la lutte contre le travail forcé et le travail des enfants dans les chaines d'approvisionnement, supra* n. 20, arts. 26–27.

34 *Ibid.*, art. 2.

35 *Ibid.*

36 *Ibid.*

37 *Ibid.*, art. 10.

mesures de transparence dans le secteur extractif[38], dont l'objectif est de réduire la corruption dans l'industrie minière grâce à des mesures de transparence accrue.

Revenons maintenant sur l'objectif phare de la *Loi sur la lutte contre le travail forcé et le travail des enfants dans les chaînes d'approvisionnement* et les critiques émises à son encontre. L'obligation de signalement, en faisant rapport sur les mesures prises pour prévenir et réduire les violations du droit du travail, ne s'accompagne étonnamment pas d'une obligation de les adopter. Dit autrement, la loi n'exige pas aux entités commerciales quelconque obligation relativement à la mise en œuvre des mesures correctives qu'elles auront elles-mêmes identifiées et déclarées. Cela signifie qu'une entreprise pourrait, en principe, se conformer à la loi en ne prenant aucune mesure ou en prenant des mesures manifestement inadéquates, c'est-à-dire en fermant volontairement les yeux sur ses propres pratiques et en poursuivant ses activités comme si de rien n'était[39]. Aux dires de la directrice des politiques au Réseau canadien sur la reddition de comptes des entreprises, cette lacune permet aux corporations « de continuer à tirer profit de la souffrance humaine et de la mise à mal de l'environnement »[40]. Il est facile pour le gouvernement, poursuit-elle dans son témoignage devant le Comité permanent des affaires étrangères et du développement international, « d'adopter une loi qui vous obligera à rendre compte de vos activités, mais sans vous obliger pour autant à mettre fin au préjudice que vous causez »[41].

Parmi les autres aspects critiqués de la loi, celle-ci n'offre aucun accès véritable à des voies de recours et à des redressements aux personnes lésées par les pratiques abusives, comme le travail forcé. C'est une raison pour laquelle de nombreuses parties prenantes auraient préféré une réponse législative qui exigerait des entités commerciales, au-delà de la transparence et la reddition de compte, un réel devoir de diligence en matière de droits de la personne.

---

38 *Loi sur les mesures de transparence dans le secteur extractif*, LC 2014, c 39, art. 376.

39 Emploi et développement social Canada, 'L'exploitation de la main-d'œuvre dans les chaînes d'approvisionnement mondiales : Rapport – Ce que nous avons entendu', (2022), <https://www.canada.ca/content/dam/esdc-edsc/documents/programs/international-affairs/reports/what-we-heard-forced-labour-global-supply-chain/Forced_Labour_WWHR(FR)-v2.pdf>. Voir aussi : J. Fudge, 'Why Labour Lawyers Should Care About the Modern Slavery Act 2015' (2018) 29:3 *King's Law J.* 377.

40 Témoignage expert de Emily Dwyer, directrice des politiques au Réseau canadien sur la reddition de comptes des entreprises, journal des débats (Hansard) du Comité des affaires étrangères de la Chambre des communes, FAAE-38, (21.11.2021), <https://www.noscommunes.ca/DocumentViewer/fr/44-1/FAAE/reunion-38/temoignages>.

41 *Ibid.*

Rappelons par ailleurs que deux formations politiques fédérales, le Nouveau Parti démocratique et le Bloc québécois, ont voté contre l'adoption de la *Loi sur la lutte contre le travail forcé et le travail des enfants dans les chaînes d'approvisionnement.*

De nombreuses personnes consultées croient que le Canada devrait envisager une législation basée sur la diligence raisonnable obligatoire relativement aux droits de la personne et au droit du travail. Dans un rapport intitulé *L'exploitation de la main-d'œuvre dans les chaînes d'approvisionnement mondiales : Ce que nous avons entendu*, le gouvernement canadien formule comme suit les résultats des consultations menées en 2019 avec des intervenants de la société civile, des représentants syndicaux, des organisations internationales, de l'industrie et des employeurs, et des universitaires :

> Il y avait… un consensus sur le fait que le Canada devrait envisager l'adoption d'une loi sur la diligence raisonnable obligatoire. Les intervenants ont également généralement convenu que la loi devrait s'inspirer des lignes directrices de l'OCDE sur le devoir de diligence et être fondée sur l'expérience des pays européens. Cela pourrait vouloir dire avoir une large portée et une perspective axée sur les droits de la personne[42].

Ces mêmes intervenants citent favorablement la loi française adoptée en 2017, la *Loi relative au devoir de vigilance des sociétés mères et des entreprises donneuses d'ordre*[43], cette dernière étant par ailleurs devenue une source d'inspiration pour la Commission européenne[44]. C'est la portée plus large de la législation française et européenne qui constitue sa force, à savoir qu'elle cible plus de types d'entreprises.

De plus, contrairement à la législation canadienne, la *Loi relative au devoir de vigilance des sociétés mères et des entreprises donneuses d'ordre* adoptée en France prévoit la possibilité d'aller devant les tribunaux pour obtenir une condamnation contre les corporations qui violent les normes internationales en matière de droits de la personne. Il s'agit là d'une lacune importante de la

42 Emploi et développement social Canada, 'L'exploitation de la main-d'œuvre dans les chaînes d'approvisionnement mondiales: Rapport – Ce que nous avons entendu' (2022), <https://www.canada.ca/content/dam/esdc-edsc/documents/programs/international-affairs/reports/what-we-heard-forced-labour-global-supply-chain/Forced_Labour_WWHR(FR)-v2.pdf>.

43 *Loi n° 2017-399 du 27 mars 2017 relative au devoir de vigilance des sociétés mères et des entreprises donneuses d'ordre*, JO, 28 mars 2017, n° 74.

44 Commission européenne, 'Proposal for a Directive on Corporate Sustainability Due Diligence and amending Directive (UE) 2019/1937 – 2022/0051' (23.02.2022).

loi canadienne que cherche justement à corriger un projet de loi subséquent déposé à la Chambre des communes, *Loi sur la responsabilité des entreprises de protéger les droits de la personne*, dont la première lecture a eu lieu le 29 mars 2022. Le projet de loi C-262, porté par le député néo-démocrate Peter Julian, prévoit des mesures législatives sur les chaînes d'approvisionnement qui se focalisent sur la prévention et la réparation des dommages, plutôt que sur la seule obligation de signaler les problèmes encourus. Une loi comme celle-ci viendrait imposer une responsabilité juridique aux entreprises multinationales de prévenir les violations contre les droits de la personne, d'en tenir compte et d'y remédier. Dans son préambule, on peut lire que : « les entités commerciales canadiennes ont la responsabilité de prévenir et d'atténuer les incidences négatives réelles ou potentielles sur les droits de la personne liées aux activités commerciales qu'elles mènent à l'étranger et qu'en conséquence, elles doivent faire preuve de diligence raisonnable » ; « le droit à réparation est un principe fondamental du système international des droits de la personne et, pour les victimes, l'accès à des voies de recours efficaces est un besoin reconnu au regard des normes internationales » ; « la responsabilité juridique des entités commerciales et l'accès des personnes touchées à une réparation efficace font partie intégrante de l'obligation de protection contre les violations des droits de la personne liées aux activités commerciales qui incombe à l'État » ; et que « des mécanismes judiciaires efficaces relevant de l'État sont essentiels pour garantir l'accès à une réparation efficace »[45].

Sans grand étonnement, ce projet de loi ne fait toutefois pas partie de l'Ordre de priorité du Parlement établi par le gouvernement Libéral au pouvoir[46]. À cet égard, le Canada ne fait pas cas d'exception : selon l'expérience à l'échelle internationale, jusqu'à présent, aucun des pays ayant adopté une loi obligeant de faire rapport sur les risques d'exploitation sur la chaîne d'approvisionnement n'avait franchi le deuxième pas, soit l'adoption d'une loi sur la diligence raisonnable ou d'une loi qui oblige les compagnies à respecter les droits de la personne et qui donne accès à des recours pour réclamer un dédommagement[47].

---

45 PL C-262, *Loi sur la responsabilité des entreprises de protéger les droits de la personne*, 1re sess, 44e lég, 2021–2022–2023 (première lecture le 29 mars 2022).

46 État d'avancement, PL C-262, <https://www.parl.ca/LegisInfo/fr/projet-de-loi/44-1/C-262?view=details#>.

47 Témoignage expert de Emily Dwyer, directrice des politiques au Réseau canadien sur la reddition de comptes des entreprises, *supra* n. 40.

3 Traite humaine et travail sous contrainte

3.1 *Légiférer contre la traite des personnes*

Le Protocole de Palerme définit la traite des personnes de sorte à englober l'exploitation sexuelle, le trafic d'organe et le travail forcé[48]. Au Canada, il existe « un réseau de lois complexe et multiscalaire »[49] qui a été conçu pour judiciariser la traite des personnes, tout particulièrement le trafic sexuel et le travail du sexe. Ces lois comprennent le Code criminel – l'art. 279 compte six infractions qui ciblent la traite des personnes[50] – les interdictions fédérales de la traite des personnes prévues par la *Loi sur l'immigration et la protection des réfugiés*[51], ainsi que les lois provinciales qui fournissent des outils pour repérer les trafiquants présumés et qui offrent des recours aux victimes. À celles-ci s'ajoutent les règlements municipaux qui régissent les activités des entreprises, comme les salons de massage et les fournisseurs d'hébergement locatif.

Dans la province de l'Ontario, des modifications législatives récentes comprennent la *Loi de 2021 sur la stratégie de lutte contre la traite des personnes*[52]. Entre autres, les objectifs déclarés de cette loi sont l'offre d'un soutien aux survivantes, notamment les femmes autochtones, et le renforcement des pouvoirs de surveillance et d'enquête de la police et des inspecteurs nommés par le ministre. Relativement aux vastes pouvoirs accordés à ces inspecteurs et à leur grande latitude d'enquêter sur ce qui est ou peut être pertinent pour une inspection, ces derniers peuvent « sans mandat ni avis et à tout moment, entrer dans tout lieu et l'inspecter »[53] et « interroger une personne sur toute question qui est ou peut être pertinente pour l'inspection »[54]. La non-conformité est une infraction punissable, sujette à une amende de 50 000 $ ou 100 000 $ pour un individu ou une société, respectivement[55]. La loi comporte aussi des précisions sur comment et quand les services de police peuvent accéder aux

48 *Protocole additionnel à la Convention des Nations Unies contre la criminalité transnationale organisée visant à prévenir, réprimer et punir la traite des personnes, en particulier des femmes et des enfants*, 15 novembre 2000, 2237 RTNU 319.

49 J. Fudge *et al.* 'Caught in the Carceral Web: Anti-Trafficking Laws and Policies and Their Impact on Migrant Sex Workers' (2021), <https://gflc.ca/wp-content/uploads/2020/10/MSW-Report-Final-Sept-26.pdf>.

50 *Code criminel*, LRC 1985,00 c. C-46, art. 279.

51 *Loi sur l'immigration et la protection des réfugiés*, LC 2001, c 27.

52 *Loi de 2021 sur la stratégie de lutte contre la traite des personnes*, LO 2021, c 21 (Ontario).

53 *Ibid.*, art. 7(3).

54 *Ibid.*, art. 7(7).

55 *Ibid.*, art. 8.

renseignements figurant dans les registres des clients des hôtels afin de dissuader la traite des personnes et d'identifier et de localiser les victimes[56].

D'autres provinces canadiennes, dont le Manitoba[57], la Saskatchewan[58], et plus récemment, l'Alberta[59], ont adopté des lois pour faciliter la capacité des victimes présumées à obtenir des ordonnances de protection contre les trafiquants et à demander une indemnisation contre ces derniers. En matière de responsabilité civile délictuelle, « les survivants doivent recourir à une mosaïque de remèdes et de protections existantes, et ils sont trop nombreux à tomber dans les failles de notre système », déplorait le ministre de la Justice de l'Alberta[60]. En 2020, l'Assemblée législative de l'Alberta a adopté la *Protecting Survivors of Human Trafficking Act*[61], conformément à laquelle les victimes d'exploitation peuvent déposer un recours civil pour obtenir un dédommagement financier. À l'instar des développements législatifs de l'Ontario, la loi albertaine veut également fournir aux forces de l'ordre une boîte à outils mieux garnie et rendre moins difficiles les interventions policières s'il y a présomption de traite humaine. Un juge provincial peut désormais lancer un mandat criminel plus rapidement afin de permettre qu'une propriété privée soit fouillée s'il y a un motif raisonnable de croire qu'ils y trouveront une victime de traite humaine[62].

En jetant un regard empirique sur l'incidence des allégations de traite humaine signalées aux forces de l'ordre, les auteurs du rapport *Caught in the Carceral Web: Anti-Trafficking Laws and Policies and their impact on Migrant Sex Workers* (2021) soulignent ce qui suit :

> Sur les 1 708 incidents de traite des personnes signalés par la police depuis 2009, la grande majorité (97 %) concernait des femmes et des filles comme victimes présumées. Selon Statistique Canada, la traite des personnes à des fins d'« exploitation sexuelle » domestique est la plus répandue, et la majorité des cas de traite humaine signalés par la police sont liés à des infractions présumées au Code criminel. Très peu de cas de traite des personnes à des fins autres que sexuelles ont été poursuivis, ce qui

56 *Loi de 2021 sur la stratégie de lutte contre la traite des personnes, supra* note 52, arts. 2 et 4.

57 *Loi sur l'exploitation sexuelle d'enfants et la traite de personnes*, C.P.L.M. c. C94 (Manitoba).

58 *Protection From Human Trafficking Act*, LS 2021, c. 23 (Saskatchewan).

59 *Protecting Survivors of Human Trafficking Act*, LA 2020, c P-26.8 (Alberta).

60 M. Djukic, 'Le gouvernement albertain veut légiférer contre le trafic d'êtres humains', *Radio-Canada*, (08.04.2020), <https://ici.radio-canada.ca/nouvelle/1691977/alberta-trafic-humain-abus-organes-sexuel-lois-juridiction>.

61 *Protecting Survivors of Human Trafficking Act, supra* n. 59.

62 *Ibid.*, art. 7.

> fait que le cadre de la traite des personnes est extraordinairement étroit et se résume presque exclusivement à la traite des personnes à des fins sexuelles domestiques, et que les abus dans d'autres secteurs du travail ne sont pas abordés[63].

Pris ensemble, les infractions criminelles, lois provinciales et règlements municipaux constituent selon ce collectif de recherche « un cadre juridique et politique qui cherche à réglementer et, en fin de compte, à éradiquer le travail du sexe, tout en bannissant de la société les travailleuses et travailleurs du sexe migrants qui travaillent dans ce secteur »[64]. Bien que le gouvernement fédéral se serve de l'argument humanitaire de la protection contre la traite humaine pour justifier l'interdiction de travailler dans l'industrie du sexe aux personnes migrantes sans statut de résident permanent, ces règlements les rendent en fait plus vulnérables à l'exploitation et à d'autres abus[65]. En raison de leur statut d'immigration précaire, « les travailleuses du sexe migrantes sont de plus en plus exposées à la violence ciblée de prédateurs qui savent qu'ils n'ont aucun recours efficace à la protection de l'État, étant donné la vulnérabilité de leur statut juridique et la criminalisation de leur travail »[66]. D'autre part, Fudge récusent l'idée même que le travail du sexe soit intrinsèquement une forme d'exploitation qui nécessite pour la dissuader une intervention punitive de l'État, car les lois destinées à lutter contre la traite des êtres humains « alimentent la panique morale entourant le travail du sexe, intensifient le profilage des travailleuses du sexe et des communautés racisées, et menacent la sûreté, la sécurité et le bien-être des travailleuses du sexe migrantes »[67]. Pour assurer une meilleure protection contre la violence et l'exploitation dans l'industrie du sexe, elle recommande qu'on se tourne plutôt vers les lois d'application générale existantes, comme les interdictions pénales contre les agressions, les agressions sexuelles, le vol, le vol qualifié, l'enlèvement et la séquestration, l'extorsion, l'intimidation, le harcèlement criminel, les menaces de mort ou de dommages physiques[68].

Selon le Centre canadien pour mettre fin à la traite des personnes, il faudrait plutôt en faire davantage pour s'attaquer aux causes sous-jacentes de la traite des personnes, car force est de constater que les lois coercitives et les pouvoirs

63 J. Fudge *et al.*, *supra* n. 49, p. 15, citant Adam Cotter, *Trafficking in persons in Canada, 2018*, Juristat, 23 juin 2020. Traduction libre.

64 *Ibid.*, p. 3. Traduction libre.

65 *Ibid.*, pp. 60–61.

66 *Ibid.*, p. 60. Traduction libre.

67 *Ibid.* Traduction libre.

68 *Ibid.*, p. 61.

accrus en matière de surveillance et d'inspection ne semblent pas apporter de solutions constructives là où elles pourraient être le plus nécessaires. Cet organisme milite pour une réaffectation des ressources au bénéfice des services sociaux, des logements abordables et des soins de santé pour les groupes les plus exposés à l'exploitation du travail[69]. Certaines populations sont plus susceptibles d'être à risque de l'exploitation du travail, dont les ressortissants étrangers, les personnes LGBTQ+ et les jeunes sans-abris, en raison des vulnérabilités créées par la pauvreté et l'endettement, l'isolement, les barrières linguistiques et la précarité du statut d'immigration[70].

3.2 *Définir la traite des personnes au sein de la jurisprudence canadienne*

Le concept multidimensionnel de la traite des personnes est défini de manière distincte au sein de la jurisprudence et des « instructions ministérielles » canadiennes. Ces instructions, issues du ministère de la Citoyenneté et de l'Immigration, dont l'objectif est de protéger les étrangers vulnérables qui sont victimes de la traite des personnes en régularisant leur statut au Canada[71], reprennent d'abord la description du concept énoncé à l'article 3 du *Protocole sur la traite des personnes des Nations Unies* (2003) des Nations Unies [le Protocole], une définition qui n'est pas subsumée dans une définition plus générale de l'esclavage, au contraire :

> L'expression « traite des personnes » désigne le recrutement, le transport, le transfert, l'hébergement ou l'accueil de personnes, par la menace de recours ou le recours à la force ou à d'autres formes de contrainte, par enlèvement, fraude, tromperie, abus d'autorité ou d'une situation de vulnérabilité, ou par l'offre ou l'acceptation de paiements ou davantage pour obtenir le consentement d'une personne ayant autorité sur une autre aux fins d'exploitation. L'exploitation comprend, au minimum, l'exploitation de la prostitution d'autrui ou d'autres formes d'exploitation sexuelle, le

---

69 The Canadian Centre To End Human Trafficking, 'The Government of Ontario's Response to Sweeping Legislation to Combat Human Trafficking Falls Short in Tackling this Crisis', <www.canadiancentretoendhumantrafficking.ca/the-government-of-ontarios-response-to-sweeping-legislation-to-combat-human-trafficking-falls-short-in-tackling-this-crisis/>.

70 *Ibid.*

71 Immigration, Réfugiés et Citoyenneté Canada, 'Instructions du Ministre sur la délivrance de permis de séjour temporaire aux victimes de la traite des personnes', tel que reprises dans *Shala c Canada* (*ministre de la Citoyenneté et de l'Immigration*), 2021 CF 326 (Cour fédérale).

travail ou les services forcés, l'esclavage ou les pratiques analogues à l'esclavage, la servitude ou le prélèvement d'organes[72].

Les instructions ministérielles indiquent ensuite que la définition des Nations Unies comporte trois « éléments clés », à savoir : (1) un acte physique : par exemple, le recrutement, le transport ou l'hébergement de personnes ; (2) des moyens coercitifs : par exemple, des menaces, la force, la contrainte ou la tromperie ; (3) un but précis : l'exploitation des victimes[73].

En 2021, la Cour fédérale a été saisie d'un cas qui a mis à l'épreuve l'application pleine et entière du Protocole et brouillé la terminologie préconisée par cette convention internationale ratifiée par le Canada. Alors que le Protocole comprend le travail forcé comme une forme d'exploitation, et que les fins d'exploitation d'une démarche sont centrales à ce que constitue la traite humaine, les autorités canadiennes ont néanmoins opté de restreindre cette définition en distinguant, sans s'appuyer sur les normes internationales sur lesquelles se fondent les instructions ministérielles, entre deux concepts qui n'apparaissent d'ailleurs aucunement dans le Protocole : « la traite des personnes à des fins de travail forcé » et « l'exploitation de la vulnérabilité des travailleurs ».

Dans l'affaire *Shala c. Canada* (*Citoyenneté et Immigration*)[74], un travailleur du Kosovo a fait valoir qu'il a été amené par la tromperie à venir au Canada et qu'une fois arrivé, il a été exploité à son lieu de travail : de très longues heures de travail dans de mauvaises conditions, six ou sept jours par semaine, sans pauses normalisées, agressions verbales, rémunération irrégulière et pour beaucoup moins d'heures que les heures travaillées. Lorsque M. Shala s'en plaignait, il a reçu des menaces de congédiement et il a été prévenu qu'il serait renvoyé au Kosovo. Il alléguait aussi que son employeur se servait d'une dette qu'il devait comme levier pour s'assurer que le travail demeure acharné, tout en faisant d'importantes retenues sur sa paie pour s'assurer que la dette ne puisse jamais être remboursée.

Dans cette demande de contrôle judiciaire, la décision contestée est celle rendue par un agent d'immigration, qui rejetait une demande de permis de séjour temporaire au Canada sur la base d'allégations de traite des personnes.

---

72 *Protocole additionnel à la Convention des Nations Unies contre la criminalité transnationale organisée visant à prévenir, réprimer et punir la traite des personnes, en particulier des femmes et des enfants*, 15 novembre 2000, 2237 RTNU 319.

73 Instructions du Ministre sur la délivrance de permis de séjour temporaire aux victimes de la traite des personnes, telles que citées dans *Shala c Canada* (*ministre de la Citoyenneté et de l'Immigration*), 2021 CF 326 (Cour fédérale) au para. 30.

74 *Shala c Canada* (*ministre de la Citoyenneté et de l'Immigration*), 2021 CF 326 (Cour fédérale).

Sur la question de savoir si M. Shala satisfait à la définition de victime de la traite des personnes à des fins de travail forcé, l'agent a énoncé celle du Protocole, précité, ainsi que celle de la Convention (n° 29) sur le travail forcé de l'OIT : « Tout travail ou service exigé d'un individu sous la menace d'une peine quelconque et pour lequel ledit individu ne s'est pas offert de plein gré »[75].

L'agent a ensuite considéré que la traite des personnes à des fins de travail forcé se produit lorsqu'un employeur oblige ou trompe un travailleur en l'incitant à travailler contre son gré, souvent en utilisant la violence, les menaces, la manipulation de la dette, le chantage ou la fraude pour forcer les victimes à travailler, tandis que l'exploitation des travailleurs décrit plutôt une situation où les employeurs profitent du traitement illégal de leurs travailleurs, mais n'exercent pas le niveau de contrôle qui caractérise la traite des personnes à des fins de travail forcé. Même si « les victimes de la traite des personnes à des fins de travail forcé sont souvent victimes de multiples formes d'exploitation des travailleurs », selon cette différenciation pour le moins questionnable, les personnes qui sont « soumises à une forme quelconque de contrainte économique qui fait qu'ils doivent accepter des conditions de travail inférieures à la norme parce qu'elles n'ont tout simplement pas d'autre choix » ne sont pas automatiquement des victimes de traite humaine ou du travail forcé[76]. En poussant ce raisonnement à son terme logique, l'agent conclut que « l'exploitation de la vulnérabilité » d'un travailleur n'est pas nécessairement l'équivalent du travail forcé, une situation dans laquelle « la coercition réelle est exercée par un tiers pour les forcer à entreprendre un travail contre leur volonté »[77]. Enfin, en ce qui concerne les heures de travail de M. Shala, les paiements irréguliers et les déductions illégitimes, l'agent d'immigration a conclu que ces éléments de preuve soutiennent plutôt une conclusion d'exploitation, et non de la traite, compte tenu de l'absence de travail forcé ou sous contrainte[78].

En appel de cette décision administrative, bien que l'exploitation soit centrale à la définition de traite humaine, la différenciation ténue entre « l'exploitation de la vulnérabilité » d'un travailleur et « la nature de la traite des personnes à des fins de travail forcé » n'a pas été récusée ou clarifiée par la Cour fédérale du Canada.

---

75 Convention (n° 29) sur le travail forcé, 1930 (OIT), art. 2, cité dans l'arrêt *Shala* au para. 32 comme : Bureau international du Travail des Nations Unies, *Human Trafficking and Forced Labour Exploitation Guidelines : for Legislation and Law Enforcement* (2005), p. 17.

76 *Shala, supra* n. 74, para. 35.

77 *Ibid.*

78 *Ibid.*, para. 36.

Dans *Manoukian c. Procureur général du Canada*[79], la Cour supérieure du Québec a fait sienne la définition suivante, considérablement plus large, du concept de la traite de personnes : « entend une situation d'exploitation et de violence, qu'elle soit physique ou psychologique »[80]. Concernant le travail forcé, selon un rapport d'expert cité favorablement par la Cour, il y a toutefois lieu de distinguer l'acte répréhensible au sens criminel de l'infraction aux normes régissant le travail :

> Bien qu'il y ait exploitation et violation des droits fondamentaux de la travailleuse dans le cas de non-respect des normes du travail, le travail forcé constitue une atteinte grave aux droits fondamentaux et une restriction de la liberté de la travailleuse. Il ne s'agit pas de bas salaires ou de mauvaises conditions de travail. [...] Dans le cas de l'infraction criminelle (ici le travail forcé lié à la traite de personnes), c'est le contrôle, l'influence exercée par le trafiquant et les moyens coercitifs employés pour exploiter la personne vulnérable qui la distinguent d'une situation de violation des droits des travailleurs. La victime de travail forcé ne peut refuser de travailler, ne peut se sauver, ne peut négocier avec son employeur. Elle a peur. [...] Les conditions de vie de la travailleuse, imposées par son employeur, deviennent de la traite de personne répréhensible au sens criminel lorsque les agissements de l'employeur portent atteinte à ses droits fondamentaux, lorsqu'elle devient un objet pour son employeur (comme une forme d'esclavage), lorsque sa liberté de mouvement et de choix, sa sécurité physique et psychologique sont entravées, lorsqu'elle ne peut refuser de faire son travail parce qu'elle a peur pour sa sécurité ou celle de ses proches. Son droit à la dignité humaine est atteint. La gravité de la peur est évaluée en tenant compte de la vulnérabilité et des caractéristiques personnelles de la victime et du contexte général[81].

Quoi qu'il en soit, la précarité englobante et la souffrance intense des personnes migrantes qui exercent un travail dans le contexte d'un rapport de servitude – ce dont nous traitons dans les lignes qui suivent – viennent brouiller la rigidité sur le plan juridique de cette distinction entre, d'une part, la traite et le travail forcé de nature criminelle et, d'autre part, la violation des normes du travail.

79 *Manoukian c Procureur général du Canada*, 2018 QCCS 30 (Cour supérieure du Québec).
80 *Ibid.*, para. 173.
81 *Ibid.*

4 Servitude transitoire des travailleurs migrants

4.1 *Programme des travailleurs étrangers temporaires*

Le Canada a une longue histoire d'exploitation à son profit des travailleurs migrants qui se perpétue malheureusement toujours aujourd'hui, en toute légalité et en pleine connaissance de cause. En dépit de l'abolition de l'esclavage historique et des efforts vers la décolonisation, l'exploitation effrénée des personnes et l'extraction débridée des ressources persistent, « à l'identique ou presque »[82], selon Maynard, qui avance par ailleurs qu'on ne peut pas aujourd'hui comprendre la dynamique des migrations vers des pays comme le Canada sans d'abord discerner les processus économiques mondiaux ayant causé le déplacement massif de populations depuis le milieu du 20e siècle : « le colonialisme et l'esclavage ont induit en leur temps une réorganisation démographique mondiale sans précédent, tout comme le néocolonialisme provoque aujourd'hui des migrations forcées considérables »[83].

L'engouement du Canada pour les programmes de migration temporaire semble constituer une tendance désormais établie ; le nombre de travailleurs étrangers temporaires est en forte hausse depuis le début du 21e siècle[84]. Chaque année, quelque 85 000 travailleurs migrants à bas salaire viennent au Canada dans le cadre du Programme des travailleurs étrangers temporaires (PTET). Dans de nombreux domaines, ces personnes effectuent un travail important, voire essentiel, dont les soins de santé, les soins à domicile, l'agriculture, la transformation des aliments, les services de nettoyage, les services de livraison et la construction. Des milliers d'autres personnes qui travaillent dans ces domaines sont, quant à elles, sans-papiers[85].

---

82 R. Maynard, *supra* n. 2, p. 82.

83 *Ibid.*, p. 88.

84 Au lieu de combler ses pénuries de main-d'œuvre par l'immigration permanente, le Canada fait augmenter de façon constante le nombre de personnes admises dans le pays détenant un permis de travail temporaire. Gesualdi-Fecteau dénote une augmentation, entre 2006 et 2012, de plus de 60 % du nombre de personnes embauchées via différents programmes-cadres fédéraux qui règlementent l'arrivée des travailleurs étrangers temporaires : D. Gesualdi-Fecteau, *L'usage par les travailleurs étrangers temporaires des ressources proposées par le droit du travail : une contribution aux études portant sur l'effectivité du droit*, thèse de doctorat, Université de Montréal, septembre 2014 [non publiée], <https://papyrus.bib.umontreal.ca/xmlui/bitstream/handle/1866/13502/Dalia_Gesualdi-Fecteau_2014_Th%c3%a8se.pdf?sequence=5&isAllowed=y>.

85 Immigration, Réfugiés et Citoyenneté Canada, 'Résidents temporaires: les détenteurs de Permis de travail du Programme de travailleurs étrangers temporaires et du Programme de mobilité internationale – Mises à jour mensuelles', <https://open.canada.ca/data/fr/dataset/360024f2-17e9-4558-bfc1-3616485d65b9>. Voir aussi : Fay Faraday, 'COVID-19's

Les programmes migratoires, dont le PTET, sont régis par la *Loi sur l'immigration et la protection des réfugiés*[86] et le Règlement sur l'immigration et la protection des réfugiés[87] ; ils sont administrés en partenariat avec Immigration, Réfugiés et Citoyenneté Canada et l'Agence des services frontaliers du Canada.

Les travailleurs étrangers temporaires sont généralement perçus comme indispensables à la croissance de l'économie du pays, car en occupant des emplois passagers et souvent dévalorisants, ils comblent le manque de main-d'œuvre lorsque des Canadiens qualifiés ne sont pas disposés à les occuper. Malgré les affirmations selon lesquelles le PTET était censé être provisoire, au fil du temps, les travailleurs migrants temporaires sont plutôt devenus une caractéristique omniprésente du marché du travail canadien[88].

Le PTET est divisé en deux catégories, soit les travailleurs hautement qualifiés et les travailleurs dont les emplois requièrent un niveau réduit de formation. Dans le cadre de cette deuxième catégorie, où les cas d'abus sont plus fréquents, il existe différentes filières : les travailleurs peu qualifiés (cuisiner ou servir des repas dans la restauration rapide, travailler dans un abattoir ou une usine de transformation de poissons), le programme des travailleurs agricoles saisonniers (cultiver les aliments dans des fermes ou les transformer dans des usines) et le programme des aides familiaux résidants (s'occuper des enfants ou des personnes ainées et des tâches domestiques connexes). Bref, les travailleurs peu qualifiés occupent des emplois difficiles et mal rémunérés que les citoyens canadiens ne veulent habituellement pas pourvoir.

Les disparités de traitement entre les groupes de travailleurs temporaires sont prononcées. Les travailleurs migrants occupant des emplois qui requièrent un niveau réduit de formation n'ont généralement pas accès à la résidence permanente, contrairement aux travailleurs migrants hautement qualifiés[89]. Ces derniers ont d'ailleurs légalement le droit d'être accompagnés de leur conjoint

---

impact on migrant workers adds urgency to calls for permanent status', The Conversation, (24.02.2021), <https://theconversation.com/covid-19s-impact-on-migrant-workers-adds-urgency-to-calls-for-permanent-status-148237>.

86 *Loi sur l'immigration et la protection des réfugiés*, LC 2001, c 27.

87 *Règlement sur l'immigration et la protection des réfugiés*, DORS 2002–227, pris conformément à la *Loi sur l'immigration et la protection des réfugiés*, LC 2001, c 27.

88 Voir: N. R. Sharma, *Home Economics: Nationalism and the Making of "Migrant Workers" in Canada*, University of Toronto Press, Toronto 2006.

89 Par exemple, sont exclus les travailleurs peu qualifiés de la Catégorie de l'expérience canadienne du Programme des résidents permanents, qui facilite toutefois le passage au statut permanent des travailleurs hautement qualifiés. Voir : Catégorie de l'expérience canadienne (CEC) : Expérience de travail admissible, dernière modification sur le 2022-11-16, <https://www.canada.ca/fr/immigration-refugies-citoyennete/organisation

et de leurs enfants, tandis que les travailleurs peu qualifiés sont catégoriquement exclus de cette possibilité[90].

Les travailleurs migrants ne peuvent pas vivre et travailler librement dans le pays comme le peuvent les citoyens canadiens et les résidents permanents, car ils ne détiennent qu'un permis de travail temporaire à l'échéance de laquelle ils doivent quitter le pays. Ce permis comporte plusieurs conditions rigoureuses, notamment celle d'être obligés de travailler pour un seul employeur à la fois, une situation qui crée un déséquilibre de pouvoir considérable et accentue les risques d'exploitation et d'abus. Bien que les travailleurs étrangers temporaires disposent des protections prévues sur le plan formel par le droit du travail, dont les lois sur les normes minimales d'emploi, leur situation demeure néanmoins extrêmement précaire. L'admissibilité à travailler légalement au Canada peut dépendre, et non dans une moindre mesure, de la capacité à rester dans les bonnes grâces de son employeur, coûte que coûte. Quiconque se plaint d'un mauvais traitement ou d'une condition de travail abusive court le risque d'étre licenciés, de perdre son logement et d'être expulsés du pays. L'absence d'un véritable pouvoir de négociation complique forcément les possibilités de dénonciation des situations dangereuses ou des conditions de travail inacceptables qui sont pourtant nombreuses : salaires impayés, horaires de travail excessifs, exigence de faire du travail qui est sans aucun rapport avec le contrat d'emploi, violence à caractère sexuelle, congédiement sans motif valable[91].

Quant aux frontières floues entre le travail et la servitude, les mauvaises conditions de travail et la perception d'un manque d'alternative face aux exigences des employeurs peuvent encore aujourd'hui être qualifiées de servitudes au regard des critères du droit international[92]. L'absence du principe de la « liberté de contracter » entrave évidemment les relations saines entre un employé et son employeur en créant un rapport de subordination qui

/publications-guides/bulletins-guides-operationnels/resdience-permanente/categories-immigration-economique/experience/experience-travail-qualifie.html>.

90 Voir par ex : Règlement sur l'immigration et la protection des réfugiés, DORS/2002-227 art. 80 (2).

91 J. Beatson et J. Hanley, 'L'exploitation des travailleurs étrangers chez nous : Examen de l'exploitation de la main-d'œuvre et du travail forcé au Canada' (2015), rapport du Comité d'action contre la traite humaine interne et internationale, <http://www.cathii.org/sites/www.cathii.org/files/lexploitation_des_travailleurs_etrangers_chez_nous.pdf>.

92 Voir par ex : B. Hastie, 'Réflexions sur les contours flous des limites entre travail domestique et servitude' (2017) 41:1 *Anthropologie et Sociétés 107*. Voir aussi : B. Hastie, 'The Inaccessibility Of Justice For Migrant Workers: A Capabilities-Based Perspective' (2017) 34:2 *Windsor Y.B. Access Justice* 20.

s'apparente à celle de la relation maître-serviteur d'antan[93]. Ne pouvant pas circuler librement sur le marché du travail comme les citoyens ou résidents permanents peuvent le faire, les travailleurs migrants temporaires dépendent entièrement d'un unique employeur pour maintenir le droit de travailler légalement au Canada. L'exigence du PTET voulant que l'employé exerce ses fonctions uniquement chez l'employeur qui a été autorisé à l'embaucher prive cette personne de sa « liberté fondamentale de démission »[94], une liberté « qui marque la différence entre l'esclavage et la conception moderne du travail »[95]. Comme l'affirment Martig et Saillant :

> [l]e phénomène du travail non libre ne se limite pas aux pays en développement. Il touche aussi les pays développés, notamment par le biais de programmes migratoires que certains n'hésitent pas à qualifier d'esclavage moderne ou de servitude transitoire. C'est le cas du Canada et de ses programmes pour travailleurs saisonniers, un cadre dénoncé d'une part et d'autre pour son caractère vulnérabilisant et asservissant[96].

Amplement de recherches universitaires, enquêtes journalistiques et films documentaires ont fait état des conditions de travail et de vie difficiles des travailleurs migrants temporaires et démontré en quoi le PTET les place dans une position de vulnérabilité vis-à-vis les risques d'exploitation et d'abus. La maltraitance des travailleurs étrangers temporaires a été largement discutée dans les médias canadiens : plus de 4150 articles traitant de ce sujet entre août 2019 et mai 2021 ont été recensés[97]. Pour ne citer qu'un exemple, dans le cadre d'une

93 À partir du 19e siècle, les juges anglais ont imposé aux employés, par le truchement des conditions fixées « implicitement » dans le contrat de travail, un « devoir de fidélité » qui a mené à la consolidation de l'autorité absolue de l'employeur de fixer pratiquement tous les aspects du travail. Pour un survol historique de la relation d'emploi « maître-serviteur » et la subordination du salarié vis-à-vis de son employeur dans les États de tradition juridique anglo-saxonne, voir par ex : D. Hay, 'Master and Servant in England: Using the Law in the 18th and 19th Centuries' dans W. Steinmetz (ed), *Private Law and Social Inequality in the Industrial Age,* Oxford University Press, Oxford 2000; I. C. Pilarczyk, 'The Law of Servants and the Servants of Law: Enforcing Masters' Rights in Montreal, 1830–1845' (2001) 46 *RD McGill* 779.

94 M. Carpentier, 'La discrimination systémique à l'égard des travailleuses et travailleurs migrants', Québec, Commission des droits de la personne et des droits de la jeunesse, 2001 à la p. 60.

95 *Ibid.*, p. 60.

96 A. Martig et F. Saillant, 'L'esclavage moderne: une question anthropologique ?' (2017) 41:1 *Journal Anthropologie et Sociétés* 9, p. 20.

97 Règlement modifiant le Règlement sur l'immigration et la protection des réfugiés (travailleurs étrangers temporaires), (2021) CP 28, Gaz C I, 155.

enquête journalistique menée par la CBC en 2022, des travailleurs étrangers temporaires ont témoigné qu'ils étaient contraints de payer leur employeur afin de recevoir leurs chèques de paie et qu'ils ne pouvaient pas se permettre d'acheter de la nourriture avec le maigre salaire qu'ils recevaient[98].

S'ils sont traités de manière abusive, les travailleurs étrangers temporaires peuvent difficilement chercher un meilleur employeur. Selon le Conseil canadien pour les réfugiés, certains travailleurs migrants qui perdent leur emploi n'ont souvent pas d'autres choix que d'essayer de se trouver un autre emploi « au noir » pour gagner un revenu, transférer des fonds à leur famille, ou même payer les frais d'un billet d'avion. Nombre d'entre eux feront désormais partie de l'économie souterraine et vivront dans la crainte des descentes policières et des contrôles d'immigration. Dans les pires cas, les travailleurs étrangers temporaires deviennent des victimes de la traite des personnes[99].

Le gouvernement fédéral a récemment reconnu l'ampleur de cette problématique et a lancé en 2019 un programme de permis de travail ouvert pour aider les travailleurs étrangers temporaires à se trouver un nouvel emploi et quitter une situation de violence de nature physique, sexuelle, financière ou psychologique. Lorsqu'il est établi qu'il a des motifs raisonnables de croire qu'un travailleur migrant est victime de violence ou risque de l'être dans le cadre de son emploi – tout comportement qui effraie, contrôle ou isole peut constituer de la violence – celui-ci pourrait devenir admissible à un « permis de travail ouvert pour travailleurs vulnérables ». Bien qu'il donne le droit à un travailleur vulnérable de travailler pour n'importe quel employeur au Canada, cette solution est de courte durée, puisque le permis prévoit une date d'expiration et ne peut être renouvelé[100].

En 2021, le gouvernement canadien a voulu prendre encore d'autres mesures pour accroitre la protection contre les situations de servitude et de maltraitance car, de son propre aveu, « le maintien du statu quo laisserait les travailleurs étrangers temporaires à la merci de l'exploitation et créerait d'autres

---

98 K. Yarr, 'Temporary foreign workers rescued from abusive situation on PEI farm', CBC, (16.08.2022), <https://www.cbc.ca/news/canada/prince-edward-island/pei-temporary-foreign-workers-open-permit-part-one-1.6534796>.

99 Conseil canadien pour les réfugiés, 'Migrant workers in Canada used and abused' (2012), <https://ccrweb.ca/sites/ccrweb.ca/files/migrantworkers4pager.pdf>.

100 Gouvernement du Canada, 'Permis de travail ouvert pour les travailleurs étrangers vulnérables victimes de violence' (03.03.2022), <https://www.canada.ca/fr/immigration-refugies-citoyennete/services/travailler-canada/permis/temporaire/travailleurs-vulnerables.html>.

vulnérabilités »[101]. L'objectif déclaré de cette ronde de modifications du *Règlement sur l'immigration et la protection des réfugiés*[102] est de mieux protéger les droits des travailleurs étrangers temporaires au Canada et de renforcer les régimes de conformité des employeurs afin de s'assurer qu'ils respectent les règles applicables à leur programme[103]. Elles imposent notamment aux employeurs des exigences et conditions supplémentaires et accroissent le pouvoir des agents de programme à mener des inspections des lieux de travail[104]. Les employeurs qui embauchent des travailleurs temporaires peuvent faire l'objet d'une inspection pour vérifier s'ils respectent leurs obligations dans le cadre du PTET, comme celle de verser régulièrement un salaire. Si un employeur est trouvé non conforme, il peut recevoir une pénalité financière et une interdiction d'embaucher d'autres travailleurs étrangers temporaires ; son nom sera placé sur une liste publique des employeurs jugés non conformes[105]. La définition d'« abus » a aussi été modifiée pour y inclure les « représailles » contre les travailleurs étrangers temporaires[106], car il est évident que ceux-ci hésitent à signaler les abus et même à coopérer avec les inspections des agents gouvernementaux par crainte de représailles. Sur ce point, entre 2016 et 2020, le PTET avait seulement reçu environ 300 signalements d'abus et de mauvais traitements par l'intermédiaire de la ligne confidentielle de Service Canada[107].

En outre, la peur des représailles, les barrières linguistiques, l'isolement social et physique résultant du lieu de travail et le manque de connaissance de leurs droits sont autant d'obstacles qui augmentent aussi la vulnérabilité des travailleurs migrants. Mais peut-être plus que toute autre exigence, l'absence de choix relativement aux conditions d'hébergement les expose à un environnement fragilisé qui se prête à des abus. De fait, les travailleurs agricoles saisonniers se voient fournir un logement par l'employeur, tandis que les personnes travaillant sous le programme des aides familiaux résidants doivent nécessairement résider chez leur employeur. Notamment à cause de la proximité physique avec le donneur d'ordre, il devient difficile de tracer une ligne

101 Règlement modifiant le Règlement sur l'immigration et la protection des réfugiés (travailleurs étrangers temporaires), (2021) CP 28, Gaz C I, 155.

102 *Loi sur l'immigration et la protection des réfugiés*, LC 2001, c 27.

103 Règlement (2021), précité n. 101.

104 *Règlement sur l'immigration et la protection des réfugiés*, DORS 2002-227, pris conformément à la *Loi sur l'immigration et la protection des réfugiés*, LC 2001, c 27.

105 Gouvernement du Canada, 'Employeurs qui ont été jugés non conformes' (01.12.2022), <https://www.canada.ca/fr/immigration-refugies-citoyennete/services/travailler-canada/employeurs-non-conformes.html>.

106 *Ibid.*

107 *Ibid.*

claire entre la vie privée et la vie professionnelle. Le travail domestique effectué dans le cadre du programme d'aide familiale canadien est d'ailleurs caractérisé par une grande présence des femmes, parmi lesquelles la majorité est originaire des Philippines. Puisque le travail s'exerce dans une résidence privée, une impression de disponibilité perpétuelle s'installe et il peut arriver que de longues heures travaillées restent impayées. La vulnérabilité particulière des aides-domestiques migrantes a d'ailleurs attiré l'attention des tribunaux, dont la Cour supérieure du Québec en 2021. À la lumière des circonstances qui incluaient le « caractère abusif du comportement à l'égard d'une employée vulnérable » et « l'importance primordiale du paiement régulier des salaires », le tribunal a octroyé le paiement de 100 000$ en dommages punitifs à une employée domestique d'origine philippine[108].

4.2 *Appel renouvelé pour un statut permanent*

Les travailleurs migrants au Canada ont beaucoup souffert pendant la crise sanitaire de la COVID-19. À peine six semaines après le début de la pandémie mondiale, les plaintes documentées de plus de 1100 travailleurs agricoles migrants faisaient déjà état des heures de travail non payées, de logements inadéquats, d'un manque d'équipement de protection individuelle, d'une alimentation insuffisante, de restrictions coercitives à leur droit à la mobilité, d'intimidation, de surveillance et d'un racisme accru[109]. Les travailleuses migrantes qui s'occupent à domicile d'enfants ou de personnes âgées ont rapporté des expériences similaires, notamment en matière de la surcharge de travail. L'ONG, *Caregivers' Action Centre*, rapporte qu'un tiers de ces travailleuses se sont même vues refuser la permission de quitter le domicile de leur employeur durant les premières vagues de la pandémie[110].

Contrairement aux travailleurs migrants hautement qualifiés, les travailleurs migrants occupant des emplois qui requièrent un niveau réduit de formation n'ont généralement pas accès à la résidence permanente. Toutefois, motivés par l'urgence et l'impact de la COVID-19, les appels à un statut permanent se

108 *P.T. c. Mohammad Naqeeb*, 2021 QCCS 1378 (CanLII). Voir aussi par ex. *PN v. FR and another (No. 2)*, 2015 BCHRT 60 (CanLII) et *O.P.T. v. Presteve Foods Ltd.*, 2015 HRTO 675 (CanLII), des arrêts dans lesquels la dissuasion et la dénonciation des actes répréhensibles, comme le harcèlement sexuel et la discrimination, dans un contexte particulier de vulnérabilité, ont justifié l'octroi de dommages punitifs importants contre les défendeurs.

109 F. Faraday, 'COVID-19's impact on migrant workers adds urgency to calls for permanent status', *The Conversation*, (24.02.2021), <https://theconversation.com/covid-19s-impact-on-migrant-workers-adds-urgency-to-calls-for-permanent-status-148237>.

110 *Ibid.*, citant 'Behind Closed Doors: Exposing Migrant Care Worker Exploitation during Covid-19' (octobre 2020), <https://migrantrights.ca/behindcloseddoors/>.

sont multipliés. Comme solution à leur exploitation, des travailleurs migrants d'un océan à l'autre ont uni leur voix pour exiger un « statut permanent pour tous »[111].

La professeure et avocate Fay Faraday résume comme suit le dénouement de cet appel renouvelé pour une voie d'accès à la résidence permanente :

> En août 2020, le gouvernement fédéral a créé une voie vers la résidence permanente pour les demandeurs d'asile qui ont travaillé en première ligne des soins de santé pendant la pandémie. Cette mesure exclut toutefois un grand nombre de travailleurs migrants et sans-papiers qui se trouvaient en première ligne et dont le travail a également été qualifié d'« essentiel » – personnel soignant, travailleurs agricoles, personnel de nettoyage, travailleurs qui garnissent les rayons des épiceries et assurent la livraison des aliments, etc. La COVID-19 a révélé l'exploitation des travailleurs migrants dans ce pays. Une exploitation qui s'est intensifiée dans des conditions pandémiques. Les travailleurs qui réclament le #StatutPourTous méritent un système d'immigration à un seul niveau plus juste. En cette année de protestations mondiales contre le racisme systémique, il est important de réfléchir à la manière dont le racisme institutionnalisé a façonné les programmes de migration temporaire de la main-d'œuvre au Canada et à la manière dont les demandes de #StatutPourTous visent à corriger cela[112].

Enfin, sur le plateau de *Tout le monde en parle*, une émission parmi les plus écoutées des francophones du pays, l'ex-représentante spéciale du Secrétaire général des Nations Unies pour les migrations, Louise Arbour, a proposé que soit régularisé le statut des sans-papiers. Mme Arbour, qui est aussi une ancienne juge de la Cour suprême du Canada, croit que la société n'aurait rien à perdre à offrir un statut juridique aux personnes migrantes qui sont déjà au Canada et qui occupent déjà des emplois, dans des conditions qui, ajoute-t-elle, sont souvent abusives[113]. La proposition de régularisation des sans-papiers, bien que soutenue par des voix influentes, n'a pas encore trouvé un écho suffisant au sein du gouvernement.

---

111 *Ibid.*

112 *Ibid.* Traduction libre.

113 Radio-Canada, 'Tout le monde en parle', (29.11.2020), <https://ici.radio-canada.ca/tele/tout-le-monde-en-parle/site/segments/entrevue/211502/lepage-louise-arbour-sans-papiers-pandemie>.

5 Conclusions

La pertinence de la voie législative afin de faire participer le secteur privé (et public) à l'endiguement de l'exploitation de la main d'œuvre est reflétée dans quelques-unes des mesures récemment mises en œuvre au Canada, dont celles qui pourraient, tant soit peu, remédier aux conséquences peut-être parmi les plus graves des formes contemporaines d'esclavage. Quant à certaines causes profondes des souffrances humaines découlant de l'exploitation du travail à l'ère du néolibéralisme – le capitalisme parasitaire, l'appauvrissement d'une grande partie de la population, les disparités de richesse faramineuses, la légalité des paradis fiscaux, les pressions spéculatives et immobilières, l'extraction déchaînée des ressources naturelles, la réfutation de l'altermondialisme et des théories de la décroissance économique, l'engouement continu pour les programmes de migration temporaire, les cadences de travail éprouvantes – ce sont là autant de raisons qui nous amènent à conclure que le Canada maintient une trajectoire qui ignore les structures de pouvoir existantes. Si l'expression « formes contemporaine d'esclavage » rappelle le caractère ininterrompu des combats politiques vers l'émancipation individuelle et collective, quelles leçons pouvons-nous tirer de la manière dont cette notion est perçue par les autorités canadiennes lorsqu'il s'agit de prendre acte des solutions à leur disposition, cette formule étant pratiquement absente de la jurisprudence, des dispositifs juridiques, des communications officielles et des sites web gouvernementaux?

En vertu de la nouvelle mouture de l'accord de libre-échange nord-américain, il est vrai que les entreprises canadiennes qui importent des marchandises produites, même en partie, par le travail forcé ou le travail d'enfants peuvent faire l'objet de sanctions administratives pécuniaires. Toutefois, la question de savoir si les grandes corporations opérant à l'extérieur des frontières nationales devraient faire face à des sanctions civiles ou pénales demeure vive. Actuellement, il n'existe pas de base législative permettant aux victimes issues des populations locales de poursuivre en justice les entreprises canadiennes pour leurs inconduites à l'étranger. Au lieu de combler le manque de mécanismes de réparation pour les individus lésés, le gouvernement a plutôt orienté ses efforts vers la création lente des voies de recours non judiciaires ou « para-judiciaires » : d'abord par l'élaboration du poste d'ombud sur la responsabilité des entreprises des industries textile, minière, pétrolière et gazière, qui manque de pouvoirs contraignants pour imposer des sanctions, ensuite par l'adoption d'une loi sur la transparence qui n'impose aux grandes corporations que des exigences de déclaration quant aux mesures prises pour prévenir et réduire le recours au travail forcé ou au travail des enfants dans les chaînes d'approvisionnement. Remarquablement, ce cadre législatif ne prévoit aucune possibilité de recours juridique ou de réparation pécuniaire aux travailleurs ayant souffert sous le joug de l'exploitation ou d'autres violations des droits de la personne. Certes, un projet de loi (C-262) visant à imposer une obligation de diligence raisonnable aux grands employeurs et à créer des mécanismes judiciaires efficaces relevant de l'État a été déposé en 2022, mais cette initiative législative d'un député de l'opposition semble déjà être vouée à l'oubli. La crainte que l'industrie minière délaisse le Canada est sans doute l'une des raisons de la réticence des gouvernements qui se succèdent à prendre position.

Les tribunaux canadiens ne se montrent pas pour autant inactifs et tracent un avenir prometteur aux interdictions émanant des normes impératives qui ont rang de *jus cogens*. Le jugement dans l'affaire *Nevsun Resources Ltd. c. Araya* représente une avancée notable en reconnaissant leur compétence pour juger des violations des droits humains commises par des entreprises à l'étranger. En effet, la Cour suprême du Canada a réitéré que l'interdiction de l'esclavage et des pratiques cruelles, inhumaines ou dégradantes analogues, dont le travail forcé, est considérée comme une norme qui informe désormais le devoir de diligence des entreprises canadiennes. Grâce à une nouvelle compréhension de la compétence des tribunaux de statuer sur les plaintes de travailleurs venant de l'étranger, la recevabilité de telles actions en justice aura sans doute pour effet de revitaliser la fonction de la responsabilité civile délictuelle dans les réclamations en droit international coutumier. Malgré cette ouverture, force est d'admettre que les recours existants demeurent néanmoins largement insuffisants et que la réparation obtenue pour le préjudice subi est rarement adéquate, efficace et rapide au regard des normes internationales. Comme dans l'affaire *Nevsun*, la réparation disposée sera le plus souvent de nature extrajudiciaire, car il s'avère que les compagnies défenderesses préfèrent conclure avec les parties lésées des ententes de règlement hors cour confidentielles, loin du regard critique de l'opinion publique. Pourtant, l'encadrement contraignant par le pouvoir judiciaire des règles de conduite et de la répartition des pertes serait bénéfique dans la mesure où les décisions rendues sont publiques, peuvent se propager dans la société, créer un effet dissuasif et régir à l'avenir les pratiques des autres acteurs dans le cadre de leurs activités commerciales. Tandis que « les procédures judiciaires transparentes permettent aux gens d'observer, de débattre, de développer, de contester et de matérialiser l'exercice du pouvoir public et privé »[114], les ententes à l'amiable

114 J. Resnick et D. Curtis, *Representing Justice, Invention, Controversy, and Rights in City-States and Democratic Courtrooms*, Yale University Press, New Haven 2011, à la p. 301, tel que cité dans *Vilardell v. Dunham*, 2012 CSCB 748 au para. 345. Traduction libre.

conclues à l'ombre de la loi ne servent généralement pas le bien-être social au-delà des intérêts des parties au litige. Les poursuites abandonnées pourraient même générer des effets négatifs, étant donné que la résolution extrajudiciaire des différends est parfois moins axée sur les droits des travailleurs que sur les intérêts purement corporatifs des parties contrevenantes.

L'effectivité des droits qui devraient servir à faciliter la dénonciation des situations de danger ou de maltraitance demeure un enjeu de taille pour les personnes migrantes qui travaillent au Canada. Il y a celles qui exercent « illégalement » la prostitution, à qui l'État refuse d'octroyer un permis de travail ou d'offrir un recours efficace à la protection de l'intégrité physique. La criminalisation du travail du sexe et la vulnérabilité du statut d'immigration contribuent pourtant à accroitre les risques de violence ciblée de prédateurs qui savent qu'il est fort improbable que les victimes de leurs méfaits dénoncent la violation des droits du travail. Il y a aussi ces nombreux individus participant au programme fédéral des travailleurs étrangers temporaires qui, même s'ils bénéficient des protections formelles prévues par les lois canadiennes en matière d'emploi malgré leur statut migratoire, sont tout de même moins enclins à signaler une infraction. Les nouvelles modifications du gouvernement fédéral accroissent le pouvoir des agents à mener des inspections des lieux de travail et permettent désormais aux travailleurs de s'extraire moins difficilement des situations violentes, mais celles-ci ne changent en rien les préceptes fondamentaux des programmes de migration temporaire depuis leur création : absence d'agentivité ou de citoyenneté politique, inaccessibilité au statut de résidence permanente et restriction de la mobilité professionnelle. Malgré le besoin flagrant de protections additionnelles pour atténuer la vulnérabilité inhérente de ces travailleurs, comme la possibilité d'avoir accès à des permis de travail ouverts, la volonté de radicalement réformer ou carrément abolir ces programmes est presque inexistante.

En somme, parmi les réponses législatives et judiciaires examinées, nombreuses d'entre elles ratent cruellement la cible dans le sens qu'elles n'assurent pas véritablement l'effectivité des droits – la réalisation du droit dans les pratiques sociales – aux personnes contraintes à l'esclavage du travail ou d'autres formes d'aliénation de la liberté humaine. Dans la mesure où « la mise en œuvre formelle du droit du travail découle généralement d'une dénonciation par les salariés de violations de leurs droits au travail »[115], bon nombre des solutions canadiennes pour contrer l'exploitation ne garantissent pas cette

115 D. Gesualdi-Fecteau, 'De l'usage du droit du travail : une contribution théorique aux études portant sur l'effectivité du droit' (2016) 1 *Revue de droit comparé du travail et de la sécurité sociale* 16, p. 27.

possibilité aux individus dont la sûreté et la sécurité sont menacées. À l'issue de cette recherche, si l'usage du droit par une travailleuse ou un travailleur dans la remédiation d'une situation d'injustice dépend notamment du pouvoir occupé dans le système d'emploi[116] – le droit du travail étant par ailleurs « plus que la plupart des autres disciplines, déterminé par le jeu des forces en présence »[117] – alors notre constat sur l'ineffectivité des droits en tant que ligne conductrice des mesures récemment mises en œuvre au Canada est d'autant plus problématique.

Remerciements

L'auteur remercie chaleureusement Samer Mishriki, étudiant en droit, pour son assistance précieuse à la réalisation de cette recherche.

Références académiques

A. Deneault, *Bande de colons, une mauvaise conscience de classe*, Lux, Montréal 2020.

A-J. Arnaud, dir, *Dictionnaire encyclopédique de théorie et de sociologie du droit*, 1ère éd, Librairie Générale de Droit et de Jurisprudence, Paris 1993.

A. Martig et F. Saillant, 'L'esclavage moderne : une question anthropologique ?' (2017) 41:1 *Journal Anthropologie et Sociétés* 9.

B. Hastie, 'Réflexions sur les contours flous des limites entre travail domestique et servitude' (2017) 41:1 *Anthropologie et Sociétés* 107.

B. Hastie, 'The Inaccessibility of Justice For Migrant Workers: A Capabilities-Based Perspective' (2017) 34:2 *Windsor Y.B. Access Justice* 20.

D. Gesualdi-Fecteau, *L'usage par les travailleurs étrangers temporaires des ressources proposées par le droit du travail : une contribution aux études portant sur l'effectivité du droit*, thèse de doctorat, Université de Montréal, 2014.

D. Gesualdi-Fecteau, 'Le droit comme rempart utile ? L'usage par les travailleurs étrangers temporaires des ressources proposées par le droit du travail' (2015) 45:2 *Revue général du droit* 531.

116 *Ibid.* Voir aussi : D. Gesualdi-Fecteau, 'Le droit comme rempart utile? L'usage par les travailleurs étrangers temporaires des ressources proposées par le droit du travail' (2015) 45:2 *Revue général du droit* 531.

117 André-Jacques Arnaud, dir, *Dictionnaire encyclopédique de théorie et de sociologie du droit*, 1ère éd, Librairie Générale de Droit et de Jurisprudence, Paris1993, *sub verbo* « Travail (Sociologie du droit du -) », à la p. 627, citant Jean Rivero et Jean Savatier, *Droit du travail*, PUF, coll, Thémis, 1993, à la p. 36.

D. Gesualdi-Fecteau, 'De l'usage du droit du travail : une contribution théorique aux études portant sur l'effectivité du droit' (2016) 1 *Revue de droit comparé du travail et de la sécurité sociale* 16.

D. Hay, 'Master and Servant in England: Using the Law in the 18th and 19th Centuries' dans W. Steinmetz (dir.), *Private Law and Social Inequality in the Industrial Age,* Oxford University Press, Oxford 2000, pp. 227–264.

J. Fudge, 'Why Labour Lawyers Should Care About the Modern Slavery Act 2015' (2018) 29:3 *King's Law J.* 377.

I. C. Pilarczyk, 'The Law of Servants and the Servants of Law: Enforcing Masters' Rights in Montreal, 1830–1845' (2001) 46 *McGill Revue de droit* 779.

J. Resnick et D. Curtis, *Representing Justice, Invention, Controversy, And Rights in City-states and democratic courtrooms,* Yale University Press, New Haven 2011.

N. R. Sharma, *Home Economics: Nationalism and the Making of "Migrant Workers" in Canada,* University of Toronto Press, Toronto 2006.

R.D.G. Kelley, *Introduction: A Poetics of Anticolonialism', Discourse on colonialism (Aimé Césaire),* Monthly Review Press, New York 2000.

R. Maynard, *NoirEs sous surveillance: esclavage, répression, violence d'État au Canada,* Mémoire d'encrier, Montréal 2018.

T. Meshel, 'From Nevsun v Araya to the Core: Taking Stock of State-based Business and Human Rights Grievance Mechanisms in Canada' (2021) 54 *University of British Columbia Law Review* 203.

Contemporary Forms of Slavery, Its Causes and Consequences: the Case of Croatia

Sandra Laleta, Marissabell Škorić and Karla Kotulovski

1 Introduction

A small medieval Croatian state, Dubrovnik Republic, was among the first in Europe to statutorily prohibit the buying and selling of slaves in 1416. Since then, Croatia has ratified all the relevant international agreements that regulate the prohibition of slavery and are part of the Croatian legal system. Following a review of the relevant Croatian legislation, the chapter analyses contemporary slavery in Croatian legislation, departing from the model of 'modern slavery' as a non-legal umbrella term and focusing more broadly on labour-law abuses.

First, it analyses the position of (seasonal) migrant workers and workers engaged in precarious forms of work (low-paid and unpaid workers, illegal employment and fixed-term workers), highlighting the issue of exploitation deriving from precarious working conditions and a lack of adequate legal protection. Second, the relevant current criminal-law regulation is analysed. The findings indicate that Croatia has recognised the problem of contemporary slavery and the need to meet the requirements for its prevention. A lot has been done at the normative level. Nevertheless, certain problems appear in criminal law practice that are, to a considerable degree, the result of a lack of appropriate and precise criminal law framework. Criminal law is just *ultima ratio societas*, while recognising vulnerable groups of people and preventing their victimisation is the key step in preventing contemporary slavery phenomena. Concerning the Croatian labour law context, it is necessary to strengthen the role of labour inspections, raise awareness of the phenomena of exploitation and precariousness and prevent them, as well to create new, high-quality jobs.

2 The Presence of the Past: Slavery as a Global Institution and Its Legacies

2.1 *The Institution of Slavery throughout Croatian History*

Croatia is a young state that declared its independence from Yugoslavia on 25 June 1991. As an independent state, Croatia has accepted numerous international agreements ratified by the former Yugoslavia, which became part of the

 | DOI:10.1163/9789004723801_007

Croatian legal system and has ratified new ones since, including documents that regulate the prohibition of slavery.

However, in the distant Croatian past, there were examples of the prohibition of slavery. Dubrovnik Republic was a small medieval state that, among the first in Europe, prohibited the buying and selling of slaves by enacting the Act on the Affiliation to Mankind in 1416.[1] The Act represented a cutting-edge contribution of Croatians to human heritage, by showing the humanity, logic and legal standards accepted in the Dubrovnik Republic. The prohibition of human trafficking seems not to be connected with racial origin because slaves were mostly white people. Even though the mentioned Act did not abolish slavery for possession for private purposes, it was gradually eradicated by the middle of the 15th century.[2]

2.2 *Legacies of the Global Institution of Slavery in the Croatian Jurisdiction*

2.2.1 International Legal Sources

Croatia became a party to the Slavery Convention (1926)[3] and Supplementary Convention on the Abolition of Slavery, the Slave Trade, and Institutions and Practices Similar to Slavery (1956) (hereinafter: Supplementary Convention),[4] as well as Protocol of 1953,[5] via notification of succession after the Socialist Federal Republic of Yugoslavia (SFRJ) ceased to exist. Therefore, Croatia has been a party to the Conventions and Protocol since 8 October 1991. Croatia has succeeded Yugoslavia as a party to the International Labour Organization's (ILO) Forced Labour Convention, 1930 (No. 29).[6] In 1996 Croatia ratified the

1 It should be noted that the prohibition of slavery trade was also prohibited by Statute four years earlier in a City of Korčula.

2 See more in: P.M. Radelj, Šest stoljeća hrvatskoga Zakona o robovima, <https://www.vjeraidjela.com/sest-stoljeca-hrvatskoga-zakona-o-robovima/>.

3 Slavery Convention, entered into force on 1 March 1927. Text is published in the Collection of the treaties of the Kingdom of Yugoslavia of 1929, p. 607. The notification of succession in: Official Gazette – International Agreements (hereinafter: NN-MU), 1/1992.

4 Text published in: Official Gazette – International Agreements of the Federal People's Republic of Yugoslavia (hereinafter: SL FNRJ-MU), 7/1958; the notification of succession in: NN-MU, 12–27/1993.

5 Text published in: SL FNRJ-MU, 6/1955; the notification of succession in: NN-MU, 12/1993.

6 The notification of succession in: NN-MU, 2/1994. Text is published in: NN-MU, 5/2000.

ILO Abolition of Forced Labour Convention, 1957 (No. 105),[7] but not Protocol No. 29 of 2014 to the Forced Labour Convention.[8]

2.2.2 Constitutional Protection

Even though the Croatian Constitution[9] does not contain an explicit prohibition of slavery, it prohibits forced and compulsory labour (Art. 23). Furthermore, it guarantees certain personal and political rights and freedoms that could be violated in case of slavery. The Constitution proclaims that "human liberty and personality shall be inviolable. No one shall be deprived of liberty, nor may liberty be restricted, except when specified by law, upon which a court shall decide". (Art. 22). In addition, it prohibits discrimination, as "… all persons in The Republic of Croatia shall enjoy rights and freedoms, regardless of race, colour, gender, language, religion, political or other opinion, national or social origin, property, birth, education, social status or other characteristics". (Art. 14(1)). It should be noted that the Croatian Constitution guarantees anti-discrimination protection based on any ground. According to Art. 14(2), all persons shall be equal before the law. The members of all national minorities in Croatia enjoy equal rights (Art. 15(1)). The Constitution further guarantees the respect for and legal protection of each person's dignity (Art. 35). In the field of economic and social rights, the right to work and freedom to work, as well as free choice of vocation and occupation, are guaranteed to everyone (Art. 54).

2.2.3 Relevant Croatian Legislation: Anti-discrimination Legislation, Criminal Law and Labour Law

2.2.3.1 *Anti-discrimination Legislation*

As an EU Member State, Croatia has implemented the European human rights and anti-discrimination standards. The purpose of the Anti-Discrimination Act is to provide for the protection and promotion of equality as the highest value of the constitutional order of Croatia,[10] to create prerequisites for the realisation of equal opportunities and to regulate protection against discrimination on different grounds, among others, on the ground of race and ethnic affiliation etc. The Anti-Discrimination Act, as a general act on discrimination, applies to

7 Decision on the promulgation of the Law of the ratification of the Convention No. 105; the Convention published in: NN-MU, 12/1996.

8 As the context and forms of forced or compulsory labour have changed since the first forced labour Convention has been adopted in 1930, Protocol and Recommendation No. 203 were adopted to adapt the standards on forced labour to a new era.

9 Constitution of The Republic of Croatia, NN, 56/1990, 135/1997, 8/1998, 113/2000, 124/2000, 28/2001, 41/2001, 76/2010, 85/2010, 5/2014.

10 Anti-Discrimination Act, NN, 85/2008, 112/2012, Art. 1(1).

work and working conditions, social insurance and health protection too. As in other EU Member States, special attention is paid to combatting racial, ethnic and sexual discrimination and the protection of the victims.

2.2.3.2 *Criminal Law*

After gaining independence, Croatia took over the legislation from the former state. The criminal offence of 'Establishing a slavery relationship and transporting persons held in slavery' was laid down in Art. 155 of the Basic Criminal Code.[11] This provision incriminated putting another in slavery or a similar relationship or holding another in such a position, or buying, selling, transferring or acting as an intermediary in the purchase, the sale or transfer of a person, or enticing another to sell his or her freedom or the freedom of a person for whom he or she is caring.

Those acts were subject to a term of imprisonment ranging from one year to ten years. The transport of persons held in slavery or servitude from one country to another was separately criminalised by imprisonment ranging from six months to five years. Furthermore, holding juvenile persons in slavery or servitude was considered a qualified form of the latter offence and was sanctioned by a minimum of a five-year imprisonment.

1997 was marked by the first significant reform of the Croatian substantive criminal law, which resulted in profound changes to the former state's legislation and led to the adoption of the new Criminal Code of The Republic of Croatia.[12] A major novelty was the introduction of the new denomination of the criminal offence, namely: 'Establishment of Slavery and Transport of Slaves', as well as a new paragraph 2. It incriminated buying, selling, transferring or acting as an intermediary in the purchase, the sale or transfer of a child or a minor for the purposes of adoption, transplantation of organs, exploitation by labour or for other illicit purposes. Those offences were punishable by a sentence of at least five years imprisonment. Some authors emphasised the latter paragraph incriminated modern ways of slavery whose objectives are fundamentally different from those of the original slavery relationship.[13]

The offence of incriminating slavery was renamed again in 2004 as 'Trafficking in human beings and Slavery'. Art. 175 incriminates three related

---

11 Basic Criminal Code, NN, 44/1976, 36/1977, 56/1977, 34/1984, 74/1987, 57/1989, 83/1989, 3/1990, 38/1990, 53/1991, 71/1991, 39/1992, 91/1992, 31/1993, 58/1993, 37/1994, 108/1995, 28/1996, 110/1997 (hereinafter: BCC).

12 Criminal Code, NN, 110/1997, 27/1998, 50/2000, 129/2000, 84/2005, 51/2001, 111/2003, 190/2003, 105/2004, 71/2006, 110/2007, 152/2008, 57/2011, 77/2011, 125/2011, 143/2012 (hereinafter: CC/97).

13 Ž. Horvatić, *Novo hrvatsko kazneno pravo*, Pravni fakultet, Zagreb 1997, p. 393.

but different things: slavery and similar relationships, forced labour and human trafficking, which is a modern form of slavery. This novelty was introduced into the Criminal Code as a result of its alignment with the Protocol to Prevent, Suppress and Punish Trafficking in Persons Especially Women and Children, supplementing the UN Convention against Transnational Organized Crime.[14] The scope of the criminal offence was extended so that paragraph 1 proscribes imprisonment from one to ten years for:

> whoever violates the rules of international law in that he or she by the use of force or of a threat to use force, by means of fraud, by abduction, by abuse of authority or of a position of helplessness or in any other manner recruits, buys, sells, hands over, transports, transfers, incites or acts as intermediary in the purchase or delivery [of a person], or harbours a person for the purposes of slavery or a similar relationship, forced labour, sexual exploitation, prostitution or illegal human-organ transplant, or who holds a person in slavery or servitude.

At the same time, however, the legislator failed to incriminate inciting another person to sell his or her freedom or the freedom of another person who is dependent on or cared for by him or her, a blatant shortcoming that was remedied in 2011 by virtue of the adoption of the new Criminal Code.[15]

As mentioned, a qualified form of this criminal offence is foreseen when it is committed against a child or a juvenile, which is punishable by a minimum of a five year imprisonment (para. 2), and when the offence is committed

14 K. Turković, 'Trgovanje ljudima i ropstvo' in P. Novoselec (ed), *Posebni dio kaznenog prava*, Zagreb 2007, p. 134. Starting from 2002 Croatia has ratified the most important international documents in the field of human trafficking. Besides the UN Convention against Transnational Organized Crime and supplementing Protocols: Protocol to Prevent, Suppress and Punish Trafficking in Persons, especially Women and Children and Protocol against the Smuggling of Migrants by Land, Sea and Air, Croatia has ratified the Convention on the Rights of the Child, Optional Protocol to the Convention on the Rights of the Child on the Involvement of Children in Armed Conflict, Optional Protocol to the Convention on the Rights of the Child on the Sale of Children, Child Prostitution and Child Pornography, and Optional Protocol to the Convention on the Rights of the Child on a Communications Procedure; the Council of Europe Convention on Action against Trafficking in Human Beings and the Directive 2011/36/EU of the European Parliament and of the Council of 5 April 2011 on preventing and combating trafficking in human beings and protecting its victims, and replacing Council Framework Decision 2002/629/JHA [2011], OJ L 101/11.

15 Criminal Code, NN, 125/2011, 144/2012, 56/2015, 61/2015, 101/2017, 118/2018, 126/2019, 84/2021 (hereinafter: the Criminal Code or CC/11).

while the perpetrator is a member of a group or a criminal organization or if it is committed against a larger number of persons or has caused the death of one or more persons, in which case the perpetrator may be punished by a minimum of a five year imprisonment or by long-term imprisonment (para. 3). As provided for under para. 4, whether or not a person engaged in forced labour or servitude, sexual abuse, slavery, to a relationship similar to slavery or to unlawful transplantation of the parts of his or her body is of no relevance to the existence of this criminal offence. In other words, the victim's consent does not eliminate the unlawfulness of this offence.

This description of the offence combining trafficking in human beings and slavery was not functional but rather rendered the provision extensive, burdensome and imprecise.[16] It was hence unsurprising that the new Criminal Code of 2011 delineated the incrimination of these offences into two provisions, so that Art. 105 addresses slavery and Art. 106 trafficking in persons for the purposes of labour and sexual exploitation, as well as other forms of exploitation. The objective of the legislator was to demarcate these two offences, in view of the fact that there was no clear demarcation between them in the single Art. 175 CC/97.[17]

It is important to point out that in 2004, the Act on the Responsibility of Legal Persons for Criminal Offences was enforced, thus enabling the sanctioning of legal persons (for example, catering establishments) who are organised in criminal activity, *inter alia* by establishing slavery or a similar relationship or trafficking in human beings. Pursuant to this Act, penalties (fine or dissolution of the legal person), a suspended sentence and security measures may be imposed against the legal persons in question.[18]

2.2.3.3 *Labour Law*

According to the Croatian Labour Act (LA),[19] some of the fundamental obligations of the employer arising from the employment relationship concern the protection of workers' dignity and anti-discrimination. The employer is entitled to determine the place and the manner of performing the work, respecting the worker's rights and dignity (Art. 7 (2)). The LA prohibits any direct or indirect discrimination in the area of labour and working conditions, including the

16 B. Herceg Pakšić, M. Jukić, 'Primjena konvencijskog prava u području zabrane ropstva i prisilnog rada: europski standardi i hrvatska postignuća', (2016) 23 *Hrvatski ljetopis za kaznene znanosti i praksu* (hereinafter: *HLJKZP*) 281, p. 303.

17 Final proposal of the Criminal Code, October 2011, Zagreb, 172.

18 Act on the Responsibility of Legal Persons for Criminal Offences, NN, 151/2003.

19 Labour Act, NN, 93/2014, 127/2017, 98/2019, 151/2022.

selection criteria and requirements for employment, advancement in employment, professional guidance, education, training and retraining, in accordance with the LA and anti-discrimination legislation. The employer should protect the worker's dignity during the work in case of acts uncalled for and contrary to LA and special legal provisions of superiors, collaborators, and persons with whom the worker contacts on a regular basis while performing his tasks (Art. 7 (4 and 5)). Moreover, the employer should ensure safe working conditions that do not have detrimental effects on the health of the worker in accordance with a special law[20] and other regulations (Art. 7 (3)). The LA does not contain a definition of discrimination and dignity, harassment and sexual harassment, but points to anti-discrimination legislation.[21]

Voluntariness is an essential element of every contractual relationship, thus of every employment contract as well.[22] "Voluntariness, i.e. the freedom of the employee to choose his or her employer, is a precondition for a contract of employment to be considered valid".[23] It concerns the contractual parties' voluntariness (consensus) about the conclusion (and, to some degree, about the termination) of the contract, duration of a contract and the choice of the other contractual party, the job to be performed and the type of employment relationship.[24] According to the Croatian obligation law, the contract is voidable when concluded under threat, i.e. if a party or a third person used unlawful threats causing justified fear in the other party inducing it to conclude a contract. Fear is deemed justified if it is evident from the circumstances that the life, limb, or other substantial good of the other party or a third person is gravely endangered. A contract concluded as a result of the use of (physical) force towards a party is void (Art. 279, Civil Obligations Act).

At the end of this part, it is possible to conclude that there is no evidence that the constitutional or human rights protection against racial discrimination in the Croatian jurisdiction is considered to be related to the legacy

20 Occupational Health and Safety Act (NN, 71/2014, 118/2014, 154/2014 , 94/2018, 96/2018). See more: I. Gović Penić, 'Procesna pravila u sporu kojim se traži zaštita od uznemiravanja/diskriminacije i mobinga' in I. Gović Penić et al. (eds), *Priručnik o diskriminaciji i mobingu na radnom mjestu (pravna i medicinska motrišta)*, Sindikat naftnog gospodarstva, Udruga za pomoć i edukaciju žrtava mobbinga, Zagreb 2018, p. 64–68.

21 It consists of Anti-Discrimination Act, the Act on Gender Equality and Act on Same-Sex Relationship.

22 A. Ravnić, *Osnove radnog prava. Domaćeg, usporednog i međunarodnog*, Pravni fakultet, Zagreb 2004, p. 514.

23 I. Grgurev, 'The Concept of 'Employee': The Position in Croatia' in B. Waas and G. Heerma van Voss (eds), *Restatement of Labour Law in Europe. Vol I: The Concept of Employee*, Hart Publishing, Oxford 2017, pp. 61–62.

24 N. Tintić, *Radno pravo, Knjiga prva: Radni odnosi (I)*, Narodne novine, Zagreb 1969, p. 356.

of slavery or, in particular, interpreted by courts and other judicial or quasi-judicial mechanisms in this light.

2.2.3.4 *Prison Labour, Duty to Work, Working Help, Military and Civilian Service*

In the Croatian, i.e. ex-Yugoslav history, there were cases of forced labour. During the Second World War, at the Croatian territory several concentration and working camps were organized by the Independent State of Croatia.[25] On the other hand, from the same territory, some 16,000 persons and from the Croatian territory under the Italian occupation ,some 20,000 persons were deported by force to Germany and Austria to perform work as forced labourers, in camps or for different employers. It seems that they found themselves in a relationship of slavery, too afraid to flee or to show resistance to their employers who exhausted them with work and hunger.[26]

After the Second World War, the Yugoslav Criminal Code prescribed different types of forced labour of the convicted person. Sanctions of forced labour (from three months to two years) were supplemented with the loss of soldier's civil honour and confiscation of the property of the convicts.[27] Thousands of sentenced people performed work in hard working conditions that caused deaths and illness of prisoners. Although forced labour was legally abolished in 1951, it continued to exist in practice.[28]

Such practice belongs to the past. Contemporary Croatian legislation regulates several types of work with some elements of compulsory labour, but they

25 This state was founded at the territory of today's Croatia, Bosnia and Herzegovina and a part of today's Serbia. Its authorities accepted a national-socialistic racist approach, which resulted in adopting several acts against Jews and Roma who were imprisoned in concentration camps, along with Serbs, as well as Croats who did not accept Ustasha politics. Nezavisna Država Hrvatska, *Hrvatska enciklopedija, mrežno izdanje*, Leksikografski zavod Miroslav Krleža, Zagreb 2022.

26 A. M. Grünfelder, *U radni stroj velikoga njemačkog Reicha*, Srednja Europa, Zagreb 2007.

27 Act on Criminal Offences against People and State (from 1945); Act on Types of Punishment (from 1945 and 1946); Criminal Act of the FPRY (1951); the Execution of the Punishments Act (1948).

28 V. Geiger, 'Lišavanje slobode i prisilni rad u hrvatskom/jugoslavenskom zakonodavstvu 1945. – 1951.' in V. Geiger, M. Grahek Ravančić and M. Karakaš Obradov (eds), *Logori, zatvori i prisilni rad u Hrvatskoj / Jugoslaviji 1941.-1945., 1945.-1951.*, Hrvatski institut za povijest, Zagreb 2010, pp. 151–54.

are exceptions in line with the ILO instruments such as the work of prisoners,[29] work in case of wartime or immediate threat,[30] and community service.[31]

3 Understanding the Causes and Consequences of Contemporary Slavery

3.1 *Contemporary Slavery in Croatia*

According to the UN Special Rapporteur on contemporary forms of slavery, "the mandate on contemporary forms of slavery includes but is not limited to issues such as traditional slavery, forced labour, debt bondage, serfdom, children working in slavery or slavery-like conditions, domestic servitude, sexual slavery, and servile forms of marriage".[32] Concerning forced labour, ILO Indicators of Forced Labour should be taken into account, as "the most common signs or 'clues' that point to the possible existence of a forced labour case":[33] abuse of vulnerability, deception, restriction of movement, isolation, physical and sexual violence, intimidation and threats, retention of identity documents, withholding of wages, debt bondage, abusive working and living conditions, and excessive overtime work.[34]

---

29 Their work should be voluntary and remunerated, in line with prisoner's health capabilities, knowledge and the possibilities of the prison, while the working conditions should be the same or similar to those of workers in an employment relationship. The Execution of Prison Sentence Act, NN, 14/2021.

30 Wartime or immediate threat justify the use of: the duty to work for workers employed in the bodies of public authority, local and regional self-government and legal entities that are especially important for defence; the duty to work of the legal entities and Croatian citizens in order to provide help to public authorities, ministries and armed forces in fulfiling their duties; serving the military service or civilian service. Defence Act, NN, 73/2013, 75/2015, 27/2016, 110/2017, 30/2018, 70/2019.

31 As measure alternative to imprisonment and fine, that is always voluntary (Art. 55 CC/11).

32 Special Rapporteur on contemporary forms of slavery, including its causes and consequences, <https://www.ohchr.org/en/special-procedures/sr-slavery>.

33 ILO Indicators on Forced Labour, International Labour Office, Geneva 2012.

34 The ILO's Special Action Programme to Combat Forced Labour, International Labour Office, 2005. It has been suggested that the presence of a single indicator in a given situation may in some cases imply the existence of forced labour. However, in some other cases only several indicators taken together, point to a forced labour practice. The ILO has also stressed that 'forced labour' encompasses activities which are more serious than the mere failure to respect labour laws and working conditions. Therefore, for example, the failure to pay a worker the statutory minimum wage does not in itself constitute forced labour. ILO, Human Trafficking and Forced Labour Exploitation: Guidance for Legislation and Law Enforcement, International Labour Office, 2005, pp. 19–21.

The approach circumscribing the term 'modern slavery' as "a broad non-legal umbrella term that refers to a range of abusive practices including, but not limited to, forced labour, bonded labour, human trafficking and child slavery" is pivotal here.[35] Beside the most severe forms of labour exploitation, to focus "on labour abuses more broadly is also important as it is not always clear at what point non-compliance with labour standards seeps into cases of criminal exploitation".[36] Therefore, our analysis firstly focuses on some of the most vulnerable groups of workers in Croatia.[37] The workers who perform some form of work marked with high precariousness are often exposed to labour abuses that deserve greater attention and which are to be encompassed by the notion of contemporary, modern slavery.[38] It is a practice that is omitted from the definition of contemporary slavery that deserves greater attention.

In the second part of this section, we deal with the criminal law aspects. According to the Global Slavery Index, it was estimated that in 2016, there were 25,000 victims of slavery in Croatia, which places Croatia at the high 54th place among 167 countries.[39] Another research shows that only 14 victims of slavery, among 16,112 of cases in Croatia, were reported, implying that a hidden number of cases amounts to 99,9%. The most common forms of slavery seem to be using minors for prostitution, for criminal offences such as burglary or other offences for the benefit of adults, as well as non-paid work.[40]

35 M. Boersma and J. Nolan, 'Modern slavery and the employment relationship: Exploring the continuum of exploitation', (2022) 64 *Journal of Industrial Relations* p. 165.

36 *Ibid.*

37 Due to space limitations, we will not deal with the discrimination of Roma that represent a historically marginalized and vulnerable group in Croatia, that is frequently faced with the problems concerning employment.

38 There is rich academic literature on the various dimensions to precariousness and its causes, e.g. G. Rodgers, 'Precarious Work in Western Europe: the State of the Debate' in G. Rodgers and J. Rodgers (eds), *Precarious Jobs in Labour Market Regulation: the Growth of Atypical Employment in Western Europe*, International Institute for Labour Studies, Geneva 1989; J. Fudge and R. Owens, 'Precarious Work, Women, and the New Economy: the Challenge to Legal Norms' in J. Fudge and R. Owens (eds), *Precarious Work, Women, and the New Economy: the Challenge to Legal Norms*, Hart Publishing, Oxford 2006.

39 Global Slavery Index 2018, p. 94, <https://cdn.walkfree.org/content/uploads/2023/04/13181704/Global-Slavery-Index-2018.pdf>.

40 One should be careful with numbers because of different methodology of collecting the data. B. Herceg Pakšić, M. Jukić, above n. 16, p. 304.

3.1.1 Migrants and Seasonal Migrant Workers

Migrants, particularly seasonal migrant workers, seem to represent one of the most marginal and vulnerable groups in Croatia exposed to discrimination, exploitation and forced labour. Especially vulnerable are migrants who requested or enjoy international protection, and are placed in shelters because they are confronted with serious problems of integration, like accommodation, employment, difficulties of language learning, adequate health protection etc.[41]

The free movement of capital, goods and labour increases migration from other EU countries and can certainly result in social dumping and disruption of working conditions. This context favours employers who can thereby gain a cheap workforce. It is justified to say that precarious work has taken root in the weaknesses, omissions and gaps in both national and international labour law regulating the employment of migrant workers. They face not only unemployment but also structurally defined shifts into more precarious working conditions. At the same time, under political and financial pressures, governments are cutting all kinds of expenditures (budgets, eliminating social protection, social support and health, education and welfare programs) that offer potential compensation for exploitative employment assisting the worker and their families to obtain basic nutrition, housing, health care and schooling.

One characteristic of Croatia and other Mediterranean countries is the demand for flexible employment. The largest proportion of fixed-term and seasonal workers can be found in agriculture and tourism.[42] As in other EU Member States, a shortage of seasonal workers is one of the key challenges of Croatian agriculture. Domestic seasonal workers are employed based on the special employment contract, voucher, but it does not cover the actual demand for workers. The new Aliens Act has introduced the labour market test as a requirement for the employment of third-country nationals in seasonal work, replacing the quota system of employment.[43]

Seasonal migrant workers are provided the same rights as Croatian citizens concerning terms of employment, working conditions, and the protection of rights arising from the employment relationship, in line with the

---

41 Unlike the great migrant crisis in 2015, in the case of the refugee wave that started from Ukraine, there are no discussions among EU Member States, including the Croatian government about who will receive how many migrants. Furthermore, some Member States, despite a restrictive migration policy have abolished quotas system showing solidarity by removing administrative barriers.

42 H. Butković and V. Samardžija (in cooperation with I. Skazlić and I. Čavar), *Nonstandard Work in Croatia: Challenges and Perspectives in Selected Sectors*, IRMO, Zagreb 2016, p. 35.

43 Aliens Act, NN, 133/2020.

Seasonal Workers' Directive.[44] Croatian regulations and collective bargaining agreements that are binding for the employer are used as the basis to equalize conditions. Croatia has not used the possibility given by the Directive to restrict equal treatment of seasonal workers regarding certain rights (family, unemployment, tax benefits etc.), but the question arises whether a seasonal worker can fulfil the conditions needed for such rights, such as the necessary qualification period. Moreover, it is doubtful whether the general protection of worker's rights can actually be an effective mechanism for the protection of the rights of such a specific group, as prescribed by the Directive. Their work and stay in Croatia are of a temporary nature and seeking protection according to the general labour-law rules may become impossible due to the complexity and duration of the procedure, as well as its expenses. This is especially true for seasonal workers in agriculture who often perform work for very short periods, of up to 90 days in a calendar year. Therefore, an appropriate, protective mechanism, tailored to fit the specific, temporary and precarious position of seasonal migrant workers, is needed *de lege ferenda* to bridge the present legislative gaps. The role of the labour inspection in regard of the protection of seasonal migrant workers' rights is crucial.[45]

The EU Common Agricultural Policy (CAP) continues to play a key role in the development of the Union's rural areas. In order to ensure subsidiarity from CAP it is necessary for farmers to respect basic human and labour rights.[46] Trade unionists point out that so far, CAP has failed to improve the working conditions of agricultural workers. They fall often victim to widespread exploitation, including undeclared work for very little money as well as to other forms of modern slavery. A large number of workers in the sector are seasonal workers facing inhumane working conditions, poor wages and unpaid overtime.[47]

---

44 Directive 2014/36/EU of the European Parliament and of the Council of 26 February 2014 on the conditions of entry and stay of third-country nationals for the purpose of employment as seasonal workers [2014] OJ L 94/390.

45 See more: K. Kotulovski and S. Laleta, 'The abuse and exploitation of foreign seasonal workers: Did the Coronavirus emergency worsen already precarious working conditions in the agricultural sector?' in D. Duić and T. Petrašević (eds), *EU and Comparative Law Issues and Challenges Series (ECLIC 5), EU 2021 – The future of the EU in and after the pandemic*, Josip Juraj Strossmayer University of Osijek, Faculty of Law Osijek, Osijek 2021.

46 European Parliament, Common agricultural policy – support for strategic plans to be drawn up by Member States and financed by the EAGF and by the EAFRD.

47 Open letter, Croatian Trade Union of Employees in Agriculture, Food and Tobacco Industry and Water Management (PPDIV), <https://ppdiv.hr/2021/04/15/otvoreno-pismo-nova-zajednicka-poljoprivredna-politika/>.

3.1.2 Are Some Precarious Forms of Work (in Croatia) Contemporary Slavery?

Discrimination and exploitation do not belong just to migrant workers. Departing from the broad interpretation of contemporary slavery, as referred to above, other precarious forms of work in Croatia deserve greater attention as well. They may be covered under the umbrella term of contemporary slavery as they often comprise (intense) human suffering and bad working conditions.

3.1.2.1 *Low-Paid and Unpaid Workers – In-Work Poverty*

In order to guarantee the minimum economic protection of workers, the statutory minimum wage is used. This legal institution is also a widely accepted practice among Croatian employers without financial problems. Low-paid (and unpaid workers) are exposed to a bigger risk of in-work poverty than other workers. In 2022 the minimum net wage amounted to ca. 500 EUR and is below 50% of the average monthly net wage, that amounted to ca. 940 EUR.[48] The share of workers with minimum wage is decreasing (8% of total employment in 2014, to 4,73% (ca. 52.000 workers) in the first quartal of 2021). There is a high share of workers that receive a wage just slightly above the minimum (in 2018, the estimated share of the wage earners that receive the amount of up to 105% of minimum wage was 10,3%).[49] As noted by some authors, working for a minimum wage does not necessarily mean living in poverty, while poverty depends on the economic status of a household, respectively the duty of the wage earner to support other persons or not.[50] But in 2014, slightly over a half of minimum wage earners were living in households that belong to 40% of the poorest in Croatia.[51]

The precarious position of low-paid workers becomes even worse if the employer does not pay the wage for the performed work.[52] The available data show that the offences concerning the timely handing over of the payslip to

48 In 2018, in Croatia the minimum wage was less than half of the median earnings (49%), Eurostat, <https://ec.europa.eu/eurostat/statistics-explained/index.php?title=Minimum_wage_statistics>.

49 *Ibid.* Proposal for the Minimum Wages Act, <https://esavjetovanja.gov.hr/ECon/MainScreen?entityId=17001>.

50 D. Nestić and S. Blažević Burić, 'Radnici na minimalnoj plaći i siromaštvo u Hrvatskoj (2018) 25 *Revija za socijalnu politiku* 235, p. 260. Cf. I. Grgurev and I. Vukorepa, 'Minimum wage as a tool in the fight against poverty: Croatian labour law perspective' in G. Löschnigg (ed), *Staatliche Eingriffe in das System der Mindestentgelte im internationalen Vergleich*, Verlag des ÖGB, Wien 2013.

51 D. Nestić and S. Blažević Burić, *ibid.*

52 Irregularities also concern unpaid overtime work, night work, work on Sundays, holidays or non-working days.

the worker and non-payment of the wage, account for the most represented offences that the Labour Inspection has to deal with. E.g., in 2020 employers did not pay minimum wage for 1.689 workers. Inspectors issued 318 charges regulated by the Minimum Wage Act.[53] One of the counteracting measures that was recently introduced is the interim measure to ensure the payment of the claim by means of confiscation and bank account preservation orders issued against the employer.[54] Such a measure seems to be an efficient instrument because in 2021 the Labour Inspection enforced interim orders for 4,670 employers (13,740 cases per year) as compared to 2017 (for 14,773 employers, 431,512 cases per year).[55]

Non-payment of wages constitutes a criminal offence under Art. 132 of the Criminal Code. Moreover, the employer can be punished for the violation of social insurance rights[56] if the employer "denies or limits the right of another that derives from pension, health or unemployment insurance established by law or withholds the payment of contributions for the employment of disabled persons, where this does not satisfy the elements of another criminal offence" (Art. 134 CC).[57] In addition, the Labour Inspection's reports show that employers often break the rules regarding working time and the right to paid annual leave and rest.[58]

53 Proposal for the Minimum Wages Act. For comparison, in 2017 inspectors registered 648 offences of non-paid minimum wage (committed against 6,680 workers). Report on the Work of the Labour Inspectorate for 2017, Labour Inspectorat, Zagreb 2018, pp. 26–29 (Report for 2017).

54 Report for 2017, p. 29.

55 Information received from the Labour Inspectorate on request, in May 2022.

56 See more: V. Grozdanić, M. Škorić and I. Martinović, 'Kaznenopravna zaštita radnika prema odredbama novog Kaznenog zakona', (2012) 19 *HLJKZP* 473, p. 479.

57 In 2021 there were 55 criminal charges for non-payment of wages, comparing to 122 in 2018 and 934 in 2017; in 2017 there were 29 criminal charges for violation of social rights, comparing to 34 registered in 2016. Report for 2018, p. 17; Report for 2017, p. 16; information on request (May 2022).

58 According to statistics, this is the case in retail sector, traditionally faced with low wages, unfavourable working conditions and bad work-life balance. Trade unionists described it as a slavery job, warning that non-paid overtime work amounted to 16.3 million working hours, or one wage per year given to employer; workers were physically and psychologically exhausted and suffered from work related stress. Z. Štulić, Kako riješiti problem nedostatka radnika u trgovini?, <https://www.sth.hr/kako-rijesiti-problem-nedostatka-radnika-u-trgovini/>; A. Vragolović, 'Pljesak herojima' ne poboljšava uvjete rada, <https://radnickaprava.org/tekstovi/clanci/ana-vragolovic-pljesak-herojima-ne-poboljsava-uvjete-rada>.

3.1.2.2 *Illegal Employment*

Other forms of work that warrant possible subsumption under the notion of contemporary slavery are illegal employment and bogus self-employment. The labour inspection registered illegal work of workers in Croatia in almost all economic activities.[59]

In Croatia, many people work based on contracts for services, which frequently accounts for precarious work also performed on long-term basis. In the latter case, the provisions of the LA do not apply. As that type of work sometimes has the characteristics of work that should be based on an employment contract, one may speak of bogus self-employment, eluding labour law by means of the frequent and illegal use of some other types of civil law contracts instead of employment contracts.[60] According to Art. 2 of the LA, in case "an assignment contract with the worker concluded by the employer has features of employment due to the nature and type of work and the employer's authority, it shall be deemed that the employment contract has been concluded with the worker unless the employer proves otherwise". The worker can seek protection from the employer afterwards before the court (declaratory action). In case of such infringement, the labour inspector may issue an administrative measure, temporarily prohibiting the employer from performing the activity and ordering him to remedy the deficiencies. Otherwise, the employer would be responsible for an offence. The shortage of such regulation is that there is no guarantee that the employer would offer the worker an employment contract, which needs to be changed *de lege ferenda*.

Moreover, inconsistent case-law[61] does not always follow the ILO Recommendation's[62] list of indicators of an employment relationship and the

59 Especially in: 'other fields' of service sector; civil-engineering; retail; provision of services and accommodation, preparation of food, processing industry, transport and warehousing; agriculture, forestry and fishery. Term 'illegal work' includes engagement of worker without written employment contract; employment based on different (fictitious) civil or commercial contracts instead on employment contract; non-application of workers on obligatory pension and health insurance; illegal employment of foreign workers (third countries nationals) or without the application to the pension and health insurance bodies; employment of seasonal workers on temporary or occasional jobs in agriculture against the regulations. It has registered 895 workers in bogus self-employment in 2017. Report for 2017, p. 28. But the hidden number is certainly higher.

60 D. Weil, *The Fissured Workplace: Why Work Became So Bad for So Many and What Can Be Done to Improve It*, Harvard University Press, Cambridge 2014, p. 9.

61 I. Grgurev, above n. 23, pp. 76ff.

62 Employment Relationship Recommendation, 2006 (No. 198) – Recommendation concerning the employment relationship, Geneva, 95th ILC session (15.06.2006).

principle of the priority of facts. Here, it should be emphasised that the Supreme Court has expressed a doubtful opinion in several cases asserting that the elements proved in trial (e.g. subordination, working hours, work performed at the employer's premises) which are indicators of an employment relationship according to the mentioned ILO Recommendation, were not relevant because they could also be conceived of as elements of a civil-law relationship, and that priority should be given to the intention of the contractual parties.[63]

3.1.2.3 *Fixed-Term Workers*

In most EU Member States, the standard employment relationship is still prevalent. Fixed-term employment[64] seems to be precarious for workers who, after the end of one or more successive fixed-term contracts, can find themselves in a precarious position, both from the legal and financial standpoint, with a very high risk of unemployment.[65] Fixed-term contracts are marked with temporal precariousness.

The Croatian LA explicitly prescribes that the fixed-term employment contract can be concluded exceptionally,[66] which "implies that such contracts are seen as an atypical form of employment and that priority should be given to standard forms of employment".[67] Nevertheless, the fixed-term contract has become the rule. Croatia belongs to the group of EU Member States with the highest growth of temporary work.[68] A quarter of Croatian employees have fixed-term contracts, while 90% of the newly employed are temporary workers.[69] The incidence of precarious casual work respective to short-term

63 Supreme Court of RC, judgments: VSRH, Revr 409/13-2, 17.12.2013; VSRH, Revr 657/14-2, 02.12.2014; VSRH, Revr 648/13-3, 09.09.2014; VSRH, Revr 177/15-2, 15.09.2015; VSRH, Revr 1536/13-3, 09.06.2015. For the employment relationship's indicators in case law see: I. Grgurev, above n. 23, pp. 76ff.

64 Directive 99/70/EC defines 'fixed-term worker' as a person having an employment contract which is determined by objective conditions such as reaching a specific date, completing a specific task, or the occurrence of a specific event.

65 P. Lokiec, 'Fixed-Terms Contracts in France', *Regulation of Fixed-term Employment Contracts, Comparative Labour Law Seminar, JILPT Report No. 9*, 2010, pp. 43–53.

66 For the purpose of taking up an employment where the end of the employment is determined by a specific date, the completion of a specific task, or the occurrence of the specific event (Art. 12 (1)), i.e. 'objective ground'.

67 I. Grgurev, 'Atypical Employment Relationships: The Position in Croatia' in B. Waas and G. Heerma van Voss (eds), *Restatement of Labour Law in Europe, vol. II, Atypical Employment Relationships*, Hart, Oxford 2019, pp. 83–84.

68 Temporary employees as percentage of the total number of employees. Source of data: Eurostat.

69 Croatian Pension Insurance Fund, <http://www.mirovinsko.hr/default.aspx?id=4298>.

temporary contracts with a maximum duration of three months (precarious temporary employment), amounts to over 30% in Croatia comparing to the stable EU average of 19%. Moreover, Croatia is one of the countries in which, in 2018, over one-third of younger workers were on short-term contracts.[70] Precarious employment is mostly present in agriculture, retail and catering activities, most notably because of the importance of tourism for the Croatian economy and because of its seasonality.[71]

According to the LA, the fixed-term employment contract between an employer and the same worker can be concluded solely when there are objective grounds (except in the case of the first fixed-term contract). However, employers often misuse this type of contract. Despite several legal presumptions that give the element of security to fixed-term workers, Croatian workers are often reluctant to claim their rights from the employer or before the court, afraid of losing their jobs. The Ombudswoman reports that "many workers have fixed-term work contracts, often concluded against the law, while employers patently exploit this institution", and aware of this and dissatisfied with their insecure employment status, "workers put up with it, hoping to be offered permanent work contracts if they prove they deserve it through their work and efforts".[72] Labour inspectors note the violations related to the illegal conclusion of the fixed-term contracts (Art. 228 (1/1)). In 2017, they amounted to 6% of the total number of violations and included 215 workers.[73]

70 Eurofound, *Labour market change: Trends and policy approaches towards flexibilisation, Challenges and prospects in the EU series*, Publications Office of the European Union, Luxembourg 2020, p. 39.

71 Trade unionists warned about the abusive practice of some employers to offer managerial contracts to all categories of tourist staff with one condition: to withdraw from the trade union membership or not join a trade union at all. Moreover, by signing such a contract, workers agreed to be available 24 hours a day without the employer's obligation to keep and maintain a working hours record. When labour inspection carried out surveillance there was no evidence of non-compliance with labour law. M. Cvitić, Turizam je najveća nevidljiva tvornica invalida rada, <https://voxfeminae.net/pravednost/marina-cvitic-turizam-je-najveca-nevidljiva-tvornica-invalida-rada/>.

72 Annual Ombudsman Report for 2018, pp. 85–89, <https://www.ombudsman.hr/en/reports/>. The situation with fixed-term contract is depicted in a complaint from "... a former employee, who had concluded 54 fixed-term work contracts with this employer during a 15-year period. Inspection found that concluding these contracts was not in contravention of the LA, and the employer received approval from the workers' council in this specific case, too".

73 Report for 2017.

The LA safeguards in line with EU employment law and the principle of equal treatment, the same rights to fixed-term workers as to the 'comparable workers' on an open-ended contract.[74] Nevertheless, in practice, they face numerous challenges concerning the opportunities for education by the employer, i.e. employability, what makes them more vulnerable on the labour market.

Based on the analysis of the fixed-term work regulation and judicature, it could be concluded that there are significant gaps in the regulation of this non-standard form of employment, enabling abuse of this type of employment on behalf of the employer and rendering it therefore even more precarious than intrinsically. As a remedy, the regulation should be changed *de lege ferenda* by introducing a detailed list of objective grounds, which are at the moment not clearly named, and a limitation to the number of successive fixed-term contracts.

As a conclusion of this part, it should be emphasised that in Croatian judicature the term 'exploitation' has been used by the County Court of Split. As a second-degree court judging in an individual labour dispute on unlawful dismissal that was based on the worker's non-fulfilment of the working norm, it has ruled that unrealistic working norms represent a severe form of exploitation of workers and set the scene for possible abuse, which is not allowed. The dismissal was based on a too-high and unrealistic norm surpassing the possibility of each worker being employed by the same employer.[75]

3.2 *Current Criminal-Law Regulation*

Pursuant to Art. 105 (1) CC/11, the criminal offence of slavery is committed by "whoever places another in a position of slavery or a similar relationship or holds another in such a position", as well as by a person who "buys, sells, transfers or mediates in the sale or transfer of a person" who is in a position of slavery or a similar relationship. Furthermore, paragraph 1 explicitly incriminates "inciting others to sell their freedom or the freedom of the person they provide for or take care of". In line with the national legislation, in order for criminal liability of the instigator to exist, it is required that the person who was instigated to the commission of the offence (as the main perpetrator) enters into the punishable stage of the commission of a certain criminal offence. Since selling one's freedom does not constitute a criminal offence, neither would instigation as a form of complicity be punishable but for the new paragraph 1. Prior to the

74 See Art. 13(1–3). For more see: I. Grgurev, above n. 67, 83, 89, 90.

75 County Court in Split, žs Gž R-765/2017-2, 18.01.2018; Municipal Court in Virovitica, OS, 12.Pr-2/2017-717, 16.05.2017.

entry into force of the current Criminal Code on 1 January 2013, inciting others to sell their freedom was not punishable.[76] The transport of slaves was prohibited in a separate paragraph 2, incriminating the transport of people who are in a position of slavery or a position similar to it. This prohibition referred to any means of transport from one country to another, as well as within one country.

The offence of slavery constitutes a so-called continuous criminal offence where the perpetrator creates an unlawful state and wilfully maintains it until he or she decides to stop the unlawful conduct or until some external circumstances end this conduct. The offence is formally completed by fulfilling all the statutory elements of the offence, i.e. as soon as the perpetrator places the person in a position of slavery or a similar position and from that moment on, the perpetrator will be punished for the complete offence. However, the offence is considered to be materially completed when that unlawful situation ends. The distinction between formal and material completion of a criminal offence bears important practical consequences. Thus, for example, in the time between the formal and material completion of the criminal offence, the new co-perpetrators and accomplices to the offence may join, and the victim has the right to self-defence. A further consequence is that the perpetrators of a formally completed criminal offence remain liable for all aggravating circumstances that may occur after the formal and before the material completion of the offence.

In order to complete the offence of slavery, it is sufficient that the offender has placed another person in slavery or a similar relationship. The duration of that unlawful state is irrelevant to the existence of the offence, but it may have an impact on the sentencing. Thus, the Supreme Court reaffirms the finding of a court of first instance that correctly took into account, when determining the sentence of the accused person, the shorter duration of the unlawful situation in regard to the injured party (from 27 March 2002 to 29 March 2002), whereas the defendant's assertion that this offence could not be committed because certain acts constituting the characteristic of that offence lasted for a single day was deemed irrelevant.[77]

The fundamental form of the offence of slavery laid down in paragraph 1 shall be subject to a term of imprisonment of between one and ten years, while the legislature has imposed a term of imprisonment of between six months and five years for the transport of people held in slavery or a similar relationship.

76 This behaviour was sanctioned under the BCC and CC/97, however, after the entry into force of the amendments and supplements to the Criminal Code of 2004 it was no longer criminalized, despite the requirement under Art. 6 of the Supplementary Convention.

77 Supreme Court of RC, VSRH, I Kž-741/04, 07.10.2004.

For qualified forms of these incriminations that exist in the event that the victim is a child, the sentence is from three to fifteen years of imprisonment.[78]

The criminal offence of slavery prescribed in Art. 105 is partly conceived as a blank criminal offence, which means that not all the elements of slavery are defined in this provision. Consequently, in order to define and properly interpret the statutory elements of a criminal offence of slavery, it is necessary to rely on the international treaties governing this issue, which Croatia has ratified, thereby committing to prescribe certain conduct in its criminal legislation as criminal offences and to impose an appropriate penalty on it.[79] Given that this offence stems from the request of the Slavery Convention of 1926 and a Supplementary Convention, the subsequent part sets out the principal provisions of the above documents.

According to Art. (1) of the Slavery Convention and Art. 7 (a) of the Supplementary Convention, 'slavery' means "the status or condition of a person over whom any or all of the powers attributable to the right of ownership are exercised". Linking slavery to a model of property or ownership, the definition does not determine the powers inherent to ownership over a person. With a view of narrowing down this concept, one may rely on the 'Report of the Secretary General on Slavery, Slave Trade and other forms of Servitude' that lists the following indicators of such a relationship: the individual may be the object of a purchase; capacity to work of the individual may be used in an absolute manner, without any restriction; the products of the labour of the individual become the property of the master without any compensation commensurate to the value of the labour; the ownership of the individual can be transferred to another person; the servile status is permanent, and it cannot be terminated by the will of the individual subject to it, and the servile status is transmitted *ipso facto* to descendants of the individual having such status.[80] Domestic courts have confirmed that the existence of slavery offence requires the existence of

78 Slavery can also be part of a criminal offence of 'Crime against humanity' in cases where it is committed as part of a widespread or systematic attack directed against any civil population, in which case the perpetrator can be punished by imprisonment for not less than five years or by long-term imprisonment. See Art. 90 (1) of the CC/11.

79 Within the Croatian legal system, international treaties have supremacy over national law adopted by the Parliament, whereas in case of discrepancies between national legislation and treaties, the courts must apply the treaty in question. Art. 134 of the Constitution prescribes: 'International treaties which have been concluded and ratified in accordance with the Constitution, published and which have entered into force shall be a part of the domestic legal order of The Republic of Croatia and shall have primacy over domestic law'.

80 UNESCO, E-2357, 27 January 1953, p. 28.

powers attributable to property rights. However, it should be pointed out that such a conceptual definition of slavery is based on the original concept of slavery, which is completely overcome since today, ownership cannot be exercised over a person. In that regard, it would be more appropriate to interpret slavery as a significant restriction of personal freedom aimed at the relationship of dependency to a significant extent and with the aim of being exploited in various ways manifesting in a significant, but not necessarily complete restriction of the freedom of movement.[81]

The following slavery-like practices are defined under Art. 1 of the 1956 Supplementary Convention: debt bondage, that is, slavery as a pay-off for a debt or as a means of debt payment; serfdom; forced marriage, including selling females for the purpose of marriage and treating women as husbands' ownership; exploitation of children including the delivery of a child to another person whether for remuneration or not, with a view to exploiting the child or its labour.[82]

To date, domestic courts have affirmed the existence of slavery offence in cases of forced begging,[83] prostitution,[84] sale for sexual exploitation and labour exploitation.[85] In doing so, in most cases the courts have correctly identified the main features of this offence: exploiting poverty and unemployment for victims, placing them in inadequate living spaces, forced work without pay, obligation to indebtedness, limiting and monitoring their movements, physical and psychological abuse and threats, while the victim often suffers from mental deficiencies and disruptive personality. However, although the results of the analysis of the case law suggest a correct understanding of slavery on behalf of Croatian courts, there are also exceptions, as confirmed by the judgement of the European Court of Human Rights (ECtHR) in the case of *S. M. v. Croatia*.[86]

Freedom from slavery and forced labour is also guaranteed by Art. 4 of the European Convention on Human Rights (ECHR), which prohibits slavery, servitude and forced labour, i.e. protects the person's right not to be in slavery or

81 B. Herceg Pakšić, M. Jukić, above, n. 16, pp. 290, 306.

82 Slavery Convention, Supplementary Convention on the Abolition of Slavery, the Slave Trade, and Institutions and Practices Similar to Slavery.

83 Supreme Court of RC, VSRH, I Kž 741/04-5, 07.10.2004.

84 Supreme Court of RC, VSRH, I Kž 703/2014-7, 02.07.2015.

85 Zagreb Municipal Criminal Court, OKS,17-KO-2728/12, Slavonski Brod County Court, ŽS, Kž-239/14-4, according to B. Herceg Pakšić, M. Jukić, above n. 16, 305.

86 *S. M. v. Croatia*, no. 60561/14.

servitude, or made to do force labour.[87] Unlike the Conventions of 1926 and 1956 which did not foresee in their provisions a judicial body in charge of interpreting the provisions of the Convention, the ECHR laid the groundwork for establishing the ECtHR whose principal task is ensuring that the states respect the rights guaranteed by the ECHR. Its judgments are legally binding on each state and bear implications for domestic legislation and case law.[88]

Until now, the ECtHR has determined one violation of Art. 4 of the ECHR by Croatia. In its judgment, *S. M. v. Croatia*, the ECtHR found that Croatia did not carry out an efficient investigation of the applicant's claims that she had been a victim of human trafficking and had been exploited for prostitution. Failures in the investigation related to these allegations led to a procedural violation of the right to a prohibition of slavery under Art. 4. However, in addition to finding a procedural violation, in the present case, the ECtHR addressed the issue of the material scope of Art. 4 which refers to three concepts: slavery, servitude and forced or compulsory labour. Since those concepts are not defined by the ECHR, the ECtHR relied on international law standards instead.

In its previous case law on the concept of *slavery*, the ECtHR referred to the definition contained in the 1926 Convention on slavery, whereas, with regard to the concept of a 'relationship similar to slavery', it took into account the earlier case-law of the European Commission on Human Rights and the 1956 Supplementary Convention, finding that the concept must be interpreted as an "obligation to provide services imposed by the use of coercion".[89] The ECtHR

87 Croatia became the 40th member of the Council of Europe on 6 November 1996, and ratified the ECHR on 22 October 1997. The ECHR entered into force (in regard to Croatia) on 5 November 1997 together with Protocols Nos. 1, 4, 6, 7 and 11. Protocols Nos. 13, 12 and 14 entered into force in 2003, 2005 and 2010, respectively.

88 Since the judgments of the ECtHR have a binding interpretative authority irrespective of the state to which they refer (*erga omnes* effect), all of its judgments are relevant for the domestic legislation. First cases before the ECtHR ascertaining a violation of Art. 4 were those against France concerning working conditions and forced labour. In the case *Siliadin v. France* the ECtHR found that the applicant worked against her will, without remuneration and days off, however, it did not find elements of slavery in light of the fact that those for whom she worked did not exercise ownership right over her by depreciating her status to an object (para. 122). In the case *C. N. and V. v. France* the ECtHR took into account the taking away of an applicant's passport and lack of remuneration for work performed as well as threats to report her to immigration services, establishing a violation of Art. 4 of the ECHR.

89 *Siliadin v. France*, no. 73316/01, §122–125.

likewise found that a relationship similar to slavery corresponds to a 'severe' form of forced or compulsory labour.[90]

As regards the definition of 'forced or compulsory work', the ECtHR pointed out that no clear guidance on the content of that concept can be found in the Council of Europe documents, and that it is evident that the wording of Art. 4 is largely based on ILO Convention No. 29.[91] As it is a document that is binding on almost all Member States of the Council of Europe, the ECtHR has held that the ILO definition of 'forced or compulsory labour', according to which that concept covers "all work or service which is exacted from any person under the menace of any penalty and for which the said person has not offered voluntarily", should be taken as the basis for interpreting Art. 4 of the ECHR.[92] The concept of 'penalty' can encompass physical violence or restraint, but it can also take subtler forms of psychological nature, such as threats to denounce victims to the police or immigration authorities when their employment status is illegal.[93] With regard to the voluntary nature of work, the ECtHR pointed out that this was a real issue which must be examined in the light of all the relevant circumstances of a case. In cases where an employer abuses the position of vulnerability of his workers in order to exploit them, this work cannot be considered voluntary, and the prior consent of the victim is not sufficient to exclude the characterisation of work as forced labour.[94]

In an earlier judgment, *Rantsev v. Cyprus and Russia*, assessing the scope of Art. 4, the ECtHR stressed that the ECHR is a living instrument which must be interpreted in the light of the present-day conditions. It emphasised that human trafficking threatens human dignity and fundamental freedoms and cannot be considered compatible with a democratic society and the values expounded in the ECHR. Because of that, human trafficking falls within the scope of Art. 4, and it is not necessary to classify it as slavery, servitude or forced and compulsory labour.[95]

90 *C. N. and V. v. France*, no. 67724/09, § 89–91.

91 *Van der Mussele v. Belgium*, no. 8919/80, § 32.

92 Art. 2 (1) of the Convention No. 29.

93 *C. N. and V. v. France*, § 77.

94 *Chowdury and others v. Greece*, no. 21884/15, § 96.

95 In case of the *Rantsev v. Cyprus and Russia* (no. 25965/04) the ECtHR considered that trafficking itself, within the meaning of Art. 3(a) of the Palermo Protocol and Art. 4(a) of the Anti-Trafficking Convention, falls within the scope of Art. 4 of the ECHR (*§* 282). Human trafficking is dependent on the presence of three constituent and cumulative elements: action, means and purpose. *Action* includes recruit, transport, transfer, harbour or receiving of persons; *means* includes threat or duress or other forms of coercion, kidnapping,

In the case *S. M. v. Croatia,* the ECtHR dealt with the question of whether exploitation for the purpose of prostitution falls within the scope of 'forced or compulsory labour' under Art. 4. There are different, often conflicting, views as to whether prostitution as such can ever be consensual or is always a coercive form of exploitation. In this regard, the ECtHR did not express its position but stressed that in the absence of coercion on a person to engage in prostitution, the application of Art. 4 of the ECHR was excluded as such work cannot be regarded as forced or compulsory labour.[96]

The ECtHR concluded that the notion of 'forced or compulsory labour' under Art. 4 aims to protect against instances of serious exploitation, such as forced prostitution, irrespective of whether, in the particular circumstances of a case, they are related to the specific human trafficking context. The question of whether a particular situation involves all the constituent elements of human trafficking and/or gives rise to a separate issue of forced prostitution is a factual question which must be examined in the light of all the relevant circumstances of a case. Moreover, any such conduct may have elements qualifying it as 'servitude' or 'slavery' under Art. 4.[97] In this context, it is important to stress that 'force' may encompass subtle forms of coercive conduct (for example, threats to denounce victims to the police when their employment status is illegal), as well as stipulated by the ILO and in other international materials.[98]

In the case of *S. M. v. Croatia,* the ECtHR finally concluded that national authorities had failed to follow obvious lines of inquiry and relied on the victim's testimony without taking into account the possible impact of psychological trauma.[99] The manner in which the criminal-law mechanisms were implemented in this case was defective to the point of constituting a violation of the State's procedural obligation under Art. 4 of the ECHR.

---

fraud, abuse of powers or vulnerability or providing or receiving payment to gain consent of a person exercising control over another person, to the purpose of exploitation, and *purpose* includes exploitation. While exploitation is not defined, it includes exploiting prostitution of others or forms of sexual exploitation, forced labour, or providing services, slavery or servitude, or removal of body organs.

96 *V.T. v. France,* no. 37194/02, § 24–27, 35.

97 *S.M. v. Croatia,* above n. 86, § 300–302.

98 For indicators, see *supra* Section 3.1.

99 For instance, they failed to investigate the circumstances of the contact via Facebook, although such contacts represent a frequent *modus operandi* of human traffickers to lure their victims; as well as the issue of whether T. M. threatened the applicant via Facebook (§ 336, 337).

4 Conclusion: Redressing and Recalibrating Contemporary Slavery

Croatia has recognised the problem of contemporary slavery and the need to meet the requirements for its prevention. To realise this important task, we need a clear legislative framework and its efficient implementation. In that direction, a lot has been done at the normative level by the accession and ratification of almost all of the most important international legal sources that prohibit such conduct and by the harmonisation of national legislation with the obligations arising therefrom. Nevertheless, certain problems appeared in criminal law practice that are, to a considerable degree, the result (consequence) of non-existing criteria for a clear determination of different forms of contemporary slavery. The judgment of the ECtHR and the concurring opinions of judges in case, *M.S. v. Croatia,* indicate just how complex this issue is.

It should be emphasized that by contemporary forms of slavery, no matter how we qualify them, the victim and her efficient protection and providing help to the victim should always be put at the forefront. Criminal law is just *ultima ratio societas*, while recognizing the vulnerable groups of people and taking measures with the aim to prevent their victimization is the key step in preventing the contemporary slavery phenomena. Therefore, it is necessary to develop and strengthen the awareness of the society about the severity of this social phenomenon, to make the public sensitive to the victims and to educate all the actors who could meet the victims in performing their work.

As mentioned, modern slavery is a very broad concept encompassing various forms of abusive practices. In the context of labour law regulation, this chapter has attempted to highlight the issue of exploitation of workers in Croatia deriving from precarious working conditions. After all, precarious work is increasingly being considered as the new *norm* to which employment and social protection systems continuously adjust. However, what are the consequences of normalising or even legitimising the existing gaps for the individual and society? Most notably, the commodification of labour and overproduction of vulnerable workers without adequate legal protection – which the ILO has been combating since 1919. The ambitious aspirations and imperatives of reducing labour costs did not outmanoeuvre a microeconomy, like Croatia. Non-standard forms of employment with a high degree of decent work deficit are spreading across the Croatian labour market. Nonetheless, the decline in work quality made insecurity in the form of precariousness present not only in all segments of the employment relationship but also in all aspects of human life. It should be pointed out that non-compliance with labour standards is a result of neoliberal logic and despondent business policies, which leads to weak enforcement of labour law (enforcement protective gaps). This specific situation implies that even those workers who are protected experience precariousness and abuse. In fact, workers are left without a right to voice their concerns and influence policy. This is seen most acutely in the customarily understaffed labour inspectorates.

In Croatia, it is thus necessary to strengthen the role of labour inspections, to raise awareness of the mentioned phenomena and to prevent them, as well, to create new, high-quality jobs. In a world in which labour is becoming a commodity, it is important to act by regulation at every level: international, regional and national, and to strengthen the social dialogue.

Academic References

A. M. Grünfelder, *Uradni stroj velikoga njemačkog Reicha*, Srednja Europa, Zagreb 2007.

A. Ravnić, *Osnove radnog prava. Domaćeg, usporednog i međunarodnog*, Pravni fakultet, Zagreb 2004.

B. Herceg Pakšić and M. Jukić, 'Primjena konvencijskog prava u području zabrane ropstva i prisilnog rada: europski standardi i hrvatska postignuća' (2016) 23 *Hrvatski ljetopis za kaznene znanosti i praksu* 281.

D. Nestić and S. Blažević Burić, 'Radnici na minimalnoj plaći i siromaštvo u Hrvatskoj' (2018) 25 *Revija za socijalnu politiku* 235.

D. Weil, *The Fissured Workplace: Why Work Became So Bad for So Many and What Can Be Done to Improve It*, Harvard University Press, Cambridge 2014.

G. Rodgers, 'Precarious Work in Western Europe: The State of the Debate' in G. Rodgers and J. Rodgers (eds), *Precarious Jobs in Labour Market Regulation: The Growth of Atypical Employment in Western Europe*, International Institute for Labour Studies, Geneva 1989, pp. 1–16.

H. Butković and V. Samardžija (in cooperation with I. Skazlić and I. Čavar), *Nonstandard Work in Croatia: Challenges and Perspectives in Selected Sectors*, IRMO, Zagreb 2016.

I. Gović Penić, 'Procesna pravila u sporu kojim se traži zaštita od uznemiravanja/diskriminacije i mobinga' in I. Gović Penić et al. (eds), *Priručnik o diskriminaciji i mobingu na radnom mjestu (pravna i medicinska motrišta)*, Sindikat naftnog gospodarstva, Udruga za pomoć i edukaciju žrtava mobbinga, Zagreb 2018, pp. 64–68.

I. Grgurev, 'The Concept of 'Employee': The Position in Croatia' in B. Waas and G. Heerma Van Voss (eds), *Restatement of Labour Law in Europe. Vol I: The Concept of Employee*, Hart Publishing, Oxford 2017, pp. 59–83.

I. Grgurev, 'Atypical Employment Relationships: The Position in Croatia' in B. Waas and G. Heerma Van Voss (eds), *Restatement of Labour Law in Europe. Vol II: Atypical Employment Relationships*, Hart, Oxford 2019, pp. 83–105.

I. Grgurev and I. Vukorepa, 'Minimum wage as a tool in the fight against poverty: Croatian labour law perspective' in G. Löschnigg (ed), *Staatliche Eingriffe in das System der Mindestentgelte im internationalen Vergleich*, Verlag des ÖGB, Wien 2013, pp. 280–308.

J. Fudge and R. Owens, 'Precarious Work, Women, and the New Economy: The Challenge to Legal Norms' in J. Fudge and R. Owens (eds), *Precarious Work, Women, and the New Economy: The Challenge to Legal Norms*, Hart Publishing, Oxford 2006, pp. 3–27.

K. Kotulovski and S. Laleta, 'The abuse and exploitation of foreign seasonal workers: Did the Coronavirus emergency worsen already precarious working conditions in the agricultural sector?' in D. Duić and T. Petrašević (eds), *EU and Comparative Law Issues and Challenges Series (ECLIC 5), EU 2021 – The future of the EU in and after the pandemic*, Josip Juraj Strossmayer University of Osijek, Faculty of Law, Osijek 2021, pp. 326–358.

K. Turković, 'Trgovanje ljudima i ropstvo' in P. Novoselec (ed), *Posebni dio kaznenog prava*, Prvo izdanje, Pravni fakultet, Zagreb 2007, pp. 134-139.

M. Boersma and J. Nolan, 'Modern slavery and the employment relationship: Exploring the continuum of exploitation', (2022) 64 *Journal of Industrial Relations* 165.

N. Tintić, *Radno pravo, Knjiga prva: Radni odnosi (I)*, Narodne novine, Zagreb 1969.

P. Lokiec, 'Fixed-Terms Contracts in France', *Regulation of Fixed-term Employment Contracts, Comparative Labour Law Seminar, JILPT Report No. 9*, 2010.

V. Geiger, 'Lišavanje slobode i prisilni rad u hrvatskom/jugoslavenskom zakonodavstvu 1945.–1951.' in V. Geiger, M. Grahek Ravančić and M. Karakaš Obradov (eds), *Logori, zatvori i prisilni rad u Hrvatskoj / Jugoslaviji 1941–1945., 1945–1951.*, Hrvatski institut za povijest, Zagreb 2010, pp. 151–54.

V. Grozdanić, M. Škorić and I. Martinović, 'Kaznenopravna zaštita radnika prema odredbama novog Kaznenog zakona', (2012) 19 *HLJKZP* 473.

Ž. Horvatić, Novo hrvatsko kazneno pravo, Pravni fakultet, Zagreb 1997.

France et esclavage contemporain : *Un phénomène enchaîné aux vicissitudes d'un pays à l' « Histoire Servile » pluriséculaire et mondiale*

Béatrice Boissard and Olivier Pluen

1 Introduction

8 500 en 2014, 12 500 en 2016, 129 000 en 2018 ... Le nombre de victimes des formes contemporaines d'esclavage en France, en hausse exponentielle entre 2016 et 2018, suscite l'effroi. Certes, ne s'agit-il là que d'évaluations. D'une part, issus des rapports[1] de la Fondation Walk Free, ces chiffres placent le pays dans la fourchette basse des autres États membres du Conseil de l'Europe et de l'Union européenne (UE). D'après les données 2018 de l'ONG, le premier espace régional comptait alors 3,104 millions de victimes et le second, 1,134 million. La France se situait ainsi légèrement au-dessus de la Norvège (1,8‰), au niveau de l'Allemagne et du Royaume-Uni (2‰ ; 2,1‰), et en dessous de l'Espagne, de l'Italie, de la Russie et de la Grèce (2,3‰ ; 2,4‰ ; 5,5‰ ; 7,9‰)[2]. D'autre part, le premier Plan d'action national contre la traite des êtres humains (2014–2016) avait été jusqu'à transposer l'évaluation du nombre de victimes de la traite des êtres humains faite par l'Organisation internationale du travail (OIT) pour l'Europe de l'Ouest en 2008 – soit 270 000 –, à la seule France[3], laissant raisonnablement penser que les autorités y estimaient déjà plausibles ces chiffres vertigineux[4].

Si les statistiques permettent d'avoir une idée de l'ampleur du phénomène, elles sont complétées par une représentation imagée. Les médias se font en ce

1 Walk Free, *Global Slavery Index*, 2014, 2016 et 2018, <https://www.walkfree.org/global-slavery-index/>.

2 *Ibid.*, 2018.

3 Voir, J.-F. Niort, O. Pluen, 'Introduction générale' dans J.-F. Niort et O. Pluen (dir.), *Esclavage, traite et autres formes d'asservissement et d'exploitation, du Code Noir à nos jours*, Dalloz, Paris 2018.

4 La question de la réalité des chiffres de l'esclavage contemporain en Europe appelle à garder à l'esprit que les autorités n'ont connaissance et ne traitent qu'une infime partie des cas, en raison du caractère officieux du phénomène. Ainsi, pour la France, la première étude annuelle conjointe du Service statistique ministériel de la sécurité intérieure (SSMSI) et du Service statistique ministériel du ministère de la Justice (SDSE), publiée le 18 octobre 2022, faisait état de l'enregistrement de seulement 1 810 victimes en 2021.

 | DOI:10.1163/9789004723801_008

sens de plus en plus fréquemment le relais des « affaires d'esclavage », offrant une vision globale des catégories de victimes et secteurs concernés. On citera ainsi pour la période récente : à propos de personnes placées auprès de diplomates ou personnalités politiques étrangers, « Esclavage moderne : l'ancien ministre du Burundi condamné ... » ; concernant des travailleurs dans certaines activités industrielles, artisanales ou agricoles, « Champagne. Des travailleurs logés comme des esclaves dans les vignes ... » ; s'agissant de personnes soumises à des réseaux de prostitution, « En France, l'exploitation sexuelle est la principale forme de traite des êtres humains » ; ou encore au sujet de victimes d'autres réseaux, « Traite des êtres humains, mendicité forcée : à Toulouse, des femmes et des hommes réduits en esclavage »[5].

Dans le cas précis de la France, de telles affaires trouvent un écho particulier du fait d'une histoire où les formes d'esclavage ont occupé une place majeure. Cela comprend le cas de la métropole, où elles ont été omniprésentes, avec par exemple : l'épopée de Spartacus et de ses lieutenants gaulois ; la réduction en esclavage des vaincus d'Alésia ; l'extinction de l'esclavage dans le royaume au XIe siècle théoriquement[6] ; l'abolition partielle du servage par Louis X « Le Hutin » en 1315 ; l'essor du système des galères et bagnes portuaires sous Louis XIV ; l'adoption du drapeau Corse à « tête de maure » ; l'abolition définitive du servage dans le domaine royal en 1787 ; l'abolition des droits féodaux dans la « Nuit du 4 août » ; la conceptualisation d'un « esclavage moderne » avec les révolutions industrielles au XIXe siècle ; et le développement du service du travail obligatoire et du système concentrationnaire pendant la Seconde Guerre mondiale.

Mais c'est surtout la situation qui a prévalu dans les deux empires coloniaux. Dans une partie des « anciennes colonies », l'esclavage a fait l'objet d'un recours « industriel » entre le milieu du XVIIe et celui du XIXe siècle, la monarchie absolue puis le Consulat légalisant la traite maritime le nourrissant, mais aussi l'esclavage lui-même avec les « Codes Noirs[7] ». La France a transporté

5 Voir, V. Mahaut, *Le Parisien, 17 février 2022* ; Agence, *Ouest France, 27 juin 2019* ; C. Calvier, *Le Figaro, 27 juin 2018* ; L. Derne, *Actu Toulouse, 15 janvier 2021.*

6 Voir, C. Gauvard, 'Le temps long de l'esclavage en Europe : histoire d'un refoulement' dans J.-P. Jean, S. Humbert, O. Pluen, A. Bendjebbar (dir.), *Justice et esclavages*, La documentation française, Paris 2021.

7 Voir, L. Salin-Molins, *Le Code noir ou le calvaire de Canaan*, PUF, Paris 1987 ; A. Castaldo, *Codes noirs, de l'esclavage aux abolitions*, Dalloz, Paris 2006 ; J.-F. Niort, *Le Code Noir. Idées reçues sur un texte symbolique,* Le Cavalier Bleu, Paris 2015. L'expression « Code Noir », souvent utilisée au singulier, peut aussi être employée au pluriel dès lors qu'elle recouvre en réalité plusieurs textes : elle a servi à désigner principalement l'ordonnance/édit royal de 1685 touchant la police des îles de l'Amérique française, mais aussi les édits de 1723 et 1724 s'en rapprochant

1,313 million d'esclaves et sa principale colonie sucrière, Saint-Domingue – aujourd'hui Haïti –, en comptera jusqu'à 550 000 en 1789, soit 85% de sa population[8]. Paradoxalement, là où on aurait pu s'attendre à ce que la volonté de la Révolution puis de la République de rompre avec l'infamie des régimes qui les ont précédé contribue à façonner une conscience collective contre l'esclavage contemporain, surtout dans un État « régénéré » où l'un des premiers actes de souveraineté a consisté à proclamer la liberté et l'égalité en 1789 et à abolir définitivement l'esclavage en 1848, c'est plutôt l'image d'une conscience à éclipse qui s'est imposée. La présidente du Comité contre l'esclavage moderne (CCEM) l'a déploré lors d'un colloque : « [En 1994], personne ne parlait en France des formes contemporaines d'esclavage… Les rares interlocuteurs rencontrés nous riaient au nez et expliquaient sèchement que l'esclavage était aboli depuis 1848 et qu'il était plus que malvenu d'en reparler en cette fin du XXe siècle[9] ». Le Président Chirac lui-même avait pourtant relevé dans son discours prononcé en 1998 pour le 150e anniversaire de l'abolition : « [S]i cette barbarie appartient au passé, ne fermons pas les yeux sur le présent ». Il parlait toutefois de l'étranger … Se doutait-il alors des chiffres qu'avancerait Walk Free vingt ans plus tard ? Face à une telle contradiction, il faut s'interroger sur les incidences de l'histoire sur la perception et la lutte contre les formes d'esclavage en France.

Un examen approfondi de la situation y révèle une appréhension tardive et perfectible des formes contemporaines d'esclavage, sous le prisme tantôt déformant, tantôt utilitaire du passé.

2 Une appréhension tardive sous le prisme déformant du passé

Entre la fin du XXe siècle et 2013, les formes contemporaines d'esclavage sont apparues comme un phénomène largement minoré, sinon ignoré. Les causes principales semblent tenir à l'existence d'un droit dogmatique et à la crainte de sa reconnaissance.

---

pour respectivement les Mascareignes et la Louisiane. Ces textes, actes de souveraineté du roi, avaient notamment vocation à régir la condition des esclaves sur ces territoires.

8 Voir, M. Dorigny, B. Gainot, *Atlas des esclavages, de l'Antiquité à nos jours*, Autrement, Paris 2022.

9 S. O'Dy, « 25 ans de combat du Comité contre l'esclavage moderne », in S. O'Dy (dir.) *Traite des Êtres Humains, esclavage moderne et travail forcé en France*, CCEM, Paris 2020, <www.esclavagemoderne.org>.

2.1 *Un phénomène longtemps minoré*

2013 est l'année de la reconnaissance par la loi française, « expression de la volonté générale »[10], des formes contemporaines d'esclavage. Avant, les pouvoirs publics sont restés timides sur le sujet.

La législation contre l'esclavage se trouve jusqu'alors construite autour de trois blocs d'importance inégale. Le premier s'inscrit dans le sillage de l'après-Seconde Guerre mondiale et du Statut du Tribunal militaire international de Nuremberg de 1945 venu créer l'infraction pénale de « crime contre l'humanité ». La « réduction en esclavage », notamment, fut alors intégrée parmi les critères de sa définition prévus à l'article 6 (c). Cela s'est traduit en droit répressif interne en 1992[11], prolongé en 1994[12] par l'entrée effective dans le « nouveau code pénal » de l'article 212–1 qui définit et réprime le crime contre l'humanité. Mais la référence à l'esclavage qui y est faite est celle d'un esclavage étatisé ou plus largement institutionnalisé. Cette intégration directe du crime contre l'humanité – incluant l'esclavage – dans le droit français se voulait ici une réponse, plusieurs décennies après le recours par l'Allemagne nazie à l'esclavage et au travail forcé, aux exactions commises dans le cadre des guerres civiles qui ont marqué l'ex-Yougoslavie et le Rwanda dans les années 1990. Le deuxième bloc fait suite au débat qui a émergé à la fin de la même décennie autour de la question de la traite transatlantique et indienne et de l'esclavage colonial. Après plusieurs initiatives parlementaires, la loi du 21 mai 2001 tendant à la reconnaissance de la traite et de l'esclavage en tant que crime contre l'humanité a été promulguée (dite loi « Taubira »). Ce texte porte sur les traites et l'esclavage perpétrés à partir du XVe siècle et qualifie ceux-ci de crimes contre l'humanité, même si cette reconnaissance doit être comprise comme ayant un caractère mémoriel[13]. Seul le dernier bloc concerne ainsi l'esclavage contemporain. De l'entrée en vigueur du nouveau code pénal de 1994 jusqu'en 2003, seules étaient sanctionnées, aux articles 225–13 et 14, les « conditions de

10 Art. 6 de la Déclaration des droits de l'homme et du citoyen de 1789.

11 Loi du 22 juillet 1992 portant réforme des dispositions du code pénal relatives à la répression des crimes et délits contre les personnes.

12 La même année, l'UNESCO lance le projet international de « La Route de l'esclave » à Ouidah (Bénin), afin de « briser le silence qui entoure la traite négrière », <https://www.unesco.org/fr/routes-enslaved-peoples>.

13 En retrait par rapport aux propositions de loi à l'origine de son adoption, dont celle de C. Taubira, la loi de 2001 revêt une fonction déclarative s'agissant précisément de la qualification de crime contre l'humanité, cette qualification n'étant pas positivement sanctionnée. Une proposition de résolution a encore été déposée début 2022 sur le bureau de l'Assemblée nationale afin de pousser à une inflexion de la législation : O. Serva (député de Guadeloupe), proposition de résolution n° 4996 du 4 février 2022, relative à l'incrimination des propos négationnistes portés sur la traite négrière et l'esclavage colonial.

travail et d'hébergement abusives » et « conditions de travail ou d'hébergement contraires à la dignité humaine »[14]. Il a fallu attendre la loi sur la sécurité intérieure du 18 mars 2003 pour que le code intègre également la traite des êtres humains, désormais régie par les articles 225-4-1 et suivants.

Il convient de souligner, à propos de ce troisième bloc, que son renforcement en 2003 est intervenu dans le contexte de l'important rapport Lazerges-Vidalies[15] et en pleine « affaire Siliadin ». Ce dernier « fiasco » judiciaire met en lumière les défaillances de la France en matière de lutte contre les formes contemporaines d'esclavage devant la Cour européenne des droits de l'homme (Cour EDH). La Convention éponyme (CEDH) prévoit parmi ses principes inconditionnels l'interdiction de l'esclavage, de la servitude et du travail forcé. Or, dans les faits, la justice répressive française avait eu à connaître la situation d'une jeune femme togolaise placée alors qu'elle était adolescente auprès d'un couple vivant en France, dans les conditions suivantes : travail sept jours sur sept et environ quinze heures par jour, absence de ressources, isolement, dépendance vis-à-vis du couple concerné, confiscation des papiers d'identité, absence de scolarisation. Malgré cela, la Cour d'appel de Versailles, suivie par la Cour de cassation[16], avait conclu à l'absence de délit de soumission d'une personne vulnérable ou en situation de dépendance à des conditions de travail et d'hébergement incompatibles avec la dignité humaine, au motif stupéfiant que « le fait de s'occuper des tâches ménagères et des enfants pendant la totalité de la journée ne saurait constituer à lui seul des conditions de travail incompatibles avec la dignité humaine, ce sort étant celui de nombreuses mères de famille »[17]. Avec l'aide du CCEM, l'affaire, portée devant la juridiction européenne, a entrainé la condamnation de la France en 2005, pour servitude[18].

2.2 *Un droit longtemps dogmatique*

Cette minoration s'explique d'abord par un droit longtemps resté dogmatique en matière de formes d'esclavage. Bien qu'elle ait incontestablement connu, pratiqué, voire régi celles-ci sur son sol, la France s'est parée avec autosatisfaction d'un titre d'État abolitionniste et porteur du flambeau de l'abolition dans le monde.

14 Ces délits subsistent, en droit positif, aux mêmes articles.
15 C. Lazerges (pdte), A. Vidalies (rap.), Rapport n° 3459 du 12 décembre 2001 au nom de la mission d'information commune sur les diverses formes d'esclavage, AN.
16 Cour de cassation, Crim., 11 décembre 2001, req. n° 00–87.280.
17 CA Versailles, 15 mai 2003.
18 CEDH, 26 juillet 2005, *Siliadin c. France*, n° 73316/01.

Au niveau interne, la France a entendu s'affirmer à partir de sa construction en tant qu'État, d'abord comme celui du « sol libre », puis comme celui de l'interdiction constitutionnelle de l'esclavage. La première expression renvoie au principe selon lequel « les esclaves ayant traversé certaines frontières territoriales se trouvent ipso facto affranchis »[19]. Dans une Europe du Moyen Âge et de la Renaissance profondément marquée par les institutions de l'esclavage et du servage, le pays s'est effectivement peu à peu distingué par l'affirmation du principe du « sol libre », qui a connu son apogée dans la pratique au début du XVIIe siècle, alors que les monarques eux-mêmes considèrent qu'il couvre y compris les nouvelles colonies. Et tandis qu'à partir du Code Noir de 1685, le roi, titulaire de la souveraineté, décide de légaliser l'esclavage dans ces mêmes colonies, tout en admettant qu'une telle décision heurtait le droit naturel, les parlements judiciaires et le tribunal de l'Amirauté vont réussir à préserver ce principe sur le sol métropolitain et à le consolider en le datant fictivement d'un édit de Louis X « Le Hutin » de 1315 qui débutait ainsi : « Comme, selon le droit de nature, chacun doit naître franc ». Avec la Révolution, l'aura du « sol libre » va ainsi jouer un rôle significatif dans le cheminement vers l'abolition. Ce principe est tour à tour consacré dans la métropole par l'Assemblée nationale révolutionnaire en 1791, puis sur l'ensemble des territoires français, même coloniaux, par le décret du Gouvernement provisoire du 27 avril 1848 – toujours en vigueur en 2023 – et la Constitution sous la Seconde République.

La France a aussi été un précurseur en prévoyant une interdiction constitutionnelle de l'esclavage[20], dans successivement ses Constitutions républicaines de l'an I, de l'an III et de 1848, ainsi que dans un Sénatus-consulte impérial de 1854. Le moment 1848, notamment et enfin, a semblé figer à tout jamais une croyance tenace : le droit interne français le plus élevé ayant consacré la fin de l'esclavage, celui-ci n'existe plus et n'appelle donc plus d'encadrement à cet échelon … Or, encore récemment, c'est précisément ce dogmatisme juridique que dix-sept députés ultramarins ont souhaité dénoncer dans un communiqué de février 2023, à la suite de l'affirmation du ministre de l'Intérieur et des Outre-mer selon laquelle : « c'est la République française qui a

---

19 Voir, S. Peabody, *"There are no slaves in France" : The political culture of race and slavery in the Ancien Régime*, Oxford University Press, New York 1996 ; O. Pluen, '1315–1946 : le mythe d'un "Empire" français sans esclaves' dans J.-P. Jean, S. Humbert, O. Pluen, A. Bendjebbar (dir.), *Justice et esclavages*, La documentation française, Paris 2021.

20 Voir, O. Pluen, 'Constitutionnaliser l'interdiction de l'esclavage et des autres formes d'exploitation des êtres humains : un impératif contemporain' dans J.-F. Niort et O. Pluen (dir.), *Esclavage, traite et autres formes d'asservissement et d'exploitation, du Code Noir à nos jours*, Dalloz, Paris 2018.

aboli l'esclavage »[21]. Ce faisant, l'hôte de la place Beauvaux a oublié que l'acte juridique d'abolition, certes étatique et républicain, est intervenu dans un certain contexte, marqué notamment par la résistance croissante des esclaves à cette condition.

Au niveau international, la France, grande puissance européenne et coloniale, a également donné l'image d'un acteur majeur de l'abolition de l'esclavage et des formes associées[22], dont certaines peuvent être aujourd'hui qualifiées de « contemporaines d'esclavage »[23]. Avant la Convention de la Société des nations (SDN) relative à l'esclavage de 1926, l'esclavage n'était toutefois perçu que sous un seul angle : celui de son vecteur qu'est la traite. Lorsque la « fièvre » coloniale a gagné l'Europe, la France a participé à l'ensemble des sommets aboutissant à l'adoption de dispositions sur l'interdiction de la traite des esclaves[24]. Ce faisant, le pays a moins agi par humanisme que dans un souci variable d'obtenir un soutien populaire, d'intégrer le concert des nations, ou encore de justifier son entreprise coloniale. L'action de la France va prendre un nouvel élan en la matière au lendemain de la Première Guerre mondiale, alors qu'elle apparaît comme le grand vainqueur du conflit et que son empire couvre un dixième de la surface du globe. Elle participe activement à la rédaction de la Convention de 1926 susmentionnée[25], plus tard amendée par le Protocole de 1953, avant de l'intégrer en droit interne par un décret en 1931. Après la Seconde Guerre mondiale, la France joue encore un rôle majeur en tant que l'une des quatre grandes puissances vainqueures et nouveau membre permanent du Conseil de sécurité de l'ONU. Elle participe à la rédaction de la Convention supplémentaire relative à l'abolition de l'esclavage, de la traite des esclaves et des institutions et pratiques analogues à l'esclavage, adoptée en 1956, ainsi que, par l'intermédiaire de René Cassin, futur Prix Nobel, à la rédaction de la

21 Voir, le texte du communiqué : « 17 députés ultramarins répondent aux propos de Gérard Darmanin », *Le Quotidien*, 5 février 2023.

22 Voir, M. Erpelding, *Le droit international antiesclavagiste des "nations civilisées" (1815–1945)*, LGDJ-IUV, Paris 2017.

23 Ce terme n'est pas employé à l'époque, mais « les institutions analogues » décrites dans la Convention supplémentaire de 1956 y renvoient. Une partie de la doctrine préfère le faire remonter à la Convention des Nations unies sur la prostitution de 1950 et une majorité au Protocole additionnel à la Convention des Nations unies contre la criminalité transnationale organisée visant à prévenir, réprimer et punir la traite des personnes, en particulier des femmes et des enfants de 2000.

24 L'Acte général de la conférence de Bruxelles de 1890, l'Acte général de Berlin de 1885, ou la Convention de Saint-Germain-en-Laye de 1919.

25 Voir, A. Bendjebbar, 'De l'esclavage au travail forcé au temps de la SDN' dans J.-F. Niort et O. Pluen (dir.), *Esclavage, traite et autres formes d'asservissement et d'exploitation, du Code Noir à nos jours*, Dalloz, Paris 2018.

Déclaration universelle des droits de l'homme de 1948. Cependant, la France a pris peu de risques pratiques dans sa participation à l'élaboration de ces textes. D'abord, la Convention de 1926 comme la Déclaration de 1948 énoncent de simples objectifs, peu contraignants pour elle. Ensuite, il faudra attendre une loi de 1963 et un décret de 1965 pour que la Convention de 1956 soit intégrée en droit interne, alors que le processus de décolonisation avait pris fin. Ainsi, la France semblait désormais ne plus avoir à se préoccuper de lutter contre les phénomènes traditionnellement associés à ses anciennes colonies ...

2.3 *Une reconnaissance longtemps crainte*

La seconde raison de cette minimisation est plus psychologique, les pouvoirs publics craignant d'ouvrir une boîte de Pandore dans le sillage des débats autour de l'adoption de la loi « Taubira » en 2001.

D'abord, l'évocation des formes contemporaines d'esclavage suppose d'être conciliée avec la question de la reconnaissance de l'esclavage issu de la traite transatlantique et indienne entre le milieu du XVIIe siècle et celui du XIXe siècle dans les « anciennes colonies ». Ces anciennes colonies regroupent encore, en 2023, environ 2,3 millions de personnes vivant en Guadeloupe, Guyane, Martinique et à La Réunion, ou résidant en métropole, mais nées dans ces territoires, sur une population française totale de près de 68 millions. Or, tandis que le principe du « sol libre » se trouvait dans une certaine mesure préservé sur le sol métropolitain avant l'abolition définitive de l'esclavage en 1848, l'État français a – au-delà des simples pratiques des colons – soumis par deux fois ces territoires à un régime juridique dérogatoire de celui de la métropole, en matière d'esclavage. Les populations noires, sauf à être affranchies, se sont trouvées juridiquement soumises aux « Codes Noirs » cités en introduction jusqu'à la première abolition républicaine de l'esclavage de l'an II, avant d'y être de nouveau soumises de 1802 sous le Consulat jusqu'à la seconde abolition de 1848[26]. Sur le plan juridique, la lutte contre les formes contemporaines d'esclavage est ainsi de nature à raviver les débats relatifs à la qualification de l'esclavage pré-1848 et à l'indemnisation des descendants de ses victimes. Le Gouvernement, représenté par la garde des Sceaux Christiane Taubira, s'est d'abord montré réticent à qualifier et réprimer les formes contemporaines d'esclavage lors de l'examen de la loi devenue celle du 5 août 2013[27]. Quant aux réparations, le refus du législateur de maintenir le dispositif initialement prévu

26 Voir, *supra* n. 7.

27 Voir, A. Lemaire, 'La loi de 2013 contre la traite et le parcours dans le cadre de la Commission des lois de l'Assemblée nationale' dans S. O'Dy (dir.) *Traite des Êtres Humains, esclavage moderne et travail forcé en France*, CCEM, Paris 2020. Voir également, l'opinion émise

à cette fin dans ce qui allait devenir la loi « Taubira » de 2001 a entrainé un important contentieux relayé par les médias. Le juge a jusqu'ici systématiquement conclu au rejet de l'application de la prescription centenaire (article 1240 du Code civil), au motif que les faits de traite et d'esclavage ont pris fin en 1848 et que les requérants n'ont pas démontré que cette prescription avait été suspendue[28]. Récemment les 18 et 25 janvier 2022, la Cour d'appel de Fort-de-France en Martinique a de nouveau rejeté des demandes du Mouvement international pour les réparations (MIR), qui portaient notamment sur une expertise de la réparation et l'indemnisation des crimes de traite négrière et de l'esclavage, puis sur une expertise aux frais de l'État pour retrouver les fosses où auraient pu être enterrés des esclaves. Malgré l'échec de ces demandes, l'UNESCO est venu susciter un espoir en 2021 en lançant la rédaction du *Rapport sur la réparation des blessures liées à la traite transatlantique des esclaves et à l'esclavage*[29]. Ce document pourrait venir démontrer qu'un passé esclavagiste mal maîtrisé dans ses conséquences peut être la cause de traumatismes intergénérationnels et commander d'opérer des changements structurels dans la société[30].

Ensuite, reconnaître l'existence de l'esclavage contemporain est susceptible d'écorner l'image construite, lors de l'abolition en 1848, puis avec la fin de la décolonisation, d'une France « civilisée » ayant éradiqué les formes d'esclavage de son territoire. Cette image se heurte pourtant à une réalité différente, dans les Outremers comme en métropole[31]. Dans les premières, entre l'abolition de l'esclavage « légal » par le décret du 27 avril 1848 et la disparition de la « Communauté » franco-africaine et malgache, la puissance coloniale a le plus

par l'ancienne ministre devant la presse, en opposition avec la parole présidentielle, lors de l'inauguration du Mémorial-ACTe en 2015.

28 Après une décennie, l'affaire des réparations rebondit devant la Cour de cassation (Cass. civ. 1re, 17 avril 2019, req. n° 18–13.894), portée notamment par le MIR et le Conseil mondial de la diaspora panafricaine (CMDPA), qui avaient initialement assigné l'État devant le tribunal de grande instance de Fort-de-France (req. n° 05/01955), puis en appel (Cour d'appel de Fort-de-France, 19 décembre 2017, req. n° 16/00185) aux fins d'obtenir une expertise pour évaluer le préjudice subi par le peuple martiniquais du fait de la traite négrière et de l'esclavage et une provision destinée à une future fondation.

29 UNESCO, 'Lancement du Rapport sur la réparation des blessures liées à la traite transatlantique des esclaves et à l'esclavage', <https://webarchive.unesco.org/web/20221005085319/https://fr.unesco.org/news/lancement-du-rapport-reparation-blessures-liees-traite-transatlantique-esclaves-lesclavage>.

30 Voir, A. Charles-Nicolas, B. P. Bowser (dir.), *L'esclavage : quel impact sur la psychologie des populations ?*, Idem Edition, Paris 2018 ; E. Fontaine, *Traumatisme historique et son expression psychopathologique dans le transgénérationnel (violences conjugales) au sein des familles réunionnaises* (thèse de doctorat en Psychologie), Université de Rouen, 2020, <https://theses.fr/2020NORMR088>.

31 O. Pluen, *supra* n. 20.

souvent toléré par traité ou de fait l'esclavage autochtone dans les nouveaux territoires inclus dans son empire. Les textes d'abolition, telles la convention franco-cambodgienne de 1884 en Indochine et la loi de 1896 à Madagascar, ont plutôt été une exception. La France a ainsi, à son tour, largement puisé dans plusieurs communautés pour développer un système de travail forcé public et son armée. C'est ainsi qu'en Afrique occidentale française, un quart de la population était asservie en 1908, tandis que les trois-quarts du contingent autochtone pendant la Première Guerre mondiale étaient composés de captifs ou anciens captifs affranchis. De même, dans les « anciennes colonies », l'esclavage a été remplacé à partir de 1848 par des dispositifs comme l'« engagisme »[32], faisant notamment appel à des travailleurs chinois, indiens ou africains. À cheval entre « nouvelles » et « anciennes » colonies, mais aussi en métropole, il convient également de mentionner les systèmes des bagnes portuaires et coloniaux[33], dont les seconds ont été progressivement instaurés en Guyane et en Nouvelle-Calédonie à partir de 1852–1854. Or, plusieurs décennies après, le recours par l'État à ces formes d'exploitation alternatives à l'esclavage a également donné lieu à une première initiative parlementaire destinée à qualifier le travail forcé de crime contre l'humanité[34].

Il persiste plus largement en France un lourd silence autour de la qualification d'une longue kyrielle de professions plaçant celles et ceux qui les exerçaient au XIXe siècle, voire pendant une partie du suivant, dans une situation

32 Système de recrutement d'une main d'œuvre étrangère « libre » par le biais de contrats de durée déterminée, dans des conditions qui n'étaient en pratique guère plus enviables que l'esclavage. V. Chaillou-Atrous, 'L'engagisme dans les colonies européennes aux XIXe siècle', Encyclopédie d'histoire numérique de l'Europe (2020), <https://ehne.fr/fr/node/12279>; S. Fuma, 'Le servilisme à la place du concept d'engagisme pour définir le statut des travailleurs immigrés ou affranchis après l'abolition de l'esclavage en 1848', *Historun* (2001), <https://www.histoire-reunion.re/le-servilisme-a-la-place-du-concept-dengagisme-pour-definir-le-statut-des-travailleurs-immigres-ou-affranchis-apres-labolition-de-lesclavage-en-1848-sudel-fuma/>. Début 2022, un journal ultramarin informait qu'un réunionnais avait engagé pour la deuxième fois une action devant la juridiction pénale afin de faire reconnaître l'engagisme vis-à-vis des populations indiennes en tant que crime contre l'humanité : L. Pinjon, 'Faire de l'engagisme indien un crime contre l'humanité', *Le Quotidien,* (15 janvier 2022), <https://www.lequotidien.re/actualites/societe/faire-de-lengagisme-indien-un-crime-contre-lhumanite/>.

33 Les bagnes portuaires étaient des ports ou des arsenaux de la Marine, et les bagnes coloniaux des lieux de relégation, en Guyane et en Nouvelle-Calédonie, dans lesquels les condamnés accomplissaient des peines de travaux forcés. L'existence de ces bagnes peut être rapprochée de la dérogation prévue au 13e amendement à la Constitution des États-Unis.

34 C. Duflot, proposition de loi n° 4640 du 10 mai 2017 relative à la reconnaissance du travail forcé comme crime contre l'humanité et à la réparation des préjudices en résultant, AN.

de dépendance et d'exploitation du fait de l'absence de réglementation ou au contraire d'une réglementation autoritaire du travail : ouvriers, mineurs, journaliers, ou domestiques. Alors que le philosophe Lamennais publie dès 1838 un texte intitulé « De l'esclavage moderne », l'attente par le gouvernement français de l'année 1965 pour ratifier la Convention de 1956 prévoyant l'abolition des institutions et pratiques analogues à l'esclavage et à la traite associée n'est certainement pas un hasard.

Enfin, parler de formes contemporaines d'esclavage se heurte à un préjugé façonné à travers le temps. D'un côté, l'esclavage renvoie à la figure étrangement « romantisée »[35] et révolue d'individus noirs, presque nus et enchainés, trimant dans les plantations de territoires lointains et tropicaux de coton, de sucre et de café. De l'autre, des situations susceptibles d'être qualifiées de formes contemporaines d'esclavage sont souvent regardées, aujourd'hui encore, comme la conséquence presque « naturelle » et donc « acceptable » de l'appartenance à certaines catégories de population et/ou à certains secteurs d'activités. Admettre qu'il puisse toujours exister en 2022 des formes d'esclavage, avec 129 000 victimes en France et 40,3 millions dans le monde en 2018 d'après Walk Free, paraît réveiller le spectre d'une « invasion migratoire » dans un pays qui a vu naître le principe du « sol libre » présenté précédemment. Il est intéressant de souligner ici que, dès l'abolition, les plus fervents défenseurs de ce principe, dont Schœlcher lui-même, se sont prononcés ou ont dû se prononcer pour une limitation de son application aux potentiels arrivants. Lors des travaux préparatoires à la Constitution de la IVe République de 1946, René Capitant défendra lui aussi une définition étroite de l'asile constitutionnel inscrit dans son préambule, par crainte de mettre un jour la France « dans l'obligation d'accueillir, non pas un nombre restreint d'individus, mais des populations entières, des milliers d'étrangers »[36]. Plus de 70 ans plus tard, le système français de l'asile, qui repose pourtant désormais largement sur la Convention de Genève de 1951 relative au statut des réfugiés, permet seulement d'accueillir à la marge les victimes de formes contemporaines (ou historiques) d'esclavage[37].

35 En référence aux œuvres picturales et littéraires du XIXe siècle. Voir, E. Saulnier Cassia, 'L'art contre l'esclavage ? Représentations graphiques de la première à la seconde abolition française' dans J.-P. Jean, S. Humbert, O. Pluen, A. Bendjebbar (dir.), *Justice et esclavages*, La documentation française, Paris 2021.

36 Propos cités dans, O. Pluen, 'De la « franchise du sol français » au droit d'asile pour cause d'esclavage : un principe inhérent à l'identité constitutionnelle de la France ?' (2020) 2:2 *Les Cahiers de la Justice* 183, p. 189.

37 *Ibid.*

3 Une appréhension perfectible sous le prisme utilitaire du passé

Si la difficulté de la France à appréhender le phénomène des formes contemporaines d'esclavage s'explique par le prisme déformant du passé, c'est paradoxalement dans ce même passé qu'elle semble en mesure de puiser les ressources destinées à lutter contre ce fléau. Ainsi, comme pour l'abolition de l'esclavage naguère, c'est par le biais de son ancrage international et régional, ainsi que par le recours aux leviers normatifs internes, qu'elle apparaît à même de poursuivre cet objectif. Et, comme naguère, une telle mobilisation ne saurait être efficace que sous réserve de trouver un prolongement dans la pratique.

3.1 *Une capacité de mobilisation liée à un ancrage international et régional important*

Bien que son droit interne doive encore être amélioré dans ce domaine, la France souscrit à un vaste réseau d'organisations et de textes internationaux et régionaux modernes en matière de lutte contre l'esclavage contemporain.

Au niveau de l'ONU (ou avant, la SDN) et au-delà des textes internationaux cités en première partie, la France a ratifié les Conventions de La Haye et de Genève relatives aux conflits armés[38], le Pacte international relatif aux droits civils et politiques et le Pacte international relatif aux droits économiques, sociaux et culturels de 1966, ainsi que la Convention des Nations Unies contre la criminalité transnationale organisée de 2000 (UNTOC) et son Protocole additionnel, dit de « Palerme », visant à prévenir, réprimer et punir la traite des personnes, en particulier des femmes et des enfants. Et si l'ONU n'a pas jugé utile d'ouvrir un bureau régional en Europe visant les États européens, hormis ceux du Sud-Est, il convient néanmoins de relever que la Conférence des Parties a adopté la résolution 9/1 ayant pour objet la création d'un mécanisme d'examen de la mise en œuvre de l'UNTOC et de ses protocoles, et la mise en place d'un groupe de travail contre la traite[39]. Un certain nombre de dispositions de la

38 Ces conventions et le Protocole additionnel I de la seconde ne reconnaissent pas explicitement l'interdiction de l'esclavage. Pour autant, les diverses dispositions des conventions de Genève de 1949 sur le travail des prisonniers de guerre et des civils en temps de guerre, ainsi que l'interdiction dans le Règlement de la Convention de La Haye de contraindre la population d'un territoire occupé à prêter serment à la Puissance ennemie présupposent cette interdiction.

39 Dans sa résolution 7/1, intitulée *Renforcement de l'application de la Convention des Nations Unies contre la criminalité transnationale organisée et des Protocoles s'y rapportant* (Vienne, 2022), la Conférence des Parties a décidé que le Groupe de travail sur la traite des personnes serait un élément constant de la Conférence.

Convention et du Protocole a ainsi été inséré dans la législation française[40]. Par ailleurs, la France participe aux partenariats mis en place par l'UNTOC, tels que l'Alliance 8.7 au sein de laquelle elle a demandé à bénéficier du statut de « pays éclaireur[41] » qui lui permet d'agir au-delà de ses frontières.

Au niveau de l'OIT, la France a ratifié toutes les conventions sur le travail forcé. Cela ne s'est cependant pas fait sans difficulté, puisque la Convention sur le travail forcé (n° 29) de 1930 se heurtait à celle de la SDN de 1926 relative à l'esclavage. En raison de la persistance de formes d'esclavage dans son empire colonial, la France a adopté une position ambiguë vis-à-vis de la question du travail forcé ou obligatoire, la conduisant finalement à s'abstenir de voter le texte final. En effet, la question principale en suspens était de savoir s'il y avait une différence de degré ou de nature entre l'esclavage et le travail forcé. Pour la France, le travail forcé n'était pas répréhensible et elle ne retenait cette expression que pour le bagne. Elle l'a tout de même ratifié en 1937, cinq ans après son entrée en vigueur. Depuis, elle a ratifié respectivement en 1969 et en 2016 la Convention n° 105 sur l'abolition du travail forcé de 1957 et le Protocole de 2014 relatif à la convention sur le travail forcé de 1930. La France informe régulièrement l'organisation de ses avancées sur la mise en œuvre des conventions et, à ce jour, aucune réclamation n'a été portée contre elle pour violation de ces dernières.

Sur le plan régional, la France est également un partenaire actif. Dans le cadre du Conseil de l'Europe d'une part, elle a ratifié en 2008 la Convention sur la lutte contre la traite des êtres humains du 16 mai 2005 et a accepté son mécanisme de suivi par le Groupe d'experts sur la lutte contre la traite des êtres humains (GRETA). Ainsi ce dernier a-t-il conclu, dans son troisième rapport sur la situation de la France en 2022, à des imperfections du système français concernant l'accès à la justice et les recours effectifs pour les victimes de la traite des êtres humains[42]. Il a également formulé des recommandations qui

40 Ex. : article 13 de la Convention sur la coopération internationale aux fins de confiscation et article 10 de la Convention sur la responsabilité des personnes morales, introduits dans le code de procédure pénale et le code pénal.

41 En qualité « d'éclaireur », la France s'engage à prendre toutes mesures internes législatives et réglementaires afin de mettre fin aux formes d'esclavages modernes et à la traite des êtres humains, de mettre en œuvre la Déclaration de Buenos Aires de la IVe Conférence mondiale sur l'éradication durable du travail des enfants (Buenos Aires, 14–16 novembre 2017) ou initiatives similaires, et à ratifier les normes internationales applicables en matière de droits de l'homme, y compris celles de travail. Voir ainsi la loi du 4 août 2021 de programmation relative au développement solidaire et à la lutte contre les inégalités mondiales.

42 La France avait déjà fait l'objet de critiques et de recommandations lors des 1er et 2nd rapports d'évaluation en 2013 et 2017 du groupe, portant sur la mise en œuvre de la Convention et notamment sur sa définition incomplète des formes modernes de la traite.

démontrent que la France doit encore progresser[43]. En effet, celle-ci étant un pays de destination des victimes de la traite des êtres humains, mais également un pays d'origine et de transit, le GRETA demande aux autorités françaises de prendre des mesures supplémentaires pour faciliter et garantir l'accès à la justice de toutes les victimes de la traite. Cet accès intègre l'allocation de montants plus conséquents alloués au titre de la réparation des préjudices qui s'appuierait sur la législation relative à la saisie et à la confiscation de biens, la spécialisation à la traite des enquêteurs et magistrats, l'amélioration des mesures de protection, le renforcement de la coopération avec le secteur privé et notamment la pleine mise en œuvre de la loi relative au devoir de vigilance des sociétés, ainsi que l'instauration d'un mécanisme national d'identification et d'orientation des victimes. À cela s'ajoutent des critiques quant à la faiblesse de la singularisation des situations des enfants, la défaillance des mesures d'assistance (le nombre d'hébergements adaptés et les fonds publics alloués aux associations d'aide aux victimes demeurent insuffisants) et la mobilisation relative de ressources financières et humaines permettant, par exemple, d'accompagner les plans nationaux contre la traite des êtres humains.

D'autre part, au sein de l'UE, la France participe indirectement au Groupe de coordination inter-institutions contre la traite des personnes (ICAT) dont elle est membre. Cette instance se présente comme un forum politique mandaté par l'Assemblée générale des Nations Unies pour améliorer la coordination entre les agences de l'organisation et d'autres organisations internationales compétentes afin de faciliter une approche globale de la prévention et de la lutte contre la traite des personnes. Plus directement, la France participe à la stratégie de la Commission européenne d'éradication de la traite des êtres humains[44] dont le dernier plan adopté couvre la période 2021–2025 et met l'accent sur la prévention de cette forme de criminalité, la traduction en justice des trafiquants et la protection et l'autonomisation des victimes.

3.2 *Une capacité de mobilisation progressive grâce à l'instrument normatif interne*

L'arrêt *Siliadin*, précité, avait été l'occasion pour la Cour EDH de relever que l'article 4 de la Convention éponyme faisait peser sur ses États parties des

43 GRETA, *L'accès à la justice et à des recours effectifs pour les victimes de la traite des êtres humains*, Rapport du troisième cycle d'évaluation, 18 février 2022, <https://www.coe.int/fr/web/anti-human-trafficking/-/greta-publishes-its-third-report-on-france>.

44 Ces stratégies s'appuient sur la Directive 2011/36/UE du Parlement européen et du Conseil du 5 avril 2011 concernant la prévention de la traite des êtres humains et la lutte contre ce phénomène ainsi que la protection des victimes, remplaçant la décision-cadre 2002/629/JAI du Conseil.

« obligations positives [commandant] la criminalisation et la répression effective » des formes contemporaines d'esclavage, consacrant ainsi l'effet horizontal de cette disposition[45]. La France a été visée par un nouvel arrêt de 2012, *C.N. et V. c. France*[46], en raison de la persistance d'une législation défaillante. Cette double condamnation en l'espace de sept ans, bien qu'elle n'ait pas réussi à susciter une volonté claire du gouvernement français de lutter contre ces atteintes, a au moins permis d'aboutir à un dispositif globalement cohérent, soit la loi du 5 août 2013.

Au regard du champ *ratione materiae* des formes contemporaines d'esclavage et des définitions afférentes, la loi du 5 août 2013 est venue clarifier l'état du droit interne. Le code pénal comprend ainsi désormais sept catégories d'atteinte, pouvant être classées par ordre de gravité, les cinq premières relevant du chapitre relatif aux « atteintes à la dignité de la personne » et les deux dernières de celui relatif aux « libertés de la personne ». Il s'agit : des conditions de travail et d'hébergement abusives (art. 225-13), des conditions de travail et d'hébergement contraires à la dignité humaine (art. 225-15), de la traite des êtres humains (art. 225-4-1), du travail forcé (art. 225-14-1), de la réduction en servitude (art. 225-14-2), de la réduction en esclavage (art. 224-1-A) et de son corollaire, l'exploitation d'une personne réduite en esclavage (art. 224-1-B). Au-delà de clarifier dans une certaine mesure ce que le droit français entend par « formes contemporaines d'esclavage », cet ensemble codifié de dispositions distingue ces dernières des « formes d'esclavage au titre du crime contre l'humanité ». En effet, une comparaison avec l'article 212-1 du même code permet de relever que ces deux formes peuvent coïncider en partie. « La réduction en esclavage », « l'emprisonnement ou toute autre forme de privation grave de liberté physique en violation des dispositions fondamentales du droit international », « la prostitution forcée, la grossesse forcée », ou « les autres actes inhumains de caractère analogue causant intentionnellement de grandes souffrances ou des atteintes graves à l'intégrité physique ou psychique », sont des éléments constitutifs du crime contre l'humanité. Ces formes se différencient toutefois par le fait que les actes doivent avoir été, dans le cadre du crime contre l'humanité, « commis en exécution d'un plan concerté à l'encontre d'un groupe de population civile dans le cadre d'une attaque généralisée ou systématique ». Plus problématique est en revanche la question de la définition donnée par l'article 224-1-B de la réduction en esclavage. Très largement inspirée de l'article

45 Cela signifie que le juge applique l'interdiction prévue à l'article 4 de la CEDH y compris dans les relations entre personnes privées, l'État étant dès lors comptable du respect par les personnes privées de cet interdit.

46 CEDH, 11 oct. 2012, *C. N. et V. c/ France*, n° 67724/09.

1er de la Convention de la SDN de 1926, cette disposition prévoit qu'elle correspond au « fait d'exercer à l'encontre d'une personne l'un des attributs du droit de propriété ». Cette définition lie malheureusement l'esclavage au droit de propriété, c'est-à-dire à un droit fondamental, qualifié de « naturel » par la Déclaration des droits de l'homme et du citoyen de 1789 et doté d'une valeur constitutionnelle en droit positif. Le risque est alors de sembler justifier l'existence de l'institution de l'esclavage dans le passé et que les esclavagistes aient pu être indemnisés lors de son abolition[47]. Elle peut également laisser penser que le code pénal criminalise uniquement l'esclavage faisant l'objet d'un acte légal et écrit de propriété, tolérant à l'inverse l'esclavage fondé sur d'autres instruments tels que la coutume ou des formes de contrainte physique ou psychologique. Malgré tout, cette définition présente pour l'heure l'avantage de pallier l'absence de reconnaissance par le droit positif international, européen et français de la notion de « formes (contemporaines) d'esclavage », en raison de la double acception[48] dont elle peut faire l'objet. Une première acceptation, stricte, désigne l'esclavage *stricto sensu* qui repose sur l'*abusus*, autrement dit le droit de disposer de la « chose ». Une seconde acceptation, large, permet au contraire de couvrir l'ensemble des formes d'esclavage, en mentionnant les autres attributs du droit de propriété que sont *fructus* – droit de percevoir les fruits de la « chose » – et l'*usus* – droit de faire usage de la « chose ». Si cette position des auteurs du présent rapport peut apparaître bien nuancée, elle l'est par défaut, faute pour le législateur français d'avoir su prendre, à leur sens, ses responsabilités. On peut en effet regretter ici que la suggestion faite par Christiane Taubira, alors ministre de la Justice, de mettre en place une commission chargée de réfléchir sur ces questions de définitions juridiques, au moment de l'examen de la proposition de loi devenue celle du 5 août 2013, ait été écartée au profit d'une adoption précipitée de ce texte qui s'est de ce fait limité à consacrer l'existant par crainte des conséquences qu'engendreraient de nouvelles définitions insuffisamment cadrées[49].

À propos ensuite des mesures destinées à lutter contre les formes contemporaines d'esclavage, celles-ci couvrent aujourd'hui de nombreux domaines, du fait

47 Consulter le site du CNRS qui a établi une base de données retraçant l'attribution et la circulation des titres d'indemnités au XIXe siècle dans les anciennes colonies esclavagistes françaises, <https://esclavage-indemnites.fr/public/>.

48 Voir, J. Allain, 'The international definition of slavery and its contemporary application' dans J.-F. Niort, O. Pluen (dir.), *Esclavage, traite et autres formes d'asservissement et d'exploitation, du Code Noir à nos jours*, Dalloz, Paris 2018.

49 Voir, O. Pluen, 'Le crime de réduction en esclavage, ou l'incrimination du "cœur de l'esclavage moderne" en droit pénal interne par la loi du 5 août 2013' (2015) 1:1 *Revue de science criminelle et de Droit Comparé* 29.

de la loi principalement, mais aussi du fait de la jurisprudence[50]. C'est ainsi que, pour la répression des auteurs d'actes d'esclavage, les cinq premières catégories d'atteintes évoquées précédemment sont qualifiées de délit et les deux dernières de crime, avec à chaque fois l'énoncé de circonstances aggravantes et des peines pouvant atteindre 30 ans de réclusion accompagnés d'une période de sûreté pour les deux formes les plus graves. En matière financière et de réparations, les dispositions du code de procédure pénale et la jurisprudence de la Cour de cassation permettent aux victimes de bénéficier de l'aide juridictionnelle gratuite dans certains cas ou de l'accompagnement d'une structure d'aide aux victimes, ainsi que de la réparation du préjudice moral et économique décidée par le juge judiciaire et la Commissions d'indemnisation des victimes d'infractions (CIVI).

En matière de protection des étrangers victimes de formes d'esclavage arrivant sur le territoire national, le code de l'entrée et de séjour des étrangers et du droit d'asile permet aux victimes de la traite des êtres humains de bénéficier d'un titre de séjour temporaire. Le tribunal administratif a progressivement reconnu sur le fondement du même code que des victimes de la traite des êtres humains et d'esclavage puissent se voir octroyer l'asile conventionnel issu de la Convention de Genève de 1951 sur le statut des réfugiés. Enfin, en matière de protection des Français et étrangers en dehors du territoire national, le juge judiciaire avait estimé dès 2006, à propos des conditions de travail d'une jeune nigériane au domicile nigérian d'un employeur britannique, que l'« ordre public international français s'oppose à ce qu'un employeur puisse se prévaloir des règles de conflit de juridiction … pour décliner la compétence des juridictions françaises[51] ». Onze ans plus tard, le Parlement a de son côté adopté la loi du 27 mars 2017 relative au devoir de vigilance des sociétés mères et des entreprises donneuses d'ordre, afin de lutter contre le recours indirect aux formes d'esclavage par les sociétés qui emploient au moins cinq mille salariés en leur sein et dans leurs filiales directes ou indirectes, dont le siège social est fixé sur le territoire français, ou au moins dix mille salariés en leur sein et dans leurs filiales directes ou indirectes, dont le siège social est fixé sur le territoire français ou à l'étranger. Concrètement, ce texte, qui rend une société comptable, y compris des activités de ses sous-traitants et fournisseurs, possède un double volet : préventif, avec l'obligation faite à ces entreprises d'élaborer et

50 *Ibid.* ; ainsi que F. Jault-Seseke et D. Porcheron, 'La protection en France de l'étranger, esclave domestique' (2020) 2:2 *Les Cahiers de la Justice* 231; V. Lasbordes de Virville, 'Quelle indemnisation pour les victimes des formes contemporaines d'esclavage ?' (2020) 2:2 *Les Cahiers de la Justice* 277; L. Moua, 'La lutte contre la traite dans les entreprises' (2020) 2:2 *Les Cahiers de la Justice* 245.

51 Cour de Cassation, Chambre sociale, 10 mai 2006, req. n° 03–46.593.

mettre en œuvre un « plan de vigilance » comprenant des « mesures de vigilance raisonnables propres à identifier les risques et à prévenir les atteintes graves envers les droits humains et les libertés fondamentales [...] » ; et répressif, en prévoyant l'engagement de leur responsabilité en cas de manquement[52]. Si cette loi, d'origine parlementaire, constitue une avancée remarquable, son évaluation par l'Assemblée nationale en 2022[53] peut donner le sentiment d'un résultat mitigé s'agissant de la lutte contre les formes d'esclavage, puisque l'expression y apparaît uniquement pour présenter l'exemple de la loi allemande du 16 juillet 2021 régissant les devoirs de diligence des entreprises dans les chaînes d'approvisionnement. Reste que la récente mise en cause du groupe de construction Vinci, en raison de soupçons de pratique d'esclavage moderne au Qatar[54], pourrait changer la donne.

3.3 *Une capacité à répondre aux besoins à parfaire dans la pratique*

Sur le plan pratique, l'effort des pouvoirs publics pour lutter contre les formes contemporaines d'esclavage s'est essentiellement traduit par une politique reposant sur deux leviers : l'un direct, avec la mise en place de plans nationaux d'action triennaux contre la traite des êtres humains ; l'autre indirect, avec la volonté de mieux faire connaître au public ce qu'est l'esclavage et de remédier à ses effets durables.

Concernant le levier « direct », le premier Plan national d'action, couvrant la période 2014–2016, comportait 23 mesures structurées au sein de trois priorités : identifier et accompagner les victimes de la traite; poursuivre et démanteler les réseaux de traite; et faire de la lutte contre la traite une politique publique à part entière. Le second Plan national pour les années 2019–2021, voulu plus ambitieux, se décline en 45 mesures articulées autour de 6 axes : informer et communiquer pour mieux prévenir le phénomène ; définir une stratégie d'identification des victimes ; protéger et accompagner les victimes de la traite ; intensifier la répression des auteurs; coordonner l'action publique de la lutte contre la traite ; et renforcer la coopération aux niveaux européen et international[55].

52 Voir, L. Moua, *supra* n. 50.

53 C. Dubost, D. Potier, rapport d'information n° 5124 du 24 février 2022 sur l'évaluation de la loi du 27 mars 2017 relative au devoir de vigilance des sociétés mères et des entreprises donneuses d'ordre, AN.

54 'Accusé d'esclavage moderne au Qatar, le groupe Vinci convoqué en vue d'une mise en examen', *Libération* (6 novembre 2022).

55 Premier Plan d'action national contre la traite des êtres humains (2014–2016) ; second Plan d'action national contre la traite des êtres humains (2019–2021), <https://www.egalite-femmes-hommes.gouv.fr/sites/efh/files/migration/2019/10/2e-Plan-action-traite-etres-humains.pdf>

Le résultat s'avère toutefois mitigé. Premièrement, tandis qu'il devrait exister une continuité entre les différents plans, deux ans ont séparé la fin du premier et le début du second, et le prochain n'est pas connu. Deuxièmement, les plans traduisent une volonté du gouvernement de singulariser l'appréhension des différentes formes contemporaines d'esclavage. Il le fait non seulement en se focalisant sur la seule traite des êtres humains au détriment de leur exploitation, mais en refusant également d'apporter une protection similaire à l'ensemble des victimes de celle-ci[56]. Dans son évaluation 2017 sur le premier Plan, la Commission nationale consultative des droits de l'homme (CNCDH)[57] a ainsi déploré que ce document privilégie la lutte contre la traite à des fins d'exploitation sexuelle et ait un champ d'application *ratione loci* essentiellement parisien[58]. Troisièmement, ces plans souffrent de leurs modalités d'élaboration et de pilotage. En effet, ceux-ci ont été confiés dès l'origine à la Mission interministérielle pour la protection des femmes contre les violences et la lutte contre la traite des êtres humains (MIPROF) placée auprès du ministre chargé du Droit des femmes. Et si, en 2014–2015 des fonctions de coordinateur du plan existaient, elles ont été remplacées en 2016 par un comité de coordination dirigé directement par le secrétaire de la MIPROF. Quatrièmement, dans le communiqué présentant son avis 2019 sur le deuxième Plan, la CNCDH a expressément déploré que celui-ci n'était « pas à la hauteur des enjeux»[59]. En des termes particulièrement vifs, la Commission a ensuite souligné que « des écueils structurels majeurs font obstacle à toute application concrète de ce plan … : sans calendrier ni budget, sa mise en œuvre est en effet illusoire », avant de recommander « vivement que le comité de coordination… définisse un plan stratégique annuel »[60].

Parmi les faiblesses de ces plans, l'une suppose que l'on s'y intéresse plus particulièrement : celle des statistiques. Depuis 2016, la MIPROF et l'Observatoire national de la délinquance et des réponses pénales (ONDRP), remplacés depuis 2021 par le Service statistique ministériel de la sécurité

56 Voir, B. Boissard, 'L'absorption de la notion de formes d'esclavage dans celle de "traite des êtres humains"' (2020) 2:2 *Les Cahiers de la Justice* 207.

57 Rapporteur indépendant depuis 2014 en application de la directive 2011/36/UE précitée et transposée par la loi du 5 août 2013 précitée.

58 CNCDH, 'Évaluation de la mise en œuvre du Plan d'action national contre la traite des êtres humains (2014–2016)', (06.07.2017), <https://www.cncdh.fr/publications/evaluation-du-plan-national-daction-national-sur-la-lutte-contre-la-traite-des-etres>.

59 CNCDH, 'Avis sur le 2nd Plan d'action national contre la traite des êtres humains (2019–2021)', JORF n°0279, (01.12.2019), <https://www.cncdh.fr/publications/avis-sur-le-2nd-plan-daction-national-contre-la-traite-des-etres-humains-2019-2021>.

60 *Ibid.*

intérieure (SSMSI), publient des chiffres relatifs au profil des victimes de traite accompagnées par les associations reconnues dans ce domaine, et l'ONDRP fait de même depuis 2019 pour les victimes et auteurs de traite identifiés par les administrations françaises. Mais ces données, très éloignées des estimations de *Walk Free*, permettent seulement de révéler la face « émergée de l'iceberg ». C'est en partie la raison pour laquelle la CNCDH a fortement recommandé, dans ses avis 2017 et 2019 précités, d'aller plus loin en créant un « véritable mécanisme national pour l'identification et l'accompagnement des victimes de traite et d'exploitation »[61], inspiré du modèle britannique. Reste que, pour gagner en fiabilité, il conviendrait qu'un tel dispositif intègre, au-delà d'indicateurs par forme d'exploitation ou secteur d'activité, des indicateurs tenant notamment compte des origines des intéressés. Or, tandis que l'utilité ou le bien-fondé d'une telle prise en compte ne pose plus question dans d'autres pays, le débat demeure vif en France. En France, le principe est l'interdiction, mais des exceptions sont admises dès lors qu'elles sont justifiées par l'existence d'un but légitime[62].

S'agissant du levier « indirect », les pouvoirs publics se sont efforcés de réconcilier la France avec son passé esclavagiste et d'essayer de mieux intégrer les descendants d'esclaves dans la communauté nationale. Pour faire progresser la connaissance du fléau qu'a été l'esclavage colonial, le pays s'est doté en 2004 d'un Comité national pour la mémoire et l'histoire de l'esclavage (CNMHE), conformément à la « loi Taubira », afin de « proposer, sur l'ensemble du territoire national, des lieux et des actions qui garantissent la pérennité de la mémoire de ce crime à travers les générations »[63]. Puis, en 2006, le Président Chirac a demandé au poète martiniquais Edouard Glissant de réfléchir à la création d'une institution autonome dédiée à cette mémoire et qui s'est concrétisée avec le Mémorial-ACTe, inauguré en 2015 en Guadeloupe. Dix ans plus tard, le Président Hollande a confié à son tour à l'ancien Premier ministre

61 CNCDH, Évaluation 2017, *supra* n. 58 ; et Avis 2019, *supra* n. 59.

62 Suite à l'adoption de la loi relative à la maîtrise de l'immigration, à l'intégration et à l'asile de 2007, le Conseil constitutionnel a été saisi de la possibilité de faire des statistiques ethniques. Le Conseil a censuré cette disposition, alors qu'il était proposé de faire contrôler cet outil par la Commission nationale de l'informatique et des libertés, commission indépendante. Si la collecte de données relatives à « l'origine ethnique ou à la race » sont interdites, la collecte de données se fondant sur le nom, l'origine géographique, la nationalité antérieure à la nationalité française, ou le « *ressenti d'appartenance* » dans le cadre de conduite d'études, est autorisée, car ces données sont considérées comme objectives et répondant de ce fait à un but légitime.

63 Loi n° 83-550 du 30 juin 1983 relative à la commémoration de l'abolition de l'esclavage et en hommage aux victimes de l'esclavage, art. unique.

du Bénin Lionel Zinsou une mission de préfiguration destinée à transformer le CNMHE en une fondation reconnue d'utilité publique. Il en est résulté la Fondation pour la mémoire de l'esclavage en 2019, dont la présidence a été confiée à l'ancien Premier ministre Jean-Marc Ayrault, avec pour triple mission de contribuer :

1. à l'histoire de la France (en faisant progresser la connaissance sur la traite et l'esclavage, les résistances qu'ils ont suscitées et le combat pour leurs abolitions en développant un récit national partagé et en expliquant la diversité française) ;
2. à la culture née de l'esclavage et de la créolisation (en célébrant la richesse des cultures, en montrant comment elles ont irrigué la culture et le patrimoine français, en promouvant les créations culturelles et artistiques contemporaines des sociétés issues de l'esclavage) ;
3. et à la citoyenneté (en promouvant les valeurs du combat pour l'émancipation dans la société actuelle : liberté, égalité, fraternité, en luttant contre les discriminations, le racisme, les préjugés et les formes contemporaines d'esclavage, enfin en organisant des cérémonies et des évènements).

Parallèlement, il faut continuer à se poser avec acuité la question des discriminations vis-à-vis des descendants d'esclaves ultra-marins et des moyens pour y remédier. Une délégation interministérielle pour la visibilité et l'égalité des chances des Français d'outre-mer[64] a ainsi été créée auprès du Premier ministre. Sa mission est, d'une part, de promouvoir et de valoriser les Outremers français sur l'ensemble du territoire national et à l'étranger, dans les domaines économique, social, culturel et sportif, et, d'autre part, de prévenir les difficultés spécifiques que rencontrent sur le territoire métropolitain les Français d'Outremer et de faciliter leurs relations avec leurs collectivités d'origine. Mais un rapport d'information parlementaire de 2019 sur les discriminations dans les départements d'Outre-mer[65] faisait encore état, selon son titre phare, de «La persistance d'inégalités et de discrimination », formulant en conséquence des propositions rarement nouvelles : élaborer une mémoire commune avec l'Hexagone et promouvoir des politiques volontaristes. Parmi ces dernières, il est possible d'évoquer les suivantes : développer des tests de situation encore insuffisamment utilisés en France en y intégrant des profils ultra-marins ; sanctuariser le volet Outre-mer au sein du Plan national d'action

64 Cette délégation remonte, avec une appellation qui a évolué, à 2007.

65 J. Manin, M. Petiti, et C. Rilhac, 'Rapport d'information n° 1793 au nom de la délégation aux outre-mer' (21.03.2019), <https://www.assemblee-nationale.fr/dyn/15/rapports/om/l15b1793_rapport-information#>.

contre le racisme ; élaborer des textes règlementaires fixant les conditions requises pour accéder à des droits, comme le congé bonifié ou les mutations, afin que les règles soient uniformes et connues de tous ; favoriser des programmes de soutien spécifiques et innovants pour lutter contre le décrochage scolaire ; et favoriser l'insertion socio-professionnelle, notamment par le service militaire adaptée (SMA).

Il n'en demeure pas moins que les progrès réalisés par les pouvoirs publics restent ici lents et parfois contradictoires, comme l'ont illustré de façon frappante la suppression de la chaine des Outremer « France ô » en 2020[66] et le résultat de l'étude « MELODI » (Mesures locales des discrimination) en 2021 dans les 4 départements d'outre-mer dans le secteur de la restauration. Le constat est assez accablant : les candidats ultramarins sont systématiquement discriminés par un candidat hexagonal dans le cadre d'une embauche dans un restaurant local (ultramarin). Trois profils de candidats fictifs ont été déterminés : un candidat originaire des DOM, qui a été formé et vit sur son territoire natif ; un candidat natif des DOM formé localement et qui vit dans un quartier prioritaire ; et un candidat natif de Paris qui vit et qui a été formé à Paris. Les candidats fictifs sont tous âgés de 22 ans, disposent du niveau de formation et du même niveau de formation professionnelle[67].

Encore en 2020, le meurtre d'un homme noir, George Floyd, par un policier blanc aux États-Unis a provoqué une onde de choc qui s'est propagée jusque dans les populations descendantes d'esclaves des « anciennes colonies » françaises. Cela s'est notamment traduit, dans ces territoires, par la destruction de statues associées au passé esclavagiste, dont une de l'abolitionniste Schœlcher à Fort-de-France, sur le socle de laquelle étaient pourtant gravés les mots : « Nulle terre française ne peut plus porter d'esclave ». Ce sentiment d'une promesse non tenue dans l'Hexagone et dans les territoires ultramarins semble malheureusement avoir été conforté ces deux dernières années, avec la

66 Cette chaîne faisait partie de la télévision généraliste française de service public France Télévisions ; elle a succédé à RFO Sat en 2005. Les raisons avancées sont son faible taux d'audience. Néanmoins, France Télévisions s'est engagée aussi à accorder une place plus importante aux programmes ultramarins sur ses autres antennes.

67 'Les candidats ultramarins systématiquement discriminés dans l'accès à l'embauche selon une étude', Outremers 360 (15.12.2021), <https://outremers360.com/bassin-atlantique-appli/les-candidats-ultramarins-systematiquement-discrimines-dans-lacces-a-lembauche-selon-une-etude>.

multiplication des cas d'ultra-marins ou personnes d'autres origines traitées[68] ou représentées sous les traits d'esclaves[69]…

Références académiques

A. Bendjebbar, 'De l'esclavage au travail forcé au temps de la SDN' dans J-F Niort et O. Pluen (dir.), *Esclavage, traite et autres formes d'asservissement et d'exploitation, du Code Noir à nos jours*, Dalloz, Paris 2018.

A. Castaldo, *Codes noirs, de l'esclavage aux abolitions*, Dalloz, Paris 2006.

A. Charles-Nicolas et B. P. Bowser (dir.) *L'esclavage : quel impact sur la psychologie des populations ?*, Idem Edition, Paris 2018.

A. Lemaire, 'La loi de 2013 contre la traite et le parcours dans le cadre de la Commission des lois de l'Assemblée nationale' dans S. O'dy (dir.), *Traite des Êtres Humains, esclavage moderne et travail forcé en France'*, CCEM, Paris 2020.

B. Boissard, 'L'absorption de la notion de formes d'esclavage dans celle de "traite des êtres humains"' (2020) 2:2 *Les Cahiers de la Justice* 207.

C. Gauvard, 'Introduction. Le temps long de l'esclavage en Europe : histoire d'un refoulement' dans J.-P. Jean, S. Humbert, O. Pluen, A. Bendjebbar, (dir.), *Justice et esclavages*, La Documentation Francaise, Paris 2021, pp. 11–17.

E. Fontaine, *Traumatisme historique et son expression psychopathologique dans le transgénérationnel (violences conjugales) au sein des familles réunionnaises* (thèse de doctorat en Psychologie), Université de Rouen 2020.

F. Jault-Seseke et D. Porcheron, 'La protection en France de l'étranger, esclave domestique', (2020) 2:2 *Les Cahiers de la Justice* 231.

J. Allain, 'The international definition of slavery and its contemporary application' dans J.-F. Niort et O. Pluen (dir.), *Esclavage, traite et autres formes d'asservissement et d'exploitation, du Code Noir à nos jours*, Dalloz, Paris 2018.

J.-F. Niort, *Le Code Noir: Idées reçues sur un texte symbolique*, Le Cavalier Bleu, Paris 2015.

J.-F. Niort et O. Pluen, 'Introduction générale' dans J.-F. Niort et O. Pluen (dir.), *Esclavage, traite et autres formes d'asservissement et d'exploitation, du Code Noir à nos jours*, Dalloz, Paris 2018.

68 Voir, pour un chauffeur de bus : B. Derveaux, *Le Parisien*, 4 février 2022 ; pour des livreurs à domicile : F. Aizicovici, *Le Monde*, 18 juin 2021 ; ou une caissière de magasin : *Sud Ouest*, 7 juin 2021.

69 En 2020, l'hebdomadaire d'extrême-droite *Valeurs actuelles* avait dépeint la députée Danièle Obono sous les traits d'une esclave dans un récit-fiction. L'année suivante, il a été condamné pour injure publique à caractère raciste.

L. Moua, 'La lutte contre la traite dans les entreprises' (2020) 2:2 *Les Cahiers de la Justice* 245.

L. Salin-Molins, *Le Code noir ou le calvaire de Canaan*, PUF, Paris 1987.

M. Dorigny et B. Gainot, *Atlas des esclavages, de l'Antiquité à nos jours,* Autrement, Paris 2022.

M. Erpelding, *Le droit international antiesclavagiste des "nations civilisées" (1815–1945)*, LGDJ-IUV, Paris 2017.

O. Pluen, 'De la « franchise du sol français » au droit d'asile pour cause d'esclavage : un principe inhérent à l'identité constitutionnelle de la France ?' (2020) 2:2 *Les Cahiers de la Justice* 183.

O. Pluen, '1315–1946 : le mythe d'un "Empire" français sans esclaves' dans J.-P. Jean, S. Humbert, O. Pluen, A. Bendjebbar (dir.), *Justice et esclavages,* La Documentation Francaise, Paris 2021, pp. 22–44.

O. Pluen, 'Constitutionnaliser l'interdiction de l'esclavage et des autres formes d'exploitation des êtres humains : un impératif contemporain' dans J.-F. Niort et O. Pluen (dir.), *Esclavage, traite et autres formes d'asservissement et d'exploitation, du Code Noir à nos jours*, Dalloz, Paris 2018.

O. Pluen, 'Le crime de réduction en esclavage, ou l'incrimination du "cœur de l'esclavage moderne" en droit pénal interne par la loi du 5 août 2013' (2015) 1:1 *Revue de science criminelle et de Droit Comparé* 29.

S. O'Dy, '25 ans de combat du Comité contre l'esclavage moderne' dans S. O'Dy (dir.), *Traite des Êtres Humains, esclavage moderne et travail forcé en France*, CCEM, Paris 2020.

S. Peabody, *There are no slaves in France: The political culture of race and slavery in the Ancien Régime*, Oxford University Press, New York 1996.

V. Lasbordes De Virville, 'Quelle indemnisation pour les victimes des formes contemporaines d'esclavage ?' (2020) 2:2 *Les Cahiers de la Justice* 277.

‘Othering’ Slavery: Germany’s Invisible Historical and Legal Involvement

Heiner Fechner

1 Introduction

“Poland shall be treated like a colony; the Poles are to be the slaves of the Greater German world empire”, Hans Frank, Hitler’s personal lawyer, the highest legal authority of the NS-regime (*Reichsrechtsführer*) and general governor of occupied Poland during World War II (1939–45), pronounced on the 3rd of October 1939.[1] Slavery was a central feature of Nazi Germany. Hitler’s election as Reich Chancellor in 1933 was not the starting point for slavery in Germany, though, and the legacies of slavery in Germany have been only partly reappraised so far from both a sociological and jurisprudential perspective.

To relate modern Germany with slavery is a recent issue. Until recently, German historians denied the existence of slaves in Germany altogether. “The Germans perceived them from afar”, a leading German historian wrote in 2000.[2] Against that, recent research has reconstructed the reception of enslaved persons by German aristocratic courts and armies in the context of trading humans of African origin. “The Holy Roman Empire [the dominion of the German emperors 962–1806] (…) was not a slave society, but it was definitely a society *with slaves*”.[3] University of Bremen’s historian Mallinckrodt observes “not merely individual cases but a system”.[4] For German territories, the historian Michael Zeuske describes the presence of servants with

1 G. Eisenblätter, *Grundlinien der Politik des Reiches gegenüber dem Generalgouvernement 1939–1945, Diss* Frankfurt a.M. Universität, Frankfurt 1969, p. 113; Translation by R. Bauer, *The Construction of a National Socialist Europe During the Second World War: How the New Order Took Shape*, Routledge, London 2019, p. 114.

2 J. Osterhammel, *Sklaverei und die Zivilisation des Westens,* Carl-Friedrich-von-Siemens-Stiftung, München 2000, p. 7.

3 R. von Mallinckrodt, J. Köstlbauer and S. Lentz, ‘Beyond Exceptionalism – Traces of Slavery and the Slave Trade in Early Modern Germany, 1650–1850’ in R. von Mallinckrodt, J. Köstlbauer and S. Lentz (eds), *Beyond Exceptionalism*, De Gruyter, Berlin 2021, p. 18.

4 R. von Mallinckrodt, ‘There Are No Slaves in Prussia?’ in F. Brahm and E. Rosenhaft (eds), *Slavery Hinterland: Transatlantic slavery and continental Europe, 1680–1850*, The Boydell Press, Woodbridge 2016, p. 121.

 | DOI:10.1163/9789004723801_009

black skin colour (*Kammermohr*) as "slaves without slavery", with systematic research concerning their situation still missing.[5]

I argue in this text that slavery – as understood from a sociological perspective – has been a common thread of German modernity serving economic development and power relations both externally and internally, whereas law, while institutionalising relations of slavery, in most cases was rather used for obfuscating.[6] Thus, slavery has not only been a relevant factor for Germany's economic system over the last 500 years, but one in which the law functionally worked towards institutionalising human exploitation based on coercion, protecting exploiters and profiteers, and steering the historical revision of these phenomena. The predecessors of the in 1871 founded German Reich also profited enormously from the transatlantic slave trade. Moreover, slavery in Germany was not only about profits – it strongly reflects narratives of racial and moral supremacy emerging in modernity.

In order to develop a critical understanding of the evolution and steps in the abolition of slavery, I use a sociological understanding of the term slavery as a point of departure, analysing slavery, forced labour and similar severe forms of exploitation. In this respect, I will not primarily use the ownership-based definition as enshrined in Art. 1 (1) Slavery Convention 1926. As Orlando Patterson shows, the legal term of ownership or property (dominion), as developed in Roman Law and adopted in German private law, rather resulted from the pre-existence of slavery and the specific needs concerning the legal conditions of a slave-based economy than preceding it.[7] It therefore neither covers the common essential features of the historical institution of slavery as it existed in virtually the whole world, nor is it capable of measuring the success of abolition. I therefore use the terminology elaborated by Patterson, who defines slavery as "the permanent, violent domination of natally alienated and generally dishonoured persons", calling natal alienation also "social death".[8] Natal alienation or social death refers to the non-recognition of institutionalised bonds such as inherited status, kinship, marriage etc.

5 M. Zeuske, *Handbuch Geschichte der Sklaverei: Eine Globalgeschichte von den Anfängen bis zur Gegenwart*, (2nd edn) De Gruyter Oldenbourg, Berlin 2020, p. 860.

6 I use the term 'othering' to describe a continuity, by which I do not mean to imply a continuity of phenomena or, indeed, an awareness of slavery on the part of the actors for the entire period covered. I use "othering" fully aware of the many different uses that the term has found in different disciplines in constructing "otherness" in terms of race, gender, class, caste etc., among others.

7 O. Patterson, *Slavery and Social Death: A Comparative Study: with a New Preface*, Harvard University Press, Cambridge 2018 [1982].

8 *Ibid.*, p. 13.

Instead of the rather unclear term 'modern slavery', for the aim of covering contemporary forms of forced exploitation I use 'servitude' defined by Patterson and Zhuo as an umbrella term, understood "as that condition in which the work, service or relationships of another person are not freely offered or, if voluntarily initiated, cannot be left or refused, and are maintained under the threat of physical or psychological coercion, violence or some other penalty".[9] The term, embracing ILO's definition of forced labour, extends this to forced marriage, thus essentially covering the phenomena called 'modern slavery' by the ILO and others.

2 Use of Slavery and Equivalent Institutions in German History

Germany's historical relationship to slavery and servitude and their legal treatment can be elaborated through six particularly noteworthy phenomena, which are developed further below, that have produced legal responses in varying degrees. The transatlantic slave trade (1500–1850) enabled the development of various economic sectors (2.1.). An advisory opinion of Prussia's supreme court (*Kammergericht*) of 1780 sheds light on the legal treatment of Africans brought to Germany as enslaved persons (2.2). The conceptual background of the advisory opinion is best understood with knowledge of the treatment of peasants in Prussia under serfdom, which makes the structural foundations of that society which interlinked traditional and new forms of servitude visible (2.3). In modern Germany, the 15th and 16th centuries witnessed in houses of correction or prisons (*Zuchthäuser*) the emergence of 'extrusive slavery', as a subcategory of (public) slavery theorised by Patterson, which linked punishment with 'education to work' and exploitation (2.4). It is not hard to recognise similarities and conceptual continuities to the time of Germany as a colonial power between 1884 and 1918, where legal treatment of traditional slavery and state-sponsored servitude can be observed (2.5). Finally, building upon these experiences and concepts, the Third Reich (1933–45) built up a complex regime of slavery and servitude from its very beginning, with a war economy based on slave labour.

2.1 *Transatlantic Slavery, Slave Trade and Slaves of African Origin*

Neither the Holy Roman Empire (800–1806; since 1512 with the appendix: 'of the Germanic Nations') and its principalities nor the German Confederation

---

9 O. Patterson and X. Zhuo, 'Modern trafficking, slavery, and other forms of servitude' (2018) 44 *Annual Review of Sociology* 407, p. 410.

(1815–1866) were among the major overseas colonisers before the Scramble for Africa began. Nevertheless, there was direct official involvement in the slavery-based economies at the very beginning of colonisation of the Americas as concession in slave trading to a German trade company by Emperor Charles v, and in a comparatively short episode of Brandenburg (later Prussia) establishing of a slavery-based trading company. Above all, German economic development between the 15th and 19th century was strongly integrated into the triangular transatlantic trade system.

The first episode of official and legally relevant participation of German actors in the transatlantic slave trade began in 1528, when Emperor Charles V., also king of Spain, passed the 'privilege' or monopoly (*asiento*) of selling 4.000 enslaved persons within four years to the colonists in the Spanish colonies,[10] a third of them female, in return for 20.000 ducats for the Crown. The beneficiary was the southern German banking and merchant company Welser. Underlying was one of several contracts between the Crown and the Welser. This contractual relation – the second asiento of the Spanish Empire – had a relevant influence on the legal structuring of the emerging *asiento* system.[11]

A second direct involvement was Brandenburg's (since 1701: Prussia's) founding of the Brandenburg African (later: African-American) Company,[12] which existed from 1682 to 1718. It was involved in the slave trade based on the Brandenburg colonies of trading posts in Africa, such as the Brandenburg/ Prussian Gold Coast, and a trading post on the Caribbean Island St. Thomas leased from the Danish Crown.[13] German trade with African actors from the Gold Coast consisted in selling cloth, iron and iron products, weapons, alcohol and other mostly European, but also Indian products in return for gold, enslaved persons, ivory and some other commodities. According to estimates, the Company temporarily reached about 15% of Gold Coast trade.[14] Slave trade was considered the "fundament of our company" as the mastermind behind

10 In 1529, additional 800 enslaved persons were allowed to be brought to Venezuela.

11 Cf. K. Haebler, *Die überseeischen Unternehmungen der Welser und ihrer Gesellschafter* Hirschfeld, Leipzig 1903, pp. 52–59, 70–89; J. Denzer, *Die Konquista der Augsburger Welser-Gesellschaft in Südamerika (1528–1556): Historische Rekonstruktion, Historiografie und lokale Erinnerungskultur in Kolumbien und Venezuela*, C.H. Beck, München 2005.

12 A trade company comparable to the British, Dutch etc. joint-stock companies such as the British East India Company.

13 C. Koslofsky and R. Zaugg, 'Ship's Surgeon Johann Peter Oettinger: A Hinterlander in the Atlantic Slave Trade, 1682–1696' in F. Brahm and E. Rosenhaft (eds), *Slavery Hinterland: Transatlantic slavery and continental Europe, 1680–1850*, The Boydell Press, Woodbridge 2016, pp. 26–30.

14 A. Weindl, *Die Kurbrandenburger im 'atlantischen System': 1650–1720*, Universität zu Köln, Köln 2001, pp. 31–32.

the Brandenburg-Prussian endeavour, the Dutch merchant and shipowner Benjamin Raule wrote.[15] In 124 voyages, 23.583 enslaved persons had been bought, while 19.240 were sold in the Caribbean.[16] The Prussian slave trade ended finally due to England's predominance in the Caribbean, which made Prussian smuggling of enslaved persons to Spanish and other colonies almost impossible, and lack of economic conditions to process colonial products in early 18th century Prussia.[17]

The triangular trade system consisted of four stages of transatlantic trade.[18] First, goods were manufactured in Europe and shipped to (mostly west) African countries. Second, these commodities were exchanged in barter trade against slaves who were shipped to the West Indies and the Americas. Third, the slaves were sold to serve primarily in the production of sugar cane and cotton, products which were then shipped to Europe. Finally, European manufacturers processed these raw materials for both domestic markets and export.

The German economy participated in all four stages from the very beginning. German manufacturers and home workers produced linen, a key product in early slave trading before cotton took over the market, and weaponry, among others. German traders, shipping companies and bankers were involved in financing and organising the slave trade, based primarily in London and Bordeaux.[19]

While Banking houses such as the Baring Brothers (London, with the founders originating from Bremen) were among the most important slave traders, German trader families such as Romberg were involved in virtually all stages of triangular trade, from the production of German linen as trading goods for slaves over the slave trade and the operation of sugar plantations in Saint-Domingue (Haiti) to sugar production in Hamburg.[20] Others settled in the colonies and organized the slave-based colonial economy. For instance, at the outset of the 19th century, Germans made up around one-third of Europeans (about 1.000) in slave-based Dutch Suriname[21] and were registered as

15 B. Raule, 'letter No. 118', in R. Schück, *Brandenburg-Preußens Kolonial-Politik unter dem Großen Kurfürsten und seinen Nachfolgern: (1647–1721)*, Grunow, Leipzig 1898, p. 303.

16 M. Zeuske, above n. 5, p. 755.

17 A. Weindl, above n. 14, p. 71.

18 K. Weber, 'Deutschland, Der Atlantische Sklavenhandel Und Die Plantagenwirtschaft Der Neuen Welt' (2009) 7:1 *Journal of Modern European History* 37.

19 *Ibid., passim.*

20 *Ibid.*

21 C. Haarnack, "Nachrichten von Surinam: Representations of a Former Dutch Colony in German Travel Literature, 1790–1900", in A. E. Martin, L. Missinne, and B. van Dam (eds), *Travel Writing in Dutch and German, 1790–1930: Modernity, Regionality, Mobility*, Routledge, Taylor & Francis, New York 2017.

slave owners in Danish and British colonies in the Americas. About 180.000 Germans returned between 1602 and 1795 with experience in slave trade from service in the Dutch *Vereenigde Oostindische Compagnie*.[22]

The legal treatment of the slave trade in Germany began in insurance legislation. The older regulation was designed as a reaction to piracy and seizure of ships by northern African 'Barbary corsairs' between the 16th and 18th centuries, for instance, in the 1731 Hamburg Insurance Ordinance.[23]

The first and only explicit regulation in German law of treating slaves as trade goods can be found in the General State Laws for the Prussian States (ALR) adopted in 1794. Concerning insurance of ships and shiploads, the law stated that slaves were to be treated like perishable goods. If perishable goods were not specified in the description of the shipload, the insurance "did not have to pay damages resulting from the perishable quality" (sec. 2048). According to sec. 2049, "[t]he same applies if slaves or living animals are not specified, but are only included in the insurance in general terms". Slaves were thus equated to animals and with them to goods, and thereby differentiated legally from human beings, whose insurance of life and freedom received particular regulation in sec. 2050f. The insurance regulation was repealed by the Commercial Code 1861.[24]

The German states, and later, the German Empire were involved in various international conventions and declarations on the abolition of the slave trade without taking a decisive role in the matter. Prussia was involved in the drafting of the Declaration on the Abolition of the Slave Trade of the Congress of Vienna 1815, which also became part of the Vienna Congress Act.[25] Prohibition of slave trade started in 1837 with the three independent port cities Bremen, Hamburg and Lübeck, which joined the British and French conventions of 1831 and 1833 on slave trade, followed by Prussia in 1844.[26] Here, the prohibition of slave trade can be interpreted as a reaction to the growing control of the sea and pressure by the British navy after prohibition of slave trade in 1807 and slavery in 1833.[27] The same direction was taken in the much more comprehensive

22 R. von Mallinckrodt, J. Köstlbauer and S. Lentz, above n. 3, pp. 9–10.

23 Der Stadt Hamburg Assecuranz-und Haverey-Ordnung, 10.09.1731, Hamburg: König, 1731.

24 Allgemeines Deutsches Handelsgesetzbuch, 31.05.1861, BGBL. Norddt. Bd. 1861, p. 601.

25 A. Forrest, 'The Hundred Days, the Congress of Vienna and the Atlantic Slave Trade' in K. Astbury and M. Philp (eds), *Napoleon's hundred days and the politics of legitimacy*, Palgrave Macmillan, Cham 2018.

26 S. Lentz, '"No German Ship Conducts Slave Trade!" the Public Controversy About German Participation in the Slave Trade During the 1840s' in R. von Mallinckrodt, J. Köstlbauer and S. Lentz (eds), *Beyond Exceptionalism*, De Gruyter, Berlin/Boston 2021, p. 290.

27 F. von Martitz, 'Das internationale System zur Unterdrückung des afrikanischen Sklavenhandels in seinem heutigen Bestande' (1885) 1:1 *Archiv des öffentlichen Rechts* 3, pp. 59–68.

'Treaty between Prussia, Austria, Russia, France and Great Britain concerning the Trade with African Negroes' of 20 December 1841,[28] which regulated in detail rules and procedures to suppress transatlantic slave trade.[29] It was transformed into national law by the 'Ordinance concerning the Punishment of Commerce with Negro Slaves' of 8 July 1844.[30]

Bremen's 1837 penal law against the slave trade,[31] Germany's first criminalisation of slavery-related economic activity, illustrates the motivation behind this legislation. The preamble emphasises the city-state's view that the slave trade had always been 'completely alien' to Bremen's commerce and shipping, whereas the objective of the law would be to bring legislation in line with the treaties between the greater sea powers.[32] The law's applicability was restricted to the supply of the Americas with "negro slaves from the African coast". In practice, the law was especially used to prevent economic damages to Bremen's and Hamburg's economies, as criminal cases against the captains, owners, helmsmen and others concerned with the barks *Julius & Eduard*, *Louise* and *Echo* show, which, according to British navy officers presumedly were involved in slave trading but in all cases found not guilty by German courts.[33] The acquittals served especially to spread the belief in the legend of abstinence from slave trade in the Hanseatic cities.[34] Although much legislation existed to prohibit the slave trade, the handling of German legislators did not suggest a serious will to combat slavery and similar practices in earnest.

2.2 *Legal Treatment of Slaves of African Origin in Germany*

The *Kammergericht* in Berlin, Prussia's highest court, had to decide in 1780 whether chattel slavery was illegal and migration to Prussia resulted in the freedom of slaves.[35] On the occasion of a petition of a black enslaved person

---

28 PGS 1844, p. 371.

29 The treaty was renewed for the German Empire by treaty with Great Britain of 29.3.1879, RGBl. 1880, p. 100.

30 PGS 1844, p. 399.

31 Strafgesetz wider den Sklavenhandel, 20.2.1837, printed in J.K. Gildemeister, *Verfahren und Erkenntniß des Bremischen Obergerichts in Untersuchungssachen wider den Capitain des Bremischen Schiffs Julius und Eduard und Cons. wegen Sklavenhandels ; Nach den Acten dargest*, Heyse, Bremen 1842, p. 2.

32 The law effectively refers to the treaties of 1831 and 1833 between Great Britain and France (cf. An Act for carrying into effect Two Conventions with the King of the French for suppressing the Slave Trade, 3&4 Will IV c. 72).

33 S. Lentz, above n. 26.

34 M. Ressel, 'Hamburg und die Niederelbe im atlantischen Sklavenhandel der Frühen Neuzeit' (2015) 66–67 *Werkstatt Geschichte* 75, p. 94.

35 Kammergericht, 12.07.1780, Beyträge zu der juristischen Litteratur in den Preußischen Staaten 1780, op. 6, pp. 296–310.

who had been bought by a Prussian nobleman in Denmark, and in the absence of an administrative court, the king asked the *Kammergericht* to deliver a legal opinion.

The *Kammergericht* saw natural law and customary international law (*ius gentium*) coincide concerning the legitimacy of slavery. *Servitus/Sklaverei* (slavery) and *Knechtschaft* (serfdom) were used synonymously. Slaves, it said, could be acquired by subjugation in war, by contract in case of need (peonage), by decision of a court, and by birth. Natural and Roman law thus would not require masters to free their slaves, whereas people trying to liberate slaves against the will of the owner would violate natural law.[36]

From the legality of enslaving people, the court deduced the lack of necessity of granting freedom. Although among Christian nations, enslavement in war would be considered illegal, the enslavement concerning 'Turks, Tartars and Blackamoors' was exempted since Muslim peoples did the same to Christians.[37] The alleged enslavement of Christians by the Ottoman Empire thus served as the pretext for the legality of the enslavement of Africans.

The court thus ruled, on the basis of natural law, that, in the case of an absence of otherwise contractual rules, the owner of a slave was free to sell him.[38] This fundamental ruling thus effectively declared chattel slavery to be legal in Germany (or at least in Prussia).

The *Kammergericht's opinio iuris* contained two noteworthy *obiter dicta*. *De lege ferenda*, the court pointed to the forces of enlightenment and religion to alleviate the situation of slaves[39] and, with reference to the legal abolition of this so-called hard serfdom (*harte Leibeigenschaft*), called the king to introduce legislation based on the Dutch model to grant manumission of slaves entering Prussian territory.[40] Describing social practice *de lege lata*, it referred to the enormous economic relevance of slavery.[41] The court thus took note of the material forces upholding slavery, legitimizing them based on natural law reasoning while passing the responsibility to ameliorate the state of slaves to individuals and social actors, and the abolition to government.

The ALR in 1794 introduced positive legislation on slavery, though ambiguous. In the chapter concerning servants (part II title 5), sections 196–208 regulated slavery. According to the law, slavery would not be tolerated, and Prussian subjects were prohibited from committing themselves to slavery. Nonetheless,

36 *Ibid.*, p. 303.
37 *Ibid.*, p. 306.
38 *Ibid.*, p. 310.
39 *Ibid.*, p. 305.
40 *Ibid.*, p. 310.
41 *Ibid.*, p. 304 f.

foreigners entering Prussia temporarily kept their rights over slaves, banning life-threatening treatment only. If slaves-accompanied persons planned to stay permanently, their enslavement ended formally, but in return, the former slave had to work off the price of their purchase, with time calculated on the base of typical servants' remuneration, enjoying servants' rights and duties. Alternatively, the owner could subdue the former slave as the subject of a country estate (sec. 207f.).

2.3 *Serfdom and 'Gutsherrschaft' until 1850*

Prior to the founding of the German Empire, the characteristic mode of exploitation based on force and coercion east of the Elbe River (i.e. about half of the territory which later formed the German Empire of 1871) was called '*Gutsherrschaft*' (manorism),[42] a form of servitude which in some contexts amounted to slavery and slave trade. At the time, large land holdings ('*Gut*', manor) coincided with a centralised economy oriented to surplus production, central administration of the territory and jurisdiction by the lord of the manor ('*Gutsherr*'; squire or estate owner). Starting in the late 15th century, *Gutsherrschaft* reached its climax in 18th century, ending with the peasant liberation in the 19th century.[43]

As of the 16th century, in Brandenburg (later Prussia), it was established by customary law for the '*Untertanen*' (subjects) to spend two days of unremunerated field service to the *Gutsherr*, supplemented by a third day of extraordinary services.[44] In return for service and loyalty, they were entitled to protection in case of calamity and other care ('*Fürsorgepflicht*'). Characteristic of *Gutsherrschaft* was the '*Gesindedienst*' introduced in 1518 (until 1763), by which children of the manor's subjects had to do compulsory work for the manors without remuneration.[45] The subjects were only allowed to leave the territory with the consent of the manor and had to name a guarantor.

Gutsherrschaft in northeastern Germany could imply market-based sale of peasants to other landlords. Knapp describes that in the 18th century, in some territories, serfs ('*Leibeigene*') were sold, given away, pawned or used as bets in

42 H. Kaak, *Die Gutsherrschaft: Theoriegeschichtliche Untersuchungen zum Agrarwesen im ostelbischen Raum*, De Gruyter, Berlin 1991, p. 4.

43 *Ibid.*, pp. 2–4.

44 H. Kaak, 'Vom Erbzinsrecht zur Leibeigenschaft – Entstehung agrarischer Zwangsformen im frühneuzeitlichen Brandenburg' (2007) 8:1 *Zeitschrift für Weltgeschichte* 71, pp. 76–77.

45 F. Großmann, Über die gutsherrlich-bäuerlichen Rechtsverhältnisse in der Mark Brandenburg vom 16. bis 18. Jahrhundert, Duncker & Humblot, Leipzig 1890, p. 14.

card games.[46] This happened apparently in accordance with the common law of the regions, as it was described as daily practice, and founded on documents.

Severe exploitation in the *Gutsherrschaft* proved to be relatively minimally productive. After the Napoleonic defeat of Prussia, beginning in 1807 and ending in 1850,[47] all peasants were declared to be free and successively liberated from feudal privileges ('*Fronden*') through the abolition of the '*Gutsuntertänigkeit*' (serfdom).

While the minority of peasants with strong rights over their territories based on purchase or heritage were liberated from personal burdens, most peasants with weak property rights only gained limited personal freedom (e.g. concerning marriage). If they stayed on their old lands, the real burdens did not change, and they still had to work for their masters without remuneration.[48] While large groups of peasants lost the territories altogether, others typically had to pay between a third and half of the territory cultivated by them, with manors enjoying the right to buy them out altogether. 'Freedom' finally meant that the former *Gutsherren* had considerably expanded their land holdings, accompanied by the proletarisation of peasants.[49]

The abolition of serfdom resulted in the guarantee of freedom of movement and its close relation to occupational freedom in the Paul's Church Constitution 1849.[50] The respective norms of this short-lived legal framework served as the blueprint for parts of the Weimar Constitution.[51] The spirit of serfdom is well recognisable in the servants' regulation as part of the *ALR* and its reform in the Servants' Ordinance 1810.[52] For instance, servants were legally obliged to tolerate insults, signs of contempt or violence, as long as these did not endanger life or health. In the case of offences against the master, servants were liable to imprisonment. Servants who left the service of their master without legal reason were to be returned to work with public coercive means.

46 G.F. Knapp, *Die Landarbeiter in Knechtschaft und Freiheit*, Duncker & Humblot, Leipzig 1891, pp. 24–25.

47 Decrees of. 09.10.1807, PGS 1807, p. 170; 14.09.1811. PGS 1811, p. 281; 29.05.1816, PGS 1816, p. 154; 07.06.1821, PGS 1821, p. 77; 02.03.1850, PGS 1850, 77.

48 H. Kaak, above n. 42, pp. 413–414.

49 *Ibid.*; G.F. Knapp, 'Die Bauernbefreiung in Oesterreich und in Preussen' (1894) 18 *Jahrbuch für Gesetzgebung, Verwaltung und Volkswirtschaft im Deutschen Reich* 409, p. 426.

50 Verfassung des Deutschen Reiches 28.03.1849, RGBl. NR 16 1849, p. 101.

51 W. Durner, 'Art 11 [Freizügigkeit]' in G. Dürig and others (eds), *Grundgesetz: Kommentar, 95. Lieferung Juli 2021*, C.H. Beck, München 2021.

52 Gesinde-Ordnung für sämmtliche Provinzen der Preußischen Monarchie. 08.11.1810, PGS 1810, p. 101.

Viewed as a whole, serfdom, as the quantitatively most common form of servitude in Germany east of the Elbe River was a system of hereditary coercive exploitation with the almost unlimited power of the *Gutsherr* over the *Untertan*. It ended not for moral but for functional considerations. Transformation towards free citizenship was a means for balancing the interests of the state and the large landowners. Abolition did not necessarily mean the improvement of conditions but rather deprivation of means of production.

2.4 *Galley-Slaves and Houses of Correction* (*Zuchthäuser*)

While serfdom as servitude and – at least in the case of the sale of serfs – slavery in Roman law terms (chattel) was a medieval instrument present in the first centuries of modernity, reformation and emerging capitalism brought about new forms of detention and forced labour. The new houses of detention, according to Patterson's definition, were centres of slavery. Patterson calls it extrusive slavery, as the enslaved persons were not kidnapped or enslaved during war from other societies (intrusive slavery) but from within the respective community or society.[53] As Patterson writes:

> [...] in France, Spain, England, and the Netherlands a severe form of enslavement of Europeans by Europeans was to develop and flourish from the middle of the fifteenth century to well into the nineteenth. This was penal slavery, beginning with galley slavery and continuing with its replacement by the *Bagnes*, or penal slavery in public works. Both were slavery in every sense of the term.[54]

Germany counted both with so-called galley-slaves (*opera publica*) and houses of correction (*Zuchthaus*) being comparable to French and Italian *bagnes/bagnos*. Although Germany had no galleys, persons condemned to public forced labour used to be called galley-slaves – first sent abroad to serve on galleys, later on staying for public works in the places where they were condemned.[55] John Howard describes conditions giving an example for the city of Hanau:

> [T]he Galley-Slaves Slaves (so called) are distinguished into *Honnêtes* and *Deshonnêtes*. The former are condemned for three, four, seven, nine,

53 O. Patterson, above n. 7, p. 43.

54 *Ibid.*, p. 44.

55 T. Krause, 'Opera publica' in G. Ammerer, F. Bretschneider and A.S. Weiß (eds), *Gefängnis und Gesellschaft: Zur (Vor-) Geschichte der strafenden Einsperrung*, Leipziger Universitätsverlag, Leipzig 2003, pp. 124–125.

> fourteen years: but the term is sometimes shortened on account of good behaviour. These wear a brown uniform; and a small chain from the girdle to one leg. The latter are for the most part such as have committed capital offences. These wear a white coat with one black sleeve; and have a chain from the girdle to each leg: they never work out of the town; and are put to the most disagreeable services in it.[56]

Galley slavery as severest form of punishment ended in steps between 1800 and 1867.[57] Impressed by the House of Correction or prison (*Rasphuis, tuchthuis*) established 1596 in Amsterdam (inspired by the London Bridewell of 1553), the German Hansa cities Bremen (1609), Lübeck (1613) and Hamburg (1618) instituted houses of correction (*Zuchthäuser*) as centres for concentrating the respective community's beggars, 'vagabonds' and other people 'unwanted', e.g. by their relatives for being wasteful. These houses of correction served as models for the introduction of work and poor houses in all parts of Germany.[58]

The German *Zuchthaus* fulfilled the same criteria as their British, Dutch or French counterparts. They evolved to be centres for the excluded in the 18th century, often including orphans, the mentally ill, prostitutes, and also prisoners. From the beginning, prisoners were forced to work, suffering hard physical punishments in case they resisted.[59] The work was exploitative, as it was expected to cover the costs of the institution – which mostly failed.[60]

Eventually serving exclusively for the retention and forced hard labour of criminals, the *Zuchthaus* became one of four types of prison in the German Reich based on the Criminal Law of 1871, next to prison (*Gefängnis*, for shorter terms, with less hard labour), short-term imprisonment for honorary offences, and fortress detention for political prisoners. It was the cruellest form of detention after the end of galley slavery. Based on the three basic criteria of Patterson, at least for the disenfranchised lifelong prisoners (sec. 32 criminal code 1871–1969), *Zuchthaus* effectively meant slavery. Prisoners were under permanent, violent domination; they lost all rights related to outside institutions, and

56 J. Howard, *The State of the Prisons in England and Wales: With Preliminary Observations and an Account of Some Foreign Prisons*, Cambridge University Press, Cambridge 2013 [1777], pp. 105–106.

57 T. Krause, above n. 55, p. 129.

58 R. von Hippel, 'Beiträge zur Geschichte der Freiheitsstrafe' (1897) 18 *Zeitschrift für die gesamte Strafrechtswissenschaft* 419, pp. 419–420.

59 *Ibid., passim.*

60 Cf. with focus on Bremen, O. Grambow, *Das Gefängniswesen Bremens*, Noske, Borna-Leipzig 1910, pp. 40–46.

they were dishonoured, as they lost their citizen rights. Temporal *Zuchthaus*, instead, equals to servitude.

During the Third Reich, since 1936, *Zuchthäuser* were part of the economic four-year plan and were used to produce weaponry, and finally, after 1942, prisoners were put into special military units. Prisoners did not enjoy human rights during their stay, as their situation was defined legally as a 'special relation of force',[61] which only in 1972 was found to be unconstitutional if not concretised by law,[62] eventually resulting in the Penitentiary System Act 1977. The *Zuchthaus* was abolished in 1970 based on a big reform of criminal law, which also abolished the loss of honorary rights.[63]

Galley slavery and *Zuchthaus* represent the transition from medieval corporal to custodial punishment.[64] The *Kammergericht* decision[65] already illustrated not only that slavery existed in Germany but also how closely related transatlantic slavery and serfdom in Prussia were, where even wording for serfdom and slavery only differed by one adjective ('hard'). Hard serfdom (*harte Knechtschaft*) was hard labour, e.g., work in stone quarries or peat extraction, as a typical form of punishment in the *Zuchthaus*.

Moreover, galley slavery and *Zuchthaus* confirm the existence of slavery and servitude on German soil not only as exceptional but as legally institutionalised. This slavery was not conceptualised as private ownership but as public forced labour. It paved the way for the law and severe exploitation in the colonies based on forced labour and punishment in the context of work and eventually to the (also legal) atrocities of the Third Reich.

The *Zuchthaus*, moreover, had an important lasting impact on German conditions of prison. It introduced the duty to work, which is valid until today in prisons. Prisoners had to work without remuneration; still, they do not enjoy the minimum wage for their work, but hourly wages pending between 1,37 and 2,30 Euros in 2022.

---

61 Besonderes Gewaltverhältnis.

62 German Constitutional Court, BVerfG 14.03.1972, decision No. 2 BvR 41/71.

63 First Act to Reform the Criminal Law, 25.06.1969, BGBL I, p. 645.

64 In Germany, the relevance of galley slavery in this respect still is discussed. Some foundational criminalists, among them v. Hippel and Radbruch, ignored galley slavery, and saw the foundation of custodial punishment in the idea of educating prisoners for the life after prison. Lately, a growing number of authors go back to the opus publicum/galley slavery as origin; T. Krause, above n. 55, pp. 117–121.

65 See above.

2.5 *Slavery and Similar Practices in the German Colonies*

It was only after the almost worldwide abolishment of slavery, between 1884 and 1919, that Germany became a colonial power, with the third largest colonial territory. In its colonies of German East Africa (henceforth GEA; today Tanzania, Ruanda and Burundi), German West Africa (Namibia), Togo and Cameroon, the German Empire dealt with pre-colonial forms of slavery and introduced new forms of similar practices.

2.5.1 Treating Traditional Slavery in the Colonies

Slavery and slave trade had existed in different forms in all German colonies in Africa before and after their acquisition.[66] The aim of its abolition served as one of the major arguments for domestic public opinion to engage in colonial expansion as a 'civilising mission'. For political decision-makers, the abolition of slavery served primarily as a means of establishing consensus and justifying considerable costs. It is therefore not surprising that the only major public campaign to abolish the slave trade occurred when the GEA Society was in distress because of its abusive practices. As dissatisfaction with (company-based) colonialism grew in Germany and Reich and Chancellor Bismarck also found himself in domestic political straits, a 'movement' was launched that served primarily to justify military expansion into the interior of GEA. From the perspective of its masterminds, its practical aim was to push back competition from Arab traders who were better entrenched in the region, and enable the establishment of colonial structures of administration and also guarantee financial means for the military.[67]

Legislation concerning the abolition of slave raiding, the slave trade and slavery was passed in all African colonies under German control. Since the colonies were not considered the territory of the Reich, the Protectorate Law (1900) ruled that the law concerning the punishment of slave raiding and slave

66 Cf. P.E. Lovejoy, *Transformations in Slavery: A History of Slavery in Africa,* (3rd edn), Cambridge University. Press, Cambridge 2011, pp. 152–154; P.E. Lovejoy and J.S. Hogendorn, *Slow Death for Slavery: The Course of Abolition in Northern Nigeria, 1897–1936*, Cambridge University Press, Cambridge 1993, pp. 263, 267; A. Brivio, '« Nos grands-pères achetaient des esclaves … »: Le culte de Mami Tchamba au Togo et au Bénin' (2008) 8 *Gradhiva. Revue d'anthropologie et d'histoire des arts* 64; Jakob Zollmann, 'Slavery and the Colonial State in German South West Africa 1880s to 1918' (2010) 7 *Journal of Namibian Studies* 85, *passim.*

67 K.J. Bade, 'Zwischen Mission und Kolonialbewegung, Kolonialwirtschaft und Kolonialpolitik in der Bismarckzeit: der Fall Friedrich Fabri' in K.J. Bade (ed), *Imperialismus und Kolonialmission: Kaiserliches Deutschland und koloniales Imperium,* Steiner, Wiesbaden 1982, pp. 124–132.

trade of 1895[68] was not applicable to the African population in the colonies. Legislation on slavery was, therefore, mostly passed by local governors.

In GEA, in 1891, an ordinance concerning the manumission of slaves was passed.[69] It regulated that a slave became free when he was resold (also by exchange, gift, etc.) to a 'non-native' and that a contract to work off the purchase price was permissible. In 1896, a governmental order concerning the prosecution and punishment of the slave trade was passed,[70] specifying the punishments for kidnapping, trade, transport and exportation of slaves. In 1899, the Governor prohibited the emigration via sea of non-adult Africans without their parents or Europeans.[71]

In 1901, an ordinance on house slavery was passed by the Reich Chancellor "to prepare the abolition of house slavery".[72] It provided that a relationship of slavery could not be newly established. Furthermore, it allowed the manumission of house slaves by paying ransom at any time and guaranteed two days of work per week for the slave's own interest, as well as the master's duty to care for the slave in case of sickness or old age. By lifting the ban on resale, the transfer of the 'master's right' was made dependent on official approval. In case of severe violation of duties against the slave, the master forfeited his master's right, and the house slave was freed without paying any compensation. In 1902, a governor's supplementary order introduced a stricter line, e.g. by establishing the death penalty as standard punishment in severe cases of professional slave traders.[73] An ordinance of the Reich Chancellor in 1904 furthermore established that children of house slaves born after 1905 were born free.[74]

Concerning Cameroon, two ordinances were passed in 1896 and 1902, the first of which concerned the protection of women from slavery,[75] whereas the

---

68 Gesetz, betreffend die Bestrafung des Sklavenraubes und des Sklavenhandels. 28.07.1895, RGBl 1895, p. 425.

69 Verordnung, betreffend den Freikauf von Sklaven. 01.09.1891, DKG I 1893, p. 431

70 Anweisung des Kaiserlichen Gouverneurs von Deutsch-Ostafrika, betr. die bei Bestrafung des Sklavenhandels usw. zu befolgenden Grundsätze. 19.08.1896, DKG II 1893–97, p. 267.

71 Gouverneurs-Verordnung, betreffend die Ausführung unerwachsener Farbiger nach dem Ausland über See. 31.05.1899, DKG 1901–02, p. 211.

72 Verordnung des Reichskanzlers, betreffend die Haussklaverei in Deutsch-Ostafrika. 29.11.1901, DKG VI 1901–02, p. 426.

73 Runderlass des Gouverneurs von Deutsch-Ostafrika, betreffend Maßnahmen zur Bekämpfung des Sklavenhandels. 10.12.1902, DKG 1901–02, p. 558.

74 Verordnung des Reichskanzlers, betr. die Haussklaverei in Deutsch-Ostafrika. 24.12.1904, DKG VIII 1904, p. 267.

75 Verordnung des Gouverneurs von Kamerun, betreffend den Schutz weiblicher Personen gegen die Sklaverei. 7.12.1896, DKG VI 1901–02, p. 138.

second dealt with house slavery.[76] The first ordinance prohibited the pledging, capturing or selling of women because of debts of others, especially their husbands. The second ordinance resembled the 1901 GEA ordinance on house slavery in prohibiting the new establishment of slavery by the same means. In Togo, in 1893, all slaves were declared free.[77] In German South-West Africa, no regulation of slavery or slave trade was made. The differences were due to differing forms and economic weight of slavery present in the territories, but also depending on the strength of colonial administration and relative power and interests of local elites.

Again, legislation on slavery showed Germany's strong interest in protecting what was considered legitimate ownership of slaves, putting strategic political interests first when treating slavery, refraining from taking responsibility and guaranteeing equal rights in territories otherwise taken by force and deceit.

2.5.2 Servitude for Colonial Exploitation

Even more illuminating is how the German government dealt with the problem of procuring labour to exploit the colonies. In practical terms, GEA is exemplary for the path between chattel slavery and free, dignified labour under colonial authorities. The assessment by Carl Peters, a pioneer of German colonialism whose racist and cruel understanding of colonial expansion served as the model for Nazi ideology, illustrates this.[78] Peters, who had organised the signatures of local chiefs for the German East African Company's 'protection contracts', wrote in 1896:

> According to our present-day views, the relationship in which the worker stands to the employer can only be the contractual relationship. We must completely eliminate slavery and serfdom from our means of coercion. Since the European world has only gradually worked its way out of slavery into a free contractual relationship through a development of centuries, it is unlikely that the black race will be able to digest our contract law provisions immediately without certain intermediate stages. Since a contract relationship is based on the assumption that the obligation is recognised by both sides, but the black is not always inclined to recognise

76 Verordnung des Reichskanzlers, betreffend die Haussklaverei in Kamerun. 21.02.1902, DKG VI 1901–02, p. 462.

77 Verordnung, betreffend die Befreiung der in Sklaverei gehaltenen Personen. 15.01.1893, DKG 1891, p. 281.

78 A. Perras, *Carl Peters and German Imperialism 1856–1918: A Political Biography,* (reprint) Clarendon Press, Oxford 2006, pp. 249–251.

> his part, I recommend for the beginning that exceptional provisions be made for the blacks. I recommend for a start that the penal laws of our protectorates be exempted from the law on breach of contract. In my view, this is the real crux of the whole question of whether black people will be good workers, and thus ultimately the decision about Africa's ability to develop at all.[79]

Peters sketched central aspects of the path taken in German colonies. Historical relations of slavery were successively abandoned, but it was not planned that dignified labour relations protecting the workers from structural inequality would replace them. Breach of labour contracts indeed was penalised. The Reich Colonial Office held that this was for "education of the natives to a workmanlike and well-behaved life", but "corporal punishment has been imposed in such a large number of cases that it is to be feared that the Reichstag and public opinion will draw unfavourable conclusions from this with regard to the success of the German cultural work in our colonies".[80] Penal law in the colonies for the autochthonous population altogether became part of administrative law; the Indigenous persons were considered children which had to be educated by prohibitions and punishments.[81] The punishments allowed to be imposed in administrative decisions without control by a second instance were "corporal punishment (caning, rod penalty), fines, prison, imprisonment with forced labour, chain imprisonment, death penalty",[82] strongly reminding of the early *Zuchthaus* punishments before reforms in the 19th century. Naucke calls this "an educative criminal policy without legal limitation", sketching the (interrupted) continuities between the 18th century and the 20th century, used in Europe already in World War I in the territories occupied by Germany, where "one says criminal law and means legally unregulated criminal power".[83]

One factor characteristic of German colonialism, and especially of GEA, was the transition from traditional slavery to contract-based labour relations. Between 1890 and 1914, official estimates observed a decrease from initially

---

79 C. Peters, 'Dr. Peters' in F. Giesebrecht (ed), *Die Behandlung der Eingeborenen in den deutschen Kolonien*, Fischer, Berlin 1898, p. 89.

80 Runderlaß der Kolonial-Abteilung, betreffend die Strafurtheile gegen Eingeborene. 12.01.1900, Dt. Kolonialgesetzgebung 1899–1900, p. 15.

81 W. Naucke, 'Deutsches Kolonialstrafrecht: 1886–1918' (1988) 7 *Rechtshistorisches Journal* 297, 303.

82 Verfügung des Reichskanzlers wegen Ausübung der Strafgerichtsbarkeit und der Disziplinargewalt gegenüber den Eingeborenen in den deutschen Schutzgebieten von Ostafrika, Kamerun und Togo, Dt.Kolonialgesetzgebung, 1893–1897, p. 215.

83 W. Naucke, above n. 81, pp. 314–315.

about 500.000 to about 160.000 persons living in conditions of traditional slavery in GEA.[84] In this time period, the colonial authorities issued 'letters of freedom' (*Freibriefe*) as certification to about 60.000 people, of which 38% redeemed themselves or were redeemed by third parties, 34% were manumitted by their owners and 24% were emancipated by the authorities.[85] Contractual freedom (*Freibriefe*) was one factor of many for reducing the slave population, next to the prohibition and severe prosecution of slave raiding which hampered replenishment of slaves, the free birth of the children of slaves since 1905 and flight from slave owners.[86] Another aspect was the Maji-Maji rebellion, which resulted in the death of between 100.000 and 300.000 persons or about one third of the total population of the affected area due mostly to famine.[87] It seems most probable that especially in case of famine, the slave population was disproportionately affected.

Deutsch estimates that half of the slaves redeemed by Europeans, and a quarter of all slaves redeemed, were ransomed by plantation owners, where former slaves had to work for 18 months without payment before receiving their *Freibriefe*. According to him, the certification policy was used to avoid abolition.[88] The colonial government thus aimed at avoiding resistance by politically powerful local actors in the context of a relatively weak administration which depended upon the cooperation of intermediary actors. It furthermore had the purpose of preventing sudden disruptions of the slave-based plantation economy, not least in the interest of economic growth and stability.[89]

The abolition of traditional slavery did not mean its abolition altogether, but rather its transformation into new forms of forced labour. The introduction of export-oriented colonial exploitation meant the need for a workforce. People willing to do wage labour not only were scarce, but also hardly present in the areas where they were wanted by investors. Instead of opting for incentives for paid labour, such as better living conditions and access to resources, which could have resulted in higher prices for exported goods, colonial

---

84 J. G. Deutsch, 'The 'Freeing' of Slaves in German East Africa: the Statistical Record, 1890–1914' (1998) 19:2 *Slavery & Abolition* 109, p. 128.

85 *Ibid.*, pp. 109–112.

86 *Ibid.*, p. 128.

87 J. Iliffe, *A Modern History of Tanganyika*, Cambridge University Press, Cambridge 1979, p. 200; A. de Juan, 'Extraction and Violent Resistance in the Early Phases of State Building: Quantitative Evidence From the "Maji Maji" Rebellion, 1905–1907' (2016) 49:3 *Comparative Political Studies* 291, p. 299.

88 J. G. Deutsch, above n. 84, p. 123.

89 This argument is used already by F.O. Karstedt, Deutsch-Ostafrikanische Zeitung 24.01.1914, p. 1.

administration opted to use force to guarantee sufficient supply, in line with other colonial powers.

The main means for the objective of mobilising labour were described for instance in 1896 by Major Boshart, an influential and especially cruel German colonial pioneer then in service for the Belgian King Leopold II in the Congo Free State. His thinking illuminates the racist social Darwinist motives behind the legislation:

> [T]here is no difference of opinion among the connoisseurs of Africa that the Negro can only be brought to work by means of coercion; but how this coercion is to be exercised without slavery or a relationship quite similar to it, which would merely give the child a different name, is probably difficult to fathom. (… A small-scale solution is in imposing) all penalties on the Negro as labour penalties or at least combined with such penalties. Taxes, too, could, where such have been introduced, be converted into labour. Finally, an attempt could be made to gradually compel the entire Negro population to work in a similar way to the way in which everyone in Europe is required to perform compulsory military service. It can be assumed that in the latter case there would frequently be unpleasantness, the after-effects of which would not be inferior to those of the former slavery.[90]

Boshart's proposals were followed in a surprisingly precise way. In 1898, hut taxes were introduced in GEA. According to the ordinance,[91] taxes of indigenous Africans could be paid in money, in oleaginous fruits or labour. Although men and women were allowed to offer their labour, female work, by law, was considered half the value of male work. In the case of non-payment, the administration was instructed to make use of force. The ordinance of 1905[92] changed some of the rules, eliminating the payment by labour, introducing poll taxes for male workers working less than six months continuously on plantations managed by Europeans, and introducing the option for the administration to set poll taxes for every adult male able to work. Other German colonies had

90 A. Boshart, 'Major Boshart' in F. Giesebrecht (ed), *Die Behandlung der Eingeborenen in den deutschen Kolonien*, Fischer, Berlin 1898, pp. 45–46.

91 Verordnung betreffend die Erhebung einer Häuser- und Hüttensteuer in Deutsch-Ostafrika. 01.11.1897, Kol.-Bl. 1998, p. 50.

92 Verordnung betreffend die Erhebung einer Häuser- und Hüttensteuer. 22.03.1905, Kol.-Bl. 1905, p. 272.

comparable rules, with frequent minor changes. Only in German South West Africa (GSWA) did this direct taxation inducing waged labour not exist.[93]

Hut and poll taxes were especially introduced to force people to take up paid labour.[94] Since non-payment was punished with forced labour, paid labour could be considered more attractive. For large parts of the colonies, labour opportunities nonetheless did not exist. The colonial need for labour existed for plantation economies, for carriers in the unexploited areas, and for exploitation of raw materials. The means to bring workers to formally paid work was managed by forms of forced labour in the context of long-term written contracts, a form of low-paid, fixed-term work secured by coercion and conditioned by brutal force.

In the case of the GEA labour ordinances 1896[95]/1897,[96] which were to be applied exclusively to African workers, all contracts with a duration of more than one month had to be in written form. The employer was allowed to reduce wages by up to a quarter as penalties. Employers were allowed to mistreat workers to the level of danger to life, damage to health or 'unusual hardship'. If the worker abandoned work, the employer could resort to governmental coercive means (fines, forced labour, physical punishment, prison) to force the continuation of the contract. Breach of contract furthermore could be punished with a fine of up to 100 rupees – an amount equal to the value of two male slaves[97]– and additional imprisonment.[98]

The GEA labour ordinance 1909 did not include penal provisions but instead resorted to the disciplinary provisions of the 'ordinance concerning the exercise of criminal jurisdiction and disciplinary authority' 1896.[99] This ordinance stipulated corporal punishment and prison for up to two weeks for breach of

93 H. Schnee, *Deutsches Kolonial-Lexikon*, Quelle & Meyer, Leipzig 1920, p. 519.

94 Concerning the complex set of legal regulation including tax, labour, administrative, penal and other areas of law used in African colonisation to introduce segmented labour markets and the interplay of regulation which eventually meant new forms of slavery cf. H. Fechner, 'Legal Segmentation and Early Colonialism in Sub-Saharan Africa: Informality and the Colonial Exploitative Legal Employment Standard' (2022) 161:4 (Special Issue on Legal Segmentation) *International Labour Review* 615.

95 Verordnung, betreffend Arbeitsverträge mit Farbigen in Deutsch-Ostafrika. 27.12.1896, Kol.-Bl. 1897, p. 160.

96 Verordnung betreffend Abschließung von Arbeitsverträgen mit Farbigen. 12.11.1897, Kol.-Bl. 1898, p. 77.

97 Cf. J.G. Deutsch, above n. 84, p. 122.

98 See sec. 6a, 8b), 10, 11 of the cited labour ordinances.

99 Verfügung des Reichskanzlers wegen Ausübung der Strafgerichtsbarkeit und der Disziplinargewalt gegenüber den Eingeborenen in den deutschen Schutzgebieten von Ostafrika, Kamerun und Togo. 22.04.1896, Kol.-Bl. 1896, 241.

contract, and judgments to be made by public administration officers. The 1909 ordinance allowed the execution of the custodial sentence to be ordered at the employer's premises with the continuation of work, which in this case was unpaid.

Forced labour was also declared permissible by the same 1896 ordinance on criminal jurisdiction, in addition to corporal punishment, fines, chain imprisonment and the death penalty.[100] In GEA, the 1905 ordinance on compulsory labour[101] furthermore imposed general duties of unpaid local public work upon male indigenous people for public roadbuilding and maintenance. The Governor was also entitled to make use of compulsory labour for general purposes.

In effect, especially fixed-term contracts for work at long distances from home amounted to labour conditions based on force or the threat of force and thus slavery in modern terms. In addition to using forced labour and prison labour, the German coloniser developed a complex set of tools to exploit the colonies within the spectre of servitude.

2.6 *Slavery, Servitude and Legislation in the Third Reich*

After coming to power in 1933, Nazi fascism developed a highly differentiated system of forced labour in Germany. Using Patterson's terminology, they oscillated between servitude (i.e. forced labour) and slavery. In 1933, the first concentration camps were introduced. While the first extermination camps, Auschwitz-Birkenau and Majdanek (Lublin), started to exist in late 1941, concentration camps from 1933/34 fulfilled Patterson's three main criteria of slavery. They were places of total physical domination, with all inmates under exclusive power and control of the SS (since 1934; before also by the SA). Second, they symbolise social death. From the beginning, for those who entered, it was unclear whether they would ever leave again. Instead of their names, they were symbolically given numbers. Family relations officially ceased to exist. Third, inmates were dishonoured on a daily base. The hair was cut, and private clothes were confiscated. Numbers representing names were put on uniforms or even incorporated as tattoos, and signs on their uniforms classified inmates, depersonalising and dividing them at the same time. Economic exploitation, though, was not the main motive of enslavement.[102]

100 *Ibid.*

101 Verordnung betreffend die Heranziehung der Eingeborenen zu öffentlichen Arbeiten. 22.03.1905, Kol.-Bl. 1905, p. 278.

102 J. Binner, 'Zwangsarbeit im Nationalsozialismus' (2012) 13:1 *Zeitschrift für Weltgeschichte* 31, pp. 33–34.

In the late 1930s, a turn to forced labour (servitude) for exploitative interests could be observed. Industrial and agricultural production was already based on forced labour shortly after the start of the war. In the territory of the German Reich alone, over 13 million forced labourers were used during the Second World War.[103]

In terms of legal and practical conditions and categorisations, several approaches illustrate Nazi means to differentiate forms of servitude. For instance, civilian forced labourers from abroad, prisoners of war and other prisoners can be distinguished.[104] In the case of civilian forced labourers, as with prisoners of war, the Nazis' racial classification played a decisive role. People from Poland, for example, who were considered 'racially inferior', had to wear a recognisable patch with the letter 'P' on their clothing, similar to the 'Jewish star', and people from the Soviet Union had to wear patches with the letters 'Ost' (East). Depending on their origin or racial categorisation, the food rations and other living conditions differed, and with them, the likelihood of survival. Later on, productivity determined the allotment of food rations. Among the prisoners obliged to perform forced labour, differences existed between concentration camp prisoners, prisoners of labour and education camps and so-called 'labour Jews', i.e. Jewish Germans forced to work.[105]

Some authors differentiate even further. Buggeln categorises Western European prisoners of war as compulsory labourers with a survival rate of 98%, while he classifies ordinary prison inmates as forced labourers due to their lower social status.[106] According to him, the category of 'slave labourers' with a survival rate of 89% includes German Jewish forced labourers, Polish and Soviet forced labourers, Polish prisoners of war and, from 1943, Italian military internees. The category 'less-than-slaves', with a survival rate of 41%, includes Polish-Jewish and Soviet prisoners of war, concentration camp prisoners, prisoners of labour education camps and so-called 'labour Jews'. From Patterson's perspective, the condition of the compulsory labourers would be considered servitude, while both the 'slaves' and 'less-than-slaves' would fall under slavery.

---

103 Cf. M. Spoerer, *Zwangsarbeit unter dem Hakenkreuz: Ausländische Zivilarbeiter, Kriegsgefangene und Häftlinge im Deutschen Reich und im besetzten Europa 1939–1945*, Dt. Verl.-Anst, Stuttgart 2001, p. 223.

104 M. Spoerer, 'NS-Zwangsarbeiter im Deutschen Reich' (2001) 49:4 *Vierteljahrshefte für Zeitgeschichte* 665, p. 665.

105 See for the whole complex M. Spoerer, *Zwangsarbeit unter dem Hakenkreuz, above* n. 103, *passim*.

106 M. Buggeln, 'Unfreie Arbeit im Nationalsozialismus' in M. Buggeln and M. Wildt (eds), *Arbeit ikm Nationalsozialismus*, Oldenbourg Wissenschaftsverlag, München 2014, pp. 240–243.

The categorisation of servitude and slavery according to racial criteria was regulated by law. The so-called 'Polish decrees' were police decrees issued by the Reich Minister of the Interior Göring on 8 March 1940 on the segregation and living conditions of Polish 'voluntary' and forced labourers in Germany. These laws represented the first comprehensive legal regulation of racially motivated discrimination for workers from other countries.[107] The 'Ordinance on the Conditions of Employment of Eastern Workers' of 30 June 1942 first explicitly stipulated, in contrast to Polish forced labourers, that 'Eastern workers' were not employees and that labour law regulations only applied to them if this was expressly ordered (sec. 2).[108] The wage to be paid was set at less than one-third of the normal wage, from which benefits for accommodation, food and transport were to be deducted (sec. 3, 5) so that at best less than one-quarter of the normal wage was to be paid if no further deductions were made. Supplements for overtime or work on Sundays and public holidays were not to be paid, nor was leave to be granted or payments due in case of sick leave (sec. 4, 6, 7).

3 The Legacies of Slavery and Modern Law

Few survivors of slave work during the Third Reich are still alive. Since Germany's understanding of slavery has always been narrow and the acceptance of historical responsibility for slavery and similar practices came late, it is not surprising that legal initiatives against global slavery for a long time did not go beyond international standards.

3.1 *Constitutional Provisions*

Article 12 (2) *Grundgesetz* (Basic Law/constitution), introduced in 1949, reads: "No one shall be compelled to perform any particular work except within the framework of a traditional general public service obligation which is the same for everyone". The provision is intended to fundamentally prevent forced labour as it existed in the Third Reich. Thus, Member of the Parliamentary Council Zinn said, "The term "forced labour" carries within it the idea of slave labour. By speaking first of compulsory service and separately of forced labour,

107 J. Binner, above n. 102, pp. 34–35.

108 RGBl. 1942 I, p. 419.

we make the contrast clear".[109] This norm stayed the only one in reference to Nazi slavery for more than 50 years.

Concerning racism, Article 3 (3) *Grundgesetz* states that "No one shall be discriminated against or given preference on account of (...) race (...)". The characteristic 'race' as well as the racially based exploitation of people did not play a prominent role during the deliberations. Incidentally, in the contemporary debate, antisemitic racism was in the foreground due to the Nuremberg Race Laws (1935) and the Holocaust.[110] German anti-Semites had constructed Jewish people based on their historical descendancies and irrespective of their religion, i.e. including atheists and converts to Christianity, as 'Jewish race'. The Nuremberg Laws on 'Protection of German Blood and German Honour'[111] and on citizenship[112] turned this racist doctrine into law. The 'blood protection law' prohibited both marriages and non-matrimonial sexual relationships between non-Jewish Germans and Jews (sec. 1–2). Sec. 2 of the Reich Citizenship Act restricted citizenship to people of 'German or related blood'. The (basic) First Decree on the Reich Citizenship Act[113] only differentiated between Jewish and other persons, ruling that Jews could not be German citizens nor have political rights or serve as German officials (sec. 4–5). The first eleven decrees concretising the law exclusively regulated the reduction of rights of Jewish people; the 12th decree in 1943 added Romani People as unable to be German citizens (sec. 4).[114]

From the communist side, an attempt was made to restrict the right of free speech by banning 'race baiting'. The other parliamentary groups rejected such a constitutional ban on racism, referring to the possibility of regulation by non-constitutional (criminal) law.[115] A reference to slavery is thus not recognisable in the constitutional legislation against racism. No links were originally made between the prohibition of racism and economic exploitation. The learning effect of the Third Reich in terms of slavery was not strong enough to withstand the forces of the Cold War. The 'othering' of slavery, again underlining that Germany had nothing to do with slavery, was now directed towards the Soviet Union.

---

109 Deutscher Bundestag and Bundesarchiv (eds), *Ausschuß für Grundsatzfragen*, Harald Boldt Verlag, Boppard 1993, p. 96.

110 D. Liebscher, *Rasse im Recht – Recht gegen Rassismus: Genealogie einer ambivalenten rechtlichen Kategorie*, Suhrkamp, Berlin 2021, pp. 338–348.

111 15.09.1935, RGBl. I p. 1146.

112 15.09.1935, RGBl. I p. 1146.

113 14.11.1935, RGBl. I p. 1333.

114 25.04.1943, RGBl. I p. 268.

115 Deutscher Bundestag and Bundesarchiv (eds), above n. 109, p. 672.

3.2 *Legal Processing of Forced Labour and Compensation for Forced Labour and Slave Labour*

Strong impulses to juridically reflect upon slavery in Germany's past came from the outside. The Nuremberg Trials (1946–49) were the first and most important example of the criminal prosecution of the enslavement of people through forced labour during the Nazi era. Article 6 lit. b) and c) of the International Military Tribunal Statute established, among others, the tribunal's jurisdiction over war crimes, including 'deportation to slave labour', as well as 'enslavement' and 'deportation' as crimes against humanity.[116] Slavery and forced labour for German companies were charges laid against industrial managers of leading German armament companies.[117]

In the 1960s and 1970s, individual cases were also dealt with by civil and administrative courts. However, claims for remuneration or compensation for forced labour regularly failed[118] due to the 1953 Agreement on German External Debts,[119] which regulated that claims by countries against the Reich which were at war with Germany, and by their nationals, were to be deferred until the final settlement of the problem of reparation. In an exceptional case, the German claimant and former Auschwitz concentration camp forced labourer Wollheim reached a deal with the chemical industry conglomerate IG Farben, which foresaw payment of 30 million DM to former forced labourers in Auschwitz-Monowitz.[120]

Due to protest notes from Western European governments about the inadequate compensation of victims, Germany concluded global agreements with various European states, which also provided funds for the compensation of forced labourers. However, Eastern European victims of servitude and slavery, especially prisoners of war, who made up the bulk of the forced labourers used in Germany, were not taken into account.[121]

After the Second World War, there were also various legal regulations for the compensation for the victims of Nazi injustice. For example, the Federal Compensation Act of 1953/1956 provided for compensation for persons who

116 Agreement for the prosecution and punishment of the major war criminals of the European Axis. Including the Charter of the International Statute of the Military Tribunal. UNTS No. 251 1951, p. 280.

117 S. Blanke, 'Der lange Weg zur Entschädigung von NS-Zwangsarbeitern' (2001) 34:2 *Kritische Justiz* 195, p. 197.

118 Cf. Federal Supreme Court BGH 19.6.1973, VI ZR 74/70; Federal Administrative Court BVerwG 12.6.1970, VII C 64.68.

119 BGBl. II 1953, p. 331.

120 W. Benz, 'Der Wollheim-Prozeß. Zwangsarbeit für IG Farben in Auschwitz' in C. Goschler and L. Herbst (eds), *Wiedergutmachung in der Bundesrepublik Deutschland,* Reprint 2018, Oldenbourg Wissenschaftsverlag, Berlin 1988.

121 S. Blanke above n. 117, pp. 197–198.

were persecuted under National Socialist (NS) tyranny because of their political convictions, race, or faith.[122] However, compensation for servitude or slavery was not provided for there – it was not even considered a Nazi-specific injustice for a long time.[123] Persons living abroad – and thus most of the forced labourers – were also excluded from compensation.

Until the early 1990s, with few exceptions,[124] forced labour during NS fascism was not taken up by researchers in the context of labour law. Compensation for servitude was discussed in labour courts only in 1999 and 2000 when several plaintiffs from Eastern Europe claimed remuneration and damages in connection with forced labour they had performed in Germany during the war, and only in the context of these legal disputes the terms slavery and slave labour entered public discourse in Germany. The complaints here focused on whether the labour courts had jurisdiction at all over issues related to forced labour. In the first and second instances, the decisions were inconsistent. Uniformly, the courts assumed the absence of an employment relationship since a voluntary contractual relationship did not exist. The Munich Regional Labour Court nevertheless assumed the existence of a dispute under labour law since remuneration for work performed in personal dependence was the subject of the dispute.[125] In the final instance, the Federal Labour Court referred these claims to the civil courts.[126]

A comprehensive compensation scheme for slavery or forced labour during NS dictatorship was introduced in Germany in 2000 by the law establishing the 'Foundation Remembrance, Responsibility and Future' for the victims of slavery and forced labour.[127] The background to the establishment of the foundation were lawsuits filed by former forced labourers against German companies in US courts based on the Alien Tort Claims Act of 1789.[128] Although a conviction was only a possibility in relation to companies such as Daimler-Benz, VW, Siemens, Hoechst and Deutsche Bank, the considerable legal and above all financial risk of the lawsuits filed as class actions was the decisive factor in urging the German government to establish a foundation.[129]

122 Originally Bundesergänzungsgesetz, 18.09.1953, BGBl. I 1953, p. 1387; reformulated as Bundesentschädigungsgesetz, 29.06.1956, BGBl. I 1956, p. 559.

123 S. Blanke, above n. 117, p. 195.

124 Cf. C.U. Schminck-Gustavus, 'Zwangsarbeitsrecht und Faschismus Zur „Polenpolitik" im „Dritten Reich"' (1980) 13:1–2 *Kritische Justiz* 1.

125 Decision of 29.11.1999, 5 Ta 352/99.

126 Decision of 16.02.2000, 5 AZB 71/99 et al.

127 Law of 02.08.2000, BGBl. I 2000, p. 1263.

128 M. Spoerer, *Zwangsarbeit unter dem Hakenkreuz* above n. 103, pp. 247–248.

129 A. Hense, 'Limitation of Economic Damages as a 'Humanitarian Gesture': The German Foundation 'Remembrance, Responsibility and the Future'' (2011) 46:2 *Journal of Contemporary History* 407, pp. 412–414.

According to the law on the establishment of the Foundation, those entitled to benefits were persons who were imprisoned in a concentration camp, ghetto or under similar conditions and forced to work, and those who were deported to Germany and forced to work for public or private institutions (Sec. 11 para. 1).

Being a prisoner of war precluded eligibility for benefits. This led, in particular, to the exclusion of Soviet prisoners of war who, along with concentration camp prisoners, suffered the worst living conditions in forced labour for racist reasons. The regulation also led to the exclusion of Italian forced labourers (so-called Italian Military Internees or IMI) who had been imprisoned as prisoners of war by the German Wehrmacht after Italy's armistice with the Allies in September 1943 but who were then treated as civilian forced labourers from August 1944 onwards on the basis of a military order.[130] At the Foundation, the view expressed by the German international law expert Tomuschat[131] prevailed: the conversion of status into civilian forced labourers was illegal under international law and thus the conditions for compensation by the Foundation were not regularly met. International law expert Fischer-Lescano showed the cynicism behind Tomuschat's argument and referred to the need to recognise the factual loss of status due to NS injustice used again against the victims today.[132]

Finally, in 2015, a fund was set up for Soviet prisoners of war, destining 'voluntary' one-time payments of 2,500 Euros.[133] A total of 1,185 former prisoners of war received such a 'recognition benefit'.[134]

3.3 *Pulling the Past to the Present*

Until recently, slavery and forced labour had not been considered a relevant issue in public debate or research. The legal treatment of slavery in the last two centuries was characterised by 'othering': servitude in the context of

130 *Ibid.*, p. 417.

131 Report by Prof. Christian Tomuschat, 'Entitlement of Italian Military Internees to Benefits under the Law Establishing a Foundation 'Remembrance, Responsibility and Future'', 31 July 2001. An English translation is available as Annex 8 to the German counter memorial in the ICJ case concerning jurisdictional immunities of the state (Germany v. Italy), of 14.12.2009, <https://www.icj-cij.org/index.php/node/141936>.

132 A. Fischer-Lescano, 'Schadensersatz bei Menschenrechtsverletzungen' (2015) 48:2 *Kritische Justiz* 210.

133 Regulated by the Directive on a Recognition Benefit to Former Soviet Prisoners of War of 30.09.2015, BAnz AT 14.10.2015 B1.

134 Answer of the Federal Government to the Small Question of the parliamentary group DIE LINKE of 3.4.2019, BT-DRS. 19/9036.

Gutsherrschaft was not considered slavery, as only chattel slavery was interpreted as such. Slaves had to be of African origin, and slave traders, slaveholders and other profiteers had to come from the great colonising empires or states from the Global South. Recruitment based on force and coercion and acceptance of traditional slavery was seen as a tribute to the dying past of 'retarded' African societies on their path to modernity. Forced labour during the Third Reich was attributed to war and 'Nazi power' as a culturally and historically encapsulated phase.

One central means for achieving this was a racist understanding of the world, which constructed, among others, African, Jewish and Slavic or East European races. These were either seen as 'retarded', thus legitimising forced labour as pedagogical, 'parasitic' and thus to be eradicated by slavery, or as 'inferiors', who stood in the way to settler colonialism in the East ('*Lebensraum*') and could thus be enslaved to open space for Germanic expansion. This racism was put into law, which in turn shaped the perceptions of the citizens. In Spoerer's words, even when officials of the arms industry asked for better treatment of forced workers for the improvement of productivity, "[t]hey could no longer get rid of the ghosts that they had awakened in the people through the discriminatory special law. Those whom the state did not protect from exploitation and arbitrariness the ordinary people did not need to worry about, either".[135]

The racist past and its legacies made it easier to confront the Soviet Union and coin slavery again as a phenomenon of the 'other', making it invisible in Germany. Functionally, it served to protect German industry and the state from the payment of wages and damages. In continuity since the end of *Gutsherrschaft*, the state's function in situations of change was to protect the 'properly acquired rights' of slave owners and exploiters against the victims demanding fair wages or ownership of the land they had been forced to work upon. This understanding of the rule of law served to secure peace under the law at the expense of the victims. This peace could only be disturbed by the threat of incredibly costly class actions initiated in US courts.

4 'Contemporary Slavery' as a Problem: Causes and Consequences

'Contemporary slavery', i.e. the existence of servitude, is only starting to be recognised as an issue in Germany. Between 2017 and 2021, the term 'modern

135 M. Spoerer, above n. 103, p. 256.

slavery' is mentioned in a total of 18 documents of the Bundestag.[136] Almost all of the statements refer to international organisations and conventions. In turn, human trafficking or child labour in supply chains has received much more attention.

A wide range of exploitative practices presently constitute servitude in Germany. Exploitation ranging from forced prostitution to care work, work in the meat industry, construction industry, forced marriage and forced labour within the marriage relationship, agriculture, forced begging and work in drug gangs is discussed here.

Forced sexual exploitation is the issue most discussed and most commonly accepted as a form of modern slavery in Germany. Among the preliminary proceedings for human trafficking and exploitation recorded by the Federal Criminal Police Office, sexual exploitation cases accounted for more than half (291 out of 465).[137] The exploitation of minors represented the second largest group, with 178 of the 193 proceedings alone involving commercial sexual exploitation.[138] In 2020, almost 80% of the victims were of European origin, about ten percent of Asian origin (with a focus on Thailand and Vietnam), while the proportion of South and Central American and African victims was in the low single digits. The vast majority of European victims came from Eastern European EU countries, especially Romania and Bulgaria.[139]

A second large sector with a considerable number of unreported cases is the area of care work and other household-related services. Here, too, it is mainly women with a migration history who are victims of enslavement and extreme exploitation. The number of female migrant workers, mainly from Eastern Europe, is estimated at 300–400,000.[140] The home care sector is very vulnerable to unlawful practices. Estimates speak of about 150,000 illegal employment relationships, some of which are characterised by severe economic exploitation and involve psychological or even physical coercion. In a care chain, Polish care workers come to Germany and are replaced by Ukrainians in Poland.[141]

---

136 Cf. Deutscher Bundestag, <https://dip.bundestag.de>, searched term 'modern slavery'.

137 Bundeskriminalamt, 'Menschenhandel und Ausbeutung: Bundeslagebild 2020' (Wiesbaden 2021) 2; 5, <www.bka.de/DE/AktuelleInformationen/StatistikenLagebilder/Lagebilder/Menschenhandel/menschenhandel_node.html>.

138 *Ibid.*, p. 20.

139 *Ibid.*, p. 8.

140 A. Satola and B. Schywalski, '"Live-in-Arrangements" in deutschen Haushalten: Zwischen arbeitsrechtlichen/-vertraglichen (Un)-Sicherheiten und Handlungsmoglichkeiten'. in K. Jacobs and others (eds), *Pflege-Report 2016: Schwerpunkt: Die Pflegenden im Fokus* Schattauer, Stuttgart 2016, p. 128.

141 E. Palenga-Möllenbeck, 'Care Chains in Eastern and Central Europe: Male and Female Domestic Work at the Intersections of Gender, Class, and Ethnicity' (2013) 11:4 *Journal of Immigrant & Refugee Studies* 364, pp. 366–367.

A widespread means of labour migration are contracts concluded in Eastern European countries, which pretend that the care workers are self-employed, while the recruiting company only claims an intermediary role. The employment of migrant women in home-care very often takes the form of live-in care with 24-hour care, which is agreed between the Eastern European recruiter and the German family. The care workers are expected to be present and available to work all the time. Many of these women barely speak German, have no networks in Germany, and have no knowledge of the German legal system. Extreme exploitation is typical in 'live-ins', as employment law is systematically violated – although the Federal Labour Court has recently underlined minimum wage application in 24-hour contracts.[142] Workers in this industry often describe the withholding of pay combined with the threat of being reported for undeclared work, being locked up in the flat and other forms of physical or psychological coercion, so that some of the literature speaks of 'modern slavery'.[143] Although Germany has ratified ILO Convention C-189, its application is extremely fragmentary.[144]

Live-in care is often linked to racist, sexist and classist stereotypes and is the object of intersectional discrimination.[145] This is vividly illustrated in the advertisement 'Oma's neue Polin'[146] (Grandma's new Polish girl/woman) on a public bus in Northern Germany in 2021. Other examples can be found in the meat industry, the construction industry or agriculture. The patterns are similar. The level of exploitation in these industries differs significantly according to the origin and legal status of the victims, with the vast majority of victims coming from Eastern Europe and the most severely exploited being undocumented persons. Jobs with low union density and difficulties in organising, such as seasonal or domestic work, and with a lot of mobility, such as the construction industry or transport, are particularly vulnerable to abuse. As for

142 Decision of 24.06.2021–5 AZR 505/20.

143 C. Molitor, 'Geschäftsmodell Ausbeutung: Wenn europäische Arbeitnehmer_innen in Deutschland um ihre Rechte betrogen werden' (Berlin, 2015) 11–14, <library.fes.de/pdf-files/id/11307.pdf>; P. Graf and A. Kupfer, 'Moderne Sklaverei und extreme Ausbeutung in globalisierten Arbeits- und Geschlechterverhältnissen – ein Blick auf Deutschland. Einleitung' (2016) 25:1 *FEMINA POLITICA – Zeitschrift für feministische Politikwissenschaft* 9, pp. 15–17.

144 V. Vogt, 'Pflegearbeit in deutschen Privathaushalten: weiblich, osteuropäisch, prekär' in K. Kappler and V. Vogt (eds), *Gender im Völkerrecht*, Nomos, Baden-Baden 2019.

145 E. Palenga-Möllenbeck, above n. 141, *passim*; P. Graf and A. Kupfer, above n. 143, p. 15.

146 Ellen Kranz, '"Grandma's new Polish girl!" causes criticism in Ammerland', 03.09.2020, <https://www.nwzonline.de/plus-ammerland/slogan-omas-neue-polin-von-procura24-pflegevermittlung-aus-cloppenburg-auf-bussen-im-ammerland-linke-oldenburg-ammerland-rassismus_a_50,9,3296416056.html>.

the countries of origin, it is characteristic that the risk of abuse increases with growing socio-economic inequality, but also in post-conflict situations.[147]

The connection to historical racism, especially in relation to people of Eastern European origin, has only been discussed sporadically so far. It is openly addressed, for example, in relation to Roma from Romania and the related discriminatory antiziganism.[148]

German companies have been profiting from servitude through often complex supply chains in the textiles, food and communication industries, among others.[149] The relevance of servitude in supply chains for German industries is on a relatively low level from a general perspective at first view. According to estimations, 1,1–1,4% of workers in different steps of the textile supply chains are enslaved, 1,1–1,3% in agriculture, forestry and fishing, or 1,0–1,2% in mining, to name a few.[150] Furthermore, with the exception of textile production, a trend towards higher levels of servitude in production chains can be observed.[151] In numbers, even 1–2% is a high incidence.

4.1 *Definition of Slavery and Related Concepts*

How prepared are German society and the legal system to confront 'modern slavery'? Slavery and servitude would hardly be present in the contemporary German legal system if not for the implementation of international and regional treaties. There is no common understanding of the terminology of 'modern slavery' yet. The relevant provisions originate from different areas of regulation with different protected interests. Originally, the legal interests of personal freedom and sexual self-determination were protected in an unconnected manner. Economic exploitation was only punishable as usury, where it was long disputed whether usury was also applicable to extreme exploitation of labour forces.[152]

---

147 P. Follmar-Otto, *Menschenhandel in Deutschland: Die Menschenrechte der Betroffenen stärken*, Deutsches Institut für Menschenrechte, Berlin 2009, p. 22.

148 R. Riegler, ‚Roma aus (Süd-) Osteuropa als Betroffene von Frauenhandel', *Welcome to Germany IV: Menschenhandel in Deutschland*, <https://www.boell.de/sites/default/files/welcome_to_germany_iv-menschenhandel.pdf> ; P. Graf and A. Kupfer, above n. 143, p. 14.

149 P. Graf and A. Kupfer, above n. 143, p. 19.

150 S. Hofmann and others, 'Soziale Standards in globalen Wertschöpfungsstrukturen: Empirische Analyse der globalen Lieferketten ausgewählter Wirtschaftszweige Deutschlands' (Düsseldorf May 2021). Working Paper Forschungsförderung 213, p. 51, <hdl.handle.net/10419/234192>.

151 *Ibid.*, 60–61.

152 A. Hohendorf, *Das Individualwucherstrafrecht nach dem ersten Gesetz zur Bekämpfung der Wirtschaftskriminalität von 1976*, Duncker & Humblot, Berlin 1982, pp. 78–80; Federal Supreme Court 22.4.1997–1 StR 701/96, *BGHSt* 43, 53.

Until 2005, legislation on slavery in criminal law, as interpreted by the Federal Supreme Court (*BGH*), was not much more than a sham regulation. According to Sec. 234 Criminal Code 1871, valid until 2005, the seizing of a person by cunning, threat or force in order to bring him into slavery or servitude was punishable.

In the central criminal case, which the *BGH* had to decide,[153] a man posing as a police commissioner had imprisoned another, physically and verbally abused him and forced him to work for several months. The *BGH* denied the existence of both slavery and servitude. It argued that slavery in terms of the Criminal Code provision was to be interpreted according to the legal definitions given in the Slavery Convention of 1926 and the Supplementary Convention of 1956. Since both in the *BGH's* understanding presupposed the victim's submission to a legal system that still knows slavery or servitude, and slavery was expressly prohibited in Germany under Article 4 ECHR and was not tolerated in practice, punishment under the law could only be considered if the victim was to be taken abroad to a country where slavery was at least tolerated by the authorities.[154] The case illustrates how the othering of slavery functions in German criminal law.

After the adoption of the Palermo Protocol of 15 November 2000,[155] the Council Framework Decision of 19 July 2002[156] and the EU Directive 2011/36/EU of 15 April 2011,[157] a comprehensive reform of criminal law was undertaken in 2005[158] and 2016[159] with regard to trafficking in human beings, but also in particular aspects of 'modern slavery' more generally. Other international agreements that have been taken into account are the Optional Protocol to the Convention on the Rights of the Child on the sale of children, child prostitution and child pornography,[160] the ILO Worst Forms of Child Labour

153 BGH 11.05.1993–1 StR 896/92, NJW 1993, 2252–2253.

154 *Ibid.*, 2252.

155 Protocol to Prevent, Suppress and Punish Trafficking in Persons Especially Women and Children, supplementing the United Nations Convention against Transnational Organised Crime, 15.11.2000, BT-Drs. 15/5150 Annex 1.

156 2002/629/JHA, Council Framework Decision of 192002.07. on combating trafficking in human beings, OJ L 203, *01/08/2002, p. 0001–0004.*

157 Directive 2011/36/EU of the European Parliament and of the Council of 05.04.2011 on preventing and combating trafficking in human beings and protecting its victims, and replacing Council Framework Decision 2002/629/JHA, OJ L 101/1.

158 37 Criminal Law Amendment Act of 11.02.2005, Federal Law Gazette I 2005, 239.

159 Act to Improve the Fight against Trafficking in Human Beings and to Amendment of the Federal Central Register Act and the Eighth Book of the Social Code of 11.10.2016, Federal Law Gazette I, 2226.

160 A/RES/54/263 of 25 May 2000; Federal Law Gazette II 2008, 1222.

Convention, 1999 (No. 182),[161] and the Council of Europe Convention on Action against Trafficking in Human Beings of 16 May 2005.[162]

Criminal liability now covers various aspects of servitude ('slavery, serfdom, debt bondage or in conditions corresponding or resembling such', forced prostitution, exploitative employment including begging), with human trafficking as one central issue, where recruitment for slave labour is punishable.[163]

The definitions are based on the relevant international conventions and thus derived from the 1926 Convention on Slavery, as amended by the 1953 Protocol, and the 1956 Supplementary Convention. According to these definitions, slavery means "the status or condition of a person over whom any or all of the powers attaching to the right of ownership are exercised, and 'slave' means a person in such condition or status"; serfdom means "the condition or status of a tenant who is by law, custom or agreement bound to live and labour on land belonging to another person and to render some determinate service to such other person, whether for reward or not, and is not free to change his status".[164] Exploitation is defined as "[e]xploitation through employment occurs when the employment is carried out of a ruthless profit motive at working conditions that are conspicuously disproportionate to the working conditions of such workers who are engaged in the same or comparable employment (exploitative employment)".[165] Especially the definitions used in the 1926 and 1956 conventions and the 1953 Protocol do not seem adequate to cover contemporary forms of servitude, as could be seen in the analysis of colonial relations, the Third Reich and the Federal Supreme Court (BGH).

5 Redressing and Recalibrating Contemporary Slavery

Germany's traditional main approach to redress contemporary servitude and slavery was almost exclusively via criminal law. It has been recalibrated in the context of EU activities against human trafficking. In the implementation of

161 BGBl. 2001 II, 1290.

162 CETS No. 197; J.uEisele, '§§ 232–241a StGB' in Schönke/Schröder (ed), *Strafgesetzbuch: Kommentar*, 30. neu bearbeitete Auflage C.H. Beck, München 2019, § 232 Rn. 2–5.

163 Sec. 232–232b Criminal Code, incorporating Article 2-4 EU directive 2011/36/EU.

164 Art. 7 a. and b. of the Supplementary Convention on the Abolition of Slavery, the Slave Trade, and Institutions and Practices Similar to Slavery of 07.09.1956.

165 Sec. 232 Criminal Code.

the EU Directive 2011/36/EU, some instruments of victim protection also have been introduced, although a general strategy is still missing.[166]

5.1 *Legal Innovations*

In recent years, victim protection has increasingly become the focus of attention. The approaches worth mentioning here come only partly from fields that focus on combating 'modern slavery'. Innovative legal measures that are worthwhile mentioning are especially situated in employment law and supply chain regulation.

5.1.1 Changes in Labour Law

German labour law still generally starts its protective function at the threshold of an employment relationship. A relevant innovation was introduced in two steps. The law on posted workers introduced successively sectoral minimum wages based on collective agreements;[167] its loopholes were filled in 2015 by the general minimum wage law.[168] The law on posted workers was the first to provide for liability provisions in the whole supply chain.[169] The relevant norm provides for the liability of an entrepreneur who sub-contracts concerning the payment of net minimum wages in the supply chain. If a sub-contractor does not pay an employee's minimum wages due for producing the works or services for the contractor, the employee is entitled to payment of the net minimum wage they would have received from the employer. This rule, originally introduced in 1996 for construction workers, was successively extended to other sectors and finally also to the universal minimum wage. The universal minimum wage, raised to 12,82 Euros in 2025,[170] applies to all employees, including trainees, but not to apprentices, prisoners and certain other groups.[171]

An important element for migrant workers is the state and union-funded institutionalisation of advisory centres for migrant workers called 'fair

166 E. Küblbeck, 'Die EU-Richtlinie gegen Menschenhandel: Situation und Umsetzung in Deutschland' (2017) *Nachrichtendienst des Deutschen Vereins für öffentliche und private Fürsorge eV* 172, p. 176.

167 Arbeitnehmerentsendegesetz. First introduced 26.02.1996, BGBl. I, p. 227; major restructuring 20.04.2009, BGBl. I, p. 799; last large reform 11.08.2014, BGBl. I p. 1348, 1356, as part of a package of laws on minimum wages.

168 Mindestlohngesetz. 11.08.2014, BGBl. I 2014, p. 1348.

169 Cf. H. Fechner, 'Posting of workers before German courts' in Z. Rasnača and M. Bernaciak (eds), *Posting of workers before national courts*, ETUI aisbl, Brussels 2020, pp. 108–109.

170 BGBl. I 2023 Nr. 321.

171 W. Däubler, '§ 1 MiLoG' in W. Däubler et al. (eds), *Arbeitsrecht: Individualarbeitsrecht mit kollektivrechtlichen Bezügen; Handkommentar*, 4. Auflage, Nomos, Baden-Baden 2017, para. 3.

mobility', which are run by the trade union federation. Here, information and advice on rights and options for action is given proactively and in the applicable native language in relevant sectors such as agriculture, meat industry, domestic care, construction, postal services and international road transport.[172] It has been successful in providing knowledge of rights and assistance close to the places where severely exploited migrant workers are living and working.

5.1.2 Due Diligence in Supply Chains

The 2011 UN Guiding Principles on Business and Human Rights (UNGP)[173] first resulted in a governmental National Action Plan passed in 2016.[174] The plan focused on aspects such as educating firms in terms of human rights and due diligence in supply chains and calling for CSR activities. It received strong criticism from NGOs for staying far behind legislation in other countries. Complaints referred to voluntariness instead of binding duties of companies, the lack of remedies for victims of human rights violations in supply chains, and the lack of political will altogether to address deficits in human rights protection in transnational contexts.[175] It is noteworthy that the German government has not been supporting the Geneva process of writing an internationally binding treaty on business and human rights, but rather sabotaging it.[176] Although with the new government a change of positions has been announced, a common strategy and joint support is still lacking.[177]

In 2021, the Bundestag passed the Law on Corporate Due Diligence in Supply Chains,[178] which was inspired by the French *Loi de vigilance*. The law establishes human rights and ecological 'due diligence standards' for big companies with at least 3.000 employees in Germany in 2023 and 1.000 starting in 2024 (sec. 1). It concretizes compliance measures (sec. 3–10), which are to be controlled by the authorities (sec. 12–18). Non-compliance can be sanctioned with fines (sec. 24)

---

172 Cf. Faire Mobilität, <https://www.faire-mobilitaet.de>.

173 UN doc A/HRC/17/31.

174 Bundesregierung, 'Nationaler Aktionsplan Umsetzung der VN-Leitprinzipien für Wirtschaft und Menschenrechte' (Berlin 2017).

175 CorA and others, 'Kein Mut zu mehr Verbindlichkeit: Kommentar deutscher Nichtregierungsorganisationen zum Nationalen Aktionsplan Wirtschaft und Menschenrechte der Bundesregierung' (February 2017), <www.germanwatch.org/de/13252>.

176 'Deutschland bremst Menschenrechte', taz, (14.10.2019), <https://taz.de/Bessere-Normen-fuer-Unternehmen/!5632860/>.

177 S. Luthango and M. Schulze, 'The EU and the negotiations for a binding treaty on business and human rights' (2023), <www.swp-berlin.org/publikation/the-eu-and-the-negotiations-for-a-binding-treaty-on-business-and-human-rights>.

178 Gesetz über die unternehmerischen Sorgfaltspflichten in Lieferketten, (16.07.2021), BGBl. I 2021, p. 2959.

and exclusion from public orders (sec. 22). As relevant human rights standards, the law refers to the ILO core labour standards conventions and the UN ICCPR and ICSECR, among others (sec. 2). Its understanding of 'risks for human rights' explicitly covers the prohibition of all forms of slavery, slave-like practices, servitude or other forms of domination or oppression in the workplace environment (sec. 2 par. 2). Furthermore, it refers to forced labour understood as any work done under the threat of punishment (sec. 2 par. 2 No. 3).

The law has received both critical and positive appraisal by the initiative of more than 125 NGOs for supply chain legislation. NGOs criticised the limitation of supply chain responsibility effectively to direct suppliers, the lack of civil liability, which would have offered damages to victims abroad, the restriction to big few corporations, ecological deficits and possible conflicts of interests of the responsible authorities. In effect, the preventive idea of the UNGP is not recognised in the supply chain. The same is true for the interests of those affected by violations against due diligence rules. Their interests in consultations and redress are not considered by the law. Gender aspects are hardly present, as well as the recognition of the rights of indigenous peoples. The administrative entity responsible for control belongs to the responsibility of the Ministry of Economy, without human rights or ecological expertise, and civil society participation is missing.[179] On the other hand, it is seen as a first step towards a generalised responsibility of firms for the respect of human rights in the whole supply chain.[180]

The passing of the law may be interpreted as suggestive of a possible change of direction in German politics towards an understanding of our own responsibility for extreme forms of exploitation in Germany and abroad. It may be seen as timid, in the tradition of putting economic interests first, but also realising that the existing economic model is bringing about dangers for human dignity in the whole supply chain. Whether this is a real change of policy or simply window dressing is not clear yet. Germany's recent (2021) participation in Alliance 8.7 as a pathfinder country for combatting child labour[181] in this context can be seen at least as a contribution to public sensitivity concerning aspects of modern slavery.

179 Initiative Lieferkettengesetz, 'What the new supply chain act delivers – and what it doesnt' (11.06.2021), <https://www.germanwatch.org/de/20324>.

180 Initiative Lieferkettengesetz, 'Stellungnahme zum Gesetzentwurf für ein Lieferkettengesetz' (Berlin March 2020), <lieferkettengesetz.de/wp-content/uploads/2021/03/Initiative-Lieferkettengesetz_Stellungnahme-zum-Gesetzentwurf.pdf>.

181 Cf. Wirtschaft & Menschenrechte, 'Alliance 8.7' (09.26.2021), <https://www.csr-in-deutschland.de/DE/Wirtschaft-Menschenrechte/Internationales/Alliance-8-7/alliance-8-7.html>.

5.2 *From 'Othering' Slavery to Decent Labour Conditions*

Germany's history is replete with forms of exploitation based on force or coercion, which, until the millennium change, had been largely ignored by using a wide array of narratives to make them a problem for others. The exploitation of lower classes and people from other territories, especially in Eastern Europe and Africa, with government support has been a common thread of Germany's economic structures. Indeed, a common thread of slavery and servitude, according to Patterson's terminology, can be seen from the 15th century until the end of World War II. Yet, legal institutionalisation has contributed to making the circle of othering invisible.

Avoiding the redressing of victims as forced workers have been functional for this. The victims had to pay with the loss of territory (serfs) for their freedom by offering unpaid labour as a redemption fee. Victims were then abandoned after 1945. Courts left the victims of forced exploitation without remedy and negated the possibility of slavery in Germany based on its prohibition of treating persons like chattel. Legalism reached the point of sorting out prisoners of war who were forced to do slave work from the definition of forced workers entitled to compensation.

The methods used by law and public narratives served to build up an understanding that, until today, has left racist prejudices and supremacist economic narratives in German society. Antiracist legislation in the Constitution obliterated slavery-related background. Even antiracist literature on legislation tends to oversee racism towards Eastern Europeans, including Russians.

Besides a need for public debates concerning the reinterpretation of the past and German co-responsibility for overcoming extreme forms of exploitation, stronger legal measures with a focus on redressing victims of servitude need to be implemented. If contemporary servitude is the tip of a pyramid of exploitation, measures have to be implemented where fair employment conditions are not met. The first steps have been the introduction of sectoral and universal minimum wages and liability in the whole supply chain in Germany. On the domestic level, the introduction of a generalised, broadly available system of labour inspection is urgent to protect workers who are not part of unions and do not enjoy the protection of works councils. The current system is highly fragmented and only works well where work councils function as supervisors. Especially smaller enterprises and those in the low-wage sector are left with little control and their workers with relatively high thresholds for labour court access.[182] Minimum wage control by the 'finance control undeclared work', a

---

182 Although labour courts in first instance are free of charge and both first advice free of charge and legal aid are available, they are hardly used by marginalised employees. In the end, both sides have to pay their costs in first instance – and legal aid has to be paid back

police unit of the customs department, is of little help, especially for unregistered workers. The expansion of representation by works councils and trade unions in small and medium-sized companies must also be a central focus.

Supply chain due diligence legislation should effectively combat human rights violations in the whole supply chain. Coverage needs to be expanded. Victims of human rights violations should be entitled to demand compensation for violation of due diligence duties in the whole supply chain, using (for Germany innovative[183]) instruments such as class action and the right of unions and associations to start proceedings on behalf of marginalised persons, including those in 'modern slavery'. The Wollheim case had great effects because of the solidarity of the claimant and the resolution of the case via settlement, but at the same time, it has shown what could be possible if the juridical means were better suited for the oppressed.[184]

Acknowledgements

Funded by the Deutsche Forschungsgemeinschaft (DFG, German Research Foundation) – Projektnummer 374666841 – SFB 1342. I thank Adelle Blacket, Laura Dehaibi, Irene Dingeldey, Andreas Fischer-Lescano, Ulrich Mückenberger, Mohammed Odusanya, Audrey Parent, Andrea Schäfer and Theresa Wobbe for their helpful comments on an earlier version of this article.

Academic References

A. Boshart, 'Major Boshart' in F. Giesebrecht (ed), *Die Behandlung der Eingeborenen in den deutschen Kolonien*, Fischer, Berlin 1898.

A. Brivio, '« Nos grands-pères achetaient des esclaves … »: Le culte de Mami Tchamba au Togo et au Bénin'(2008) 8 *Gradhiva. Revue d'anthropologie et d'histoire des arts* 64.

A. De Juan, 'Extraction and Violent Resistance in the Early Phases of State Building: Quantitative Evidence From the "Maji Maji" Rebellion, 1905–1907' (2016) 49:3 *Comparative Political Studies* 291.

later if the situation of need ceases. Advice on site which could be presented by labour inspectors is missing. Cf. E. Kocher, *Effektive Mobilisierung von Beschäftigtenrechten: Das Arbeitsrecht in der betrieblichen Praxis*, Hans-Böckler-Stiftung, Düsseldorf 2009.

183 In civil law and public law, class action and the right of unions and associations to sue wrongdoers without individual mandate has been introduced in some areas via EU directives; in labour law, these instruments are practically unavailable, especially in areas of severe exploitation.

184 See above.

A. Fischer-Lescano, 'Schadensersatz bei Menschenrechtsverletzungen' (2015) 48:2 *Kritische Justiz* 210.

A. Forrest, 'The Hundred Days, the Congress of Vienna and the Atlantic Slave Trade' in K. Astbury and M. Philp (eds), *Napoleon's hundred days and the politics of legitimacy*, Palgrave Macmillan, Cham 2018, pp. 163–181.

A. Hense, 'Limitation of Economic Damages as a 'Humanitarian Gesture': The German Foundation 'Remembrance, Responsibility and the Future'' (2011) 46:2 *Journal of Contemporary History* 407.

A. Hohendorf, *Das Individualwucherstrafrecht nach dem ersten Gesetz zur Bekämpfung der Wirtschaftskriminalität von 1976*, Duncker & Humblot, Berlin 1982.

A. Perras, *Carl Peters and German Imperialism 1856–1918: A Political Biography*, (reprint) Clarendon Press, Oxford, 2006.

A. Satola and B. Schywalski, '"Live-in-Arrangements" in deutschen Haushalten: Zwischen arbeitsrechtlichen/-vertraglichen (Un)-Sicherheiten und Handlungsmoglichkeiten' in K. Jacobs, A. Kuhlmey, S. Greß, J. Klauber, and A. Schwinger (eds), *Pflege-Report 2016: Schwerpunkt: Die Pflegenden im Fokus*, Schattauer, Stuttgart 2016, pp. 127–138.

A. Weindl, *Die Kurbrandenburger im ‚atlantischen System': 1650–1720*, Universität zu Köln, Köln, 2001.

B. Grambow, *Das Gefängniswesen Bremens*, Borna-Leipzig, Noske 1910.

B. Raule, 'Letter No. 118' in R. Schück, *Brandenburg-Preußens Kolonial-Politik unter dem Großen Kurfürsten und seinen Nachfolgern: (1647–1721)*, Grunow, Leipzig 1898.

C. Haarnack, "'Nachrichten von Surinam': Representations of a Former Dutch Colony in German Travel Literature, 1790–1900", in A. E. Martin, L. Missinne, and B. van Dam, *Travel Writing in Dutch and German, 1790–1930: Modernity, Regionality, Mobility*, Routledge, Taylor & Francis, New York 2017, pp. 114–138.

C. Koslofsky and R. Zaugg, 'Ship's Surgeon Johann Peter Oettinger. A Hinterlander in the Atlantic Slave Trade, 1682–1696' in F. Brahm and E. Rosenhaft (eds), *Slavery Hinterland: Transatlantic slavery and continental Europe, 1680–1850*, The Boydell Press, Woodbridge 2016, pp. 25–44.

C. Peters, 'Dr. Peters' in F. Giesebrecht (ed), *Die Behandlung der Eingeborenen in den deutschen Kolonien*, Fischer, Berlin 1898.

C.U. Schminck-Gustavus, 'Zwangsarbeitsrecht und Faschismus. Zur "Polenpolitik" im "Dritten Reich"' (1980) 13:1–2 *Kritische Justiz* 1.

D. Liebscher, *Rasse im Recht–Recht gegen Rassismus: Genealogie einer ambivalenten rechtlichen Kategorie*, Suhrkamp, Berlin 2021.

E. Kocher, *Effektive Mobilisierung von Beschäftigtenrechten: Das Arbeitsrecht in der betrieblichen Praxis*, Hans-Böckler-Stiftung, Düsseldorf 2009.

E. Küblbeck, 'Die EU-Richtlinie gegen Menschenhandel: Situation und Umsetzung in Deutschland' (2017) *Nachrichtendienst des Deutschen Vereins für öffentliche und private Fürsorge eV* 172.

E. Palenga-Möllenbeck, 'Care Chains in Eastern and Central Europe: Male and Female Domestic Work at the Intersections of Gender, Class, and Ethnicity' (2013) 11:4 *Journal of Immigrant & Refugee Studies* 364.

F. Großmann, *Über die gutsherrlich-bäuerlichen Rechtsverhältnisse in der Mark Brandenburg vom 16. bis 18. Jahrhundert*, Duncker & Humblot, Leipzig 1890.

F. von Martitz, 'Das internationale System zur Unterdrückung des afrikanischen Sklavenhandels in seinem heutigen Bestande' (1885) 1:1 *Archiv des öffentlichen Rechts* 3.

G. Eisenblätter, *Grundlinien der Politik des Reiches gegenüber dem Generalgouvernement 1939–1945*, Diss Frankfurt a.M. Universität Frankfurt 1969; Translation by R. Bauer, *The Construction of a National Socialist Europe During the Second World War: How the New Order Took Shape*, Routledge, London 2019.

G.F. Knapp, 'Die Bauernbefreiung in Oesterreich und in Preussen' (1894) 18 *Jahrbuch für Gesetzgebung, Verwaltung und Volkswirtschaft im Deutschen Reich* 409.

G.F. Knapp, *Die Landarbeiter in Knechtschaft und Freiheit*, Duncker & Humblot, Leipzig, 1891.

H. Fechner, 'Legal Segmentation and Early Colonialism in Sub-Saharan Africa: Informality and the Colonial Exploitative Legal Employment Standard' (2022) 161:4 (Special Issue on Legal Segmentation) *International Labour Review* 615.

H. Fechner, 'Posting of workers before German courts' in Z. Rasnača and M. Bernaciak (eds), *Posting of workers before national courts*, ETUI, Brussels 2020, pp. 105–126.

H. Kaak, *Die Gutsherrschaft: Theoriegeschichtliche Untersuchungen zum Agrarwesen im ostelbischen Raum*, De Gruyter, Berlin, 1991.

H. Kaak, 'Vom Erbzinsrecht zur Leibeigenschaft – Entstehung agrarischer Zwangsformen im frühneuzeitlichen Brandenburg' (2007) 8:1 *Zeitschrift für Weltgeschichte* 71.

H. Schnee, *Deutsches Kolonial-Lexikon*, Quelle & Meyer, Leipzig 1920.

J. Binner, 'Zwangsarbeit im Nationalsozialismus' (2012) 13:1 *Zeitschrift für Weltgeschichte* 31.

J. Denzer, *Die Konquista der Augsburger Welser-Gesellschaft in Südamerika (1528–1556): Historische Rekonstruktion, Historiografie und lokale Erinnerungskultur in Kolumb ien und Venezuela*, C.H. Beck, München 2005.

J. Eisele, '§§ 232–241a StGB' in Schönke/Schröder (ed), *Strafgesetzbuch: Kommentar*, 30 neu bearbeitete Auflage, C.H. Beck, München 2019.

J.G. Deutsch, 'The 'Freeing' of Slaves in German East Africa: the Statistical Record, 1890–1914' (1998) 19:2 *Slavery & Abolition* 109.

J. Howard, *The State of the Prisons in England and Wales: With Preliminary Observations and an Account of Some Foreign Prisons*, Cambridge University Press, Cambridge 2013 [1777].

J. Iliffe, *A Modern History of Tanganyika*, Cambridge University Press, Cambridge 1979.

J.K. Gildemeister, *Verfahren und Erkenntniß des Bremischen Obergerichts in Untersuchungssachen wider den Capitain des Bremischen Schiffs Julius und Eduard und Cons. wegen Sklavenhandels; Nach den Acten dargest*, Heyse, Bremen 1842.

J. Osterhammel, *Sklaverei und die Zivilisation des Westens*, 2nd ed, Carl-Friedrich-von-Siemens-Stiftung, München, 2000.

J. Zollmann, 'Slavery and the Colonial State in German South West Africa 1880s to 1918' (2010) 7 *Journal of Namibian Studies* 85.

K. Haebler, *Die überseeischen Unternehmungen der Welser und ihrer Gesellschafter*, Hirschfeld, Leipzig, 1903.

K.J. Bade, 'Zwischen Mission und Kolonialbewegung, Kolonialwirtschaft und Kolonialpolitik in der Bismarckzeit: der Fall Friedrich Fabri' in K.J. Bade (ed), *Imperialismus und Kolonialmission: Kaiserliches Deutschland und koloniales Imperium*, Steiner, Wiesbaden 1982, pp. 103–141.

K. Weber, 'Deutschland, Der Atlantische Sklavenhandel Und Die Plantagenwirtschaft Der Neuen Welt' (2009) 7:1 *Journal of Modern European History* 37.

M. Buggeln, 'Unfreie Arbeit im Nationalsozialismus' in M. Buggeln and M. Wildt (eds), *Arbeit im Nationalsozialismus*, Oldenbourg Wissenschaftsverlag, München 2014, pp. 231–252.

M. Ressel, 'Hamburg und die Niederelbe im atlantischen Sklavenhandel der Frühen Neuzeit' (2015) 66–67 *Werkstatt Geschichte* 75.

M. Spoerer, 'NS-Zwangsarbeiter im Deutschen Reich' (2001) 49(4) *Vierteljahrshefte für Zeitgeschichte* 665.

M. Spoerer, *Zwangsarbeit unter dem Hakenkreuz: Ausländische Zivilarbeiter, Kriegsgefangene und Häftlinge im Deutschen Reich und im besetzten Europa 1939–1945*, Dt. Verl.-Anst., Stuttgart 2001.

M. Zeuske, *Handbuch Geschichte der Sklaverei: Eine Globalgeschichte von den Anfängen bis zur Gegenwart*, 2nd edn, De Gruyter Oldenbourg, Berlin, 2020.

O. Grambow, *Das Gefängniswesen Bremens*, Noske, Borna-Leipzig 1910, pp. 40–46.

O. Patterson, *Slavery and Social Death: A Comparative Study: with a New Preface*, Harvard University Press, Cambridge 2018 [1982].

O. Patterson and X. Zhuo, 'Modern trafficking, slavery, and other forms of servitude' (2018) 44 *Annual Review of Sociology* 407.

P. Follmar-Otto, *Menschenhandel in Deutschland: Die Menschenrechte der Betroffenen stärken*, Deutsches Institut für Menschenrechte, Berlin 2009.

P. Graf and A. Kupfer, 'Moderne Sklaverei und extreme Ausbeutung in globalisierten Arbeits- und Geschlechterverhältnissen – ein Blick auf Deutschland. Einleitung' (2016) 25:1 *Femina Politica – Zeitschrift für feministische Politikwissenschaft* 9.

P.E. Lovejoy, *Transformations in Slavery: A History of Slavery in Africa* (3rd edn), Cambridge University Press, Cambridge, 2011.

P.E. Lovejoy and J.S. Hogendorn, *Slow Death for Slavery: The Course of Abolition in Northern Nigeria, 1897–1936*, Cambridge Univ. Press, Cambridge, 1993.

R. von Hippel, 'Beiträge zur Geschichte der Freiheitsstrafe' (1897) 18 *Zeitschrift für die gesamte Strafrechtswissenschaft* 419.

R. von Mallinckrodt, J. Köstlbauer and S. Lentz, 'Beyond Exceptionalism – Traces of Slavery and the Slave Trade in Early Modern Germany, 1650–1850' in R. Mallinckrodt, J. Köstlbauer and S. Lentz (eds), *Beyond Exceptionalism*, De Gruyter Oldenbourg, Berlin, Boston, 2021.

R. von Mallinckrodt, 'There Are No Slaves in Prussia?' in F. Brahm and E. Rosenhaft (eds), *Slavery Hinterland: Transatlantic slavery and continental Europe, 1680–1850*, The Boydell Press, Woodbridge, 2016.

S. Blanke, 'Der lange Weg zur Entschädigung von NS-Zwangsarbeitern' (2001) 34:2 *Kritische Justiz* 195.

S. Lentz, '"No German Ship Conducts Slave Trade!" the Public Controversy About German Participation in the Slave Trade During the 1840s' in R. Mallinckrodt, J. Köstlbauer and S. Lentz (eds), *Beyond Exceptionalism*, De Gruyter, Berlin/Boston 2021, pp. 286–311.

T. Krause, 'Opera publica' in G. Ammerer, F. Bretschneider and A.S. Weiß (eds), *Gefängnis und Gesellschaft: Zur (Vor-) Geschichte der strafenden Einsperrung*, Leipziger Universitätsverlag, Leipzig, 2003.

V. Vogt, 'Pflegearbeit in deutschen Privathaushalten: weiblich, osteuropäisch, prekär' in K. Kappler and V. Vogt (eds), *Gender im Völkerrecht*, Nomos, Baden-Baden 2019.

W. Benz, 'Der Wollheim-Prozeß. Zwangsarbeit für IG Farben in Auschwitz' in C. Goschler and L. Herbst (eds), *Wiedergutmachung in der Bundesrepublik Deutschland*, Reprint 2018, Oldenbourg Wissenschaftsverlag, Berlin 1988.

W. Däubler, '§ 1 MiLoG' in W. Däubler et al. (eds), *Arbeitsrecht: Individualarbeitsrecht mit kollektivrechtlichen Bezügen; Handkommentar*, 4 Auflage, Nomos, Baden-Baden 2017.

W. Durner, 'Art 11 [Freizügigkeit]' in G. Dürig et al (eds), *Grundgesetz: Kommentar, 95. Lieferung Juli 2021*, C.H. Beck, München 2021, pp. 12 17.

W. Naucke, 'Deutsches Kolonialstrafrecht: 1886–1918' (1988) 7 *Rechtshistorisches Journal* 297.

Troubled Waters: Exploitative Child Labour in the Ghanaian Fisheries Industry

Julia Selman Ayetey

1 Introduction

Target 8.7 of the Sustainable Development Goals seeks the implementation of immediate and effective measures to eliminate the worst forms of child labour and end all forms of child labour by 2025. In certain Ghanaian communities, cultural practices, such as Trokosi and Kayayei – viewed by some as unlawful forms of child labour – continue to be practised.[1] Significant numbers of Ghanaian children are also unlawfully engaged in quarrying, domestic servitude, cocoa production and mining. However, exploitative child labour in the Ghanaian fishing industry, particularly on Lake Volta, has attracted significant media attention locally and globally.[2]

1 Trokosi has evolved into the practice of young girls being given to Fetish Priests at local shrines. Their purpose is to serve the gods and fetish priests as a means of atonement for crimes committed by a family member. For a historical account of the practice see, E.K. Quashigah, 'Legislating Religious Liberty: The Ghanaian Experience' (1999) 1999:2 *Brigham Young University Law Review* 58. Kayayei are manual labourers, almost always female, who typically work in markets and transport goods on their heads, usually in a large pan. See, S. Buske, 'Prostitutes, Orphans and Entrepreneurs: The Effect of Public Perceptions of Ghana's Girl Child Kayayei on Public Policy' (2013) 20:2 *William and Mary Journal of Women and the Law* 295; For further reading see, A. S. Bilyeu, 'Trokosi – The Practice of Sexual Slavery in Ghana: Religious and Cultural Freedom vs. Human Rights' (1999) 9:2 *Indiana International & Comparative Law Review* 458. A.N. Botchway, 'Abolished by Law—Maintained in Practice: The Trokosi as Practiced in Parts of the Republic of Ghana' (2008) 3:2 *Florida International University Law Review* 369. R. Atuguba, 'Human Trafficking in Ghana: A Review of Legislation', International Labour Organisation, (2005). These practices exist despite the constitutional prohibition of cultural practices which are dehumanizing or harmful, see Article 26(2) of the *1992 Constitution of the Republic of Ghana*.

2 See for example, D. Patta, 'Children forced into slavery risk lives deep-dive fishing in Ghana – CBS News', *CBS News*, (28.09.2021), <https://www.cbsnews.com/news/ghana-lake-volta-child-slavery/>; L. Kristine, 'On Ghana's Lake Volta, child slavery is in plain sight', *CNN*, (03.07.2021), <https://www.cnn.com/2021/07/03/opinions/lisa-kristine-lake-volta-spc-intl/index.html>; Free the Slaves, 'New Research Indicates High Prevalence of Child Trafficking and Slavery-Like Conditions in Ghana Fishing Villages', *Free the Slaves*, (28.02.2017), <https://freetheslaves.net/new-research-indicates-high-prevalence-of-child-trafficking-and-slavery-like-conditions-in-ghana-fishing-villages/>'.Child Labour in Fishing on the Increase in

 | DOI:10.1163/9789004723801_010

This chapter will highlight the incidence and cultural acceptability of child fishing labour in Ghana, examine the circumstances under which it becomes exploitative and outline the legislative framework available to address it. Whilst it is not possible to undertake an exhaustive examination of this multi-faceted social issue, this chapter will identify and analyse four factors which contribute to its persistence: (i) poverty and socio-cultural dynamics (ii) agency (iii) a lack of reliable and independent data and (iv) a lack of enforcement. The chapter concludes by suggesting measures that could be adopted to enhance the effectiveness of anti-child labour laws.

2 Child Labour and Exploitative Child Labour in the Fisheries Industry

As will be evinced in the discussion below, the treatment some children are subjected to in the Ghanaian fishing industry may be tantamount to what is now commonly termed 'contemporary (or modern) slavery'. Combatting exploitative child labour is a critical aspect of reducing unfair and harmful labour practices, both of which are key objectives of the 'contemporary slavery' agenda. However, domestically, there is no criminal offence with that nomenclature. Moreover, as a country directly impacted by the transatlantic slave trade, the term slavery brings an intensely sensitive period in the region's history to the fore. To separate this term from its historical and institutional context would be to trivialize the ineffable suffering and colossal economic impact on the region's people, past and present.[3] For these reasons, this chapter uses specific terminologies that refer to concrete scenarios rather than the broad term of 'contemporary slavery', which is both vague and carries multi-generational and multifaceted historical trauma.

As a legal term, 'child labour' carries no negative connotation in Ghana. Unlike the International Labour Organisation (ILO), which conceptualises child labour as work which deprives children of their "potential and their dignity", under the *Children's Act, 1998 (Act 560)* (*'Children's Act'*), the term 'child labour' appears to simply mean children in work.[4] This is in contrast to Western discourse distinguishing between child work and child labour, the latter of which is "dangerous and intolerable" and associated with exploitation and the

Ghana' *Modern Ghana,* (27.08.2009), <https://www.modernghana.com/news/235046/child-labour-in-fishing-on-the-increase-in-ghana.html>.

3 A. Blackett, 'Slavery is not a Metaphor' (2018) 66:4 *American Journal of Comparative Law* 927.

4 ILO, <https://www.ilo.org/topics/child-labour/what-child-labour>.

former which is not.[5] Thus, the phrase 'exploitative child labour', defined in the *Children's Act* as labour through which a child is "deprived of health, education or development", is used throughout this chapter as an umbrella term to cover children in (paid or unpaid) work that is unlawful and has harmful, abusive or exploitative aspects.[6]

Ghana has a long history of working children.[7] An ILO report explained that,

> From a historical perspective, child work is part and parcel of the fabric of Ghanaian society. Children are viewed as an investment, with the legitimate expectation that they will contribute to the family income ...[8]

It is perhaps thus foreseeable that Ghana is amongst the countries with the highest incidences of child labour. Almost 22% of children between the ages of 5–17 participate in some form of child labour.[9] This equates to approximately one in every five children. The 2017–2021 National Plan of Action for the Elimination of the Worst Forms of Child Labour reported that more than one in ten children (14.2%) were engaged in the worst forms of child labour, and six in

---

5 A. Bhukuth, 'Defining Child Labour: A Controversial Debate' (2008) 18:3 *Development in Practice*, 385. Bhukuth notes the position in English-language writings is different from French discourse which generally sees all child work as damaging. In June 2023 the province of Quebec in Canada implemented, for the first time, a minimum working age of 14 (with a few exceptions). Prior to its enactment, *Bill 19* (*An Act respecting the regulation of child labour*) encountered resistance from the restaurant and farming industry which laid bare the disjunction between discourse and practice in parts of the world where academics and policymakers distinguish between child work and child labour. See, "Quebec introduces new exception to child labour laws", CBC *News* (24.05.2023), <https://www.cbc.ca/news/canada/montreal/quebec-introduces-new-exception-to-child-labour-laws-1.6852806>; H. Jouan, 'In Quebec, a new law will regulate child labor', *Le Monde*, (01.04.2023), <https://www.lemonde.fr/en/economy/article/2023/04/01/in-quebec-a-new-law-will-regulate-child-labor_6021387_19.html>.

6 Section 87, *Children's Act.*

7 As is the case with many countries. Britain, for example, did not view child labour as a problem until the 19th century, see J. Humphries, *Childhood and Child Labour in the British Industrial Revolution*, Cambridge University Press, Cambridge 2010; H. Cunningham, 'The Employment and Unemployment of Children in England c.1680–1851' (1990) 126:1 *Past & Present* 115. In Ghana, a child is anyone below the age of 18 years, see Section 1, *Children's Act, 1998* (*Act 560*).

8 "Girl Child Labour in Agriculture, Domestic Work and Sexual Exploitation: Rapid Assessments on the Cases of the Philippines, Ghana and Ecuador" in *Girl Child Labour Studies 1* (International Labour Organisation, 2004).

9 Ghana Living Standards Survey, Round 6 (Ghana Statistical Service, 2014).

ten children were involved in hazardous work.[10] Over the last decade, the Ghanaian government has made significant efforts to reduce child labour, a feat recognised by academics and foreign governments alike.[11] Yet child labour generally and exploitative child labour, in particular, remains seemingly endemic in the fisheries industry.[12]

The fishing industry employs about 20% of those in active labour (over 6 million people) in all age groups.[13] Official data on the number of children involved in the fishing industry has not been updated since the 2003 estimate of 49,000 published in the Ghana Child Labour Survey.[14] Nevertheless, fishing has consistently been listed as one of the most problematic industries concerning forced and exploitative child labour.[15] Whilst large-scale fishing trawlers operate in Ghanaian waters, most fishing in the country is undertaken on an informal small-scale basis using canoes and small motorised boats. In addition to catching fish, daily tasks include paddling the fishing boats, untangling nets above and under water, casting or collecting nets out of the water, repairing nets, unloading and transporting heavy loads of fish, scaling, salting, smoking and drying fish, and otherwise preparing fish to be sold.[16] Besides the potential emotional and psychological impact of working in the fishing industry, such as underdeveloped social skills, nightmares, anxiety, depression and

10 National Plan of Action for the Elimination of the Worst Forms of Child Labour in Ghana 2017–2021 (Phase II – NPA2): Towards Achieving Sustainable Development Goal SDG 8.7 (Government of Ghana, UNICEF, ILO and the International Cocoa Initiative, 2017). As of the end of 2022, it is unclear as to whether the government intends to establish an NPA3 and the intended National Plan of Action for the Elimination of Human Trafficking in Ghana 2022–2026 has yet to be published.

11 *Trafficking in Persons Report: Ghana* (United States of America, Department of State, 2022).

12 *Report of the FAO Workshop on Child Labour in Fisheries and Aquaculture in cooperation with ILO*, Report. No. 944 (Rome, Italy: Food and Agriculture Organization of the United Nations, 2010).

13 *The Fisheries Sector in Ghana: A Political Economy Analysis*, by W. Akpalu, S.S. Eriksen & G.K. Vondolia (Norwegian Institute of International Affairs, 2018). The fishing industry here includes activities related to aquaculture, fishing and the processing, distribution and selling of fish.

14 *Ghana Child Labour Survey* (Accra, Ghana: Ghana Statistical Service, 2003).

15 *Ibid.*; *Child Labour Report*, Ghana Living Standards Survey Round 6 (Accra, Ghana: Ghana Statistical Service, 2014); O. Adonteng-Kissi, 'Child Labour Versus Realising Children's Right to Provision, Protection, and Participation in Ghana' (2021) 74:4 *Australian Social Work* 464.

16 *A Qualitative Study of Child Labour in Ghana's Fishing Communities Along the Volta Lake*, by The Commission on Human Rights and Administrative Justice (CHRAJ) (Ghana, 2021).

other signs of trauma, children risk harm or injury to their physical health and safety by using sharp and heavy tools and working in hot temperatures often with insufficient breaks, food or clean drinking water.[17]

There is evidence that children are trafficked across the West African sub-region to work in the fishing industry.[18] Some children are sent or taken under false pretence from Togo, Benin and Cote D'Ivoire to Ghanaian fishing communities, rendering this a transnational issue. Locally, others are sold or relocated from their homes to coastal villages or cities.[19] This has led to an increased focus on trafficked children and several joint efforts between government agencies and NGOs to rescue victims from Lake Volta.[20] Yet Lawrance deems unwarranted what he has identified as the shift in focus from a "child labor problem" to a "child trafficking crisis".[21] Similarly, Mensah and Okyere, argue that,

> The fact is, cases that should be described or defined at best as "child labour" are deliberately being distorted to tell fantastic stories of "child slavery" and "child trafficking", feeding into stereotypes of supposed primitiveness and backwardness of African communities.[22]

Mensah and Okyere have thus sought to highlight this distinction and suggest that reports of widespread child trafficking and child slavery in communities along Lake Volta are inaccurate and without context.

For exploitative child labour to be given the consideration it deserves, a distinction must be drawn between difficult work on the one hand and work

17 *Child Trafficking into Forced Labor on Lake Volta, Ghana: A Mixed-Methods Assessment*, by K. Singleton, K.B. Stone & J. Stricker (International Justice Mission, 2016).

18 E.S. Hamenoo and C.A. Sottie, 'Stories from Lake Volta: The Lived Experiences of Trafficked Children in Ghana' (2015) 40 *Child Abuse & Neglect* 103. *Child Trafficking into Forced Labour on Lake Volta, Ghana: A Mixed-Methods Assessment* (International Justice Mission, 2016).

19 Friends of the Nation, (2015), *Anti-Child Labor and Trafficking Field Survey Report.* The USAID/Ghana Sustainable Fisheries Management Project (SFMP), Coastal Resources Center, Graduate School of Oceanography, University of Rhode Island. Narragansett, RI: <https://www.crc.uri.edu/download/gh2014_pol040_fon_fin508.pdf>.

20 International Justice Mission, '10 Boys Rescued from Slavery on Ghana's Lake Volta', <https://www.ijm.org/news/10-boys-rescued-from-slavery-on-ghanas-lake-volta>.

21 B.N. Lawrance, 'From Child Labor 'Problem' to Human Trafficking 'Crisis': Child Advocacy and Anti-Trafficking Legislation in Ghana' (2010) 78 *International Labor and Working-Class History* 63.

22 B. Mensah & S. Okyere, 'How CNN reported on child slaves who were not really enslaved', *Al Jazeera*, (18.03.2019), <https://www.aljazeera.com/opinions/2019/3/18/how-cnn-reported-on-child-slaves-who-were-not-really-enslaved/>.

involving abuse and exploitation on the other. It is important to acknowledge that child engagement in appropriate forms of work can provide essential "life skills for their future and contribute to intergenerational knowledge transfer and families' livelihoods".[23] It is equally important to acknowledge that abuse and exploitation do occur and, as Manful rightly notes, culture and context should not permit harm to be overlooked.[24] Any lawful child labour that has shifted to exploitative child labour must be recognised, perpetrators punished and efforts made to reduce its incidence.

3 The Legislative Framework Governing Child Labour

Ghana was the first country to ratify the *UN Convention on the Rights of the Child* (CRC).[25] It is also a State Party to several international treaties related to child labour, including the *African Charter on the Rights and Welfare of the Child, ILO Convention on Minimum Age, 1973* (*Convention No. 138*), *Worst Forms of Child Labour Convention, 1999* (*No.182*), and *Protocol to Prevent, Suppress and Punish Trafficking in Persons, Especially Women and Children, supplementing the United Nations Convention against Transnational Organized Crime*.

The *1992 Constitution of the Republic of Ghana* ('the Constitution') is the supreme law. It applies to all organs of government and, where applicable, to all natural and legal persons within the jurisdiction. The Ghanaian government is required by *Article 36* of the *Constitution* to safeguard the health, safety, and welfare of all persons in employment. In addition to the prohibition of slavery, servitude and forced labour in *Article 16*, other fundamental rights and freedoms provided by the *Constitution* mitigate against exploitative child labour. These include, but are not limited to, the right to personal liberty and dignity, the right not to be subjected to torture, cruel, inhuman or degrading treatment, the freedom of movement, the economic right to work under satisfactory, safe and healthy conditions, the right to rest, leisure and reasonable limitation of working hours and remuneration for personal and

23 *Accelerating action to help to end child labour in agriculture in Africa*, (Background Paper) (Rome, Italy: Food and Agriculture Organization of the United Nations, 2021) at 6.

24 K. Manful, 'Ghana Child Slavery: When Seeking Context Overlooks Harm', *Al Jazeera*, (01.04.2019), <https://www.aljazeera.com/opinions/2019/4/1/ghana-child-slavery-when-seeking-context-overlooks-harm>.

25 Though other countries signed the Convention earlier, Ghana was the first to ratify it (date of ratification: 5 February 1990), see United Nations, "Convention on the Rights of the Child": *Status of Treaties, Treaty Collection* <https://treaties.un.org/pages/ViewDetails.aspx?src=IND&mtdsg_no=IV-11&chapter=4&clang=_en>.

public holidays. Whilst all the general human rights and freedoms enunciated in the *Constitution* apply to children, it also provides specific protections for children.[26]

There are number of statutory provisions that seek to protect children.[27] The *Children's Act* permits children to engage in "light work" from the age of 13.[28] Light work is defined as work which "is not likely to be harmful to the health or development of the child and does not affect the child's attendance at school or the capacity of the child to benefit from school work".[29] Apart from this exception, children are not permitted to engage in employment until the age of 15. The *Children's Act* also prohibits children from working at night, yet they often work before dawn and sometimes after dusk in the fishing industry.[30] As mentioned above, the *Children's Act* prohibits "exploitative child labour", and bans children from undertaking "hazardous work", namely work that "poses a danger to the health, safety or morals of a person".[31] Working at sea is one of the few scenarios explicitly listed as hazardous work.[32] For most offences pertaining to child labour under the *Children's Act*, the punishment is a fine of up to 10 million cedis, a maximum term of two years imprisonment or both.[33]

Under the *Labour Act*, 2003 (*Act 651*) ('Labour Act'), workers must have a weekly 48-hour rest period, yet children in the fishing industry often work six days a week.[34] The *Labour Act* also demands equal pay for equal work "without distinction of any kind".[35] However, children and young people are recruited into the fishing industry precisely because they are cheaper to employ than adults. Children are also less likely to attempt to assert their legal right to be paid for personal leave and public holidays which are usually not paid in the informal sectors.

To enforce the *Labour Act's* provisions relating to health, safety, welfare, and the "employment of young persons", labour inspectors have broad powers of

26 For example, see *Articles 28*(2) and *37*(2)(*b*) of the Constitution.

27 The *Human Trafficking Act, 2005* (*Act 694*) contains provisions relevant to children in exploitative labour. Due to the word limit, trafficking is not discussed in detail.

28 Section 90, *Children's Act.*

29 Section 90(2), *Children's Act.*

30 Section 88, *Children's Act.*

31 Sections 87, 91(1) and 91(2), *Children's Act* respectively.

32 Section 91(3), *Children's Act.*

33 See the exception under s. 94(2) *Children's Act.*

34 E.K.A. Agbényiga, 'Child Labor and Child Well-Being: The Case of Children in Marine Fishing in Ghana' in D.J. Johnson, D.L. Agbényiga and R.K. Hitchcock (eds) *Vulnerable Children: Global Challenges in Education, Health, Well-Being, and Child Rights*, Springer, New York 2013.

35 Section 68, *Labour Act.*

inspection. Under s.122(c) and (d) of the *Labour Act,* inspectors are also encouraged to raise defects in, or "unfair labour practices or abuses not specifically provided …" by, the statute with the Labour Department or Labour Commission. Employers may be penalised for non-compliance with an order of labour inspectors.[36] An employer convicted of exacting or permitting forced labour is liable for a maximum fine of 3,000 Ghana cedis.[37] Additionally, under s.124(6) of the *Labour Act* employers may be ordered to pay compensation to any person who proves that they suffered loss, damage or injury due to the employer's non-compliance. Other penalties under the *Labour Act* range from 12 months to 3 years imprisonment and/or a fine between 1,200 to 12,000 Ghana cedis.[38] For example, a person who employs a young person in hazardous work, which is contrary to s.58(1) of the *Labour Act,* is liable on summary conviction to a maximum fine of 1,200 Ghana cedis as per s.58(4).

In addition to its international legal obligations, constitutional requirements and statutory provisions which seek to protect children, Ghana has implemented various policies to reduce exploitative child labour.[39] Though the application of labour protections can be challenging in the informal economy, of which the fishing industry forms part, in theory, the existing national legal architecture should be sufficient to achieve that objective. Whilst a few legislative gaps remain, these gaps are unlikely to account for the perceived high incidence of exploitative child labour in the fisheries industry.[40] Contributing factors are discussed below.

36 Section 124(6), *Labour Act.*

37 This is currently equivalent to approximately 270 US dollars. Maximum of 250 penalty units and each penalty unit is 12 Ghs.

38 Fines under the Act range from 100–1000 penalty units, which, at the current exchange rate, is equivalent to approximately 105 US Dollars to 1,058 US Dollars.

39 *ECOWAS Child Policy 2019–2030 (ECOWAS Commission, 2020); Strategy on Anti-Child Labour and Trafficking in Fisheries: Towards the Eradication of Child Labour and Trafficking in Ghanaian Fishing Communities (Accra, Ghana: Ministry of Fisheries and Aquaculture Development, 2018).* ECOWAS *Strategic Framework for Strengthening National Child Protection Systems to Prevent and Respond to Violence, Abuse and Exploitation Against Children in West Africa: (Ecowas, 2017).* There are also statutory victim support mechanisms and government agencies and bodies such as the Commission on Human Rights and Administrative Justice (CHRAJ) and the Domestic Violence and Victim Support Unit (DOVVSU), which have a role to play but are not discussed here due to word limitations.

40 For example, Ghana is neither a State Party to the *United Nations Convention on the Rights of the Child's Optional Protocol on the Sale of Children, Child Prostitution and Child Pornography* nor does Ghanaian legislation proscribe the use of children for illegal activities.

4 Failure to Meet Objectives

4.1 *Poverty and Socio-cultural Factors*

Most children in the fisheries industry live in rural areas which, unlike the cities of Accra, Kumasi or Sekondi-Takoradi, do not have many employment options. According to 2020 data from the United Nations Development Programme, Ghana has a poverty rate of about 46%.[41] Thus, amongst a population of approximately 31 million, an estimated 14 million Ghanaians are considered poor.[42] About 12% of young people aged 15–35 in Ghana are unemployed, and more than 50% are underemployed.[43] Many children and young people are thus desperate for employment "to supplement family income and to take care of their basic needs, including education".[44] This renders them vulnerable to circumstances involving forced, hazardous or the worst forms of child labour.[45]

The socio-cultural history of the country is an equally important contributor to exploitative child labour in Ghana. Tsikata notes that the fishing industry, along with other problematic sectors, is "regulated by customary practices".[46] Adonteng-Kissi contends that despite the various efforts to eliminate exploitative child labour in the fishing industry, it is sustained mainly due to culture.[47] Many local communities are accustomed to parents sending children and young people to live with and work for family, friends or strangers to improve the economic status of the entire family. Children, parents and community members typically don't view this as trafficking, where the relocation of the child has occurred without the exchange of money.[48] Generations of fishermen endured similar treatment when they were younger. Consequently,

41 *Multi-dimensional Poverty – Ghana*, by Francis Bright Mensah et al. (Accra, Ghana: Ghana Statistical Service, 2020).

42 The term 'poor' goes beyond financial poverty and refers to a list of 12 indicators of deprivation including those related to health, education and general living standards, see, UNDP Ghana, 'New data looking at poverty in different dimensions in Ghana show reduction over time' (2020), Sustainable Development Goals, <https://www.gh.undp.org/content/ghana/en/home/presscenter/pressreleases/2020/new-data-looking-at-poverty-in-different-dimensions-in-ghana-sho.html>.

43 C.E. Dadzie, M. Fumey and S. Namara, 'Youth Employment Programs in Ghana: Options for Effective Policy Making and Implementation' (2020), World Bank, Washington, DC.

44 E.K.A. Agbényiga, above n. 34.

45 This is especially so in the case of orphans, as the traditional extended family support culturally engrained in Ghana is being eroded.

46 D. Tsikata, "Promoting Change in Domestic Work Conditions from Outside the State in a Context of Regulatory Inertia: The Case of Ghana", (2018) LLDRL Working Paper Series, WP #9.

47 *Ibid.*; O. Adonteng-Kissi, above n. 15.

48 B. Koomson and D. Abdulai, 'Putting Childhood in its Place: Rethinking popular discourses on the conceptualisation of child trafficking in Ghana' (2021) 16 *Anti-Trafficking Review* 28.

it is viewed by some as a form of training and providing skills for economic independence as an adult. These practices have thus traditionally been considered unproblematic.

Some of the very law enforcement officials responsible for enforcing the law prohibiting exploitative child labour may be reluctant to do so because of cultural norms and resistance to the imposition of foreign conceptualisations of childhood. In a study by Koomson and Abdulai, one participant, described as a 'Community Child Protection Member', stated:

> I believe that one ceases to be a child when the person turns 13 years old. Generally when an individual attains 13 years of age, they are not considered as a child anymore within this community.[49]

Another participant, a mother, said, "When a person attains the age of 12, they have crossed the stage of childhood. In this community, even children as little as nine years are seen at the seashore working".[50] There is thus a dichotomy between the legal age of a child under the CRC, the *African Charter on the Rights and Welfare of the Child* and the *Children's Act* on the one hand and how local fishing communities seemingly define a child and childhood on the other hand. For laws and policies to be effective against exploitative child labour, they must either be adapted to, or seek to change, the conceptualisation of childhood and socialisation of children in Ghana, which, in some respects, is at variance with that in the West.

4.2 *Agency*

The term agency refers to one's ability to make decisions, participate in society, affect outcomes, exert control and have a purpose in life which they have had a hand in creating.[51] In studying children and young people there is a need to consider agency to recognise that children and young people have "… a mind of their own … and thereby acknowledge their self-efficacy and personal control".[52] Children that work in the Ghanaian fishing industry often relinquish their wages to their parents or guardians. In turn, these adults will give the children money for food, transport, school fees or uniforms. Twum-Danso suggests this "immediate transfer of earnings to parents/guardians reduces

49 *Ibid.*

50 *Ibid.*

51 For an interesting discussion on childhood and the role of children as social agents, see A. James, 'Agency' in J. Qvortrup, W.A. Corsaro and M.S. Honig (eds) *The Palgrave Handbook of Childhood Studies*, Palgrave Macmillan UK, London 2009; B. Mayall (ed) *Children's Childhoods: Observed and Experienced*, Falmer Press, London 1994.

52 S. Gurdal and E. Sorbring, 'Children's agency in parent – child, teacher – pupil and peer relationship contexts' (2018) 13 *International Journal of Qualitative Studies on Health and Well-being* 1.

any autonomy or control" a child labourer may have.[53] This practice warrants further study.

More research should be undertaken on the link between agency and exploitative child labour in the fisheries industry, either at the expense of their education or to fund their education. Schools available to many children in the fisheries industry, particularly those residing in rural fishing villages, have scarce resources, a high teacher turnover, poor or no sanitation amenities, deteriorating infrastructure and are located far from home.[54] Relatedly, some children and young people need money to attend school, whether for fees, transport, lunch, uniforms or learning materials. Thus, some children may make a conscious decision to work in the fishing industry to fund their educational expenses. In other cases, some decide that it is more worthwhile to work and earn money for themselves or their family rather than go to school, particularly where the school lacks basic resources or teachers do not attend consistently. In one study, when discussing her working children in an interview, a mother asked,

> What should I do with my two children whose school fees I have paid and yet they prefer to fish? When I insist, they attend school, both of them decided to move from Ada to unknown communities to engage in fishing.[55]

Lawrance notes that reports of child labour often "whitewash complexity", including "the relationship between school fees and work".[56] Bellwood-Howard and Abubakari suggest the focus on trafficking "conflates movement and harm" and "overrides even the possibility of children's agency expressed as autonomous migration for work".[57] Indeed, in a report jointly published by the

---

53 *Ibid.*; A. Twum-Danso, 'The Construction of Childhood and the Socialisation of Children in Ghana: Implications for the implementation of Article 12 of the CRC' in B. Percy-Smith & N.P. Thomas (eds) *A Handbook of Children and Young People's Participation: Perspectives from Theory and Practice*, Routledge, London 2009.

54 *Findings on the Worst Forms of Child Labor – Ghana* (Bureau of International Labor Affairs, United States Department of Labor, 2021).

55 CHRAJ, above n. 16 at p. 23.

56 B.N. Lawrance, above n. 21.

57 I. Bellwood-Howard and A. Abubakari, 'Children's Harmful Work in Ghana's Lake Volta Fishery: Beyond Discourses of Child Trafficking' in J. Sumberg and R. Sabates-Wheeler (eds) *Children's Work in African Agriculture: The Harmful and the Harmless*, Bristol University Press, Bristol 2023.

ILO and the United Nation's Food and Agricultural Organisation, it was noted that for some children,

> No one is stealing their childhood or coercing them, but they have made the choice, given the socio-economic context in which they live, to pursue an opportunity that appears to hold more promise for their future.[58]

In instances of exploitation, abuse or a hazardous working environment, such agency neither displaces children's legal rights nor the criminal liability of the adults involved. Indeed, the *Human Trafficking Act* expressly excludes the recognition of agency in trafficking scenarios.[59] However, understanding the role of agency is an essential ingredient in fostering effective legislation, policies and programmes aimed at reducing exploitative child labour.

4.3 *Lack of Reliable and Conflict-Free Data*

The impact of legislation is difficult to assess objectively where there is a lack or absence of independent and reliable data. Despite the media's insistence on the high incidence of exploitative child labour, there is a paucity of recent and reliable in-depth data on child labour generally and exploitative child labour in the fishing industry particularly. Admittedly, it can be challenging to obtain qualitative data in this industry. One such attempt found that,

> [E]ven though the relevant consent was sought, it was observed in some communities that parents kept their children indoors and prevented them from being interviewed. It came to the fore during the course of the fieldwork that attempts to obtain information about children's involvement in fishing endeavours in some respects were seen as a threat to the livelihood of communities.[60]

The qualitative data that does exist requires further interrogation. For example, one study found that children who are sent to live and work in the fishing industry with relatives and family friends endure less abuse and exploitation than those who are sent to live and work with strangers.[61] However, it is unclear whether strangers abuse child fishers more than relatives and family friends or children feel more able to report abuse when the perpetrator is a stranger.

58 *Report of the FAO Workshop on Child Labour in Fisheries and Aquaculture in cooperation with ILO. FAO Fisheries and Aquaculture*, Report No. 944 (Rome, Italy: Food and Agricultural Organisation and International Labour Organization, 2010).

59 See section 1(4) of the *Human Trafficking Act, 2005 (Act 694)*.

60 CHRAJ, above n. 16.

61 B. Koomson & D. Abdulai, above n. 48.

Quantitative data, particularly official government data, which should be more easily obtainable, has also been difficult to acquire.[62] Whilst statistics from the police have improved recently, data from other government agencies lag. For example, there doesn't appear to be any official data on how many children, if any, were removed from exploitative situations by labour inspectors. Figures on how many employers were sanctioned under *s.124(6)* of the *Labour Act* and paid a fine or compensation also appear unavailable. There is also little publicly available data on the effectiveness of the Ghana Child Labour Monitoring System.

More effort needs to be made by various government agencies, particularly the Ghanaian Statistical Service, Immigration, Education and Judicial Services, the Attorney General's Office, the Department of Social Welfare, the Ministry for Fisheries and the Ministry of Labour to collect, evaluate and publish data consistently. This can then be used to assess the efficacy of existing laws, justify amendments and contribute to prosecutions. Such data would also aid in addressing the root causes of exploitative child fishing labour by contributing to the creation and implementation of evidence-based programmes and policies, thus reducing its incidence.

It is important to note that much of the available data has been published by NGOs, foreign governments and foreign media.[63] This results in a narrative significantly framed by non-locals, who may not have access to what is happening on the ground or have a sufficient socio-cultural context to understand the nuances of the situations reported. Though a broad cross-section of stakeholder engagement is necessary and their addition to the literature commended, it cannot be ignored that these stakeholders have a potentially conflicted interest in the resulting data. Huijsmans and Baker have described NGOs, for example, as having a direct interest in promoting certain narratives.[64] Such reports should be complemented by increased research undertaken by independent academics and local thinktanks to improve the scientific veracity and reliability of exploitative child labour data.

---

62 One researcher identified the lack of reference to government data as a limitation of his study: "I could not get adequate information and appropriate statistics from governmental agencies to support my arguments and findings", see S. Bukari, 'Working Experience Among School-going Children in the Ekumfi-Narkwa Fishing and Farming Community, Ghana' (2022) 8:1 *Cogent Social Sciences* 1.

63 For example, see D. Patta, above n. 2; L. Kristine, above n. 2; Free the Slaves, above n. 2.

64 R. Huijsmans and S. Baker, 'Child Trafficking: 'Worst Form' of Child Labour, or Worst Approach to Young Migrants?' (2012) 43:4 *Development and Change* 919; See also, I. Bellwood-Howard & A. Abubakari, above n. 57; S. Okyere, 'Shock and Awe: A Critique of the Ghana-centric Child Trafficking Discourse' (2017) 9 *Anti-Trafficking Review* 92.

4.4 *Lack of Enforcement*

Another reason exploitative child labour in the fishing industry persists is "… weak enforcement of laws and implementation of national policies and plans".[65] Concerning the enforcement of labour laws, anecdotal evidence suggests that labour investigations are often hampered by a lack of transportation to sites where exploitative child labour exists. The inability of labour inspectors to travel to locations where children are engaged in work reduces the number of inspections. For 2022, the government has not reported the number of children removed from exploitative labour situations by labour inspectors, despite most fishing work occurring in plain sight. For 2020, available data suggests that just 213 labour inspections relating to children were conducted in which only eight child labour violations were identified.[66] Additionally, a forced labour training manual for labour inspectors which was drafted with the aid of donors remains unimplemented.[67]

Enforcement under criminal law is not much better. The number of prosecutions for exploitative child labour is negligible. In 2021, just three defendants were convicted of exploitative child labour under the *Children's Act*, all of which were fined.[68] For breaches of provisions relating to child labour under the *Children's Act*, there is a specific enforcement mechanism to tackle exploitative child labour in the informal sector.[69] Data on how often this mechanism is instituted is not easily accessible, if at all available. A contributing factor to low numbers of investigations, prosecutions and convictions is the insufficient communication and coordination between the labour inspectorate and criminal justice actors, including police investigators, police prosecutors, state attorneys and relevant government bodies. Additionally, given the nature of small fishing communities, threats to enforcement officials or other stakeholders sometimes account for a failure to investigate or undertake arrests.[70] Structural or institutional barriers to enforcement must be improved.

On the rare occasions that a complaint to the police is lodged or prosecutions are initiated, they often result in a simple caution or are withdrawn at the

65 D.K. Awushi, 'Let's eliminate child trafficking in Ghana', (2015) *Graphic Online*, <https://www.graphic.com.gh/features/features/let-s-eliminate-child-trafficking-in-ghana.html>.

66 *Findings on the Worst Forms of Child Labor – Ghana* (Bureau of International Labor Affairs, United States Department of Labor, 2021). It is not known whether any of these relate to children in the fishing industry.

67 *Trafficking in Persons Report* (United States of America, Department of State, 2022).

68 *Ibid.*

69 See s.96 of the *Children's Act*.

70 CHRAJ, *supra* note 16.

behest of parents, family members and friends.[71] This results in limited public awareness of the issue.[72] Where the courts impose convictions, the punishment given is generally lenient – often a small fine, rarely imprisonment. These outcomes are neither commiserate with the seriousness of exploitative child labour nor do they serve as a deterrent.

5 Recommendations

Measures aimed at poverty reduction in coastal villages would reduce exploitative child labour. The government must find the means of augmenting funding for such measures, including increased availability of appropriate social support. Failure to consider agency and cultural history when designing laws and policies will likely result in local communities rejecting the changes sought by the government, NGOs and the wider international community. Indeed, ingrained cultural practices render the total elimination of child workers in the fishing industry unrealistic. Given the socio-economic realities of local areas where exploitative child labour occurs, the suggestion that anti-child labour programmes would be most effective if they shifted "… from an abolitionist agenda to a protectionist one that reduces the risk of harm for children rather than removing them completely …" is supported.[73] Cultural training, public awareness campaigns, wide consultation and initiatives informed by worker-children, their parents and the fishermen who employ such children would facilitate a reduction in exploitative child labour.[74] Where relevant government agencies do not adequately enforce laws or implement applicable policies, Dowuona-Hammond *et al.* have proposed the implementation of a litigation strategy, including judicial review.[75] Such a strategy would hold relevant state institutions accountable and raise public awareness of the issue.[76] Additional

71 D. Tsikata, above n. 46.

72 Government of Ghana, UNICEF, ILO, International Cocoa Initiative National Plan of Action to Eliminate the Worst Forms of Child Labour, (2017), *Working together to achieve SDG Goal 8.7*, <https://www.unicef.org/ghana/reports/national-plan-action-eliminate-worst-forms-child-labour>.

73 *Ibid.*; B. Koomson & D. Abdulai, above n. 48.

74 G. LeBaron, *Combatting Modern Slavery: Why Labour Governance Is Failing and What We Can Do about It*, Polity, Cambridge 2020.

75 C. Dowuona-Hammond, R.A. Atuguba and F.X.D. Tuokuu, 'The Child Labour Quagmire in Ghana: Root Causes and Ephemeral Solutions' (2021) 6:1 *Business and Human Rights Journal* 163.

76 *Ibid.*

and scientifically robust empirical research, which explores the role of agency, should be undertaken. Such analysis by academics with no conflict of interest in the outcome of such studies would complement similar research undertaken by governments and NGOs. Relatedly, monitoring and evaluation of relevant criminal and labour laws and policies should be conducted to inform future amendments.

6 Conclusion

Addressing the causes of exploitative child labour is crucial to avoiding its perpetuation, accelerating the country's socio-economic development and achieving target 8.7 of the Sustainable Development Goals. Until there are viable alternatives to working in the fishing industry which are perceived by children and their families as more beneficial, statutory mechanisms aimed at countering such practices will continue to have a limited impact. Whilst the lack of enforcement contributes to its persistence, enforcement alone will not significantly reduce the incidence of exploitative child labour. Achieving that objective requires a holistic approach that includes consultation at the grassroots level, consideration of culture and agency, the availability of reliable data and the implementation of measures targeted at reducing poverty. Failure to do so will not only keep Ghana's waters troubled but also its children and future generations of adults.

Acknowledgements

The author is thankful to Adelle Blackett and Laura Dehaibi for comments on an earlier draft of this chapter. The usual disclaimer applies.

Academic References

A. Bhukuth, 'Defining Child Labour: A Controversial Debate' (2008) 18:3 *Development in Practice*, 385.

A. Blackett, 'Slavery is not a Metaphor' (2018) 66:4 *American Journal of Comparative Law* 927.

A. James, 'Agency' in J. Qvortrup, W.A. Corsaro and M.S. Honig (eds) *The Palgrave Handbook of Childhood Studies*, Palgrave Macmillan UK, London 2009, pp. 34–45.

A.N. Botchway, 'Abolished by Law—Maintained in Practice: The Trokosi as Practiced in Parts of the Republic of Ghana' (2008) 3:2 *Florida International University Law Review* 369.

A.S. Bilyeu, 'Trokosi – The Practice of Sexual Slavery in Ghana: Religious and Cultural Freedom vs. Human Rights' (1999) 9:2 *Indiana International & Comparative Law Review* 458.

A. Twum-Danso, 'The Construction of Childhood and the Socialisation of Children in Ghana: Implications for the implementation of Article 12 of the CRC' in B. Percy-Smith & N.P. Thomas (eds) *A Handbook of Children and Young People's Participation: Perspectives from Theory and Practice*, Routledge, London 2009, pp. 133–140.

B. Koomson and D. Abdulai, 'Putting Childhood in its Place: Rethinking popular discourses on the conceptualisation of child trafficking in Ghana' (2021) 16 *Anti-Trafficking Review* 28.

B. Mayall (ed) *Children's Childhoods: Observed and Experienced*, Falmer Press, London 1994.

B.N. Lawrance, From Child Labor 'Problem' to Human Trafficking 'Crisis': Child Advocacy and Anti-Trafficking Legislation in Ghana' (2010) 78 *International Labor and Working-Class History* 63.

C. Dowuona-Hammond, R.A. Atuguba and F.X.D. Tuokuu, 'The Child Labour Quagmire in Ghana: Root Causes and Ephemeral Solutions' (2021) 6:1 *Business and Human Rights Journal* 163.

E.K.A. Agbényiga, 'Child Labor and Child Well-Being: The Case of Children in Marine Fishing in Ghana' in D.J. Johnson, D.L. Agbényiga and R.K. Hitchcock (eds) *Vulnerable Children: Global Challenges in Education, Health, Well-Being, and Child Rights*, Springer, New York 2013, pp. 139–149.

E.K. Quashigah, 'Legislating Religious Liberty: The Ghanaian Experience' (1999) 1999:2 *Brigham Young University Law Review* 58.

E.S. Hamenoo and C.A. Sottie, 'Stories from Lake Volta: The Lived Experiences of Trafficked Children in Ghana' (2015) 40 *Child Abuse & Neglect* 103.

G. Lebaron, *Combatting Modern Slavery: Why Labour Governance Is Failing and What We Can Do about It*, Polity, Cambridge 2020.

H. Cunningham, 'The Employment and Unemployment of Children in England c.1680–1851' (1990) *Past & Present* 115.

I. Bellwood-Howard and A. Abubakari, 'Children's Harmful Work in Ghana's Lake Volta Fishery: Beyond Discourses of Child Trafficking' in J. Sumberg and R. Sabates-Wheeler (eds) *Children's Work in African Agriculture: The Harmful and the Harmless*, Bristol University Press, Bristol 2023, pp. 273–295.

J. Humphries, *Childhood and Child Labour in the British Industrial Revolution*, Cambridge University Press, Cambridge 2010.

O. Adonteng-Kissi, 'Child Labour Versus Realising Children's Right to Provision, Protection, and Participation in Ghana' (2021) 74:4 *Australian Social Work* 464.

R. Huijsmans and S. Baker, 'Child Trafficking: 'Worst Form' of Child Labour, or Worst Approach to Young Migrants?' (2012) 43:4 *Development and Change* 919.

S. Bukari, 'Working Experience Among School-going Children in the Ekumfi-Narkwa Fishing and Farming Community, Ghana' (2022) 8:1 *Cogent Social Sciences* 1.

S. Buske, 'Prostitutes, Orphans and Entrepreneurs: The Effect of Public Perceptions of Ghana's Girl Child Kayayei on Public Policy' (2013) 20:2 *William and Mary Journal of Women and the Law* 295.

S. Gurdal and E. Sorbring, 'Children's agency in parent – child, teacher – pupil and peer relationship contexts' (2018) 13 *International Journal of Qualitative Studies on Health and Well-being* 1.

S. Okyere, 'Shock and Awe: A Critique of the Ghana-centric Child Trafficking Discourse' (2017) 9 *Anti-Trafficking Review* 92.

Slavery *in/and* the Netherlands: Past, Present and Future Regulatory Initiatives Concerning Slavery and Forced Labour

Bas Rombouts

1 Introduction

This chapter explores a number of recent regulatory efforts and instruments that are directed at combatting modern slavery – primarily in the shape of forced labour – linked to the Netherlands.[1] To come to terms with the specific Dutch context, this chapter starts with tracing the history of slavery (regulation) as concerns the Netherlands – primarily in relation to the transatlantic slave trade – and exploring its legacy in modern times. It is argued that recent years have witnessed an increased understanding of slavery as a global institution, to which several recent developments testify. Subsequently, the international instruments to which the Netherlands is bound related to slavery and forced labour are examined. Subsequently, the focus shifts to a number of relevant and recent regulatory instruments that aim to combat forced labour and modern forms of slavery, including labour exploitation.

This contemporary part is divided in two sections. The first section investigates modern slavery *in* the Netherlands and describes current issues and challenges. Subsequently, this part identifies weaknesses in the current national regulatory framework – with respect to the closely related concepts of forced labour, human trafficking and labour exploitation – and explores recently

1 Modern slavery is not a legal term in the Netherlands. Following the International Labour Organization (ILO) definitions, modern slavery comprises both forced marriages and forced labour. This chapter focuses on forced labour. See: Global Estimates of Modern Slavery: Forced Labour and Forced Marriage, ILO, Walk Free, and International Organization for Migration (IOM), Geneva, 2022, p. 2. Labour exploitation is also a related (legal) term, and all forms of forced labour include labour exploitation, while not all forms of labour exploitation necessarily constitute instances of forced labour under Dutch (criminal) law. See: S.M.A. Lestrade, *De strafbaarstelling van arbeidsuitbuiting in Nederland. Een toetsing op basis van internationale mensenrechten, internationale en Europese anti-mensenhandelregelgeving en de grondslagen van het strafrecht* (*Labour Exploitation under Dutch Criminal Law* […]) (Staat en Recht nr. 39) (PhD Thesis, Nijmegen), Wolters Kluwer, Deventer 2018, pp. 325–326. Also see: Adelle Blackett & Laura Dehaibi, in this volume: “Combining all forms of exploitation under a vaguely defined concept with limited legal applicability is at best unhelpful, and at worst, turns attention away from addressing systemic causes”, at p. 30.

 | DOI:10.1163/9789004723801_011

suggested improvements. The second section of the contemporary part relates to modern slavery *and* the Netherlands. This section will explore recent regulatory efforts in relation to combatting forced labour and modern slavery in global supply chains in which the Netherlands may be involved. A number of recent initiatives that assign responsibilities to the private sector are examined. These include the Dutch International Responsible Business Conduct (IRBC) Sector Agreements, the Duty of Care for Child Labour Act (2019) and the most recent proposals from the Dutch Social-Economic Council (SER), parliament and government to develop broad human rights due diligence legislation. The latest developments at the EU level are also taken into account.

In order to understand these largely national initiatives, the chapter will also explain the underlying international normative framework and will briefly analyse the system of the UN Guiding Principles on Business and Human Rights and related instruments in the framework of the OECD and the ILO. The current developments in the European Union in relation to responsible corporate behaviour for possible violations of the prohibition of forced labour will also be touched upon since these have a profound impact on Dutch regulatory efforts. In this way, the paper aims to sketch the architecture of current regulatory efforts to combat forced labour and modern slavery from a Dutch perspective but with a strong international dimension.

The overarching questions that are examined are, therefore: What is the legacy of the Dutch involvement in the transatlantic slave trade, and how is this legacy addressed? Which types of modern slavery presently exist in the Netherlands, how are these legally defined, and in what way does the legislative framework aim to combat these types? Which new regulatory tools have been/are developed to address adverse human rights impacts – especially regarding forced labour – in the global supply chains of multinational enterprises?

This chapter provides a sketch of the past, present, and future of addressing slavery and forced labour in the context of the Netherlands, and provides a critical assessment of contemporary regulatory developments. It is argued that the current developments towards more mandatory regulation of private actor responsibilities for negative human rights impacts related to their activities are especially invaluable for effectively addressing present day problems with forced labour in the Netherlands and beyond.

2 Slavery and the Netherlands: the Colonial Past and Its Legacy

The Netherlands, as a former colonial power, was heavily involved in the transatlantic and Indian Ocean slave trade even though at the end of the sixteenth and beginning of the seventeenth century, the Republic had been opposed to slavery.[2] Profit prevailed over people and around 1630 the Dutch Republic through its West-India Company (WIC), started to engage in slave trade, following the Portuguese and – before that – Arab examples. In 1624, the WIC conquered a part of Portuguese Brazil and, since there was a shortage of forced labourers, devised a scheme to exploit enslaved Africans to work on the – mainly sugarcane – plantations.[3] In 1636, the first thousand enslaved Africans were transported from the Gold Coast to Brazil.[4] The Dutch conquered Castelo da Mina (present-day Ghana) from the Portuguese in 1637, which became a central hub for the slave trade under the name Fort Elmina. There, enslaved Africans were detained, awaiting their transportation to the Americas.[5]

In the Dutch East-Indies – present-day Indonesia and some other areas – as well as in other parts of Southeast Asia, slavery was present long before the Dutch (17th century) or other Europeans (15th century) arrived.[6] The Dutch East India Company also became very active on the slave market in Asia, which was quite diverse and extended beyond chattel slavery on plantations. Slaves also worked (more often than in the Americas) as domestic servants, dockworkers and craftsmen.[7] A consequence of the diverse nature of slavery in 'the East' is that up until today "a history of silence" prevails and very little is known about it.[8] The diverse nature and lack of more precise data,[9] make this aspect

2 M. Vink 'Freedom and Slavery: The Dutch Republic, the VOC World, and the Debate over the 'World's Oldest Trade"(2007) 59:1 *South African Historical Journal* 19.

3 Although urban slavery was also widespread in the Dutch Colonies, see: K. Fatah-Black, 'Introduction: Urban Slavery in the Age of Abolition' (2020) 65:S28 *International Review of Social History* 1.

4 National Archives Online, *Ending a Sad History of Slavery (1863)*, (nationaalarcief.nl, Einde aan een treurige geschiedenis van slavernij (1863)).

5 National Archives Online, *Fort Elmina in Ghana*, (nationaalarcief.nl, Fort Elmina in Ghana).

6 National Archives Online, Slavery and slave trade in the Dutch East-Indies (1820–1900) (nationaalarcief.nl, Zoekhulp Slavernij en slavenhandel in Nederlands-Indië (1820–1900).

7 National Archives Online, above n. 6.

8 M. Vink, "The World's Oldest Trade': Dutch Slavery and Slave Trade in the Indian Ocean in the Seventeenth Century" (2003) 14:2 *Journal of World History* 131, p. 133.

9 Dutch Prime Minister Mark Rutte reaffirmed in his formal apology about the role of the Dutch government in the slave trade that the exact scope of the slave trade in Asia under the authority of the Dutch East-India Company is still unknown, but estimates are that this concerned between 660.000 and 1 million people. See: Rijksoverheid, 'Toespraak van minister-president Mark Rutte over het slavernijverleden' (19.12.2022), <https://www.rijksoverheid.nl/documenten/toespraken/2022/12/19/toespraak-minister-president-rutte-over-het-slavernijverleden>.

of Dutch involvement in slavery much less tangible, visible and well-known.[10] Many more details are known about the transatlantic slave trade in former Dutch colonies in the Caribbean.

In 1634, the Caribbean island of Curaçao was conquered by the WIC to support the Dutch trading position. It became an important slave market. In 1654, the Brazilian territories were lost, but in 1667, Suriname was taken by the Republic and turned into a plantation colony, supported mainly by forced labour from enslaved Africans. The indigenous peoples, as elsewhere in the Americas, suffered too much from virgin soil epidemics to be effectively exploited. After arrival in Paramaribo, the slaves – who were commonly referred to as "salt water negroes" – were publicly auctioned, and the initials of their new master were branded on their skin.[11]

The planters readily found a divine excuse for using slaves in the book of Genesis, where Ham, one of Noah's sons, was cursed to live in servitude. According to 'planter theology', Ham was the ancestor of all black people, and therefore, all black people were predestined to a life of slavery.[12] Hugo Grotius had explained in his *De jure belli ac pacis* that victors of just wars could decide on the fates of their prisoners of war and either kill or enslave those persons.[13] Hans Buddingh comments in his authoritative book *The History of Suriname*, that merchants and planters did not care much whether slaves were captured in just wars or not, and regarded slaves as an essential tool for the continuation of the plantations.[14] Different racial theories also emerged together with the institution of slavery, all of them asserting the superiority of the white race.[15]

Approximately 200.000 slaves were brought to Suriname in total, partly by the WIC and partly by other slave traders. The Dutch meticulously kept track of every person that was transported to Suriname. For example, in 1854, almost a decade before slavery was finally formally abolished in 1863, they recorded 38.545 slaves working and living in Suriname: 17.884 on sugar plantations, 5584 on coffee plantations, 4550 in the cotton sector and 4396 in other areas.[16]

10 National Archives Online, above n. 6.

11 H. Buddingh, *De Geschiedenis van Suriname* (*The History of Suriname*), Nieuw Amsterdam – NRC Boeken publishers, Amsterdam 2012, p. 83. This Chapter is not the place for summing up the atrocities, deprivations and hardships the enslaved Africans had to suffer in Suriname, for a number of examples see: *Ibid.*, pp. 79–118.

12 *Ibid.*, p. 79.

13 *Ibid.*, p. 80.

14 *Ibid.*, p. 81.

15 *Ibid.*, p. 81.

16 *Ibid.*, p. 85.

Work on the sugar plantations was by far the most intensive, especially during harvest season. A Colonial Commissioner calculated in 1838 that slaves only had 6 hours to eat and sleep in a period of 48 hours.[17] An estimated total number of 550.000 enslaved Africans were brought to the Americas by the Dutch, of which approximately 460.000 survived the journey.[18] Although exact figures about the Dutch involvement in the slave trade in the Indian Ocean are hard to provide,[19] the numbers may be similar or even higher than those of the transatlantic trade, with recent estimates by the Dutch government ranging between 660.000 and one million people.[20]

The Netherlands was late in abolishing both the slave trade and slavery. While the slave trade was formally abolished in 1814, it would take until 1860 for parliament to prohibit slavery in 'the East' and 1863 to abolish slavery in 'the West.'[21] To make matters worse, only the slaveholders received compensation, and the slaves were not free in practice, since they were placed under a system of 'state monitoring' and obliged to serve for another period of ten years on the plantations.[22] Every slave between 15 and 60 years old was compelled to sign an employment contract and could only be released from this decade-long obligation on the basis of "proper behaviour."[23] For this reason, many regard July 1, 1873 as the real date on which slavery was abolished in the Dutch territories.[24] Suriname and the large Surinamese community in the Netherlands celebrate and commemorate Keti Koti (the breaking of the chains) yearly on July 1st.

---

17 *Ibid.*, p. 86.

18 Estimates are that a total of about 12.5 million slaves were brought to the Americas, of which about 10.7 million survived the journey, see: R. v. Welie. 'Slave trading and slavery in the Dutch colonial empire: A global comparison' (2008) 82:1–2 *New West Indian Guide/Nieuwe West-Indische Gids* 47, p. 52. The Dutch government mentioned a number of 600.000 victims of the transatlantic slave trade, see: Rijksoverheid, above n. 9.

19 For a better understanding of the scope, drivers and diversity of the slave trade in the East, see: M. Vink, above n. 8.

20 R. v. Welie, above n. 18, pp. 72–73. Also see Rijksoverheid, above n. 9.

21 P.C. Emmer, *Geschiedenis van de Nederlandse Slavenhandel* (*History of the Dutch Slave trade*), Nieuwamsterdam, Amsterdam (fifth edition) 2021, p. 235. Noteworthy, in 1860 the immensely influential novel 'Max Havelaar' was published, which contained an indictment against Dutch colonial rule in the Dutch East Indies.

22 National Archives Online, above n. 4.

23 H. Buddingh, above n. 11, p. 202.

24 This is also the reason why 2023 and not 2013 will be a special year in which numerous activities will take place to commemorate the abolition of slavery 150 years ago.

The effects of the colonial slave trade are still visible in present-day Dutch society in the shape of systemic racism.[25] The still present effects of this "most extreme social power relation possible in a society,"[26] lead to discrimination and exclusion, for instance on the labour market, but also for example in relation to access to bars, restaurants, and schools. The Committee on the Elimination of Racial Discrimination, the body supervising the International Convention on the Elimination of All Forms of Racial Discrimination, has examined these issues in several recent reports.[27] While the Committee welcomes a number of recent regulatory initiatives, it also expresses its concern in relation to online hate speech, racial profiling, discrimination in recruitment and job selection and access to health care. Specifically in relation to people of African descent, the Committee recommends the Netherlands "firmly combat stereotypes and develop and implement specific measures and policies" to address the "historically rooted racial discrimination" still present in Dutch society.[28] The Committee suggested that the State issue a formal apology for its role in the slave trade, that it continues to raise awareness about the lasting impact of colonialism on people from African descent and that awareness about the negative impact of the figure of Black Pete[29] is increased.[30] Discriminatory elements within certain traditions – such as the Black Pete figure in the

25 Human Rights Commission of the Netherlands, 'Why should we commemorate the past of Slavery?' (30.06.2023), <https://www.mensenrechten.nl/actueel/toegelicht/toegelicht/2023/waarom-moeten-we-het-slavernijverleden-herdenken>.

26 K. Fatah-Black, 'The Dominant Narrative about Slavery is still Painfully Colonial' (23.11.2021), <https://decorrespondent.nl/12932/het-dominante-verhaal-over-slavernij-is-nog-pijnlijk-koloniaal-terwijl-een-eerlijker-verhaal-allang-voor-het-oprapen-ligt/4991030769428-254d24cb>.

27 CERD/C/NLD/CO/19-21, Committee on the Elimination of Racial Discrimination, Concluding observations on the nineteenth to twenty-first periodic reports of the Netherlands, 28 August 2015. CERD/C/NLD/22-24, Twenty-second to twenty-fourth periodic reports submitted by the Netherlands under article 9 of the Convention, due in 2019, 4 March 2019. CERD/C/NLD/CO/22-24, Concluding observations on the combined twenty-second to twenty-fourth periodic reports of the Kingdom of the Netherlands, 16 November 2021.

28 CERD/C/NLD/CO/22-24, par. 28.

29 Black Pete (Zwarte Piet) is a blackface character in Dutch folklore that accompanies Saint Nicholas during the yearly children's feast of 'Sinterklaas'. In recent years, 'black' has been removed from songs and other use and 'Pete' no longer has a blackface appearance.

30 CERD/C/NLD/CO/22-24, par. 28.

Saint Nicolas tradition[31] – are, slowly, being removed. The Committee's recommendations were appreciated by the Dutch government, which regards those recommendations as a welcome addition to current efforts to combat racism and discrimination.[32]

The last few years have witnessed increased attention for the slave trade and its victims. National museums devote more attention to the slave trade and to other crimes related to the colonial past.[33] Academic research on the topic is increasing and has revealed insights into the role of the state, major cities and financial institutions in the slave trade.[34] This has led the cities of Amsterdam, Rotterdam and Utrecht to publicly apologize for their roles in the slave trade in 2021 and 2022.[35]

Most recently, on December 19, 2022, the Dutch government officially and publicly apologised for its role in the slave trade.[36] While there was some controversy about the timings of the speech by the prime minister as well as about the consultations with affected parties and organisations, the apologies were generally well received. The government concluded on the need and manner of the apologies after having studied the findings of the report Chains of the

31 For a historical analysis about the link between Zwarte Piet and Blackface, see: E. Koning, 'Zwarte Piet, een blackfacepersonage, Een eeuw aan blackfacevermaak in Nederland (Black Pete, a Representation of Blackface)' (2018) 131:4 *TVGESCH* (*Journal of History*) 551.

32 Ministry of Social Affairs, Letter to the Second Chamber of Parliament on the Recommendations of the Committee on the Elimination of Racial Discrimination, 11 November 2021.

33 The Dutch National Museum hosted a large exposition on the colonial slave trade (see <https://www.rijksmuseum.nl/en/whats-on/exhibitions/past/slavery>) and more recently about the anti-colonial revolution in Indonesia (see <https://www.rijksmuseum.nl/en/whats-on/exhibitions/past/revolusi>).

34 See: International Institute for Social History 'Slavery in the East and West, The Amsterdam Research (De Slavernij in Oost en West: Het Amsterdam Onderzoek)' (29.10.2020), <https://iisg.amsterdam/en/blog/de-slavernij-oost-en-west-het-amsterdam-onderzoek>. Royal Netherlands Institute of Southeast Asian and Carbbean Studies, 'The Colonial and Slavery Past of Rotterdam (Het koloniale en slavernijverleden van Rotterdam)', <https://www.kitlv.nl/research-projects-het-koloniale-en-slavernijverleden-van-rotterdam/>. DUIC, 'Five Questions about the Research Project into the Slavery Past of Utrecht (Vijf vragen over het onderzoek naar het slavernijverleden van Utrecht)' (07.12.2021), <https://www.duic.nl/algemeen/vijf-vragen-over-het-onderzoek-naar-het-slavernijverleden-van-utrecht/>.

35 The city of Middelburg, which had a very prominent role in the transatlantic slave trade, has also issued a public apology.

36 Rijksoverheid, above n. 9. Also see: Response of the Dutch Government to the Second Chamber of Parliament regarding the findings of the Advisory Committee dialogue on the past of slavery "Chains of the Past" (Second Chamber of Parliament, item 35570-VII nr. 106), 19 December 2022.

Past by the Advisory Committee dialogue on the past of slavery.[37] The Prime Minister stated that "we can only look upon this past, to which we are all connected, with horror, remorse and shame" in which there were "no limits to cruelty and arbitrariness" and to "injustices and sheer fear."[38] The goal of these apologies is to contribute to a "society in which there is no place for discrimination and racism."[39] The Advisory Committee, after extensive consultations with many affected people and institutions, recommended a strategy based on three pillars: recognitions, apologies and restoration.[40] As part of the government's strategy and plans, a State Commission against Discrimination and Racism was installed in 2021 mandated to conduct interdisciplinary research on fundamental issues underpinning discrimination and racism in all layers of Dutch society.[41] Furthermore, the National Programme against Discrimination and Racism aims to implement preventive and protective measures to combat discrimination and a National Coordinator Against Discrimination and Racism was appointed in 2021.[42] The range of measures the Dutch governments intends to implement in the coming years are meant to provide a sustainable basis to policies that serve knowledge and awareness raising, recognition and remembrance and an enhanced understanding of how the past practices of slavery influence the present.[43] Examples of these measures are the creation of a national slavery museum, adaptation of the public school curricula, a special national programme in 2023 to commemorate the abolition of slavery 150 years ago and a special fund to address negative effects of the colonial past in the present.[44] While the action to address the legacy of slavery across the entire spectrum of Dutch society in recent years is to be welcomed, numerous issues of institutional racism, often linked to the colonial past, remain.

37 Ketenen van het Verleden (Chains of the Past), Rapport van Bevindingen Adviescollege Dialooggroep Slavernijverleden (26.07.3032), <https://www.rijksoverheid.nl/documenten/rapporten/2021/07/01/ketenen-van-het-verleden>.

38 Rijksoverheid, above n. 9.

39 Response of the Dutch Government to the Second Chamber of Parliament regarding the report of the Advisory Committee dialogue on the past of slavery "Chains of the Past," above n. 36.

40 Ketenen van het Verleden (Chains of the Past), above n. 37.

41 Response of the Dutch Government to the Second Chamber of Parliament regarding the report of the Advisory Committee dialogue on the past of slavery "Chains of the Past," above n. 36, p. 6.

42 *Ibid.*, p. 13.

43 *Ibid.*, p. 7.

44 *Ibid.*, pp. 7–12.

3 Core International Legal Obligations

This section describes the main international legal instruments the Netherlands is bound to in relation to the prohibition of slavery and forced labour. The Netherlands has a good track record when it comes to ratifying and implementing international human rights treaties and is bound to promote the international legal order under article 90 of its constitution.[45] Although the Dutch constitution does not include a provision on the prohibition of slavery, the Netherlands has ratified the vast majority of international instruments dealing with the subject.[46] The Slavery Convention was ratified on January 7, 1928,[47] and its protocol on July 7, 1955.[48] The Supplementary Convention on the Abolition of Slavery, the Slave Trade, and Institutions and Practices Similar to Slavery was ratified on December 3, 1957.[49]

With respect to international human rights law, the Netherlands is party to and has endorsed several instruments that include slavery-related provisions. The Universal Declaration of Human Rights (UDHR) contains the prohibition of slavery and servitude in article 4.[50] Article 8 of the International Covenant on Civil and Political Rights (ICCPR) echoes article 4 of the UDHR and adds a prohibition of forced and compulsory labour.[51] Article 6 of the Convention on the Elimination of All Forms of Discrimination against Women calls for the suppression of trafficking, exploitation and prostitution of women.[52] The

45 The Constitution of the Kingdom of the Netherlands, lastly amended 2018, art. 90.

46 The Netherlands has a limited monist system of applicability of international law, which means that only 'generally binding' provisions in international treaties have direct effect. Transposition into domestic law is not necessary for international norms to become valid in the national legal system.

47 Slavery, Servitude, Forced Labour and Similar Institutions and Practices Convention of 1926 (Slavery Convention of 1926), 60 L.N.T.S. 253, entered into force March 9, 1927. Noteworthy, forced labour was eventually not included in the Convention, see: Adelle Blackett & Laura Dehaibi, IACL General Report, in this volume, p. 4.

48 Protocol amending the Slavery Convention, 182 U.N.T.S. 51, entered into force December 7, 1953.

49 Supplementary Convention on the Abolition of Slavery, the Slave Trade, and Institutions and Practices Similar to Slavery, 226 U.N.T.S. 3, entered into force April 30, 1957.

50 Universal Declaration of Human Rights, G.A. res. 217A (III), U.N. Doc A/810 at 71 (1948)

51 International Covenant on Civil and Political Rights, G.A. res. 2200A (XXI), 21 U.N. GAOR Supp. (No. 16) at 52, U.N. Doc. A/6316 (1966), 999 U.N.T.S. 171, entered into force Mar. 23, 1976, art. 8.

52 Convention on the Elimination of All Forms of Discrimination against Women, G.A. res. 34/180, 34 U.N. GAOR Supp. (No. 46) at 193, U.N. Doc. A/34/46, entered into force Sept. 3, 1981, art. 6.

Convention of the Rights of the Child contains a prohibition of the abduction, sale and trafficking of children in article 35.[53] Furthermore, the Netherlands has ratified the Palermo Protocol to the UN Convention Against Transnational Organized Crime, which aims to suppress trafficking in persons, especially women and children.[54]

At the regional level, the Netherlands is a party to the European Convention on Human Rights, which prohibits slavery and forced labour in Article 4.[55] The Charter of Fundamental Rights of the European Union includes a similar provision in its Article 5.[56] Moreover, the Netherlands has ratified the 2005 Council of Europe Convention on Action against Trafficking in Human Beings.[57]

Considering that this Chapter focuses on forced labour, the relevant ILO Conventions to which the Netherlands is a party are examined in a bit more detail. The Netherlands has ratified both fundamental conventions dealing with forced labour, the Forced Labour Convention, 1930 (No. 29) and the Abolition of Forced Labour Convention, 1957 (No. 105).[58] Additionally, the Netherlands has also ratified the 2014 Protocol to the Forced Labour Convention (Protocol to Convention No. 29) and the Worst Forms of Child Labour Convention, 1998 (No. 182), which contains a prohibition of slavery and all practices similar to slavery in article 3.[59] Forced labour is closely related to the prohibition of slavery, which is a peremptory norm under public international law. The 1926 Slavery Convention defines slavery as "the status or condition of a person over whom any or all of the powers attaching to the right of ownership

53 Convention on the Rights of the Child, G.A. res. 44/25, annex, 44 U.N. GAOR Supp. (No. 49) at 167, U.N. Doc. A/44/49 (1989), entered into force Sept. 2 1990, art. 35.

54 Protocol to Prevent, Suppress and Punish Trafficking in Persons, Especially Women and Children, Supplementing the United Nations Convention Against Transnational Organized Crime, G.A. Res. 25, annex II, U.N. GAOR, 55th Sess., Supp. No. 49, at 60, U.N. Doc. A/55/49 (Vol. I) (2001), entered into force Dec. 25, 2003.

55 Convention for the Protection of Human Rights and Fundamental Freedoms, 213 U.N.T.S. 222, entered into force Sept. 3, 1953, as amended by Protocols Nos 3, 5, 8, and 11 which entered into force on 21 September 1970, 20 December 1971, 1 January 1990, and 1 November 1998 respectively, art. 4.

56 Charter of Fundamental Rights of the European Union, (2012/C 326/02), art. 5.

57 Council of Europe Convention on Action against Trafficking in Human Beings, (ETS No. 197), Warsaw, 16.V.2005.

58 C029 – Forced Labour Convention, 1930 (No. 29). C105 – Abolition of Forced Labour Convention, 1957 (No. 105).

59 P029 – Protocol of 2014 to the Forced Labour Convention, 1930. C182 – Worst Forms of Child Labour Convention, 1999 (No. 182), art. 3(1).

are exercised."[60] According to Convention No. 29, forced labour refers to work performed involuntarily and under the menace of a sanction.[61] The ILO further specifies that it refers to "situations in which persons are coerced to work through the use of violence or intimidation, or by more subtle means such as manipulated debt, retention of identity papers or threats of denunciation to immigration authorities."[62] Exceptions to the general prohibition are allowed under five specific grounds of justification: (a) compulsory military service; (b) normal civic obligations; (c) prison labour; (d) work in emergency situations and; (e) minor communal services.[63]

Particularly relevant for this chapter are the 2014 Protocol to Convention No. 29 and the accompanying Recommendation (Recommendation No. 203).[64] These instruments aim to adjust the normative framework so that it is better suited to address contemporary forms of slavery and forced labour. The preamble to the Protocol to Convention No. 29 explains that: "the context and forms of forced or compulsory labour have changed and trafficking in persons for the purposes of forced or compulsory labour, which may involve sexual exploitation, is the subject of growing international concern and requires urgent action for its effective elimination."[65] The Protocol to Convention No. 29 includes detailed provisions on education, labour inspection, recruitment, public and private due diligence, remedies and compensation and legal protection for the victims of forced labour.[66] Recommendation No. 203 offers guidance related

---

60 Slavery, Servitude, Forced Labour and Similar Institutions and Practices Convention of 1926 (Slavery Convention of 1926), 60 L.N.T.S. 253, entered into force March 9, 1927, Article 1(1).

61 C029 – Forced Labour Convention, 1930 (No. 29), art. 2(1).

62 ILO, 'What is forced labour, modern slavery and human trafficking', <http://www.ilo.org/global/topics/forced-labour/definition/lang--en/index.htm>.

63 C29 – Forced Labour Convention, 1930 (No. 29), Article 2(2). See ILO, Fundamental rights at work and international labour standards, Geneva, International Labour Office, 2003, pp. 39–44. For further interpretation of the scope of the exceptions, see the work of the ILO Committee on Freedom of Association: Freedom of Association. Compilation of decisions of the Committee on Freedom of Association/International Labour Office – Geneva: ILO, 6th edition, 2018.

64 P029 – Protocol of 2014 to the Forced Labour Convention, 1930. R203 – Forced Labour (Supplementary Measures) Recommendation, 2014 (No. 203).

65 P029 – Protocol of 2014 to the Forced Labour Convention, 1930, preamble. The European Court of Human Rights has also interpreted human trafficking as closely related to slavery and forced labour and under the scope of article 4 of the European Convention of Human Rights. A. Blackett and L. Dehaibi, IACL General Report, in this volume, p. 15. ECtHR, Rantsev v. Cyprus and Russia, no. 25965/04, ECHR 2010 para. 280–281.

66 P029 – Protocol of 2014 to the Forced Labour Convention, 1930, Articles 2–4.

to preventive measures, protective action, remedies, enforcement and international cooperation.[67] It suggests different measures and remedies, such as awareness raising campaigns, skills training, social security benefits, adequate penalties, adequate and accessible complaint mechanisms, compensation schemes and legal advice.[68] Protocol to Convention No. 29 and Recommendation 203 take a victim-oriented approach in order to combat modern forms of forced labour.

When modern slavery occurs, it is not only the prohibition of slavery and forced labour that is violated, but a range of human rights, such as the right to equality (art. 26 ICCPR, art. 14 ECHR, art. 21 EU Charter of Fundamental Rights), the right to liberty of movement (art. 12 ICCPR), the right to just and favourable conditions of work (art. 7 International Covenant on Economic Social and Cultural Rights (ICESCR)) and the right to an adequate standard of living (art. 11 ICECSR).

Along with ratifying key instruments on the prohibition of slavery and forced labour, the Netherlands is a pathfinder country for Alliance 8.7, a global partnership that aims to secure UN Sustainable Development Goal target 8.7 which includes ambitious objectives to end child and forced labour.[69] Pathfinder countries accelerate their efforts to achieve target 8.7 by developing and implementing improved legislation, translating their public commitments into concrete action and actively work towards ratification of relevant international human rights and labour standards.[70] The next section examines the domestic legal framework and assesses whether this framework is adequate to address modern slavery, forced labour and labour exploitation problems in the Netherlands.

4 Current Regulatory Challenges and Developments: Modern Slavery in the Netherlands

While a constitutional prohibition of slavery is absent, the Netherlands is bound to the international instruments described above. Under Article 94 of the Constitution of the Kingdom of the Netherlands, provisions of treaties or

67 R203 – Forced Labour (Supplementary Measures) Recommendation, 2014 (No. 203).

68 *Ibid.*, par. 3–13.

69 ILO, 'The Netherlands becomes an Alliance 8.7 pathfinder country' (15.02.2022) <https://www.ilo.org/brussels/information-resources/news/WCMS_837351/lang--en/index.htm>. Also see: Aliance 8.7, 'Pathfinder Countries', <https://www.alliance87.org/pathfinder-countries/>.

70 Aliance 8.7, Pathfinder Countries, <https://www.alliance87.org/pathfinder-countries/>.

resolutions by international institutions that are considered "binding on all persons" prevail over national legislation.[71] A central legal provision is article 273f of the Criminal Code, which contains the prohibition of human trafficking and exploitation including "exploitation of another person in prostitution, other forms of sexual exploitation, forced or compulsory labour or services, slavery or practices similar to slavery or servitude."[72] Specific protection of employees is furthermore safeguarded under different national labour laws such as the Working Conditions Act, the Minimum Wage Act and the General Equal Treatment Act.[73]

While the precise extent to which labour exploitation and modern slavery related-practices occur in the Netherlands is difficult to assess, it is clear that victims are mainly migrants, especially with regard to cases of labour exploitation. Recent examples are the debt bondage and exploitation of migrants working in Asian restaurants,[74] exploitation and retention of identity papers of Eastern European and Asian workers on river cruise ships[75] and Polish workers who were brought to the Netherlands to work in the mushroom farming sector, where they were threatened, intimidated, fined, and exploited.[76]

A 'Team Protection Labour Migrants' under the leadership of Emile Roemer (former MP and longtime leader of the Socialist Party) was installed by the government and produced a groundbreaking report with detailed data and recommendations on how to address abuse of migrant workers in the Netherlands in October 2020.[77] The majority of labour migrants come from within the EU, mostly from the 'new' member states and end up in low or unskilled jobs in logistics, construction, agriculture and the food industry, and work for minimum wages.[78]

---

71 The Constitution of the Kingdom of the Netherlands 2018, art. 94.

72 Criminal Code (Wetboek van Strafrecht), Art. 273f(2).

73 Arbeidsomstandighedenwet, Wet minimumloon en minimumvakantiebijslag, Algemene wet gelijke behandeling.

74 Investico, 'Uitbuiting in de Aziatische horeca' (27.03.2021), <https://www.platform-investico.nl/artikel/aziatische-koks-uitgebuit-in-nederland/>.

75 The Netherlands Court of Audit, Perpetrators go free, no help for the victims, problems regarding labour exploitation (Algemene Rekenkamer, Daders vrijuit, slachtoffers niet geholpen), 2021, p. 9.

76 Openbaar Ministerie, 'Prison sentences of up to 4.5 years for labor exploitation at mushroom farm' (22.09.2016), <https://www.om.nl/actueel/nieuws/2016/09/22/gevangenisstraffen-tot-45-jaar-voor-arbeidsuitbuiting-bij-champignonkwekerij>.

77 Team Protection Labour Migrants, 'No Second Range Citizens, Recommendations to Remedy Abuse of Labour Migrants in the Netherlands' (Aanjaagteam Bescherming Arbeidsmigranten, Geen tweederangsburgers, Aanbevelingen om misstanden bij arbeidsmigranten in Nederland tegen te gaan), 30 October 2020.

78 *Ibid.*, p. 12.

In 2000, a National Rapporteur on Human Trafficking was installed, which is mandated to research the nature and scope of human trafficking (which includes different types of exploitation) in the Netherlands and provides recommendations on how to help victims and how to deal with perpetrators.[79] The main report of the National Rapporteur – the Victim Monitor Human Trafficking 2016–2020 – contains the most recent and reliable information on the scope of the problem in the Netherlands. In the period 2016–2020, a total number of 5186 cases of human trafficking were reported to the Coordination Centre Human Trafficking (CoMensha).[80] Of this number, 1.274 cases concerned labour exploitation, 927 reports concerned sexual exploitation in the Netherlands, 1.892 dealt with transnational sexual exploitation, 672 with criminal exploitation, 12 with forced organ removal and for 409, it is unclear.[81] The number of reported cases for labour exploitation has increased significantly in recent years and was the most reported form of exploitation in 2020, making up 43% of the total number of reported cases.[82] The Special Rapporteur's report indicates that this increase is caused by the COVID-19 pandemic, in which many people lost their jobs. This in turn caused many of those people to report their situation. The Rapporteur explains that this way, many cases of exploitation were revealed, that otherwise would have remained hidden.[83] The number of registered cases forms only a small part of the actual number of victims. Estimates are that yearly between 5.000 and 7.500 people are victims of human trafficking.[84]

Although the Dutch approach to human trafficking is internationally regarded as among the best according to the Human Slavery Index 2018 and the 2021 Trafficking in Persons report by the U.S. government, it is presently criticized at the domestic level.[85] A large problem hampering addressing labour exploitation effectively is the grey area between the strict criminal code definition of exploitation and other types of harmful behaviour against workers.[86] Oftentimes it is difficult for Criminal Court judges to come to a conviction on

79 Nationaal Rapporteur Mensenhandel en Seksueel Geweld tegen Kinderen, 'Over Mensenhandel', <https://www.nationaalrapporteur.nl/mensenhandel>.

80 National Rapporteur Human Trafficking, Victim Monitor 2016–2020, December 2021, p. 25.

81 *Ibid.*

82 *Ibid.*

83 *Ibid.*

84 *Ibid.*, p. 21.

85 Walk Free Foundation, Global Slavery Index 2018, p. 41. US Department of State, Trafficking in Persons Report, June 2021, p. 67.

86 Dutch Ministry of Justice and Security, Letter to the Second Chamber of Parliament, Addressing Human Trafficking (Motie en toezeggingen mensenhandel), 1 July 2021.

the basis of article 273f of the Criminal Code, since not all necessary elements of that article can be proven.[87] To effectively deal with exploitation, criminal law alone is insufficient. Therefore, the Dutch Labour Inspectorate implemented the policy program 'Labour Exploitation' in 2017 to address labour exploitation in an integral manner, not exclusively based on the narrow definition within criminal law. In 2018, the government also adopted the policy program 'Together Against Human Trafficking', which contains five integrated 'action lines.' One is to expand and reinforce the approach against labour exploitation in consultation with workers' and employers' organisations and in line with the approach included in the 2014 Protocol to Convention No. 29.[88]

In February 2021, this strategy was further specified in the report 'Guidance integral approach labour exploitation' by the Centre for Crime Prevention and Security.[89] Cases of labour exploitation that could escape the criminal law system can also be addressed under administrative law by the Labour Inspectorate. Administrative sanctions are possible under different labour laws, such as the Working Conditions Act, Working Hours Act, Minimum Wage Act and Foreign Workers Act.[90] There are also options under tax law and civil law to address malicious employers.[91] In September 2021, the Netherlands Court of Audit issued a very critical report with the illustrative title 'Perpetrators go free, no help for the victims, problems regarding labour exploitation' in which it highlights several issues that prevent effectively combatting modern slavery and labour exploitation.[92] The report concludes that the Labour Inspectorate is not well-equipped to help victims of labour exploitation, since there are insufficient legal possibilities under administrative law. Although the Inspectorate takes more and more cases under consideration, only a few of those are

87 The Netherlands Court of Audit, Perpetrators go free, no help for the victims, problems regarding labour exploitation (Algemene Rekenkamer, Daders vrijuit, slachtoffers niet geholpen), 2021, p. 5.

88 Ministry of Justice and Security, Ministry of Social Affairs and Employment, Ministry of Public Health, Well-being and Sports and Ministry of Foreign Affairs, Together against Human Trafficking, and integrated approach for addressing sexual, labour and criminal exploitation, November 2018 (Samen tegen mensenhandel Een integrale programma-aanpak van seksuele uitbuiting, arbeidsuitbuiting en criminele uitbuiting).

89 Centre for Crime Prevention and Security, Guidance integral approach labour exploitation, Cooperation in Practice (CCV, Handreiking integrale aanpak Arbeidsuitbuiting, Samenwerken in de praktijk), 2021.

90 *Ibid.*, p. 9.

91 *Ibid.*

92 The Netherlands Court of Audit, Perpetrators go free, no help for the victims, problems regarding labour exploitation (Algemene Rekenkamer, Daders vrijuit, slachtoffers niet geholpen), 2021.

adjudicated in Court under the criminal prohibition of exploitation.[93] Under administrative law, the penalties for employers that are guilty of seriously injuring workers are insufficient to end violations since for malicious employers the profit made by the exploitative situations easily covers the possible cost of fines.[94] Additionally, the Inspectorate only has knowledge of a very limited amount of victims and cooperation between the Inspectorate and its partners is insufficient to effectively help victims.[95] Especially the process of referring victims by the Inspectorate to the relevant institutions that provide aid and assistance needs to be improved.[96] Generally, the report concludes, the Inspectorate and ministry of Social Affairs have insufficient access to information needed to stop violators and help victims of labour exploitation.[97] The Court of Audit report recommends that the Dutch government improves the legal instruments available and intensifies collaboration between the Inspectorate, its partners and aid agencies.[98] Moreover, it is vital to get a more complete picture of the extent of the problem of labour exploitation by increasing the willingness to report situations by the Inspectorate and its partners.

The Dutch government has acknowledged the issues raised – including the feasibility and desirability to amend article 273f of the Criminal Code – and has promised to address them.[99] The government has furthermore committed itself in its coalition agreement of 15 December 2021 to address labour exploitation and related issues such as inadequate housing conditions, unfair competition and displacement of workers. These governmental policy objectives are based on the recommendations of the Team Protection Labour Migrants mentioned above.[100]

While the existing domestic legal architecture for addressing forced labour and similar practices of exploitation is far from perfect, considerable efforts are directed towards addressing modern slavery, different types of exploitation and human trafficking. Present-day victims of labour exploitation in the Netherlands mostly come from the EU-11 countries and some other countries outside

---

93 *Ibid.*, p. 52.
94 *Ibid.*, p. 31.
95 *Ibid.*, p. 54.
96 *Ibid.*
97 *Ibid.*, p. 53.
98 *Ibid.*, p. 52.
99 *Ibid.*, pp. 52–54. Dutch Ministry of Justice and Security, Letter to the Second Chamber of Parliament, Addressing Human Trafficking (Motie en toezeggingen mensenhandel), 1 July 2021, pp. 2–3.
100 Coalition Agreement 2021–2021, Looking out for each other, looking forward into the future (Omzien naar elkaar, vooruitkijken naar de toekomst), 15 December 2021, p. 42.

the EU, such as Ukraine, and these problems are therefore not directly linked to the former colonial territories.[101] Hopefully, the increased funding, efforts and attention will lead to better protection of the victims of modern slavery and more effective ways to deal with the perpetrators in the Netherlands.

5 Current Developments in Relation to International Responsible Business Conduct: Modern Slavery and the Netherlands

Forced labour and other forms of labour exploitation are substantial problems within the Netherlands. However, there is also a lot of attention on problems related to these and other human rights issues in the global supply chains of Dutch corporations and corporations that produce goods and services for the Dutch and EU markets. According to the most recent available estimates of the ILO, approximately 49,6 million people worldwide are in modern slavery, of which 27,6 million are trapped in forced labour.[102]

A number of significant regulatory developments that are relevant beyond the Dutch context are taking place. Therefore, this section will assess the regulatory tools that exist and those that are being developed in the Netherlands. Those tools aim to address corporate responsibilities for violations of the prohibition of forced labour related to business activities of corporations themselves and those of actors in their supply chains.[103] This survey will illustrate an evolution from voluntary norms for IRBC towards binding due diligence legislation.[104] First, the underlying normative international instruments and concepts – included in the UN Guiding Principles on Business and Human Rights (UNGPs) and OECD Guidelines for Multinational Enterprises – are briefly explained as well as their relevance for addressing issues of forced labour and modern slavery. Secondly, the development towards (more) mandatory norms

101 The EU-11 countries are those that became a member of the EU after 2004: Bulgaria, Romania, Estonia, Hungary, Croatia, Latvia, Lithuania, Poland, Slovenia, Slovakia and the Czech Republic.

102 ILO, 'Forced labour, modern slavery and human trafficking', <https://www.ilo.org/topics/forced-labour-modern-slavery-and-trafficking-persons>.

103 Self-regulatory approaches by the private sector to address modern slavery are increasingly seen as ineffective, see: A. Blackett and L. Dehaibi, IACL General Report, in this volume, pp. 32–40.

104 Different terminology is used by different organisations to describe corporate responsibilities in relation to sustainability and human rights issues, such as: 'Business and Human rights,' 'Corporate Social Responsibility' (CSR), and Environmental, Social, Governance (ESG).

is illustrated by examining a number of consecutive domestic initiatives, firstly, the Dutch IRBC Sector Agreements, secondly, the Duty of Care for Child Labour Act and thirdly, the most recent efforts for determining the 'building blocks' for broad and effective mandatory due diligence legislation and a legislative proposal – the Responsible and Sustainable International Business Act – in November 2022.

A brief explanation of the workings of the UNGPs and the OECD Guidelines – especially the Human Rights Due Diligence (HRDD) system – seems in place to comprehend the recent regulatory initiatives developed in the Netherlands since they both take these international instruments as their normative foundation and entail HRDD requirements. The UNGPs are widely regarded as a ground-breaking instrument to attribute responsibilities to corporations in relation to human rights violations related to their business activities.[105] They comprise 31 foundational and operational principles based on the "protect, respect and remedy" framework devised by Special Representative John Ruggie and his team in 2008.[106] Under this framework, states have the duty to protect human rights while companies have the duty to respect human rights and make sure that they address violations in which they are involved. Both states and corporate actors should make sure there are effective remedies available for victims of human rights violations. Noteworthy, the UNGPs explicitly mention the International Bill of Human Rights (the UDHR, ICCPR and ICESCR) and the ILO Fundamental Principles and Rights at Work as the minimum norms that need to be respected.[107] As discussed above, the prohibition of forced labour is one of those fundamental ILO norms. The central mechanism by which corporations should assess the – potential and actual – human rights risks related to their activities is the HRDD process. The key purpose of HRDD is described in Principle 13 of the UNGPs:

> The responsibility to respect human rights requires that business enterprises: (a) Avoid causing or contributing to adverse human rights impacts through their own activities, and address such impacts when they occur; (b) Seek to prevent or mitigate adverse human rights impacts that are

105 HR/PUB/11/04, UN Guiding Principles on Business and Human Rights, Implementing the United Nations "Protect, Respect and Remedy" Framework, (UNGPs) 2011.

106 A/HRC/8/5, Protect, Respect and Remedy: a Framework for Business and Human Rights, Report of the Special Representative of the Secretary-General on the issue of human rights and transnational corporations and other business enterprises, John Ruggie, Human Rights Council, 7 April 2008.

107 HR/PUB/11/04, UNGPs, pp. 13–14.

> directly linked to their operations, products or services by their business relationships, even if they have not contributed to those impacts.[108]

This HRDD process was incorporated in the OECD Guidelines for Multinational Enterprises in 2011. The OECD Guidelines contain 'non-binding principles and standards for responsible business conduct in a global context consistent with applicable laws and internationally recognised standards.'[109] Currently, 50 governments adhere to the guidelines, which, according to the OECD, represents 85% of the world's foreign direct investment.[110] The content of the HRDD process is explained in the UNGPS, OECD Guidelines and related documents.[111]

HRDD is an iterative process that helps companies assess and address adverse human rights risks linked to their business operations through a risk analysis that takes into account the severity and likelihood and which can include a prioritisation of risks.[112] At its core, it includes six main steps. Firstly, corporations should include responsible business conduct in their policies and management systems.[113] Secondly, the actual and potential risks need to be assessed.[114] Thirdly, corporations should cease, prevent and mitigate adverse human rights impacts.[115] Fourthly, corporations should track the implementation and effectiveness of their HRDD process, in order to take the lessons learned into account for future HRDD improvements.[116] Fifthly, it is required to communicate relevant information on how the impacts are addressed in an appropriate and accessible manner.[117] Finally, corporations have to cooperate in the remediation of adverse impacts, in cases where they have caused or contributed to these impacts.[118]

While the UNGPS, OECD Guidelines and other international instruments, such as the ILO Tripartite Declaration of Principles Concerning Multinational Enterprises and Social Policy,[119] have a voluntary character, and

108 HR/PUB/11/04, UNGPS, Principle 13.

109 OECD (2011), OECD Guidelines for Multinational Enterprises, OECD Publishing, p. 3.

110 OECD Website, 2011 Update of the OECD Guidelines for Multinational Enterprises.

111 Especially: OECD (2018), OECD Due Diligence Guidance for Responsible Business Conduct.

112 OECD (2018), OECD Due Diligence Guidance for Responsible Business Conduct, p. 17.

113 *Ibid.*, p. 27.

114 *Ibid.*, p. 25.

115 *Ibid.*, pp. 29–30.

116 *Ibid.*, p. 32.

117 *Ibid.*, p. 33.

118 *Ibid.*, p. 34.

119 ILO Tripartite Declaration of Principles concerning Multinational Enterprises and Social Policy, 2017 version.

an international binding treaty on business and human rights is still being negotiated,[120] there are a number of progressive instruments created or being developed at the national and regional (EU) level that include binding due diligence requirements for corporate actors.[121] Well known examples include the UK Modern Slavery Act, the French Vigilance Law and the German Duty of Care in Supply Chains Act.[122]

The Netherlands is also contributing significantly to the development of more effective due diligence regulations. This development towards binding norms for corporations to respect human rights and particularly fundamental labour standards – including the prohibition of forced labour – can be illustrated by examining three recent types of initiatives. First, this subsection will explain the IRBC Sector Covenants. Secondly, a brief overview of the Duty of Care for Child Labour Act will be provided, and thirdly, the most recent studies and proposals for a broad mandatory due diligence law will be analysed in order to provide an overview of the 'smart mix' of current tools to promote international responsible business conduct.

An important first step towards more binding obligations for corporations to respect fundamental labour standards and other human rights was taken by the creation of the IRBC Sector Covenants. These sector-specific agreements involve partnerships between businesses, trade associations, governments, trade unions and NGOs. They establish collaborative systems to address issues such as labour exploitation, environmental damage and other sustainability challenges.[123] They are based on a recommendation from 2014 by the Dutch Social and Economic Council – an important advisory body to the

120 See: Business & Human Rights Resource Centre, 'UN Binding Treaty', <https://www.business-humanrights.org/en/big-issues/binding-treaty/>.

121 About the need for mandatory due diligence legislation, see: Human Rights Council: A/HRC/47/39 (2021), Guiding Principles on Business and Human Rights at 10: taking stock of the first decade, Report of the Working Group on the issue of human rights and transnational corporations and other business enterprises, par. 114: "The persistence of business-related abuses is a major concern and a source of deep frustration, and should be a matter of urgent priority attention by States and business. The last decade has underscored the point made in the Guiding Principles: voluntary approaches alone are not enough. The rise of mandatory measures will undoubtedly accelerate both uptake and progress."

122 Modern Slavery Act 2015; LOI n° 2017–399 du 27 mars 2017 relative au devoir de vigilance des sociétés mères et des entreprises donneuses d'ordre; Gesetz über die unternehmerischen Sorgfaltspflichten in Lieferketten, 2021.

123 Dutch Social and Ecnomic Council (SER), 'International RBC Agreements', <https://www.imvoconvenanten.nl/en>.

government – and a sector risk analysis by consultancy firm KPMG.[124] Based on the framework of the UNGPs and OECD Guidelines, the IRBC Agreements fall in the middle between voluntary and binding instruments. They involve a 'firm commitment' for those companies that have acceded to the agreements and often also contain binding conflict settlement mechanisms.[125] The main ideas behind the IRBC Agreements are that collaboration between different stakeholders will improve the effectiveness of addressing human rights risks in global supply chains, and that a sector-specific approach will enable targeted solutions.[126] Presently there are 11 IRBC Agreements in force, for industries such as gold, natural stone, textiles and banking, sectors in which forced labour issues arise. An example of this is the debt bondage that migrant workers in the sandstone industry in Rajasthan, India, are suffering from. The parties to the TruStone IRBC Agreement are collaborating with local suppliers to promote transparent wages and help local organisations provide workers with access to their earnings.[127] Although the approach of the IRBC Agreements, according to the Ministry of Foreign Affairs, has proven to be an innovative and fruitful way of promoting human rights and sustainability goals in corporate policy, the 5-year evaluation in 2020 also concluded that the Agreements by themselves are insufficient for incorporating human rights due diligence processes in business practice.[128] They are, however, an important element of the 'smart-mix' of measures needed to promote sustainable supply chains.

A second noteworthy development is the adoption in 2019 of the Duty of Care for Child Labour Act, since this is the first piece of binding legislation that obliges companies in the Netherlands or that access the Dutch market

124 Recommendation 14/04 of the Social Economic Council, IRBC Agreements (Sociaal-Economische Raad, Advies 14/04, "IMVO-Convenanten") April 2014. Also see: KPMG Sustainability, IRBC Sector Risk Analysis, Focal Points for Dialogue (MVO Sector Risico Analyse, Aandachtspunten voor Dialoog), (01.09.2014), <https://www.rijksoverheid.nl/documenten/rapporten/2014/09/01/mvo-sector-risico-analyse>.

125 Dutch Social and Ecnomic Council (SER), above n. 123.

126 *Ibid.*

127 For the TruStone initiative, see: <https://www.imvoconvenanten.nl/en/trustone/initiatief>. For the risk assessment of sandstone and black granite in India, see: Study of Natural Stone Sector: Sandstone (Rajasthan) & Black Granite (Telangana) | Association For Stimulating Knowhow : <https://www.imvoconvenanten.nl/en/trustone/initiatief/publicaties>.

128 Ministry of Foreign Affairs of the Netherlands, from information to obligation, a new impuls for IRBC, 16 October 2020 (Ministerie van Buitenlandse Zaken, Van voorlichten tot verplichten, een nieuwe impuls voor internationaal maatschappelijk verantwoord ondernemen).

(physically or online), to conduct human rights due diligence in their supply chain.[129] This Act is specifically directed at combatting child labour and contains a risk assessment obligation for corporations when a reasonable suspicion that child labour is used arises. It also contains possible sanctions under administrative and criminal law.[130] Importantly, according to the ILO, about 1 in 4 victims of modern slavery are children, and ILO Convention No. 182 explicitly recognises slavery and forced labour as one of the worst forms of child labour.[131] The Duty of Care for Child Labour Act has been adopted but has not been implemented yet. The current plans are to integrate it into the broader Responsible and Sustainable International Business Act.[132] Incorporating due diligence requirements in respect of modern slavery, exploitation, and forced labour in general legislation seems more in line with the spirit and purpose of the UNGPs, which is to protect all human rights instead of focusing on specific issues.

The final regulatory initiative that is covered concerns the development and components of – or in the words of the minister of foreign affairs, 'building blocks' – mandatory due diligence legislation.[133] While the Dutch government has emphasised that European legislation on this topic is most desirable, the delay of the European Commission to come up with a proposal has led the Dutch government to initiate a domestic legislative process on mandatory due diligence legislation; a private members bill covering the same ground was already under construction.[134] European legislation is still the end goal since this will promote a level playing field for companies and will prevent fragmentation of due diligence requirements.

On the 23rd of March, 2022 the long-awaited Commission Proposal for a Directive on Corporate Sustainability Due Diligence was published.[135] While the European Proposal covers similar ground, the Dutch proposals can be

129 Duty of Care for Child Labour Act 2019 (Wet zorgplicht kinderarbeid 2019, Wzk).

130 Duty of Care for Child Labour Act 2019, art. 7 and 9.

131 ILO, above n. 102. C182 – Worst Forms of Child Labour Convention, 1999 (No. 182), art. 3(a).

132 Explanatory Memorandum to the Responsible and Sustainable International Business Act, Nr. 35 761, p. 31.

133 For some preliminary research on the impact of mandatory human rights due diligence legislation, see: A. Lafarre and B. Rombouts, 'Towards Mandatory Human Rights Due Diligence: Assessing Its Impact on Fundamental Labour Standards in Global Value Chains' (2022) 13:4 *European Journal of Risk Regulation* 567.

134 See explanatory memorandum to the proposed Responsible and Sustainable International Business Act, Item 35 761, p. 21.

135 Proposal for a Directive of the European Parliament and of the Council on Corporate Sustainability Due Diligence and amending Directive (EU) 2019/1937, Brussels, 23.2.2022, COM(2022) 71 final, 2022/0051 (COD).

regarded as more ambitious in terms of scope and better aligned with the UNGPs and OECD Guidelines. The Dutch government and the Social Economic Council have developed a number of elements that ambitious mandatory due diligence legislation – national or regional – should include.[136] These elements or building blocks concern the scope, due diligence requirements, enforcement, and a general duty of care. Firstly, the Dutch proposals aim for a broad scope under which all major corporations with 250 or more employees are obliged to conduct HRDD. In comparison, the German and French laws are only applicable to businesses with 3000 and 5000 employees, respectively. Additionally, to promote a level playing field, corporations outside the EU that produce goods or services for the internal market, should also fall under the scope of the legislation.[137]

The second element is that the system of UNGPs and OECD guidelines including the six steps of a HRDD process described above, have to be followed, since they are broadly supported internationally and will promote legal certainty.[138] Thirdly, in respect of monitoring and enforcement, the Dutch proposals suggest administrative law tools and an independent monitoring mechanism. Individual liability of managers is not recommended, since IRBC strategies call for "bravery and ambition" of corporate managers.[139] A culture of 'positive supervision' should be promoted instead of a system of repressive sanctions, although such measures will remain available. A final building block concerns a general duty of care for all corporations, irrespective of their size. This will be a more general and less detailed duty than the one for the larger sized enterprises (250+ employees).[140] This would mean that under the Dutch proposals every corporation has to take some responsibility for respecting human rights and addressing forced labour, exploitation and modern slavery linked to its activities and supply chains.

---

136 Ministry of Foreign Affairs, Building Blocks for IRBC Legislation, 5 November 2021 (Ministerie van Buitenlandse Zaken, Kamerbrief inzake Bouwstenen voor IMVO-wetgeving). Dutch Government, Mandatory due diligence: Building blocks for effective and ambitious European due diligence legislation, non-paper for the European Commission, 5 November 2021. Recommendations 20/08 of the Social Economic Council, Together towards sustainable supply chain impact, Futureproof policies for IRBC, 2020 (SER Advies 20/08). Recommendation 21/11 of the Social Economic Council, Effective European due diligence legislation for sustainable supply chains, 2021 (SER Advies 21/11).

137 Ministry of Foreign Affairs, above n. 136, p. 5.

138 Ministry of Foreign Affairs, above n. 136, p. 2.

139 Recommendation 21/11 of the Social Economic Council, p. 13.

140 Second Chamber of Parliament, Item 26485, nr. 345 (Kamerstukken II 2020–2021, 26485, nr. 345).

Parallel to the development of the building blocks, a private members bill ('initiatiefwet') has been created ,which was re-proposed to parliament after review by the Council of State – an advisory body to the legislature – in November 2022.[141] The proposed 'Responsible and Sustainable International Business Act' ('Wet verantwoord en duurzaam internationaal ondernemen'), takes into account the building blocks discussed above and also proposes ambitious and broad HRDD requirements that align largely with the government plans.[142]

As mentioned, the Netherlands is in favour of EU legislation on HRDD to guarantee a level playing field in the Member States. The Dutch (legislative) proposals, therefore, also have the explicit purpose to influence and speed up the EU process.[143] It is believed that without a strong and ambitious domestic proposal, it will be harder for the Netherlands to have a strong impact on the European legislative process.[144] Several of the building blocks mentioned are also reflected in the Commission's proposal. The scope of the proposal is more narrow than the Dutch proposals, targeting only companies of over 500 employees and over 250 employees for specific designated high-risk sectors.[145] The proposal refers to the UNGPs and the OECD Guidelines and includes the different steps for a HRDD process detailed above.[146] The Annex to the Commission's proposal includes a list of human rights that should be protected under the Directive and explicitly refers to forced labour, slavery and human trafficking.[147]

However, there are also a number of concerns regarding the proposed EU directive. Most importantly, the Netherlands finds that the proposed directive is not properly aligned with the OECD Guidelines and UNGPs, since it limits certain obligations to "established business relationships" and does not include the distinction between cause, contribute and directly linked, which is included in the international frameworks and facilitates a prioritisation of risks.[148] Additionally, access to remedy for victims, one of the pillars of the

141 Proposed legislation, Responsible and Sustainable International Business Act, Item 35 761, Nr. 9, 1 November 2022.

142 Explanatory memorandum to the proposed Responsible and Sustainable International Business Act, Item 35 761, p. 21. The initiators therefore also suggest that their proposed Act could serve as the basis for legislation to be created by the government. See p. 19 for an overview of the differences between the 'building blocks' and the proposed Act.

143 Explanatory memorandum to the proposed Responsible and Sustainable International Business Act, Item 35 761, p. 21.

144 *Ibid.*

145 COM(2022) 71 final 2022/0051 (COD), art. 2.

146 *Ibid.*, preamble par. 12, 26. Art. 4.

147 Annex to COM(2022) 71 final 2022/0051 (COD), par. 12–14.

148 Second Chamber of Parliament, Item 22112, Nr. 3393, p. 5.

UNGPs and also a key component of HRDD under the OECD model, is insufficiently addressed in the current proposal.[149] For an effective and coherent due diligence regime, it seems desirable to keep domestic or regional legislative due diligence initiatives as much as possible in line with the international instruments and procedures.

6 Closing Remarks: Adequacy of the Regulatory Framework in and outside the Netherlands

While the effects of the colonial past – including discrimination and exclusion – are still visible in Dutch society, the Netherlands could be slowly coming to terms with its history as a slave-trading nation. In particular, the last few years have witnessed more initiatives, academic studies, improved education programmes, political movements, cultural events, public apologies and media attention on the history and present legacies of slavery. With respect to the international legal framework, the Netherlands is a party to the vast majority of treaties and conventions that address (modern) slavery and forced labour.

Present-day problems with forced labour and exploitation are generally not directly related to the groups that suffered from the global institution of slavery in the past. Inside the Netherlands, a substantial number of people – mainly migrant workers – continue to suffer from exploitation, unfair wages, intimidation and forms of forced labour such as debt bondage. While the regulatory framework to combat these issues is internationally perceived as one of the most advanced ones, domestically, there is a strong impetus to improve the legislative tools to better protect victims and more effectively confront perpetrators. Especially in the situation that certain types of labour exploitation cannot be effectively addressed under criminal law. The effectiveness of the labour inspectorate to deal with labour exploitation have to be – and fortunately are already to some extent – addressed.

The largely voluntary nature of the international regulatory architecture to hold corporations responsible for forced labour and modern slavery in their supply chains is insufficient to tackle the problem. Nevertheless, the voluntary instruments – the UNGPs and OECD Guidelines – do provide the normative vantage point for the development of mandatory due diligence legislation. The Netherlands is involved in the development of different progressive IRBC instruments and is a strong advocate of ambitious European legislation that

149 *Ibid.* An overreliance on contractual cascading is another concern the Dutch government has expressed, see *ibid.*, pp. 6–7.

is currently being developed. Such mandatory due diligence legislation, combined with other IRBC instruments in a 'smart mix,' may lead to a more effective approach towards tackling forced labour and modern slavery worldwide.

Academic References

A. Lafarre and B. Rombouts, 'Towards Mandatory Human Rights Due Diligence: Assessing Its Impact on Fundamental Labour Standards in Global Value Chains' (2022) 13(4) *European Journal of Risk Regulation* 567.

E. Koning, 'Zwarte Piet, een blackfacepersonage, Een eeuw aan blackfacevermaak in Nederland' (Black Pete, a Representation of Blackface) (2018) 131:4 *TVGESCH* (*Journal of History*) 551.

H. Buddingh, *De Geschiedenis van Suriname* (*The History of Suriname*), NRC Boeken – Nieuw Amsterdam, Amsterdam 2012.

K. Fatah-Black, 'Introduction: Urban Slavery in the Age of Abolition' (2020) 65:S28 *International Review of Social History* 1.

M. Vink, 'Freedom and Slavery: The Dutch Republic, the VOC World, and the Debate over the 'World's Oldest Trade' (2007) 59:1 *South African Historical* Journal 19.

M. Vink, "The World's Oldest Trade': Dutch Slavery and Slave Trade in the Indian Ocean in the Seventeenth Century', (2003) 14:2 *Journal of World History* 131.

P.C. Emmer, *Geschiedenis van de Nederlandse Slavenhandel* (*History of the Dutch Slave Trade*), 5th ed., New Amsterdam, Amsterdam 2021.

R.V. Welie, 'Slave trading and slavery in the Dutch colonial empire: A global comparison' (2008) 82(1–2) *New West Indian Guide/Nieuwe West-Indische Gids*, 47.

S.M.A. Lestrade, *De strafbaarstelling van arbeidsuitbuiting in Nederland. Een toetsing op basis van internationale mensenrechten, internationale en Europese anti-mensenhandelregelgeving en de grondslagen van het strafrecht*, Wolters Kluwer, Deventer 2018.

Asservissement, capitalisme et économie minière au Pérou

Laura Dehaibi

1 Introduction

Dans une récente décision phare, la Cour suprême du Canada reconnaissait la compétence des tribunaux canadiens pour entendre des plaintes contre des entreprises canadiennes opérant à l'étranger en fonction du droit international coutumier, en l'occurrence de l'interdiction du travail forcé et de l'esclavage[1]. L'entreprise en question était une compagnie minière opérant en Érythrée où les travailleurs étaient recrutés au moyen d'un régime de conscription forcée. Bien que la Cour ne s'attarde pas sur la nature des activités économiques de l'entreprise, le cas semblait parfaitement choisi pour aborder la question du droit en matière d'esclavage contemporain. En effet, le secteur minier à travers le monde possède un bilan médiocre à cet égard[2]. Étant donné la nature transnationale de l'industrie minière, il n'est pas étonnant que des réflexions sur la trans-territorialité des obligations internationales en matière d'esclavage soient ressorties dans cette décision.

Le présent rapport s'intéresse au droit en matière d'esclavage contemporain au sein de l'économie minière avec une étude de cas au Pérou. L'attrait d'étudier l'esclavage contemporain en utilisant l'exemple de l'économie extractive est double. D'abord, il permet de démontrer que l'esclavage contemporain n'est pas un phénomène marginal commis par des criminels parias, mais est plutôt intégré dans le commerce mondial, reflétant ainsi une continuité historique de la dualité asservissement/accumulation de capital. Ensuite, étant donné que les zones riches en ressources minérales sont souvent éloignées physiquement des centres de pouvoir, l'exemple de l'économie minière peut révéler le rôle de la géographie dans l'asservissement et l'exploitation, permettant d'approfondir la réflexion sur l'idée d'aliénation comme modalité de l'esclavage.

Le Pérou possède de riches ressources minières. Selon les données de l'Institut National de Statistiques et d'Informatique du Pérou (INEI) pour l'année

1 *Nevsun Resources Ltd.* v. *Araya*, 2020 SCC 5.

2 Notamment au sein de l'exploitation minière aurifère, voir : Verité, 'The Nexus of Illegal Gold Mining and Human Trafficking in Global Supply Chains – Lessons from Latin America' (2016), <https://verite.org/resources/verite-publications/>.

 | DOI:10.1163/9789004723801_012

2019, l'industrie extractive représentait près de 18% du produit intérieur brut du pays et les produits miniers représentaient 58,9% des exportations totales[3]. Sans compter les nombreuses mines illégales, 14% du territoire péruvien est affecté à l'exploitation minière[4]. Le Pérou est parmi les leaders mondiaux dans la production de cuivre, d'argent, de zinc, de plomb et d'or. Le secteur minier a également attiré près de 25% des investissements directs étrangers au pays dans les dix dernières années. La production et l'exportation de minéraux au Pérou n'ont pas ralenti pendant la pandémie, d'autant plus que les grandes entreprises minières faisaient partie de la première vague de réactivation économique[5]. Il s'agit donc d'une industrie de haute importance pour l'économie péruvienne. Il faut également mentionner que l'emploi dans le secteur minier au Pérou est souvent informel[6]. Les travailleurs, en marge du droit étatique, sont ainsi plus vulnérables à l'exploitation.

Nous proposerons dans les lignes qui suivent que l'économie minière prise dans son ensemble crée des conditions propices à l'exploitation humaine par son isolement sociogéographique et son insertion dans une économie capitaliste transnationale qui favorise l'exploitation agressive des ressources naturelles. Nous porterons particulièrement notre attention sur l'économie minière informelle, qui fait un usage accru de main-d'œuvre bon marché par rapport à la machinerie[7].

Pour illustrer comment l'isolement géographique favorise l'exploitation, ce rapport s'intéresse tant au travail forcé dans les mines qu'à celui qui se développe en périphérie des mines, au sein de villes minières artificiellement plantées dans des milieux autrement hostiles à la colonisation humaine. Bien que l'activité minière soit présente sur la presque totalité du territoire péruvien, nous nous concentrerons sur deux départements, Madre de Dios et Puno, où se retrouvent le plus grand nombre de mines dites informelles ou illégales.

---

3 Instituto nacional de estadística e informatica del Peru, 'Économía', : <https://www.inei.gob.pe/estadisticas/indice-tematico/economia/> ; valeurs à prix constants de 2007.

4 Verité, 'Risk Analysis of Indicators of Forced Labor and Human Trafficking in Illegal Gold Mining in Peru' (2013), <https://verite.org/resources/verite-publications/>.

5 La Gestión, 'Reactivación de la gran minería generará más de 68,000 empleos directos, estima Minem', (08.05.2020), <https://gestion.pe/economia/coronavirus-peru-reactivacion-de-la-gran-mineria-generara-mas-de-68000-empleos-directos-estima-minem-covid-19-nndc-noticia/>.

6 Perú, *Estrategia sectorial para la formalización laboral 2018–2021*, Resolución Ministerial No. 071-2018-TR, p. 36.

7 D. Cortés-McPherson, 'Digging into the Mining Subculture: The Dynamics of Trafficking in Persons in the Artisanal and Small-Scale Gold Mining of Peru's Madre de Dios' dans Y. Zabyelina & D. van Uhm (dir.), *Illegal Mining, Organized Crime, Corruption, and Ecocide in a Resource-Scarce World*, Palgrave MacMillan, Cham 2020, p. 364.

Puno étant une des régions les plus pauvres du pays, elle est également un des principaux points de départ des travailleurs migrants dans l'industrie minière informelle[8]. Les exemples que nous présenterons plus bas nous mèneront à constater l'influence du milieu géographique sur la faiblesse des institutions étatiques en zone rurale, ce qui favorise la dérogation à l'état de droit.

Dans les lignes qui suivent, nous expliquerons d'abord la pertinence d'une approche des phénomènes contemporains d'exploitation humaine sévère par la géographie et par le concept d'aliénation sociale. Nous poursuivrons avec un parcours de l'histoire de l'esclavage et du travail forcé au Pérou dans le contexte de l'exploitation des ressources naturelles, ainsi qu'un aperçu de la persistance de pratiques d'asservissement au 21e siècle dans le secteur minier informel. Finalement, après avoir décrit le cadre législatif péruvien pour la lutte contre l'esclavage contemporain, nous évaluerons si ce cadre répond à l'héritage laissé par l'esclavage dans le pays.

2 Cadre d'analyse : aliénation sociale et géographie dans un contexte capitaliste

Dans les lignes qui suivent, nous nous intéresserons à l'idée d'aliénation sociale comme modalité de renforcement de la perte effective de liberté et d'autonomie qu'implique les pratiques d'esclavage et comme effet de l'asservissement. Nous soumettons que l'aliénation sociale est favorisée par l'isolement géographique. À travers l'histoire de l'esclavage, le mouvement dans l'espace, les migrations ont souvent été utilisés afin d'engendrer ce qu'Orlando Patterson a décrit comme l'aliénation natale ou la mort sociale de l'esclave[9]. Pour Patterson, l'idée de la mort sociale exprime le processus par lequel l'esclave est déraciné, désocialisé et dépersonnalisé[10]. Perdant tous ces repères sociaux et culturels, l'esclave en terres inconnues devient étranger, vulnérable et donc

8 Verité, *supra* n. 4, p. 10.

9 O. Patterson, *Slavery and Social Death: A Comparative Study*, Harvard University Press, Cambridge 1982. Patterson décrit l'aliénation comme le fait de perdre un lien d'appartenance. Cette aliénation, pour Patterson, est « natale » du fait que, à travers l'histoire, l'esclavage est renforcé par la perte de liens intergénérationnels et le déracinement ; *Ibid.*, p. 7. La traite transatlantique d'Africains est une illustration criante de l'usage des migrations comme stratégie d'aliénation, voir C.J. Robinson, *Black Marxism: The Making of the Black Radical Tradition*, University of North Carolina Press, Chapel Hill 2000, p. 23.

10 O. Patterson, *supra* n. 9, p. 38.

plus facile à contrôler physiquement et psychologiquement[11]. Le concept de mort sociale a été critiqué, puisqu'il semble ignorer les différentes formes historiques de résistance à la violence et de socialisation[12]. Cependant, l'idée de mort sociale ou d'aliénation natale visait surtout dans les propos de Patterson à décrire le processus symbolique utilisé par l'asservisseur pour asseoir son autorité de « propriétaire », son *dominium*[13]. Le concept décrit la perspective du propriétaire cherchant à réduire l'humain à un objet plutôt que la perspective de la personne asservie cherchant à affirmer son humanité. Bien que l'absence de cette perspective soit un manque (admis par l'auteur)[14], les idées de Patterson résonnent du fait de la continuité dans le temps des moyens utilisés pour renforcer l'exploitation humaine, la propriété légale n'étant finalement qu'un outil parmi une gamme de stratégies d'aliénation.

Ainsi, nous verrons que l'aliénation *sociale*—entendue comme la perte d'un sentiment d'appartenance par la perte des repères sociaux d'une personne—semble sciemment utilisée afin de favoriser l'exploitation des travailleurs, notamment à travers des processus migratoires et la manipulation de l'identité et de la citoyenneté. En effet, la vaste majorité des travailleurs dans les mines aurifères péruviennes sont migrants. Ce déplacement a évidemment des motivations commerciales, puisque l'idée est de fournir une main-d'œuvre là où elle fait défaut[15]. Il sert également, encore de nos jours, à renforcer le contrôle exercé sur les personnes asservies en diminuant leurs points de repère et donc leur capacité d'action. Ainsi, l'environnement

---

11 F.P. Bowser, *The African Slave in Colonial Peru, 1524–1650*, Stanford University Press, Stanford 1974, p. 7.

12 Pour un résumé de ces critiques voir R. Mawani, 'From Slave Revolts to Social Death' (2019) 48 *Theory and Society* 835, p. 836. L'auteure note que la théorisation de la mort sociale par Patterson doit se lire dans le contexte plus large de ses écrits antérieurs et postérieurs qui abordent plus directement la « subjectivité » des personnes asservies (*ibid.*, p. 837). Les formes de résistances des personnes asservies font de plus en plus l'objet de l'étude historique de l'esclavage, voir par exemple C.L.R. James, *The Black Jacobins: Toussaint L'Ouverture and the San Domingo Revolution*, Penguin, London 2001; C.J. Robinson, *supra* n. 9; et dans le contexte péruvien, M.A. McKinley, *Fractional Freedoms: Slavery, Intimacy, and Legal Mobilization in Colonial Lima*, Cambridge University Press, New York 2016.

13 O. Patterson, *supra* n. 9, pp. 31–32, et 38.

14 Une faille qui est d'ailleurs récurrente dans les études historiques de l'esclavage compte tenu de la rareté des archives décrivant la résistance des personnes asservies. Patterson reconnaît ce fait tout en notant différentes circonstances dans lesquelles même les propriétaires d'esclave admettaient l'agentivité des personnes asservies (*Ibid.*, pp. 200–208).

15 E. Williams, *Capitalism & Slavery*, University of North Carolina Press, Chapel Hill 1994, pp. 2–3.

physique est utilisé activement pour asseoir l'autorité du patron et créer un sentiment d'absence d'alternative.

Les deux régions à l'étude, Puno et Madre de Dios, possèdent une géographie distincte, la première se retrouvant aux plus hauts sommets des Andes péruviennes alors que la deuxième est en plein cœur de la forêt amazonienne. Pour des raisons tant naturelles que structurelles, elles sont toutes deux isolées géographiquement et socialement du reste du pays, ce qui a, comme nous tenterons de le démontrer, un impact tant sur la facilitation de l'esclavage que sur la réponse nationale au problème. Notre hypothèse est que l'emplacement des mines dans des zones rurales éloignées a un impact direct sur la mise en œuvre de mesures juridiques pour éradiquer l'esclavage. Non pas que l'esclavage est inexistant dans les centres urbains. Historiquement, le Pérou possédait une forte proportion d'esclaves dans les centres urbains, pour le travail domestique ou l'artisanerie. Cependant, il existait un contraste marqué entre la capacité des personnes asservies d'obtenir leur liberté en zones rurales et en zones urbaines puisque les occasions pour développer des relations sociales et juridiques favorables étaient beaucoup plus importantes dans ces dernières[16]. De nos jours, l'éloignement des centres urbains pose les mêmes problèmes d'accès à des réseaux d'entraide et d'accès à la justice, ce qui renforce la vulnérabilité des personnes et favorise leur exploitation[17].

L'isolement géographique n'est pas strictement du ressort de la nature : il est en bonne partie structurel. Le fait que certaines mines se retrouvent dans des zones inhospitalières n'a pas empêché qu'on s'y rende pour développer des centres miniers. Cependant, si l'intérêt économique motive l'exploration des ressources naturelles en régions hostiles, la volonté politique ne suit pas, et les villes minières vont souvent manquer de services élémentaires. De plus, la structure même de l'entreprise minière, la manière dont l'espace de l'entreprise est divisé et géré, contribue à l'isolement. Les mines occupent de grands

16 C. Aguirre, *Breve historia de la esclavitud en el Perú*, Fondo editorial del Congreso del Perú, Lima 2005, pp. 135–136; F.P. Bowser, *supra* n. 11, pp. 298–299; McKinley explique que la majorité des cas de manumissions était générée par l'auto-rachat, M.A. McKinley, *supra* n. 12, p. 12.

17 Le Médiateur public péruvien note par exemple que les nombre de refuges pour femmes en zones rurales ne correspond pas aux chiffres de violence domestique dans ces régions, démontrant une disjonction entre les besoins des femmes en région et les services offerts. Voir Defensoria del Pueblo, *Supervision a los hogares de refugio temporal para mujeres victimas de violencia, Reporte de Adjuntia No 002-2019-DP/ADM*, 2019, p. 13, <https://www.defensoria.gob.pe/deunavezportodas/wp-content/uploads/2019/08/Supervisi%C3%B3n-Hogares-de-Refugio-Temporal-2019-Defensor%C3%ADa-del-Pueblo.pdf>.

espaces, et souvent les travailleurs vont vivre directement sur le site de la mine, dont les propriétaires peuvent contrôler les entrées et les sorties[18]. Le territoire de la mine, qu'il soit acquis par droits de propriété, par licences exclusives ou de manière informelle, devient une quasi-juridiction créant des frontières physiques avec le monde extérieur. Ces « frontières » sont souvent protégées par des gardes de sécurité, renforçant encore plus l'isolement des mines[19].

À cette invisibilité géo-sociale s'ajoute une autre couche d'opacité, soit celle de l'informalité, qui est endémique au Pérou. En effet, selon les données de 2019 de l'INEI, 72,7% des emplois au Pérou étaient informels[20]. En 2020, la première année de la pandémie, ce taux avait augmenté à 75,3%[21]. Le secteur minier n'échappe pas à cette réalité[22]. L'informalité pour le travailleur des mines comporte une double invisibilité, puisqu'elle maintient une aliénation des espaces tant physiques que juridiques. Cette invisibilisation implique également l'impunité pour les agresseurs, renforçant leur contrôle sur la main-d'œuvre.

3 Économie minière au pérou : une histoire de l'asservissement au service du développement

Potosí est une ville située à plus de 4000 mètres d'altitude en Bolivie, connue comme le Haut Pérou à l'époque de la colonisation espagnole. Dès sa fondation en 1545, elle attire les colons par ses riches ressources en argent, un métal précieux déjà bien connu des peuples locaux, et, en moins de deux ans, sa population aurait atteint les 14 000 habitants pour ensuite dépasser les 100 000

18 Une stratégie similaire est observable à la lecture des faits dans la première décision de la Cour interaméricaine des droits de l'homme sur la prohibition de l'esclavage, *Trabajadores de la Hacienda Brasil Verde v. Brasil* (2016), Inter-Am Ct HR (Ser C) No 318, para. 113–114.

19 Voir par exemple la description des conditions dans une mine illégale à Madre de Dios dans Verité, *supra* n. 4, pp. 68–69.

20 INEI, *Produccion y Empleo Informal en el Peru – Cuenta Satélite de la Economia Informal 2007–2020*, INEI 2020, p. 101, <https://www.inei.gob.pe/media/MenuRecursivo/publicaciones_digitales/Est/Lib1828/>.

21 Observatorio de la formalización del Trabajo, Ministerio del Trabajo y de la Promoción del Empleo del Perú, <https://www2.trabajo.gob.pe/estadisticas/observatorio-de-la-formalizacion-laboral/tableros-interactivos/tablero-interactivo-del-empleo-informal-observatorio/>.

22 Perú, *Estrategia sectorial para la formalización laboral 2018–2021*, Resolución Ministerial No. 071-2018-TR, p. 36.

habitants en 1611[23]. L'existence du Pérou et l'essor commercial de l'Espagne ont tous deux dépendu de la découverte de ces mines d'argent et de bien d'autres ressources extractives de la région[24]. Selon les dires d'un historien, l'environnement de Potosí était si inhospitalier que, n'eût été des ressources minières, elle serait encore déserte[25]. Or l'exploitation minière et le développement colonial du Pérou dépendront massivement de l'asservissement tant des Africains emmenés de force dans la région par la traite transatlantique que de la population autochtone des Andes[26]. Le développement économique capitaliste, associé au commerce transnational et à la traite transatlantique d'esclaves[27], est à l'origine de cette violence et nous verrons qu'elle ne se limite pas à l'époque coloniale, mais perdurera sur le territoire péruvien jusqu'à nos jours.

3.1 *La traite transatlantique et le Pérou*

L'asservissement dans l'histoire du Pérou est multiforme et découle du contact de diverses cultures et de différents mouvements migratoires. Au Pérou, comme ailleurs en Amérique, l'existence même du pays dépend dans une très grande mesure de la traite transatlantique[28]. Bien que la Couronne espagnole ne se soit pas engagée elle-même de manière intensive dans la traite transatlantique, elle en bénéficie substantiellement, grâce à son proche allié portugais[29]. Il est difficile d'évaluer exactement le nombre d'esclaves africains amenés au Pérou, étant donné les nombreux canaux par lesquels ils pouvaient être vendus, mais les estimations oscillent autour de 100 000 durant l'époque coloniale[30]. Aux débuts de la colonie, les esclaves sur la côte péruvienne com-

---

23 B. Moses, *The Spanish Dependencies in South America: An Introduction to the History of Their Civilisation*, Smith, Elder & Co, London 1914, pp. 2–6.

24 J.E. Inikori, 'Atlantic Slavery and the Rise of the Capitalist Global Economy' (2020) 61:S22 *Current Anthropology* S159, p. S163.

25 J.A. Cole, *The Potosí Mita, 1573–1700, Compulsory Indian Labor in the Andes*, Stanford University Press, Stanford 1985, p. 5.

26 F.P. Bowser, *supra* n. 11, p. VIII.

27 E. Williams, *supra* n. 15.

28 J. Allain, *Slavery in International Law: Of Human Exploitation and Trafficking*, Martinus Nijhoff, Boston 2013, p. 29; C.J. Robinson, *supra* n. 9, pp. 109–111.

29 F.P. Bowser, *supra* n. 11, pp. 1–4; M.A. McKinley, *supra n. 12*, p. 32. À noter que les royaumes d'Espagne et du Portugal se fusionnèrent vers la fin du 16e siècle jusqu'en 1640, facilitant l'approvisionnement des colonies espagnoles d'esclaves par la traite transatlantique.

30 C. Aguirre, *supra* n. 16, p. 21; Bowser note que jusqu'à 1640, il y aurait eu quelque 30 000 esclaves amenés vers le Pérou : F.P. Bowser, *supra* n. 11, p. 75.

posent près de 50% de la population totale, et cette proportion descend progressivement jusqu'à la fin de l'ère coloniale[31].

L'historien Bowser affirme que l'esclavage africain au Pérou est si omniprésent dès le 16e siècle qu'il aurait été impossible que la colonie espagnole fonctionne sans[32]. À titre d'exemple de son étendue, les artisans péruviens, en tant que groupe, étaient parmi les plus grands propriétaires d'esclaves au Pérou[33]. Les deux autres secteurs ayant eu le plus recours à l'esclavage africain étaient l'agriculture et le travail domestique, deux secteurs qui encore aujourd'hui sont associés avec la pauvreté et l'exploitation[34].

Les esclaves d'origine africaine étaient toutefois moins présents dans le secteur minier, ce que la géographie explique partiellement. Les mines d'argent de l'époque coloniale étaient principalement dans les Andes et les colons espagnols estimaient que les personnes d'origine africaine ne supporteraient pas le climat dans ces régions. Ainsi, on retrouvait plus d'esclaves dans les mines d'or à plus basse altitude, où le climat était plus clément[35]. Il semble toutefois que cette justification ait surtout servi de prétexte pour renforcer la division sociale entre Africains et Autochtones, en s'assurant qu'ils ne se côtoient pas dans leur milieu de travail[36]. De plus, les coûts associés avec l'acquisition et le transport d'esclaves vers les mines semblaient prohibitifs[37]. Ainsi, les populations d'esclaves se sont traditionnellement plus concentrées sur la côte et le travail dans les mines était surtout réservé aux populations autochtones.

Que les esclaves africains aient joué un rôle moindre dans l'exploitation minière ne signifie pas que cette industrie est marginale dans la facilitation de la traite transatlantique vers le Pérou. Comme nous l'avons déjà mentionné, le principal attrait de la région était ses ressources minérales et les besoins en main-d'œuvre d'autres secteurs n'auraient pas existé, n'eût été cet appât économique. Le commerce de l'argent, principalement extrait du travail forcé des Autochtones, alimente directement le commerce transatlantique, incluant la

31 C. Aguirre, *supra* n. 16, p. 22; J. Lockhart, *Spanish Peru, 1532–1560: A Social History*, University of Wisconsin Press, Madison 1994, p. 203; M.A. McKinley, *supra* n. 12, p. 31.

32 F.P. Bowser, *supra* n. 11, p. 109.

33 J. Lockhart, *supra* n. 31, pp. 111–112.

34 C. Aguirre, *supra* n. 16, pp. 50–52. Aguirre révèle qu'à une certaine époque, la Compagnie de Jésus était la plus importante propriétaire d'esclaves dans le Pérou colonial, *ibid.*, pp. 17, 55–57.

35 F.P. Bowser, *supra* n. 11, p. 13.

36 R.S. O'Toole, *Bound Lives: Africans, Indians, and the Making of Race in Colonial Peru*, University of Pittsburg Press, Pittsburg 2012, p. 18.

37 F.P. Bowser, *supra* n. 11, pp. 13–15.

traite des esclaves au sein des colonies espagnoles[38]. Ainsi, le travail forcé et l'esclavage sont interreliés.

3.2 *Le travail forcé des populations andines conquises*

La population autochtone sur le territoire du Pérou n'a pas été formellement soumise à un régime d'esclavage, les peuples andins étant considérés comme des vassaux[39]. Les autochtones n'en étaient toutefois pas moins asservis[40]. La gestion de la colonie péruvienne était soumise au système des *encomiendas*, où les diverses régions du territoire étaient confiées à un *encomendero* dont une des responsabilités principales était de récolter les tributs dus par les populations autochtones. Ce tribut était de deux natures : d'une part, les nouveaux sujets espagnols devaient fournir des produits de consommation, et d'autre part, ils devaient, comme vassaux, fournir leur labeur au souverain.

La Couronne espagnole était initialement très réticente à forcer les populations autochtones à travailler dans les mines, en bonne partie pour éviter les désastreuses pertes en vie humaine des populations locales vécues dans leurs colonies antillaises et sur la côte péruvienne[41]. Elle consent tout de même rapidement à l'usage d'un système de travail forcé au Pérou[42]. Deux raisons principales auraient mené à cette décision. Premièrement, l'Espagne avait dramatiquement besoin de revenus pour financer de nombreuses campagnes en cours en Europe. Les mines d'argent péruviennes étaient exploitées au moyen de licences royales qui garantissaient à la Couronne un cinquième

38 La transnationalité des gains économiques tirés de l'esclavage est bien documentée, notamment en ce qui concerne l'Angleterre par E. Williams, *supra* n. 15; voir également C.J. Robinson, *supra* n. 9, p. 113 et, pour l'exemple français, C.L.R. James, *supra* n. 12, pp. 47–50.

39 F.P. Bowser, *supra* n. 11, p. 12. Bowser explique que les Espagnols en sont venus à construire une image de l'Autochtone comme un « noble sauvage », alors que les personnes d'origine africaine étaient plus aisément peintes comme un ennemi à contrôler par leur proximité géographique et historique avec les Européens, (*ibid.*, pp. 26–27). Dans un même ordre d'idée, Robinson suggère que la construction du « Noir » visait à poser les Africains comme inférieurs et serviles, alors qu'auparavant ils étaient plutôt craints par les Européens dû à leur association avec des civilisations supérieures ou antagonistes, tel que l'Islam, C.J. Robinson, *supra* n. 9, p. 82.

40 R.S. O'Toole, *supra* n. 36, pp. 20–21.

41 Voir, F.P. Bowser, *supra* n. 11, pp. 116–117. Bowser rapporte qu'entre 1525 et 1571, la population autochtone aurait baissé de 6 à 1.5 millions. Ces pertes affectent surtout la côte, où il est estimé qu'environ 90% de la population autochtone avait disparu dès la fin des années 1540.

42 *Ibid.*, p. 12 ; J.A. Cole, *supra* n. 25, p. 3.

des revenus, donc une production soutenue lui était hautement bénéfique[43]. Deuxièmement, les populations locales ne s'offrant pas volontairement pour travailler dans les mines, Potosí fit vite face à des pénuries de main-d'œuvre. L'envoi de main-d'œuvre était une mesure nécessaire afin de motiver les propriétaires des mines à investir dans l'exploitation commerciale des mines d'argent et à maintenir leur rythme de production[44].

Les Espagnols s'inspirèrent d'un système de travail forcé développé par l'administration Inca, le système de la *mita*. Il consistait à diviser les populations en groupes qui devaient, de manière périodique et rotative, se rendre disponibles pour travailler au service de l'empereur, après quoi, les travailleurs pouvaient retourner à leur vie quotidienne jusqu'à ce que leur tour revienne[45]. Similaire à un système de conscription, la *mita* était intégrée dans le système des *encomiendas* afin d'assurer un accès soutenu à la main-d'œuvre. Chaque *ayllus* (communautés regroupant plusieurs familles) devaient fournir un certain nombre de travailleurs pour une durée moyenne d'un an, durant laquelle, contre rémunération, ils étaient obligés à travailler trois semaines consécutives suivies de deux semaines libres, et ainsi de suite pour le reste de l'année[46]. La *mita* a été instaurée en 1573 et fut abolie en 1825. En 1775, c'est plus de 14 000 travailleurs qui prennent la route de force vers Potosí[47].

Durant les 250 ans d'existence de la *mita*, les besoins d'une production toujours plus intensive et le déclin des ressources ont contribué à la dégradation des conditions de travail des *mitayos*. Les travailleurs étaient soumis à des quotas de production, pouvaient être fouettés ou battus et subissaient parfois des déductions salariales pour payer des équipements et outils nécessaires à leur travail[48]. Il est à noter que la dégradation des conditions de travail n'était pas le résultat de politiques publiques formelles, mais de la gestion des responsables des mines. Bien que l'abolition du système fût suggérée à de nombreuses

43 J.A. Cole, *supra* n. 25, pp. 7–8, 20, 66.

44 *Ibid.*, pp. 17–18.

45 F.P. Bowser, *supra* n. 11, p. 19; B. Moses, *supra* n. 23, pp. 5–7; *Ibid.*, p. 9.

46 J.A. Cole, *supra* n. 25, pp. 9, 12. La durée des rotations pouvait changer selon les modifications qui étaient amenés au système au fil des ans, mais le principe demeurait le même. Les deux semaines libres pouvaient être utilisées pour le repos, mais les travailleurs pouvaient également s'offrir pour travailler contre rémunération durant cette période. Après un certain temps, il arrivait également que les travailleurs soient forcés à travailler également durant leur période de repos.

47 *Ibid.*, pp. 9, 17.

48 *Ibid.*, pp. 23–25.

reprises, la nécessité de maintenir les revenus miniers venait toujours freiner les élans humanistes des gouverneurs de la colonie[49].

Les dimensions migratoires de la *mita* sont multiples. D'abord, les travailleurs de la *mita* provenaient de diverses régions et devaient parfois voyager plusieurs jours à pied pour pouvoir se rendre à leur poste, même si, en principe, le recrutement se faisait dans les régions environnantes[50]. Il arrivait également que les *mitayos* ne soient pas retournés à leur *ayllu* à la fin de leur service, mais qu'ils soient plutôt replacés dans des villages où l'instruction religieuse et la collecte des tributs étaient plus faciles à contrôler[51]. Ensuite, étant donné les conditions de travail et de vie déplorables dans les mines andines, plusieurs décidaient de s'exiler, c'est-à-dire de ne pas retourner à leur *ayllu* pour éviter les prochaines conscriptions et chercher une nouvelle vie ailleurs, généralement dans les villes[52]. Ainsi, d'une manière ou d'une autre, la *mita* a mené à un déracinement profond des populations andines, sans compter les nombreuses morts causées par ce régime de travail forcé[53].

Pour les colonisateurs, la *mita* a permis l'accumulation des richesses tirées des ressources naturelles[54]. Si l'on accepte, comme le suggère Robinson, que les migrations de la main-d'œuvre font partie intégrante du développement des économies européennes, on comprend que la *mita* n'était pas une anomalie dans le contexte commercial de l'époque, mais une stratégie intégrée et complémentaire à la traite transatlantique[55]. L'historien Cole résume bien le lien entre travail forcé et développement économique colonial, expliquant que "*without the mita there would be no Potosí, and without Potosí there would be no Peru*"[56]. Étant donné que la Couronne espagnole dépendait grandement de ces revenus miniers, on peut également conclure que, sans la *mita*, l'Espagne ne serait pas la même aujourd'hui.

49 *Ibid.*, p. 22.

50 *Ibid.*, p. 9.

51 *Ibid.*, p. 2.

52 *Ibid.*, pp. 26–27; J. Lockhart, *supra* n. 31, p. 235.

53 Moses fait état de possiblement huit millions d'Autochtones ayant péris dans les mines du Pérou, B. Moses, *supra* n. 23, p. 7.

54 *Ibid.*, pp. 8–10.

55 C. J. Robinson, *supra* n. 9, p. 23.

56 J.A. Cole, *supra* n. 25, p. 20.

3.3 *Abolition et continuation*

L'abolition de la traite des esclaves est en vigueur dès 1821 au Pérou, et l'esclavage y est aboli en 1855[57]. L'abolition de l'esclavage s'est concrétisée législativement par la conversion de l'esclave d'objet de propriété à sujet de droit : ainsi, un des nombreux décrets présidentiels adoptés par l'État péruvien (indépendant depuis 1821) pour mettre en œuvre l'abolition prévoyait une compensation financière pour les propriétaires frustrés de leurs biens, équivalente à la valeur marchande d'un esclave à l'époque[58]. Aucune mesure compensatoire n'est toutefois envisagée pour les personnes libérées ; les personnes d'origine africaine se voient souvent forcées de quitter les *haciendas* où ils travaillaient sans pour autant se faire accorder les pleins bénéfices de la citoyenneté[59]. Cependant, dès le milieu du 19e siècle, le Pérou a de plus en plus recours à des migrants chinois pour combler les besoins de main-d'œuvre en agriculture, à travers des contrats de servitude[60]. La combinaison des compensations financières reçues par les anciens maîtres d'esclaves et l'usage du travail forcé des Chinois contribuera à renforcer l'accumulation des richesses des élites péruviennes agricoles, pavant la voie à leur domination politique[61].

Malgré la sympathie des leaders indépendantistes du Pérou à la cause abolitioniste, un des arguments invoqués contre une abolition drastique était l'impact que cela aurait sur l'économie agricole[62]. Cette position démontre ce que plusieurs auteurs concluent de l'esclavage : ce sont surtout des impératifs économiques qui sont à la base de l'asservissement, un « mal nécessaire » qui devient plus facile à justifier du fait que certaines personnes sont par nature, selon le colon blanc, inférieures[63]. Comme l'explique Bowser dans le contexte de l'esclavage: « *the idea of African inferiority, always vaguely present*

57 C. Aguirre, *supra* n. 16, p. 161.

58 M. Arrelucea, 'Historia de la esclavitud africana en el Peru desde la Conquista hasta la Abolición' (2004) 14 *Arqueología y Sociedad* 239, pp. 275–276.

59 *Ibid.*, pp. 89–90, 193–194.

60 Jusqu'en 1874, il est estimé que quelques 100 000 Chinois ont été soumis à un régime de travail par contrats de servitude au Pérou : M. J. Gonzales, 'Chinese Plantation Workers and Social Conflict in Peru in the Late Nineteenth Century' (1989) 21:3 *Journal of Latin American Studies* 386.

61 *Ibid.* Voir aussi, C. Aguirre, *supra* n. 16, p. 189, qui explique que les propriétaires terriens créèrent un conglomérat pour mettre en commun les compensations financières et les réinvestir dans les plantations, créant une "puissante ploutocratie côtière" (notre traduction).

62 C. Aguirre, *supra* n. 16, pp. 162–168.

63 Voir, par exemple, E. Williams, *supra* n. 15, pp. 2–3.

in the European mind, was given impetus by colonial need for labor»[64]. Ce qui lie le traitement des personnes d'origine africaine, des Autochtones et des migrants chinois est donc cet impératif économique requis par une exploitation capitaliste des ressources de la terre.

Or, les systèmes d'exploitation du travail hérités de l'époque coloniale ont contribué à ancrer dans la culture péruvienne une hiérarchie sociale et raciale persistante[65]. Les Espagnols semblaient obsédés par la classification raciale (*castas*) et ont très tôt développé un vocabulaire pour distinguer les personnes sur la base de leur niveau de « blancheur »[66]. Ce système de caste utilisé par la société coloniale servait surtout d'outil idéologique pour diviser la population et favoriser les colons blancs[67]. Ces désignations perdurent aujourd'hui, comme le terme *Cholo* (indiquant un héritage autochtone), parfois utilisé comme terme dérogatoire, parfois comme terme affectueux, parfois comme forme de résistance[68]. Cependant, nous verrons plus loin que l'État péruvien n'aborde que superficiellement cette racialisation de la société dans ses lois et ses politiques en lien avec l'esclavage contemporain. Nous nous tournons maintenant vers ces formes d'exploitation sévère dans l'économie minière contemporaine.

4 La ruée vers l'or péruvien et l'esclavage contemporain

La Rinconada est une ville minière dans le département de Puno, au Pérou, considérée, du haut de ses 5100 mètres d'altitude, comme la ville la plus élevée

64 F.P. Bowser, *supra* n. 11, p. 325. Williams s'accorde à suggérer que l'esclavage ne naît pas du racisme, mais que le racisme est né de l'esclavage, E. Williams, *supra* n. 15, pp. 4, 14.

65 C. Aguirre, *supra* n. 16, p. 16.

66 *Ibid.*, pp. 43–45; J. Lockhart, *supra* n. 31, p. 198. La rhétorique du 'blanchiment' et du métissage racial a continué à se développer après l'indépendance des pays d'Amérique latine, notamment par le droit, tel que décrit par T.K. Hernández, *Racial Subordination in Latin America: The Role of the State, Customary Law, and the New Civil Rights Response*, Cambridge University Press, New York 2013. L'auteure note que l'idée de métissage est utilisée de nos jours dans les pays d'Amérique latine pour nier la présence de racisme, *ibid.*, p. 2; cependant, les politiques de métissage découlent de la prémisse de la supériorité de la race blanche, *ibid.*, p. 34.

67 M.A. McKinley, *supra* n. 12, pp. 113–115; C. Aguirre, *supra* n. 16, p. 46; R.S. O'Toole, *supra* n. 36, pp. 18–19.

68 Voir, Marco Avilés, *De donde venimos los cholos*, Planeta Peru, Lima 2018, où l'auteur explore les différents usages du terme 'cholo' au sein de la société péruvienne. Hernández note qu'il est commun en Amérique latine d'utiliser un langage racialisé comme termes affectueux, « which unconsciously invoke the paternalism of slavery's past » ; voir T.K. Hernández, *supra* n. 66, p. 7.

au monde. La ville doit son existence à la présence de ressources aurifères, sans quoi la zone est considérée comme pratiquement inhabitable. En espagnol, une « rinconada » est l'angle entrant qui se forme entre deux maisons, routes ou montagnes ; le nom décrit donc bien l'emplacement de la ville entre le Mont Ananea et le glacier Auchita. « Rinconada » est également cousin du mot « rincón », généralement traduit comme un « coin », un mot qui représente souvent l'idée d'un endroit retiré, caché, presque oublié. Pour les travailleurs qui y sont exploités, le nom de la ville représente cette idée d'invisibilisation.

À La Rinconada, il n'y a aucune mine légale. L'or est une des principales ressources extraites des mines illégales au Pérou et son exploitation est liée avec le crime organisé et le travail forcé[69]. L'exploitation illégale[70] de l'or emploierait entre 250 000 et 500 000 personnes au pays[71]. Cette exploitation n'est pas marginale et bénéficie directement à l'économie péruvienne : entre 2015 et 2019, bien que le Pérou ait officiellement produit 720 tonnes d'or, il en a exporté 2242 tonnes, ce qui indique que près de 70% de la production d'or durant cette période n'était pas comptabilisée[72].

Ces mines sont propices à l'exploitation humaine. Selon la *Politique Nationale de lutte contre la traite des personnes et ses formes d'exploitation d'ici 2030*, les départements de Madre de Dios et Puno, connus pour la forte présence de mines informelles, sont parmi les cinq départements du pays avec le plus grand nombre de dénonciations de traite des personnes[73]. Il n'existe toutefois pas de chiffres précis sur le nombre de victimes de la traite des personnes destinées vers les marchés miniers, ni même sur le nombre de victimes de la traite en général, les cas étant largement sous-répertoriés[74]. L'ONG CHS Alternativo

69 OAS, *On the Trail of Illicit Gold Proceeds: Strengthening the Fight against Illegal Mining Finances* (2021), en ligne: <https://www.oas.org/en/sms/dtoc/docs/On-the-trail-of-illicit-gold-proceeds-Peru-case.pdf>; Verité, *supra* n. 4.

70 Selon le droit péruvien, une exploitation minière illégale inclut toute activité minière utilisant des équipements et de la machinerie non conformes à l'activité et sans remplir les exigences réglementaires ou qui est réalisée dans une zone où l'activité minière est interdite. L'exploitation informelle en est une qui, bien que non conforme, est en processus de formalisation (*Decreto Legislativo N° 1105 que establece disposiciones para el proceso de formalizacion de las actividades de pequena mineria y mineria artesanal*, 19.11.2012).

71 Verité, *supra* n. 4, pp. 13–14.

72 OAS, *On the Trail of Illicit Gold Proceeds: Strengthening the Fight against Illegal Mining Finances* (2021), p. 19, en ligne: <https://www.oas.org/en/sms/dtoc/docs/On-the-trail-of-illicit-gold-proceeds-Peru-case.pdf>.

73 Perú, *Politica Nacional frente a la Trata de personas y sus formas de explotacion al 2030*, Decreto Supremo N° 009-2021-IN.

74 Voir, R. Valdés, C. Basombrio et D. Vera, *Las economias criminales y su impacto en el Peru: ¿Cuáles? ¿Cuánto? ¿Cómo? ¿Dónde?*, Capital Humano y Social, Lima 2021, pp. 77–78. Voir

note également que les efforts au Pérou se sont surtout concentrés sur la traite des personnes avec comme finalité l'exploitation sexuelle, laissant un grand vide dans la compréhension du lien entre traite des personnes et travail forcé dans l'économie informelle[75].

4.1 *Les travailleurs informels des mines d'or*

Bien que la majorité des victimes péruviennes de la traite des personnes sont des femmes, les personnes soumises à un régime de travail forcé dans le secteur minier entendu de manière étroite (extraction et traitement des produits de l'extraction) sont majoritairement des hommes[76]. De plus, les mines illégales sont reconnues pour employer des dizaines de milliers d'enfants même si le droit péruvien interdit formellement le travail des enfants dans le secteur minier[77].

Une pratique commune d'exploitation à La Rinconada est le mécanisme de « *cachorreo* » au sein duquel le travailleur offre ses services dans les mines d'or à titre gratuit ou à salaire réduit pendant un certain nombre de jours, en échange desquels les jours restants il peut garder l'or extrait pour lui-même à titre de rémunération[78]. Les travailleurs dans ce système ne sont pas nécessairement victimes de coercion : ce qui justifie leur soumission à un système de travail sans rémunération est la promesse d'or. Cependant, ces promesses sont souvent enflées par des fables d'hommes ayant fait fortune grâce à ce système, alors que dans les faits la possibilité de faire des gains est surtout une question de chance. Il est fréquent qu'un travailleur ne réussisse pas à extraire de l'or pour lui-même et qu'il se retrouve donc à travailler sans rémunération pendant des périodes prolongées. Ce faisant, le travailleur se voit contraint à emprunter pour survivre, créant un cycle d'endettement qui renforce le contrôle des

aussi T. Sanz, *Caracterización de las condiciones de trabajo forzoso en la minería de oro en Madre de Dios y una aproximación a los factores de riesgo*, OIT, Lima 2015, p. 9.

75 R. Valdés, C. Basombrio et D. Vera, *supra* n. 74, p. 80; Verité, *supra* n. 4, p. 56.

76 Perú, *Plan Nacional para la Lucha contra el Trabajo Forzoso 2019–2022*, Decreto Supremo, N° 015-2019-TR ; Verité, *supra* n. 4, p. 22; D. Cortés-McPherson, *supra* n. 7, pp. 367–368.

77 *Codigo de los ninos y adolescentes*, Decreto Ley N° 26102, 29.12.1992, arts. 51 et 58. Voir UN, *Report of the Special Rapporteur on contemporary forms of slavery, including its causes and consequences, Gulnara Shahinian*, UN Doc A/HRC/18/30/Add.2, 15.08.2011, para. 40; Verité, *supra* n. 4, p. 22; Cette situation s'est d'ailleurs empirée avec la pandémie et l'abandon scolaire qu'elle a causé, R. Valdés, C. Basombrio et D. Vera, *supra* n. 74, p. 95.

78 R. Valdés, C. Basombrio & D. Vera, *supra* n. 74, p. 82. Certains comptes rendus parlent d'une rotation mensuelle (28 jours de travail pour 2 jours à son compte), d'autres d'une rotation hebdomadaire (6 jours de travail pour 1 journées à son compte).

employeurs miniers. Des rumeurs de sacrifices humains rituels contribuent aussi à développer une culture de peur au sein des travailleurs[79].

À Madre de Dios, le département où se retrouverait le plus grand nombre de mines illégales d'or, un système commun est l'*habilitación-enganche* (ou simplement *enganche*). Le travailleur y accumule des dettes auprès de son employeur avant même de commencer à travailler dans les mines, créant une situation de servitude[80]. Les recruteurs peuvent présenter comme cadeaux des outils, du transport et même de l'argent aux recrues, mais en exigent ensuite le remboursement, menant donc à la création de dettes. Des entrevues menées par l'organisation Verité rapportent le cas de deux personnes ayant été « vendues » par des membres de leur famille (ayant reçu de l'argent en échange de leur recrutement), le prix de la vente devant ensuite être remboursé par 90 jours de travail, qui peuvent dans les faits s'étendre sur plusieurs mois[81]. À la fin de ces « contrats », les travailleurs doivent en principe être payés, mais il arrive souvent que la dette accumulée consomme la quasi-totalité de la rémunération promise. Le système *enganche* affecte également les populations autochtones de la région, et certaines sources ont rapporté l'accumulation de dettes pouvant être transmises de génération en génération[82].

Cette servitude est renforcée par le fait que les mines illégales de la région de Madre de Dios sont extrêmement isolées géographiquement, perdues au milieu de la dense forêt amazonienne. La plupart du territoire de la région n'est accessible que par des voies maritimes qui sont peu contrôlées, sinon par les propriétaires miniers[83]. Le contrôle des voies maritimes par les propriétaires miniers facilite le trafic illicite de personnes vers les zones minières et renforce l'isolement géographique des victimes de la traite une fois rendues sur place.

De plus, la plupart des travailleurs pris dans ce système sont migrants, emmenés surtout des départements de Puno et Cuzco sous la promesse d'argent, ce qui exacerbe leur vulnérabilité à leur arrivée[84]. Environ 40% de la population de Madre de Dios est migrante[85]. Ces travailleurs sont souvent sans document officiel d'identité, soit parce qu'ils n'ont jamais possédé

79 Verité, *supra* n. 4, pp. 58–59.

80 *Ibid.*, p. 21; T. Sanz, *supra* n. 74, pp. 11–14.

81 Verité, *supra* n. 4, pp. 39–40.

82 CHS Alternativo, *La Trata de Persona en la región de Madre de Dios*, Capital Humano y Social, Lima 2012, pp. 35–36.

83 Verité, *supra* n. 4, pp. 37, 47.

84 *Ibid.*, pp. 37–38.

85 CMP Flora Tristan, 'Diagnostico sobre trata de mujeres, niños y niñas en ocho ciudades del Perú' (2015), p. 13, <https://www2.congreso.gob.pe/sicr/cendocbib/con2_uibd.nsf/201B9608F142AF730525765C0070DB1F/$FILE/larrain.pdf>.

un certificat de naissance ou parce que leur document leur a été retiré. Cela maximise leur aliénation sociale et facilite leur exploitation. Patterson mentionne d'ailleurs cet effacement de la personnalité juridique comme élément de la mort sociale, ce qui s'observe d'une certaine manière dans un contexte de défaillance institutionnelle à garantir le droit à l'identité. L'isolement est finalement complété par la menace de violence ou d'extorsion, d'autant plus que ces travailleurs sont souvent forcés de s'engager dans des activités illicites telles que la contrebande[86].

Il est important de noter que ce ne sont pas tous les travailleurs des mines aurifères informelles ni tous les travailleurs migrants qui sont soumis à des régimes de travail forcé. L'absence de chiffres précis dans le secteur rend difficile cette analyse, cependant, sur la base de diverses enquêtes sur le terrain on peut conclure que le phénomène n'est pas marginal. Par exemple, sur 202 travailleurs des mines de Madre de Dios interviewés en 2014, 77 cas ont été identifiés comme présentant des indices de travail forcé[87]. Sans nécessairement représenter un échantillon représentatif, ces chiffres laissent toutefois supposer une situation alarmante.

4.2 *Les économies périphériques*

La particularité du secteur minier est qu'il attire le développement d'une économie informelle autour de lui. Selon des chiffres rapportés par l'État péruvien en 2012, pour chaque mineur illégal se créaient quatre emplois dans des services périphériques[88]. Ces services périphériques sont souvent requis étant donné l'isolement géographique des mines et la nécessité d'avoir accès aux services de base à proximité. En effet, il existe peu de services formels (éducation, santé) à La Rinconada et encore moins de présence gouvernementale et policière, faisant en sorte que la mise en œuvre du droit y est limitée[89]. On constate donc que la distance physique entre La Rinconada et les centres du pouvoir engendre en parallèle une distance institutionnelle.

Cette informalité mène à l'exploitation. Les entreprises minières illégales de Madre de Dios et de Puno engagent souvent des femmes comme cuisinières, lesquelles sont ensuite obligées à fournir des services sexuels aux mineurs[90]. Des enfants sont également massivement employés dans ces services

86 Verité, *supra* n. 4, pp. 41–42.

87 T. Sanz, *supra* n. 74, p. 30.

88 Verité, *supra* n. 4, p. 21.

89 CMP Flora Tristan, 'Diagnostico sobre trata de mujeres, niños y niñas en ocho ciudades del Perú' (2015), p. 34, <https://www2.congreso.gob.pe/sicr/cendocbib/con2_uibd.nsf/201B9608F142AF730525765C0070DB1F/$FILE/larrain.pdf>.

90 Verité, *supra* n. 4, pp. 20, 62.

périphériques, par exemple pour travailler dans les restaurants et les bars[91]. Les villes minières regroupent de nombreux « prostibars », établissements destinés à la prostitution où se retrouvent de nombreuses filles et jeunes femmes issues de familles pauvres[92]. Selon des estimations de 2010, certaines régions de Madre de Dios comportaient plus de 100 bordels où 60% des travailleuses étaient âgées de moins de 18 ans[93]. Il existe également de nombreux prostibars à La Rinconada. Les travailleuses des prostibars sont souvent soit victimes de traite, au moyen de réseaux nationaux et internationaux de proxénétisme, ou recrutées par de fausses annonces de travail. Elles sont ensuite forcées à se prostituer sous la menace de représailles et leurs mouvements sont grandement contrôlés.

Sachant qu'en 2015, près de 50% des femmes en zones rurales ne possédaient pas de documents d'identification officiels, on comprend qu'ici encore l'aliénation sociale passe par l'effacement civique[94]. D'autres part, les victimes de traite qui possèdent des documents d'identité se les font généralement retirer[95]. Des femmes travaillant dans les bars de La Rinconada ont également rapporté se faire escompter arbitrairement des sommes de leur salaire déjà maigre[96].

Une dernière particularité de l'asservissement dans l'économie minière informelle au Pérou, tant pour les travailleurs miniers que périphériques, est le fait que, bien que migrants, ils sont souvent recrutés au moyen de réseaux locaux, communautaires, voire même familiaux, qui leur font miroiter des rémunérations avantageuses[97]. C'est-à-dire que plusieurs travailleurs asservis dans les mines informelles péruviennes s'y rendent de leur propre gré, quoique sur la base de mensonges et de tromperies. Une fois sur place, l'employeur exerce sur ces personnes une forme de contrôle (accumulation de dettes

91 *Ibid.*, p. 43.

92 CHS Alternativo, *supra* n. 82, pp. 31–32; CMP Flora Tristan, 'Diagnostico sobre trata de mujeres, niños y niñas en ocho ciudades del Perú' (2015), p. 34, <https://www2.congreso.gob.pe/sicr/cendocbib/con2_uibd.nsf/201B9608F142AF730525765C0070DB1F/$FILE/larrain.pdf>.

93 Verité, *supra* n. 4, pp. 45–46; CHS Alternativo, *supra* n. 82, pp. 25–26.

94 *Ibid.*, p. 58.

95 UN, *Report of the Special Rapporteur on contemporary forms of slavery, including its causes and consequences, Gulnara Shahinian*, UN Doc A/HRC/18/30/Add.2, 15.08.2011, para. 42; CHS Alternativo, *supra* n. 82, p. 30.

96 CMP Flora Tristan, 'Diagnostico sobre trata de mujeres, niños y niñas en ocho ciudades del Perú' (2015), p. 69, <https://www2.congreso.gob.pe/sicr/cendocbib/con2_uibd.nsf/201B9608F142AF730525765C0070DB1F/$FILE/larrain.pdf>.

97 D. Cortés-McPherson, *supra* n. 7, pp. 372–375; Voir aussi T. Sanz, *supra* n. 74, p. 10.

ou menaces de violence) renforcée par l'aliénation sociale qui, ensemble, réduisent leur capacité d'action et leur libre arbitre.

5 Réponse contemporaine du pérou à l'esclavage contemporain : l'économie minière dans la mire

Selon le Global Slavery Index, l'indice de l'esclavage au Pérou est faible. Les dernières estimations font état d'environ 80 000 personnes soumises à l'esclavage moderne, pour un taux de 2,56 pour 1000 habitants[98]. Cela étant, le portrait ci-haut de l'exploitation humaine dans le secteur minier illégal démontre que l'exploitation sévère persiste. Les développements récents du cadre législatif et administratif de l'esclavage contemporain au Pérou démontrent une prise de conscience de l'étendue du problème et de la nécessité de l'aborder. Toutefois, deux problèmes subsistent. Premièrement, au niveau de la forme, on observe un manque de ressources pour mettre en œuvre les plans audacieux d'élimination de l'esclavage au Pérou, carences qui affectent en particulier les zones rurales éloignées où le problème est pourtant le plus criant. Deuxièmement, au niveau du fond, on note l'absence d'une reconnaissance de la continuité des pratiques d'esclavage, notamment du rôle de l'économie minière transnationale dans la perpétuation de pratiques dégradantes envers l'être humain.

5.1 *Droit international et le Pérou*

Le pays n'a pas ratifié la *Convention relative à l'esclavage* de 1926[99], ni la *Convention supplémentaire relative à l'abolition de l'esclavage, de la traite des esclaves et des institutions et pratiques analogues à l'esclavage* (1956), qu'il a pourtant signée le jour de son adoption[100]. Il est toutefois parti à la *Convention* (*n°29*)

98 Global Slavery Index (2018), <https://www.walkfree.org/global-slavery-index/map/>.

99 *Convention relative à la suppression de la traite des esclaves et de l'esclavage*, 25 septembre 1926, 60 L.N.T.S. 253 No. 1414.

100 *Convention supplémentaire relative à l'abolition de l'esclavage, de la traite des esclaves et des institutions et pratiques analogues à l'esclavage*, 7 septembre 1956, 266 RTNU 3. La raison pour laquelle le Pérou n'a pas ratifié les deux conventions n'est pas claire. La Rapporteuse générale sur les formes contemporaines d'esclave suite à sa visite en 2011 mentionne ce fait et demande d'y remédier, sans élaborer sur les raisons de cette non-ratification, voir UN, *Rapport de la Rapporteuse spéciale sur les formes contemporaines d'esclavage, y compris leurs causes et leurs conséquences, Mme Gulnara Shahinian, Mission au Pérou*, UN Doc A/HRC/18/30/Add.2, 15.08.2011. Une demande d'accès à l'information envoyée au ministère des relations extérieures du Pérou le 9 novembre 2022 et répondu le 23 novembre 2022 n'a pas amené d'indications supplémentaires pour élucider cette question. Le Pérou n'a pas participé à la rédaction de la Convention de 1926, mais a été plus active au niveau

sur le travail forcé (1930), à la *Convention (n°105) sur l'abolition du travail forcé* (1957) et la *Convention (n°182) sur les pires formes de travail des enfants* (1999) de l'OIT et est parmi les premiers pays à avoir ratifié le Protocole de Palerme sur la traite des personnes[101]. En juin 2021, le Pérou a également ratifié le *Protocole de 2014 relatif à la convention sur le travail forcé, 1930* de l'OIT. Outre les diverses conventions des Nations Unies sur les droits de la personne, le Pérou est également parti à la *Convention Américaine relative aux droits de l'homme,* qui prévoit à son article 6 l'interdiction de l'esclavage, de la servitude, de la traite des esclaves, de la traite des femmes et du travail forcé[102].

Le Pérou a fait l'objet de divers suivis internationaux, dont une visite en 2011 de la Rapporteuse spéciale sur les formes contemporaines d'esclavage, y compris leurs causes et leurs conséquences[103] et diverses observations de la Commission d'experts de l'OIT pour la mise en œuvre des conventions et recommandations. Le rapport de Mme Gulnara Shahinian identifie le secteur minier comme étant un des secteurs avec le plus grand nombre de cas d'esclavage contemporain, aux côtés du travail domestique et des activités forestières[104]. Parmi les causes de ces pratiques, elle nomme la disparité entre les zones rurales et urbaines, la discrimination envers les personnes d'origine andine et les hauts taux de pauvreté[105]. Le rapport recommande entre autres que le Pérou revoie son cadre législatif et ratifie les deux conventions sur l'esclavage, qu'il prenne toutes les mesures nécessaires pour formaliser l'économie minière, et qu'il augmente les inspections en milieu de travail. La Commission d'experts de l'OIT identifie également le secteur minier parmi les principaux secteurs responsables de la prévalence du travail forcé au Pérou et recommande

---

des débats en lien de la Convention de 1956, tel qu'illustré dans les travaux préparatoires compilés dans J. Allain, *The Slavery Conventions : The Travaux Préparatoires of the 1926 Leave of Nations Convention and the 1956 United Nations Convention,* Martinus Nijhoff, Leiden 2008.

101 *Protocole additionnel à la Convention des Nations Unies contre la criminalité transnationale organisée visant à prévenir, réprimer et punir la traite des personnes, en particulier des femmes et des enfants*, 15 novembre 2000, 2237 RTNU 319.

102 *Convention Américaine relative aux droits de l'homme*, 22 novembre 1969, 1144 RTNU 143.

103 UN, *Rapport de la Rapporteuse spéciale sur les formes contemporaines d'esclavage, y compris leurs causes et leurs conséquences, Mme Gulnara Shahinian, Mission au Pérou,* UN Doc A/HRC/18/30/Add.2, 15.08.2011. La visite a été faite à l'invitation du gouvernement péruvien, malgré le fait que le Pérou n'ait pas ratifié les deux conventions des Nations unies relatives à l'esclavage. Le rapport souligne toutefois que le Pérou est partie à de nombreux instruments internationaux en lien avec l'élimination des formes contemporaines d'esclavage, tel que ceux relatifs aux droits des enfants et les conventions de l'OIT sur le travail forcé, voir *ibid.*, para 14.

104 *Ibid.*, para 8.

105 *Ibid.*, para 31.

le renforcement des mesures législatives pour mettre fin aux diverses formes de travail forcé[106]. Nous verrons dans les prochaines lignes que l'État péruvien a répondu à ces appels en modifiant son code pénal et en établissant des plans d'action pour combattre le travail forcé et la traite des personnes.

5.2 *Cadre législatif*

Le Pérou possède un système législatif développé vis-à-vis de la lutte contre l'esclavage contemporain. La Constitution politique du pays interdit l'esclavage, la servitude et la traite des personnes sous toutes ses formes à l'article 2(24)b) et consacre le principe du droit au travail libre à l'article 2(15)[107]. L'article 23 de la Constitution vient renforcer les droits fondamentaux au travail, mentionnant qu'aucun travailleur ne peut être forcé à travailler sans rémunération ou sans son libre consentement. Cela étant, les lois péruviennes adressent surtout les défis de l'esclavage contemporain dans le domaine pénal plutôt que dans celui du travail.

Dans les dernières années, le Code criminel péruvien a énormément changé quant à la typification des crimes de traite, d'esclavage, d'exploitation sexuelle et autres pratiques s'apparentant à l'esclavage, en écho aux demandes répétées de la Commission d'experts de l'OIT. En 2007, le Code pénal a été modifié pour inclure une définition plus complète de la traite des personnes[108], puis, en 2017 ont été introduits les délits d'exploitation sexuelle, d'esclavage et de travail forcé[109]. Finalement, en 2021, le législateur péruvien a apporté des changements pour systématiser les différents crimes liés à l'esclavage contemporain sous toutes ses formes. Différents délits (traite, exploitation sexuelle, esclavage, travail forcé) sont regroupés sous une nouvelle division du Code pénal, les crimes contre la dignité humaine, alors qu'ils étaient auparavant considérés comme des crimes attentant à la liberté individuelle[110].

---

106 Voir, par exemple, les rapports pour l'année 2004 (Conférence internationale du Travail, 92e session, 2004, Rapport III (Partie 1A), 2004/1A); 2006 (Conférence internationale du Travail, 95e session, 2006, Rapport III (Partie 1A), 2006/1A); 2011 (Conférence internationale du Travail, 100e session, 2011, Rapport III (Partie 1A), 2011-100-1A) et 2013 (Conférence internationale du Travail, 102e session, 2013, Rapport III (Partie 1A), 2013-102-1A).

107 *Constitución política del Perú de 1993*, promulgué le 29 décembre1993.

108 Voir *Ley N° 28950 Contra la Trata de Personas y el Tráfico Ilícito de Migrantes*, 16.01.2007.

109 Voir *Decreto Legislativo N° 1323 que fortalece la lucha contra el feminicidio, la violencia familiar y la violencia de género*, 5.01.2017.

110 Voir *Ley N° 31146 que modifica el código penal, el código procesal penal y la ley 28950, ley contra la trata de personas y el tráfico ilícito de migrantes, con la finalidad de sistematizar los artículos referidos a los delitos de trata de personas y de explotación, y considerar estos como delitos contra la dignidad humana*, 30.03.2021.

Le nouvel article 129 du Code pénal élabore sur les différentes modalités de crimes contre la dignité humaine[111]. Durant les discussions sur le projet de loi ayant mené à ce changement, plusieurs intervenants, dont le représentant du Ministère public, ont suggéré que l'idée de dignité humaine transcende la liberté personnelle et fait appel à la « dégradation permanente » que constitue la traite des personnes[112]. Ainsi, le concept de dignité humaine vise à combattre l'instrumentalisation de l'être humain.

La traite des personnes y est définie selon les principes du droit international, et une attention particulière est accordée à l'exploitation sexuelle[113]. En effet, en 2018, 89,2% des victimes de la traite des personnes enregistrées par la police nationale étaient de sexe féminin (incluant enfants et adultes) et, dans 75,2% des cas, ces victimes étaient destinées à l'exploitation sexuelle[114]. L'article 129-Ñ prévoit des peines spécifiques pour les cas d'esclavage ou analogues à l'esclavage, telle que la servitude, sans toutefois définir ces termes[115]. Le travail forcé, toutefois, est défini à l'article 129-O comme la soumission ou l'obligation envers une personne, peu importe le moyen ou contre sa volonté, à réaliser un travail ou à fournir un service, qu'il soit rémunéré ou non. L'esclavage et l'exploitation sexuelle constituent les deux délits comportant les peines minimales les plus élevées, sous réserve des nombreux facteurs aggravants mentionnés dans le Code pour chaque délit. Cela étant, le fait que l'esclavage ne soit pas défini laisse penser que, dans la pratique, cette disposition sera moins utilisée que d'autres.

Notons finalement que la traite des personnes, le travail forcé et l'esclavage contemporain sont également abordés, directement ou indirectement, dans

111 *Código penal del Perú* (*Decreto Legislativo 635*), promulgué le 3 avril 1991.

112 Voir commentaire du Fiscal Superior Rosario Lopez Wong, durant les discussions sur le projet de loi, dans Comisión de Justicia y Derechos Humanos, *Periodo Anual de sesiones 2020–2021*, Proyecto de Ley 5556/2020-CR (10.12.2020).

113 *Código penal del Perú* (Decreto Legislativo 635), Article 129-A: "*El que mediante violencia, amenaza u otras formas de coacción, privación de la libertad, fraude, engaño, abuso de poder o de una situación de vulnerabilidad, concesión o recepción de pagos o de cualquier beneficio, capta, transporta, traslada, acoge, recibe o retiene a otro, en el territorio de la República o para su salida o entrada del país con fines de explotación* […]"

114 INEI, 'Peru: Estadisticas de Trata de Personas, 2012–2019' (2019), <https://www.inei.gob.pe/media/MenuRecursivo/boletines/boletin_trata_de_personas_4.pdf>. Les chiffres sont similaires pour 2019 et 2020; voir, Peru, *Politica Nacional frente a la Trata de personas y sus formas de explotacion al 2030*, Decreto Supremo N° 009-2021-IN.

115 Cela dit, le Plan National contre le travail forcé, 2019–2022 définit l'esclavage comme l'exercice des attributs de la propriété sur une personne (Perú, *Plan Nacional para la Lucha contra el Trabajo Forzoso 2019–2022*, Decreto Supremo, N° 015-2019-TR).

diverses lois nationales[116]. L'esclavage et le travail forcé ne sont cependant pas abordés par les lois du travail.

5.3 *Politiques et actions gouvernementales*

En plus de mettre à jour ses lois, le gouvernement du Pérou a développé dans les dernières années de nombreuses politiques afin de combattre les diverses formes d'esclavage contemporain ainsi que leurs causes. Nous pouvons mentionner ici des actions liées au travail forcé, à la traite des personnes et à l'informalité.

Au niveau du travail forcé, le plus récent « Plan National contre le travail forcé, 2019–2022 », élaboré avec le soutient de l'OIT, note d'emblée que le Pérou manque d'information et de statistiques complètes sur l'ampleur du phénomène au pays, tout en identifiant l'exploitation forestière, le secteur minier et le travail domestique comme trois secteurs préoccupants[117]. Parmi les facteurs de risque du travail forcé identifiés dans le Plan National se retrouvent la discrimination systémique sur la base de genre, du statut migratoire et de l'origine ethnique, le niveau inadéquat d'éducation, et la pauvreté. L'inaccessibilité géographique est également citée par le Plan National comme facteur de risque. Sur la base de ces facteurs de risque, le Plan National identifie différentes stratégies afin de diminuer la prévalence du travail forcé, et préconise une approche tenant compte des droits de la personne, des approches de genre, du principe de protection spéciale des enfants et des principes d'intersectionnalité et d'interculturalité.

Le gouvernement péruvien a également adopté en 2021 la *Politique Nationale de lutte contre la traite des personnes et ses formes d'exploitation d'ici 2030*[118] faisant suite au *Plan National contre la traite des personnes applicable pour la*

116 Il s'agit notamment de lois d'intervention auprès des personnes disparues, dont plusieurs finissent par être victimes de la traite (*Ley N° 28022 que crea el Registro Nacional de Información de Personas Desaparecidas* ; *Ley N° 29685 – establece medidas especiales en casos de desaparición de niños, niñas, adolescentes, personas adultas mayores y personas con discapacidad mental, física o sensorial*), de la législation en lien avec la lutte contre le crime organisé (*Ley N° 30077 contra el crimen organizado*) la lutte contre la violence faite aux femmes (*Ley N° 30364 Ley para prevenir, sancionar y erradicar la violencia contra las mujeres y los integrantes del grupo familiar*) ou la protection des enfants comme groupe vulnérable (*Codigo de los ninos y adolescentes*).

117 Perú, *Plan Nacional para la Lucha contra el Trabajo Forzoso 2019–2022*, Decreto Supremo, N° 015-2019-TR.

118 Perú, *Politica Nacional frente a la Trata de personas y sus formas de explotacion al 2030*, Decreto Supremo N° 009-2021-IN.

période 2017–2021[119]. La nouvelle Politique Nationale reconnait l'association entre traite et secteur minier illégal et insiste sur l'importance d'une action concertée sur les facteurs de risque menant à la traite (genre et âge, notamment). Ce faisant, la Politique Nationale identifie trois objectifs prioritaires, soit l'augmentation des mesures de prévention, en particulier auprès des populations vulnérables et en situation de risque ; l'amélioration du système de poursuite et de sanction pénale pour lutter contre la traite des personnes; et le renforcement des services de réintégration des victimes. Ces objectifs sont également développés en diverses stratégies, lignes d'action et cibles chiffrées[120].

Ainsi, on constate que le Pérou a répondu à l'appel de la Rapporteuse spéciale et de la Commission d'experts de l'OIT en bonifiant son cadre législatif et en adoptant des politiques de lutte contre l'esclavage contemporain[121]. Cependant, la conversion de ces avancements en actions concrètes tarde, notamment au niveau de l'allocation budgétaire[122]. À titre d'exemple, seuls neuf gouvernements locaux avaient alloué des budgets pour la lutte contre la traite des personnes en 2019[123]. La Politique Nationale de 2021 reconnaît d'ailleurs les manques budgétaires comme un des principaux problèmes dans la mise en œuvre du Plan National de 2017–2021. Aussi, la formation des intervenants concernés est lacunaire. Des entrevues menées en 2015 par l'ONG Flora Tristan auprès de divers opérateurs de service dans les régions les plus affectées par la traite des personnes ont par exemple démontré leur connaissance limitée du concept de traite des personnes[124]. De manière générale, l'ONG CHS

119 Perú, *Plan Nacional contra la trata de personas 2017–2021*, Decreto Supremo N° 012 -2017-IN.

120 Perú, *Politica Nacional frente a la Trata de personas y sus formas de explotacion al 2030*, Decreto Supremo N° 009-2021-IN, p. 130.

121 Voir additionnellement l'adoption en 2019 d'un Guide pour l'élaboration de Plans de réintégration individuelle pour les personnes affectées par la traite des personnes (Decreto supremo No 009-209-MIMP) et de la *Ley N° 30925* visant à renforcer la mise en œuvre d'espace de refuge temporaire pour les victimes de la traite des personnes et de l'exploitation sexuelle.

122 L'ONG CHS Alternativo a évalué de manière concrète la mise en œuvre du Plan d'action de lutte contre la traite des personnes pour la période 2017–2021, notant que seulement le tiers des objectifs avaient été atteints, voir R. Valdés, C. Basombrio et D. Vera, *supra* n. 74, p. 88.

123 CHS Alternativo, *Balance de la sociedad civil sobre la situación de la trata de personas en el Perú 2018–2019*, Capital Humano y Social Alternativo, Lima 2020, pp. 19, 40, <http://chsalternativo.org/wp-content/uploads/2015/12/VII-Informe-Alternativo-Resumen-Ejecutivo.pdf>.

124 CMP Flora Tristan, 'Diagnostico sobre trata de mujeres, niños y niñas en ocho ciudades del Perú' (2015), p. 11, <https://www2.congreso.gob.pe/sicr/cendocbib/con2_uibd.nsf/201B9608F142AF730525765C0070DB1F/$FILE/larrain.pdf>.

Alternativo rapportait en 2022 que plusieurs gouvernements successifs depuis 2018 avaient failli à la tâche de rendre des comptes périodiquement sur l'avancement de la mise en œuvre du Plan National contre la traite des personnes applicable pour la période 2017–2021[125].

L'exploitation par le travail au Pérou est intimement liée à l'informalité et montre des failles non seulement dans la condamnation des formes les plus sévères d'exploitation, mais également dans la capacité de l'État péruvien de protéger les travailleurs par des lois sociales sensibles à la réalité économique et sociale du pays. Si les travailleurs informels se retrouvent en plus grand nombre dans les centres urbains du pays, ils sont proportionnellement beaucoup plus présents en zones rurales, où 93% des emplois en 2016 étaient informels[126]. Les causes de l'informalité sont évidemment multiples : des niveaux de scolarité bas et des taux de pauvreté élevés, un développement économique faible, un manque de connaissance du travail formel et le manque d'inspections en milieu de travail sont souvent pointés du doigt. Une des actions entreprises par l'État péruvien a été de créer en 2013 un organisme de supervision du travail, SUNAFIL, dans le but de contribuer à la formalisation du travail grâce à une supervision plus serrée de l'application des lois du travail et des lois sociales. La SUNAFIL a adopté en 2016 un Protocole relatif à la marche à suivre en matière de travail forcé et, en 2018, un groupe spécialisé d'inspecteur a été créé pour traiter directement des cas de travail forcé et de travail des enfants[127].

La lutte contre l'informalité spécifiquement dans le secteur minier a également été abordée par l'État péruvien au moyen de divers décrets législatifs adoptés en 2012. Ces décrets visent à interdire l'exploitation minière illégale et à établir un processus de formalisation des petites mines et des mines artisanales[128]. Par ailleurs, le gouvernement péruvien a adopté en 2014 une Stratégie

---

125 CHS Alternativo, 'Desde hace 5 anos, 13 gabinetes no rinden cuentas sobre las acciones contra la trata de personas en el Peru, pese a que es obligatorio', note de presse, <https://chsalternativo.org/desde-hace-5-anos-13-gabinetes-no-rinden-cuentas-sobre-las-acciones-contra-la-trata-de-personas-en-el-peru-pese-a-que-es-obligatorio/>.

126 Perú, *Estrategia sectorial para la formalización laboral 2018–2021*, Resolución Ministerial No. 071-2018-TR, p. 21.

127 SUNAFIL, *Protocolo de Actuación en materia de Trabajo Forzoso*, Resolucion de superintendia N° 001-2016-SUNAFIL; SUNAFIL, *Crean Grupo Especializado de Inspectores del Trabajo en materia de Trabajo Forzoso y Trabajo Infantil de la SUNAFIL*, Resolución Directoral N° 05-2018-SUNAFIL. Voir aussi Perú, *Estrategia sectorial para la formalización laboral 2018–2021*, Resolución Ministerial No. 071-2018-TR.

128 Voir notamment *Decreto Legislativo N° 1100 que regula la interdiccion de la mineria ilegal en toda la republica y establece medidas complementarias* (18.02.2012) et *Decreto Legislativo N° 1105 que establece disposiciones para el proceso de formalización de las actividades de pequena mineria y mineria artesanal* (19.11.2012).

nationale pour l'interdiction de l'exploitation minière illégale où il est fait état de l'augmentation de ce type d'exploitation[129]. La Stratégie vise à éradiquer les principales enclaves de l'exploitation minière illégale et à réduire de manière significative sa prévalence à l'échelle nationale ainsi que les crimes reliés à cette pratique, dont la traite des personnes. Pour ce faire, il prévoit des efforts concertés de différentes institutions étatiques. Les principales enclaves identifiées dans cette Stratégie nationale se retrouvent dans les départements de Puno, Cusco et Madre De Dios.

Selon un rapport de l'Organisation des États américains, plus de 90 000 mineurs au Pérou ont initié le processus de formalisation dans les quatre dernières années, mais seulement 2% l'ont formellement complété[130]. Ces chiffres montrent une difficulté institutionnelle à appliquer promptement le processus, d'autant plus que les mineurs artisanaux sont dépendants des propriétaires de concessions minières pour pouvoir se formaliser. En effet, selon la loi, les propriétaires doivent accorder l'autorisation d'opérer sur leurs terres pour compléter le processus de formalisation et certains monnaient ces permissions à coûts élevés, rendant les mineurs autonomes vulnérables à des situations de servitude pour dettes[131].

Force est de constater, donc, que les actions entreprises jusqu'à maintenant en matière de formalisation ne portent pas fruit. Si bien il est vrai que l'État péruvien va au-delà de l'approche punitive en tentant de remédier à un facteur de risque à l'exploitation, elle le fait dans une perspective étroite et corporative qui met l'accent sur la formalisation technique des entreprises plutôt que sur l'agentivité des travailleurs. En effet, les décrets peignent un portrait incomplet de la réalité en distinguant entre les 'bonnes' mines artisanales et les 'méchantes' mines illégales, sans aborder de manière plus approfondie les causes et les mécanismes de l'informalité dans un pays où l'exploitation des ressources naturelles s'est toujours accompagnée d'une division inégale des richesses. Dans un contexte de pauvreté extrême, accentué par la pandémie[132], l'attrait de la formalisation est minime si le processus pour y arriver est lourd et si les bénéfices en matière d'amélioration du niveau de vie tel que

129 Peru, *Estrategia Nacional para la Interdiccion de la Mineria Ilegal*, Decreto Supremo N° 003-2014-PCM.

130 OAS, *On the Trail of Illicit Gold Proceeds: Strengthening the Fight against Illegal Mining Finances* (2021), p. 18, <https://www.oas.org/en/sms/dtoc/docs/On-the-trail-of-illicit-gold-proceeds-Peru-case.pdf>. Pour une discussion détaillée du processus de formalisation des mines illégales, voir R. Valdés, C. Basombrio et D. Vera, *supra* n. 74.

131 Verité, *supra* n. 4, pp. 18–19.

132 Selon les données de l'Institut National de Statistiques et d'Informatique du Pérou (INEI), le taux de pauvreté au Pérou aurait augmenté de plus de 5% entre 2019 et 2021, voir INEA,

l'accession à des protections sociales—ne sont pas évidents[133]. Ce faisant, les facteurs de risque pouvant mener à des formes extrêmes d'exploitation ne sont pas adéquatement abordés.

5.4 *Traitement judiciaire des cas d'esclavage contemporain*

Au niveau du traitement judiciaire des cas d'esclavage contemporain, on retrouve surtout des décisions en lien avec la traite des personnes, les délits de travail forcé et d'esclavage n'ayant été introduits qu'en 2017. Or, malgré un cadre législatif et des plans d'action élaborés, la poursuite des cas de traite des personnes est déficiente. En 2018, l'ONG CHS Alternativo évaluait que seulement 4,8% des cas rapportés de traite des personnes s'étaient conclus avec une condamnation criminelle[134]. Quant au traitement de ces cas, plusieurs stéréotypes persistent au sein de l'appareil judiciaire péruvien, notamment vis-à-vis des femmes. Par exemple, dans un cas rapporté dans un rapport conjoint de l'Ombudsman péruvien et de l'ONG CHS Alternativo sur le traitement judiciaire de la traite des personnes, un juge a déterminé qu'une jeune fille qui était exploitée sexuellement n'était pas victime de traite puisqu'elle pouvait sortir une heure par jour du bar où elle travaillait[135]. Tout en reconnaissant qu'elle devait payer une amende de 400 soles[136] en cas de retard, le juge a estimé qu'elle n'était pas « séquestrée ». Le rapport conjoint fait également état de stéréotypes de genre dans les décisions judiciaires sur la traite, et rapporte quelques décisions où le tribunal retient le fait qu'une victime ait déjà travaillé

'Cifras de pobreza 2021' (2021), <https://www.gob.pe/institucion/inei/informes-publicaciones/3149908-cifras-de-pobreza-2021>.

133 D'autant plus que l'économie informelle possède son propre système normatif et réussit ainsi à gérer de manière efficace les activités économiques du quotidien et les relations sociales qui s'y rattachent, voir A. Blackett, *Everyday Transgressions: Domestic Workers' Transnational Challenge to International Labor Law*, Cornell University Press, Ithaca 2019, p. 40. Bonilla-Maldonado utilise plutôt l'expression d''extra-légalité' pour décrire des systèmes normatifs en marge du droit formel, dans le contexte de la propriété informelle en Amérique latine, voir D. Bonilla-Maldonado, 'Extralegal Property, Legal Monism, and Pluralism' (2009) 40:2 *U Mia Inter-Am L Rev* 213.

134 CHS Alternativo, *Balance de la sociedad civil sobre la situación de la trata de personas en el Perú 2018–2019*, Capital Humano y Social Alternativo, Lima 2020, p. 37, <http://chsalternativo.org/wp-content/uploads/2015/12/VII-Informe-Alternativo-Resumen-Ejecutivo.pdf>.

135 Defensoria del Pueblo y CHS Alternativo, 'Abordaje Judicial de la Trata de Personas', Informe N° 001-2020-DP/ADHPD (2020), p. 41, <https://www.defensoria.gob.pe/wp-content/uploads/2020/06/INFORME-TRATA-DE-PERSONAS.pdf>.

136 L'équivalent d'environ 40% du salaire minimum mensuel péruvien.

dans des bars comme dame de compagnie comme signifiant qu'elle ne peut pas être victime de traite[137].

Le Tribunal constitutionnel du Pérou (TC) s'est prononcé brièvement en 2019 sur l'importance de la lutte contre la traite des personnes dans une demande d'habeas corpus soumises par deux personnes condamnées pour le délit de traite envers des enfants. Le TC note l'importance d'aborder le problème de manière coordonnée, ce qui inclut le système judiciaire[138]. Bien que la décision sur le fond soit courte, plusieurs opinions séparées se sont attardées sur le thème de la traite des personnes. Le juge Miranda Canales, par exemple, souligne qu'il s'agit d'un phénomène mondial ayant ses sources dans la traite des esclaves, mais qui s'en distingue du fait qu'elle s'intègre dans le processus de mondialisation, dans lequel les personnes sont vues comme fongibles[139]. Le juge Espinosa-Saldaña Barrera, quant à lui, met en lumière le fait que le phénomène semble s'empirer au Pérou et que l'économie extractive illégale constitue « un terreau propice à la multiplication des activités liées à la traite des personnes »[140]. Le juge note qu'il existe à l'échelle nationale plusieurs lois et politiques visant à affronter le problème, mais qu'il reste beaucoup à faire pour protéger les personnes en situation de vulnérabilité et renforcer les institutions.

5.5 *Actions transnationales*

Depuis 2019, le Pérou est également un des 26 pays pionniers de l'Alliance 8.7, une initiative transnationale créée en 2016 visant à mettre en œuvre l'éradication immédiate du travail forcé et du travail des enfants en conformité avec les Objectifs de développement durable des Nations Unies. Depuis, l'OIT a accordé une assistance technique au Pérou afin de mettre en place divers programmes et mécanismes, surtout axés vers le travail des enfants. Ceux-ci sont principalement mis en œuvre par le Ministère du travail et de promotion de l'emploi (MTPE). On peut noter parmi ces programmes une coordination multisectorielle accrue aux niveaux nationaux et régionaux, l'adoption d'un

137 Defensoria del Pueblo y CHS Alternativo, 'Abordaje Judicial de la Trata de Personas', Informe N° 001-2020-DP/ADHPD (2020), p. 92, <https://www.defensoria.gob.pe/wp-content/uploads/2020/06/INFORME-TRATA-DE-PERSONAS.pdf>.

138 EXP. No 00208-2018-PHC/TC, 24.02.2020, Lima (Julia Teresa Benavente Tenemas y Otro), para 4 et 6, <https://tc.gob.pe/jurisprudencia/2020/>.

139 *Ibid.*, opinion du juge Miranda Canales, para 1.

140 *Ibid.*, opinion du juge Espinosa-Saldaña Barrera, para 8 et 11 (notre traduction).

modèle d'identification des risques liés au travail des enfants, et la création d'une catégorie « exempt de travail des enfants »[141].

Cependant, ni les politiques nationales ci-haut mentionnées ni la Politique nationale multisectorielle pour les enfants et les adolescents[142] ne font référence à l'Alliance 8.7 même si la plupart ont été adoptées après 2019, ce qui semble dénoter un manque de coordination entre les actions transnationales et nationales. Cela dit, en tant que pays pionnier, le Pérou est appelé à rendre compte de manière annuelle de son avancement en matière de lutte contre le travail forcé et le travail des enfants ainsi que des défis auxquels le pays fait face, ce qui encourage un engagement systématique dans cette lutte. Le fait que la coordination au niveau national s'articule autour du MTPE permet également d'aborder le problème au-delà de l'angle traditionnel de la criminalisation. À titre d'exemple, le Pérou s'est engagé à développer un programme de réinsertion au travail pour les victimes de travail forcé et de traite des personnes[143].

6 Asservissement et discrimination : un mal nécessaire pour le commerce mondial?

Ce rapport s'est concentré sur le cas de l'esclavage dans le secteur minier au Pérou tout en insérant ce thème dans le contexte historique et législatif plus large de la lutte contre l'esclavage contemporain dans ce pays. Le bref résumé historique montre la relation entre l'exploitation commerciale des ressources naturelles et l'asservissement. Pour Bowser, l'esclavage et la *mita* étaient deux institutions complémentaires et persistantes rendues nécessaires par la réalité économique et géographique du pays[144]. Les exemples d'esclavage contemporain de Madre de Dios et de Puno visaient quant à eux à démontrer la persistance de cette corrélation entre capitalisme et exploitation, contestant le

141 Alliance 8.7, 'Peru – Informe de progeso anual de Pais Pionero' (2021–2022), <https://www.alliance87.org/sites/default/files/2023-06/ES_Progress_Report_PERU_21-22_FINAL.pdf>.

142 Perú, *Política Nacional Multisectorial para las Niñas, Niños y Adolescentes al 2030*, Decreto Supremo N° 008-2021-MIMP.

143 Alliance 8.7, 'Peru – Informe de progeso anual de Pais Pionero' (2021–2022), p. 13, <https://www.alliance87.org/sites/default/files/2023-06/ES_Progress_Report_PERU_21-22_FINAL.pdf>.

144 F.P. Bowser, *supra* n. 11, p. 124.

discours commun de 'nouvelles' formes d'esclavage et de travail forcé qui crée une rupture avec le passé[145].

Bien que le Pérou ait répondu aux appels internationaux pour lutter contre l'esclavage contemporain, il semble que la réponse nationale soit incomplète. D'abord, le Pérou ne tient pas compte dans ses plans d'action de la corrélation entre le développement économique, le commerce transnational et l'exploitation des personnes. Ensuite, il ne tient pas suffisamment compte du rôle de la discrimination raciale dans la persistance de l'informalité et de l'exploitation par le travail qui maintiennent la marginalisation socio-spatiale des populations andines.

Le Pérou n'est certainement pas le seul pays où l'économie minière mène à l'esclavage. L'organisation Verité fait état de 32 pays où l'extraction d'or mène soit au travail forcé, au travail des enfants ou aux deux[146]. La corrélation entre l'industrie minière, la traite des personnes et l'exploitation sexuelle a également été observée dans divers pays[147]. L'extraction d'or, un produit principalement destiné à l'exportation, est intégrée dans une chaîne globale d'approvisionnement. La production aurifère péruvienne ne fait pas exception à la règle : de tous les investissements dans le secteur minier péruvien en 2012, seulement 3% étaient domestiques, alors que la majorité était financée par la Chine, les États-Unis, le Canada, l'Australie et la Suisse[148]. Quand on sait que le développement d'une économie globale a été facilité par l'exploitation humaine de masse[149], on doit se demander si la nature transnationale des échanges commerciaux ne doit pas être également mise en cause dans les formes extrêmes d'exploitation au 21e siècle[150].

Bien que le cas d'étude de l'exploitation minière au Pérou démontre une continuité historique, le modèle économique capitaliste transnational—dont

145 A. Blackett et A. Duquesnoy, 'Slavery is Not a Metaphor: U.S. Prison Labor and Racial Subordination Through the Lens of the ILO's Abolition of Forced Labor Convention' (2021) 67 *U.C.L.A. Law Review* 1504, pp. 1506–1507, 1519. C. Aguirre, *supra* n. 16, p. 14.

146 Verité, 'Countries Where Gold is Reportedly Produced with Forced Labor and/or Child Labor', <https://www.verite.org/project/gold-3/>.

147 Voir par exemple K. Bales, *Disposable People: New Slavery in the Global Economy*, University of California Press, Berkeley 2012, p. 4.

148 Verité, *supra* n. 4, p. 17. Ces pays sont également parmi les principaux pays importateurs de l'or péruvien.

149 E. Williams, *supra* n. 15, pp. 44–50, 77, 83; C.J. Robinson, *supra* n. 9, pp. 81, 113–114; Voir aussi J.E. Inikori, *supra* n. 24, pp. s161–163. Allain suggère d'ailleurs que la défense de l'institution de l'esclavage par divers penseurs et juristes entre le 16e et 18e siècle s'explique mieux dans le contexte de la nécessité de la traite transatlantique pour l'avancement des colonies européennes (J. Allain, *supra* n. 28, p. 55).

150 Voir généralement K. Bales, *supra* n. 147.

le développement dépend en bonne partie de la traite transatlantique d'esclave[151]—n'est pas mentionné dans les facteurs de risque de l'esclavage contemporain au Pérou. Ce facteur aiderait pourtant à comprendre que c'est le besoin d'une main-d'œuvre accessible et à faible coût qui justifiait hier et qui justifie encore aujourd'hui le recours au travail forcé. Nous avons mentionné que la principale motivation historique du recours au travail forcé des peuples autochtones était la nécessité d'assurer une production soutenue dans un contexte où le travail des mines était boudé par les populations locales. Or, cette situation n'a pas changé. Des enquêtes auprès de diverses personnes s'étant volontairement engagées à travailler dans les mines informelles de Madre de Dios démontrent que, si la rémunération qu'ils peuvent aller chercher est séduisante, les conditions de travail et de vie y sont extrêmement dures ce qui explique probablement le fait qu'en moyenne ces personnes ont travaillé moins d'un an dans les mines[152]. La main-d'œuvre est difficile à trouver dans les mines informelles, bien que les besoins soient constants, voire augmentent avec l'augmentation du prix de l'or et la diminution des réserves[153]. Ce faisant, le recours à des pratiques d'esclavage devient un mal nécessaire. L'amélioration des conditions de travail ne semble pas considérée comme une option, ni par l'employeur ni par l'État.

Tout comme à l'époque de la traite transatlantique, cette situation est directement tributaire de la nature transnationale de l'économie. Le Pérou a adopté une posture néo-libérale qui crée pour les entreprises étrangères un accès facile aux ressources naturelles du pays[154]. Ces entreprises étrangères ne sont pas illégales : pour pouvoir accéder aux ressources, elles doivent se conformer à de nombreuses exigences juridiques et administratives, incluant par exemple, celle de consulter les populations autochtones[155] et d'appliquer les législations du travail. Cela n'empêche pas leur participation dans le marché informel péruvien : d'une part, l'économie informelle peut s'installer autour de ces

151 Voir généralement E. Williams, *supra* n. 15. Voir aussi G. Grandin, 'How Slavery Made the Modern World' (2014) *The Nation,* <https://www.thenation.com/article/archive/how-slavery-made-modern-world/>.

152 T. Sanz, *supra* n. 74, pp. 29, 31.

153 Verité, *supra* n. 4, pp. 15–16.

154 J. Bury et A. Kolff, 'Livelihoods, Mining and Peasant Protests in the Peruvian Andes' (2002) 1:1 *Journal of Latin American Geography* 3.

155 Le Pérou a ratifié la *Convention (No 169) relative aux peuples indigènes et tribaux (1989)* (OIT) dès 1994, et en 2011 le Congrès l'a officiellement mise en œuvre en droit national en adoptant la *Ley N° 29785 del derecho a la consulta previa a los pueblos indigenas u originarios, reconocido en el Convenio 169 de la Organización internacional del Trabajo* (OIT).

mines, et d'autre part, les entreprises minières légales peuvent s'engager directement avec les entreprises illégales pour leur avancement mutuel[156] ou même embaucher des travailleurs de manière informelle[157]. Comme l'expliquent les auteurs van der Valk, Bisschop et van Swaaningen, la chaîne globale d'approvisionnement de l'industrie minière informelle de l'or au Pérou est si complexe et multidimensionnelle que l'évaluation de la légalité ou de l'illégalité d'une activité ne peut être clairement réalisée[158].

Le fait qu'une exploitation minière soit informelle ou illégale ne l'empêche pas d'être intégrée au sein du commerce international. Au contraire, les chaînes globales d'approvisionnement contribuent précisément à cacher l'origine illicite de la production[159]. Un rapport de l'OEA démontre que, presque systématiquement, les importations d'or rapportées des principaux pays importateurs de l'or péruvien étaient plus élevées que les exportations rapportées par le Pérou[160]. La production illégale d'or atteint donc sans problème le marché mondial. Or, cette dimension est pratiquement absente des discussions nationales péruviennes, qui n'abordent pas la problématique de la traite et du travail forcé dans son contexte transnational. C'est dire que le fondement du développement économique du pays sur une violence originelle est ignoré et donc perdure[161].

D'autre part, les lois et politiques péruviennes en matière de lutte contre l'esclavage contemporain se concentrent principalement sur les caractéristiques des "victimes" comme étant vulnérables, pauvres et en manque

156 Voir OAS, *On the Trail of Illicit Gold Proceeds: Strengthening the Fight against Illegal Mining Finances* (2021), p. 31, <https://www.oas.org/en/sms/dtoc/docs/On-the-trail-of-illicit-gold-proceeds-Peru-case.pdf>.

157 N. van der Valk, L. Bisschop et R. van Swaaningen, 'When Gold Speaks, Every Tongue Is Silent: The Thin Line Between Legal, Illegal, and Informal in Peru's Gold Supply Chain' dans Y. Zabyelina & D. van Uhm (dir.), *Illegal Mining, Organized Crime, Corruption, and Ecocide in a Resource-Scarce World*, Palgrave MacMillan, 2020, pp. 319–321.

158 *Ibid.*, pp. 318–319.

159 Verité, *supra* n. 4, p. 48; Voir à l'échelle régionale : <https://globalinitiative.net/wp-content/uploads/2016/03/Organized-Crime-and-Illegally-Mined-Gold-in-Latin-America.pdf>; pour une description détaillée des éléments de la chaîne d'approvisionnement globale de l'or péruvien, voir N. van der Valk, L. Bisschop et R. van Swaaningen, *supra* n. 157, pp. 299–327.

160 OAS, *On the Trail of Illicit Gold Proceeds: Strengthening the Fight against Illegal Mining Finances* (2021), pp. 20–21, <https://www.oas.org/en/sms/dtoc/docs/On-the-trail-of-illicit-gold-proceeds-Peru-case.pdf>.

161 A. Blackett, 'Follow the Drinking Gourd: Our Road to Teaching Critical Race Theory and Slavery and the Law, Contemplatively, at McGill' (2017) 62:4 *McGill Law Journal* 1251, pp. 1268–1269.

d'alternatives d'emplois sans poser de questions sur le rôle de l'État et de l'industrie minière dans la perpétuation de pratiques discriminatoires structurelles. Si les personnes afro-péruviennes, les peuples andins et la communauté sino-péruvienne, entre autres, continuent d'être considérés comme des citoyens de seconde main, et si les élites continuent de s'approprier les ressources sur la base de cette hiérarchie sociale construite dès les tous débuts de la colonie[162], alors peu de changements concrets pourront s'observer dans la lutte contre l'esclavage contemporain.

Nous devons garder à l'esprit que le contrôle exercé sur un autre être humain a une motivation économique, et que cette motivation économique s'appuie sur le maintien de divisions raciales et genrées. Ben que mentionnée dans les politiques nationales en matière d'éradication de l'esclavage contemporain, la lutte contre la discrimination systémique ne semble pas avoir été articulée en actions tangibles. On sait par exemple que la pauvreté affecte en majorité les zones rurales où se retrouve une plus grande proportion de populations autochtones ou andines[163]. Or, cette corrélation est pratiquement ignorée dans les politiques nationales. La Rapporteuse spéciale en 2011 soulignait pourtant le rôle de la discrimination systémique dans l'esclavage contemporain. La racialisation de la société péruvienne introduite par le système hiérarchique des castes perdure à ce jour et, sachant que ces hiérarchies et divisions ont été développées dans le contexte de l'esclavage précisément pour favoriser l'accumulation primitive des ressources, il est fondamental d'évaluer l'impact qu'elles ont sur les formes contemporaines d'exploitation au travail[164].

D'autre part, étant donné que la forte majorité des victimes de la traite sont des femmes, il est tout autant fondamental d'adopter une perspective genrée intersectionnelle. Nous avons vu que les stéréotypes de genre persistent dans l'application du droit. Cela nécessite, comme le suggère l'auteure Andrea Querol, une intervention paradigmatique à la base, au moyen d'une éducation

162 Sur la continuation des divisions raciales et sociales au sein de la société péruvienne, voir C. Aguirre, *supra* n. 16, pp. 193–195.

163 À noter que bien que la définition d'autochtone est étroite au Pérou, la langue maternelle (comme le quechua ou l'aymara, toutes deux associées avec la désignation « andin ») constitue une donnée importante pour mesurer la corrélation entre origine ethnique et pauvreté : voir E.R. Baldarrago Estremadoyro, *Dinamicas Etnicas en el Peru : Hacia una Caracterizacion y Tipologia para el Diseno de Politicas Publicas*, INEI 2017, p. 37, <https://www.inei.gob.pe/media/MenuRecursivo/investigaciones/dinamicas_etnicas_6_web.pdf>.

164 C.J. Robinson, *supra* n. 9, pp. 26–27; A. Blackett et A. Dusquenoy, *supra* n. 145, pp. 1534–1535.

inclusive[165]. Ce changement contribuerait également à adresser un autre facteur de risque, soit la violence au sein du milieu familial qui, encore une fois, possède une dimension genrée et pousse plusieurs femmes à quitter leur milieu de vie, ce qui les rend plus vulnérables à l'exploitation.

Mentionnons en conclusion que le secteur minier en général possède un bilan médiocre en matière de conformité aux lois du travail et aux lois environnementales. Au Pérou, de nombreux conflits sociaux sont en cours entre des communautés autochtones ou rurales et des entreprises minières qui suivent de manière superficielle les législations environnementales[166]. L'exploitation de ressources minières s'accompagne souvent de déforestations massives et de contaminations des sols et de l'eau. Les mines illégales sont aussi un terreau fertile pour les activités criminelles organisées[167]. Le processus de consultation des peuples autochtones affectés par les chantiers miniers est souvent superficiel, voire complètement ignoré[168]. C'est donc une culture générale de déni des droits des populations locales qui est en place dans l'économie minière, sous le couvert d'un langage développementaliste : les entreprises minières répètent un discours des bénéfices socio-économiques que les mines amèneront aux communautés voisines[169]. D'ailleurs, les politiques de formalisation des mines artisanales adoptées par l'État péruvien semblent suivre cette logique développementaliste plutôt que de sérieusement considérer le rôle des entreprises formelles dans la perpétuation des formes contemporaines d'esclavage.

Une solution durable au problème est donc une solution intégrée et coordonnée à divers niveaux de gouvernance, qui adresse tant la réalité des petites mines informelles que le rôle des grandes compagnies minières; qui responsabilise tant les acteurs transnationaux de la chaîne d'approvisionnement mondiale de l'or que les réseaux locaux de recrutement; et qui combat tant la pauvreté qui pousse des gens à vendre des membres de leur famille que les

165 A. Querol, *Buscando Justicia: Trata de personas, violencia y explotación: 40 testimonios*, Capital Humano y Social, Lima 2020, pp. 162–163.

166 Verité, *supra* n. 4, p. 24 ; J. Bury et A. Kolff, *supra* n. 157.

167 A. Valencia, *Human Rights Trade-Offs in Times of Economic Growth : The Long-Term Capability Impacts of Extractive-Led Development*, Palgrave Macmillan, New York 2016; OAS, *On the Trail of Illicit Gold Proceeds: Strengthening the Fight against Illegal Mining Finances* (2021), <https://www.oas.org/en/sms/dtoc/docs/On-the-trail-of-illicit-gold-proceeds-Peru-case.pdf>.

168 CHS Alternativo, *supra* n. 82, p. 35; L. Wiener Ramos, *Gobernanza y Gobernabilidad: El Caso las Bambas*, CooperAccion, Lima 2018.

169 B. Meyersfeld. 'Empty Promises and the Myth of Mining: Does Mining Lead to Pro-Poor Development?' (2017) 2:1 *Business and Human Rights Journal* 31.

systèmes économiques racialisés et genrés qui maintiennent cette pauvreté. Une approche intégrée doit également tenir compte des dimensions géographiques de l'esclavage (aliénation sociale, accès restreint aux services publics de base, aux moyens de communication et aux opportunités d'emploi en zones rurales) et de l'impact du racisme sur la faiblesse institutionnelle dans les régions géographiquement isolées. La plus récente politique nationale pour combattre la traite des personnes, mentionnée ci-haut, semble consciente de la nécessité d'une telle approche intégrée, du moins au niveau national ; il reste donc à voir si elle sera concrètement appliquée.

Références académiques

A. Blackett et A. Dusquenoy, 'Slavery is Not a Metaphor: U.S. Prison Labor and Racial Subordination Through the Lens of the ILO's Abolition of Forced Labor Convention' (2021) 67 *U.C.L.A. Law Review* 1504.

A. Blackett, 'Follow the Drinking Gourd: Our Road to Teaching Critical Race Theory and Slavery and the Law, contemplatively at McGill' (2017) 62:4 *McGill Law Journal* 1251.

A. Blackett, *Everyday Transgressions: Domestic Workers' Transnational Challenge to International Labor Law*, Cornell University Press, Ithaca 2019.

A. Querol, *Buscando Justicia: Trata de personas, violencia y explotación: 40 testimonios*, Capital Humano y Social, Lima 2020.

A. Valencia, *Human Rights Trade-Offs in Times of Economic Growth: The Long-Term Capability Impacts of Extractive-Led Development*, Palgrave Macmillan, New York 2016.

B. Meyersfeld. 'Empty Promises and the Myth of Mining: Does Mining Lead to Pro-Poor Development?' (2017) 2:1 *Business and Human Rights Journal* 31.

B. Moses, *The Spanish Dependencies in South America: An Introduction to the History of Their Civilisation*, Smith, Elder & Co, London 1914.

C. Aguirre, *Breve historia de la esclavitud en el Perú*, Fondo editorial del Congreso del Perú, Lima 2005.

C.J. Robinson, *Black Marxism: The Making of the Black Radical Tradition*, University of North Carolina Press, Chapel Hill 2000.

C.L.R. James, *The Black Jacobins: Toussaint L'Ouverture and the San Domingo Revolution*, Penguin, London 2001.

D. Bonilla-Maldonado, *'Extralegal Property, Legal Monism, and Pluralism'* (2009) 40:2 *U Mia Inter-Am L Rev* 213.

D. Cortés-McPherson, 'Digging into the Mining Subculture: The Dynamics of Trafficking in Persons in the Artisanal and Small-Scale Gold Mining of Peru's Madre de

Dios' dans Y. Zabyelina et D. Van Uhm (dir.) *Illegal Mining, Organized Crime, Corruption, and Ecocide in a Resource-Scarce World*, Palgrave MacMillan, Cham 2020, pp. 359–386.

E. Williams, *Capitalism & Slavery*, University of North Carolina Press, Chapel Hill 1994.

F.P. Bowser, *The African Slave in Colonial Peru, 1524–1650*, Stanford University Press, Stanford 1974.

J.A. Cole, *The Potosí Mita, 1573–1700, Compulsory Indian Labor in the Andes*, Stanford University Press, Stanford 1985.

J. Allain, *The Slavery Conventions: The Travaux Préparatoires* of *the 1926 League of Nations Convention and the 1956 United Nations Convention*, Martinus Nijhoff, Leiden 2008.

J. Allain, *Slavery in International Law: Of Human Exploitation and Trafficking*, Martinus Nijhoff, Boston 2013.

J. Bury et A. Kolff, 'Livelihoods, Mining and Peasant Protests in the Peruvian Andes' (2002) 1:1 *Journal of Latin American Geography* 3.

J.E. Inikori, 'Atlantic Slavery and the Rise of the Capitalist Global Economy' (2020) 61:S22 *Current Anthropology* S159.

J. Lockhart, *Spanish Peru, 1532–1560: A Social History*, University of Wisconsin Press, Madison 1994.

K. Bales, *Disposable People: New Slavery in the Global Economy*, University of California Press, Berkeley 2012.

L. Wiener Ramos, *Gobernanza y Gobernabilidad: El Caso las Bambas*, CooperAccion, Lima 2018.

M.A. McKinley, *Fractional Freedoms: Slavery, Intimacy, and Legal Mobilization in Colonial Lima*, Cambridge University Press, New York 2016.

M. Arrelucea, 'Historia de la esclavitud africana en el Peru desde la Conquista hasta la Abolición' (2004) 14 *Arqueología y Sociedad* 239.

M. Avilés, *De donde venimos los cholos*, Planeta Peru, Lima 2018.

M.J. Gonzales, 'Chinese Plantation Workers and Social Conflict in Peru in the Late Nineteenth Century' (1989) 21:3 *Journal of Latin American Studies* 386.

N. Van Der Valk, L. Bisschop et R. Van Swaaningen, 'When Gold Speaks, Every Tongue Is Silent: The Thin Line Between Legal, Illegal, and Informal in Peru's Gold Supply Chain' dans Y. Zabyelina et D. Van Uhm (dir.), *Illegal Mining, Organized Crime, Corruption, and Ecocide in a Resource-Scarce World*, Palgrave MacMillan, London 2020, pp. 299–328.

O. Patterson, *Slavery and Social Death: A Comparative Study*, Harvard University Press, Cambridge 1982.

R. Mawani, 'From Slave Revolts to Social Death' (2019) 48 *Theory and Society* 835.

R.S. O'Toole, *Bound Lives: Africans, Indians, and the Making of Race in Colonial Peru*, University of Pittsburg Press, Pittsburg 2012.

R. Valdés, C. Basombrio et D. Vera, *Las economias criminales y su impacto en el Peru: ¿Cuáles? ¿Cuánto? ¿Cómo? ¿Dónde?*, Capital Humano y Social, Lima 2021.

T.K. Hernánez, *Racial Subordination in Latin America: The Role of the State, Customary Law, and the New Civil Rights Response*, Cambridge University Press, New York 2013.

T. Sanz, *Caracterización de las condiciones de trabajo forzoso en la minería de oro en Madre de Dios y una aproximación a los factores de riesgo*, OIT, Lima 2015.

Preventing and Combating Modern Forms of Slavery in Poland: Historical Background and Current Challenges

Dagmara Skupień and Łukasz Pisarczyk

1 Introduction

According to the 1926 Slavery Convention, slavery is 'the status or condition of a person over whom any or all of the powers attaching to the right of ownership are exercised'.[1] The above-mentioned definition refers to the classical form of slavery, namely chattel slavery, and as such is less useful in describing contemporary forms of exploitation of human beings. At present, slavery mostly takes on other forms, including forced labour, debt bondage, and human trafficking, especially concerning undocumented migrants.[2]

Slavery was known on the territory of the newly created Polish state in the early Middle Ages, but it did not exist in the following centuries in this form.[3] Yet, there have been certain social and economic phenomena, such as serfdom, which exhibited characteristics similar to slavery. Serfdom seriously impacted the social structure of the state, and according to some contemporary opinions, could also exert an influence on contemporary economic relationships,[4] as well as the situation of specific social groups, in particular women.[5]

Polish legislation combating modern slavery is strongly influenced by international and European law, especially conventions of the UN, the ILO and the Council of Europe, as well as the *acquis* of the European Union. Most cases of modern slavery bear the features of forced labour and are related to human trafficking. Poland is, at the same time, a country of origin, a country of transit

1 Article 1(1) of the 1926 Slavery Convention.

2 ILO and Walk Free Foundation, *Global Estimates of Modern Slavery: Forced Labour and Forced Marriage*, Geneva, 2017, p. 9, <https://www.ilo.org/wcmsp5/groups/public/@dgreports/@dcomm/documents/publication/wcms_575479.pdf>.

3 See A. Brückner, *Dzieje kultury polskiej* (*History of Polish culture*), Książka i Wiedza, Warszawa 1957, pp. 92–94.

4 See A. Leszczyński, *Ludowa historia Polski* (*People's history of Poland*), W.A.B., Warszawa 2020, extensively with further references, and especially pp. 528–532.

5 See J. Kuciel-Frydryszak, *Chłopki. Opowieść o naszych babkach* (*Peasants. A story of our grandmothers*), Marginesy, Warszawa 2023.

 | DOI:10.1163/9789004723801_013

and a country of destination for victims of human trafficking.[6] Such victims can be either persons of foreign origin or Poles, regardless of their place of residence.

In Poland, a relatively strong social differentiation is observed what influences the labour market (a large number of individuals of poor negotiating position, are forced to commence unsatisfactory employment). The organization and functioning of the labour market have contributed to deepening inequality. Two phenomena must be indicated in this context. First, a large scale of abuse in the use of atypical forms of employment (civil law employment). Non-employees enjoy very limited work-related rights. This exacerbates their precarious situation. At the same time, Polish law does not offer an efficient mechanism to counteract the abuse. Second, the coverage of collective bargaining is very limited.[7] As a result, working conditions are set up mainly by individual (either employment or civil law) contracts. It deepens inequality in the distribution of national income.

In the case of precarious workers, the risk of abuse increases. It concerns both: the basis of employment (civil law contracts instead of employment relationships) and working conditions. Although such a situation does not constitute forced labour in a strict sense, it nevertheless threatens the realization of fundamental freedoms and human rights and, as a result, also human liberty.[8] Precarious workers, due to their position, have to accept an inappropriate basis of employment and unfavourable working conditions. Due to their legal and factual situation they have to work long hours (usually without extra payments). They often have limited opportunities to change jobs. As a result, some features of forced labour can be seen here.[9] Moreover, the deepening of such a situation will result in an increase in the number of people whose employment in many aspects is not fully voluntary. Considering the scale of these phenomena (larger than in other European Union countries), it would be difficult to completely disregard this issue.

In this chapter, we will discuss the legal framework and measures aiming at preventing and combating slavery, forced labour, trafficking in humans, sanctioning employers using work of undocumented migrants as well as labour law

6 Krajowy Plan Działań Przeciwko Handlowi Ludźmi na lata 2020–2021 (The National Action Plan against Trafficking in Human Beings for 2020–2021), p. 2.

7 See, e.g. Ł. Pisarczyk, 'The Crisis of the Collective Bargaining System in Poland' (2019) 35:1 *International Journal of Comparative Labour Law and Industrial Relations* 57.

8 Cf. R. Alexy, *A Theory of Constitutional Rights*, Oxford University Press, Oxford 2010, p. 223 ff.

9 B. Faracik (ed), *Praca przymusowa* (*Forced labour*), Minister Funduszy i Polityki Regionalnej, Warszawa 2020, p. 23.

measures adopted in order to guarantee decent conditions of work and prevent exploitation at the workplace.

2 Slavery

2.1 *'Old' Forms of Slavery, Personal Dependency and Feudal Service*

The Polish state dates back to 966.[10] In 1386, Poland and Lithuania concluded an agreement creating a personal union (two separate states with a common king) between these two states. The union (in 1569 converted into a real one with common state institutions) existed until the collapse of the Polish-Lithuanian Commonwealth in 1795, when it was partitioned by neighbouring states: Russia, Prussia and Austria.[11] For centuries, it was one of the largest states in Europe. It was never a colonial country in a strict sense, as no territorial expansion beyond Europe ever took place. However, in the 14th century, the territorial expansion to the East began. First, western Ukraine (Red Ruthenia) was annexed to the Kingdom of Poland. At the turn of the 16th and 17th centuries Polish-Lithuanian Commonwealth covered an area of nearly 1 million square kilometers and the territories of contemporary countries, such as Poland, Lithuania, Ukraine, Belarus, Latvia and Western Russia.[12] The Polish-Lithuanian Commonwealth was an agricultural country with the nobility and peasantry playing a key role. Peasants constituted (depending on the period) between 70 and 80% of the society.[13]

Slavery known in the early Middle Ages (using slave labour on-site, selling people to Spain and the Middle East) did not exist in the following centuries. Nevertheless, certain social and economic phenomena occurred that can be compared to slavery and that seriously affected the social structure. Some scholars conclude that their effects are still felt today.[14]

---

10 About the history of Poland see, e.g. A. Zamoyski, *Poland. A History*, Harper Press, New York 2009; A. Prazmowska, *A History of Poland*, Palgrave Macmillan, London 2011.

11 Encyclopedia Brittanica, *Partitions of Poland*, <https://www.britannica.com/event/Partitions-of-Poland>.

12 See e.g. Encyclopedia Brittanica, *The State of Jagiellonians*, <https://www.britannica.com/place/Poland/The-states-of-the-Jagiellonians>.

13 For the structure of the society in 1791 see J. Bardach, B. Leśnodorski, M. Pietrzak, *Historia ustroju i prawa polskiego* (*History of the Polish political system and law*), Lexis Nexis, Warsaw 1998, p. 290.

14 See more M. Gliński, *Kolonializm po polsku, czyli długi cień pańszczyzny*, (*Colonialism in Polish or the long shadow of serfdom*), <https://culture.pl/pl/artykul/kolonializm-po-polsku-czyli-dlugi-cien-panszczyzny>; A. Leszczyński, above n. 4, p. 528.

The peasants did not own the land they worked on. The land belonged to the nobility, clergy or the state.[15] Moreover, the peasants were personally dependent on the owners of the land. Their ability to leave the village and move to another place was very limited. They were also obliged to provide the so-called serfdom work (feudal service, corvée) for the sake of the lord. This was unpaid work for the owner of the land.[16] Since the 16th century, the number of days of serfdom gradually increased. In the 16th century, the burden was comparable with or even lower than its equivalent in Western Europe,[17] and certain historians state it was supportable for the peasant families (since they enjoyed landlord protection and could take advantage of economic surpluses).[18] However, in the following centuries, a very heavy burden was put on the peasants. In some parts of the territory it amounted to ten days of work per family per week in the 18th century.[19]

Since the 15th century, considerable development of enormous estates owned by landlords belonging to the highest stratum of the nobility (magnates)[20] had taken place in the eastern part of the Polish-Lithuanian Commonwealth inhabited mostly by a Cossack Community (consisting of the local Ruthenian people and fugitives and peasant migrants from other parts of the country who have created an autonomous, self-governed militarised community on this territory).[21] The biggest estates (feudal latifundia), weakly

15 For the percentage of peasants living on the lands owned by these different entities, see J. Bardach, B. Leśnodorski, M. Pietrzak, above n. 13, p. 290.

16 See e.g. W. Kuligowski, 'A history of Polish serfdom' (2016) 3 *Czas Kultury* 1, <https://www.eurozine.com/a-history-of-polish-serfdom/>. The dependency of peasants is sometimes perceived even as a form of slavery. Compare A. Leszczyński, above n. 4, and M. Gliński, '*Slavery vs. Serfdom, or Was Poland a Colonial Empire?*', <https://culture.pl/en/article/slavery-vs-serfdom-or-was-poland-a-colonial-empire>.

17 See R. Frost, *The Oxford History of Poland-Lithuania. Volume 1 – The Making of the Polish-Lithuanian Union, 1385–1569*, Oxford University Press, New York 2015 – in translation into Polish: *Oksfordzka historia Unii Polskiej-Litewskiej, Powstanie i rozwój 1385–1569, tom I*, Rebis, Poznań 2018, pp. 410–411.

18 See J. Bardach, B. Leśnodorski, M. Pietrzak, above n. 13, p. 203.

19 See G. J. Lerski, *Historical Dictionary of Poland, 966–1945*, Westport 1996, p. 86.

20 G.J. Lerski, above n. 19, pp. 86–87; J. Bardach, B. Leśnodorski, M. Pietrzak, above n. 13, p. 194; M. Hruszewski, *Szlachta ukraińska na przełomie XVI i XVII w.* (*Ukrainian nobility at the turn of the 16th and 17th centuries*) in vol. 6 *Historia Ukrainy-Rusi* (*History of Ukraine and Russia*), chapter III. *Stosunki kulturalne i narodowe: skład narodowościowy i narodowe żywioły* (*Cultural and national relations: national composition and national elements*), Kiev, Lviv 1907 in Polish translation, pp. 29–30, 33, 37, 42.

21 See e.g. Encyclopedia Brittanica, *The Cossacks of Poland*, <https://www.britannica.com/place/Poland/The-Cossacks>; A. Leszczyński, above n. 4, pp. 211–220.

controlled by the Commonwealth authorities, resembled states, with their own private armies, courts and thousands of peasants submitted to the power of the magnate.[22] The gradual inflow of Polish-Lithuanian clergy and nobility into these territories is perceived by certain researchers as comparable to colonization, showing some similarities to the colonization of India by the British Empire.[23] This approach has been severely criticized.[24] However, recently, a more balanced approach has been advocated. It highlights the existence of colonial elements in the Polish rules in Ukraine (economic exploitation, polonization of local elites).[25] Since the 16th century, social, national and religious tensions in the Polish-Lithuanian state had grown significantly, notably causing a series of Cossack and Ukrainian peasants' rebellions, including the most famous Chmielnicki Uprising in 1648.[26]

Personal dependence and serfdom were abolished as late as the 19th century. Due to the partitions of Poland, the abolition of serfdom and the enfranchisement of the peasants occurred gradually: in the so-called Polish Kingdom within the Russian Empire, in 1861 and 1864; in Prussia, gradually in the years

22 See J. Bardach, B. Leśnodorski, M. Pietrzak, above n. 13, p. 232.

23 J. Sowa, *Fantomowe ciało króla. Peryferyjne zmagania z nowoczesną formą* (*The phantom body of a king. Peripheral struggles with modern form*), TAiWPN Universitas, Kraków 2011; M. Gliński, above n. 16. On the other hand, occupied Poland experienced attempts of colonialisation by Prussia and Russian Empire during the period of partitions in the 19th and early 20th centuries; compare N. Davies, *Europa* (*Europe*), Znak, Kraków 2002, p. 909; or D. Trześniowski, *Rusyfikacja jako pozorne zagrożenie. O nieskuteczności rosyjskiego projektu kolonialnego w Polsce* (*w XIX w.*) [Russification as an apparent threat. About the ineffectiveness of the Russian colonial project in Poland (in the 19th century)] in K. Stępnik and D. Trześniowski (eds) *Studia postkolonialne nad literaturą i kulturą polską* (*Postcolonial studies on Polish literature and culture*), Wydawnictwo UMCS, Lublin 2010.

24 J. Kieniewicz, *O perspektywę dla Polski* (*For a perspective for Poland*) and H. Grala, *Rzeczpospolita szlachecka – twór kolonialny?* (*The Commonwealth of the Nobility – a colonial creation?*) in J. Kieniewicz (ed) *Perspektywy postkolonializmu w Polsce, Polska w perspektywie postkolonialnej* (*Prospects of postcolonialism in Poland. Poland in the postcolonial perspective*), Wydział "Artes Liberales" Uniwersytet Warszawski, Warszawa 2016.

25 T. Stryjek, *Czy Polska rządziła Ukrainą jak kolonią? O potrzebie wielości perspektyw w historiografii i relacjach polsko-ukraińskich* (*Did Poland rule Ukraine like a colony? About the need for multiple perspectives in historiography and Polish-Ukrainian relations*), Warszawa 2021, <https://www.batory.org.pl/wp-content/uploads/2021/10/T.Stryjek_Czy.Polska.rzadzila.Ukraina.jak_.kolonia.pdf>.

26 See e.g. Internet Encyclopedia of Ukraine, *Cossack-Polish War*, <http://www.encyclopediaofukraine.com/display.asp?linkpath=pages%5CC%5CO%5CCossack6PolishWar.htm>.

1807–1850; and in Austria, in 1848.[27] On the occasion of the 150th anniversary of the abolition of serfdom discussions were raised as to whether the peasants' legal successors should receive some form of compensation for centuries of economic exploitation.[28] It began to be argued that the (slavery-like) labour of the peasants has never been compensated.[29]

The scope of personal dependence and serfdom, as well as their long duration, had a serious impact on the social structure. The Polish territories (with the exception of certain areas belonging to Prussia, later Germany) were less industrialized and urbanized than Western Europe, and a strong middle class had not developed. Much of the society, though formally free, lived in poverty and was prone to economic dependence on landowners and owners of the means of production. One of the solutions was mass economic emigration, including to the United States of America.[30] Poland did not manage to overcome the inheritance of the feudal era in its short period of independence between the First and the Second World War (1918–1939),[31] even though agrarian reforms[32] and improved conditions of work in the industry were legislated.[33] The communist regime, which governed Poland after the Second World War II until 1989 in theory supporting working groups, continued to exploit workers and peasants.[34]

2.2 *Combating Slavery*

Having regained independence in 1918 after more than a hundred years of partitions, Poland immediately became involved in the works of the League

---

27 K. Janicki, *Zniesienie pańszczyzny. Najważniejsza data w historii polskich chłopów* (*Abolition of serfdom. The most important date in the history of Polish peasants*), Wielka Historia, (20.12.2022), <https://wielkahistoria.pl/zniesienie-panszczyzny-najwazniejsza-data-w-historii-polskich-chlopow/>.

28 M. Gliński, above n. 16.

29 See, e.g. P. Kozak, *Pańszczyzna. Sprawa niedokończona* (*Serfdom. Unfinished history*), Krytyka Polityczna, (23.02.2014), <https://krytykapolityczna.pl/kraj/panszczyzna-niedokonczona-sprawa/>.

30 See J. Bardach, B. Leśnodorski, M. Pietrzak, above n. 13, p. 402.

31 Despite reforms undertaken in this period, Poland was hit by grave economic and social problems. Especially the eastern part of the country (so-called Poland "B") remained underdeveloped (see e.g. <https://www.britannica.com/place/Poland/The-Second-Republic>).

32 J. Bardach, B. Leśnodorski, M. Pietrzak, above n. 13, pp. 526–528.

33 See J. Bardach, B. Leśnodorski, M. Pietrzak, above n. 13, pp. 573–574; or M. Święcicki, *Instytucje polskiego prawa pracy w latach 1918–1939* (*Institutions of Polish Labour Law in years 1918–1939*), PWN, Warszawa 1960, pp. 78–99.

34 See more A. Leszczyński, above n. 4, p. 477 et seq.

of Nations.[35] Our country was among 35 countries originally signing the Slavery Convention of 1926. Poland subsequently ratified the Convention in 1930.[36] Poland also ratified the International Convention for the Suppression of the White Slave Traffic, signed at Paris on 4 May 1910.[37]

The Constitution of 1921, in its Article 95, guaranteed the protection of freedom to everyone independently of origin, nationality, language, race or religion.[38] In the context of Polish obligations to combat slavery resulting from public international law, the following regulations, ratified by Poland, should also be mentioned: the UN 1956 Supplementary Convention on the Abolition of Slavery; the Slave Trade, and Institutions and Practices Similar to Slavery adopted on 30 April 1956;[39] as well as Article 8 of the International Covenant on Civil and Political Rights (1966),[40] which states that: no one shall be held in slavery; that slavery and the slave-trade in all their forms shall be prohibited; and that no one shall be held in servitude.

As a member of the Council of Europe since 1991, Poland ratified in 1993 the European Convention of Human Rights,[41] which states in Article 4(1) that no one shall be held in slavery or servitude. These two concepts were interpreted by the European Court of Human Rights in the judgment in *Siliadin v. France*.[42] The concept of 'slavery' was defined by the European Convention on Human Rights (ECHR) in a strict sense, corresponding to the 'classic' meaning of slavery as practiced for centuries, related to the exercise by one person of a genuine right of legal ownership over another one, thus reducing this person to the status of an 'object'.[43] According to the ECHR, servitude instead meant an obligation to provide one's services that are imposed through the use of coercion.

35 J. Beck, *Wspomnienia o polskiej polityce zagranicznej 1926–1939* (*Memories of Polish Foreign Policy 1926–1939*), Wingert, Warszawa-Kraków 2015, p. 56.

36 Polish Journal of Laws of 1931, No. 4, item 21.

37 Polish Journal of Laws of 1922, No. 87, item 783.

38 Ustawa z dnia 17 marca 1921 r. – Konstytucja Rzeczypospolitej Polskiej. Polish Journal of Laws of 1921, No. 44, item 267.

39 Polish Journal of Laws of 1963, No. 33, item 185.

40 Polish Journal of Laws of 1977, No. 38, item 167.

41 Polish Journal of Laws of 1993, No. 61, item 284.

42 *Siliadin v. France No.* 73316/01, ECHR, 26 July 2005, para. 122–123.

43 Compare J. Allain, 'The International Legal Regime of Slavery and Human Exploitation and its Obfuscation by the Term of Art: "Slavery-like Practice"' (2012) 10 *Cahiers de la recherche sur les droits fondamentaux* 27, para. 12.

Correspondingly, at Article 115 § 23 of the Polish Penal Code,[44] slavery is strictly defined as "a state of dependency in which a person is treated as an object of property". Poland ratified the Statute of the International Criminal Court in 2001,[45] approving its jurisdiction over the most serious crimes as enumerated in the Statute. At Article 7 para. 1 (c), enslavement is classified as a form of crime against humanity.

Article 8 of the Act of 6 June 1997 – Provisions introducing the Penal Code, penalizes with the penalty of deprivation of liberty of no less than 3 years conducts which consist in submitting a person into slavery, keeping a person in the position of slavery or perpetrating trafficking in slaves. According to Article 118a § 2 of the Penal Code:

> whoever, while taking part in a widespread attack or at least in one of the systematic attacks against a population, conducted with the purpose of implementing or supporting a policy of a state or an organization 1) creates or maintains enslavement of a person, 2) deprives a person of liberty for a period exceeding 7 days or couples it with special torment [...] 6) deprives a person of liberty and refuses to provide information regarding this person or this person's whereabouts, or provides false information regarding this person or this person's whereabouts, with an intent to deprive such person of legal protection for a prolonged period of time, is subject to the penalty of deprivation of liberty for no less than 5 years or the penalty of deprivation of liberty for 25 years.

Moreover, the Penal Code provides for the criminal offence of unlawful deprivation of liberty in Chapter XXIII, 'Crimes against liberty'. According to Article 189 § 1–3 of this Code, whoever deprives a human of liberty is subject to the penalty of deprivation of liberty for between 3 months and 5 years. If the deprivation of liberty lasts longer than 7 days, the perpetrator is subject to the penalty of deprivation of liberty for between 1 year and 10 years. If the deprivation of liberty concerns a human who is incapacitated due to their age or mental or physical condition, the perpetrator is subject to the penalty of deprivation of liberty for between 2 and 12 years. If the deprivation of liberty referred to above was coupled with special torment, the perpetrator is subject to the penalty of deprivation of liberty for no less than 3 years.

---

44 Ustawa z dnia 6 czerwca 1997 r., Kodeks karny consolidated text of 2024.01.04, Polish Journal of Laws 2024.17.

45 Polish Journal of Laws of 2003, No. 78, item 708.

3 Trafficking in Human Beings

Trafficking in human beings in Poland concerns both Poles sent by criminal groups to work in exploitative conditions abroad, and foreigners brought to work under conditions of exploitation in Poland. It is usually carried out by international criminal networks. This procedure, which brings shame to humanity, began in contemporary Poland about 20 years ago on a bigger scale.[46]

The 1990s marked the beginning of Poland's political transformation from a totalitarian country with virtually closed borders to a member of the European Union (EU) (2004), cooperating economically with Western Europe. The opening of borders, largely recognized as beneficial in terms of doing business and seeking work abroad, has also resulted in negative phenomena. The largest number of cases of human trafficking involved the referral of women into prostitution in Germany and the Netherlands at the turn of the 21st century. Only a small group of these persons had knowledge of the real purpose of their migration as criminal groups generally lured their victims with offers of well-paid work abroad.[47]

Another example of human trafficking at the time was the recruitment of Poles for extremely exploitative work in dire conditions in southern Italy in work camps organised by international criminal networks.[48] This sort of criminal activity was punished by Polish and Italian courts.[49] The condemnation of members of the organised criminal network for acts of human trafficking and maintaining in the enslavement of Polish citizens in Southern Italy (lured for agricultural work in the farms) was a judicial success on the European scale.[50]

46 Z. Lasocik, 'O handlu ludźmi w Polsce, czyli o ewolucji zjawiska i budowie systemu jego eliminowania' (*Human trafficking in Poland, or the evolution of the phenomenon and the construction of a system to eliminate it*) (2012) 34 *Archiwum Kryminologii* 481, p. 486.

47 For details about human trafficking in this period see: Z. Lasocik, 'Human Trafficking in Poland - Evolution of the Devil' in L.E. Sullivan (ed), *Criminal Justice and Law Enforcement Annual: Global Perspectives*, Ams Press Inc, New York 2014.

48 See the media release entitled: 'Kraków: Wyroki w procesie ws. „obozów pracy" we Włoszech' (*Sentences in the trial on 'labour camps' in Italy*), <https://www.money.pl/archiwum/wiadomosci_agencyjne/pap/artykul/krakow;wyroki;w;procesie;ws;obozow;pracy;we;wloszech,223,0,1420511.html>.

49 See for example judgment of the Polish Supreme Court of 21 December 2021 in case IV KK 54/20 or the decision of the Polish Supreme Court of 4 July 2017 in case IV K 86/17.

50 See judgment No. 198/2008 of the Tribunal of Bari, <https://www.osservatoriointerventitratta.it/wp-content/uploads/2016/01/GUP-Bari-sentenza-n.-198_2008.pdf>. The terrifying fate of modern slaves trafficked from Poland to Italian Puglia was described in: A. Leogrande, *Uomini e caporali. Viaggio tra i nuovi schiavi nelle campagne del Sud*, Feltrinelli Editore, Milan 2016.

The scope of trafficking in human beings diminished due in part to the investigative institutions' engagement (coordinated efforts of Polish and foreign police).[51] In addition, the unemployment rate in Poland declined and better opportunities for legal work in EU countries emerged after the transitional period. Nevertheless, Polish citizens are still being trafficked for forced labour, especially men for work in agriculture or the construction sector abroad.[52] With the extension of the free movement of persons within the EU to Eastern European countries such as Romania and Bulgaria, with the accession of these countries to the EU and the facilitation of entry of persons from the former USSR, especially from Belarus and Ukraine, Poland also became a destination and transit country for trafficking in human beings. Cases of trafficking in human beings from those countries concerned, in particular the provision of sexual services or forced begging (in particular Romanian citizens, including minors).[53]

The first legislative acts ratified by Poland concerning the fight against human trafficking were:[54] the International Agreement for the 1904 Suppression of the White Slave Traffic,[55] the 1910 International Convention for the Suppression of the White Slave Traffic,[56] the 1933 International Convention for

51 In years 1995–2002 criminal proceedings ended with condamnation of criminals responsible for trafficking of women in the sex business abroad. See Krajowy Program Zwalczania i Zapobiegania Handlowi Ludźmi (National Action Plan to Combat and to Prevent Trafficking in Human Beings) 2003/2004, p. 4, <https://www.gov.pl/web/handel-ludzmi/krajowy-program-zwalczania-i-zapobiegania-handlowi-ludzmi-na-lata-2003-2004>.

52 See 'Krajowy Plan Działań przeciwko Handlowi Ludźmi na lata 2022–2024' (National Action Plan Against Trafficking in Human Beings 2022–2024), p. 2, <https://www.gov.pl/web/handel-ludzmi/krajowy-plan-dzialan-przeciwko-handlowi-ludzmi-na-lata-2022-2024>.

53 Compare Krajowy Plan Działań Przeciwko Handlowi Ludźmi na lata 2009/2010 (National Action Plan against Trafficking in Human Beings), p. 1–2, <https://www.gov.pl/web/handel-ludzmi/krajowy-plan-dzialan-przeciwko-handlowi-ludzmi-na-lata-2009-2010>.

54 For more about this subject see e.g. Z. Latosik E. Rekosz-Cebula, and Ł. Wieczorek, *Filling the Gaps in the System of Combating Human Trafficking in Poland – Research Report*, Human Trafficking Studies Center – University of Warsaw, Warsaw 2015, p. 33; B. Klebeko, *Handel ludźmi jednym z największych współczesnych zagrożeń dla realizacji idei praw człowieka* (*Human trafficking Human trafficking as one of the greatest contemporary threats to the realization of human rights*) in M. Jabłoński, T. Jurczyk and P. Gutierrez (eds), *Międzynarodowa ochrona praw człowieka – współczesne problemy na świecie* (*International protection of human rights – contemporary problems in the world*), E-Wydawnictwo. Prawnicza i Ekonomiczna Biblioteka Cyfrowa., Wrocaw 2015.

55 Polish Journal of Laws of 1922, No. 87, item 783.

56 Polish Journal of Laws of 1922, No. 87, item 783.

the Suppression of the Traffic in Women of Full Age,[57] and the 1921 International Convention for the Suppression of the Traffic in Women and Children.[58] Contemporary measures for combating trafficking in human beings in Poland result from various international and European Union obligations. The following crucial acts of international law (UN) ratified by Poland should be mentioned: the Protocol to Prevent, Suppress and Punish Trafficking in Persons, especially Women and Children,[59] and the Protocol against the Smuggling of Migrants by Land, Sea and Air (supplementing the United Nations Convention against Transnational Organized Crime).[60] Both documents (called the Palermo protocols) were signed by the then European Community.[61]

Poland is also party to the 2005 Council of Europe Convention on Action against Trafficking in Human Beings (Warsaw Convention), ratified by Poland in 2008. A special body, the Group of Experts on Action against Trafficking in Human Beings (GRETA), was set up to monitor the implementation of the Convention.[62] The European Union has also responded with legislation binding on all the Member States to prohibit this severe type of criminality. Trafficking in human beings is specifically prohibited by Article 5 of the Charter of

57 Compare Z. Latosik E. Rekosz-Cebula, and Ł. Wieczorek, above n. 54, p. 33.

58 Polish Journal of Laws 1925, No. 125, item 893.

59 Polish Journal of Laws 2005, No. 18, item 160.

60 Polish Journal of Laws 2005, No. 18, item 162.

61 Council Decision (2006/618/EC) of 24 July 2006 on the conclusion, on behalf of the European Community, of the Protocol to Prevent, Suppress and Punish Trafficking in Persons, Especially Women And Children, supplementing the United Nations Convention Against Transnational Organised Crime concerning the provisions of the Protocol, in so far as the provisions of this Protocol fall within the scope of Articles 179 and 181a of the Treaty establishing the European Community, OJ L 262, 22.9.2006, pp. 44–50; Council Decision of 24 July 2006 (2006/616/EC) on the conclusion, on behalf of the European Community, of the Protocol Against the Smuggling of Migrants by Land, Sea and Air, supplementing the United Nations Convention Against Transnational Organised Crime concerning the provisions of the Protocol, in so far as the provisions of this Protocol fall within the scope of Articles 179 and 181a of the Treaty establishing the European Community, OJ L 262, 22.9.2006, pp. 24–33; Council Decision of 24 July 2006 (2006/617/EC) on the conclusion, on behalf of the European Community, of the Protocol Against the Smuggling of Migrants by Land, Sea and Air, supplementing the United Nations Convention Against Transnational Organised Crime concerning the provisions of the Protocol, in so far as the provisions of the Protocol fall within the scope of Part III, Title IV of the Treaty establishing the European Community, OJ L 262, 22.9.2006, pp. 34–43.

62 Compare N. Ollus and A. Jokinen, 'Trafficking for Forced Labour and Labour Exploitation – Setting the Scene', in A. Jokinen, N. Ollus, K. Aromaa, *Trafficking for Forced Labour Exploitation in Finland, Poland and Estonia*, United Nations European Institute for Crime Prevention and Control (HEUNI), Helsinki 2011, pp. 21–22.

Fundamental Rights of the EU. The following important EU legal act should be mentioned: Directive 2011/36/EU of the European Parliament and of the Council of 5 April 2011 on preventing and combating trafficking in human beings and protecting its victims, and replacing Council Framework Decision 2002/629/JHA (the gender perspective).[63] The Directive 2004/81/EC on the residence permit issued to third-country nationals who are victims of trafficking in human beings or who have been the subject of an action to facilitate illegal immigration, who cooperate with the competent authorities has also been adopted.[64] The aim of the latter act is especially to define the conditions for granting residence permits of limited duration to third-country nationals who cooperate in the fight against trafficking in human beings.

Combating trafficking in human beings was part of the Stockholm Programme for years 2010–2014 – An Open and Secure Europe Serving and Protecting Citizens[65]– which provided a 'roadmap' for EU work in the area of justice, freedom and security. An important basis for transnational actions is the EU Strategies on Combatting Trafficking in Human Beings, adopted for a 4-year period. On 14 April 2021, the Commission adopted a new EU Strategy on Combatting Trafficking in Human Beings (2021–2025).

The Palermo Protocols and Warsaw Convention influenced Polish law. The definition of the act of trafficking in human beings in the Polish Penal Code is compliant with the concept of trafficking in human beings stemming from Article 4 a-c of the Warsaw Convention as well as from the UN Protocol to Prevent, Suppress and Punish Trafficking in Persons, especially Women and Children.

According to Article 115 § 22 of the Polish Penal Code, the definition of trafficking in persons consists of three elements. The first one is an *act*, which may take the form of the recruitment, transportation, delivery, transfer, harbouring, or receipt of a person. The second one is the use of one or more following *means*: 1) violence or unlawful threat, 2) abduction, 3) deception, 4) misrepresentation or exploitation of an error or incapacity to comprehend an intended action, 5) abuse of a relationship of dependence, exploitation of a critical position or a state of helplessness, or 6) giving or accepting a financial or personal benefit or the promise thereof to a person exercising care or supervision over another person. The third one is the *purpose* of the *act*, which is exploitation, even with the person's consent, in particular in prostitution, pornography or

63 OJ L 101, 15.4.2011, pp. 1–11.

64 OJ L 261, 6.8.2004, pp. 19–23.

65 OJ C 115 of 4.5.2010.

other forms of sexual exploitation, in forced labour or services, in begging, slavery or other forms of exploitation degrading human dignity or in order to obtain cells, tissues or organs in violation of the law. If the perpetrator's conduct involves a minor, it constitutes trafficking in human beings even if the methods or means listed in items 1–6 are not used. According to Article 189a § 1 of the Polish Penal Code, the acts of trafficking in persons are punished with the penalty of imprisonment between three and twenty years.

Since 2003, every two years, the Polish Council of Ministers has developed the National Action Plan Against Trafficking in Human Beings. The last publicly available document concerns years, 2022–2024. The fight against human trafficking is said to rely upon '5Ps' namely prevention, protection, prosecution, punishment and partnership/promotion.[66] The institutional framework consists of the National Consulting and Intervention Centre for the Victims of Trafficking (NCIC) as well as the Regional Teams for Counteracting Human Trafficking. The important element of the system is the cooperation with non-governmental organizations.

In the years 2009–2020, 2270 persons (941 Polish citizens and 1329 foreign nationals) benefited from the support of the NCIC. Available support covers such measures as providing accommodation in a secure centre, food, basic medical care, psychological support, legal consultations, assistance in contacting law enforcement authorities and the assistance of an interpreter. NCIC also runs shelters, ensures that victims of human trafficking exercise their rights, supports state and local government institutions in identifying and working with victims of human trafficking, and provides preventive counselling to individuals and consultation to institutions providing assistance to victims.[67]

4 Forced Labour

4.1 *Forced Labour of Poles under Nazi German and Soviet Regimes*

Forced labour was a special feature of the totalitarian regimes – the Third Reich and the Soviet Union – which occupied Polish territories on the basis of the German-Soviet pact, which enabled the two powers to partition Poland

---

66 See Z. Lasocik et. al., above n. 54, pp. 36–37.

67 Compare National Action Plan Against Trafficking in Human Beings 2022–2024, pp. 3–4, <https://www.gov.pl/web/handel-ludzmi/krajowy-plan-dzialan-przeciwko-handlowi-ludzmi-na-lata-2022-2024>.

in 1939.[68] Polish territories occupied by Germany were divided into two parts: General gouvernement (General Government) and territories directly incorporated into the Third Reich. First, in all occupied territories there was an obligation to work, which also stood for children from 14 years old. Second, around 2.5 million civilians[69] and hundreds of thousands of prisoners of war[70] performed forced labour for the Third Reich (agriculture, industry, etc.).[71] In the majority of cases, they were detained and transported to Germany by force.[72] Polish forced labourers were granted a special legal status and did not enjoy numerous workers' rights arising from German labour law (the right to annual leave, social allowances, etc.).[73] They were paid much less favourably than the Germans, and some of them even worked without pay. Their freedoms and personal rights were significantly restricted (living in separate barracks, prohibition to leave a specific area, restriction of access to public places and contacts with local people, and the obligation to wear the letter P).[74] Contrary to the Nazi doctrine, which treated the employment of Poles as a special form of providing services, it can be considered an example of forced[75] or even slave labour. The most tragic situation leading to death or purposeful extermination

68 Ribbentrop-Molotov Pact of 23 August 1939, for more details see J. Bardach, B. Leśnodorski, M. Pietrzak, above n. 13, p. 583.

69 J. Baczała, *Około 2,5 miliona Polaków zmuszono do pracy w III Rzeszy* (*Approximately 2.5 million of Poles were forced in the III Reich*) <https://www.pap.pl/aktualnosci/news%2C1386493%2Cokolo-25-mln-polakow-zmuszono-do-pracy-w-iii-rzeszy-blisko-150-tysiecy>.

70 U. Herbert, 'Forced Laborers in the Third Reich: An Overview' (2000) 58 *International Labor and Working-Class History* 192, p. 194.

71 D. Kaliński, *Deportacje Polaków na roboty przymusowe do Rzeszy. Niemcy wywieźli co najmniej 2,5 miliona ludzi* (*Deportations of Poles for forced labor to the Reich. The Germans deported at least 2.5 million people*), Wielka Historia, (10.06.2022), <https://wielkahistoria.pl/deportacje-polakow-na-roboty-przymusowe-do-rzeszy-niemcy-wywiezli-co-najmniej-25-miliona-ludzi/>.

72 More than half of Polish civilian forced labourers were women. See U. Herbert, above n. 70, p. 199.

73 See e.g. H. Szurgacz, *Polscy pracownicy w Niemczech 1880–2004. Studium historyczno-prawne* (*Polish workers in Germany 1880–2004. A historical and legal study*), Willy Brandt Centre for German and European Studies at University of Wrocław (CSNE), Wrocław 2022, p. 200 et seq.

74 See more H. Szurgacz, 'Die rechtliche Lage der Polnischen Arbeiter im nationalsozialistischen Staat 1933–1945' in U. Becker, B. Baron von Maydell, H. Szurgacz (eds) *Die Realisierung der Arbeitnehmerfreizügigkeit im Verhältnis zwischen Dutschland und Polen aus arbeits- und sozialrechtlicher Sicht*, Nomos, München 2012, p. 43 et seq; and H. Szurgacz, above n. 73, p. 195 et seq. The 'Polish deployment model' assumed 'a two-tiered society based on a hierarchy of "racial" criteria' (U. Herbert, above n. 70, p. 194).

75 H. Szurgacz, above n. 73, pp. 233–238.

was the enslaved work of prisoners in the concentration camps as well as of persons of Jewish origin in the ghettos.[76] The history of 13.5 million slave (forced) labourers from territories occupied by the Third Reich and their families has not finished yet.[77]

The German state, on the basis of the Federal Compensation Act and further regulations,[78] paid over DM 120 billion to victims of the Nazi regime (with significant personal limitations concerning third-party citizens). Unfortunately, these payments did not apply, as a rule, to victims living in Central and Eastern Europe, including Poland. Mainly because, according to the German side, the states that received war reparations took over the obligation to compensate individual victims. The Polish side did not accept such an approach and distinguished between reparations for the states and individual compensation.[79] The situation started changing in the 1970s when the Federal Republic of German recognized the People's Republic of Poland (a loan for Poland with favourable terms, mutual recognitions of pension claims in 1975).[80]

The collapse of the communist system in Central and Eastern Europe opened a new chapter in Polish-German relationships. The problem of slave (forced) labour was discussed in Two-Plus-Four negotiations (1990)[81] and regulated in the Polish-German agreement (1991) providing payment of compensation for the forced labour of the Poles.[82] According to the Polish-German agreement of 1991 Poland established the 'Polish-German Reconciliation Foundation'[83] while the German government transferred to it the sum of DM 500 million in order to help the particularly affected victims of Nazi crimes, including deported to forced labour for the Third Reich for a period of at least 6 months.

---

76 See more U. Herbert, above n. 70, pp. 200–206.

77 See A. von Plato, A. Leh, C. Thonfeld (eds), *Hitler's Slaves: Life Stories of Forced Labourers in Nazi-occupied Europe*, Berghahn Books, Oxford/New York 2010 (describing the situation of various victim groups).

78 BEG – Bundesentschädigungsgesetz of 18 September 1953.

79 U. Herbert, above n. 70, p. 208.

80 U. Herbert, above n. 70, p. 214. In Poland the agreement was criticized because it could lead to a loss of personal indemnification.

81 *Two Plus Four Treaty*, <https://www.deutschland.de/en/topic/politics/germany-europe/two-plus-four-treaty>.

82 Forced Labor 1939-1945, 'Compensation – Background Information', <https://www.zwangsarbeit-archiv.de/en/zwangsarbeit/entschaedigung/entschaedigung-2/index.html>; Fundacja Polsko-Niemieckie Pojednanie 'Historia wypłat świadczeń', <https://www.fpnp.pl/Wyp%C5%82aty-%C5%9Bwiadcze%C5%84.html>; U. Herbert, above n. 70.

83 Fundacja Polsko-Niemieckie, <http://www.fpnp.pl/home.html>.

In the late 1990s, a new period of compensating slave (forced) labour began. In the face of class action lawsuits against German companies (especially in the United States of America), German businesses together with the German government, launched a new initiative aimed, *inter alia*, at compensating slave (forced) labour. In years 1999/2000, after long international negotiations (with the USA but also with countries of Central and Eastern Europe – the German side was accused of discriminating forced labourers from the East), a compromise was achieved. As a result, the German Parliament enacted the law establishing the Foundation 'Remembrance, Responsibility and Future'.[84] The law of 2000 provided for individual humanitarian payment to be made to the victims of National Socialism, including formerly enslaved and forced labourers as well as their families.[85] The disbursement of the payments commenced in 2001 and finished in 2007 (in Poland via the Polish-German Reconciliation Foundation).[86] An analogous institution, the 'Reconciliation, Peace and Cooperation Fund', was established in 2000 in Austria.[87]

However, many forced labourers or their heirs have not met the criteria established in compensation programs and have not received adequate compensation. As a result, it has been disputable whether and to what extent the compensation programs may exclude unsatisfied individual claims.[88] Poles, although they are one of the largest injured groups, received only about 2–3% of compensation.[89] It is assumed that the vast majority of Polish claims have not been satisfied and their pursuit is still possible.[90]

---

84 The Law of 2 August 2000 on the Creation of a Foundation 'Remembrance, Responsibility and Future', Federal Law Gazette I 1797.

85 See: *Origins of the EVZ Foundation*, <https://www.stiftung-evz.de/en/who-we-are/history/founding-history/>.

86 About the history of payments and the institutions responsible see <https://www.zwangsarbeit-archiv.de/en/zwangsarbeit/entschaedigung/entschaedigung-2/index.html>; *Historia wypłat świadczeń* (*Benefit payment history*), <https://www.fpnp.pl/Wyp%C5%82aty-%C5%9Bwiadcze%C5%84.html>.

87 See: <http://reconciliationfund.at/index-2.html>.

88 M. Behrens, *Forced labour compensation scheme faces difficulties*, Eurofound 2001, <https://www.eurofound.europa.eu/de/publications/article/2001/forced-labour-compensation-scheme-faces-difficulties>.

89 *Niemcy nadal płacą odszkodowania za wojnę. Polacy otrzymali około 2 proc. z całości odszkodowań za II wojnę światową* (*The Germans still pay compensation for the war. Poles have obtained around 2% of payments*), <https://www.gazetaprawna.pl/wiadomosci/artykuly/1063648,niemcy-nadal-placa-odszkodowania-za-wojne.html>.

90 *260 miliardów. Adwokat oferuje pomoc w dochodzeniu odszkodowań od Niemiec za pracę przymusową* (*260 billion. The lawyer offers assistance in seeking compensation from*

Large-scale forced labour also affected Poles in the Soviet Union. Millions of people were deported to the Eastern (including Asian) part of the country (Polish citizens as well as Poles living in the Soviet Union before the Second World War).[91] They were treated formally or at least factually as prisoners and forced to work in mines, industries and agriculture. Some of them were imprisoned in special camps (*Gulag*). In many cases, they had to work in very difficult (even murderous) conditions. Extremely difficult living conditions and a harsh climate resulted in numerous diseases and very high mortality. The problem of slave labour in the Soviet Union and possible compensation have not been comprehensively solved. Neither the Soviet Union nor the Russian Federation created a program that allowed compensation.

The Polish state, at least to some extent, sought to compensate for forced labour performed for totalitarian regimes. The key element of the compensation system is the law of 31 May 1996 on persons deported for forced labour and imprisoned in labour camps by the Third Reich and the Union of Soviet Socialist Republics.[92] The law provides special allowances for those who were deported and performed forced labour (for both the Third Reich and the Soviet Union). The allowances are granted to persons detained in labour camps for political, national, racial and religious reasons or deported to Germany or to the Soviet Union to perform forced labour unless they are entitled to other cash benefits (e.g. as war veterans).

Another phenomenon is the various forms of forced labour in communist Poland (1944–1989). An important example is an alternative military service for soldiers who were compulsorily employed in coal mines, quarries, uranium ore plants and construction battalions (1949–1959). Former forced labourers are entitled to cash benefits and other services.[93]

The amount of benefits for forced labourers (either abroad or in Poland) depends on the duration of forced labour. Periods of forced labour are also

---

Germany for forced labor), <https://www.tysol.pl/a50683-260-miliardow-adwokat-oferuje-pomoc-w-dochodzeniu-odszkodowan-od-niemiec-za-prace-przymusowa>.

91 See e.g. G. Kucharczyk, *Deportacje Polaków na Syberię* (*Deportations of Poles to Siberia*), <https://www.nck.pl/upload/deportacje_polakw_na_syberi_w_xx_wieku433.pdf> and <https://www.polska1918-89.pl/polityka-okupanta-sowieckiego-na-ziemiach-polskich-w-latach-1939%E2%80%931941,30.html>.

92 Polish Journal of Laws 2021, item 1818.

93 The Law of 2 September 1994 on substitute military service soldiers forced to labour in coal mines, quarries, uranium ore plants and construction battalion, Polish Journal of Laws 2021, item 1774.

recognized by social security law.[94] Periods of forced labour performed: a) for the Third Reich, b) in the territory of the Soviet Union, c) on the orders of the Allied authorities until December 31, 1945, d) in coal mines, quarries, plants uranium ore extraction and enrichment and construction battalions during military service in the Polish Army are treated as contribution periods and taken into account for social insurance benefits (e.g. pensions). There were also some special rights, for example, the right to an early retirement for the soldiers who had performed forced labour.

4.2 *Regulations concerning Forced Labour in Poland*

Work under the communist system established in Poland after the Second World War went beyond the role ascribed to it in free market economies. Work was a duty of citizens and a 'question of honour'.[95] The Polish People's Republic[96] ratified both the ILO Forced Labour Convention, 1930 (No. 29)[97] and the ILO Abolition of Forced Labour Convention, 1957 (No. 105).[98] However, refraining from work was a source of disapproval. The authorities intended to integrate citizens into society through work.[99] In certain sectors crucial to the economy, workers had limited rights to leave their positions of their own will for a set duration of time (so-called orders of work).[100]

94 See The Social Insurance Act of 17 December 1998, Polish Journal of Laws 2021, item 291, as amended and the Law of 20 December 1990 of social insurance of farmers, Polish Journal of Laws 2021, item 266, as amended.

95 Compare Article 14 (1) of the Constitution of the Polish People' Republic of 1952. 'Praca jest prawem, obowiązkiem i sprawą honoru każdego obywatela' (Work is a right, a duty and a question of honour of every citizen).

96 PRL – the official name of Poland in the years 1952–1989.

97 Polish Journal of Laws of 1959, No. 20, item 122.

98 Polish Journal of Laws of 1959, No. 39, item 240. See Z. Lasocik, E. Rekosz-Cebula, Ł. Wieczorek, *Human Trafficking for Forced Labour in Poland – Effective Prevention and Diagnostics of Mechanisms*, Human Trafficking Studies Center – University of Warsaw, Warsaw 2014, pp. 18–21.

99 See M. Seweryński and D. Skupień, 'The Martial Law and its Impact on Labour Relations in Poland' (2017) 102 *Studia Prawno-Ekonomiczne* 107, p. 108.

100 Act of 7 March 1950 on Preventing the Outflow of Workers in Professions or Specialties of Particular Importance to the Socialized Economy (Ustawa z dnia 7 marca 1950 o zapobieżeniu płynności kadr pracowników w zawodach lub specjalnościach szczególnie ważnych dla gospodarki uspołecznionej), Polish Journal of Laws of 1950, No. 10, item 106 and 107.

The Decree on Martial Law of 12 December 1981,[101] the legal basis for the military coup d'état in Poland,[102] allowed the government to introduce forced labour during the period of martial law. The forced labour conditions applied to men aged 18–45, with some derogations. Even once martial law was lifted in 1983, the authorities retained forced labour under conditions resulting from the Law on the Proceedings against Persons Refraining from Work of 1982 (repealed in 1989) for men aged 18–45.[103] According to the above-mentioned law, notorious work evasion resulted in enrolment in a special list held by the administrative authorities. Persons included in the list could be forced to perform work for public needs.[104]

Contemporarily, Poland is bound by the forced labour prohibition expressed in Article 4(2) of European Convention of Human Rights and Article 5(2) of the Charter of Fundamental Rights of the European Union, mentioned above.[105] The prohibition of forced labour results indirectly from Article 65 para. 1 of the Constitution of the Republic of Poland.[106] It guarantees the freedom to choose an occupation and a place of work allowing for derogations which should obligatorily result from acts of legislative rank. Similarly, in the light of Article 10 § 1 of the Labour Code,[107] everyone has the right to freely chosen work. According to Article 11 of this Code, the establishment of an employment relationship and the determination of the terms and conditions of work and pay requires a consensual statement of intent by the employer and the employee.

Certain derogations from the constitutional freedom to choose an occupation and a place of work concern work for social purposes as a criminal penalty

---

101 Dekret z dnia 12 grudnia 1981 r. o stanie wojennym, Polish Journal of Laws of 1981, No. 29, item 154.

102 The military coup d'état of 1981 put an end to democratic developments in Poland which followed the conclusion of the August Agreements (1980) by the communist government with the representatives of the workforce. It suspended the functioning of trade unions, and especially the trade union organization independent from the State – NSZZ Solidarność (NSZZ Solidarity). For more details see M. Seweryński, *Polish Labour Law from Communism to Democracy*, Dom Wydawniczy ABC, Warsaw 1999, pp. 75–78; or J. M. Bloom, *Seeing through the eyes of the Polish revolution. Solidarity and the Struggle Against Communism in Poland*, Brill, Leiden-Boston 2013, pp. 287–305.

103 Ustawa z dnia 26 października 1982 r. o postępowaniu wobec osób uchylających się od pracy, Polish Journal of Laws of 1982, No. 35, item 229.

104 See M. Seweryński, D. Skupień, above n. 99, pp. 116–117.

105 For details about the legal framework concerning the prohibition of forced labour see Z. Lasocik, E. Rekosz-Cebula, Ł. Wieczorek, above n. 98, pp. 18–24.

106 Polish Journal of Laws of 1997, No. 78, item 483.

107 Ustawa z dnia 26 czerwca 1974 r. Kodeks pracy, consolidated text: Polish Journal of Laws of 2023, item 1465.

and work in case of natural disasters,[108] or for the reasons of state defence.[109] These derogations appear to be compliant with Article 8(3a) of the UN International Covenant on Civil and Political Rights and with Article 65 para. 1 of the Constitution.

In light of Art. 34 of the Polish Penal Code,[110] the penalty of restriction of liberty together with a fine is a less onerous penalty than that of imprisonment. Article 34 § 1a of the Penal Code states that the penalty of restriction of liberty shall consist in the obligation to perform unpaid, controlled work for social purposes or a deduction of 10% to 25% of monthly remuneration for work for a court-designated community purpose. Unless otherwise provided by law, the term of restriction of liberty shall be a minimum of one month and a maximum of two years. According to Article 35 § 1 of the Penal Code, unpaid, controlled work for social purposes shall be performed at the rate of 20 to 40 hours per month. In light of Article 35 § 2 of the Penal Code, a deduction of wages may be ordered against a person who is employed. During the period for which the deduction is ordered, the convicted person may not terminate the employment relationship without the court's approval.

5 Protection of Vulnerable Groups against Exploitation

5.1 *Special Protective Measures against Exploitation of Women and Juvenile Workers*

According to ILO estimates, women and children are persons who are the most vulnerable to different forms of modern slavery.[111] Turning back to the 19th century, the exploitation of women was prevalent in agriculture, industry and domestic work. In the latter group such negative phenomena like very long working hours with no days off, low remunerations, corporal punishment and cases of sexual abuse took place.[112] In 1918 the newly established Polish State

108 Compare Law of 18 April 2002 on the state of natural disaster (ustawa z dnia 18 kwietnia 2002 o stanie klęski żywiołowej).

109 Article 200 section 1 of the Act of November 21st, 1967 on general obligation of defending the Republic of Poland.

110 Ustawa z dnia 6 czerwca 1997 r. Kodeks karny, Polish Journal of Laws 2024.17, consolidated text of 2024.01.04.

111 ILO, Walk Free and IOM, Global Estimates of Modern Slavery. Forced Labour and Forced Marriage, Geneva 2022, p. 2, <https://www.ilo.org/wcmsp5/groups/public/---ed_norm/---ipec/documents/publication/wcms_854733.pdf>.

112 B. Nowak, 'Sytuacja służących kobiet w kontekście winy, kary i działań pomocowych na obszarach Krakowa w XIX wieku (*Situation of serving women in the context of guilt,*

granted women the right to vote as one of the first countries in the world. It was one of the factors that improved the position of women in the society. The equality of all citizens before the law was introduced in 1921 on the basis of Article 96 of the Constitution.[113] Legislation concerning the protection of pregnancy and the working time was introduced.[114] The above-cited provisions helped to improve the situation of women and to overcome their subordination and vulnerability to exploitation at work.

The Presidential Decree of 16 March 1928 on the employment contract of physical workers did not cover domestic workers.[115] However, Title XI Section I (employment contract) of the Code of Obligations of 1933 applied to them. Certain provisions of the Code of Obligations reflected the specificity of domestic work (*i.e.*, employer's obligations in case of worker's illness or duty to grant a domestic worker adequate time for rest and religious practice). The Code of Obligations established the guarantee of remuneration in cash, paid in regular intervals (Article 450–451), and the right of a worker to terminate the employment contract with notice (Article 468), as well as without notice in the case of important reasons (Article 470). Unfortunately, working time was not regulated in the Code of Obligations. The annual leave was very short, that is, one week after one year of work (Article 465). These regulations did not significantly improve the factual situation of domestic workers. In practice, domestic workers – in their great majority single women – were still very dependent on their employers.[116] After the Second World War, the Polish Labour Code, in its initial version of 26 June 1974 allowed for certain derogations from the general labour provisions for domestic workers. Special provisions concerning, in particular, working time and the termination of employment relationships were introduced by a decree of the Council of Ministers of 20 November 1974, on employment relationships where the employer is a natural person, and were in force until 1996.

At present, domestic workers are not explicitly excluded from the Labour Code provisions. Polish labour and social security laws theoretically apply to domestic workers as to 'all other' workers. However, national regulations do not take into account the specificity of domestic work. Polish law is not compliant with the ILO Domestic Workers Convention No. 189, 2011 (not ratified by

punishment and relief activities in the Krakow area in the 19th century)', Annales Universitatis Paedagogicae Cracoviensis, Studia Sociologica VIII (2016) 2 *Annales Universitatis Paedagogicae Cracoviensis, Studia Sociologica VIII* 177; A. Leszczyński, above n. 4, p. 365.

113 Polish Journal of Laws of 1921, No. 44, item 267.

114 See also M. Święcicki, above n. 33, pp. 86–93.

115 Rozporządzenie Prezydenta Rzeczypospolitej z dnia 16 marca 1928 o umowie o pracę robotników, Polish Journal of laws of 1928, No. 35, item 323 and 324.

116 See M. Święcicki, above n. 33, pp. 86–93, 150.

Poland), and it does not provide this group of workers with effective protection against discrimination, breaches of law, and abuses. Furthermore, Polish legislation does not establish effective measures to reduce the scale of illegal domestic worker employment. To avoid social security and labour law obligations, as well as formalities related to the employment of a worker, domestic work is often carried out in Polish households without a contract and is not legalized.

Problems concerning inequalities between men and women have been gradually eradicated in contemporary Poland. However, the gender pay gap was still at the level of 4.5% in 2021 to the disadvantage of women.[117] The trafficking of women and young girls still takes place, even though not on such a scale as in the 1990s. Polish women are victims of sexual exploitation, including forced prostitution or in the pornography industry, both abroad and within the country.[118]

Children are more vulnerable than adults and therefore at greater risk of becoming victims of trafficking in human beings or of exploitation. Therefore, the guarantees of protection for them are particularly important. The Constitution of 1921 prohibited the work of children under the age of 15.[119] However, the work of juvenile persons remained a fact, especially in agriculture, leading to many workplace accidents. It also continued after the Second World War, in the communist times. Nowadays, according to Article 64 para. 4 of the Constitution of the Republic of Poland (1997), permanent employment of children under 16 years of age is prohibited. The types and nature of admissible employment are specified by legislative acts only. Any employment of children under the age of 15 is prohibited, with exception of work within professional education.[120] Apart from this exception, in light of Article 304^5 § 1 of the Labour Code, a child under 16 may only work for entities carrying out cultural, artistic, sporting or advertising activity. Such work requires the prior consent of the child's legal representative or guardian, and a permit from the competent labour inspector. Breaches of these regulations by employers may

117 See Eurostat, <https://ec.europa.eu/eurostat/statistics-explained/index.php?title=Gender_pay_gap_statistics>.

118 See National Action Plan Against Trafficking in Human Beings 2022–2024, p. 3, <https://www.gov.pl/web/handel-ludzmi/krajowy-plan-dzialan-przeciwko-handlowi-ludzmi-na-lata-2022-2024>.

119 Ustawa z dnia 17 marca 1921 r. – Konstytucja Rzeczypospolitej Polskiej, Polish Journal of Laws of 1921, No. 44, item 267.

120 Article 190 § 2 the Labour Code. Poland has ratified ILO Minimum Age Convention of 1973, No. 138 in 1978.

be sanctioned with fines. In recent years, the protection of juvenile persons at work has improved *inter alia* under the influence of the EU legislation.[121]

5.2 *Combating Illegal Employment of Foreigners*

5.2.1 Factual Situation

After decades of being a migrant-origin country, Poland now hosts hundreds of thousands of foreign workers. In 2021, nearly 1 million migrants worked in Poland (871,000 in October 2021, around 5% of the whole workforce).[122] Currently, the Polish labour market attracts workers from countries that formed the Polish-Lithuanian Commonwealth in the past. Workers from Belarus and Ukraine enjoy preferential access to employment in Poland.[123] They form the largest migrant groups in Poland (especially Ukrainians whose number in Poland was estimated to be around 2,2 million people by the end of 2022).[124] There is also migration from Asian and African countries. Lacking supportive networks, migrants are particularly vulnerable to exploitation. First, illegal employment is more common among migrant workers. As a result, they do not enjoy any guarantees in terms of working conditions and remuneration. Second, the police reported some cases of human trafficking and modern slavery among foreigners:[125] work in illegal camps in agriculture,[126] forced begging or

---

121 Council Directive 94/33/EC of 22 June 1994 on the protection of young people at work, OJ L 216, 20.8.1994, pp. 12–20.

122 See the online publication entitled '*Polski rynek pracy idzie po kolejny rekord. Te dane pokazują, jak ważni są pracownicy spoza kraju*' (*Polish labor market goes for another record. These figures show how important workers from outside the country are*) <https://businessinsider.com.pl/twoje-pieniadze/praca/polski-rynek-pracy-idzie-po-kolejny-rekord-te-dane-pokazuja-jak-wazni-sa-pracownicy/zpdfx11>. Figures based on data published by ZUS (The Social Insurance Institution). The statistics include workers and self-employed individuals who are covered by mandatory social insurance (the total amount is around 16 million).

123 For more details see J. Cichoń, *Legalność zatrudnienia cudzoziemców* (*Legality of employment of foreign nationals*), Państwowa Inspekcja Pracy, Warszawa 2019.

124 M. Duszczyk, *Pomiędzy dwoma kryzysami migracyjnymi: Czego się nauczyliśmy, a co może nas czekać w przyszłości* (*What we have learnt, and what may await us in the future*), Dziennik Gazeta Prawna, (11.11.2022), <https://www.gazetaprawna.pl/wiadomosci/kraj/artykuly/8585718,migracje-duszczyk-raport-ukraincy-granica-polsko-bialoruska.html>.

125 See also P. Dąbrowski, *Praca przymusowa cudzoziemców w Polsce. Analiza zjawiska w wybranych grupach imigranckich* (*Forced labor of foreigners in Poland. Analysis of the phenomenon in selected migrant groups*), Wydawnictwo Uniwersytetu Warszawskiego, Warszawa 2014.

126 R. Woś, *Czy mamy w Polsce obozy pracy dla migrantów z Ukrainy* (*Do we have labour camps in Poland for migrants from Ukraine*), Polityka, (28.02.2018), <https://www.polityka.pl

forced sexual labour.[127] Forced labour was detected in various sectors of the economy: agriculture and food processing, construction or heavy industry.[128] Forced labour (in various fields, including begging but also agriculture) is organized by criminal groups.[129] In the worst cases, foreigners were detained, deprived of money and documents, they could not leave their working spaces and finally, they were forced to work. Sometimes living and working conditions are very poor and foreign workers are remunerated at a very low level, often below minimum standards.[130] In some cases, they do not receive any remuneration (e.g. remuneration is 'deducted' against the alleged debts). Similar problems concern Polish workers in Western countries. Third, common phenomena for foreigners in Poland are generally less favourable conditions of work and pay.[131] Theoretically, there are legal mechanisms to prevent abuse,[132] but practically their use is limited. Recently, there were prognoses of movement of workers from Ukraine and Belarus to Germany, and an increase in the number of workers from Africa and Asia to Poland was also expected.[133] However, the situation of these last groups is less favourable due, for example, to language barriers. In many cases, migrants are exploited with the support of foreign criminal organizations, often of the same national origin as the victim, which pretend to guarantee assistance in the transfer abroad.[134] In fact, the

---

/tygodnikpolityka/rynek/1739324,1,czy-mamy-w-polsce-obozy-pracy-dla-migrantow-z-ukrainy.read>.

127 See 'Krajowy Plan Działań przeciwko Handlowi Ludźmi na lata 2022–2024' (National Action Plan Against Trafficking in Human Beings 2022–2024), p. 2, <https://www.gov.pl/web/handel-ludzmi/krajowy-plan-dzialan-przeciwko-handlowi-ludzmi-na-lata-2022-2024>.

128 Z. Lasocik, J. Filipowicz, Ł. Wieczorek, *Handel ludźmi do pracy przymusowej w Polsce* (*Human trafficking for forced labour in Poland*), Human Trafficking Studies Center – University of Warsaw, Warszawa 2010, p. 23.

129 *Ibid.*, p. 15–17, 29, 56.

130 R. Woś, above n. 126.

131 M. Keryk, *Working in Poland: violations of the labour rights of Ukrainian migrants in the construction and services sectors*: Foundation Our Choice 2018, <https://pl.naszwybir.pl/wp-content/uploads/sites/2/2018/03/raport-online-en.pdf>.

132 See e.g. Act of 15 June 2012 on the consequences of entrusting work to foreigners residing in the territory of the Republic of Poland in violation of the law (Polish Journal of Laws 2021, item 1741).

133 See the online publication: *Rąk do pracy może zabraknąć. Na ratunek pracownicy z Afryki i Azji* (*There may not be enough hands for work. Workers from Africa and Asia to the rescue*), <https://businessinsider.com.pl/twoje-pieniadze/praca/kto-zastapi-bialorusinow-i-ukraincow-wyjezdzajacych-do-niemiec/mmyq4ro >.

134 E. Szczepańska, *Rozbito zorganizowaną grupę przestępczą* (*An organized crime group has been broken up*), <https://www.strazgraniczna.pl/pl/aktualnosci/8053,Rozbito-zorganizowana-grupe-przestepcza.html >.

first case concerning human trafficking outside sex business in Poland concerned a Vietnamese person exploited by Vietnamese nationals.[135]

The Russian invasion of Ukraine in February 2022 led to a huge influx of refugees to Poland, the consequences of which are visible in the labour market.[136] Persons fleeing the war are obviously particularly vulnerable. Automatic legalisation of stay and work in Poland for persons fleeing from war in Ukraine is supposed to support them in settling in Poland and preventing exploitation in the labour market.[137]

5.2.2 Legal Framework to Combat Illegal Employment of Foreigners

Being without status puts undocumented migrants at particular risk of exploitation, forced labour or trafficking for forced labour.[138] The fear of being deported may lead people to tolerate abusive conditions of work, which in the worst cases may vest different forms of modern slavery.

Illegal employment of third-country nationals is combated especially based on the Act of 15 June 2012 on the consequences of entrusting work to foreigners residing in the territory of the Republic of Poland in violation of the law which implements into the Polish legal system the EU Employers' Sanctions Directive (2009/52/EC).[139] This act establishes a system of sanctions for employers illegally employing persons from countries other than the EU/EEA and Switzerland, as well as persons other than members of the family of the latter group as they do not require residence permit to stay in another EU Member State. Illegally employed third-country nationals are entitled to claim

135 Z. Lasocik, above n. 47, p. 226.

136 According to the estimates, around 900 000 persons who fled from the war in Ukraine and 1,2 million Ukrainian citizens who have migrated before the the outbreak of the war stayed in Poland in 2022, see: M. Duszczyk, above n. 124. Number of Ukrainians residing in Poland in September 2023 was estimated at 2.5–3 million, see J. Piekutowski, *Migracje: Niewykorzystana (na razie) szansa Polski.* Report [*Migration: Poland's (so far) untapped opportunity*], Warsaw Enterprise Institute, September 2023 p. 18, <https://wei.org.pl/2023/aktualnosci/jarema/raport-migracje-niewykorzystana-na-razie-szansa-polski/>.

137 Compare especially Article 2 and 22 of the Law on assistance to citizens of Ukraine in connection with the armed conflict on its territory (ustawa z dnia z dnia 12 marca 2022 r. O pomocy obywatelom Ukrainy w związku z konfliktem zbrojnym na terytorium tego państwa), Polish Journal of Laws of 2022, item 583.

138 Compare also ILO, Walk Free and IOM UN Migration, Global Estimates of Modern Slavery. Forced Labour and Forced Marriage. Executive Summary, September 2022, pp. 1, 81 <https://www.ilo.org/global/topics/forced-labour/publications/WCMS_854795/lang--en/index.htm>.

139 Directive 2009/52/EC of the European Parliament and of the Council of 18 June 2009 providing for minimum standards on sanctions and measures against employers of illegally staying third-country nationals, OJ L 168, 30.6.2009, pp. 24–32.

back the payment of outstanding wages. The act facilitates access to justice for undocumented migrant workers and enhances access to labour inspections. Severe sanctions and penalties are provided for especially in the cases of: (1) submitting workers to "particularly exploitative working conditions";[140] (2) profiting from the work of victims of human trafficking; or (3) using child labour. It should be noted, however, that in its recent report, the EU Agency for Human Rights indicates the low effectiveness of measures provided for by the above-cited directive. It links it with a lack of incentives for foreigners to come forward, lack of awareness about their rights, a fear of being detected as illegally staying, being detained or returned, or losing the job.[141] The weakness of EU legislation also consists in fact, that the prolongation of legal stay for victims of human trafficking being undocumented migrants depends on their willingness to cooperate with prosecution authorities.[142]

Criminal law provisions should also be mentioned; they apply to the abuse of rights of all employees, irrespective of their nationality. According to Article 219 of the Penal Code, whoever violates the provisions of the social insurance law by failing to report the required data, even with the consent of the person concerned, or by reporting false data affecting the right to benefits or the amount thereof, shall be subject to a fine, penalty of restriction of liberty or imprisonment for up to 2 years. Article 218 of the Penal Code criminalizes malicious or persistent violation of employee rights.

6 Combating Exploitative Working Conditions

The specific social and economic development determined the Polish labour market after 1989, when the communist system collapsed. Poland started restoring the free market economy. The reforms relied heavily on the neoliberal model. There were collective redundancies in restructured enterprises

140 According to the definition formulated in Article 2(i) of the EU Employers' Sanctions Directive, 'particularly exploitative working conditions' means working conditions, including those resulting from gender based or other discrimination, where there is a striking disproportion compared with the terms of employment of legally employed workers which, for example, affects workers' health and safety, and which offends against human dignity.

141 For more details see: European Union Agency for Fundamental Rights, *Protecting Migrants in Irregular Situation from Labour Exploitation. Role of the Employers Sanctions Directive. Report*, Luxembourg 2021, p. 5, <https://fra.europa.eu/sites/default/files/fra_uploads/fra-2021-employers-sanctions-directive-report_en.pdf>.

142 Compare Article 6 of the Directive 2004/81/EC.

(including agriculture enterprises) and a dramatic increase in the unemployment rate. It was necessary to attract foreign investment. Poland became a country of cheap labour. A large part of the society did not benefit from the effects of the reforms. The sphere of poverty and social exclusion was widening. As a result, a very large group of people found themselves in an extremely unfavourable situation in the labour market. They had to accept precarious forms of employment as well as extremely unfavourable working and pay conditions, which made their situation even worse.[143] An example is doing very long working hours (exceeding adopted norms) without appropriate remuneration.

In the years following the economic transformation of 1989, numerous workers had to accept work outside the employment relationship – formally on the basis of civil law contracts.[144] There are two types of civil law employment. First, workers are treated just as civil law contractors (a party to a contract for services). Second, they are entrepreneurs, so they conclude civil law contracts as part of their businesses (self-employment). In both cases workers are deprived of labour law protection. At the same time, many of them perform work in conditions similar to those of employees (false self-employment).

Not being employees, workers and self-employed individuals were deprived of labour law protection (including working time, annual leaves, as well as the protection against termination of the contract).[145] In civil law, employment parties were free to determine the amount of remuneration. As a result, in many cases, it was set at a very low level (e.g. the hourly rate of EUR 1). Theoretically, Polish law provides that work-bearing features typical of an employment relationship (in particular subordinate work) creates an employment relationship, regardless of the name given to the contract. However, the mechanism adopted in the Polish law seems to be inefficient.[146] As a result, there is a significant discrepancy between the theoretical model of the employment relationship and its practical meaning.

---

143 See e.g. M. Kramer, 'Polish Workers and the Post-Communist Transition 1989–93' (1995) 47:4 *Europe-Asia Studies* 669.

144 See e.g. P. Sula, *Poland: Self-employed workers*, Eurofound 2006.

145 Over the recent years the Polish labour law has undergone a number of significant reforms. There were two main driving forces of the changes: the global crisis and the need to resolve demographic problems. See more D. Skupień, M. Łaga and Ł. Pisarczyk, *'Polish labour law: the impact of the economic crisis and demographic problems'* (2016) *Hungarian Labour Law E-Journal* 1.

146 The worker must apply to the labour court to declare the existence of the employment relationship. Due to many reasons (fear of losing the job, the court procedure) workers only rarely decide to requalify their contracts. Although the procedure can be initiated also by labour inspectors, in practice they do not utilise their competences.

In recent years, however, workers and self-employed individuals have been provided with some forms of protection. First, the minimum hourly rate (HMR) for non-employees was established (2017). It has gradually increased from around EUR 3 in 2017 to around EUR 7 in 2025. Second, for many decades, freedom of association in trade unions had been guaranteed for employees only. Poland was accused of violating the fundamental ILO conventions (Nos. 87 and 98). In 2015, the Constitutional Tribunal ruled that the statutory limitation of union freedoms to employees is inconsistent with the Constitution.[147] The amending law, finally enacted in 2018 (it came into force on 1 January 2019), extended trade union freedoms to workers (non-employees) who meet specific criteria: they perform paid work for another person or entity, do not employ other persons and have collective interests that can be represented by a trade union. They also enjoy the right of collective bargaining and the right to go on strike.[148] However, the practical importance of the reform (due to the factual weakness of the social dialogue) remains limited. To summarise, the abuse of bogus self-employment still poses a serious threat to the social security of the employed. This is one of the biggest problems still facing Polish legislation.

Some forms of exploitation occurred even in typical employment (based on the employment contract). It is true that employees were covered by protective labour legislation, but their actual position was influenced by low (or even very low) levels of wages. In 2004 (Poland's accession to the EU), the statutory minimum wage was around EUR 200. Such a low level of wages could lead to poverty and social exclusion. However, since 2004, the minimum wage has increased significantly (around EUR 1000 in 2024). It has been a result of both economic growth and general pay rise, as well as the state policy, which interferes to a greater extent with economic and social relations.[149]

Polish international companies play a rather limited role in globally shaping working conditions, mainly because their position and supply chains are usually regional. Nevertheless, they use raw materials or semi-finished products from regions affected by modern slavery (also as a part of international companies or groups of companies). Polish companies have also employed workers recruited (by employment agencies/temporary work agencies) in countries/

147 Judgment of the Constitutional Court of 2 June 2015, K 1/13.

148 The statutory provisions on collective agreements and resolving collective disputes that concern employees apply *mutatis mutandis* to workers performing paid work.

149 See, T. Gyulavári and Ł. Pisarczyk, '*Populist labour law reforms in Hungary and Poland: Same Song, Different Melodies*' (2023) 39:4 *International Journal of Comparative Labour Law and Industrial Relations* 49.

regions where fundamental workers' rights are not respected. Recruited employees are not properly informed about their future situation (employment basis, salary, working hours) and are even misled.[150]

The COVID-19 pandemic brought new challenges to the world of work. Polish law on counteracting COVID-19 distinguishes a category of critical infrastructure.[151] It covers systems necessary for the proper functioning of public administration as well as of institutions and businesses.[152] The regulations adopted during the pandemic allowed for special rules of work organization for employees working in the critical infrastructure. This concerned, *inter alia*, extending working hours or taking rest periods at a place determined by the employer. Although justified by extraordinary situations, it interfered with workers' freedoms and rights (a kind of compulsion to work in certain conditions). A particular example was the medical staff. Healthcare workers could be assigned to work to combat the epidemic.[153] The assignment was made by way of an administrative decision. An unjustified refusal was treated as a misdemeanour. An administrative fine of up to PLN 30,000 (approximately EUR 7000) could also be imposed on the worker.[154] Since the application scope of the regulations was very broad, the law was challenged from the constitutional perspective (also from the perspective of the constitutional principle of freedom of work).[155]

Various negative phenomena, having their source in the social structure and status of an individual (e.g. less favourable working conditions for vulnerable groups of workers), can be, at least in theory, eliminated or mitigated thanks to the use of anti-discrimination mechanisms. Poland has developed comprehensive legislation protecting against discrimination in employment. There

150 B. Faracik (ed), above n. 9, pp. 17–18.

151 See the Law of 2 March 2020 on counteracting COVID-19, Polish Journal of Laws 2021, item 2095, as amended. Available at: <https://isap.sejm.gov.pl/isap.nsf/download.xsp/WDU20200000374/U/D20200374Lj.pdf>.

152 Ustawa z dnia 26 kwietnia 2007 r. o zarządzaniu kryzysowym (Law on Crisis Management), Polish Journal of Laws 2007, No. 89, item 590.

153 See Art. 47 of the Law of 5 December 2008 on the prevention and counteracting infections and infectious diseases in humans, Polish Journal of Laws 2022, item 1657, as amended. The law provides for exceptions (workers who cannot be assigned), e.g. workers of retirement age, workers taking care of children up to 14.

154 See also R. Kubiak, 'Skierowanie lekarza do pracy przy zwalczaniu pandemii wirusa SARS-CoV-2 (*Referring a physician to work against the SARS-CoV-2 pandemic*)' (2020) 12:4 *Medycyna Paliatywna* 174.

155 Cf. M. Waszak, '*Skierowanie do pracy przy zwalczaniu epidemii. Blaski i cienie regulacji* (*Referring to work in combating epidemics. Pros and cons of legal regulation*)' (2020) 14 *Medyczna Wokanda* 93, pp. 99–100.

are, however, two standards of protection: for employees (regulated by the Labour Code),[156] and for other workers.[157] The labour law (employees) provides for an open catalogue of discriminatory reasons.[158] As a result, all criteria concerning worker's features (gender, age, ethnic origin, nationality, religion or other grounds) can be treated as potential source of discrimination. Employees affected by discrimination may claim fair, non-discriminatory conditions of work as well as compensation. Moreover, the burden of proof is regulated in a special manner (the reverse burden of proof). The employee is expected to make the unequal treatment plausible (e.g. differentiation in the level of remuneration). Next, this is the employer who must prove that the different treatment has been justified by objective reasons.[159] Otherwise the employer is responsible for discrimination.

In the case of workers who are not employees, the reverse burden of proof applies as well. Workers who have faced discrimination may claim compensation. However, in the case of other workers (non-employees), the law lists the discriminatory criteria: gender, race, ethnicity, nationality, religion, disability, age and sexual orientation. Moreover, the practical use of anti-discrimination mechanisms outside the employment relationship is limited.[160] This is especially true of the most vulnerable groups of workers, including migrant workers. The main reason is low awareness of the available protection measures. This applies, in particular, to the rights of non-employees. Added to this is the practice of the courts, which often dismiss anti-discrimination claims.[161]

156 See, extensively with further references, Z. Hajn, L. Mitrus, *Poland* in R. Blanpain (ed.) *International Encyclopaedia of Laws: Labour Law and Industrial* Relations, Kluwer Law International, Alphen aan den Rijn 2016, p. 67–78.

157 The Law of 3 December 2010 implementing some EU standards in the field of equal treatment, Polish Journal of Laws, 2020, item 2156.

158 Arts. 11^3 and 18^{3a} § 1 of the Labour Code.

159 Art. 18^{3b} of the Labour Code.

160 See also Rzecznik Praw Obywatelskich, *Ochrona przed dyskryminacją w Polsce. Stan prawny i świadomość społeczna. Wnioski i rekomendacje* RPO (*Protection against discrimination in Poland. Legal status and social awareness. Conclusions and recommendations of the Ombudsman*), Warszawa 2020, <https://bip.brpo.gov.pl/sites/default/files/Ochrona_przed-_dyskryminacja_w_Polsce.pdf>.

161 Ł. Guza, *Brak wiedzy ułatwia dyskryminację w zatrudnieniu* (*Lack of knowledge facilitates discrimination in employment*), Dziennik Gazeta Prawna, (18.012021), <https://praca.gazetaprawna.pl/artykuly/8070891,dyskryminacja-w-zatrudnieniu-prawa-pracownika.html>.

7 Redressing Modern Forms of Slavery in Poland

In Poland, there are a number of institutions dealing with contemporary forms of slavery from various angles. An important role is played by bodies analysing and combating criminal activity, especially in the field of human trafficking. An example is the Human Trafficking Research Center – a research and educational institution operating within the Faculty of Political Science and International Studies at the University of Warsaw. The Center is considered to be an independent academic centre dealing with all forms of scientific, training, didactic, and information activity related to modern forms of slavery. The Center organises debates and seminars, and is involved in publications on human trafficking.[162] The Centre is among partners of the Alliance 8.7.[163] The activities of the Center are a form of scientific support for institutions combating trafficking in human beings. They also contribute to educating specialists and raising awareness in this area.[164] An important output are publications.[165]

As for the implementation of the United Nations Guiding Principles on Business and Human Rights (2011), the National Action Plans (NAP) were adopted by the government. The first edition (2017) covered the period 2017–2021 while the second edition (2021) the period 2021–2024. The NAP was based on the three pillars included in the Guiding Principles: 1. The state's duty to protect human rights; 2. The corporate responsibility to respect human rights; 3. Access to remedies.[166] The state's duty to protect human rights covers the prohibition of forced or compulsory labour, the prevention of economic exploitation of children, the freedom of association and the right to a fair wage.

By describing the government's actions to promote corporate social responsibility, as well as referring to strategic documents in this area, the NAP demonstrated a deliberate state policy of supporting businesses while stressing the need for human rights.[167] The NAP underlined the role of the National Labour

162 Available at: Human Trafficking Studies Center 'About us', <https://wnpism.uw.edu.pl/en/obhl-about/>.

163 Available at: Alliance 8.7, 'Network for Change', <https://www.alliance87.org/partners/>.

164 Above n. 162.

165 See, e.g. Z. Lasocik, J. Filipowicz, Ł. Wieczorek, above n. 128.

166 Ministry of Foreign Affairs Republic of Poland, 'Polish NAP for the Implementation of the UN Guiding Principles on Business and Human Rights', <https://www.gov.pl/web/diplomacy/polish-nap-for-the-implementation-of-the-un-guiding-principles-on-business-and-human-rights>.

167 *Ibid.*

Inspectorate, especially in the field of combating human trafficking and forced labour.[168] For instance, labour inspectors check whether there are indications of forced labour at an inspected establishment. In order to identify potential victims of trafficking, a number of criteria are taken into account, i.e., the circumstances of taking up and performing work, which may indicate that the employee is a victim of this type of crime. In combating human trafficking and forced labour, the National Labour Inspectorate collaborates with other public institutions, including the Police and Border Guard.[169] The Labour Inspectorate and the Police and Border Guard exchange information. They also carry out joint inspections.[170]

Of particular importance is cooperation with the Border Guard, which controls the Eastern and Northern borders of Poland (with Ukraine, Belarus and the Russian Federation). It is also the external border of the EU, through which people from third countries who are forced to work in conditions of coercion can be transported.

8 Conclusions

Although Poland has been gradually rejoining the Western European community since the 1990s, it still bears the features of a country divided between the East and West, together with other Central European countries. The difficult situation of Polish society, especially of the peasants and physical workers, was exacerbated by numerous wars and the exploitation of the Polish people by occupying states at different times in history and by the Communist regime.

The 1990s brought economic liberalization and the opening of borders. However, these generally positive developments also opened the way for negative phenomena such as human trafficking, forced labour or the exploitation of workers in private companies, both concerning Polish and foreign citizens. Since the 1920s, Poland has introduced, especially under the influence of international law, regulations designed to combat these negative phenomena. Today, Poland's membership of the Council of Europe and the EU is significant

168 See more, Z. Lasocik, J. Filipowicz, Ł. Wieczorek, above n. 128, p. 11 et seq.

169 Polish NAP for the Implementation of the UN Guiding Principles on Business and Human Rights available at: <https://www.gov.pl/web/diplomacy/polish-nap-for-the-implementation-of-the-un-guiding-principles-on-business-and-human-rights>.

170 Z. Lasocik, J. Filipowicz, Ł. Wieczorek, above n. 128, p. 11.

in this respect. The legal acts of these two organizations primarily influence criminal law instruments for combating trafficking in human beings and the exploitation of foreigners illegally residing within the Polish territory.

The Polish government, through National Action Plans against Trafficking in Human Beings, developed since 2003, has been taking measures, including the participation of NGOs, to prevent and combat trafficking in human beings and forced labour. The situation still leaves much to be desired. In particular, the foreigners' fear of being forcibly expelled to their country of origin often results in a conspiracy of silence and impedes effective controls of the relevant authorities.[171] It seems that preventing and combating modern forms of slavery in Poland, as in other countries, requires more effective controls of the competent inspections as well as the cooperation of public authorities, including at the local level, with entrepreneurs and raising the ethical level of the latter. International actions, including the cooperation of law enforcement bodies in order to detect transnational criminal networks, are not without significance.

The long-term goal and the ideal for the international community as a whole is the improvement in living conditions, a guarantee of personal safety, independence and a high level of education for people and especially for women in the global scale. Most often, in the history of the human race, people who have been uneducated, deprived of ownership of land or means of production, in a state of poverty, dependency or danger, have been prone to slavery and exploitation.[172] It seems that everyone, in their working environment as a manager or a business owner, has a moral duty to have a small part in making working conditions decent and human. As a good example of solidarity in the enterprise, we may indicate the Presidential Decree of 1932 concerning the limitation of excessive corporate pay, which, during times of economic crisis, mitigated the wages of the management to make it proportional to the

171 Compare European Union Agency for Fundamental Rights, *Protecting Migrants in Irregular Situation from Labour Exploitation. Role of the Employers Sanctions Directive*, Report, Luxembourg2021,p.5<https://fra.europa.eu/sites/default/files/fra_uploads/fra-2021-employers-sanctions-directive-report_en.pdf>.

172 Compare ILO, Walk Free and IOM UN Migration, Global Estimates of Modern Slavery. Forced Labour and Forced Marriage. Executive Summary, September 2022, p. 1, <https://www.ilo.org/global/topics/forced-labour/publications/WCMS_854795/lang--en/index.htm>.

financial outcome of the enterprise and the overall level of remunerations of workers.[173]

Academic References

A. Brückner, *Dzieje kultury polskiej* (*History of Polish culture*), Książka i Wiedza, Warszawa 1957.

A. Leogrande, *Uomini e caporali. Viaggio tra i nuovi schiavi nelle campagne del Sud*, Feltrinelli Editore, Milan 2016.

A. Leszczyński, *Ludowa historia Polski* (*People's history of Poland*), W.A.B., Warszawa 2020.

A. Prazmowska, *A History Of Poland*, Palgrave Macmillan, London 2011.

A. Von Plato, A. Leh and C. Thonfeld (eds), *Hitler's Slaves: Life Stories of Forced Labourers in Nazi-occupied Europe*, Berghahn Books, Oxford/New York 2010.

A. Zamoyski, *Poland. A History*, Harper Press, New York 2009.

B. Faracik (ed.), *Praca przymusowa* (*Forced labour*), Minister Funduszy i Polityki Regionalnej, Warszawa 2020.

B. Klebeko, 'Handel ludźmi jednym z największych współczesnych zagrożeń dla realizacji idei praw człowieka (*Human trafficking Human trafficking as one of the greatest contemporary threats to the realization of human rights*)' in M. Jabłoński, T. Jurczyk and P. Gutierrez, *Międzynarodowa ochrona praw człowieka – współczesne problemy na świecie* (*International protection of human rights – contemporary problems in the world*), E-Wydawnictwo. Prawnicza i Ekonomiczna Biblioteka Cyfrowa, Wrocław 2015.

B. Nowak, 'Sytuacja służących kobiet w kontekście winy, kary i działań pomocowych na obszarach Krakowa w XIX wieku (*Situation of serving women in the context of guilt, punishment and relief activities in the Kraków area in the 19th century*)' (2016) 2 *Annales Universitatis Paedagogicae Cracoviensis, Studia Sociologica VIII* 177.

D. Skupień, M. Łaga and Ł. Pisarczyk, 'Polish labour law: the impact of the economic crisis and demographic problems' (2016) 1 *Hungarian Labour Law E-Journal* 1.

D. Trześniowski, 'Rusyfikacja jako pozorne zagrożenie. O nieskuteczności rosyjskiego projektu kolonialnego w Polsce (w XIX w.) (*Russification as an apparent threat. About the ineffectiveness of the Russian colonial project in Poland (in the 19th century)*)' in K. Stępnik and D. Trześniowski (eds) *Studia postkolonialne nad literaturą*

173 Polish Journal of Laws of 1922, No. 87, item 783.

i kulturą polską (*Postcolonial studies on Polish literature and culture*), Wydawnictwo UMCS, Lublin 2010, pp. 159–174.

G. J. Lerski, *Historical Dictionary of Poland, 966–1945*, Greenwood, Westport 1996.

H. Grala, *Rzeczpospolita szlachecka – twór kolonialny?* (*The Commonwealth of the Nobility – a colonial creation?*) in J. Kieniewicz (ed.), *Perspektywy postkolonializmu w Polsce, Polska w perspektywie postkolonialnej* (*Prospects of postcolonialism in Poland. Poland in the postcolonial perspective*), Wydział "Artes Liberales" Uniwersytet Warszawski, Warszawa 2016.

H. Szurgacz, 'Die rechtliche Lage der Polnischen Arbeiter im nationalsozialistischen Staat 1933–1945' in U. Becker, B. Baron von Maydell and H. Szurgacz (eds), *Die Realisierung der Arbeitnehmerfreizügigkeit im Verhältnis zwischen Dutschland und Polen aus arbeits- und sozialrechtlicher Sicht*, Nomos, München 2012.

H. Szurgacz, *Polscy pracownicy w Niemczech 1880–2004. Studium historyczno-prawne* (*Polish workers in Germany 1880–2004. A historical and legal study*), Willy Brandt Centre for German and European Studies at University of Wrocław (CSNE), Wrocław 2022.

J. Allain, 'The International Legal Regime of Slavery and Human Exploitation and its Obfuscation by the Term of Art: "Slavery-like Practice"' (2012) 10 *Cahiers de la recherche sur les droits fondamentaux* 27.

J. Bardach, B. Leśnodorski and M. Pietrzak, *Historia ustroju i prawa polskiego* (*History of the Polish political system and law*), Lexis Nexis, Warszawa 1998.

J. Beck, *Wspomnienia o polskiej polityce zagranicznej 1926–1939* (*Memories of Polish Foreign Policy 1926–1939*), Wingert, Warszawa-Kraków 2015.

J. Kieniewicz, *O perspektywę dla Polski* (*For a perspective for Poland*) in J. Kieniewicz (ed.), *Perspektywy postkolonializmu w Polsce, Polska w perspektywie postkolonialnej* (*Prospects of postcolonialism in Poland. Poland in the postcolonial perspective*), Wydział "Artes Liberales" Uniwersytet Warszawski, Warszawa 2016.

J. Kuciel-Frydryszak, *Chłopki. Opowieść o naszych babkach* (*Peasants. A story of our grandmothers*), Marginesy, Warszawa 2023.

J. M. Bloom, *Seeing through the eyes of the Polish revolution. Solidarity and the Struggle Against Communism in Poland*, Brill, Leiden-Boston 2013.

J. Sowa, *Fantomowe ciało króla* (*The phantom body of a king*), TAiWPN Universitas, Kraków, 2011.

Ł. Pisarczyk, 'The Crisis of the Collective Bargaining System in Poland' (2019) 35:1 *International Journal of Comparative Labour Law and Industrial Relations* 57.

M. Hruszewski, *Szlachta ukraińska na przełomie XVI i XVII w.* (*Ukrainian nobility at the turn of the 16th and 17th centuries*) in *Historia Ukrainy-Rusi* (*History of Ukraine and Russia*), Vol. 6, Lviv, Kiev 1907.

M. Kramer, 'Polish Workers and the Post-Communist Transition 1989–93' (1995) 47:4 *Europe-Asia Studies* 669.

M. Seweryński and D. Skupień, 'The Martial Law and its Impact on Labour Relations in Poland' (2017) 102 *Studia Prawno-Ekonomiczne* 107.

M. Seweryński, *Polish Labour Law from Communism to Democracy*, Dom Wydawniczy ABC, Warsaw 1999.

M. Święcicki, *Instytucje polskiego prawa pracy w latach 1918–1939* (*Institutions of Polish Labour Law in years 1918–1939*), PWN, Warszawa 1960.

M. Waszak, 'Skierowanie do pracy przy zwalczaniu epidemii. Blaski i cienie regulacji (*Referring to work in combating epidemics. Pros and cons of legal regulation*)' (2020) 14 *Medyczna Wokanda* 93.

N. Davies, *Europa* (*Europe*), Znak, Kraków 2002.

N. Ollus and A. Jokinen, 'Trafficking for Forced Labour and Labour Exploitation – Setting the Scene', in A. Jokinen, N. Ollus, K. Aromaa (eds), *Trafficking for Forced Labour Exploitation in Finland, Poland and Estonia*, United Nations European Institute for Crime Prevention and Control (HEUNI), Helsinki 2011, pp. 11-30.

P. Dąbrowski, *Praca przymusowa cudzoziemców w Polsce. Analiza zjawiska w wybranych grupach imigranckich* (*Forced labor of foreigners in Poland. Analysis of the phenomenon in selected migrant groups*), Wydawnictwo Uniwersytetu Warszawskiego, Warszawa 2014.

R. Alexy, *A Theory of Constitutional Rights*, Oxford University Press, Oxford 2010.

R. Frost, *The Oxford History of Poland-Lithuania. Volume 1 – The Making of the Polish-Lithuanian Union, 1385–1569*, Oxford University Press, New York 2015.

R. Kubiak, 'Skierowanie lekarza do pracy przy zwalczaniu pandemii wirusa SARS-CoV-2 (*Referring a physician to work against the SARS-CoV-2 pandemic*)' (2020) 12:4 *Medycyna Paliatywna* 174.

T. Gyulaváriand and Ł. Pisarczyk, '*Populist labour law reforms in Hungary and Poland: same song, different melodies*'(2023) 39:1 *International Journal of Comparative Labour Law and Industrial Relations* 49.

U. Herbert, 'Forced Laborers in the Third Reich: An Overview' (2000) 58 *International Labor and Working-Class History* 192.

W. Kuligowski, 'A history of Polish serfdom' (2016) 3 *Czas Kultury* 1.

Z. Hajn and L. Mitrus, 'Poland' in R. Blanpain (ed.), *International Encyclopaedia of Laws: Labour Law and Industrial Relations,* Kluwer Law International, Alphen aan den Rijn 2016, p. 67–78.

Z. Lasocik, 'O handlu ludźmi w Polsce, czyli o ewolucji zjawiska i budowie systemu jego eliminowania' (*Human trafficking in Poland, or the evolution of the phenomenon and the construction of a system to eliminate it*) (2012) 34 *Archiwum Kryminologii* 481.

Z. Lasocik, 'Human Trafficking in Poland - Evolution of the Devil' in L. E. Sullivan (ed), *Criminal Justice and Law Enforcement Annual: Global Perspectives*, Ams Press Inc, New York 2014, pp. 222–275.

Z. Lasocik, J. Filipowicz and Ł. Wieczorek, *Handel ludźmi do pracy przymusowej w Polsce* (*Human trafficking for forced labour in Poland*), Human Trafficking Studies Center – University of Warsaw, Warszawa 2010.

Z. Lasocik, E. Rekosz-Cebula, and Ł. Wieczorek, *Human Trafficking for Forced Labour in Poland – Effective Prevention and Diagnostics of Mechanisms*, Human Trafficking Studies Center – University of Warsaw, Warsaw 2014.

Z. Lasocik, E. Rekosz-Cebula, and Ł. Wieczorek, *Filling the Gaps in the System of Combating Human Trafficking in Poland – Research Report*, Human Trafficking Studies Center – University of Warsaw, Warsaw 2015.

Contemporary Forms of Slavery, including Causes and Consequences: Slovenia

Darja Senčur Peček

1 Introduction

Slovenia is one of the countries historically not burdened by slavery. It is, however, faced with various forms of contemporary slavery, especially as a destination and transit country in the case of human trafficking. The legal regulation of the prohibition of slavery derives primarily from international legal acts that Slovenia ratified or took over from the former Yugoslavia. The paper discusses the development of the legal regulation of slavery, the actual situation regarding the incidence of individual forms of contemporary slavery in Slovenia, the national legal definition of forms of contemporary slavery, the protection of victims from the point of view of criminal, labour and immigration law, various preventive and protective measures implemented at the national level and various activities coordinated at the supranational level, in which Slovenia actively participates. Based on the analysis of the current (relatively adequate) legal regulation, the paper also points out some shortcomings, and possible solutions are also indicated.

2 The Historical Background of the Prohibition of Slavery in the Slovenian Legal System

As a preliminary remark, the Republic of Slovenia (Slovenia) is a young country that became independent in 1991. Countries of which the Slovenian territory was part in the past (the Kingdom of Yugoslavia before the Second World War and the Socialist Federal Republic of Yugoslavia after the Second World War) were never part of the transatlantic slave trade, unlike other European countries. Slavery and the African slave trade did not exist in Yugoslavia.[1]

1 Nonetheless, if we go further back in History (way before the establishment of Yugoslavia and Slovenia's independence in 1991) the majority of Slovenia's nowadays territory was for several centuries under the rule of the Austrian Habsburg Empire. For the latter Empire, there is evidence that it (its traders) participated in the international colonial trade system (including slave trade). On this matter see: W. Sauer, 'Habsburg Colonial: Austria-Hungary's

 | DOI:10.1163/9789004723801_014

2.1 *The Influence of International Legal Acts*

In 1929, the Kingdom of Yugoslavia ratified the Slavery Convention (1926, adopted by the League of Nations), which was supplemented in 1953 by a special protocol. In 1958, Yugoslavia also ratified the Supplementary Convention on the Abolition of Slavery, the Slave Trade, and Institutions and Practices Similar to Slavery (1956). Slovenia confirmed to be bound by the latter Convention as Yugoslavia's successor.

Article 112 of the Slovenian Criminal Code (KZ-1) criminalizes the offence of Enslavement, which is committed by a person who, in violation of the rules of international law, places or holds another person in a slave or slave-like relationship or mediates in the sale of such a person.[2] In Slovenia, in practice, there have been only a few cases of offences under this article (which does not cover forced labour and trafficking in human beings and forced marriages, which are otherwise covered as a form of slave labour under the 1956 Convention).

The International Labour Organisation (ILO) Forced Labour Convention (1930 No. 29), which entered into force in 1932, was ratified by the Kingdom of Yugoslavia in the same year.[3] The Convention is binding on Slovenia by virtue of the Act of Notification of Succession.[4] The ILO Convention No. 105 concerning the Abolition of Forced Labour (1957) which is an amendment to Convention No. 29, was not ratified by Yugoslavia,[5] but was ratified by Slovenia in 1997.[6]

Socialist Yugoslavia, which was bound by ILO Convention No. 29, introduced (with criminal and misdemeanour legislation) the punishments of forced labour (either with or without deprivation of liberty), correctional work and community service during the 1945 to 1951 period. These penalties were imposed by the courts or administrative authorities on the perpetrators – including political opponents of the authorities – of criminal offences or

Role in European Overseas Expansion Reconsidered' (2012) 20 *Austrian Studies* 5, pp. 12–14. Nonetheless, *Sauer* at the same time emphasises that colonial experience and colonialist interests in Habsburg lands developed at a slower pace and were regarded less important than in some other West European countries (*ibid*, p. 13).

2 See K. Filipčič, 'Spravljanje v suženjsko razmerje' in D. Korošec, K. Filipčič and S. Zdolšek (eds), *Veliki komentar posebnega dela Kazenskega zakonika*, Uradni list Republike Slovenije, Ljubljana 2018.

3 Slovenske novine, No. 297-CXI/32.

4 OJ RS, No. 54/92-MP.

5 The obstacles to ratification are said to lie in criminal law. See R. Kyovsky and R. Radovan, *Konvencije in priporočila MOD s komentarjem*, Centar za samoupravno normativno dejavnost, Ljubljana 1975, p. 63.

6 Act on the ratification of the Convention on the Abolition of Forced Labour (OJ RS – International Treaties, No. 10/97).

misdemeanours. There is a view in the part of the Slovenian public that these penalties violated the provisions of the latter Convention.[7] In 1996, Slovenia adopted the Law on the Reparation of Injustice,[8] under which former political prisoners, as well as those who were sentenced to community service for political reasons, have the right to compensation and to recognition of pensionable service for that period. The system of redress in Slovenia is thus not linked to the prohibition of slavery, nor does it derive from the prohibition of forced labour as such, but rather redresses injustices committed by politically motivated convictions.[9]

Moreover, the constitutional and legal prohibition of discrimination,[10] which includes the prohibition of racial discrimination, is not rooted in the abolition of slavery. In the Slovenian legal order, the prohibition of discrimination is in line with the international human rights instruments binding on Slovenia. It follows from the reports of the monitoring bodies that the issues of the Roma people (as a specific community in Slovenia) and migrants or asylum seekers are relevant from the perspective of racial discrimination and racism.[11] Furthermore, there is no constitutional or statutory exception to the prohibition of slavery and forced labour in the Slovenian legal system, which would allow slavery or forced labour under certain circumstances (e.g. prison labour).

Under the Enforcement of Criminal Sanctions Act (ZIKS-1),[12] persons serving a prison sentence may work. However, this is not forced labour since convicted persons are allowed to work (within their means),[13] but they are not ordered to work as a sanction, nor are they obliged to work while serving a

---

7 See K. Zajc, *Primerjava ustavnih ureditev prepovedi suženjstva in prepovedi prisilnega dela: Magistrsko delo*, Master's Thesis, New University European Law Faculty, Nova Gorica, 2018, pp. 97 ff. and the references cited in this section.

8 OJ RS, No. 70/05, 89/07 – odl. US and 92/07.

9 In the same way, the Law on Victims of War Violence (OJ RS, No. 18/03, 54/04 – ZDoh-1, 68/05 – odl. US, 61/06 – ZDru-1, 114/06 – ZUTPG, 72/09, 40/12 – ZUJF, 21/18 – ZNOrg, 174/20 – ZIPRS2122 and 159/21) recognised the rights of Slovenian citizens who were sent to forced labour by the German, Hungarian or Italian occupying forces during World War II for political, national, racial or religious reasons.

10 See Article 14 of the Slovenian Constitution and see the Protection Against Discrimination Act, OJ RS, No. 33/16 and 21/18 – ZNOrg.

11 See European Commission against Racism and Intolerance Report on Slovenia, fifth phase of monitoring, (05.06.2019), <https://www.coe.int/en/web/european-commission-against-racism-and-intolerance/slovenia>.

12 See ZIKS-1 (OJ RS, No. 110/06, 76/08, 40/09, 9/11 – ZP-1G, 96/12 – ZPIZ-2, 109/12, 54/15, 11/18 in 200/20 – ZOOMTVI), Articles 45 to 57a.

13 According to the 2020 report of the Penitentiary Enforcement Board, it was not possible to provide work to all prisoners who wanted to work, p. 95, <https://www.gov.si/assets/organi-v-sestavi/URSIKS/Dokumenti/Letna-porocila-/Letno-porocilo-2020.pdf>.

prison sentence. In the event that convicted persons do work (usually in a public economic institution, which is part of the prison, or in the prison – housework), they are entitled to a monetary remuneration,[14] to some days of annual leave and to other work-related rights. In Slovenian case law, there have been cases where prisoners have claimed compensation from the State on the grounds that such work is a form of forced labour and unequal treatment compared to employees in regular employment. The courts rejected these claims, as there was no basis for concluding that the State was exploiting prisoners, who were forced to work for an indecent wage. Work during a sentence is a right, not an obligation, of the convicted person. Nor are the employee and the prisoner in the same situation requiring the same legal regulation since, unlike the convicted person, the employee must provide for his or her own basic subsistence, and his relationship with the employer is of economic nature – whereas for the work of convicted persons, the rehabilitation aspect of the work is of primary importance. It follows that Article 54 of the ZIKS-1, which establishes the initial remuneration relationships for prisoners' work, is not incompatible with the Constitution.[15]

3 Recognition of the Problem of Contemporary Slavery

In the Slovenian legal sphere, the term contemporary slavery is usually associated with the term 'trafficking' in human beings. In general, Slovenia is a destination country for trafficking in human beings and also a transit country for persons from South-Eastern Europe to other European Union (EU) Member States.[16] Most often, trafficking in human beings in Slovenia is linked to prostitution. However, relatively few cases have been detected.[17]

In the 10-year period from 2010 to 2020, 186 people were suspected of trafficking in human beings, 107 were charged, and 63 were convicted in Slovenia.

14 Rules on payment for the work of persons sentenced to prison, OJ RS, No. 27/16 and 4/20. The remuneration is, however, lower than the remuneration for regular (non-incarcerated) workers.

15 Ljubljana Higher Court (VSL) Judgment II CP 3067/2012, of 21.08.2013; Ljubljana Higher Court (VSL) Judgment II CP 1090/2018 of 12.06.2019, paras. 17–20.

16 Inter-ministerial Working Group for Combating Trafficking in Human Beings, Report for year 2020, p. 10, <https://www.gov.si/zbirke/delovna-telesa/medresorska-delovna-skupina-za-boj-proti-trgovini-z-ljudmi/>.

17 N. Kogovšek Šalamon and K. Filipčič, 'Trgovina z ljudmi' in D. Korošec, K. Filipčič and S. Zdolšek (eds), *Veliki komentar posebnega dela Kazenskega zakonika*, Uradni list Republike Slovenije, Ljubljana 2018, p. 247.

There were 389 cases of victims of traffickers, of whom 344 were women, four were minors, and only 41 were men. In 89% of the cases, they were victims of sexual exploitation, 8% were forced to commit crimes, and 3% were exploited in other ways (forced labour, servitude, forced begging). Most victims, one in five, were from Ukraine, 15% from Romania, 9% from Hungary, and a significant proportion of Chinese victims – 8.5%. Just under 6% of victims were from Slovenia.[18]

Čurin indicates that in Slovenia, trafficking in human beings is intertwined with other areas of social life, such as migration issues and the exploitation of (mainly foreign) workers. The increase in forced criminal offences as one of the purposes of trafficking in human beings, general security issues, and the problem of children – especially unaccompanied children (applicants for international protection), abused minors forced into begging or girls in servitude under the disguise of forced marriages.[19] All of this makes the problem of trafficking in human beings a multifaceted one that needs to be approached in a comprehensive and coordinated manner.

Trafficking in human beings is defined as the recruitment and disposition of vulnerable individuals or groups (within or outside a country) for the purpose of exploitation (in the form of prostitution or other forms of sexual abuse, forced labour, slavery, servitude and the forced commission of criminal acts), based on payment or other consideration, and on the use of physical force or other violence, fraud, deception, emotional abuse, abuse of social vulnerability – so as to obtain the consent of or control over the victim.[20] Trends in recent years show that the basis of action is no longer physical violence, but psychological violence and emotional blackmail of vulnerable victims who 'voluntarily' enter into a relationship with members of criminal gangs and, because of the financial straitjacket in which they find themselves, are forced to stay and persist in the relationship.[21] Recruitment of victims is also increasingly carried out via the internet and social networks.[22]

Data from the Ministry of the Interior over the last three years show that the predominant type of trafficking offences detected is still that of sexual

18 See P. Malovrh, *Vsaka peta žrtev pri nas je iz Ukrajine*, Delo, (18.10.2021), <https://www.delo.si/novice/slovenija/vsaka-peta-zrtev-pri-nas-je-iz-ukrajine/>.

19 See S. Čurin, 'Kritičen pogled na problematiko trgovine z ljudmi v Sloveniji ob upoštevanju mednarodnih priporočil in evropskega pravnega reda' (2016) 3 *Pravosodni bilten* 87, p. 88.

20 See Ministry of the Interior, *Trgovina z ljudmi*, (09.09.2022), <https://www.gov.si/zbirke/projekti-in-programi/boj-proti-trgovini-z-ljudmi/trgovina-z-ljudmi/>.

21 Inter-ministerial Working Group, Report for year 2020, p. 16, <https://www.gov.si/zbirke/delovna-telesa/medresorska-delovna-skupina-za-boj-proti-trgovini-z-ljudmi/>.

22 *Ibid.*

exploitation of women.[23] These are predominantly third-country nationals from Eastern and South-Eastern Europe who are exploited in prostitution in Slovenia.[24] The 2018 report of the Inter-ministerial Working Group for Combating Trafficking in Human Beings (Inter-ministerial Working Group) notes that the vulnerability of the victims is caused by various personal factors, such as unemployment, poor job prospects, low level of education, low earnings, indebtedness, the obligation to support minor children, disabled or unemployed partners, the obligation to support the extended family, serious illnesses in the family, martial law, etc.[25]

Although human trafficking for forced labour is hardly ever detected by law enforcement authorities, various reports and surveys show that (mainly) foreign workers often work in highly exploitative conditions bordering on forced labour.[26] This is particularly true for industries that employ many unskilled and relatively low-paid foreign workers, such as construction, catering, agriculture, transport, logistics, forestry and food processing. Employers in these sectors also subcontract extensively to Slovenian or foreign companies and

---

23 In 2020, all 27 victims of trafficking were adult women for sexual exploitation (prostitution and sexual abuse), of whom 24 were from Ukraine, 2 from Moldova, and 1 from Romania (*Ibid.*, p. 11). In 2019, victims of trafficking were identified in both sexual exploitation and servitude, with victims also coming from Asia and Africa (China, Taiwan, Madagascar) (Inter-ministerial Working Group, Report for year 2019, p. 15, <https://www.gov.si/zbirke/delovna-telesa/medresorska-delovna-skupina-za-boj-proti-trgovini-z-ljudmi/>). In 2018, alongside sexual exploitation, victims of trafficking for forced labour and forced begging were also detected. Victims also came from countries in Eastern and Southern Europe (Bulgaria, Hungary, Poland, Romania, Slovakia, Ukraine) and Central and South America (Venezuela, Dominican Republic) (101 victims in total). Of these, 67 were victims of trafficking for sexual exploitation (Inter-ministerial Working Group, Report for year 2018, p. 16–17, <https://www.gov.si/zbirke/delovna-telesa/medresorska-delovna-skupina-za-boj-proti-trgovini-z-ljudmi/>,

24 In addition, women from EU countries (such as Romania) are also victims of so-called 'apartment prostitution'. These women do not have a temporary residence permit, are not employed and therefore do not have adequate social and health insurance.

25 Inter-ministerial Working Group, Report for year 2018, above n. 23, p. 24.

26 See D. Frangež and A. Bučar Ručman, 'Specific forms of human trafficking in Slovenia: Overview and preventive measures' (2017) 18:3 *Police Practice and Research* 230. This is also reported in the media – see, for example: M. Zabukovec, 'Trgovina z ljudmi: Zakonodaja naj se prilagodi razmeram' (28.05.2013), <https://old.delo.si/novice/slovenija/trgovina-z-ljudmi-zakonodaja-naj-se-prilagodi-razmeram.html>; M. Zabukovec, 'Migrantski delavci v Sloveniji: Življenje na robu' (15.02.2015), <https://old.delo.si/ozadja/migrantski-delavci-v-sloveniji-zivljenje-na-robu.html>; D. Levpušček, 'Prisilno delo: kako hitro bi vi našli pot ven?' (18.10.2018), <https://www.24ur.com/novice/slovenija/prisilno-delo-kako-hitro-bi-vi-nasli-pot-ven.html>; IUS-INFO, 'Vnovični val tujih delavcev odpira vprašanja o izkoriščanju' (03.06.2019), <https://www.iusinfo.si/medijsko-sredisce/v-srediscu/243404>.

consequently have less control over the working conditions of these workers.[27] As a result, there may be a risk that a particular company is linked to trafficking in human beings for the purpose of forced labour.

Reports from the Workers' Advisory (*Delavska svetovalnica*) – a Slovenian NGO working to help vulnerable groups in the labour market – show that workers in these industries report a number of serious breaches of labour law, such as: severe overwork, unpaid overtime, unpaid social security contributions, work-related injuries, unpaid wage compensation for sickness absences etc.[28] Migrant workers tolerate these violations because their livelihoods and the livelihoods of their families depend on their work in Slovenia.[29] These workers (who come mainly from the former Yugoslav republics)[30] also depend on their employer in Slovenia because of their immigration status, which is temporarily linked to their employment with that employer.[31] Moreover, it is interesting to note that all the annual reports (for 2020, 2019 and 2018) of the Inter-ministerial Working Group identify a very high number of criminal offences in the area of violations of the fundamental rights of workers under Article 196 KZ-1, in which elements of labour exploitation of the victims have been identified.[32] However, at the same time, these reports explicitly state that no elements of forced labour as a form of exploitation of victims of trafficking (under Article 113 KZ-1) were detected in the pre-trial proceedings, nor were

27 Ministry of the Interior, 'Preprečite prisilno delo, priročnik za delodajalce', p. 5, <https://www.gov.si/assets/vladne-sluzbe/UKOM/Boj-proti-trgovini-z-ljudmi/Dokumenti/Prirocnik-za-delodajalce.pdf>.

28 2019 Workers' Advisory Report about the activities carried out on the »PO-MOČ« project and guidelines or recommendations for social partners, especially employers in industries where labour exploitation is most perceived.

29 *Ibid.*, pp. 6–7. Or from working in another European country (e.g. Germany) where Slovenian companies send workers as intermediaries. See D. Frangež and A. Bučar Ručman, above n. 26, p. 238.

30 In October 2019, 101,200 foreigners were working in Slovenia (49,600 from Bosnia and Herzegovina, 12,900 from Serbia, 9,600 from Kosovo, 6,600 from North Macedonia and 8,300 from Croatia (which is now a member of the EU, so its citizens have free access to the Slovenian labour market). Most foreign workers worked in construction (27%), manufacturing (24%), transport and storage (17%) and other miscellaneous business activities (9%), see <https://pxweb.stat.si/SiStat/en>.

31 The research, which included structured interviews with relevant stakeholders, also found that foreign workers were dependent on their employers precisely because of migration legislation. D. Frangež and A. Bučar Ručman, above n. 26, pp. 231, 234–235.

32 Inter-ministerial Working Group, Report for year 2020, p. 12, provides statistics on the treatment of these offences for the period 2016–2020: 3,042 offences of violation of the fundamental rights of workers under Article 196 KZ-1 were processed in 2016; 1,329 in 2017; 1,518 in 2018; 2,384 in 2019 and 2,177 in 2020.

these elements detected in subsequent criminal proceedings.[33] Forced criminality related to trafficking in human beings is also less frequently detected.[34] The police occasionally detect the presence of organised groups or criminal gangs that are suspected of exploiting trafficked persons for the purpose of coercing them to commit crimes.[35] The victims are mainly foreign nationals. In 2018, a total of 32 victims of trafficking in human beings were under consideration for these practices.[36]

A high-profile case in the media and more widely known in recent years is the case of illegal call centres, which resulted in a conviction (for trafficking in human beings under Article 113 KZ-1) of those involved.[37] The accused (three Slovenian citizens, and four persons from Taiwan) locked the victims (at least sixty-three, predominantly from Taiwan) in call centres. They restricted their freedom of movement, isolated them from their surroundings, confiscated their personal documents, money and telephones, and through various instructions, threats and punishments, induced them to commit frauds.[38]

As regards human trafficking for the purpose of forced begging, a study by Frangež and Bučar Ručman has found that victims are also children, minors, elderly or people with disabilities.[39] The perpetrators take advantage of their social hardship. The victims are usually of Romanian or Slovak nationality.[40] However, research also shows that the rapid response of social services and

33 Inter-ministerial Working Group, Report for year 2019, p. 17.
34 Inter-ministerial Working Group, Report for year 2020, p. 10.
35 Inter-ministerial Working Group, Report for year 2019, p. 17.
36 Inter-ministerial Working Group, Report for year 2020, p. 17.
37 In this case, a total of 23 years of imprisonment, fines of EUR 16,000, confiscation of over EUR 110,000 in unlawful gains and deportation of 4 foreigners for 5 years were the result of the proceedings. See Inter-ministerial Working Group, Report for year 2020, p. 17.
38 See: Ministry of the Interior, '*Prva obsodilna sodba zaradi kaznivega dejanja trgovine z ljudmi v primeru nezakonitih klicnih centrov*', (7.10.2019), <https://www.gov.si/novice/2019-10-07-prva-obsodilna-sodba-zaradi-kaznivega-dejanja-trgovine-z-ljudmi-v-primeru-nezakonitih-klicnih-centrov/>; and IUS-INFO, '*Sojenje za nezakonite klicne centre počasi h koncu*', (18.2.2020), <https://www.iusinfo.si/medijsko-sredisce/dnevne-novice/257793>. Moreover, it follows from the additional known circumstances of the case that the victims arrived in Europe on the basis of an advertisement for casual work abroad. The offer and the promised earnings were very tempting. They contacted the provider who bought them the plane ticket. Transport was waiting for them in Vienna. They didn't know where they were being taken, and their documents, phones and money were taken from them. See: T. Klipšteter, Dnevnik, '*Afera klicni centri: Za kazen so po več ur zrli v steno*, 6.4.2020', <https://www.dnevnik.si/1042926542>.
39 D. Frangež and A. Bučar Ručman, above n. 26, pp. 236–237.
40 *Ibid.*, pp. 236–237.

the police to appeals from the population reporting such begging as unwanted makes Slovenia an unsuitable country for forced begging by children.[41] In addition, according to Inter-ministerial Working Group reports, organised groups of beggars (from Slovakia, Bulgaria and Romania) are only occasionally present in the territory of Slovenia, but they do not identify themselves as victims of trafficking in human beings or forced begging and do not want to cooperate with the police. In 2018, 2 victims of forced begging were identified in Slovenia.[42]

Children in Slovenia are less exposed to human trafficking due to institutional care and support from the social services. If they are not living with their original family, children are systematically placed with a foster family. However, cases of forced marriages between children can be found in the context of traditional Roma marriages, where under-age Roma girls get married. These girls do not identify themselves as victims. However, members of Roma communities are also adapting to the Slovenian system and are not marrying before the age of 15,[43] or are simply leaving Slovenia and marrying in countries where they are not prevented by law from doing so (e.g. in Bosnia & Herzegovina).[44] It is worth noting that such Roma marriages may be qualified differently depending on the circumstances – in some cases it is not a criminal offence or a forced marriage (the so-called 'early marriages' or 'Roma style marriages'). In other cases, the legal elements under Article 132a KZ-1 (Forced Marriage), or trafficking in human beings under Article 113 KZ-1 (also in connection with servitude) are fulfilled.[45]

In general, Slovenia is neither a country where transnational corporations have their headquarters or centre of gravity nor a country whose citizens are victims of contemporary slavery in the production (or supply) chain of these corporations. Nor is it a country of origin or destination in the context of global supply chains. Moreover, the migration of Slovenian nationals to more

41 *Ibid.*, p. 237.

42 Inter-ministerial Working Group, Report for year 2020, pp. 17 and 20.

43 In general, the legal age for marriage is 18. Only exceptionally (under certain conditions) the legal age for marriage is 15.

44 D. Frangež and A. Bučar Ručman, above n. 26, pp. 235–236.

45 A guide on how to identify and intervene in cases of early and forced marriage in the Roma community, 2021, pp. 3–5, <https://www.gov.si/assets/vladne-sluzbe/UN/SIFOROMA-4/Urad-za-narodnosti_Nacionalna-platforma-za-Rome_prirocnik_165x240mm.pdf>.

developed countries (mostly to Germany and Austria) for mainly economic reasons are in general not connected to the problem of contemporary slavery.[46]

4 Definition of (Contemporary) Slavery in the Slovenian System

4.1 *The Constitutional Aspects*

The Constitution does not explicitly prohibit slavery. However, the chapter on human rights and fundamental freedoms guarantees freedom of labour in Article 49, which, inter alia, prohibits forced labour in paragraph 4. The Constitution does not define forced labour. The Constitutional Court has also not yet considered any acts that would constitute a violation of human rights on the grounds of forced labour.[47]

According to Blaha, the interpretation of Article 49 of the Constitution takes into account that freedom of labour has its roots in the time and history of the efforts to abolish the most extreme forms of forced labour – slavery, servitude, as well as forced and compulsory labour, as defined in international documents. Although the Constitution explicitly mentions only forced labour, according to Blaha, in view of the obligations under international instruments and the general definition of the constitutional right as the right to freedom of labour, it is undoubtedly clear that the Constitution guarantees protection against any form of unfree labour.[48] There is a unanimous view that the content of the provision of Article 49(4) of the Constitution must be filled in by taking into account the international instruments so that the prohibition of slavery and servitude is an integral part of the prohibition.[49]

4.2 *The Impact of International Legal Sources in the Slovenian System*

Among the international documents that bind Slovenia are the Slavery Convention (1926), which prohibits slavery and the slave trade, and the Supplementary

46 The only mentioned notable exception are the rare (Slovenian national) victims of forced prostitution (exploited in Germany and Italy). Migrants & Refugees, 'Country Profiles: Slovenia', pp. 1, 3, <https://migrants-refugees.va/country-profile/slovenia/>.

47 E. Korpič-Hovat, 'Pravica do dela' (The right to work) (2018) 4:1–2 *Anali PAZU HD* 25, p. 35, <http://hd.anali-pazu.si/sites/default/files/Etelka_K.Horvat.pdf>.

48 M. Blaha, 'Svoboda dela', in L. Šturm (ed), *Komentar Ustave Republike Slovenije*, Faculty of Government and European Studies, Kranj 2010, p. 506. See also: E. Korpič-Hovat, above n. 47.

49 L. Zore, 'Svoboda dela', in M. Avbelj (ed), *Komentar Ustave Republike Slovenije*, New University: European Law Faculty, Nova Gorica 2019, para. 11.

Convention on the Abolition of Slavery (1956) adopted by the UN, which also prohibits slavery-like relationships.

Importantly, the Universal Declaration of Human Rights (1948) states in Article 4 that "no one shall be held in slavery or servitude; slavery and the slave trade in any form shall be prohibited". Slovenia is also bound by both UN Covenants. In addition to prohibiting slavery, the slave trade and servitude, Article 8 of the International Covenant on Civil and Political Rights (1966) stipulates that no one shall be subjected to forced or compulsory labour. The International Covenant on Economic, Social and Cultural Rights (1976), in Article 6, obliges States Parties to recognise the right to work, which includes the right to the opportunity to earn an income through work freely chosen or accepted, and to protect it by appropriate measures.

The UN Convention for the Suppression of the Traffic in Persons and of the Exploitation of the Prostitution of Others (1949) does not contain a definition of trafficking in human beings. Trafficking in women and exploitation of the prostitution of women is also explicitly addressed in the UN Convention on the Elimination of All Forms of Discrimination against Women (1979), which also binds Slovenia. Moreover, Slovenia has also ratified the Protocol to Prevent, Suppress and Punish Trafficking in Persons, especially Women and Children (Palermo Protocol, 2003), which supplements the UN Convention against Transnational Organised Crime. The Palermo Protocol defines trafficking in human beings in Article 3 as:

> the recruitment, transportation, transfer, harbouring or receipt of persons for the purpose of exploitation, by means of the threat or use of force or other forms of coercion, of abduction, of fraud, of deception, of the abuse of power or of a position of vulnerability, or receiving of payments or benefits to achieve the consent of a person having control over another person. Exploitation shall include, at a minimum, the exploitation of prostitution of others or other forms of sexual exploitation, forced labour or services, slavery or practices similar to slavery, servitude or the removal of organs.

The Protocol sets out minimum obligations for States Parties in terms of criminalisation of such practices, their prevention and assistance to victims of trafficking. Slovenia has also ratified the ILO Forced Labour Convention, 1930 (No. 29) and the ILO Abolition of Forced Labour Convention, 1957 (No. 105). ILO Convention No. 29 defines forced labour in Article 2, which states: "Forced or compulsory labour shall mean all work or service which is exacted from any person under the menace of any penalty and for which the said person has not offered himself voluntarily". Furthermore, Slovenia submitted the Forced Labour (Supplementary Measures) Recommendation, 2014 (No. 203).[50] Slovenia has also ratified the ILO Convention concerning the Prohibition and Immediate Action for the Elimination of the Worst Forms of Child Labour, 1999 (No. 182), which defines in Article 3 the worst forms of child labour, including all forms of slavery or slavery-like treatment.[51]

As a member of the Council of Europe, Slovenia is bound by the ECHR, which stipulates in Article 4 that no one shall be held in slavery or servitude or be required to perform forced or compulsory labour. The European Court of Human Rights (ECtHR) has developed a rich body of case law on this provision.[52] While it has not found a violation of the prohibition of slavery, it has identified elements of servitude and forced labour in several cases. Slovenia has also ratified the Council of Europe Convention on Action against Trafficking in Human Beings (2005), which defines trafficking in human beings in the same way as the Palermo Protocol. The Convention builds on that Protocol and applies to all forms of trafficking in human beings, whether national or transnational, linked to organised crime or not, and to all victims of trafficking (women, men and children).

As an EU member, EU acts are also important for Slovenia. The EU Charter of Fundamental Rights, which is part of the EU's primary law, states in Article 5 (Prohibition of slavery and forced labour) that no one shall be held in slavery or servitude, no one shall be required to perform forced or compulsory labour, and that trafficking in human beings shall be prohibited. Directive 2011/36/EU on preventing and combating trafficking in human beings and protecting its victims lays down minimum rules on the definition of offences and penalties in the field of trafficking in human beings,[53] introduces common provisions to strengthen the prevention of offences and the protection of victims of trafficking in human beings – while taking into account a gender perspective.

Starting from the international and regional documents that bind Slovenia, it is clear that Slovenia has undertaken the obligation to prohibit slavery and

---

50 Nonetheless, Slovenia has not ratified the Protocol of 2014 (P029) to the Forced Labour Convention, 1930.

51 See Article 3(a).

52 See, *inter alia*, cases: *Siliadin v. France*, No. 73316/01, ECLI:CE:ECHR:2005:0726JUD007331601; *J. and others v. Austria*, No. 58216/12, ECLI:CE:ECHR:2017:0117JUD005821612; *L.E. v. Greece*, No. 71545/12, ECLI:CE:ECHR:2016:0121JUD007154512; *Chowdury and others v. Greece*, No. 21884/15, ECLI:CE:ECHR:2017:0330JUD002188415.

53 Directive 2011/36/EU of the European Parliament and of the Council of 5 April 2011 on preventing and combating trafficking in human beings and protecting its victims, and replacing Council Framework Decision 2002/629/JHA, OJ L 101, 15.04.2011, p. 1–11.

the slave trade, slavery-like relationships, servitude, forced and compulsory labour and trafficking in human beings. These international instruments have had a significant impact, particularly on criminal law (see section 4.3.). However, like most other countries, Slovenia has not fully complied with all its obligations under the international instruments.[54] The offences of enslavement or slavery-like relationships (including slave trade), trafficking in human beings and, in particular, forced marriage, are defined as criminal offences. Nevertheless, servitude and forced labour, and individual acts that fall within the scope of slavery-like practices are not specifically criminalised. All of these practices are covered only under the constitutional prohibition of slavery, and some are also covered in relation to trafficking in human beings (servitude, forced labour).

4.3 *The Legislative Definition of (Contemporary) Slavery*

4.3.1 Slavery and Slavery-Like Relationships

Article 112 KZ-1 establishes the offence of 'Enslavement', which is committed by:

> whoever, in violation of international law, forces another person into slavery or a similar condition, or keeps another person in such a condition, or buys, sells or delivers another person to a third party, or brokers the buying, selling or delivery of another person, or incites another person to sell his or her freedom or the freedom of a person he or she supports or looks after.[55]

It is therefore a blanket offence, since the perpetrator must be in breach of the rules of international law. Slovenian legal doctrine and jurisprudence rely primarily on the definition in the Slavery Convention (1926) and the Supplementary Convention (1956) to interpret the concept of slavery and slavery-like relationships.[56] One of the few decisions of the courts concerning this offence states:

---

54 See K. Schwarz and J. Allain, 'Antislavery in domestic legislation, An empirical analysis of national prohibition globally', *University of Nottingham*, 2020, p. 11, <https://www.nottingham.ac.uk/research/beacons-of-excellence/rights-lab/resources/reports-and-briefings/2020/february/antislavery-legislation-report.pdf>.

55 The slave or slave-like relationship must already exist at the time the acts are committed. If such a relationship has not yet been established, but this is the aim of the perpetrator's acts, the offence of trafficking in human beings is committed under Article 113 KZ-1, which criminalises the disposition of a person for the purpose of slavery.

56 See K. Filipčič, above n. 2, p. 240.

> Under the rules of international law, slavery is defined as the state or condition of a person over whom all or certain rights are exercised, deriving primarily from the right of property, and consisting in the owner being able to dispose of the person, that is to say, to sell him, to give him as a gift, to lease him, to destroy him, etc.[57]

A person who is placed in a relationship of slavery or a similar relationship is therefore merely an object intended solely for economic exploitation, and his or her freedom is completely restricted.[58] The unlawful situation is thus established when the perpetrator acquires ownership or possession of the person.[59]

The criminalization under Article 112 KZ-1 also covers slavery-like relationships, which, taking into account the Supplementary Convention (1956), include debt bondage, serfdom, the sale of a woman for marriage, the handing over of a woman to another person for a certain equivalent, a situation where a woman belongs to another person after the death of her husband, the handing over of a child to another person by a parent or guardian for the purpose of exploitation of the child and the child's labour.[60] This offence does not include forced labour.[61] The Supplementary Convention does not list it as a slavery-like situation. The Forced Labour Convention (1926) provides that measures must be taken to prevent forced labour from degenerating into a slavery-like situation. Forced labour is therefore not in itself slavery. It is also clear from ECtHR case *Siliadin v France* in relation to Article 4 ECHR that the exploitation of workers (forced labour) may constitute slavery if it is accompanied by other elements of a slavery relationship, such as humiliation, restriction of liberty and the treatment of a person as an object.[62]

---

57 Higher Court in Ljubljana (VSL) judgment I Kp 1596/2006 of 20.12.2007.

58 In the present case, the Court found that the circumstances were not such as to constitute a slave-like or slavery-like relationship. All the girls had their own mobile phones, the flat in which they lived had a landline telephone, the girls were not locked in the flat but could move freely outside it, e.g., to go shopping in the city, and all the girls were paid the same wages for their work. According to the Court, slavery could only be established if the purchase of the victims as objects could be proven and, at the same time, the new 'owner' prevented them from moving freely and, therefore, the women were in a situation which they could not change without the owner's consent. See Higher Court in Ljubljana (VSL) judgment I Kp 1596/2006 of 20.12.2007.

59 K. Filipčič, above n. 2, p. 242.

60 *Ibid.*, p. 240.

61 *Ibid.*, pp. 240–241.

62 See *Siliadin v France,* No. 73316/01, ECLI:CE:ECHR:2005:0726JUD007331601.

4.3.2 Trafficking in Human Beings

The concept of exploitation is key to the definition of trafficking in human beings. Article 113 KZ-1 provides that the offence is punishable:

> Whoever purchases, takes possession of, accommodates, transports, sells, delivers or uses another person in any other way, or recruits, exchanges or transfers control over another person or acts as a broker in such operations, for the purpose of exploiting prostitution or other forms of sexual exploitation, forced labour, slavery, servitude, or committing the criminal offences of trafficking in organs, human tissue or blood.[63]

It follows from the above definition that the two key elements of the offence are the various acts of disposing of the victim and their purpose, which is to exploit the victim.[64] This is either the exploitation of the victim's prostitution, forced labour, slavery, servitude, the commission of a crime or the trafficking of organs.

The aforementioned offence of trafficking in human beings was introduced into Slovenian KZ-1 in 2004 as a result of the implementation of the Palermo Protocol and later amended several times due to other international instruments in this area. However, until recently, there were speculations as to whether the phenomenon of trafficking in human beings was even present in Slovenia. Given that the most common form of trafficking in human beings perceived in Slovenia is related to prostitution, such acts were often treated as mere abuse of prostitution[65] – due to the ease of provability of this crime and the interconnectedness of these acts.[66] This approach neglected other forms of human trafficking.

An analysis of the case law shows that the crime of trafficking in human beings (Article 113 KZ-1) is often treated together with the crime of abuse of prostitution (Article 175 KZ-1), and the Supreme Court has already pointed out the importance of the distinction between the two.[67] As is clear from the

---

63 The law makes it clear that the victim's consent does not exclude criminality. The reason is that due to the victims' economic and social situation it is impossible to argue that their actions are voluntary (they are being forced to do so due to hardship).

64 N. Kogovšek Šalamon and K. Filipčič, above n. 17, p. 248.

65 According to Article 175 KZ-1, the offence of abuse of prostitution is committed by "Whoever participates for exploitative purposes in the prostitution of another or instructs, obtains or encourages another to engage in prostitution by force, threats or deception."

66 See S. Čurin, above n. 19, p. 88.

67 See the judgment of the Supreme Court XI Ips 11586/2015–241 of 24.04.2015.

judgment of the Supreme Court X Kp 13636/2016, the crime of trafficking in human beings is a crime against humanity, while the crime of abuse of prostitution is a crime against sexual integrity. The essential distinction between the two is the position of the victim, who, in the crime of trafficking in human beings, has the status of an object, a dehumanised individual without free will (regardless of any consent she may have given). Whereas in the crime of the abuse of prostitution, she still has the status of a subject (she retains a certain degree of autonomy and sexual self-determination).[68] Only if the court finds that:

> forced prostitution (physical or psychological) exists and, in particular, that the various forms of coercion render prostitution a condition which the victim cannot or dare not resist for reasons of economic, physical, intellectual or other reasons which demonstrate her vulnerability and powerlessness, can the offence of trafficking in human beings be committed. The essence of the offence of trafficking in human beings is therefore that the individual is disposed of as a commodity.[69]

In this context, it is also worth recalling the ECtHR's decision in *Rantsev v. Cyprus and Russia,*[70] in which the ECtHR clearly interpreted the scope of Article 4 of the ECHR as including the prohibition of trafficking in human beings. The Court found that trafficking in human beings is very similar to slavery in that the traffickers have power equivalent to ownership (although not ownership in the legal sense). It also found that trafficking in human beings threatens the human dignity and fundamental freedoms of the victims and cannot be understood as compatible with the principles of a democratic society and the values expressed in the ECHR.[71] In doing so, the ECtHR confirmed the jurisprudence of the International Criminal Tribunal for the former Yugoslavia (ICTY),[72] that trafficking in human beings is in fact a contemporary form of

68 See para. 111 of the grounds of the judgment. Similarly, see the judgment of the Higher Court in Ljubljana (VSL) II Kp 11523/2016 of 14.12.2018.

69 See paragraphs 112 and 113 of the reasoning of the judgment of Higher Court in Ljubljana (VSL) X Kp 13636/2016 of 29.06.2020. See also the judgment of the Supreme Court I Ips 2897/2009 of 10.11.2011, where the elements of trafficking in human beings were established.

70 *Rantsev v. Cyprus and Russia,* No. 25965/04, ECLI:CE:ECHR:2010:0107JUD002596504.

71 See S. Čurin, above n. 19, p. 91.

72 See ICTY, Prosecutor v. Kunarac, Vukovic and Kovac, Judgment of 12.06.2002.

slavery.[73] As the ICTY *Kunarac* case makes clear, the elements that may constitute contemporary slavery are:

> control of someone's movement, control of physical environment, psychological control, measures taken to prevent or deter escape, force, threat of force or coercion, duration, assertion of exclusivity, subjection to cruel treatment and abuse, control of sexuality and forced labour.[74]

4.3.3 The Concepts of Servitude and Forced or Compulsory Labour

As mentioned above, the offence of trafficking in human beings (Article 113 KZ-1) covers the various dispositions of human beings with a view to their exploitation, whether for prostitution, slavery, servitude, forced labour or other purposes. The concepts of servitude and forced labour are not defined in Slovenian legislation, and it is, therefore, necessary to take into account the definitions of these concepts as derived from the international instruments binding on Slovenia (ECHR, UN Covenant, ILO Conventions on forced labour). In accordance with Article 8 of the Constitution, ratified and published international treaties are directly applicable, and Slovenian legislation must comply with the generally applicable principles of international law and with the international treaties binding on Slovenia. Given that Slovenia is bound by all relevant regional and global international legal sources in the relevant field, these institutions are recognised as peremptory norms at international law, as the national legal order does not provide for any derogations from international standards in any case.

The ECtHR's decisions make it clear that, unlike slavery, where someone owns the other person completely (in legal terms), servitude is about other, less far-reaching forms of control over the individual, which the individual cannot avoid or change.[75] As is clear from the *Siliadin* case, where the ECtHR found the existence of servitude, the latter is characterised by a particular form of

73 A. Tratnik, 'Trgovina z ljudmi je samostojno prepovedano dejanje' (2010) *Pravna praksa*, 2010, 8, pp. 26–27.

74 See ICTY, Prosecutor v. Kunarac, Vukovic and Kovac, Judgment of 12.06.2002, para. 119. See also V. Mantouvalou, 'The Prohibition of Slavery, Servitude and Forced and Compulsory Labour under Article 4 ECHR' in F. Dorssemont, K. Lörcher and I. Schömann (eds), *The European Convention on Human Rights and the Employment Relation*, Hart Publishing, London 2013, p. 149.

75 M. Blaha, above n. 48, p. 509.

coercion.[76] The person is unfree, does the work of a servant, lives with another person, and cannot escape because he would become an undocumented immigrant.[77] When defining this relationship as servitude, the ECtHR considered it crucial that it was a "particular serious form of denial of freedom".[78]

The definition of trafficking in human beings for the purpose of exploiting servitude is based on one of the few decisions of this kind in the Supreme Court judgment XI Ips 17546/2017. The Court identified the latter in the conduct of the perpetrators who recruited the victims as nannies lured them to Slovenia for the purpose of performing unpaid or underpaid work. It was established that the perpetrators deceived the victims about the pay and the nature of the work and abused the subordinate (dependent) position and vulnerability of the victims. The latter stemmed from the adverse socio-economic situation in Serbia, Bosnia and Herzegovina and Croatia – manifested in poverty, lack of social inclusion and poor employability of the victims. Moreover, the victims were required to work all days of the week and for a significant part of the day – more than 15 hours –, with mental and physical ill-treatment and restriction of movement.

Although the Constitution prohibits forced labour, neither criminal nor labour legislation in Slovenia concretises this prohibition. Thus, the legislation does not define forced labour, and there are no (published) court decisions defining forced labour in relation to trafficking in human beings. In Slovenian legal doctrine, forced labour is defined in accordance with the definition set out in Article 2 of ILO Convention No. 29 and Article 4 of the ECHR (as defined by the ECtHR). The ILO Convention definition consists of two elements, namely that the work is performed under threat of punishment and that it is not voluntary/freely chosen. The ILO supervisory bodies define the first element to include not only punishment of a criminal offence but also in the form of loss of rights or privileges, financial penalties, loss of employment, and registration as an undocumented (illegal) migrant. The second element is represented by various forms of external or indirect coercion (e.g., the worker is not free to stop working, the person is kidnapped or sold to another, physical

76 A girl (minor) from Togo lived with a family in France, where she had to do housework, for which she was not paid. She was also without documents and money.

77 E. Korpič-Hovat, above n. 47, p. 33.

78 V. Mantouvalou, above n. 74, p. 146.

confinement in a room, false promises as to the nature of the work and working conditions, non-payment of wages, withholding of identity documents etc.).[79]

A similar definition can be drawn from the decisions of the ECtHR.[80] The forms of threats can be different: financial (non-payment of wages or low wages, non-payment of social security contributions, loss of employment, loss of privileges, etc.), physical (the person is kidnapped, works in impossible conditions, has his/her documents taken away, performs dangerous work without security protection and in an unhealthy working environment, lives in inadequate premises etc.), and psychological (threatening to report the person to the police etc.). As regards voluntariness, it is crucial that the person does not perform the work voluntarily. The person works in such exploitative conditions and in a situation where basic human rights are violated because he/she has no other choice.[81] Unlike servitude, forced labour is of a temporary nature.[82]

4.3.4 Indicators of Contemporary Slavery

The concept of contemporary slavery is not mentioned and not defined in Slovenian legislation. At the national level, the concept of trafficking in human beings, which is referred to as contemporary slavery, is highlighted in this regard.[83] The Government's website on combating trafficking in human beings states that:

> the most common and widely recognised definition of trafficking in human beings is the trafficking of women and children, as particularly vulnerable categories of persons, for the purpose of sexual abuse and exploitation. However, trafficking in human beings is also intended to serve the needs of modern-day slavery, labour exploitation, begging, organ trafficking and so on.[84]

Contemporary slavery, therefore, encompasses various forms of exploitation of human beings that make them commodities (objects of disposition), such

79 M. Novak, P. Končar, A. Bubnov Škoberne (eds) *Konvencije Mednarodne organizacije dela s komentarjem*, GV Založba, Ljubljana 2006, p. 82.

80 In addition to those already mentioned, see for example *Chowdury and Others v Greece*, No. 21884/15, ECLI:CE:ECHR:2017:0330JUD002188415; *J and Others v Austria*, No. 58216/12, ECLI:CE:ECHR:2017:0117JUD005821612.

81 E. Korpič-Hovat, above n. 47, pp. 34–35.

82 M. Blaha, above n. 48, p. 509.

83 See Ministry of Internal Affairs, 'Trgovina z ljudmi' *Republika Slovenija*, <https://www.gov.si/zbirke/projekti-in-programi/boj-proti-trgovini-z-ljudmi/trgovina-z-ljudmi/>.

84 *Ibid.*

as prostitution (especially of women and children) or other forms of sexual abuse, forced labour, slavery, servitude, the commission of crimes, forced begging, and others.

Indicators of the different forms of contemporary slavery can be found in the 'Handbook on the Identification, Assistance and Protection of Victims of Trafficking in Human Beings' (2016),[85] which was prepared by the Interministerial Working Group.[86] The Handbook is intended for state bodies and institutions as well as NGOs that deal with trafficking in human beings in their work. It also contains indicators to facilitate the identification of potential victims of trafficking in human beings.[87] In addition to general indicators[88] and behavioural indicators,[89] indicators for the identification of trafficked minors are also presented, as well as indicators regarding the specific forms of exploitation – sexual exploitation, forced begging or the commission of criminal offences and forced labour.[90]

---

85 Handbook on the Identification, 'Assistance and Protection of Victims of Trafficking in Human Beings', 2016, <https://www.gov.si/assets/vladne-sluzbe/UKOM/Boj-proti-trgovini-z-ljudmi/Dokumenti/Prirocnik-o-identifikaciji-pomoci-in-zasciti-zrtev-trgovine-z-ljudmi.pdf>.

86 It is based on the Report on the implementation of the Council of Europe Convention on Action against Trafficking in Human Beings in Slovenia and the list of GRETA recommendations.

87 Handbook on the Identification, Assistance and Protection of Victims of Trafficking in Human Beings, 2016, pp. 21–28. In addition, indicators have been added to identify the perpetrators of trafficking in human beings (see *ibid.*, p. 29).

88 For example, the person does not know which country he/she is in; he/she does not know the address where he/she will be staying; if several people are travelling, they have similar clothes or similar travel bags; he/she is in possession of a forged travel document or a forged residence permit etc.

89 For example, a person arrives at a border checkpoint as part of a group, but at the check point presents himself as an individual traveler, pretends not to know the other people travelling with him, acts very passive, especially if separated from the group leader/officer; is visibly restless; acts scared; behaves as instructed etc.

90 Regarding forced labour, the Handbook makes it clear that all labour exploitation is not human trafficking for the purpose of forced labour. The offence of trafficking in human beings under Article 113 KZ-1 is committed if there are indicators of the act (disposing of the person) and the means used (for example, threat), combined with indicators of forced labour (for the purpose of which the person is disposed of). These indicators are: the worker is required to perform work/hazardous work without adequate safety protection; the worker does not have adequate training and experience to work safely; the worker lives in the area where the work is being performed; there is a perceived increased presence of workers of one ethnic group in the work environment; the worker is forced to perform unauthorised and degrading work; the worker is working in an unhealthy working environment, the workers appear to be exhausted; the standards for working conditions are severely violated and are not in compliance with labour legislation; the workers are

4.4 *The Importance of the Concept of Contemporary Slavery*

In my opinion, the term contemporary slavery may be an appropriate label for various forms of restriction of human freedom to work and to earn a livelihood. However, the fact that the content of this umbrella term is not clearly defined at the international (much less national) level may have a negative impact on the prevention and elimination of such phenomena. In the Slovenian legal order, it is mainly associated with trafficking in human beings, leaving other forms (such as forced labour and servitude) in the background, even though Slovenia is bound by international instruments, which also prohibit them all. Therefore, in my view, the interpretation of this concept should be sufficiently universal and dynamic to cover the different forms that are emerging.[91] It is also necessary to spread awareness about the content of this concept.[92] Currently, no specific discussion or activity in Slovenia regarding the definition of this concept is to be found.

5 Slovenia's Approach to Contemporary Slavery

5.1 *The Legal Framework to Address Contemporary Slavery*

At the level of human rights, Article 49 of the Constitution (freedom to work) is of particular importance in the Slovenian legal order. Freedom to work implies an obligation to prevent impermissible interference with this right. According to the ECtHR,[93] this right also requires the State, in particular regarding the

---

not paid or are paid less than normal; the worker is required to work when ill or heavily pregnant; the employer does not provide the employment contract at the time of the inspection; the employer does not pay contributions; the worker is required to work overtime without adequate pay; working hours are very loosely defined or not defined at all; the worker must be available 24 hours a day, seven days a week to carry out the work; the worker carries out the work in the employer's private residence; the worker cannot take a break, a day off or a holiday. Indicators for other forms of exploitation are defined in a similar way.

91 See K. Bales, 'Addressing contemporary forms of slavery in EU external policy', Briefing paper, European Parliament, 2013, p. 5, <https://www.europarl.europa.eu/RegData/etudes/note/join/2013/433703/EXPO-DROI_NT(2013)433703_EN.pdf>.

92 See S. Scarpa and J. Cabot, 'Contemporary forms of slavery', European Parliament, 2018, p. 6, <https://www.europarl.europa.eu/RegData/etudes/STUD/2018/603470/EXPO_STU(2018)603470_EN.pdf>.

93 See, *inter alia*, cases: *Siliadin v. France*, No. 73316/01, ECLI:CE:ECHR:2005:0726JUD007331601; *J. and others v. Austria*, No. 58216/12, ECLI:CE:ECHR:2017:0117JUD005821612; *L.E. v. Greece*, No. 71545/12, ECLI:CE:ECHR:2016:0121JUD007154512; Chowdury and others v. Greece, No. 21884/15, ECLI:CE:ECHR:2017:0330JUD002188415.

prohibition of forced labour, to take certain positive measures to deter infringements of that prohibition or to protect individuals affected by infringements. The prohibition of forced labour is binding on the widest possible range of potential violators (e.g. the state, private subjects etc.) of this right.[94]

There is no specific law in Slovenia that comprehensively covers all forms of contemporary slavery, prevents them, and provides for the protection of victims. The legal prohibition of specific forms of contemporary slavery in Slovenia and the protection of victims is mainly the result of the implementation of binding international instruments in the field of criminal and immigration law. Criminal law is key to regulating contemporary forms of slavery in Slovenia (see section 5.2.). Labour law does not explicitly prohibit forced labour, nor does it specifically regulate the protection of workers in particularly exploitative working conditions. These workers are also only protected by general labour law. Only the Foreigners Act[95] and the Employment, Self-employment and Work of Foreigners Act (- ZZSDT)[96] provide for specific protection for foreign workers who are victims of trafficking in human beings (see section 5.3.). It should be noted, however, that Slovenia is also active in raising awareness of the problem of trafficking in human beings and other forms of contemporary slavery and their prevention, as well as systematically providing assistance to victims of crime (see section 5.4.).

5.2 *Criminal Law Protection*

In the case of the offence of slavery or slavery-like relationship (Article 112 KZ-1), the offender is sentenced to imprisonment for a term of 1 to 10 years, and in the case of a qualified form (if the victim is a minor), for a term of 3 to 15 years. It is also a criminal offence to transport a person in a slavery or slavery-like relationship from one country to another, punishable by imprisonment for a term of 6 months to 5 years.

The offence of trafficking in human beings (Article 113 KZ-1) covers offences committed both on national and international level, which is very important given that it is a global phenomenon and that the victims are very often foreign nationals.[97] The perpetrator is liable to imprisonment for between 1 to 10 years

94 L. Zore, above n. 49, para. 16.

95 OJ RS, No. 91/21 and 95/21.

96 OJ RS, No. 91/21 – official consolidated text.

97 N. Kogovšek Šalamon and K. Filipčič, above n. 17, p. 247.

and a fine. If the act is committed in a particularly reprehensible manner it is punishable by a prison sentence of 3 to 15 years of imprisonment.[98]

It can be observed that the Slovenian regime is stricter than the regime in Directive 2011/36/EU and in the Protocol. The perpetrator fulfils the legal elements of the offence of trafficking in human beings, even if he does not use force, threat, persuasion, abduction or similar means, which are included in the basic definition of trafficking in human beings in the Protocol and the Directive. However, by using such means, the perpetrator commits a qualified form of the offence under the Slovenian KZ-1. Furthermore, under KZ-1, the consent of the victim is in any case not taken into account (neither in the case of the basic nor in the case of the qualified form of the offence).[99] Article 113(3) KZ-1 also specifically criminalises preparatory acts for the offence of trafficking in human beings – withholding, taking, concealing, damaging or destroying documents proving the identity of the victim (passport, identity card).[100] The user of services of a victim of trafficking in human beings is also liable to a penalty (up to 3 years imprisonment) if he/she knows that the service provider is a trafficking victim.[101]

Since 2015, Article 132a KZ-1 defines a specific offence of forced marriage. A perpetrator who, by means of force or threat of force or by abuse of a position of subordination or dependence, forces another to enter into a marriage or to establish a similar union, is liable to imprisonment for up to 3 years, or, if the act is committed in the case of a minor or a person who is frail, to imprisonment for up to 5 years.[102] In this respect, our legal system also takes into account Article 42 of the Istanbul Convention, according to which culture,

---

98 If the act is committed against a minor or by means of force, threat, deception, abduction or abuse of a position of subordination or dependence, or by giving or receiving payments or benefits in order to obtain the consent of a person having control over another person, or with the intent to coerce pregnancy or artificial insemination.

99 Such an explicit legal provision reflects the fact that victims of trafficking in human beings often 'voluntarily' choose to participate in trafficking due to their difficult socio-economic situation – making it difficult to speak of true voluntariness. See Maribor Higher Court (VSM) Judgment II Kp 54529/2010 of 14.12.2017, para. 21. See also N. Kogovšek Šalamon and K. Filipčič, above n. 17, p. 251.

100 It is the implementation of Article 20 of the Council of Europe Convention on Action against Trafficking in Human Beings.

101 This implements Article 18 of Directive 2011/36/EU. See also N. Kogovšek Šalamon and K. Filipčič, above n. 17, p. 247.

102 According to Slovenian legal doctrine, Article 37 of the Istanbul Convention has thus been properly implemented. See B. Novak, K. Filipčič and N. Kogovšek Šalamon 'Prisilna sklenitev zakonske zveze ali vzpostavitev podobne skupnosti' in D. Korošec, K. Filipčič and S. Zdolšek (eds), *Veliki komentar posebnega dela Kazenskega zakonika*, Uradni list Republike Slovenije, Ljubljana 2018, pp. 550–551.

custom, religion, tradition or so-called 'honour' shall not be considered as a justification for forced marriages and other impermissible practices. This is also confirmed by case law.[103]

In the context of trafficking in human beings for the purpose of exploitation of forced labour, the offence under Article 199 KZ-1 regarding undeclared/illegal employment (of both domestic and foreign workers) is also relevant. The second paragraph of this Article criminalises illegal employment of foreigners,[104] while the third paragraph criminalises the qualified form of conduct referred to in the second paragraph – if it is committed by employing workers under particularly exploitative conditions or by exploiting a victim of trafficking in human beings. In this case, the penalty is imprisonment for up to 3 years. The third paragraph also implements the requirements of Directive 2009/52/EC,[105] although Slovenian legal doctrine points out that the implementation is inconsistent. The Directive obliges States to criminalise the employment of an illegally staying third-country national who is a victim of trafficking in human beings. Given that Articles 199(1) and (2) KZ-1 refer only to the employment of two or more workers, the qualified form of the third paragraph is also committed only in the case of the employment of two or more victims of trafficking in human beings (and not in the case of the employment of a single victim).[106] On the other hand, it is to be welcomed that KZ-1 provides for a

103 In the case of a forced marriage of a minor the Court ruled (before the enactment of the specific offence under Article 132a KZ-1), that this act was trafficking in human beings (for the purpose of slavery and servitude) under Article 113 KZ-1, and that no conduct, nor tradition and custom, could justify what had happened to the victim. In the case at hand the three accomplices (father, mother and son) bought an under-age girl in Macedonia for EUR 6,000, with the intention that she would marry their son. The purchase price was handed over to her father in Macedonia, where the perpetrator and the victim were immediately married. Upon arrival in Slovenia, the victim's movement, contact and communication were restricted. She was exploited as a domestic servant, doing domestic work for all members of her family, working unpaid on construction sites and farms. The consequences of the physical and psychological violence placed the victim in a position of total subordination and dependence, as she was influenced by religious customs that demanded female obedience (Supreme Court Judgment I Ips 5830/2014 of 23.11.2017).

104 The offence is committed by anyone who "subsequently or permanently or in significant numbers employs foreigners who are not EU citizens and reside illegally in the territory of the Republic of Slovenia". The provision implements Directive 2009/52/EC.

105 Directive 2009/52/EC of the European Parliament and of the Council of 18 June 2009 providing for minimum standards on sanctions and measures against employers of illegally staying third-country nationals, OJ L 013 p. 133–141.

106 K. Filipčič and L. Tičar, 'Zaposlovanje na črno' in D. Korošec, K. Filipčič and S. Zdolšek (eds), *Veliki komentar posebnega dela Kazenskega zakonika*, Uradni list Republike Slovenije, Ljubljana 2018, pp. 379–380.

higher prison sentence for the qualified forms of the offence under paragraph 3 than under paragraphs 1 and 2 (although this is not explicitly required by Directive 2009/52/EC).

It should also be noted that in Slovenia, victims of trafficking in human beings who have been forced to commit a crime are generally not prosecuted. This is based on Article 23 KZ-1, which provides that an act committed under the influence of force which the perpetrator was unable to resist is not a criminal offence.[107]

5.3 *Protection of Victims of Contemporary Forms of Slavery from the Perspective of Labour and Immigration Law*

Victims of the various forms of contemporary slavery have mainly criminal law protection. However, workers also have general labour law protection and the possibility to initiate misdemeanour and inspection procedures through the infringements of labour law and legislation on the employment of foreigners, on undeclared work and on the posting of workers. Control of infringements is carried out by the Labour Inspectorate and by the Financial Administration. Although access to specialised labour courts in Slovenia is guaranteed to all workers, foreign workers are even more likely than nationals to be unaware of their rights and to fear enforcing protection or reporting violations due to the prospect of losing their jobs and, thus, their residence permits.[108]

With regard to the participation of victims of trafficking in human beings[109] in criminal proceedings, given the fact that the victims are usually foreign nationals, the immigration legislation is also relevant, as it allows them to legally reside in Slovenia during this period (Article 50 Foreigners Act).[110] A victim of trafficking in human beings who is residing illegally in Slovenia is permitted by the police, at the victim's request or ex officio, to stay in Slovenia for a period of 90 days in order to decide whether to participate as a witness in criminal proceedings.[111] During the period of permitted stay, they also have the right to free translation and interpretation, and the police and NGOs must inform them about the possibility and conditions for obtaining a

107 S. Čurin, above n. 19, p. 96.

108 See D. Frangež and A. Bučar Ručman, above n. 26, p. 235.

109 And also victims of illegal employment (employment of illegally staying third-country nationals). These are victims of the offences under Article 199(2) and (3) KZ-1 (which implement Directive 2009/52/EC).

110 This provision implements the provisions of the Istanbul Convention and Article 14(1) of the Council of Europe Convention on Action against Trafficking in Human Beings.

111 The victim is also not penalised for any illegal border crossing.

residence permit. A temporary residence permit may be issued to a victim of trafficking in human beings if he/she is willing to participate as a witness in criminal proceedings and if there are personal circumstances justifying his/her stay in Slovenia.[112] A victim of trafficking in human beings who has no means of subsistence is also exempted from the payment of the administrative fee, the cost of printed materials and the costs of interpretation and translation in the procedure for issuing a temporary residence permit. The temporary residence permit is issued for the duration of the criminal proceedings or personal circumstances for up to 1 year (with the possibility of subsequent 1-year extensions). A victim of trafficking in human beings who has been granted a temporary residence permit and has no means of subsistence is also entitled to emergency health care and financial assistance. A victim of trafficking in human beings may also work in Slovenia, in accordance with Article 6 ZZSDT.[113]

However, under the current legal framework, not all victims of trafficking in human beings can claim the right to compensation under the Crime Victim Compensation Act,[114] as this law only allows Slovenian nationals or other EU Member States nationals to do so. GRETA calls on Slovenia to amend its legislation accordingly in this respect.[115] In this connection, it should also be noted that an employer or contracting authority who has been convicted of the offence of enslavement or trafficking in human beings is prohibited from employing or working with foreigners for five years from the date on which the conviction becomes final (Article 42 ZZSDT).

5.4 *Preventive and Protective Measures*

Slovenia became actively involved in the fight against trafficking in human beings in 2002 with the creation of the Inter-ministerial Working Group[116] and

112 In this case, the foreign national, who is a victim of trafficking in human beings, is assigned a legal residence at the address of the social work centre (if he/she is not required to register his/her permanent or temporary residence under the provisions of Residence Registration Act, OJ RS, No. 52/16, 36/21 in 3/22 – ZDeb). This legal amendment to Residence Registration Act, introduced in 2021, represents one of the bureaucratic reliefs for victims of trafficking in human beings.

113 They have free access to the labour market, which means they do not need a single permit as is the case for non-EU nationals.

114 Crime Victim Compensation Act, OJ RS, No. 101/05, 114/06 – ZUE and 86/10.

115 GRETA, 'Report concerning the implementation of the Council of Europe Convention on Action against Trafficking in Human Beings by Slovenia', 2018, p. 30–31, <https://rm.coe.int/greta-2017-38-fgr-svn-en/168078919e>.

116 The work of the Inter-ministerial Working Group involves representatives of nine ministries and government offices, the Police, the Financial Office and the Labour Inspectorate.

the appointment of the National Coordinator for Combating Trafficking in Human Beings.[117] They are also professionally supported by the Office for Preventing and Combating Trafficking in Human Beings of the Ministry of the Interior.[118] In its regular annual reports, the Inter-Ministerial Working Group informs the Government, the National Assembly,[119] and the public about the activities carried out. In its two-year action plans, it defines its specific tasks in the areas of legislation, prevention, detection, investigation and prosecution of crimes, assistance and protection of victims, and cooperation in the framework of regional and international organisations.[120] The State also regularly finances the activities resulting from the Action Plan.

To prevent violations, a number of manuals have also been adopted for different stakeholders on the issue of contemporary slavery, including:
- Handbook on the identification, assistance and protection of victims of trafficking in human beings[121]
- Guide for employers: Prevent forced labour[122]
- A guide on how to identify and intervene in cases of early and forced marriage in the Roma community[123]

Representatives of the Specialised State Prosecutor's Office, National Assembly, *Ključ* Association, Slovenian Caritas, Slovenian Philanthropy, Legal Centre for the Protection of Human Rights and the Slovenian Free Trade Unions Association also participate in the work of the group as independent external members.

117 It manages the Inter-ministerial Working Group and coordinates the work of the competent state bodies, NGOs and humanitarian organisations in the field of preventing and combating trafficking in human beings.

118 Inter-ministerial Working Group Report for year 2020, p. 3.

119 Annual reports and action plans are presented to the National Assembly's Committee on Petitions, Human Rights and Equal Opportunities.

120 Ministry of the Interior, 'Medresorska delovna skupina za boj proti trgovini z ljudmi', <https://www.gov.si/zbirke/delovna-telesa/medresorska-delovna-skupina-za-boj-proti-trgovini-z-ljudmi/>.

121 The manual covers the rights of victims of trafficking in human beings, the procedures for dealing with identified victims in care programmes, the police procedures for assisting and ensuring the safety of victims, and the rights and obligations of (towards) victims in relation to international protection procedures and their return to their country of origin, see Ministry of the Interior, 'Pomoč in zaščita žrtev trgovine z ljudmi', <https://www.gov.si/zbirke/projekti-in-programi/boj-proti-trgovini-z-ljudmi/pomoc-in-zascita-zrtev/>.

122 Ministry of the Interior, 2020, 'Prevent Forced Labour, A Guide for Employers', <https://www.gov.si/assets/vladne-sluzbe/UKOM/Boj-proti-trgovini-z-ljudmi/Dokumenti/Prirocnik-za-delodajalce.pdf>.

123 The Handbook is a necessary and useful tool for institutions and organisations working with the Roma community. It contains information gathered in one place, namely general facts and experiences. The issues and legislation are presented in a brief and clear way, the existing procedures for action, concrete examples of how the procedures have been dealt with in practice, and contacts of the most experienced NGOs working in the fields related

Further preventive measures include direct outreach to groups potentially at risk of trafficking (for example, adolescents in Roma centres)[124] and raising awareness (and providing advice and advocacy) for potential victims of labour exploitation and forced labour.[125]

In 2019, prevention activities focused on four target groups: the general public, target risk groups, potential service users and the professional public. To this end, the Government co-financed five projects by NGOs and humanitarian organisations for a total of EUR 30,000. In addition to the regular annual training of civil servants whose work is related to the issue of trafficking in human beings, awareness-raising and training of health professionals was also carried out within the framework of a project funded by the Ministry of Health.[126] Awareness-raising and training of the professional public (criminologists, police officers, social workers, inspectors, public prosecutors, judges, ministry staff) is also carried out on a regular basis.[127]

In the context of work with victims of trafficking in human beings, a number of projects and social programmes are underway to protect and assist victims.[128] Firstly, 'Programme for the care of victims of trafficking in human beings' – crisis accommodation (provides all support to the victim, from accommodation to psychosocial counselling. 24-hour availability of a professional worker is guaranteed for persons in crisis accommodation). Secondly, 'Project care for victims of trafficking in human beings' – accommodation in a safe space' (implemented by the NGO *Ključ* Association – two victims were included in the programme in 2020). Thirdly, 'Project reintegration of victims of trafficking in human beings' (support in all aspects of the victim's reintegration and functioning in society). Fourthly, 'Project information for victims of trafficking in human beings, sexual and gender-based violence' performed within procedures for granting international protection.

However, the 2020 report highlights as an important issue that, due to the COVID-19 epidemic, prevention activities have been carried out to a much

to this issue are listed – to which institutions, other organisations and individuals can turn for help or cooperation. See: Office of the Government of the Republic of Slovenia for Nationalities, 'Priročnik o prepoznavanju zgodnjih in prisilnih porok v romski skupnosti in o ukrepanju v teh primerih', <https://www.gov.si/zbirke/projekti-in-programi/krepitev-nacionalnega-posvetovalnega-procesa-nacionalna-platforma-za-rome-siforoma-3/prirocnik-o/>.

124 Inter-ministerial Working Group Report for year 2020, p. 7.

125 Inter-ministerial Working Group Report for year 2019, p. 9.

126 *Ibid.*, p. 31.

127 Inter-ministerial Working Group Report for year 2020, p. 9.

128 See Inter-ministerial Working Group Report for year 2019, pp. 9 and 31, Inter-ministerial Working Group Report for year 2020, pp. 9, 22–23.

lesser extent than in the past, particularly in the area of training of professionals dealing with trafficking in human beings and awareness-raising among vulnerable groups.[129]

6 Coordinated Initiatives on Contemporary Slavery and Slovenia

Slovenia participates in the informal Network of Anti-Trafficking Coordinators of South-East Europe (NATC SEE), which is specifically focused on trafficking. It was established in 2010 at the initiative of Slovenia. This network exchanges information, good practices and experiences.[130] From the perspective of Slovenia, the network is a particularly important contribution to strengthening regional cooperation in the fight against trafficking in human beings.[131]

An informal network of EU National Rapporteurs on Preventing Trafficking in Human Beings was established by a 2009 EU Council Decision, which provides the basis for annual meetings of EU Member States' representatives. These meetings are important for the monitoring and implementation of common EU policies to combat trafficking in human beings. For many years, Slovenia has been paying special attention to the Western Balkans region, which was also one of the priorities of the Slovenian Presidency of the Council of the EU (in the second half of 2021 – when Slovenia was also the organiser of the Network's meetings).[132]

Slovenia has ratified the Council of Europe Convention on Action against Trafficking in Human Beings, which also provides a mechanism to monitor the implementation of the provisions of the Convention (GRETA). The first round of Slovenia's evaluation took place in 2012 and 2013, the second round in 2016 and 2017, and the third round started in 2021. Based on the country's responses to the questionnaire and the GRETA visit, a report with recommendations is prepared each time. It was acknowledged by GRETA that Slovenia has been responsive to GRETA's recommendations – the legal framework in Slovenia has been further developed with, *inter alia*, appropriate Criminal

---

129 Inter-ministerial Working Group Report for year 2020, p. 27.

130 See: International Centre for Migration Policy Development, 'Network of Anti-Trafficking Coordinators of South-East Europe (NATC SEE)', <https://www.icmpd.org/our-work/capacity-building/anti-trafficking-programme/network-of-anti-trafficking-coordinators-of-south-east-europe-natc-see>.

131 Ministry of the Interior, 'Hojs believes an integrated approach is needed in the fight against human trafficking', (06.12.2021), https://www.gov.si/en/news/2021-12-06-hojs-believes-an-integrated-approach-is-needed-in-the-fight-against-human-trafficking/.

132 *Ibid.*

Code amendments, victims of trafficking holding temporary residence permits have been granted access to the labour market etc.[133]

Moreover, the Conference of the UNTOC Parties in October 2020 established a mechanism to review the implementation of the United Nations Convention against Transnational Organised Crime and its Protocols (including the Palermo Protocol). The review process is conducted through a self-assessment of Member States, with two countries reviewing each other, each serving as a reviewer for at least one and up to four countries. Slovenia also participates in the review procedures.

The second aspect of international cooperation is operational, mainly as a reflection of the cooperation of individual institutions (police, public prosecutor) in concrete cases of detection and prosecution of trafficking in human beings. These tasks are also defined within the EU Plan on best practices, standards and procedures for preventing and combating trafficking in human beings. Cooperation takes place within Europol, Interpol and Eurojust.

In November 2018, the Government adopted the National Action Plan on Respect for Human Rights in Business, which aims to ensure the implementation of the UN Guiding Principles on Business and Human Rights. Moreover, it aims to contribute to ensuring respect for human rights in economic activities throughout the value chain and to further develop cooperation between the State, businesses and business associations, trade unions, NGOs, and other stakeholders.[134] The latter National Action Plan is based on three pillars, which are also foreseen in the UN Guiding Principles: the responsibility of the State to put in place an appropriate legal framework; the responsibility of business to respect human rights; and the responsibility of the State to sanction violations.

Furthermore, the annex to the National Action Plan includes the Guidelines for human rights due diligence in business.[135] The Guidelines define human rights due diligence as a process undertaken by business enterprises to identify, prevent and mitigate negative human rights impacts and report on ways to reduce such impacts. The implementation of human rights due diligence is to be carried out in five steps, which include making a commitment to respect human rights throughout the business process; establishing a structure for conducting due diligence in all internal as well as in external relationships;

133 Council of Europe, 'GRETA publishes second report on Slovenia', (15.02.2018), <https://www.coe.int/en/web/anti-human-trafficking/-/greta-publishes-second-report-on-slovenia> (the full report is accessible here).

134 See: Ministry of Foreign and European Affairs, 'Človekove pravice v gospodarstvu', <https://www.gov.si/teme/clovekove-pravice-v-gospodarstvu/>.

135 National Action Plan of the Republic of Slovenia for the Respect of Human Rights in Business, p. 42, <https://www.gov.si/teme/clovekove-pravice-v-gospodarstvu/>.

analysing priorities; conducting due diligence through mechanisms for detecting and responding to violations; and monitoring and reporting on due diligence and respect for human rights.[136]

So far, 18 Slovenian companies have taken the first step towards due diligence by signing the Commitment to Respect Human Rights in Business. They have committed to implement the measures set out in the Due Diligence Guidelines within three years of signing the commitment.

Slovenian Sovereign Holding (SDH), which exercises the State's shareholder role in state-owned companies, also signed this commitment in 2019 – and called on all state-owned companies to do the same. Although the majority (10) of the 18 companies listed are state-owned, there are still more than 80 such companies that have not signed the commitment. The literature, therefore, points out that it would be crucial for all state-owned enterprises to sign the commitment, as this would send a clear message from the State to all other companies on Slovenian territory to strictly respect human rights.[137]

It can be concluded that the National Action Plan on Respect for Human Rights in Business and the Due Diligence Guidelines represent an important step towards respect for human rights in business, especially for state-owned enterprises. A specific law obliging companies to do so would undoubtedly be more effective in this respect. This will certainly happen if the Directive on Corporate Sustainability Due Diligence and amending Directive (EU) 2019/1937 is adopted at EU level. It should be noted that Slovenia has already partially intervened in this area with some legislative changes resulting from the implementation of EU directives. Article 75 of the Public Procurement Act,[138] which follows Directives 2014/24/EU and 2014/25/EU,[139] provides that the contracting authority must exclude an economic entity from participation in a public procurement procedure if that entity or a member of its management or supervisory body has been the subject of a final judgment for certain criminal offences (including, inter alia, offences under Articles 112 and 113 KZ-1). In 2017, the introduction of Article 70c of the Companies Act,[140] which follows

136 *Ibid.*, p. 44.

137 T. Rozman, 'Business and Human Rights – Implementing the United Nations Guiding Principles on Business and Human Rights in Slovenia' (2020) 12:1 *Lexonomica* 51, pp. 71–72.

138 OJ RS, No. 91/15, 14/18, 121/21 in 10/22.

139 Directive 2014/24/EU of the European Parliament and of the Council of 26 February 2014 on public procurement and repealing Directive 2004/18/EC, OJ L 94, 28.3.2014, p. 65–242; Directive 2014/25/EU of the European Parliament and of the Council of 26 February 2014 on procurement by entities operating in the water, energy, transport and postal services sectors and repealing Directive 2004/17/EC, OJ L 94, 28.3.2014, p. 243–374.

140 OJ RS, No. 65/09, 33/11, 91/11, 32/12, 57/12, 44/13 – odl. US, 82/13, 55/15, 15/17, 22/19 – ZPosS, 158/20 – ZIntPK-C in 18/21.

Directive 2014/95/EU,[141] made it mandatory for larger companies (with more than 500 employees), which are also "public interest entities",[142] to include in their business report a statement on their non-financial performance, including, inter alia, information on respect for human rights.

7 Conclusion

Although Slovenia has ratified all the key international instruments prohibiting specific forms of contemporary slavery, the focus at the legislative and operational levels is on trafficking in human beings. While there is also room for individual improvements in this area (as suggested by the supervisory authorities),[143] the regulations are generally adequate. On the other hand, there is no specific definition of the offence of servitude or forced labour. Moreover, prevention and protection activities in relation to these (and other) forms of contemporary slavery are only carried out in the context of trafficking in human beings.[144] In this context, it would be appropriate for Slovenia to ratify the Protocol of 2014 to the Forced Labour Convention (1930) and, in accordance with it, to take appropriate measures to prevent and eliminate forced labour, to protect victims and to punish perpetrators (including by amending labour and criminal legislation) – and to focus activities to prevent contemporary slavery more broadly than just in relation to trafficking in human beings (e.g. through an action plan to prevent contemporary slavery).

Last but not least, I believe that the UN, ILO, Council of Europe and EU documents – together with the positions of the monitoring bodies and the judgments of the courts (ECHR, Court of Justice of the EU), which ensure that they are interpreted appropriately in changing circumstances – constitute an adequate legal framework for combating contemporary slavery. However, it is to agree with the arguments that, in order to eliminate and prevent such acts

141 Directive 2014/95/EU of the European Parliament and of the Council of 22 October 2014 amending Directive 2013/34/EU as regards disclosure of non-financial and diversity information by certain large undertakings and groups, OJ L 330, 15.11.2014, pp. 1–9.

142 According to the legislation, this means a company whose securities are traded on a regulated securities market; a credit institution; an insurance company; a pension company; and a company subject to statutory audit in which the State or the municipalities, jointly or severally, directly or indirectly, hold a majority shareholding.

143 See Action Plan for years 2021–2022, p. 25.

144 However, as the Inter-ministerial Working Group reports show, law enforcement authorities generally do not identify elements of trafficking for forced labour, even when they identify violations of workers' fundamental rights (and it is a fundamental workers' rights offence).

more effectively and to protect victims, it would be necessary to link or harmonize the standards arising from the international instruments on the prohibition of slavery with those contained in the international instruments on the prohibition of forced labour and trafficking in human beings.[145]

Academic References

A. Tratnik, 'Trgovina z ljudmi je samostojno prepovedano dejanje' (2010) *Pravna praksa* 8.

B. Novak, K. Filipčič and N. Kogovšek Šalamon 'Prisilna sklenitev zakonske zveze ali vzpostavitev podobne skupnosti' in D. Korošec, K. Filipčič and S. Zdolšek (eds), *Veliki komentar posebnega dela Kazenskega zakonika*, Uradni list Republike Slovenije, Ljubljana, 2018.

D. Frangež and A. Bučar Ručman, 'Specific forms of human trafficking in Slovenia: overview and preventive measures' (2017) 18:3 *Police Practice and Research* 230.

D. Korošec, K. Filipčič and S. Zdolšek (eds), *Veliki komentar posebnega dela Kazenskega zakonika*, Uradni list Republike Slovenije, Ljubljana, 2018.

E. Korpič-Hovat, 'Pravica do dela' (2018) 4:1–2 *Anali Pazu HD* 25.

K. Filipčič, 'Spravljanje v suženjsko razmerje' in D. Korošec, K. Filipčič and S. Zdolšek (eds), *Veliki komentar posebnega dela Kazenskega zakonika*, Uradni list Republike Slovenije, Ljubljana, 2018.

K. Filipčič, and L. Tičar, 'Zaposlovanje na črno' in D. Korošec, K. Filipčič and S. Zdolšek (eds), *Veliki komentar posebnega dela Kazenskega zakonika*, Uradni list Republike Slovenije, Ljubljana, 2018.

K. Zajc, *Primerjava ustavnih ureditev prepovedi suženjstva in prepovedi prisilnega dela: Magistrsko delo*, Master's Thesis, New University European Law Faculty, Nova Gorica, 2018.

L. Zore, 'Svoboda dela', in M. Avbelji (ed), *Komentar Ustave Republike Slovenije*, New University: European Law Faculty, Nova Gorica, 2019.

M. Blaha, 'Svoboda dela', in L. Šturm (ed), *Komentar Ustave Republike Slovenije*, Faculty of Government and European Studies, Kranj, 2010.

M. Novak, P. Končar, A. Škoberne (eds) *Konvencije Mednarodne organizacije dela s komentarjem* in GV Založba, Ljubljana, 2006.

145 See S. Scarpa and J. Cabot, 'Contemporary forms of slavery', European Parliament, 2018, p. 6, <https://www.europarl.europa.eu/RegData/etudes/STUD/2018/603470/EXPO_STU(2018)603470_EN.pdf>.

N. Kogovšek Šalamon and K. Filipčič, 'Trgovina z ljudmi' in D. Korošec, K. Filipčič and S. Zdolšek (eds), *Veliki komentar posebnega dela Kazenskega zakonika*, Uradni list Republike Slovenije, Ljubljana, 2018.

R. Kyovsky and R. Radovan, *Konvencije in priporočila MOD s komentarjem*, Centar za samoupravno normativno dejavnost, Ljubljana, 1975.

S. Čurin, 'Kritičen pogled na problematiko trgovine z ljudmi v Sloveniji ob upoštevanju mednarodnih priporočil in evropskega pravnega reda' (2016) 3 *Pravosodni bilten* 87.

T. Rozman, 'Business and Human Rights – Implementing the United Nations Guiding Principles on Business and Human Rights in Slovenia' (2020) 12:1 *Lexonomica* 51.

V. Mantouvalou, 'The Prohibition of Slavery, Servitude and Forced and Compulsory Labour under Article 4 ECHR', in F. Dorssemont, K. Lörcher and I. Schömann (eds), *The European Convention on Human Rights and the Employment Relation*, Hart Publishing, London, 2013, pp. 143–157.

W. Sauer, 'Habsburg Colonial: Austria-Hungary's Role in European Overseas Expansion Reconsidered' (2012) 20 *Austrian Studies* 5.

Slavery in Swedish Law – Past and Present: Productive Judicial Framing, Silencing, and Exceptionalisation

Niklas Selberg and Amin Parsa

1 Introduction

Sweden, located in the global North-West of Europe, took part in the centuries-long and largely legal global institution of slavery. In this chapter, we chart the received narrative on slavery in Swedish legal discourse by analysing its historical trajectories in three legal institutions: constitutional protection and human rights discourse, criminalisation, and recognition and reparation to enslaved persons. This allows us to illuminate the legacy of slavery in the contemporary Swedish legal system and provide a discussion of the legal definition of slavery operational in contemporary Sweden.

We focus on the following questions: How are Sweden's colonial endeavours expressed in the nation's legislation regarding slavery? What does 'Scandinavian exceptionalism' in relation to colonial history imply for the (contemporary) regulation of slavery? What are the historical trajectories particular to Sweden, and what effects have they had on the present-day Swedish law on slavery? The history of slavery can be told through the lens of national legal texts and sources, legislation, cases, and *travaux préparatoires*. Our understanding of both the present national legislation on slavery and contemporary forms of slavery deepens through historicising the legal developments.

This chapter contributes to the examination of slavery in the context of global racial capitalism by first rendering clear the contours of the mechanisms through which the Swedish legislator underemphasises the relevance of any deep-cutting engagement with slavery and forced labour as a historically relevant matter for the past, present, and future of the Swedish labour organisation. The Scandinavian exceptionalism has taken a judicial form in which ratification of human rights and international labour instruments goes hand in hand with framing slavery as an *irrelevant* and *meaningless* topic of engagement for the legislature. The chapter charts the extent to which Sweden has ratified international human rights law on slavery and forced labour and describes the national definition of these phenomena. Furthermore, the chapter describes the 2018 criminalisation of so-called 'human exploitation', which applies to situations of exploitation in the labour market.

 | DOI:10.1163/9789004723801_015

The structure of the chapter is as follows. First, Swedish colonial history is introduced together with a discussion of the Swedish relationship to remembrance of this part of national history. A legal section divided into two parts follows, describing the Swedish constitutional and human rights discourse on slavery as well as the criminal law perspective on slavery. This is followed by a description of processes on formal recognition of Sweden's colonial past and the issue of reparations. The chapter concludes with a summary and a reflection on slavery in the Swedish legal system.

2 Swedish Colonial History: St. Barthélemy 1784–1878

Serfdom was, as historian Fredrik Thomasson reminds us, abolished in Sweden in the 14th century, but with the acquisition of the Caribbean Island of St. Barthélemy in 1784, Sweden would become, and remain for almost a century, a slaveholding nation. This period ended when Sweden sold the island back to France in 1878 and paid reparations to slave owners. During Sweden's possession of St. Barthélemy, both Swedish law and French colonial law, known as the *Code Noir,* were applicable on the island. When Swedish colonisers arrived at St. Barthélemy, the island had a population of approximately 700. During the Swedish colonial regime, the population grew so that in 1800, the capital Gustavia— named after King Gustav III—had 5000 inhabitants, making it Sweden's fifth or sixth largest town. A mixed legal system upheld the atrocities levelled at enslaved persons on the part of the Swedish state. Sweden, quite simply, was doing what many other European nations were doing in the Caribbean. Very little research has been carried out regarding the Swedish period of the island's history, and in present-day Sweden, there is little public knowledge of Swedish slavery in St. Barthélemy.[1]

Within the silences of the national history, however, resides a longer trajectory of the Swedish ambition to take part in European colonial ventures. In 1628— more than a century before purchasing St. Barthélemy from France in exchange for staple rights to French ships in the harbour of Göteborg[2]—the then Swedish King Gustav II signed a contract with the Duke of Buckingham

1 F. Thomasson, 'Thirty-Two Lashes at Quatre Piquets: Slave Laws and Justice in the Swedish Colony of St. Barthélemy ca. 1800' in H. Weiss (ed), *Ports of Globalisation, Places of Creolisation. Nordic Possessions in the Atlantic World during the Era of the Slave Trade*, Brill, Leiden 2016; F. Thomasson, *Svarta Saint-Barthélemy. Människoöden i en svensk koloni 1785–1847*, Natur & Kultur, Stockholm 2022.

2 F. Thomasson, above n. 1.

to buy the Caribbean island of Jamaica in exchange for transferring ten percent of the profits from the gold mines in Jamaica.[3] This contract was never fulfilled as the Duke was murdered soon after, but nevertheless, the Swedish government continued its dream of becoming a colonial power. A central figure in keeping this desire alive was none other than Axel Oxenstierna—the author of the Swedish constitution (known as the Instrument of Government) and one of the most revered statesmen in Sweden's history. At the same time as he was defining the foundations of constitutional democracy in Sweden, Oxenstierna fantasised about establishing Swedish colonies from Florida to Newfoundland—some 100 years before the formation of the United States of America.[4]

Beyond its colonial ambitions, Sweden is also linked to the Transatlantic slave trade through the vital logistical role it played in the upkeep of violence across the ocean. As historians Chris Evans and Göran Rydén point out, the Baltic iron, specifically the high-quality Oregrounds iron originating from the Swedish county, Uppland (*Bergslagen*), dominated the British market from the mid-seventeenth to mid-nineteenth century:[5]

> The merchant fleet and British Royal Navy alike owed their seaworthiness to bolts and hoops of Swedish iron not to mention Swedish tar. It mattered not whether the vessels were built in Shadwell or Salem, Massachusetts; their timbers were shaped by adzes and axes that had been edged with steel of Swedish ancestry.[6]

This link between Sweden and the global commodity chain built around the Transatlantic slave trade and European colonialism indicates the 'Atlanticity' of Sweden.[7] By the end of the seventeenth century, this linkage became more pronounced as the Swedish Tar Company established itself as the exclusive provider of tar—an essential product for the construction, repair, and maintenance of the naval fleet and the production of ropes—to the British Navy.[8] Later, and in the mid-nineteenth century (1840), Sweden established its own

3 H. Lindqvist, 'Drömmen om ett svenskt imperium', *Aftonbladet,* (8.11.2014), <https://www.aftonbladet.se/nyheter/kolumnister/a/WLJyag/drommen-om-ett-svenskt-imperium>.

4 *Ibid.*

5 C. Evans and G. Rydén, *Baltic Iron in the Atlantic World in the Eighteenth Century*, Brill, Leiden 2007, p. 294.

6 *Ibid.*

7 *Ibid.*, p. 293.

8 M. Airaksinen, 'Tar Production in colonial North America' (1996) 2:1 *Environment and History*, p. 115.

direct link to the United States' market and, as such, acquired its own direct link to the accumulation of capital through enslaved labour that took place on a large scale in the United States of America.[9] Swedish iron and tar played an indispensable role in the colonial exploits of the British Navy as well as the plantation economy of the United States through the production of guns, blades, ropes, shackles, and hardware. It is through this logistical upkeep of violence of the Atlantic powers that Sweden has left its own singular and distinct mark in global racial capitalism.

3 'Scandinavian Exceptionalism' – Remembering (?) Sweden's Colony St. Barthélemy

Historian Lill-Ann Körber characterises the narrative of colonialism in Sweden as 'Scandinavian exceptionalism', defined as "a self-perception as good when others are bad, as innocent when others are guilty, as peaceful and friendly when others are violent, as marginal when others are at the centre, as small when others are big, as complicit when others are perpetrators".[10] This exceptionalism has, according to Körber, four dimensions. First, Sweden's role in slavery was small in scale, marginal, without effects and consequently not relevant. *Smallness* seems to imply a lesser degree of responsibility. Even critical historians who traced Swedish iron across the Atlantic to the shackles of the kidnapped and enslaved people do not miss the opportunity to mention how "tiny" St. Barthélemy is,[11] or that in comparison to its European rivals—the Dutch, the Spanish, the Portuguese, and the British—or even its Scandinavian neighbour, Denmark—the Swedish colonial history is a "sorry record" of minimal proportion.[12] It appears that the failure to partake in the Transatlantic slave trade in a monumental manner is an exonerating factor. Second, the present-day claims of friendly relations with the former colony are mobilised as immunity against accusations of racism and as a show of 'innocence', while the past is marred only by a lack of attention and simple ignorance. Third, Sweden's 'benevolence' is evidenced by its postcolonial attitude and better contribution

9 C. Evans and G. Rydén, above n. 5, p. 294.

10 L.A. Körber, 'Exceptionalisms and Entanglements. Legacies and Memories of Scandinavian Colonial History' in J. Bjerring-Hansen, T. Jelsbak & A.E. Mrozewicz (eds) *Scandinavian Exceptionalisms, Culture, Society, Discourse*, Nordeuropa-Institut der Humboldt-Universität, Berlin 2021.

11 C. Evans and G. Rydén, above n. 5, p. 292.

12 *Ibid.*

to sustainable development and equality when compared to some other countries. Fourth, Sweden is a 'homogeneous' society since, in Sweden, nationality and ethnicity/race are often conflated: 'ethnic Swede' is equal to White. This conflation, combined with benevolence and innocence, writes Körber, often results in colour-blindness and claims that race is irrelevant and that racism is non-existent. In relation to slavery, this process of homogeneity leads to the universalisation of the perspective of the 'national majority': "we do not have any experience with slave trade".[13]

One can argue that the Swedish brand of colour-blindness has been pioneering the contemporary process of 'exceptionalisation' of racism in the public discourses of Western liberal democracies. In *Faces at the Bottom of the Well*, and while writing on the failures of liberal intellectuals to acknowledge racism as a structural matter, Derrick Bell refers to none other than Gunnar Myrdal—the Swedish social scientist and the (together with spouse Alva Myrdal) foremost public intellectual of Swedish social democracy. In his mid-century study, *The American Dilemma*, Gunnar Myrdal describes racism as "a terrible and inexplicable anomaly stuck in the middle of our liberal democratic ethos".[14] As Bell points out, this conceptualisation of racism as an anomaly reduces racial oppression to "merely an odious holdover from slavery", rather than part and parcel of what made liberal democracies (specifically the United States) possible.[15] This legacy of exceptionality of racism persists to date in the form of Swedish colour-blind anti-discrimination legislation. In 2008, the Swedish legislator removed all traces of the term 'race' from its legislation. This move was promoted as an affirmation that 'race' is a scientifically debunked and erroneous mode of differentiation. Consequently, race and racism in anti-discrimination legislation were replaced by terminology of ethnic origin/affiliation and ethnic discrimination. The result, as Leila Brännström has shown in her study of two decades of Swedish anti-discrimination case law, is an extreme exceptionality of proving unfavourable treatment based on 'ethnic affiliation'. As Brännström notes, it is virtually impossible to prove unfavourable treatment on the basis of ethnic origin unless such acts are "verbally related to ethnic affiliation" of a person or when the case at hand involves "an unambiguous

---

13 *Ibid.*, p. 292. See also L.A. Körber, 'Sweden and St. Barthélemy: Exceptionalisms, Whiteness, and the Disappearance of Slavery from Colonial History' (2019) 91:1–2 *Scandinavian Studies*, 74.

14 G. Myrdal, *An American Dilemma: The Negro Problem and Modern Democracy*, Harpers & Brothers, New York 1944, p. XIX.

15 D. Bell, *Faces at the Bottom of the Well: The Permanence of Racism*, Basic Books, New York 1992, p. 34 (e-book version).

and well witnessed discrimination due to appearance in certain areas of social life".[16] In adopting a colour-blind approach to racial discrimination, the Swedish legislator effectively codified the 'anomaly thesis' that saw racism as an exceptional element of Western liberal democracy.

4 Slavery and the Swedish Constitution and Human Rights Discourse

4.1 *Introduction*

How do the top echelons of the Swedish national legal system deal with the issue of slavery? And how has Sweden anchored the prohibition against slavery in national human rights discourse? This section describes the national legal processes in relation to international—global, and regional—norms on slavery, as well as national developments regarding the constitutional protection of human rights. The aim is to shed light on the processes of reception of the definition of slavery and to focus on legal form rather than to explain the definition of slavery operational in Sweden—a definition found in international sources. Constitutional developments have always occurred in light of the presence of some type of criminalisation of slavery and a labour law regime. Criminal law aspects of slavery will be described and analysed in a following section.

4.2 *The International Labour Organization*

Sweden ratified the 1930 International Labour Organization (ILO) Forced Labour Convention (no. 29) in 1931. However, the Swedish employers' organisation suggested that the convention was irrelevant since Sweden did not own any colony. The government agreed with the employers and stated that the convention was "completely irrelevant" for Sweden but nonetheless favoured its ratification and integrated the corresponding recommendation without any amendment to national law.[17] In doing so, Sweden joined a large group of states that claimed it was important to provide principled support to the prohibition of forced labour.[18]

The government, as well as the social partners (the trade union federation, *Landsorganisationen* [LO], and the national employers' organisation), all

16 L. Brännström, 'The Terms of Ethnoracial Equality: The Swedish Courts' Reading of Ethnic Affiliation, Race and Culture' (2018) 27:5 *Social & Legal Studies* 616, p. 627.

17 Government Bill 1931:32, p. 5.

18 *Ibid.*

favoured ratifying the 1957 ILO Abolition of Forced Labour Convention (no. 105) stating that none of the practices mentioned in the instrument occurred in Sweden. The Government commented that the text adopted by the International Labour Conference (ILC) "completely lacked practical meaning as far as our country is concerned".[19] Offering principled support for the Convention went hand in hand with denying any involvement in the practices addressed in the instrument. The Swedish government pointed to the fact that it, together with the Danish government, had proposed to the ILC that the definition of forced labour should explicitly include the use of concentration camps, deportation of national minorities as a means of exerting political pressure or schooling or punishment of those dissenting to the prevailing political, social, or economic system in place. The Swedish government noted that this proposal was not adopted by the ILC because the Secretary-General of the United Nations had stated that these issues were included in the competency of the UN, not the ILO.[20] Instead, this matter was included in a resolution adopted by the ILC.[21] The proposal put forward by Sweden and Denmark at the 1957 ILC linked these states to the larger strategy of directing the struggle against forced labour towards the Eastern Bloc and including it in the political conflict between North-Western states and the Soviet Union.[22]

In 2017, when the government proposed that Sweden approve the Protocol of 2014 to the Forced Labour Convention (No. 29), the Instrument of Government was not mentioned at all. The government invoked as grounds for approval of the Protocol Sweden's ratification of the Forced Labour Convention and the 2000 Palermo Protocol to Prevent, Suppress, and Punish Trafficking in Persons, Especially Women and Children, supplementing the United Nations Convention against Transnational Organized Crime[23] and the EU directive 2011/36 on preventing and combatting trafficking in human beings and protecting

---

19 *Ibid.*

20 *Ibid.*

21 Resolution concerning the Abolition of Concentration Camps and the Deportation of National Minorities, Submitted by the Committee on Forced Labour. See International Labour Office, The fortieth session of the International Labour Conference: Geneva, June 1957, in *International Labour Review*, Vol. 76(3), 1957, pp. 217–243.

22 On this conflict, see e.g. S.M. Schwebel, 'The United States Assaults the I.L.O'. (1971) 65:1 The American Journal of International Law 136.; D. Maul, *The International Labour Organization. 100 years of global social policy*, De Gruyter Oldenbourg, 2019, p. 97; D. Maul, "Help Them Move the ILO Way': The International Labour Organization and the Modernization Discourse in the Era of Decolonization and the Cold War' (2009) 33:3 *Diplomatic History* 387.

23 Government Bill 2003/04:111.

its victims, and replacing Council Framework Decision 2002/629/JHA. The government argued, in sum, that the international and regional definitions of forced labour had already been successfully integrated into valid Swedish criminal law on human trafficking.[24]

4.3 *Regional European Human Rights Instruments as the Swedish Prohibition of Slavery*

The regional European human rights instrument, the 1950 Convention for the Protection of Human Rights and Fundamental Freedoms, prohibits slavery, servitude, and forced labour:

> 1. No one shall be held in slavery or servitude.
> 2. No one shall be required to perform forced or compulsory labour.
> 3. For the purpose of this Article the term "forced or compulsory labour" shall not include:
>   a. any work required to be done in the ordinary course of detention imposed according to the provisions of Article 5 of this Convention or during conditional release from such detention;
>   b. any service of a military character or, in case of conscientious objectors in countries where they are recognised, service exacted instead of compulsory military service;
>   c. any service exacted in case of an emergency or calamity threatening the life or well-being of the community;
>   d. any work or service which forms part of normal civic obligations.[25]

Sweden ratified the European Convention, reporting no discrepancy between Article 4 and national laws or practices.[26] While the 1961 European Social Charter (revised 1996) does not contain a prohibition against slavery and forced labour, it protects "the effective exercise of the right to work", which includes: "to protect effectively the right of the worker to earn his living in an occupation freely entered upon".[27] Sweden has ratified the Charter without reporting any discrepancies between the instrument and national practices.[28]

---

24 Government Bill 2016/17:93, p. 9; Ch. 4, Sect. 1 a of the Criminal Code of 1965.

25 Council of Europe, Convention for the Protection of Human Rights and Fundamental Freedoms, 1950 (ETS No. 5); Article 4.

26 Government Bill 1951:165, p. 11.

27 Council of Europe, European Social Charter (revised), 1996 (ETS No. 163); Part II, Article 1.

28 Government Bill 1962:175, Government Bill 1997/98:82.

4.4 *Global Instruments and United Nations Covenants*

Sweden is a member of the United Nations and has been bound by the 1948 Universal Declaration of Human Rights[29] and, as of 1954, the 1926 Slavery Convention as amended in 1953. The 1966 United Nations International Covenant on Civil and Political Rights, including its prohibition against slavery, servitude and forced or compulsory labour, was ratified by Sweden. The government made clear that no practices on the Swedish labour market met the criteria for forced labour and emphasised that national provisions enabling ratification could be found in the general Criminal Code.[30]

The 1966 United Nations International Covenant on Economic, Social and Cultural Rights lacks a prohibition against slavery and forced labour but protects instead the right to work, including "the right of everyone to the opportunity to gain his living by work which he freely chooses or accepts".[31] The state parties to the covenant are required to take appropriate steps to safeguard this right. However, Sweden has ratified this provision without any amendments to national law.[32]

4.5 *1974 Swedish Instrument of Government (1974:152)*

The present constitution of Sweden—the 1974 Instrument of Government—does not explicitly prohibit slavery, serfdom, and forced labour. The provision closest to such a prohibition was added in 1976 and is found in the chapter on Fundamental rights and freedoms: "Everyone shall be protected in his or her relations with the public institutions against deprivations of personal liberty".[33] The government explains in the *travaux préparatoires* the strategy not to provide explicit constitutional protection against slavery, serfdom, and forced labour. First, it was suggested that human rights protection was altogether not very important:

> The hitherto development in our country as regards human rights shows that it is hardly necessary to enhance the protection of rights under normal circumstances. It is highly unlikely that the Riksdag [Parliament] would in times of inner and outer calm abuse its powers.[34]

29 General Assembly Resolution 217 A, December 10, 1948.
30 Government Bill 1971:125, p. 30.
31 General Assembly Resolution 2200A (XXI); Article 6.
32 Government Bill 1971:125, p. 27.
33 Ch. 2, Sect. 8 of the Instrument of Government (1974:152).
34 Government Bill 1975/76:209, p. 84 f.

Second, the government points to technical difficulties in defining rights protection as complementing the usual regulation of relations between private parties. It would be difficult to describe in detail the scope of the prohibitions and what the consequences of transgressions would be—and this regulation would easily come to encroach upon private law (i.e. contract law and ownership). Therefore, the protection of rights is, in our reading of the *travaux préparatoires*, firmly embedded in a vertical worldview in which rights apply solely between the state and private subjects. The constitutional protection implies nothing more than that the constitution must be changed before the legislator can intervene in areas defined as covered by human rights, effectively making it more time-consuming for the legislator to intervene in topics defined as rights.[35] Third, the *travaux préparatoires* seem to prioritise rights pertaining to freedom to form and express opinions above rights relating to freedom of movement and the like. The government first explains that what is referred to as 'corporal human rights' largely function as support to rights protecting freedom of opinion. Only after this statement is it explained that 'corporal human rights' are "an expression of the respect of the individual person's integrity that defines a society in which rule of law prevails".[36] In sum, the position seems to be that protecting freedoms of opinion secures rights to bodily integrity. Fourth, and most importantly, protection against slavery, serfdom, and forced labour was clearly deemed as entirely unimportant. The government states that prohibiting slavery, serfdom, and depravation of freedom because of failure to pay a debt would "obviously not imply any enhancement of the protection of citizens".[37]

While the Parliamentary Ombudsman has suggested that the Swedish constitution should explicitly reflect the wording of Article 4 of the European Convention and its prohibition against slavery, servitude, and forced or compulsory labour, it has done so for purely legal-technical reasons. The Ombudsman raised concerns that the partial transformation of international human rights protection into national constitutional protection would invite conclusions *e contrario*, i.e. that rights not directly transformed into national law were not covered by the national constitutional protection.[38] Reacting to this proposal to explicitly prohibit slavery when expanding the constitutional protection

35 *Ibid.*, p. 85 f.

36 Government Bill 1975/76:209, p. 119 f.

37 *Ibid.*, p. 120.

38 *Ibid.*, p. 249.

of human rights, the then Minister of Justice commented in the *travaux préparatoires*:

> The constitutional regulation on rights should in my opinion be chiefly designed to not comprise more rules than those that must be considered to be of fundamental importance for the democratic form of government or for individuals' personal freedom and safety. [...] To include, as has been suggested, in the Instrument of Government a prohibition against such phenomena as slavery, serfdom, prohibition of imprisonment for debt, would, for example, obviously not imply any real enhancement of the protection afforded individuals.[39]

This line of reasoning assumes that slavery does not exist in Sweden and that there is no real risk that it could come into existence. Furthermore, the position that clear constitutional protection against slavery does not add anything of value to the legal system arguably reflects the notion that the newly implemented labour law scheme is both far-reaching and efficient, in effect leaving no need for any more protection for workers. Another tacit assumption behind the constitutional human rights protection seems to be that slavery is understood through a vertical lens focusing on the responsibility of the state: If the state itself does not engage in slavery, this will not come about. Since the government assumes the Swedish state will be eternally benign and progressive, it suggests that there is no need for constitutional protection against slavery. In sum, the government seems to argue that private law—of which labour and employment law is a part—is enough to protect citizens from one another and that the (assumed) absence of slavery, serfdom, and forced labour on the Swedish labour market implies that these phenomena could never reappear unless orchestrated by the state itself. It might be of interest to note that the government at the time was formed by Social Democrats and that the Minister for Justice, Lennart Geijer, was a Ph.D. in labour law. Social Democrats had just launched an extensive reform of labour law —Democracy at work[40]— and were, perhaps, disposed to view labour law as the sole regulator of labour and as a sufficient response to severe forms of oppression in the labour market.

This ambiguous way of dealing with the matter of slavery in the constitution seems to have, in the early 2000s, given rise to some kind of afterthought and attempts at re-writing the *travaux préparatoires* from the 1970s. The government suggested in 2001 that Sweden should ratify the ILO Convention no. 182

39 *Ibid.*, p. 119 f.

40 SOU 1975:1, Government Bill 1975/76:105.

on Worst Forms of Child Labour, and in doing so, it stated in the new *travaux préparatoires* that:

> The travaux préparatoires to the Instrument of Government state that this provision [i.e. Ch. 2, Art. 8] shall be understood as unambiguously forbidding circumstances similar to slavery or forced labour, even though the provision not explicitly was designed as such a prohibition.[41]

The Swedish government had apparently changed its views on the need for clear human rights protection against slavery and forced labour. During the 1970s, it was argued that protection against slavery and forced labour in the form of human rights was largely unnecessary, while in the 2000s, it was argued that these practices were 'unambiguously' forbidden by human rights provisions in the constitution. The international development of human rights protection against oppressive and exploitative work relations combined with a decline in the national level of labour protection in the form of private (labour and employment) law comprise a likely legal explanation for the government's change in view on prohibitions against slavery in the form of human rights.

4.6 *Summing-Up: Slavery and the Constitution*

Sweden has ratified all international and regional instruments on the prohibition of slavery, serfdom, and forced labour, but this has always been done under the assumption that these labour market phenomena are not and never will be present here. Sweden, therefore, assumes that the prohibition of slavery is relevant because of events that happened or are currently happening in other nations.

The definition of slavery operational in Sweden is entirely a product of Sweden's reaction to international legal developments. Labour protection has always occupied a prominent place on the government agenda, and labour law is advanced in Sweden. However, Sweden has not significantly engaged in any attempts to further develop the legal analysis regarding slavery. Slavery seems to have been understood as a self-evident or unimportant concept. A proposal for the ratification of an international instrument on the prohibition of slavery has been on the agenda many times in Sweden but never has the government seized the opportunity to develop a more advanced analysis of slavery.

41 Government Bill 2000/01:93, p. 22.

The reform of the human rights protection in the constitution took place during the heyday of the development of Swedish labour and employment law during the mid-1970s.[42] During an intense process of reshaping working conditions in Sweden and with a successful labour movement, the issue of slavery did not get more than a bare minimum of attention on the part of the national legislator. Furthermore, it seems as if the legislator could not envision a labour market with inequalities so stark that they could give rise to relations similar to those of slavery between private parties. Slavery was understood and discussed as an entirely vertical relationship, and since the state was benign—a welfare state—there was no need for a conversation on slavery in Sweden. To be clear, the international definition of slavery is presently operational in Sweden. This definition is also relevant in criminal law, which will be discussed in the following section.

5 Slavery and Forced Labour as a Matter of Swedish Criminal Law

5.1 *Introduction*

How is slavery perceived in terms of criminalisation? Which actions towards another private party are so heinous that they also amount to a transgression against the state? The criminalisation of slavery in Sweden has shifted significantly. This section will describe these shifts in chronological order. The contemporary legislation criminalising 'human exploitation' will be analysed in more detail.

5.2 *The 1864 Penal Code*

The Penal Code, valid law for almost a century between 1864 and 1965, explicitly criminalised, in its chapter 'On offences against liberty', slave trade and slavery using very specific language:

> 1 § A person who with intent enslaves someone, or trades in negroes or someone else, to put him in and keep him in such a state, or takes on-board, detains or incarcerates on a ship to abduct him into slavery, is to be sentenced to hard labour for life, and the ship used for such a purpose, together with its cargo, is forfeited to the Crown.
>
> 2 § A person who took up service on a ship knowing it was to be used for slave trade or the abduction of slaves, and if the ship is used for this

42 See e.g. R. Fahlbeck, *Nothing Succeeds Like Success. Trade Unionism in Sweden*, Juristförlaget i Lund, Visby 1999.

purpose while he is employed there, is to be sentenced as an aid following Ch. 3, Art. 4, even though he did not meet or engaged the slaves in any way.

3 § A person who supplies, rents out or provides a ship for slave trade or the abduction of slaves, is to be sentenced to hard labour for between four and eight years, even though the ship was not used for this purpose.

4 § Moneys, or their value, that was used for or asked for slave trade or the provision of a ship for the purpose of the abduction of slaves, or to supplies for the ship mentioned in 3 §, is forfeited to the Crown.[43]

The criminalisation of slavery was put forward first in the chapter protecting liberty, framing slavery as the negation of liberty and the most heinous crime against it. The criminal provisions were also explicit in their reference to persons of African descent. The reasons for referencing persons of African descent were treated as a matter of course and were not made explicit. The state assumes jurisdiction over slavery: Any winnings and any paraphernalia related to slavery were forfeited to the state. The focus on maritime travel and ships suggests that the legislation did not have events taking place on mainland Sweden as its primary objective.

5.3 *The 1965 Criminal Code*

In the legislative process aimed at modernising Swedish criminal law during the beginning of the 1960s, the crime of slavery, found in the 1864 Penal Code, was referred to as a qualified instance of unlawful deprivation of liberty.[44] The government proposed scrapping the provisions found in Ch. 15, Art. 1–4 of the 1864 Penal Code, referring to them as "from a practical point of view nowadays insignificant particular rules".[45] An overarching policy of using fewer and broader criminalizations rather than having many specific provisions guided the government.[46]

At the same time as the explicit criminalisation of slavery, with its reference to persons of African descent, was removed, two changes to the criminal law were proposed. First, the crime of 'kidnapping' was amended with the addition of a variant consisting of coercing someone into service.[47] Second, a new crime was proposed. It was intended to suppress the phenomena covered by

43 Ch. 15, Sects. 1–4 of The Penal Code of 1864.
44 Government Bill 1962:10.
45 Government Bill 1962:10 B, p. 99.
46 SOU 1953:14.
47 Ch. 4, Sect. 1 of the 1965 Criminal Code. RH 2014:38, prop. 1962:10 B p. 99, pp. 417.

the older law, while also combatting the phenomenon historically referred to as 'white slave trade', i.e. trade with women and children for sexual (forced prostitution) purposes from Europe to the Americas, Africa, and Asia.[48] The new provision was worded:

> A person who otherwise […], by unlawful coercion or deceit, causes the entry of someone into military or work service or other similar condition of restraint or induces someone to go or remain in a place abroad where he or she may be in danger of being exposed to persecution or exploited for casual sexual relations or otherwise fall into distress, shall be sentenced for *placing a person in a distressful situation* [sic] to imprisonment for at least one and at most ten years.[49]

The scope of criminalisation is thus unchanged: the actions that were criminalised as slavery with explicit reference to persons of African descent are still a crime, but with a new heading that does not link to the historical atrocities. The purpose of combatting the slave trade for—white, as is tacitly assumed by the legislator— women and children is added to the criminalisation of slavery with its strong link to persons of African descent and Transatlantic kidnappings. The crime of placing a person in a distressful situation was scrapped in 2004 and replaced with the criminalisation of trafficking in human beings.[50] This further linked the prohibition of slavery to the issue of sexualised and gendered exploitation in relation to sex work.

5.4 *The Criminalization of Practices Similar to Slavery outside the Scope of Human Trafficking*

Practices similar to slavery are criminalised in several provisions, together arguably amounting to an indirect criminalisation of slavery.[51] A person who, by assault, by violence, or by threat of a criminal act, coerces another person to perform work is guilty of 'unlawful coercion' and is sentenced to a fine or imprisonment for at most two years.[52] A person who confines a person or deprives them of their liberty in some other way is guilty of 'unlawful

48 A. Hallner, 'Från vit slavhandel till trafficking. En studie om föreställningar kring människohandel och dess offer' (2003) 129:3 *Historisk tidskrift* 429.

49 Ch. 4, Sect. 3 of the Criminal Code of 1965.

50 SOU 2016:70, p. 223, Government Bill 2003/04:111.

51 Government Bill 2017/18:123, p. 35 f, SOU 2016:70, p. 199 ff.

52 Ch. 4, Sect. 4 of the Criminal Code of 1965.

deprivation of liberty' and is sentenced to imprisonment for at least one year and, at most, ten years.[53] Also, 'procuring' could be mentioned here: promoting or, in an improper manner, financially exploiting another person's engagement in casual sexual relations in return for payment.[54] Seizing and confining someone with the intent to injure them physically or harm their health, to coerce them into service, or to practice extorsion amounts to 'kidnapping'.[55]

Furthermore, a person who inflicts bodily injury, illness, or pain on another person, renders them helpless, or some other similar state is guilty of assault and is sentenced to imprisonment for at most two years or, if the offence is minor, to a fine or imprisonment for at most six months.[56] A person who, by deception, induces someone into an action that involves gain for the perpetrator and loss for the person deceived or someone they represent is guilty of fraud and is sentenced to imprisonment for at most two years.[57] Finally, a person who exploits someone else's distress or position of dependence when entering into an agreement or some other action with legal consequences to obtain a benefit that is manifestly disproportionate to the consideration or for which no consideration is to be paid, is guilty of usury and is sentenced to a fine or imprisonment for at most two years.[58] Demanding that the worker pay the 'employer' money for some kind of 'service' can be covered by this provision.

The practice of slavery, the government proposes dryly, would likely entail poor working conditions, dangerous workplaces, and long periods of work without rest. Slavery, therefore, also constitutes violations of laws on health and safety at work[59] and working time regulation.[60] This strategy for criminalising slavery divides it into several discrete instances—coercion, restriction to freedom and movement, violence, and wage theft—which are handled in separate provisions. Dividing slavery into smaller events risks obfuscating the total experience of the person affected. Furthermore, the law will fail to address and name the event in its entirety.

53 Ch. 4, Sect. 2 of the Criminal Code of 1965.
54 Ch. 6, Sect 12 of the Criminal Code of 1965.
55 Ch. 4, Sect 1 of the Criminal Code of 1965.
56 Ch. 3, Sect. 5 of the Criminal Code of 1965.
57 Ch. 9, Sect. 1 of the Criminal Code of 1965.
58 Ch. 9, Sect. 5 of the Criminal Code of 1965.
59 Work Environment Act (1977:1160).
60 Working Hours Act (1982:673).

5.5 *Criminalization of Practices Similar to Slavery in the Context of Human Trafficking*

Acts not amounting to kidnapping are criminalised as human trafficking with the following definition:

> A person who, in cases other than those referred to in Section 1, by:
> 1. unlawful coercion;
> 2. deception;
> 3. exploitation of another person's vulnerable situation that severely restricts that person's alternatives; or
> 4. other such improper means that severely restrict another person's alternatives, recruits, transports, transfers, harbours or receives a person in order for that person to be exploited for sexual purposes, the removal of organs, military service, forced labour or some other activity in a situation that involves distress for that person is guilty of *trafficking in human beings* and is sentenced to imprisonment for at least two and at most ten years.[61]

One of the purposes required for an event to be branded as human trafficking is forced labour. This concept is to be defined according to international legal sources. The *travaux préparatoires* define forced labour as a situation in which the victim is "forced to against his or her will perform actions that are unjustified or comprising an element of oppression or an avoidable hardship", while at the same time, there are no "justified or legally recognized social interests" present.[62] The criminalisation also covers situations where the victim has "some other kind of obligation to perform or endure a not only short period of a state of total dependency, which the individual cannot influence or escape".[63] Essentially, what is to be covered by this provision are situations in which the victim is forced to carry out "unjustified" work or work which is characterised by "an element of oppression or avoidable hardship" and also situations in which the victim "is under some kind of obligation to perform in or endure a not very brief state of total unavoidable or unchangeable dependency".[64]

The Swedish political discourse and policy, perhaps taking its cue from the 2014 Protocol No. 29 to the ILO Forced Labour Convention (1930),

61 Ch. 4, Sect. 1 a of the Criminal Code.

62 Government Bill 2003/04:111, p. 45. The provision has since been amended several times; see *e.g.* prop. 2004/05:45, prop. 2009/10:152, prop. 2017/18:123.

63 Government Bill 2003/04:111, p. 45.

64 Government Bill 2003/04:111, p. 45.

predominantly formulates contemporary references to forced labour and slavery through the framework of combatting the crime of trafficking in humans.[65] The crime of trafficking does not require an international border crossing as its constitutive element. However, folding forced labour into the matter of trafficking has likely been driven by a policing agenda that ultimately justifies evermore harsh border control practices at the national and European levels.[66]

The significance of this symbiotic relation between the framing of 'modern' slavery as a matter of border policing is that it simultaneously dislocates and reinforces racial ordering with regard to forced labour within the European context. The turn to trafficking as *the* main cause of so-called modern slavery initially contributes to a sense of benevolence as the governments find a way to highlight their "positive role in preventing forced labour".[67] This framing further bolsters a self-affirming illusion that the evil of forced labour and slavery always originates from the other side of the border and not where the legislator (here, the Swedish) is standing. Such a framing moreover delinks slavery and forced labour from national, regional, and global histories of racial capitalism—hence the adjectives such as 'modern' and 'contemporary'—and directs focus toward the criminalised actions of individual traffickers and trafficking organisations. Lastly and more insidiously, the laws and practices of border control—in Europe and beyond—have been unpacked as foremost a mechanism of racial ordering of national spaces.[68]

Yet mobilising efforts against slavery through the legal prism of trafficking act as a double entendre that further re-energizes the racial function of borders in producing the very condition of 'il-legalization', which in turn allows for casting certain bodies as vulnerable to conditions of forced labour, slavery,

65 *E.g.* The National Audit Office, Government initiative to combat labour exploitation: Regulations, inspection, information and support to victims, a Performance audit report from the Swedish National Audit Office, 2020/11/30, Ref. No. 3.1.1 2019-1075, RIR 202:27.

66 The European Border and Coast Guard Agency, Frontex, continuously frames its mission as one of saving lives and fighting cross-border crimes such as trafficking in humans. Frontex is currently the most lavishly funded European agency with a recently approved standing corps of its own. Frontex, *Standing corps*, <https://www.frontex.europa.eu/about-frontex/standing-corps/standing-corps/>. See also Nidžara Ahmetašević, 'Frontex: When great power comes with no responsibility', *Aljazeera*, (12.07.2023), <https://www.aljazeera.com/opinions/2023/7/12/frontex-when-great-power-comes-with-no-responsibility>.

67 A. Blackett and A. Duquesnoy, 'Slavery Is Not a Metaphor: U.S. Prison Labor and Racial Subordination through the Lens of the ILO's Abolition of Forced Labour Convention' (2021) 67 *USLA Law Review* 1504, p. 1526.

68 See, N. Sharma, *Home Rule: National Sovereignty and the Separation of Natives and Migrants*, Duke University Press, Durham 2020.

and trafficking in the first place. In other words, the same move that turns trafficking into the dominating location of slavery and forced labour, at once gestures to the combat against 'modern' slavery while at the same time lays the groundwork for casting masses of people—who are considered legally 'undocumented'—as an unfree labour force. This move, perhaps, is the completing move in a full circle in which exceptionalism in the Scandinavian countries in relation to their history of racism comes to its formidable conclusion. At first, the historical role of slavery in primitive accumulation of national wealth is denied, then slavery and racism are framed as external problems brought into the national realm by illegalised border crossings, all at the same time as the anti-migration policies and increasing investments in policing prepare the ground for the possibility of valuing certain human lives as il-legalized, violable, and as Ruth Wilson Gilmore says; vulnerable to premature death.[69]

5.6 *2018 Criminalization of 'Human Exploitation'*

As an explicit response to the approach of dividing exploitation on the labour market into many crimes, a subsidiary crime to human trafficking was legislated in 2018. The new crime is called 'human exploitation':

> A person who, in cases other than those referred to in Section 1 or 1a, by unlawful coercion, deception or exploitation of another person's position of dependence, defencelessness or difficult situation, exploits another person in forced labour, labour under clearly unreasonable conditions or begging is guilty of *human exploitation* and is sentenced to imprisonment for at most four years.[70]

Three criteria must be fulfilled for the provision to apply, the first being the particular means, i.e. coercion and deception. The lowest threshold is, however, the exploitation of another person's position of dependence, defencelessness, or difficult situation. This is defined in the *travaux préparatoires* as a situation arising from "financial debt or employment or subordination".[71] Financial duress, refugee status, or drug addiction are examples provided by the government.[72] Crucially, there is no demand that the exploitation of the victim's position results in duress or any significant delimitation of the victim's options.

69 R. Wilson-Gilmore, *Golden Gulag: Prisons, Surplus, Crisis, and Opposition in Globalizing California*, University of California Press, Berkeley 2007, p. 28.
70 Ch. 4, Sect. 1 b of the Criminal Code of 1965.
71 Government Bill 2017/18:123, p. 59 f.
72 *Ibid.*, p. 59 f.

This is an important difference in relation to the crime of human trafficking. The crime of human exploitation does not presuppose that the victim lacked a true or acceptable option besides accepting the exploitation.[73] Second, there must be exploitation, which is discussed by the government in the *travaux préparatories*: "The term exploitation implies, as is the case with human trafficking, an undue utilization of the victim. This means that exploitation is not at hand in every type of utilization of a person. Instead, it is presupposed that the utilization of the person on the basis of an assessment in the individual case appears as undue".[74] The victim must have suffered an attack on his or her freedom and peace. Third, the exploitation must be in one of the enumerated forms—either forced labour, labour under clearly unreasonable conditions, or begging. Forced labour is defined using the 1930 ILO Forced Labour Convention. Furthermore, threats from the 'employer' covered by this provision include not only violence and deprivation of freedom but also the reporting of undocumented migrants to the authorities, threats of withholding salaries, or a general delimitation of the victim's liberty. This lack of voluntariness does not need to be present from the beginning of the work, implying that the provision also covers situations in which an employee voluntarily entered into the employment contract but was subsequently subjected to threats, violence, and delimitations of freedom.[75]

The lowest threshold in this regard is the criterion "labour under clearly unreasonable conditions", which refers to actual circumstances at work or terms and conditions that are "detrimental to the extent that, following an objective overall assessment of the circumstances in the individual case, they blatantly differ negatively from what can be deemed acceptable on the labour market".[76] Examples of clearly unreasonable conditions are extremely low or no wages at all, long working days, risks for personal safety, high deductions from salaries for food and housing, etc.[77] The standard of clearly unreasonable conditions seems to be quite unclear and might even appear to be over-inclusive. An effect of a broad criminalisation of exploitation at work could be a shift in mandate in addressing inequalities from trade unions to crime-fighting agencies such as the police, prosecutors, and criminal courts. Historically,

73 *Ibid.*
74 *Ibid.*
75 *Ibid.*
76 *Ibid.*
77 *Ibid.*

autonomous regulation and enforcement of labour rights have been the lode star of the Swedish labour market model.[78]

Furthermore, Sweden has an extensive regime of labour and employment law covering all aspects of the work relationship. For every sector of the Swedish labour market, there is a comprehensive collective bargaining agreement concluded by the labour market parties on the sectoral level. It is, therefore, surprising that the *travaux préparatoires* do not refer to the labour market regulation in defining 'clearly unreasonable conditions'. Labour Law scholar Erik Sjödin comments:

> … the object of comparison is what is acceptable on the labour market. In order to establish that something is obviously unreasonable, it is necessary to know with some certainty what is acceptable. […] the introduction of the crime of 'human exploitation' is a criminalisation that does not take place in a void that lacks any pre-existing standards. Labour law defines what is acceptable on the labour market. Exploitation is relative to the extent that it must be compared to norms and standards otherwise applicable, and those are not provided by criminal law.[79]

The clearest example of this problem concerns wages. There is no law on minimum wages in Sweden, and freedom of contract prevails *de facto*. What can be considered an unacceptably low wage when the legislator has not decided what is the lowest possible wage? It is up to the courts to decide these complex matters.

In the first and only precedent from the Supreme Court regarding the new offence of human exploitation, handed down on February 15, 2022, the Court affirmed the position of Sjödin: the point of reference in deciding what is unacceptable on the labour market is labour legislation and relevant collective bargaining agreements.[80] Very few cases have been taken to court.[81] It is not clear why it took so long before a case reached the Supreme Court. In all instances, the Supreme Court specifies the type of exploitation that is to be covered by the crime of human exploitation: the purpose of this provision is, according to the Court, to sanction behaviour that constitutes an attack on somebody else's

---

78 *Ibid.*

79 E. Sjödin, 'Criminalisation as a response to low wages and labour market exploitation in Sweden' (2021) 12:4 *European Labour Law Journal* 529, p. 540.

80 Supreme Court Case NJA 2022 s. 23, para. 21.

81 A. Sonnsjö Andersson, 'Straffbar exploatering i arbete? Arbetet i restaurangen' (2022/2023) 23 *Juridisk tidskrift* 604.

peace and human dignity. This implies that the exploitation must comprehend "a not insignificant dimension of violation of a person's integrity" to constitute human exploitation.[82] If the actions of the perpetrator are "essentially limited to economic exploitation which is not a violation of personal integrity", then other crimes might have taken place, such as fraud or usury.[83] The criteria described above apply. 'Deception' is fulfilled if the perpetrator never had the intention of honouring his or her relevant obligations. *In casu*, the difficult situation the victims found themselves in was a result of them only recently having arrived in Sweden and the fact that they did not have housing arrangements besides those provided by the perpetrator. The court finally states that when terms and conditions differ significantly from 'normal conditions', the criterion of 'clearly unreasonable conditions' is met. This criterion is exemplified by the facts of the case. In terms of pay, the workers/victims had received remuneration in the form of free meals and housing, which the court translates into an hourly wage of 19 SEK (appr. USD 1,85) and 56 SEK (appr. USD 5,43), to be compared to the wage level stipulated in the applicable collective bargaining agreement of 124 SEK (appr. 12 USD). Both these sums are considered to be clearly unreasonable. In terms of the amount of work performed, the court states that an average amount of work of 69 hours per week, to be compared to the 40-hour work week provided for by the Working Hours Act constitutes unreasonable conditions. The element of 'exploitation' in the actions of the perpetrator consisted of the motive to make a profit, the prolonged nature of this relationship and comments made by the perpetrator to the victims that he could have them deported from Sweden. These circumstances constituted a violation of the victims' personal integrity, amounting to exploitation.[84]

5.7 *Summing Up: Slavery and Criminal Law*

The legacy of slavery has been visible in different ways in the Swedish Penal Code and has shifted significantly over the years. Between 1864 and 1965, explicit reference was made in the Penal Code to both slavery and its racial aspect. These explicit references were scrapped in the 1965 criminal law reform, which found that it was unnecessary to criminalise slavery in a single specific provision. The crime of kidnapping and placing a person in a 'distressful situation', together with several other crimes against freedom and liberty, was put in slavery's stead, amounting to an indirect criminalisation of slavery. Subsequent to international legal developments regarding the trafficking of human beings,

82 Supreme Court Case NJA 2022 s. 23.

83 *Ibid.*

84 *Ibid.*

the criminalisation of slavery became closely linked to this specific provision. This was eventually followed by the criminalisation of human exploitation, which serves to render some particularly unequal working relationships into crimes, even though they are in some respect 'voluntary' on the part of the worker. While the actual term 'slavery' is not used in any valid Swedish legislation, the criminalisation of forced labour and slavery must be said to be sufficient at present. The need for criminal law in the labour market has also been re-assessed: the crime of human exploitation would have been perceived as quite out of place—redundant—during the heyday of the trade union movement in the 1970s and 1980s. This criminalisation has today proven itself to be a measure needed to complement the usual private law mechanisms (not least trade union enforcement) for securing decent working conditions in the Swedish labour market. Discourses on contemporary slavery or forced labour are most often connected to migrant workers in Sweden,[85] enforcing the casting of these types of work relations as something fundamentally alien and external to the Swedish labour market.

6 The Issue of Remembrance, Apology, and Reparations

6.1 *Introduction*

The fact that Swedish society has not accepted its colonial past and role in the slave trade does not imply that no initiatives have been taken through formal channels, such as motions for Acts of Parliament. Furthermore, a process is underway to demand reparations from Sweden.

6.2 *Remembrance and Apology: an Act of Parliament?*

Between 2001 and 2012, the issue of remembrance and apologies for Sweden's part in the slave trade was on the agenda of the Swedish Parliament. Several proposals have been put forward by individual members of Parliament—all of whom were from the Left Party, Social Democrats, and Green Party. In every instance, the motion was rejected. It is not unlikely that the United Nations' 2001 World Conference against Racism, Racial Discrimination, Xenophobia and Related Intolerance contributed to creating momentum for these actions.

In 2001, a motion from the Left Party suggested that the extent to which Sweden took part in the Transatlantic slave trade should be investigated and

85 C. Woolfson, P. Herzfeld Olsson and C. Thörnqvist, 'Forced Labour and Migrant Berry Pickers in Sweden' (2012) 28:2 *The International Journal of Comparative Labour Law and Industrial Relations* 147.

that this project should form the basis for an apology on the part of Sweden.[86] In rejecting the motion, Parliament stated that slavery and the slave trade were "a shameful part of human history".[87] It continued, "it is important not to forget or belittle what took place. Knowledge about history is important not least to be able to understand current events and to prevent similar tragedies from occurring again. In this respect schools are important".[88] The motion was rejected by Parliament with reference to the initiatives included in the Durban Declaration from the 2001 World Conference against Racism, Racial Discrimination, Xenophobia and Related Intolerance and the Slave Route Project of UNESCO. These initiatives would suffice to effectuate what the member had asked for, Parliament argued.

The following year, a Social Democratic member of parliament—Joe Frans—motioned for Parliament to improve teaching and learning as well as school materials on Sweden's role in slavery and the slave trade. Learning more about slavery would be the most dignified way of taking responsibility for the suffering caused by slavery, the member argued.[89] Parliament did not respond in the same serious and solemn tone as the member. Instead, it reminded the member that schools were allowed to cover slavery in their history classes—the curricula in force did not hinder teaching about Sweden's role in slavery. Frans put the same motion forward the following year and got an identical response.[90] He would, for the coming four years, try different ways to convince Parliament to act in relation to the historical practice of slavery. In 2003, Frans suggested that Sweden join the United Nation's efforts to remember and honour victims of the slave trade. Parliament, however, responded by emphasising the importance of remembering slavery but nevertheless decided that an Act of Parliament was not called for.[91] Frans once again tried to persuade Parliament to act in relation to Sweden's slaving years. This time, he suggested initiating a research programme to investigate the scope of Sweden's involvement in the slave trade in order to create better teaching materials for schools. Parliament again refused to decide in accordance with the proposal: this research was important but would probably be addressed in some of the academic history departments in Sweden anyway.[92] The last time the Social

86 Motion 2001/02:U220, betänkande 2001/02:UU8.
87 Motion 2001/02:U220, betänkande 2001/02:UU8.
88 Motion 2001/02:U220, betänkande 2001/02:UU8.
89 Motion 2002/03:Ub396, betänkande 2002/03:UbU11.
90 Motion 2003/04:Ub386, betänkande 2003/04:UbU11.
91 Motion 2003/04:Ub386, betänkande 2003/04:KU15.
92 Motion 2004/05:Kr336, betänkande 2004/05:KrU7.

Democrat attempted to get an Act of Parliament regarding slavery, he did not get a reasoned response.[93]

It was not until March 25, 2007, that the Swedish government, for the first time, officially acknowledged Sweden's role in the slave trade. In a speech on the International Day of Remembrance of the Victims of Slavery and the Transatlantic Slave Trade, then Minister for Integration and Gender Equality Nyamko Sabuni (Liberal Party) stated: "Herewith the Swedish government acknowledges that Sweden also took part in slavery [...]. All states that participated must make up with the past [...]. We must shed light on this dark part of Swedish history and understand its underlying mechanisms".[94] This amounts to a fairly strong statement, albeit not from the Prime Minister.

In 2010 and 2012, elected officials from the Green Party tried to persuade Parliament that it should act in favour of Sweden 'processing' its role and participation in the slave trade. It was suggested that Sweden should join the efforts of the United Nations, disseminate information about the slave trade nationally, and also issue an official apology for Sweden's slaving years. Parliament responded that a teaching material was presently highlighting Sweden's role in slavery. The proposal for an apology was not met with a response.[95]

6.3 *Reparations*

The Caribbean Reparations Commission (CRC) issued in December 2020 a demand that former European slaving nations pay their debts. It argues that the Caribbean people are still affected by the legacy of slavery and that it is necessary to compensate for the damages caused.[96] Professor Verene Shepherd, vice chairman of the CRC, is quoted as saying: "Sweden and the Swedish royal family made a profit from slavery. We demand an apology from the Swedish government and the royal family to the people of the Caribbean".[97] She adds: "[a]s a nation proud of its efforts to further human rights and equality Sweden

93 Motion 2005/06:U366, betänkande 2005/06:UU15.

94 Speech at Anti-Slavery Event, <https://web.archive.org/web/20080218105838/http://www.regeringen.se/sb/d/7613/a/93574>.

95 Motion 2010/11:Kr328, betänkande 2010/11:KrU10, motion 2012/13:KrU9/13:Kr317, betänkande 2012/13:KrU9.

96 Caribbean Countries Call on Former European Slave Nations to Pay Back their Debts, <https://caricomreparations.org/caribbean-countries-call-on-former-european-slave-nations-to-pay-back-their-debts/>.

97 Slave Trade in the Swedish Colony – She Demands an Apology from the King, <https://www.expressen.se/nyheter/slavhandeln-i-svenska-kolonin-hon-kraver-ursakt-av-kungen-/>.

cannot be comfortable with this part of its history. Sweden should do the right thing and apologize, even if it is not formally obliged to do so".[98] In relation to this intervention, the Swedish government has responded that it has noted the processes within the CRC, but since it has not received a formal request, it has not taken a position regarding reparations and apology.[99] Verene Sheperd is working to pressure *inter alia* the Swedish government for a meeting about the issue of reparations.[100]

6.4 *Summing Up: the Non-issue of Apology and Reparations*

Implementing measures serving to process Sweden's participation in the slave trade is not a priority for the government. Not much has been done in this respect. The discourse of 'Scandinavian exceptionalism' is mirrored in the official positions and actions on the part of the government. Feminist scholars have pointed out the central role of discourses around exceptionalism in Swedish foreign policy. Annika Bergman Rosamond, for example, has described how Swedish foreign policy has been focused on "projecting [Sweden] as a neutral partner of small and medium-sized postcolonial states in need of foreign assistance" and seeking "to disperse democratic and peaceful ideas, as well as contributing to economic development across the globe".[101] Furthermore, domestic social and political processes of change in Sweden interplay with foreign policy stances on the part of Sweden. Solidarity, according to Bergman Rosamond, is "viewed as a universal value" with wider appeal than that of the working class, and domestic practices and discourses of solidarity have "helped to constitute Sweden's self-narrative and sense of ethical obligation to distant others".[102]

The national self-image of being a force for good in the international arena does not seem to imply a need for any particularly forceful measures in dealing with a colonial past. Sweden still perceives itself as being external or alien to historical processes of exploitation and colonialism. The relative success of the labour movement and Social Democracy in reshaping the Swedish labour

98 *Ibid.*

99 *Ibid.*

100 Slavery Reparations in the Caribbean: What to Expect?, <https://www.americasquarterly.org/article/slavery-reparations-in-the-caribbean-what-to-expect/>.

101 A. Bergman Rosamond, 'Swedish Internationalism and Development Aid', in Jon Pierre (ed.) *The Oxford Handbook of Swedish Politics*, Oxford University Press, Oxford 2015, p. 467.

102 *Ibid.*, p. 466.

market and Swedish society into a welfare state might have fuelled these discourses on Swedish exceptionalism in relation to the global arena.

In sum, the Swedish government has had many opportunities to accept proposals in Parliament for apologies, remembrance, education, and reparations in relation to Sweden's role in the slave trade. The parliamentarians who put forward the proposals that were rejected have been members of the party in government. The last word has probably not been said about the issue of reparations. A process seems to be underway in the community of Caribbean states, and the issue is unresolved.

7 Concluding Remarks

This chapter has illustrated Sweden's past as a slave nation and what its 'exceptionalist' stance towards this history implies for processing this past. Slavery has been underemphasised in domestic constitutional debates and remains not explicitly prohibited by constitutional norms. The prohibition of slavery operational today in Sweden is thus found in its obligations to other states and the international community. This constitutional situation neatly mirrors the exceptionalist stance towards Sweden's role in slavery.

This stance likely has contributed to the understanding of so-called 'contemporary slavery' or human exploitation, which is coded as an entirely marginal phenomenon in the labour market and as a result of external forces in the form of migration to Sweden. In this respect, there is a continuity of historical practices in the Swedish labour market. The criminalisation of unequal and oppressive work relations has, to some extent, gone full circle in Sweden: from explicitly referencing slavery and people of African descent to a notion of prohibition against slavery being irrelevant to linking it to trafficking of human beings and sexual exploitation of women, to a very inclusive definition of 'human exploitation' lacking reference to people of African descent. The criminalisation of human exploitation is quite inclusive and overlaps with conflicts regulated by purely private law mechanisms.

The general discourse which renders Sweden's past as a slave nation invisible is reflected in official government policy. The state has acknowledged its past but has not moved beyond this. Silencing history through legal formations is, in many ways, a productive tactic. Exceptionalising Sweden in the history of global racial capitalism and the Transatlantic slave trade is the externalisation of the violence and violent actors attached to these practices. This exceptionalising, in turn, has manifested itself in dealing with forced labour and slavery as a matter exclusively linked to trafficking. This framing on the one hand—and internally—confirms the self-image of the Swedish innocence and the supposed meaninglessness of dealing with slavery in a substantial manner, while on the other hand, it establishes the violence of slavery and forced labour as an external threat linked to borders and border crossers. Furthermore, this framing is legally and politically productive. Externalizing slavery allows the state to mobilize its legal forces, resources, and mechanisms of control not to address its internal labour relations (past and present) but under the pretext of combatting the criminal offence of trafficking to enforce and bolster the ongoing European border politics of *non-entrée*. This is to say that forced labour/slavery enters the imagination of the Swedish legislature only when it has something to offer for the purpose of managing the composition of its demography through exclusion at the borders. What makes people vulnerable to conditions of forced labour in the Swedish labour market today is the militarized enforcement of the border regime through criminal law, which is based on the differentiation of people through their migratory status as irregular migrant workers, seasonal migrant workers, or non-citizens.

Academic References

A. Bergman Rosamond, 'Swedish Internationalism and Development Aid' in J. Pierre (ed) *The Oxford Handbook of Swedish Politics*, Oxford University Press, Oxford 2015, pp. 462–478.

A. Blackett and A. Duquesnoy, 'Slavery Is Not a Metaphor: U.S. Prison Labor and Racial Subordination through the Lens of the ILO's Abolition of Forced Labour Convention' (2021) 67 *USLA Law Review* 1504.

A. Hallner, 'Från vit slavhandel till trafficking. En studie om föreställningar kring människohandel och dess offer' (2003) 129:3 *Historisk tidskrift* 429.

A. Sonnsjö Andersson, 'Straffbar exploatering i arbete? Arbetet i restaurangen' (2022/2023) 23 *Juridisk tidskrift* 604.

C. Evans and G. Rydén, *Baltic Iron in the Atlantic World in the Eighteenth Century*, Brill, Leiden 2007.

C. Woolfson, P. Herzfeld Olsson and C. Thörnqvist, 'Forced Labour and Migrant Berry Pickers in Sweden' (2012) 28:2 *The International Journal of Comparative Labour Law and Industrial Relations* 147.

D. Bell, *Faces at the Bottom of the Well: The Permanence of Racism*, Basic Books, New York 1992.

D. Maul, "Help Them Move the ILO Way': The International Labour Organization and the Modernization Discourse in the Era of Decolonization and the Cold War' (2009) 33:3 *Diplomatic History* 387.

D. Maul, *The International Labour Organization. 100 Years of Global Social Policy*, De Gruyter Oldenbourg, 2019.

E. Sjödin, 'Criminalisation as a response to low wages and labour market exploitation in Sweden' (2021) 12:4 *European Labour Law Journal* 529.

F. Thomasson, 'Thirty-Two Lashes at Quatre Piquets: Slave Laws and Justice in the Swedish Colony of St. Barthélemy ca. 1800' in H. Weiss (ed), *Ports of Globalisation, Places of Creolisation. Nordic Possessions in the Atlantic World during the Era of the Slave Trade*, Brill, Leiden 2016, pp. 280–305.

F. Thomasson, *Svarta Saint-Barthélemy: Människoöden i en svensk koloni 1785–1847*, Natur & Kultur, Stockholm 2022.

G. Myrdal, *An American Dilemma: The Negro Problem and Modern Democracy*, Harpers & Brothers, New York 1944.

L.A. Körber, 'Exceptionalisms and Entanglements. Legacies and Memories of Scandinavian Colonial History' in J. Bjerring-Hansen, T. Jelsbak and A.E. Mrozewicz (eds) *Scandinavian Exceptionalisms, Culture, Society, Discourse*, Nordeuropa-Institut der Humboldt-Universität, Berlin 2021, pp. 183–204.

L.A. Körber, 'Sweden and St. Barthélemy: Exceptionalisms, Whiteness, and the Disappearance of Slavery from Colonial History' (2019) 91:1–2 *Scandinavian Studies* 74.

L. Brännström, 'The Terms of Ethnoracial Equality: The Swedish Courts' reading of Ethnic Affiliation, Race and Culture' (2018) 27:5 *Social & Legal Studies* 616.

M. Airaksinen, 'Tar Production in colonial North America' (1996) 2:1 *Environment and History* 115.

N. Sharma, *Home Rule: National Sovereignty and the Separation of Natives and Migrants*, Duke University Press, Durham 2020.

R. Fahlbeck, *Nothing Succeeds Like Success. Trade Unionism in Sweden*, Juristförlaget i Lund, Visby 1999.

R. Wilson-Gilmore, *Golden Gulag: Prisons, Surplus, Crisis, and Opposition in Globalizing California*, University of California Press, Berkeley 2007.

S.M. Schwebel, 'The United States Assaults the I.L.O'. (1971) 65:1 *The American Journal of International Law* 136.

Contemporary Forms of Slavery, Causes and Consequences: United Kingdom

Shahrzad Fouladvand

1 Introduction

The United Kingdom has always asserted a leadership role in the global campaign against slavery. Despite itself profiting handsomely from the conduct of the slave trade for over 200 years, it nevertheless became one of the first nations to outlaw slave trading, and since the enactment of the 1807 *Slave Trade Abolition Act*, it has conducted a vigorous abolitionist campaign, supported first by its maritime dominance and latterly by its role in the League of Nations and other international bodies. However, slavery remains stubbornly resistant to abolition. In a comprehensive evidence review chaired by the Centre for Social Justice (CSJ) in their 2013 policy report 'It Happens Here: Equipping the United Kingdom to fight modern slavery', it was noted that "there are still slaves in our sophisticated society today".[1] Moreover, the Global Slavery Index suggests that up to 50 million people suffer under various forms of modern slavery,[2] an appalling form of oppression which targets the vulnerable and voiceless, representing a grave violation of human rights and basic dignity.

It was submitted in the 2013 Report of the Modern Slavery Bill Evidence Review that in response to the complexity of modern slavery, new legislation was needed to establish Britain as "a world leader in fighting the insidious curse of slavery", which is hidden underground and difficult to detect.[3] The resulting UK *Modern Slavery Act 2015* is a historic piece of legislation, claimed to be the first of its kind in Europe to address this problem. Following the three internationally recognised themes of prevention, protection, and prosecution,[4] the

1 The 2013 Report by Centre for Social Justice (CSJ) 'It Happens Here: Equipping the United Kingdom to fight modern slavery', p. 12, <www.centreforsocialjustice.org.uk/wp-content/uploads/2013/03/CSJ_Slavery_Full_Report_WEB5.pdf>.

2 Global Slavery Index, <https://www.walkfree.org/global-slavery-index/map/>.

3 UK Parliament, Establishing Britain as a world leader in the fight against modern slavery: Report of the Modern Slavery Bill Evidence Review, Chaired by Rt Hon Frank Field MP, p. 1, <https://www.centreforsocialjustice.org.uk/wp-content/uploads/2018/03/modern-slavery_text_final-for-web.pdf>.

4 Article 2 of the 2000 United Nations Protocol to Prevent, Suppress and Punish Trafficking in Persons, Especially Women and Children (United Nations Trafficking Protocol).

 | DOI:10.1163/9789004723801_016

United Kingdom has again, so it is argued, led the way towards the eradication of all forms of slavery by its legislative measures in a single Act to "counter this growing evil".[5] This short analysis examines the basis for these claims and enquires whether slavery was ever really eradicated by the measures outlined above and whether the UK's *Modern Slavery Act* represents a viable way forward in the campaign to abolish these practices.

2 The Presence of the Past

Various forms of slavery emerged in different parts of the world and were developed particularly in the regions of the Mediterranean Sea (today's Europe and the Middle East). Slavery in the Western Roman Empire continued on a large scale, and some laws were also enacted for the enslavement of criminals who could not pay financial penalties for their crimes.[6] Enslaved labourers were used in ancient Egypt, Greece, Imperial Rome, and Islamic societies in the Middle East and North Africa for construction, the armed forces, agriculture, industry, and domestic service. Slaves were mostly recruited through kidnapping or capture during warfare with their own and neighbouring societies around the Mediterranean, with Cairo serving as a large emporium for the slave trade to the Mediterranean.[7] During the Middle Ages, slavery existed across the Mediterranean world, Russia and other Slavic lands, Africa, and Asia.[8] Africa became the main source of slaves, and during the Arab slave trade, or the 'trans-Saharan trade', around 9.5 million Africans were shipped out by the Arabs into the Mediterranean world.[9] The Seljuk Empire established slave posts on the East African coast, where they shipped the enslaved to the Persian Gulf and India.[10] Slave routes in the intercontinental slave trade were not stable, and during the Ottoman period, they stretched from Kyiv westwards towards Slavic lands and southwards to Istanbul and various ports on

5 UK Parliament, above n. 3.

6 D. A. Pargas, and J. Schiel, *The Palgrave Handbook of Global Slavery throughout History*. Springer International Publishing, New York 2023, p. 304.

7 K. Morgan, *Slavery and the British Empire: From Africa to America*, Oxford University Press, New York 2007, p. 1.

8 *Ibid.*

9 D. Clarke, *Slaves & Slavery*, Grange, London 1998. See also Recalling Africa's harrowing tale of its first slavers – The Arabs – as UK Slave Trade Abolition is commemorated, <https://newafricanmagazine.com/16616/>.

10 K. Morgan, above n. 7.

the southern shores of the Black Sea.[11] The demand for labour had become apparent in the 14th century in Europe due to the decline of serfdom and as the rural population became more mobile to satisfy that demand.[12] The growth of the Transatlantic Slave Trade was a response to the problem of labour.[13]

With the European discovery of America, the slave trade shifted towards the West.[14] Slavery as an institution in the transatlantic world was well established in the New World (the Atlantic World) during the 15th and 16th centuries by the Portuguese and the Spanish.[15] The Portuguese explorations of the West African coast opened up colonial Atlantic Slavery, which gave rise to a massive coastal slave trade route from West Africa to the Americas.[16] Portugal was the first European nation to become involved in transatlantic slave trafficking. England followed the Spanish, Dutch, and French, shipping large numbers of enslaved Africans across the Atlantic. Slavery was transplanted to Central and South America and the Caribbean in the 16th century for forced labour on plantations.[17] England's involvement received royal endorsement in 1663,[18] and the concentration of slaves in British colonies based on plantation labour began primarily in the Caribbean islands, including Jamaica, Grenada, Barbados, Dominica, St. Vincent, and Trinidad and Tobago. It later expanded to the North American mainland—in Virginia, Maryland, Massachusetts Bay—and subsequently to the South Atlantic and Indian Oceans.[19]

The failure of indigenous slavery and an increasing unwillingness of European labourers to emigrate under certain terms and conditions of their contract—particularly in the British, French, Dutch, and Spanish colonies—resulted in the importation of enslaved Africans and a massive Atlantic slave trade, which serviced the cultivation of sugarcane and the production of

11 H. G. Özkoray, 'Slavery in the Ottoman Empire' in D. A. Pargas, and J. Schiel, *The Palgrave Handbook of Global Slavery Throughout History*, Springer International Publishing, New York 2023, p. 246.

12 J. Walvin, *Slavery and the Slave Trade: A Short Illustrated History*, The Macmillan Press, London and Basingstoke 1983, p. 19.

13 K. Morgan, above n. 7, p. 12.

14 D. Clarke, above n. 9.

15 K. Morgan, above n. 7, p. 5.

16 D. Clarke, above n. 9.

17 K. Morgan, above n. 7, p. 12.

18 Charter granted to the Company of Royal Adventurers of England Trading into Africa, 1663, British Library.

19 K. Morgan, above n. 7, p. 8.

colonial commodities for European and, increasingly, global markets.[20] The Royal African Company, based in London, was established by a royal charter granted by Charles II in 1672[21] which gave it a monopoly on the British slave trade between Africa and the West Indies[22] and transported an average of 5,000 slaves a year. In addition to slaves, the Royal African Company had a monopoly on exporting gold, ivory, malaguetta (pepper), and redwood from Africa.[23] However, its monopoly charter was ended by an Act of Parliament after 1689, and the slave trade was opened to private merchants.[24]

Slavery and the slave trade became a way of supplying inhabitants to maintain the sugar plantations in the Caribbean and to support the maritime strength of the British Empire.[25] A social and economic historian of the British Atlantic world, Kenneth Morgan, claims the first known example of English slave trading in Africa was between 1564–69 when British maritime explorers were interested in trading opportunities in Africa and the New World.[26] The defeat of the Spanish Armada in 1588 launched the English colonisation of the Americas by destroying Spanish naval dominance. By the end of the 17th century, around 350,000 English people had crossed the Atlantic.[27] Abigail Swingen, in her book 'Comparing Visions of Empire',[28] argues that the English government's endorsement of open trade for African slaves indicated its acceptance of slavery as an institution. Consequently, "a colonial planter vision of empire, wherein local Indigenous peoples were systematically dispossessed and murdered, and Africans were enslaved and brought to the Americas for forced plantation labour, was developed in the 1650s".[29]

Enslaved persons were taken from Africa on European ships arriving in European colonies in the Americas during 1501–1866, in a period when many Europeans held racist attitudes towards black people and accepted the racial

---

20 M. Zeuske 'The Rise of Atlantic Slavery in the Americas' in D. A. Pargas, and J. Schiel, *The Palgrave Handbook of Global Slavery throughout History*, Springer International Publishing, New York 2023, p. 382.

21 K. Morgan, above n. 7, p. 56.

22 A. Carlos, A. M. and J. B. Kruse 'The Decline of the Royal African Company: Fringe Firms and the Role of the Charter' (1996) 49:2 *The Economic History Review* 291.

23 *Ibid.*, p. 292.

24 K. Morgan, *Slavery, Atlantic Trade and the British Economy, 1660–1800*, Cambridge University Press, Cambridge 2000, p. 9.

25 *Ibid.*, p. 148.

26 K. Morgan, above n. 7, p. 53.

27 K. Morgan, above n. 24, p. 6.

28 A. L. Swingen, *Competing Visions of Empire: Labor, Slavery, and the Origins of the British Atlantic Empire.* New Haven, Yale University Press, 2015.

29 *Ibid.*, p. 171.

nature of black slavery.[30] In England, racial thinking developed during the Elizabethan period and was shaped by beliefs about skin colour, religion, nationality, class, money, and gender.[31] Africans, North African Moors, and Jewish people were the three main community groups who were treated differently. They were perceived as 'the Other' and considered to be capable of less moral conduct than Christians. Therefore, as Ania Loomba notes, race was utilised as an instrument to wield power over a variety of minority groups.[32] Before 1750, blackness was associated with a range of negative factors, including heathenism and paganism.[33] The presence of Africans in Elizabethan England has been explored by some scholars such as Kim Hall and Ania Loomba,[34] who note that the majority of the black population were African domestic slaves —male and female—and some were Moors, mostly from North Africa, such as Morocco. In addition, the Portuguese New Christians, who were forcibly converted Jews and wealthy merchants, sought refuge in English Ports during the 1540s, keeping their slaves and maintaining their old elite lifestyle.[35]

The British government offered no legislative or other guidance on the status and treatment of slaves. All thirteen British North American colonies were allowed to formulate their own slave codes.[36] British colonies enacted laws on slavery after 1660 in support of white slave owners, giving them complete control over the movement and punishment of their slaves, which stigmatised Africans as racially inferior. For example, Morgen, in his study of 'Slavery and British Empire: From Africa to America' notes that the Barbados Slave Code of 1661—which became the model for slave laws in Jamaica and elsewhere—emphasised the wickedness caused by black "Disorder, Rapines and Inhumanities to which they are naturally prone and inclined".[37] Another example is

30 D. Wilkins, 'Reparations, Restorative Justice, and the impact of the 2007 Bicentenary of the Abolition of the British Slave Trade' in D. Bulla (ed) *Why Slavery Endures: Its Past, Present and Future*, Cambridge Scholars Publishing, Cambridge 2020, p. 102.

31 A. Loomba, *A Shakespeare, Race, and Colonialism*, Oxford University Press, New York 2002.

32 *Ibid.*

33 K. Morgan, above n. 7, p. 148.

34 For example: K. F. Hall, *Things of Darkness: Economies of Race and Gender in Early Modern England Cornell*, University Press, Ithaca 1995; A. Loomba, above n. 31; G. Ungerer, 'The Presence of Africans in Elizabethan England and the Performance of "Titus Andronicus" at Burley-on-the-Hill, 1595/96'. (2008) 21 *Medieval & Renaissance Drama in England* 19; T. Hahn, 'The Difference the Middle Ages Makes: Color and Race before the Modern World' (2001) 31:1 *Journal of Medieval and Early Modern Studies* 1.

35 G. Ungerer, above n. 34, p. 32.

36 K. Morgan, above n. 7, p. 112.

37 *Ibid.*, pp. 113–114.

Virginia's first major slave code, which passed in 1680 and degraded the status of non-Europeans in the colony to slaves, asserting that "all servants imported into the Country ... who were not Christians in their native Country ... shall be accounted and be slaves. All Negro, mulatto and Indian slaves within this dominion ... shall be held to be real estate".[38]

3 The Transatlantic Slave Trade

An estimated 12 million Africans were victims of the Transatlantic Slave Trade.[39] Between 1660 and 1807, it is estimated that Britain transported 3.4 million Africans to the Americas, mainly from Senegambia, Sierra Leone, the Windward Coast, the Gold Coast, the Bight of Benin, the Bight of Biafra, and West-central Africa.[40] In addition, the estimated number of slaves in India acquired by Britain was between 8 and 9 million.[41] Particularly in Bengal, as part of the British Empire in the East, there were slaves in the military, trade, and domestic servitude.[42] However, the heart of British involvement with slavery and the slave trade was in the operation of the triangular trade with Africa and the Americas.[43]

The European discovery of America and the Cape route to India, as economic historian Eric Willims notes, were "the two greatest and most important events recorded in the history of mankind".[44] The cost and financing of the Nine Years' War against France (1689–1697) have also been mentioned as one important aspect of Britain's involvement in the slave trade.[45] Furthermore, according to Williams,[46] slavery helped finance the Industrial Revolution in England. Catherine Hall et al., in their study 'Legacies of British Slave-Ownership', found that slaveowners in the West Indies were influential in the

38 *Ibid.*, p. 112.
39 M. Zeuske, above n. 20, p. 383.
40 J. Oldfield, 2021, Abolition of the slave trade and slavery in Britain, British Library.
41 K. Morgan, above n. 7, p. 18.
42 *Ibid.*
43 *Ibid.*, p. 203.
44 Cited in E. E. Williams, *Capitalism & Slavery*, University of North Carolina Press, Chapel Hill 1994, p. 51.
45 A. L. Swingen, above n. 28, p. 159.
46 E. E. Williams, above n. 44.

rise of industrial capitalism, as they were able to finance it.[47] They made an essential contribution to the Industrial Revolution in the late 18th century when cotton machinery and steam engines in coal mines emerged.[48] Through the slave trade, plantation owners, shipbuilders, and merchants established the banking industry in Europe and gradually expanded powerful ideas of capitalism worldwide.[49] Allegedly, eleven former governors and 16 directors of the Bank of England owned slaves or directly profited from the trade between the 18th and 19th centuries. The Royal Bank of Scotland, Barclays Bank, Lloyds Banking Group, HSBC, and Royal Mail have all been linked to slavery.[50]

The Transatlantic Slave Trade was subject to losses as well as financial gains.[51] Textiles, beads, firearms, and metalware were shipped to West Africa and sold in exchange for Africans. The historical record reveals that slaves were packed tight into the holds of ships for the Atlantic crossing and subsequently sold in the Americas. In the last part of the triangular slaving voyage, staple commodities from the Americas were loaded aboard ships for the voyage home and the prospects of sale in the ships' port of origin.[52] The costs of operating slave-trading voyages were substantial. For example, British slave merchants invested about £200,000 in Liverpool's slave trade in 1750 (about £55 million today) and more than £1 million in 1800 (about £104 million today), resulting in very substantial profit.[53] Between 1630 and 1807, Britain's slave merchants made a profit of about £12 million (about £ 1 billion) from participation in the slave trade.[54] Former slave owners made their fortune from the slave trade and contributed to the transformation of the British economy.[55] For example, Edward Colston of Bristol made his fortune with the Royal African Company (RAC), which was the leading provider of slaves transported in English vessels from the West Coast of Africa to the Americas in the 17th century. The

47 C. Hall, et al., *Legacies of British Slave Ownership: Colonial Slavery and the Formation of Victorian Britain*, Cambridge University Press, Cambridge 2014, p. 9.

48 *Ibid.*

49 *Ibid.*

50 'Blood money—how wealth created by slavery bankrolled capitalist Britain', *Socialist Worker*, (06.03.2021), <https://socialistworker.co.uk/features/blood-money-how-wealth-created-by-slavery-bankrolled-capitalist-britain/>.

51 K. Morgan, above n. 7, p. 66.

52 K. Morgan, above n. 24, p. 9.

53 K. Morgan, above n. 7, p. 79.

54 'Britain and the Caribbean Financial Considerations', <https://www.bbc.co.uk/bitesize/guides/zjyqtfr/revision/7>.

55 C. Hall, et al., above n. 47, p. 79.

company shipped about 84,000 enslaved Africans to serve as the labour force for plantations in North America and the Caribbean.[56]

In the late 18th century, Britain's Atlantic empire comprised thirteen colonies in North America, as well as the Caribbean islands of Grenada, Dominica, St Vincent, and Tobago, which were ceded to the British by the Treaty of Paris in 1763. Victory in the Seven Years' War greatly increased Britain's dominance in trade. In addition, Britain acquired more colonies that had slave labour. For example, Trinidad was taken from the Spanish under the Peace of Amiens in 1802.[57] Jamaica was the largest West Indian Island to come into British possession, and its sugar plantations sector expanded massively during the 18th century.[58] Some planters were residents in the Caribbean and occasionally visited Britain. Other planters acted as merchants and spent their time between the West Indies and Britain, however, gradually, by 1775, absentees owned most of the sugar plantations.[59]

Merchants from London, Bristol, and Liverpool were dominant in the English slave trade until the abolition of the slave trade in 1807. For example, 63 slave vessels were cleared from Bristol in 1725, and Bristol became the leading English slave-trading port until the 1740s. Liverpool increased its slave trade, surpassing Bristol to become the nation's leading slave-trading port. Between 1773 and 1804, 107 slave ships cleared from Liverpool.[60] Other British ports, such as Lancaster and Whitehaven, participated in the Transatlantic Slave Trade on a smaller scale. Economic gain was the main motive of the merchants and planters for the slave trade. For example, sugar planting was a profitable enterprise and was the most lucrative import brought into Britain, worth £2,360,000 in 1772.[61] Every sale at the end of the voyage meant revenue for the state and profits for the traders.[62] Planters initially owned the Royal African Company in Barbados, Jamaica, and the Leewards, but due to serious financial and operational problems, they eventually lost their prestige and power. They survived the abolition of the British slave trade in 1807, but the Parliamentary Act in 1821 dissolved the Royal African Company.[63] Slavery, however, remained

56 W. A. Pettigrew, *Freedom's debt: The Royal African Company and the politics of the Atlantic slave trade, 1672–1752*, The University of North Carolina Press, Chapel Hill 2013.

57 K. Morgan, above n. 7, p. 8.

58 *Ibid.*, p. 15.

59 *Ibid.*, p. 46.

60 *Ibid.*, p. 62.

61 *Ibid.*, p. 34.

62 S. Drescher, *From Slavery to Freedom: Comparative Studies in the Rise and Fall of Atlantic Slavery*, Macmillan Press, New York 1999, p. 321.

63 K. Morgan, above n. 7, p. 59.

a lawful form of commerce until the parliamentary approval of the abolition of slavery in 1833, which took effect in 1834.[64]

It was not until the 19th century that gradual emancipation started to occur, particularly in the British Caribbean, due to the decline of the plantation system[65] and, more broadly, the rise of industrial capitalism.[66] Consequently, anti-slavery campaigners in Britain lobbied for many years to end the slave trade, resulting in the enactment of the *Abolition of the Slave Trade Act* on March 25th, 1807. Subsequently, the British government passed the *Slavery Abolition Act of 1833*, which formally freed 800,000 enslaved Africans, predominantly in the Caribbean and South Africa.[67]

4 The Abolition of the Slave Trade and Slavery

Negative attitudes and intellectual and religious attacks on slavery began to be developed by philosophers, lawyers, political, and religious figures in the second half of the 18th century.[68] As Oldfield—a social historian—and Kaplan—a feminist critic with strong interests in both race and class—note, abolitionists condemned transatlantic slavery on moral grounds and its dehumanising impact on Africans.[69] Events such as the case of *Somerset v. Steward* in 1772, although unsuccessful in ending slavery in Britain, served as forceful encouragement to the abolitionists.[70] The *Somerset* case is a good example of two contradictory legal systems: English law's emphasis on the extension and maintenance of liberties while 'the Atlantic slave empire' was based on the denial of liberty to millions of Africans.[71] Lord Mansfield's ruling, which was handed down before the American Declaration of Independence, also had an impact on the Americas and "became part of a newly developing American

64 A. Tewari, 'The Reform Bill (1832) and the Abolition of Slavery (1833): A Caribbean Link' (2012) 73 *Proceedings of the Indian History Congress*, 1140.

65 T. Burnard 'Plantation Slavery in the British Caribbean' in D. A. Pargas, and J. Schiel, *The Palgrave Handbook of Global Slavery throughout History*, Springer International Publishing, New York 2023, p. 406.

66 C. Hall, et. al., above n. 47, p. 9.

67 Slavery Abolition Act 1833, Minutes of the Committee for the abolition of the slave trade, British Library.

68 *Ibid.*, 149.

69 J. Oldfield and C. Kaplan (eds), *Imagining Transatlantic Slavery*, Palgrave Macmillan 2010, p. 2.

70 A. Tewari, above n. 64.

71 J. Walvin, *The Zong : A Massacre, the Law and the End of Slavery*, Yale University Press, New Haven 2011, p. 118.

common law".[72] In this very important case, Lord Mansfield maintained that '(t)he air of England is too pure to be breathed by an enslaved person'.[73] He went on:

> The state of slavery is of such a nature, that it is incapable of being introduced on any reasons, moral or political, but only by positive law, ... It is so odious, that nothing can be suffered to support it, but positive law. Whatever inconveniences, therefore, may follow from the decision, I cannot say this case is allowed or approved by the law of England; and therefore, the black must be discharged.[74]

The Zong is another important case which provoked a public outcry because of the massacre of 132 enslaved Africans, which occurred aboard a ship in 1781 and had a significant influence on the abolitionist movement.[75] The Zong was a slave cargo vessel commanded by Luke Collingwood, a former surgeon with extensive experience of the Atlantic crossing. The owners took out insurance "upon the whole of the Ship and on Goods ... valuing Slaves at £30 Sterling per head" and covering everything for £8,000.[76] The Zong, with 442 slaves aboard, left the West African coast bound for Jamaica. When water resources ran low because of a navigational error, the captain decided to throw one-third of the Slaves overboard to save the rest. The issue in this case was whether enslaved persons were considered insured property. Instead of bringing to justice those responsible for murdering the slaves, the owners of the ship argued that it was necessary to throw the slaves overboard due to a lack of water, and they made an insurance claim for the value of the lost 'human cargo'.[77] The first trial found that the insurance company was liable for the damages.[78] The insurers, however, refused to pay compensation to the ship owner.[79] Lord Mansfield addressed the question of a 'Policy of Insurance' upon the ship: how could such

72 W. R. Cotter, 'The Somerset Case and the Abolition of Slavery in England' (1994) 255:79 *History* 31.

73 D. A. Webb, 'The "Somerset" Effect: Parsing Lord Mansfield's Words on Slavery in Nineteenth Century America' (2014) 32:3 *Law and History Review* 455, p. 485.

74 Cited in W. M. Wiecek, 'Somerset: Lord Mansfield and the Legitimacy of Slavery in the Anglo-American World' (1974) 42:1 *The University of Chicago Law Review* 86, p. 86.

75 J. Walvin, above n. 71, p. 137.

76 *Ibid.*, p. 70.

77 J. Krikler, 'The Zong and the Lord Chief Justice' (2007) 64 *History Workshop Journal* 29, p. 29.

78 'Zong slave ship trial: insurance loss or mass murder?', <https://www.history.com/this-day-in-history/zong-slave-ship-trial>.

79 J. Walvin, above n. 71, p. 138.

mass killings be justified for insurance?[80] The Chief Justice believed, based on a growing abolitionist sentiment, that the captain and the crew of the Zong had acted wrongfully, and he ordered a retrial, which never took place. This case highlighted the ill-treatment of slaves and brought together the supporters of the abolition of the slave trade, including Granville Sharp and Olaudah Equiano.[81] The religious motivations of abolitionists can be seen in the central role played by the Quakers and other evangelicals, particularly those who were active in the Parliament. The Quakers were a politically prominent religious faction in 18th-century England. In 1787, they established a Society for Effecting the Abolition of the Slave Trade, and during their twenty-year campaign, they presented information and petitions to the House of Commons proposing measures to abolish the slave trade.[82] William Wilberforce, the leading British antislavery spokesman and the county MP for Yorkshire after 1784, played an important role in leading the anti-slave trade campaign in Parliament and actively raising the call for a general abolition of the slave trade.[83] In addition, some authors, such as Thomas Clarkson, began publishing evidence about slavery and the slave trade, which became a concern of British abolitionists during the 1780s and 1790s. This was not a purely European campaign. Former slaves, such as Olaudah Equiano and Ottobah Cugoan, also played an important role in the British abolition movement and appealed for human equality. Olaudah Equiano publicised the facts of the 1781 Zong massacre, and his writing was used as evidence in the House of Commons.[84] Equiano, in his 'Thoughts and Sentiments on the Evils of Slavery', originally published in 1787, wrote compellingly about the horrors of slavery and of his own experiences.[85] Cugoan and Olaudah were both members of an abolitionist group formed by Africans in Britain called the Sons of Africa, which had close connections with the first organised anti-slavery society in Britain, the Society for Effecting the Abolition of the Slave Trade (SEAST) founded in May 1787.[86]

Several attempts were made to ban the slave trade. For example, the Slave Trade Act of 1788 was proposed by Sir William Dolben, who was a close ally of William Wilberforce in Parliament. During debates on the Bill, he raised

80 *Ibid.*, p. 145.
81 'Zong slave ship trial: insurance loss or mass murder?', <https://www.history.com/this-day-in-history/zong-slave-ship-trial>.
82 K. Morgan, above n. 7, p. 149.
83 *Ibid.*, p. 154.
84 UK Parliament, The Transatlantic Slave Trade, <https://heritagecollections.parliament.uk/stories/the-transatlantic-slave-trade/>.
85 J. Oldfield and C. Kaplan, above n. 69, p. 2.
86 J. Oldfield, The Abolition of the Slave Trade and Slavery in Britain, (2021), British Library.

concerns about the appalling conditions in the 'Middle Passage', during which slaves were transported from the West Coast of Africa to West Indian ports.[87] The Slave Trade Act of 1788 was one of the first measures that legally restricted the number of slaves that could be carried on British vessels to five slaves for every three tons up to 200 tons. Under this Act, slave ships were required to keep a log of illness and mortality.[88] Subsequently, due to the political atmosphere at Westminster when Britain went to war against France in 1773 and amidst slave revolts in French colonies, abolition of the slave trade was adopted as a government policy issue. Following the Royal Proclamation of 1805, Wilberforce introduced a bill in Parliament in 1806 to prevent the supply of slaves by British ships to foreign and colonial territories.[89] The *Abolition of the Slave Trade Act* was passed in March 1807 and was the direct result of one of the most successful public campaigns in history.[90] The passage of the Act marked the official end of the British slave trade. Although the slave trade ended, the House of Commons had voted for gradual emancipation rather than immediate freedom for slaves.[91] The *1832 Reform Act* made electoral changes and gave many more people the right to vote,[92] influencing the process of ending slavery in Britain and its Atlantic colonies.[93] The *Emancipation Act* was passed on 31 July 1833, and slavery in the British Empire officially ended in 1834. Around 800,000 slaves were freed.[94] The Royal Naval West African Squadron played an important role in suppressing slave trafficking by the British and other nations as they exercised their power to search and seize the slave ships.[95] In early 1840, the suppression of the Transatlantic Slave Trade at the high seas brought together European and American abolitionist societies in London to unite international abolitionist forces in the fight for emancipation. This resulted in

87 J. W. LoGerfo, 'Sir William Dolben and "The Cause of Humanity": The Passage of the Slave Trade Regulation Act of 1788' (1973) 6:4 *Eighteenth-Century Studies* 431.

88 K. Morgan, above n. 7, p. 160.

89 *Ibid.*, p. 165.

90 Parliament and the British Slave Trade, <www.parliament.uk/about/living-heritage/transformingsociety/tradeindustry/slavetrade/#:~:text=Throughout%20the%2017th%20and%2018th,successful%20public%20campaigns%20in%20history>.

91 S. Drescher, above n. 62, p. 5.

92 T. S. Aidt and R. Franck, 'Democratization Under the Threat of Revolution: Evidence from the Great Reform Act of 1832' (2015) 83:2 *Econometrica* 505.

93 Jason Kelly, 'Anti-Slavery Movement in Britain', IUPUI ScholarWorks, Indiana University, <https://scholarworks.indianapolis.iu.edu/items/6fa795fc-1c2f-4734-b78e-1881478b2078>.

94 K. Morgan, above n. 7, p. 191.

95 A. Sullivan, *Britain's War Against the Slave Trade: The Operations of the Royal Navy's West Africa Squadron 1807–1867*. Frontline/Pen and Sword Books, Barnsley 2020.

the 1840 World Anti-Slavery Convention, which also marked the beginning of the sustained movement for women's rights as the Convention's negotiations excluded women abolitionists, such as Lucretia Mott and Elizabeth Cady Stanton, from being present in the delegates' discussions.[96]

When slavery ended, the slave economy was no longer essential to the British imperial economy, and inefficient modes of production had also become obstacles to progress.[97] Some of the former slave owners and West India merchants specified that the money raised from their property in the Caribbean should be invested in railway construction, maritime insurance, banking, or other companies "in England, Wales, Scotland or Ireland or any of the British colonies".[98] Cecil Rhodes, a former slave owner who also served as Prime Minister of the Cape Colony in the 1890s, profited from slavery, particularly from the diamond fields of Kimberley in South Africa.[99] He left a substantial fortune to fund his ideas, which were formed in Oxford, to set up a society to promote imperial expansion and the 'Rhodes Scholarship'.[100] Furthermore, vessel owners such as those based in Liverpool redeployed their slave fleet into other avenues of African and Atlantic trade. Bristolians concentrated on other European and American trades and the palm oil trade with Africa, in particular, Nigeria.[101] Attention also shifted to India and the Australian agricultural sector.[102]

5 Compensation Scheme and Reparations for Slavery

It is also important to consider the effects of slavery and the slave trade on people's 'afterlife of slavery'. Saidiya Hartman, in her book 'Lose Your Mother: A Journey Along the Atlantic Slave Route' coined the phrase 'the afterlife of

96 D. H. Maynard, 'The World's Anti-Slavery Convention of 1840' (1960) 47:3 *The Mississippi Valley Historical Review* 452, p. 452.
97 S. Drescher, above n. 62, p. 7.
98 C. Hall, et al., above n. 47, p. 4.
99 R. I. Rotberg, *The Founder: Cecil Rhodes and the Pursuit of Power*, Oxford University Press, Oxford 1988.
100 G. Walker, "So Much to Do': Oxford and the Wills of Cecil Rhodes' (2016) 44:4 *The Journal of Imperial and Commonwealth History* 697, p. 697.
101 K. Morgan, above n. 7, p. 171.
102 C. Hall, et al., above n. 47, p. 8.

slavery', signifying that enslaved people had to live with a variety of suffering.[103] The longing for an unattainable past and the unfulfilled promise of emancipation demonstrate slavery's enduring presence in the twenty-first century, where we can still find evidence of an incomplete freedom project.[104]

Under the *Slavery Abolition Act 1833*, the government offered a loan of £20 million to planters in compensation "for the loss of their slaves' labour" and to "buy freedom for slaves in Empire".[105] Compensation was paid to slave owners[106] instead of any compensation for the enslaved, and this was equivalent to approximately 40% of the Government's total annual expenditure in 1833.[107] Slave children aged under six were freed, but adults became 'apprentices'.[108] In this way, the slaveowners received compensation and benefited from the system of 'apprenticeship' in which formerly enslaved people were compelled to work for a further six years for field slaves and four years for domestic slaves.[109] The apprenticeships were designed to prepare former slaves for independent living. However, abolitionists felt apprenticeship was 'another name for slavery', and as a result of public pressure, this scheme was abolished in 1838.[110] It is interesting to note that according to the Treasury,[111] British taxpayers finished paying off borrowed money for the *Abolition Act* in 2014. The significance of British Caribbean slave ownership has been explored by University College London in the project 'Legacies of British Slave-Ownership'.[112]

---

103 S. V. Hartman, *Lose Your Mother: A Journey Along the Atlantic Slave Route* (first edition), Farrar, Straus and Giroux, New York 2007.

104 A. Womack, 'Visuality, Surveillance, and The Afterlife of Slavery' (2017) 29:1 *American Literary History* 191, p. 194.

105 HM Treasury, Information Rights Unit 'Freedom of Information Act 2000: Slavery Abolition Act 1833', <assets.publishing.service.gov.uk/government/uploads/system/uploads/attachment_data/file/680456/FOI2018-00186_-_Slavery_Abolition_Act_1833_-_pdf_for_disclosure_log__003_.pdf>.

106 The National Archives, <https://discovery.nationalarchives.gov.uk/details/r/C11249>.

107 HM Treasury, Information Rights Unit 'Freedom of Information Act 2000: Slavery Abolition Act 1833', <assets.publishing.service.gov.uk/government/uploads/system/uploads/attachment_data/file/680456/FOI2018-00186_-_Slavery_Abolition_Act_1833_-_pdf_for_disclosure_log__003_.pdf>.

108 K. Morgan, above n. 7, p. 190.

109 C. Hall, et al., above n. 47, p. 6.

110 P. Scanlan, 'Slaves and Peasants in the Era of Emancipation' (2020) 59:3 *Journal of British Studies* 495.

111 HM Treasury, Information Rights Unit 'Freedom of Information Act 2000: Slavery Abolition Act 1833' assets.publishing.service.gov.uk/government/uploads/system/uploads/attachment_data/file/680456/FOI2018-00186_-_Slavery_Abolition_Act_1833_-_pdf_for_disclosure_log__003_.pdf

112 The Centre for the Study of the Legacies of British Slavery, <https://www.ucl.ac.uk/lbs/>.

Reparations are commonly associated with the compensation owed to people of African descent for the impact of the slave trade. The issue of reparation for people of African descent is an ongoing call all over the world. For example, the 'slave trade reparation' was discussed in the World Conference against Racism, Racial Discrimination, Xenophobia and Related Intolerance in 2001. A Declaration emerged from this conference, acknowledging that "slavery and the slave trade are a crime against humanity ... Africans and people of African descent, Asians and people of Asian descent and Indigenous people were victims of these acts and continue to be victims of their consequences".[113]

In the case of England, the disclosure regarding the paid compensation under the *Slavery Abolition Act of 1833* encouraged public discussions to pay reparations to people of African descent in the UK. For example, in 2013 and 2014, Caribbean countries called on the UK and other European countries—particularly the Netherlands, Spain, and Norway—to pay reparations. Although the UK has expressed its regret for the slave trade, reparations have never been paid.[114] Jamaica, for instance, requested compensation from Britain. However, the British High Commissioner to Jamaica dismissed the claim, raising the concern of "who do we pay it to? ... the people who were harmed directly are no longer there".[115] Interestingly, some British companies, such as the large pub chain Greene King and the insurance firm Lloyd's of London, which received compensation as former slave owners, have acknowledged paying back 'large sums' to Black, Asian, and minority ethnic communities.[116]

Developments in British museums and revisions to the national schools' curricula, associated with the 2007 Bicentenary of the Abolition of the British Slave Trade, have been some of the initiatives of educational reform aimed at addressing racial discrimination and reparations for people of African descent, as well as facilitating the truth-telling processes.[117] Museums and galleries across the country started a dialogue between community representatives[118] and presented the history of transatlantic slavery and its abolition, which also

113 F. Brennan and J. Packer (eds) *Colonialism, Slavery, Reparations and Trade: Remedying the Past?*, Routledge, London 2012.

114 H. S. Stevens, 'What Are Reparations And What Forms Can They Take?', <https://eachother.org.uk/what-are-reparations-and-what-forms-can-they-take/>.

115 'British High Commissioner dismisses Jamaica's £7 Billion reparations claim 21 July 2021', <https://www.voice-online.co.uk/news/2021/07/21/british-high-commissioner-dismisses-jamaicas-7-billion-reparations-claim/>.

116 H. S. Stevens, above n. 114.

117 D. Wilkins, above n. 30, p. 100.

118 University of Hull, 'Remembering 1807, <https://www.hull.ac.uk/research/institutes/wilberforce/remembering-1807>.

led to changes to the national curriculum.[119] In addition, several projects were funded by the government to help charitable organisations develop educational resources through an active agency and citizenship model.[120]

6 The 1926 League of Nations Slavery Convention and the 1956 Supplementary Convention on the Abolition of Slavery

Although slavery was abolished in Britain in 1833, France in 1848, the Netherlands in 1861, Cuba in 1886, and Brazil in 1888,[121] different forms of unfree and bonded labour persist across the world. It was not until the 1920s that the League of Nations established the Temporary Slave Commission to address the problem of slavery. British activists played a key role at the League of Nations to publicise information about slavery and to pressure civil servants for an international response.[122]

Following up on the anti-slavery efforts of the 19th century, negotiations began among member and non-member states of the League of Nations. The United Kingdom maintained the lead role in the first half of the 20th century in addressing the abolition of slavery and the slave trade by proposing a draft Convention to the 1925 League of Nations Draft Convention.[123] The British Delegate to the League of Nations, Viscount Cecil of Chelwood, made a significant effort in the drafting process in 1925 to include the suppression of slavery and the slave trade. He noted that "[the slavery] Convention will free tens or hundreds of thousands of unhappy beings from conditions which closely resemble slavery and which now exist".[124]

In addition, the British Delegate proposed a provision in the Slavery Convention, requiring the slave trade at sea to be considered an act of 'piracy'. However, other delegations did not support this idea, and it was removed from

119 D. Wilkins, above n. 30, p. 109.

120 *Ibid.*, p. 110.

121 'Who banned slavery when?', <https://www.reuters.com/article/world/chronology-who-banned-slavery-when-idUSMOL058960/>.

122 A. R. Forclaz, *Humanitarian Imperialism: The Politics of Anti-Slavery Activism, 1880–1940*, Oxford University Press, New York 2015, p. 47.

123 J. Allain, *The Slavery Conventions: The Travaux Préparatoires of the 1926 League of Nations Convention and the 1956 United Nations Convention*, Martinus Nijhoff Publishers 2008, p. 7.

124 League of Nations, Question of Slavery: Report of the Sixth Committee; Resolution, League of Nations Official Journal (Special Supplement 33) Records of the Sixth Assembly: Text of Debates, Nineteenth Plenary Meeting, 26 September 1925, p. 157.

the draft Convention.[125] Nevertheless, the 1925 British Draft Convention, which was a "watered-down version of the treaty", was considered by the Assembly of the League of Nations,[126] and a definition of slavery appeared in an international instrument for the first time.[127] The Slavery Convention also defined 'the slave trade' in Article 1(2), and 'forced labour' was defined in Article 5.

Similarly, the United Kingdom had a leading role in amending the Slavery Convention by proposing a draft resolution entitled 'the Draft Supplementary Convention' to the Sixth Committee of the General Assembly.[128] In this process, an *Ad Hoc* Committee of Experts on Slavery was appointed in 1949 by the United Nations Economic and Social Council (ECOSOC) to consider whether the definition in the Slavery Convention covered the full range of slavery practices[129] and to transfer to the United Nations the functions undertaken by the League of Nations under the 1926 Slavery Convention.[130] The 1953 Draft Resolution proposed by the United Kingdom was adopted by the Sixth Committee of the General Assembly.[131] Subsequently, a supplementary convention was recommended by the Committee. The Supplementary Convention on the Abolition of Slavery, the Slave Trade and Institutions and Practices Similar to

125 Hansard UK Parliament, Slavery Volume 235: debated on Wednesday 12 February 1930, <https://hansard.parliament.uk/commons/1930-02-12/debates/ee794fec-fe51-4dd8-b3c7-1f0b5e927a30/Slavery>.

126 S. Miers, 'Slavery and the Slave Trade as International Issues 1890–1939' (1998) 19:2 *Slavery and Abolition* 16, p. 28.

127 OHCHR Abolishing Slavery and its Contemporary Forms, <https://www.ohchr.org/sites/default/files/Documents/Publications/slaveryen.pdf>. Article 1(2) of the 1926 Slavery Convention defined slavery as "the status or condition of a person over whom any or all of the powers attaching to the right of ownership are exercised". It further defined the slave trade as "all acts involved in the capture, acquisition or disposal of a person with intent to reduce him to slavery; all acts involved in the acquisition of a slave with a view to selling or exchanging him; all acts of disposal by sale or exchange of a slave acquired with a view to being sold or exchanged, and, in general, every act of trade or transport in slaves" (art. 1(2)). The Convention also distinguished forced labour, stipulating that "forced labour may only be exacted for public purposes" and requiring States parties "to prevent compulsory or forced labour from developing into conditions analogous to slavery" (art. 5).

128 J. A. C. Gutteridge, 'Supplementary Slavery Convention, 1956' (1957) 6:3 *The International and Comparative Law Quarterly* 462.

129 M. Awad, Report of the Special Rapporteur of the Sub-Commission on Prevention of Discrimination and Protection of Minorities, "Question of slavery and the slave trade in all their practices and manifestations, including the slavery-like practices of apartheid and colonialism", United Nations document E/CN.4/Sub.2/322 (1971), para. 12.

130 J. Allain, above n. 123, p. 190.

131 *Ibid.*, p. 202.

Slavery of 1956 (the Supplementary Convention)[132] "went further and covered more ground than the 1926 Convention".[133]

7 The ILO Forced Labour Convention, 1930 (No. 29) and the ILO Abolition of Forced Labour Convention, 1957 (No. 105)

To regulate the use of forced or compulsory labour, a Committee of Experts on Labour was appointed by the ILO Governing Body in 1926. The main issue was that the Slavery Convention 1926 did not cover the grounds for the 'prohibition of forced or compulsory labour', which was recommended by the Temporary Slavery Commission at the time. Therefore, the ILO took the initiative to address this matter before its Governing Body and the International Labour Conference (ILC) in 1930.[134] A draft convention was put before the governments' delegations but also the Employers' and Workers' representatives. British Government adviser, Mr Vernon, was the Reporter of the Committee on Forced Labour who presented the draft convention to the tripartite representatives, emphasising that the draft was not on behalf of any single country or any group or countries but that it was "a piece of active and constructive co-operation on the part of three Groups".[135] Twenty-two Governments, including Great Britain, replied to the ILO questionnaire on Forced or Compulsory Labour and a draft proposal in February 1930. The United Kingdom delegation, in its input, emphasised that a draft convention should be "applied to the colonies and protectorates of all the signatory states without the reserves or modifications provided for in Article 421 of the Treaty of Versailles".[136] The Committee on Forced Labour held 16 sittings, and the replies from the Governments showed that they were prepared to support a convention for the suppression

132 Supplementary Convention on the Abolition of Slavery, the Slave Trade and Institutions and Practices Similar to Slavery of 1956 (the Supplementary Convention), United Nations Treaty Series, vol. 226, p. 3; entered into force on 30 April 1957.

133 M. Awad, above n. 129.

134 Forced Labour, ILO International Labour Conference, Fourteenth Session Geneva 1930, 30B09, <ilo.primo.exlibrisgroup.com/discovery/delivery/41ILO_INST:41ILO_V2/1246629800002676>.

135 Forced Labour Discussion, ILO International Labour Conference (ILO) 1929, Twelfth Session, <ilo.primo.exlibrisgroup.com/discovery/delivery/41ILO_INST:41ILO_V2/1246629820002676>.

136 Forced Labour, ILO International Labour Conference, Fourteenth Session Geneva 1930, 30B09, p. 13., <ilo.primo.exlibrisgroup.com/discovery/delivery/41ILO_INST:41ILO_V2/1246629800002676>.

of forced and compulsory labour.[137] The United Kingdom was among the first countries to ratify the Forced Labour Convention, 1930 (No. 29), in 1931, and the Abolition of Forced Labour Convention, 1957 (No. 105), in 1957.[138]

Although the ILO Forced Labour Convention was adopted in 1930, it was primarily concerned with forced labour practices arising in non-metropolitan territories. Therefore, a wider discussion on forced labour and its abolition was examined by the ILO jointly with the United Nations. An *ad hoc* Committee on Forced Labour was set up by the decision of the Economic and Social Council in 1951.[139] The United Kingdom again made an influential effort in the drafting process. Its Workers' adviser, Mr Geddes, on behalf of the Workers on the Committee on Forced Labour, for instance, mentioned that "all the workers in the world should know that we, the Workers, were determined to see the abolition of forced labour throughout the world".[140]

8 Conclusion

Although transatlantic African slavery was supposedly consigned to history in the 19th century, new forms of slavery have been developed in the modern world, which presents even more difficult challenges to the international community. The persistence of slavery into the contemporary period requires us to ask whether there are lessons to be learned from the historical abolitionist process which could assist the contemporary struggle against modern slavery. For example, was the ending of this form of slavery the result of abolitionist campaigning by activists such as Wilberforce and Equiano, of legal action in cases such as *Somerset* and *The Zong*, or simply a reflection of changes in the global economy, which was seeking increased profitability by moving from a feudal to a market-based system of labour? Was change possible only through the actions of a globally dominant power, such as Great Britain in the 19th century, or can the modern institutions of international cooperation, such as the United Nations, offer more robust prospects of complete global abolition?

137 *Ibid.*, p. 122.

138 ILO Forced Labour Convention: United Kingdom joins renewed fight to end forced labour, <https://www.ilo.org/resource/news/united-kingdom-joins-renewed-fight-end-forced-labour>.

139 ILO International Labour Conference Thirty-Ninth Session, Geneva 1956, Record of Proceedings, p. 501. <ilo.primo.exlibrisgroup.com/discovery/delivery/41ILO_INST:41ILO_V2/1246512840002676>.

140 *Ibid.*

And were the changes achieved under UK leadership largely cosmetic, given the toxic racist legacy of slavery around the world?

These are important questions to be considered when assessing the success and impact of legislation such as the UK's *Modern Slavery Act 2015* and its potential role as a model for other countries. New forms of slavery demand new strategies to combat them, but difficult lessons learned in over two centuries of struggle against this scourge and the historical context of current forms of oppression should never be forgotten.

Academic References

A. Loomba, *A Shakespeare, Race, and Colonialism*, Oxford University Press, New York 2002.

A. L. Swingen, *Competing visions of empire: Labor, slavery, and the origins of the British Atlantic empire.* Yale University Press, New Haven 2015.

A. M. Carlos and J. B. Kruse 'The Decline of the Royal African Company: Fringe Firms and the Role of the Charter' (1996) 49:2 *The Economic History Review* 291.

A. R. Forclaz, *Humanitarian Imperialism: The Politics of Anti-Slavery Activism, 1880–1940,* Oxford University Press, New York 2015.

A. Sullivan, *Britain's War Against the Slave Trade: The Operations of the Royal Navy's West Africa Squadron 1807–1867*, Frontline/Pen and Sword Books, Barnsley 2020.

A. Womack, 'Visuality, Surveillance, and The Afterlife of Slavery' (2017) 29:1 *American Literary History* 191.

C. Hall, N. Draper, K. McClelland, K. Donington and R. Lang, *Legacies of British Slave-Ownership: Colonial Slavery and the Formation of Victorian Britain*, Cambridge University Press, Cambridge 2014.

D. A. Pargas, and J. Schiel (eds), *The Palgrave Handbook of Global Slavery throughout History*, Springer International Publishing, New York 2023.

D. A. Webb, 'The "Somerset" Effect: Parsing Lord Mansfield's Words on Slavery in Nineteenth Century America'. (2014) 32:3 *Law and History Review* 455.

D. Clarke, *Slaves & Slavery*, Grange, London 1998.

D. H. Maynard, 'The World's Anti-Slavery Convention of 1840' (1960) 47(3) *The Mississippi Valley Historical Review* 452.

D. Wilkins, 'Reparations, Restorative Justice, and the impact of the 2007 Bicentenary of the Abolition of the British Slave Trade' in D. Bulla (ed) *Why Slavery Endures: Its Past, Present and Future*, Cambridge Scholars Publishing, Cambridge 2020, pp. 100–135.

E. E. Williams, *Capitalism & Slavery*, University of North Carolina Press, Chapel Hill 1994.

F. Brennan and J. Packer (eds) *Colonialism, Slavery, Reparations and Trade: Remedying the Past?*, Routledge, London 2012.

G. Ungerer, 'The Presence of Africans in Elizabethan England and the Performance of "Titus Andronicus" at Burley-on-the-Hill, 1595/96'. (2008) 21 *Medieval & Renaissance Drama in England* 19.

G. Walker, "So Much to Do': Oxford and the Wills of Cecil Rhodes' (2016) 44:4 *The Journal of Imperial and Commonwealth History* 697.

H. G. Özkoray, 'Slavery in the Ottoman Empire' in D. A. Pargas, and J. Schiel (eds), *The Palgrave Handbook of Global Slavery throughout History*, Springer International Publishing, New York 2023, pp. 243–258.

J. A. C. Gutteridge, 'Supplementary Slavery Convention, 1956' (1957) 6:3 *The International and Comparative Law Quarterly* 462.

J. Allain, *The Slavery Conventions: The Travaux Préparatoires of the 1926 League of Nations Convention and the 1956 United Nations Convention*, Martinus Nijhoff Publishers, Leiden 2008.

J. Krikler, 'The Zong and the Lord Chief Justice' (2007) 64 *History Workshop Journal* 29.

J. Oldfield and C. Kaplan (eds), *Imagining Transatlantic Slavery*, Palgrave Macmillan, London 2010.

J. Walvin, *Slavery and the Slave Trade: A Short Illustrated History*, The Macmillan Press, London and Basingstoke 1983.

J. Walvin, *The Zong: A Massacre, the Law and the End of Slavery*, Yale University Press, New Haven 2011.

J. W. Logerfo, 'Sir William Dolben and "The Cause of Humanity": The Passage of the Slave Trade Regulation Act of 1788' (1973) 6:4 *Eighteenth-Century Studies* 431.

K. F. Hall, *Things of Darkness: Economies of Race and Gender in Early Modern England*, Cornell University Press, Ithaca 1995.

K. Morgan, *Slavery and the British Empire: From Africa to America*, Oxford University Press, New York 2007.

K. Morgan, *Slavery, Atlantic Trade and the British Economy, 1660–1800*, Cambridge University Press, Cambride 2000.

M. Zeuske 'The Rise of Atlantic Slavery in the Americas' in D. A. Pargas, and J. Schiel (eds), *The Palgrave Handbook of Global Slavery throughout History*. Springer International Publishing, New York 2023, p. 379–393.

P. Scanlan, 'Slaves and Peasants in the Era of Emancipation' (2020) 59:3 *Journal of British Studies* 495.

R. I. Rotberg, *The Founder: Cecil Rhodes and the Pursuit of Power*, Oxford University Press, Oxford 1988.

S. Drescher, *From Slavery to Freedom: Comparative Studies in the Rise and Fall of Atlantic Slavery*, Macmillan Press, New York 1999.

S. Miers, 'Slavery and the Slave Trade as International Issues 1890–1939' (1998) 19:2 *Slavery and Abolition* 16.

S. V. Hartman, *Lose Your Mother: A Journey Along the Atlantic Slave Route* (first edition), Farrar, Straus and Giroux, New York 2007.

T. Burnard 'Plantation Slavery in the British Caribbean' in D. A. Pargas, and J. Schiel (eds), *The Palgrave Handbook of Global Slavery throughout History*, Springer International Publishing, New York 2023, pp. 395–412.

T. Hahn, 'The Difference the Middle Ages Makes: Color and Race before the Modern World' (2001) 31:1 *Journal of Medieval and Early Modern Studies* 1.

T. S. Aidt and R. Franck, 'Democratization under the Threat of Revolution: Evidence from the Great Reform Act of 1832' (2015) 83:2 *Econometrica* 505.

W. A. Pettigrew, *Freedom's Debt: The Royal African Company and the Politics of the Atlantic Slave Trade, 1672–1752*, The University of North Carolina Press, Chapel Hill 2013.

W. M. Wiecek, 'Somerset: Lord Mansfield and the Legitimacy of Slavery in the Anglo-American World' (1974) 42:1 *The University of Chicago Law Review* 86.

W. R. Cotter, 'The Somerset Case and the Abolition of Slavery in England' (1994) 255:79 *History* 31.

Contemporary Forms of Slavery, including Causes and Consequences: United States

Lolita Buckner Inniss

1 Introduction

The United States and its predecessor sovereigns have a long and complex history of enslavement of Africans and their descendants.[1] Much of this history centres on the enslavement of Africans, dating from their arrival in the Americas in the 1600s to the general emancipation of enslaved African descendants effectuated by the stop of the US Constitution.[2] Understanding the social and legal beginnings and endings of United States slavery, has, like many other topics in law, been subject to narrative choices. This is not unique; as many scholars have noted, law is about telling stories, stories that must have beginnings, middles, and ends.[3] This is true whether law takes place in the courtroom, in the legislature, or in the constitutional convention. It is even more true when law begins outside of formal legal renderings or occurs in legal voids, where there are neither prescriptions nor proscriptions. So, in several accounts, United States African slavery is viewed as having started in 1619, designated as the first arrival of enslaved Africans in the Americas: this is frequently taken as a beginning of the institution of African enslavement in what is now the United States. However, the group of 'twenty and odd' captive Africans who arrived in the Virginia Colony in 1619 might not have been the first such African captives

1 Some Indigenous people in the Americas were enslaved before the enslavement of Africans became a widespread practice. However, this fell into disfavour, and pronouncements against Indigenous slavery were enacted. In one of the more complex U.S. stories of enslavement, Indigenous peoples themselves later adopted the practice of enslaving African descendants. See e.g., L. Buckner Inniss, 'Cherokee Freedmen and the Color of Belonging' (2015) 5 *Colum. J. Race & L.* 100.

2 The Thirteenth Amendment of the United States Constitution states that "neither slavery nor involuntary servitude, except as a punishment for crime whereof the party shall have been duly convicted, shall exist within the United States, or any place subject to their jurisdiction." U.S. Const. Amend. XIII.

3 P. Brooks, 'Narrative in and of the Law' in J. Phelan & P. J. Rabinowitz (eds) *A Companion to Narrative Theory*, Blackwell, Oxford 2008.

 | DOI:10.1163/9789004723801_017

in the colony. Some studies have suggested that the Spanish brought almost two dozen captive Africans to colonial South Carolina in 1526, for example.[4] The ultimate fate of these captives is unknown.

Just as the ascribed beginning of African enslavement in what is now the United States is subject to a narrative choice, so, too, is the ending of United States slavery. Slavery is said to have definitively ended for most enslaved people between 1863 and 1865, the first year being the date of the Emancipation Proclamation and the latter being the time when the last known groups of enslaved people were officially told of their freedom.[5] Between these choices of the beginnings and the ends of the practice, it is clear that the eighteenth century saw the height of the institution of slavery in the United States. The slave trade peaked at unprecedented numbers in history: in the last quarter of this century, an average of 80,000 captives were transported each year from Africa to America, the Caribbean, and the West Indies.[6] The economies of the Western world were deeply tied to this trade, and almost all countries practised slave transport from their ports or supported the manufacture and trade of goods and services that made the trade possible.

An important aspect of the legal narratives of the stops and starts of African slavery is the stops and starts that, though grounded in law and law-like norms, are less frequently discussed. One example is the termination of slavery that occurred via purchased emancipation. An example of a 'start' is constitutional and legal norms that purported to stop slavery and instead promoted it. Still another example is a 'start' allowed by recapture provisions.

---

4 Gillian Brockell, 'Before 1619, There Was 1526,' *The Washington Post*, (07.09.2019), <https://www.washingtonpost.com/history/2019/09/07/before-there-was-mystery-first-enslaved-africans-what-became-us/>.

5 Most African descendant formal enslavement in the United States ended with the Emancipation Proclamation, which took effect on January 1, 1863. Abraham Lincoln, "Emancipation Proclamation," January 1, 1863. However, in Texas, the end of slavery was not announced until June 19, 1865, two and a half years after the Emancipation Proclamation took effect. June 19 was recently created as a national holiday in the United States The White House, *Remarks by President Biden at Signing of the Juneteenth National Independence Day Act*, (17.06.2021), <https://www.whitehouse.gov/briefing-room/speeches-remarks/2021/06/17/remarks-by-president-biden-at-signing-of-the-juneteenth-national-independence-day-act/>.

6 P. H. Franses and W. van den Heuvel, 'Aggregate Statistics on Trafficker-Destination Relations in the Atlantic Slave Trade,' (2019) 31:3 *The International Journal of Maritime History* 624, p. 625.

2 Purchased Emancipations

Antebellum manumission of slaves is often thought of as the generous act of a kind slave master.[7] However, some research shows that many emancipations occurred when owners were paid to free their slaves, with the payment often coming from slaves themselves.[8] For example, in 1839, over forty per cent of the free blacks in Cincinnati, Ohio, had purchased their own freedom.[9] Many antebellum emancipations are steeped in myths that feature emancipated people as fortunate beneficiaries of a series of generous and just actions crowned by the indulgence of owners willing to accept a price for an enslaved person's liberty. However, these acts, far from being benevolent, may have been part of the harsh and spare reality of a world where slavery was a vital economic engine. As scholar Edward Baptist shows in *The Half Has Never Been Told: Slavery and the Making of American Capitalism*, United States slavery was also fundamental in creating conditions for the country's initial and ongoing geographic and economic growth.[10] In a context where slavery was so vital an economic indicator, manumission without payment would have been counter to the entire enterprise.

3 "Stop-Start" Constitutional Provisions

As several scholars have noted, the Fugitive Slave Clause of the United States Constitution gave slave owners the right to reclaim escaped enslaved people, thereby constituting a restart of enslavement where it had ended via the enslaved person's action of self-liberation.[11] And post-slavery U.S. Constitutional amendments meant to liberate enslaved Africans and their descendants give evidence of the potential for ongoing slavery-like conditions, or for the

7 L. Buckner Inniss, *The Princeton Fugitive Slave*, Fordham University Press, New York 2019, p. XI.

8 See e.g. R. Olwell, 'Becoming Free: Manumission and the Genesis of a Free Black in South Carolina, 1740–90' (1996) 17:1 *Slavery and Abolition* 1.

9 L. Buckner Inniss, above n. 7.

10 E. Baptist, *The Half Has Never Been Told: Slavery and the Making of American Capitalism*, Basic Books, New York 2012.

11 See generally H. R. Barker, 'The Fugitive Slave Clause and the Antebellum Constitution' (2012) 30:4 *Law and History Review* 1133; L. A. Hudley, 'A Profile of Runaway Slaves in Virginia and South Carolina from 1730 through 1787' (2012) 30:4 *Law and History Review* 1133; E. Foner, *Gateway to freedom: the hidden history of America's fugitive slaves*, Oxford University Press, Oxford 2015.

restart of such conditions even where they might have ended. The Thirteenth Amendment, meant to explicitly bar "involuntary servitude," leaves an exception for uncompensated prison labour.[12] This meant that those convicted of a crime could be made to work with little or no compensation. This constitutional exception, combined with the mass incarceration of Black people that persisted even during recent decades, has been a key means by which slavery-like conditions have been perpetuated in the United States. As one scholar notes, the Fourteenth Amendment no sooner recognised Black people as citizens than a proliferation of laws "began to criminalize Blackness, chipping away at Black citizenship and belonging, and exiling Black people from various communities and forums of civic engagement."[13] This sort of "social death" is arguably a potent form of enslavement, given the way that such exclusion limits human possibilities.[14]

Most traditional narratives about African descendant slavery in the United States do not address the history of servitude-like conditions that African descendants endured after the general emancipation and well into the twentieth century.[15] Jim Crow laws limited Black rights for decades.[16] This included schemes like vagrancy laws that made it unlawful for an individual to be unemployed. These laws were largely aimed at the formerly enslaved and their descendants, and those arrested under such provisions were frequently forced into uncompensated labour via convict leasing.[17] There was also the process of peonage, which involved incarcerating indebted Black people and forcing them to work without pay to repay the debt.[18] The United States Supreme

12 U.S. Const. amend. XIII.

13 D. Archer, 'Exile from Main Street' (2019) 55 *Harvard Civil Rights-Civil Liberties Law Review* 30.

14 Social death concerns people existing in situations of poverty, isolation or suffering from other serious privations (see O. Patterson, *Slavery and Social Death: A Comparative Study*, Harvard University Press, Cambridge 1982).

15 See, e.g. I. Berlin, *Generations of Captivity: A History of African-American Slaves*, Harvard University Press, Cambridge 2003; E. Tawil, *The Cambridge Companion to Slavery in American Literature*, Cambridge University Press, Cambridge 2016. But see N. Hannah-Jones, *The 1619 Project: A New Origin Story*, Random House, New York 2021.

16 M. Alexander, *The New Jim Crow: Mass Incarceration in the Age of Colorblindness*, New Press, New York 2020, pp. 30–35 (discussing the rise of Jim Crow laws as a response to the abolition of slavery and as an attempt to put American Blacks into subordinate positions); D. A. Blackmon, *Slavery by Another Name: The Re-enslavement of Black Americans from the Civil War to World War Two*, Icon Books, London 2012.

17 J. G. Pope, 'Mass Incarceration, Convict Leasing, and the Thirteenth Amendment: A Revisionist Account' (2019) 94 *N.Y.U. L. Rev.* 1465, p. 1470.

18 M. Goodwin, 'The Thirteenth Amendment: Modern Slavery, Capitalism, and Mass Incarceration' (2019) *104 Cornell L. Rev.* 899, p. 935.

Court eventually outlawed peonage.[19] Peonage persisted, nonetheless, as state and local authorities refused to act to end it.[20]

Anti-Black practices recalling enslavement continue to limit Black freedom even into the twenty-first century. The early decades of the twenty-first century have witnessed the ongoing instances of vigilante and police detentions, assaults, and killings of black people who find themselves charged with running afoul of formal legal norms and, just as often, informal, unarticulated norms that seem to apply only to Black people.[21] Recent years especially have witnessed an overwhelming outcry from activists who have assailed unequal treatment of Black people in both civil justice and criminal justice settings.[22] These complaints sometimes make little headway, as many people in the United States seem to think that if non-racial reasons can explain these inequalities, no harm is done. This kind of thinking ignores the more subtle, pervasive legacy of African enslavement in the United States that perpetuates economic and social disenfranchisement: discrimination against Blacks in hiring, in obtaining rental housing and homes for sale, in mortgage lending processes, in interactions with supervisors, peers and subordinates, store clerks, and in a host of other daily activities.[23]

---

19 Clyatt v. United States, 197 U.S. 207, 215 (1905); United States v. Reynolds, 235 U.S. 133, 139–40 (1914).

20 T. R. Birckhead, 'The New Peonage' (2015) 72 *Wash. & Lee L. Rev.* 1595, p. 1612 (citing D. A. Novak, *The Wheel of Servitude: Black Forced Labor After Slavery*, University Press of Kentucky, Lexington 1978, pp. 2–3).

21 See generally T. Aiello, *The Routledge History of Police Brutality in America*, Routledge, New York 2023; C. Chancy and R. V. Robertson, 'Racism and Police Brutality in America' (2013) 17 *J. Afr. Am. Stud.* 480; D. W. Carbado, 'From Stopping Black People to Killing Black People: The Fourth Amendment Pathways to Police Violence' (2017) 105 *Calif. L. Rev.* 125; M. Alexander, above n. 16 (describing the "web of laws, regulations, and informal rules" by which people who have been incarcerated are "confined to the margins of mainstream society and denied access to the mainstream economy" p. 5); B.W. Smith and M.D. Holmes, 'Community Accountability, Minority Threat, and Police Brutality: An Examination of Civil Rights Criminal Complaints' (2003) 41 *Criminology* 1003, p. 1037 (explaining that "[i]nformal norms of police work define extralegal sanctions, particularly excessive force, as normal and essential instruments of control for handling individuals perceived as challenging officers' authority, who pose a threat to their wellbeing, or who are otherwise discredited").

22 See e.g. Leila Rafei, *Meet the Activists Fighting to Free People from LA Jails*, ACLU, (10.03.2021), <https://www.aclu.org/news/criminal-law-reform/meet-the-activists-fighting-to-free-people-from-la-jails>; *see also* M. Alexander, above n. 16, (describing "new generations of activists who are working courageously at the intersections of our systems of control" p. XIII).

23 See e.g. M. Baradaran, *The Color of Money*, Harvard University Press, Cambridge 2018; S. K. Kang, K. A. DeCelles, A. Tilcsik & S. Jun, 'Whitened Résumés: Race and Self-Presentation

Even the most obvious and alarming instances of slavery's legacy in the United States—that is, unjustified police and vigilante detentions, assaults, and killings of Black people—frequently fail to garner much attention outside of affected communities and far too often fail to result in legal redress for victims and their families.[24] These tragedies cross class and gender lines, as Black people from all walks of life seem at all times prone to being summarily judged and even executed by agents of the state or by self-deputized private citizens.[25] Nonetheless, these virulently racially motivated injustices are too often deftly ignored, hastened into obscurity by the combined effects of postulated abstract neutrality and studious silence.[26] A key example was the killing of George Floyd.[27] Floyd died as a police officer kneeled upon his neck

---

in the Labor Market,' (2016) 61 *Admin. Sci. Q.* 469; P. Kline, E. K. Rose and C. R. Walters, 'Systemic Discrimination Among Large U.S. Employers,' (2022) 137 *Q. J. Econ.* 1963; D. Aaronson, D. Hartley and B. Mazumder, *The Effects of the 1930s HOLC "Redlining" Maps*, Federal Reserve Bank of Chicago (revised 2020), <https://www.chicagofed.org/publications/working-papers/2017/wp2017-12>; T. Y. Henderson and J. Jefferson-Jones, '#LivingWhileBlack: Blackness as Nuisance' (2020) 69 *AM. U. L. Rev.* 863, p. 863; P. Christensen, I. Sarmiento-Barbieri and C. Timmins, 'Racial Discrimination and Housing Outcomes in the United States Rental Market' (2021) *Nat'l Bureau Econ. Rsch.*, Working Paper No. 29516; C. Pittman, '"Shopping while Black": Black consumers' management of racial stigma and racial profiling in retail settings' (2017) 20 *J. Consumer Culture* 3.

24 *See, e.g.*, K. Benner, *Eric Garner's Death Will Not Lead to Federal Charges for N.Y.P.D. Officer, N.Y. Times*, (16.07.2019), <https://www.nytimes.com/2019/07/16/nyregion/eric-garner-daniel-pantaleo.html>; Rep. of the U.N. High Comm'r for Hum. Rights, U.N. Doc. A/HRC/47/53 (2021) (calling on States to end impunity for human rights violations by law enforcement officials in the wake of the murder of George Floyd).

25 P. Iron, *White Men's Law: The Roots of Systemic Racism*, Oxford University Press, New York 2022; L. Buckner Inniss, 'Race, Space, and Surveillance: A Response to #livingwhileblack: Blackness as Nuisance' (2020) 69 *Am. U. L. Rev.* 213.

26 As some scholars have suggested, there is no valueless neutral position, despite such claims. A policy is often described as 'neutral' if its "anticipated effects are equally desirable, no matter the conception of the good by which this desirability is evaluated." G. Moreno-Riaño, *Tolerance in the Twenty-First Century: Prospects and Challenges*, Lexington Books, Lanham 2006, p. 58. Fugitive slave and anti-slavery activist Samuel Ringgold Ward described the "studious silence" of Northern religious figures who actively avoided commentary on the wrongfulness of slavery, deciding instead to keep a careful silence on the matter or to condemn only "slavery in the abstract." S. R. Ward, *Autobiography of a fugitive negro*, John Snow, London 1855.

27 C. Hauser et al., *'I Can't Breathe': 4 Minneapolis Officers Fired After Black Man Dies in Custody, N.Y. Times*, (26.05.2020), <https://www.nytimes.com/2020/05/26/us/minneapolis-police-man-died.html>. Several subsequent articles focused on Floyd's "troubled" past. *E.g.*, K Sheehy, *'George Floyd Had 'Violent Criminal History': Minneapolis Police Union Chief,' N.Y. Post*, (02.06.2020), <https://nypost.com/2020/06/02/george-floyd-had-violent-criminal-history-minneapolis-union-chief>.

for almost nine minutes, asphyxiating him as he called out "I can't breathe" and called for his dead mother. Floyd's death sparked widespread protests that, while centred on his killing, were also fueled by the seemingly endless stream of Black deaths at the hands of state and non-state actors reaching back to the post-Civil War period.[28]

In the contemporary United States, hypervigilant inner-city policing and rhetoric that demand 'law and order' have fueled the mass incarceration of Black people that continues as a dominant feature of Black life in the United States.[29] Much of the framework for this incarceration began with the 1970s 'war on drugs,' which was allegedly an effort to reduce criminality by the creation of stringent local, state and federal laws to limit the use of illegal drugs. While one of the asserted goals of the war was to create a 'drug-free' United States, much research suggests that this goal could never have been realised.[30]

The United States was born out of a grand impulse of freedom and liberty. One of the United States founding documents, the Constitution, was correspondingly meant to embody the political and legal norms that grow out of these values and was seen as a break not only from monarchy or peony but from the entire European imperial project.[31] A Constitution is, in the words of one founder, "a charter of power founded by liberty."[32] The United States polity was thus envisioned as a set of "equal, rights-bearing citizens, united in patriotic

---

28 For an account of black massacre during the reconstruction period, see Equal Justice Initiative, Reconstruction in America, 2020, <https://eji.org/wp-content/uploads/2005/11/reconstruction-in-america-rev-111521.pdf>.

29 P. Butler, *Let's Get Free: A Hip-Hop Theory of Justice*, New Press, New York 2009, p. 21. Butler's hip-hop theory of justice includes some explicitly spatial concerns ("Hip hop music contains a powerful analysis of the criminal justice system by the people who know if from the inside out." at p. 21.) Butler cites R. D. G. Kelley for the proposition that prisons are not meant to discipline but to corral bodies labeled menaces to society; policing is not meant to stop or reduce crime in inner-city communities. R. D. G. Kelley, 'Kickin' Reality, Kickin' Ballistics: 'Gangsta Rap' and Postindustrial Los Angeles' in W.E. Perkins (ed) *Droppin' Science: Critical Essays on Rap Music and Hip Hop Culture*, Temple University Press, Philadelphia 1996, pp. 117–118.

30 L. Buckner Inniss, 'A Moving Violation-Hypercriminalized Spaces and Fortuitous Presence in Drug Free School Zones' (2003) 8 *Tex J on C.L. & C.R.* 51.

31 Butler, above n. 29.

32 "In Europe, charters of liberty have been granted by power. America has set the example and France has followed it, of charters of power granted by liberty." James Madison, "For the National Gazette, 18 January 1792," Founders Online, National Archives, <https://founders.archives.gov/documents/Madison/01-14-02-0172>. Original source: R. A. Rutland and T. A. Mason, The Papers of James Madison, vol. 14, 6 April 1791–16 March 1793, University Press of Virginia, Charlottesville 1983.

attachment to a shared set of political practices and values."[33] Along with this vision, there has been an insistence on a United States exceptionalism that places the country and its founding documents outside of the contested social and political histories of some of its European forebears.[34] But despite often being held up as the first modern Constitution to embrace such human rights ideals, it is also the first modern constitution that addressed the enslavement of human beings.[35]

The United States Constitution, though not unreservedly endorsing slavery, condoned its practice. This is not unusual, for the United States was not, and is not, unique in having inherent in its national ideals a fundamental disagreement about the principles of freedom and equality.[36] And the fact that the United States is a relatively young nation with a republican form of government makes this conflict no more surprising. Indeed, the question of freedom is one more specific to modernity than to antiquity, notwithstanding the tendency for many modern writers to confuse concepts like democracy and republic with freedom.[37] The eighteenth century heralded an age wherein there was an embrace of intellectual inquiry and belles letters, along with an increase in theorising about values like equality and freedom. But this atmosphere was suffused with a major contradiction: pervasive support for the Black inequality and enslavement that made such lifestyles possible.[38] Most of the drafters of the Constitution owned slaves, and the Constitution itself, besides standing for liberty, also embraced and promoted slavery.

Perhaps one of the best-known United States Constitutional provisions on slavery is the Migration or Importation clause of Article I, Section 9, which

33 M. Ignatieff, *Blood and Belonging: Journeys into the New Nationalism*, Farrar, Straus and Giroux, New York 1993, pp. 3–4.

34 A. Rana, 'Colonialism and Constitutional Memory' (2015) 5 *UC Irvine L. Rev.* 263.

35 The preamble of the French Constitution of Year III (1795), known as the Declaration of Rights and Duties of Mankind, contained an explicit ban on slavery. Some have argued, however, that other language in the document left slavery in place, or created new barriers to Black freedom. L. Semley, *To Be Free and French: Citizenship In France's Atlantic Empire*, Cambridge University Press, New York 2017.

36 *Ibid.*

37 It is entirely possible, for example, for democracies and republics to be repressive and to inhibit the freedom of some people within their bounds. T. Chaimowicz, *Antiquity as the Source of Modernity: Freedom and Balance in the Thought of Montesquieu and Burke*, Routledge, New York 2018.

38 As one scholar writes, ideas of high culture, aesthetic sensibilities, taste and politeness were often closely intertwined with the brutality and inhumanity of slavery. See S. Gikandi, *Slavery and the Culture of Taste*, Princeton University Press, Princeton 2011.

prohibited the importation of slaves into the United States after 1808.[39] Some opponents of slavery envisioned the Migration or Importation Clause as a bar to further transatlantic slavery and a way of ultimately ending slavery in the United States. The Migration or Importation Clause did not, however, end slavery. It may, in fact, have helped to reshape how slavery was practised. Instead of looking continually to new arrivals, many United States slaveholders transitioned from merely holding enslaved people in bondage to creating a system that rendered enslaved people into self-regenerating commodities.[40] The presence of a domestically born class of enslaved people engendered, however, a new set of problems and trenchant ironies. For instance, the appearance and proliferation of race-based commodity enslavement was tied to a concomitant growth in urban lifestyles and cosmopolitan ideals of justice and human rights to which enslaved labour did not correspond.[41] This was especially true in mid-Atlantic states like Maryland, where multigenerational enslavement existed right alongside the largest population of free Blacks in the country.[42] It was also a problem in free states closely adjacent to slave states like Pennsylvania and New Jersey. Not only did more white people in U.S. society begin to embrace the idea of liberty, but so, too, did the enslaved. And so, they fled enslavement. The drafters of the U.S. Constitution, in creating a legal system wherein an entire class of people were enslaved at birth, also anticipated the need for and created a regulatory regime for recapturing enslaved people who sought to slip the bonds of servitude. The United States became a country that gave birth to its own asylum seekers.

4 The Fugitive Slave Clause of the United States Constitution

Envisioning the possibility of flight by the enslaved, the United States Constitution provided a means whereby slaveholders could recover escaped slaves. The Fugitive Slave Clause, enacted with the ratification of the Constitution in 1789, declared that "No Person" (avoiding the word slave as did other parts of the

39 U.S. Const. art. 1, § 9, cl. 1.

40 N. Sublette and C. Sublette, *American Slave Coast: A History of the Slave-Breeding Industry*, Laurence Hill Books, Chicago 2016. See G. D. Smithers, *Slave Breeding: Sex, Violence, and Memory in African American History*, University Press of Florida, 2012; T. A. Foster, *Rethinking Rufus: Sexual Violations of Enslaved Men*, University of Georgia Press, Athens 2019.

41 O. Patterson, 'Freedom in the Making of the Western Culture' (1991) 28:1 *Arethusa* 87.

42 L. Buckner Inniss, above n. 7, pp. 23–24.

Constitution) held to service or labour in one state and would be discharged from that labour, but instead would be delivered up on the claim of the person to whom the service or labour was due.[43] But though the Fugitive Slave Clause of the United States Constitution guaranteed the right to reclaim fugitive slaves, it did not establish a mechanism for executing the law. To address this void, on February 12, 1793, the Second Congress passed 'An act respecting fugitives from justice, and persons escaping from the service of their masters,' better known as the Fugitive Slave Act of 1793. The Act was, according to some, not only a means to address the absence of slave recapture procedures but also a response to the proliferation of anti-slavery societies and the emergence of the Underground Railroad.[44]

There were attempts by several states to evade the Fugitive Slave Act of 1793, largely by the creation of personal liberty laws that created more rights for escaped enslaved people.[45] Personal liberty laws employed a number of methods to avoid returning escapees to their enslavers, including requiring a verdict from a jury in a trial before rendition.[46] Other states prohibited the use of local jails or state action to facilitate the capture or return of the enslaved.[47]

43 Article IV, Section 2 of the United States Constitution. The clause reads: "No person held to service or labour in one state, under the laws thereof, escaping into another, shall, in consequence of any law or regulation therein, be discharged from such service or labour, but shall be delivered up on claim of the party to whom such service or labour may be due."

44 The Underground Railroad was a network of people, routes and places that helped enslaved people in the United States South escape to the North. The name "Underground Railroad" was used metaphorically, not literally. W. H. Siebert, *The Underground Railroad: From Slavery to Freedom*, Russel and Russel, New York 1967.

45 Personal liberty laws provided a means for an alleged fugitive to contest his seizure (see C. G. Fritz, *Monitoring American Federalism: The History of State Legislative Resistance*, Cambridge University Press, New York 2023).

46 L. Buckner Inniss, above n. 7, p. 81.

47 D. E. Fehrenbach and W. McAfee, *The Slaveholding Republic: An Account of the United States Government's Relations to Slavery*, Oxford University Press, Oxford 2001, p. 222; T. D. Morris, *Free Men All: The Personal Liberty Laws of the North, 1780–1861*, The Johns Hopkins University Press, Baltimore 1974, p. 118 (describing Pennsylvania's Personal Liberty Law of 1847, which, among other things, prohibited state officials from using any jail or prison for the detention of anyone claimed as a fugitive); N. L. Rosenberg, 'Personal Liberty Laws and Sectional Crisis: 1850–1861' (1971) 17 *Civil War History* 25, p. 28 (describing a Massachusetts law of 1843 which forbade the use of state jails for detention of fugitive slaves).

5 The Transatlantic Slave Trade and International Commerce

The transatlantic movement of captured Africans "was a key component in shaping African enslavement in the Americas."[48] From the fifteenth through the nineteenth centuries, European and American ships transported over twelve million captive Africans to the Americas.[49] Slavery in what is now the United States is far from the first instance of the enslaving of Africans.[50] However, maritime trade in captive Africans and their ultimate enslavement in the Americas expanded the scale, scope, geography, and social and economic complexity of human enslavement. This expansion occurred both inside and outside of the continent of Africa in ways that make it unique in the history of human enslavement.[51]

The 'Middle Passage,' the ocean transit of captured Africans, featured violence, brutal conditions, and, frequently, grave injury or death for large numbers of the captives.[52] Relatively little scholarship has addressed how the transatlantic slave trade made the United States and other parts of the Atlantic world a vital framework for the development of international commerce and the corresponding system of laws that governed that commerce, notwithstanding the vastness of the human tragedy wrought by transatlantic slavery.[53] Historians have given substantial attention to the abolition of slavery while

48 Lolita Buckner Inniss, 'Ships' Ballast' in J. Hohmann and D. Joyce (eds), *International Law's Objects*, Oxford University Press, Oxford 2019, p. 437; G. J. Heuman and J. Walvin, 'Introduction' in G. J. Heuman and J. Walvin (eds), *The Slavery Reader*, Routledge, New York 2003, p. 437.

49 P. H. Franses and W. Van Den Heuvel, above n. 6; P. D. Curtin, *The Atlantic Slave Trade: A Census*, University of Wisconsin Press, Madison 1972.

50 For a discussion of slavery among Africans of various regions, see generally S. Miers and I. Kopytoff (eds) *Slavery in Africa: Historical and Anthropological Perspectives*, University of Wisconsin Press, Madison 1977.

51 F. U. Ohaegbulam, *Towards an Understanding of the African Experience from Historical and Contemporary Perspectives*, University Press of America, Lanham 1990, p. 142; M. E. Modupe Kolawole, 'An African View of Transatlantic Slavery and the Role of Oral Testimony in Creating a New Legacy,' in A. Tibbles (ed), *Transatlantic Slavery: Against Human Dignity*, Liverpool University Press, Liverpool 2005, p. 101.

52 Lolita Buckner Inniss, above n. 48, p. 437.

53 R. Blackburn, *The Making of New World Slavery: From the Baroque to the Modern, 1492–1800*, Verso, London 2010, pp. 177–180. One researcher concluded, for example, that Aetna Insurance had insured the lives of slaves for the benefit of their owners and thereby profited from slavery. She also determined that predecessors to one financial services institution, JP Morgan Chase, had "accepted approximately 13,000 enslaved individuals as collateral on loans and took possession of approximately 1,250 enslaved individuals."

offering few accounts of how the abolition of slavery figures in the history of commercial regulations.[54] Yet, few other issues in the nineteenth century shaped the evolution of United States maritime, insurance, and contract law, as did the slave trade.[55] The conduct of the sea-faring slave trade and its eventual interdiction was the source of much of the legal intercourse between and among established European powers, colonial entities, and fledgling republics in the New World.[56] Despite the uncertainty and complexity that occurred with the transition from colonies to independent states, the slave trade was a steadying institutional presence that, while often differently practised, had similarities even across borders and distinct geographies and cultures. Slavery's persistence thus helped to enhance the growth of the economies in many newly independent states, such as the United States.[57]

The transatlantic slave trade and its subsequent practice in the United States and in its predecessor colonies combined sovereign and private power, conquest, empire-building, settler colonialism, and slavery.[58] From this combination, there developed several new economic tools, such as more complex forms of barter than had been previously seen, commercial credit and insurance.[59] The United States insurance industry was especially enhanced by the slave trade, as owners sought to protect their human investments with the purchase of insurance policies.[60] When the United States closed off the legitimate import of enslaved people from Africa, it met and exceeded any deficits in enslaved labour with the growth of a domestic slave-breeding industry that generated a whole other set of slavery-related industries, such as textiles and foodstuffs.[61]

N. Mathiason, 'British Firms Could Be Sued for Slave Trade,' *The Observer*, (01.07.2007), <https://www.theguardian.com/business/2007/jul/01/theobserver.observerbusiness4>.

54 J. Martinez, 'Antislavery Courts and the Dawn of International Human Rights Law' (2008) 117 *Yale Law Journal* 550. According to Martinez, "The abolition of chattel slavery remains perhaps the most successful episode ever in the history of international human rights law. Slavery is one of the few universally acknowledged crimes under international law," at p. 555.

55 J. Allain, *Slavery in International Law: Of Human Exploitation and Trafficking*, Martinus Nijhoff, Leiden 2013, p. 57.

56 L. Bucker Inniss, above n. 48, p. 437.

57 *Ibid.*

58 *Ibid.*

59 *Ibid.*

60 S. A. Murphy, 'Securing Human Property: Slavery, Life Insurance, and Industrialization in the Upper South' (2005) 25:4 *The Journal of the Early Republic* 615.

61 California Department of Insurance, Slavery Era Insurance Registry, 2002 at 616–617.

Purchasing policies of insurance on the health and lives of enslaved Black people worked much as did the insurance of other personal property. It typically involved a contract between a policyholder and an insurance company in which the insurer promised to pay a sum of money upon the death of an enslaved person. In the three decades leading up to the United States Civil War (1861–1865), such policies became widespread in southern states.[62] Some of the largest insurance firms in the country, New York Life, AIG, and Aetna, sold policies that ensured slave owners would be compensated if the slaves they owned were injured or killed.[63]

The slave trade in the United States was also a key element in developing agriculture, as plantation owners forced the West African captives to instruct them on the cultivation of plants like rice and other commodities.[64] As one observer notes, it is not a coincidence that a number of the agricultural practices seen in parts of Africa are also present in parts of the United States.[65]

6 Slavery-Related Reparations

There has never been a widespread, systemic effort at paying slavery-related reparations to enslaved Africans or their descendants in the United States. There have been, over the decades, several cases seeking reparations for slavery.[66] In

62 S. A. Murphy, above n. 60, p. 618–619.

63 *Ibid*, p. 635–636.

64 J. Carney, *In the Shadow of Slavery: Africa's Botanical Legacy in the Atlantic World*, University of California Press, Oakland 2011.

65 M. W. Twitty, *The Cooking Gene*, Amistad, New York 2017.

66 See generally Obadele v. United States, 52 Fed. Cl. 432, 433 (2002) (stating that Plaintiffs sought compensation from the United States to redress wrongs that their ancestors suffered as a result of being African-American); Bell v. United States, 2001 U.S. Dist. Lexis 14812 (N.D. Texas 2001) at 2 (explaining that petitioners are bringing their suit as a special damage claim for slavery reparation); Cato v. United States, 70 F.3d 1103, 1103 (9th Cir. 1995) (listing the elements of plaintiff's claim arising out of wrongdoings from slavery); Berry v. United States, 1994 U.S. Dist. Lexis 9665 (N.D. Cal. 1994) at 9 (discussing plaintiff's claim for compensation from wrongs from slavery); Johnson v. McAdoo, 45 U.S. App. D.C. 440 (1916) (seeking to sue the United States over the rate charged for the exportation of sugar). But see Pigford v. Glickman, 185 F.R.D 82 (1999) (describing black farmers' claims of redress for the federal government's failure to fund farm loans as it pledged to do, which resulted in a capitulation by the government and a settlement on behalf of black farmers whose plight in many ways resulted from slavery and Jim Crow; however, the merits of the case did not rely upon injuries from slavery, but rather from the government's actions dating from the late twentieth century: the judge who approved the settlement suggested the slavery connection in his opinion, referencing 'Forty Acres and a Mule' and

one significant case, *In Re African-American Slave Descendants*,[67] plaintiff Deadria Farmer-Paellmann sought reparations by suing. Her story of involvement in the suit is compelling. Having developed an interest in the notion of reparations generally, she first looked at suing the federal government for its role in creating and sustaining the enslavement of Africans and their descendants. When her research suggested that this would be difficult given the failure of other such suits, she turned instead to researching the role of private entities. She attended law school to further her research and gain the skills necessary to prosecute such a suit. In the course of her work, she uncovered evidence that Aetna Insurance had insured the lives of slaves for the benefit of their owners and thereby profited from slavery. She also determined that predecessors to one financial services institution, JP Morgan Chase, had "accepted approximately 13,000 enslaved individuals as collateral on loans and took possession of approximately 1,250 enslaved individuals."[68] Her work led to Aetna's offer of a public apology for its involvement in slavery. Ms. Paellmann's discovery also led the state of California and other state and municipal jurisdictions to compel other companies to search their records for involvement in slavery and to make this information available to the public.[69]

There have also been several scholarly calls for a system of reparations to be paid to the descendants of enslaved Africans in the United States. Despite these calls, there have been few actual efforts at making repayments to African descendants in circumstances of specific harm, such as the payments made to victims of the Rosewood, Florida destruction and massacre.[70] Similar efforts at compensating victims of white violence have been less successful.[71] A very

the government's broken promises to blacks, but noted that the specific promises in dispute came well after the period of slavery; R. L. Brooks, 'The Slave Redress Cases' (2005) 27 *N.C. Cent. L.J.* 130, pp. 162–166 (providing a discussion of Pigford v. Glickman). For a broad discussion of the various theories employed in reparations cases see E. K. Yamamoto, S. H. Y. Kim, and A. Holden, 'American Reparations Theory and Practice at the Crossroads' (2007) 44 *Cal. W.L. Rev.* 1.

67 In re African-Am. Slave Descendants Litig., 375 F. Supp 2d. 721, 726 (N.D. Ill. 2005).

68 N. Mathiason, above n. 53.

69 J. Levy, 'Slavery Disclosure Laws: For Financial Reparations or for "Telling the Truth?"' (2009) 2009:2 *Colum. Bus. L. Rev.* 468.

70 In 1923 an all-white mob burned the town to the ground. They killed at least six people. In 1994 the Florida legislature passed a law allowing descendants of Rosewood to attend Florida colleges tuition-free. The law is regarded as the first instance of a legislative body in the United States giving reparations to African Americans. C. P. Henry, *The Politics of Racial Reparations*, NYU Press, New York 2009, pp. 67–68.

71 *Ibid.* The city of Tulsa, Oklahoma has made similar efforts at obtaining reparations for Black people and their descendants who were harmed by white rioters who destroyed much of the Black section of Tulsa and killed hundreds. A.L. Brophy, *Reconstructing the*

narrow effort at redressing Black enslavement has been seen in some colleges and universities who, having recognised the benefits that accrued to them from Black enslavement, have called for some benefits to be made available to the descendants of some enslaved Blacks.[72] However, to date, only a few colleges and universities have attempted to make amends for their past engagement with slavery. Such involvement included directly enslaving people, benefitting from enrolling slaveholding students, supporting themselves from slavery-related property or activity, or taking advantage of the relative penury in which many Black people lived in the decades after the general emancipation. Some schools have, for example, established special programs of study that interrogate their engagement in Black oppression.[73] Others have made efforts at recognition and reconciliation of their actions. And yet other schools have offered direct apologies.[74]

7 Legacies of the Global Institution of Slavery

There are many legacies of the global institution of slavery present in the United States, including as described above. In response, the United States has adopted some domestic norms whose purpose is to combat these harms. However, even though the legacies of slavery persist, the United States has not to date fully embraced international legal norms, such as those promulgated by the International Labour Organization (ILO), a United Nations agency that "includes governments, employers, and workers in the fabric of its representative structure, [which] outlived the beleaguered League of Nations to become

Dreamland: The Tulsa Riot of 1921: Race, Reparations, and Reconciliation, Oxford University Press, Oxford 2002 (noting the Massacre destroyed thirty-five city blocks and 1,000 homes); R. Krehbiel, *Tulsa 1921: Reporting a Massacre*, University of Oklahoma Press, Norman 2019.

72 In a specific instance of attempting to compensate descendants of enslaved people, Georgetown University pledged to address harms to people they enslaved, including 272 enslaved people owned by the school who in 1838 were sold to save the institution from financial ruin. L. Buckner Inniss and Skyler Arbuckle, 'Slavery and the Postbellum University: The Case of SMU' (2021) 74 *SMU L. Rev.* 723.

73 See I. Buckner Inniss, above n. 7, pp. 131–132.

74 *Ibid.* at 131. One exception is Virginia Theological Seminary, an academic institution that recently began a program of direct cash payments to the descendants of Black people whom it enslaved or subjected to compulsory labour after the general emancipation and into the twentieth century. W. Wright, '*Seminary Built on Slavery and Jim Crow Labor Has Begun Paying Reparations*,' *N.Y. Times*, (31.05.2021), <https://www.nytimes.com/2021/05/31/us/reparations-virginia-theological-seminary.html>.

the first specialized agency of the United Nations in 1946."[75] The ILO's mission is to unite state actors with employers and workers within Member States in order to collaboratively promote rights at work, encourage the creation of jobs that provide an adequate living for workers, develop social protection, and enlarge conversations about the meaning and nature of work. In 1930, the ILO adopted the Forced Labour Convention 1930 (No. 29) (Convention No. 29).[76] The United States did not ratify the Convention then and, as of 2022, has not done so.[77]

In 2014, the ILO adopted the Protocol of 2014 to the Forced Labour Convention, 1930 (Protocol of 2014), which replaced several articles of Convention No. 29 not previously mentioned.[78] The Protocol of 2014 offers educative and preventive features whereby it emphasises the ratifiers' duties to educate persons who may be most vulnerable to forced labour and to enforce laws that prevent future forced labour.[79] The Protocol of 2014 also has a causative focus.[80] To date, there is no binding United States law that has incorporated or fully adopted Convention No. 29. The Convention is addressed in a bill titled Congressional Commission on the Abolition of Modern-Day Slavery Act, however, to date, the Act has not moved forward in the legislative process since its introduction in 2008.[81]

The United States has adopted, along with 175 other member-nations, the ILO's Abolition of Forced Labour Convention, 1957 (No. 105) (Convention No. 105).[82] Convention No. 105 calls for ILO members to enact "immediate and complete abolition" of five forms of pervasive forced labour: (a) coercion, education or punishment for holding or expressing political views, (b) purposes of economic development, (c) discipline, (d) punishment for having participated in strikes, and (e) means of discrimination. Convention No. 105 is referenced

75 A. Blackett & A. Duquesnoy, 'Slavery Is Not a Metaphor: U.S. Prison Labor and Racial Subordination Through the Lens of the ILO's Abolition of Forced Labor Convention' (2021) 67 *UCLA L. Rev.* 1504, p. 1507.

76 Convention Concerning Forced or Compulsory Labour (No. 29), June 28, 1930 39 U.N.T.S. 55 (entered into force May 1, 1932).

77 A. Blackett & A. Duquesnoy, above n. 75, p. 1515.

78 Protocol of 2014 to the Forced Labour Convention, 1930 (No. 29), 53 I.L.M. 1227 (entry into force Nov. 9, 2016).

79 *Ibid.*

80 *Ibid.*

81 H.R. 2522, 110th Cong. (2008).

82 S.J. Rombouts, 'The International Diffusion of Fundamental Labour Standards: Contemporary Content, Scope, Supervision and Proliferation of Core Workers' Rights under Public, Private, Binding, and Voluntary Regulatory Regimes' (2019) 50 *Colum. Human Rights L. Rev.* 78.

in the findings of the Trafficking Victims Protection chapter of the U.S. Code, enacted to "combat trafficking in persons, a contemporary manifestation of slavery ..., to ensure just and effective punishment of traffickers, and to protect their victims."[83] Convention No. 105 is also referenced in the Clean Economy Jobs and Innovation Act, which in part "[provides] grants to certain businesses to pay the wages of employees when they are receiving training for jobs in the renewable energy."[84] The Convention was also referenced in other bills.

8 What Is the State of Contemporary Slavery in the United States?

Addressing the nature of contemporary slavery requires exploring the meaning of slavery itself. Slavery in the United States has traditionally been defined via the lens of enslaved Africans and Afro-descendant people. In this context, discourse around slavery was largely rights-based and focused on the enslaver perspective. The United States legal definition of slavery before 1865 emphasised the property rights of the enslaver rather than the human rights of the enslaved person.[85] Supreme Court Justices of the time likened enslaved people to "articles of merchandise."[86] Justice Taney in *Dred Scott* defined them as "a form of private property explicitly recognized and protected by the Constitution and federal law. His analysis precluded seeing slaves as persons."[87]

In the decades after the enactment of the Thirteenth Amendment of the United States Constitution, courts began to shape a definition of slavery that was not necessarily, or at all, race-based and that focused on the deprivation of rights in the oppressed person.[88] Judicial pronouncements concluded that "the [Thirteenth] amendment ... [was] intended to eradicate not merely the formal system of slavery that had existed in the southern states prior to the Civil War, but all forms of compulsory, involuntary service."[89]

83 22 U.S.C. § 78.

84 H.R. 4447, 116th Cong. (2020).

85 *Dred Scott v. Sandford*, 60 U.S. 393, 411 (1857).

86 *Ibid.*

87 P. Finkelman, 'Slavery in the United States: Persons or Property' in J. Allain, *The Legal Understanding of Slavery: From the Historical to the Contemporary*, Oxford University Press, Oxford 2012.

88 See *United States v. Booker*, 655 F.2d 562, 566 (4th Cir. 1981) (in which the Court states this definition as "generally accepted.") This definition is as follows: "A slave is a person who is wholly subject to the will of another, one who has no freedom of action and whose person and services are wholly under the control of another, and who is in a state of compulsory service to another." *United States v. Ingalls*, 73 F. Supp. 76, 78 (S.D. Cal. 1947).

89 *Booker*, 655 F.2d at 564. See also *Aragon v. Ku*, 277 F. Supp. 3d 1055, 1067 (D. Minn. 2017).

Increasingly, notions of contemporary slavery began to foreground people, often women and children trafficked for sexual exploitation. While this is a vast problem, focus on compulsory sex work fails to account for the potentially millions more who suffer in forced labour that is greatly under- or uncompensated, those who suffer in debt bondage, or those whose civil rights are so delimited or curtailed that they have no meaningful participation in modern society.

9 Conclusion

This report, in assessing some of the ways in which the history of African descendant slavery in the United States offers a framework for how contemporary slavery should be understood, does not suggest that there has been no progress for Black people in the United States since the days of historic enslavement. There have undoubtedly been, dating from the United States Civil War to the present, many legal and social gains for Blacks in the United States, even in circumstances where success seemed little likely.[90] These gains have, however, been tempered by an equal or greater amount of retrenchment of Black civil rights.[91] Much scholarship has addressed the nature of and causes for this breach.[92] This report, however, departs from some previous work by focusing on how historic and contemporary anti-Black practices in the United States should not only be understood as artefacts of slavery but also as forms of contemporary slavery. This framework lays a foundation for greater understanding.

Academic References

A. Blackett and A. Duquesnoy, 'Slavery Is Not a Metaphor: U.S. Prison Labor and Racial Subordination Through the Lens of the ILO's Abolition of Forced Labor Convention' (2021) 67 *UCLA L. Rev.* 1504.

90 See M. Milewski, *Litigating Across the Color Line: Civil Cases Between Black and White Southerners from the End of Slavery to Civil Rights*, Oxford University Press, New York 2017, (addressing the successes of southern Blacks who litigated against southern whites).

91 The 1967 Kerner Commission asserted, for example, that the United States was moving "towards two societies, one black, one white—separate and unequal." National Advisory Commission on Civil Disorders, Report of the National Advisory Committee on Civil Disorders 1 (1968).

92 See e.g. S. Sternberg Greene, 'Race, Class, and Access to Civil Justice,' (2016) 101 *Iowa L. Rev.* 1234.

A. L. Brophy, *Reconstructing the Dreamland: The Tulsa Riot of 1921: Race, Reparations, and Reconciliation*, Oxford University Press, Oxford 2002.

A. Rana, 'Colonialism and Constitutional Memory' (2015) 5 UC Irvine L. Rev. 263.

B. W. Smith and M. D. Holmes, 'Community Accountability, Minority Threat, and Police Brutality: An Examination of Civil Rights Criminal Complaints' (2003) 41 *Criminology* 1003.

C. Chaney and R. V. Robertson, 'Racism and Police Brutality in America' (2013) 17 *J. Afr. Am. Stud.* 480.

C. G. Fritz, *Monitoring American Federalism: The History of State Legislative Resistance*, Cambridge University Press, New York 2023.

C. P. Henry, *The Politics of Racial Reparations*, NYU Press, New York 2009.

C. Pittman, '"Shopping while Black": Black consumers' Management of Racial Stigma and Racial Profiling in Retail Settings,' (2017) 20 *J. Consumer Culture* 3.

D. A. Blackmon, *Slavery by Another Name: The Re-enslavement of Black Americans from the Civil War to World War Two*, Icon Books, London 2012.

D. A. Novak, *The Wheel of Servitude: Black Forced Labor After Slavery*, University Press of Kentucky, Lexington, 1978.

D. Archer, 'Exile from Main Street' (2019) 55 *Harvard Civil Rights-Civil Liberties Law Review* 30.

D. E. Fehrenbach and W. McAfee, *The Slaveholding Republic: An account of the United States Government's Relations to Slavery*, Oxford University Press, Oxford 2001.

D. W. Carbado, 'From Stopping Black People to Killing Black People: The Fourth Amendment Pathways to Police Violence' (2017) 105 *Calif. L. Rev.* 125.

E. Baptist, *The Half Has Never Been Told: Slavery and the Making of American Capitalism*, Basic Books, New York 2012.

E. Foner, *Gateway to Freedom: the Hidden History of America's Fugitive Slaves*, Oxford University Press, Oxford 2015.

E. K. Yamamoto, S. H. Y. Kim, and A. Holden, 'American Reparations Theory and Practice at the Crossroads' (2007) 44 *Cal. W.L. Rev.* 1.

E. Tawil, *The Cambridge Companion to Slavery in American Literature*, Cambridge University Press, Cambridge 2016.

F. U. Ohaegbulam, *Towards an Understanding of the African Experience from Historical and Contemporary Perspectives*, University Press of America, Lanham 1990.

G.D. Smithers, *Slave Breeding: Sex, Violence, and Memory in African American History*, University Press of Florida, Gainesville 2012.

G. J. Heuman and J. Walvin, 'Introduction' in G. J. Heuman and J. Walvin (eds), *The Slavery Reader*, Routledge, New York 2003.

G. Moreno-Riaño, *Tolerance in the Twenty-First Century: Prospects and Challenges*, Lexington Books, Lanham 2006.

H. R. Barker, 'The Fugitive Slave Clause and the Antebellum Constitution' (2012) 30:4 *Law and History Review* 1133.

J. Allain, *Slavery in International Law: Of Human Exploitation and Trafficking*, Martinus Nijhoff, Leiden 2013.

J. G. Pope, 'Mass Incarceration, Convict Leasing, and the Thirteenth Amendment: A Revisionist Account' (2019) 94 *N.Y.U. L. Rev.* 1465.

J. Carney, *In the Shadow of Slavery: Africa's Botanical Legacy in the Atlantic World*, University of California Press, Oakland 2011.

J. Levy, 'Slavery Disclosure Laws: For Financial Reparations or for "Telling the Truth?"', (2009) 2009:2 *Colum. Bus. L. Rev.* 468.

J. Martinez, 'Antislavery Courts and the Dawn of International Human Rights Law' (2008) 117 *Yale Law Journal* 550.

I. Berlin, *Generations of Captivity: A History of African-American Slaves*, Harvard University Press, Cambridge 2003.

L. A. Hudley, 'A Profile of Runaway Slaves in Virginia and South Carolina from 1730 through 1787' (2012) 30:4 *Law and History Review* 1133.

L. Buckner Inniss, 'A Moving Violation-Hypercriminalized Spaces and Fortuitous Presence in Drug Free School Zones' (2003) 8 *Tex J on C.L. & C.R.* 51.

L. Buckner Inniss, 'Cherokee Freedmen and the Color of Belonging' (2015) 5 Colum. J. Race & L. 100.

L. Buckner Inniss, 'Race, Space, and Surveillance: A Response to #livingwhileblack: Blackness as Nuisance' (2020) 69 *Am. U. L. Rev.* 213.

L. Buckner Inniss, 'Ships' Ballast' in J. Hohmann and D. Joyce (eds), *International Law's Objects*, Oxford University Press, Oxford 2019, pp. 431–442.

L. Buckner Inniss, *The Princeton Fugitive Slave*: *The Trials of James Collins Johnson*, Fordham University Press, New York 2019.

L. Buckner Inniss and S. Arbuckle, 'Slavery and the Postbellum University: The Case of SMU' (2021) 74 *SMU L. Rev.* 723.

L. Semley, *To Be Free and French: Citizenship in France's Atlantic Empir*e, Cambridge University Press, New York 2017.

M. Alexander, *The New Jim Crow: Mass Incarceration in the Age of Colorblindness*, New Press, New York 2020.

M. Baradaran, *The Color of Money*, Harvard University Press, Cambridge 2018.

M. Goodwin, 'The Thirteenth Amendment: Modern Slavery, Capitalism, and Mass Incarceration' (2019) *104 Cornell L. Rev.* 899.

M. E. Modupe Kolawole, 'An African View of Transatlantic Slavery and the Role of Oral Testimony in Creating a New Legacy,' in A. Tibbles (ed), *Transatlantic Slavery: Against Human Dignity*, Liverpool University Press, Liverpool 2005, pp. 107–106.

M. Ignatieff, *Blood and Belonging: Journeys into the New Nationalism*, Farrar, Straus and Giroux, New York 1993.

M. Milewski, *Litigating Across the Color Line: Civil Cases Between Black and White Southerners from the End of Slavery to Civil Rights*, Oxford University Press, New York 2017.

M. W. Twitty, *The Cooking Gene*, Amistad, New York 2017.

N. Hannah-Jones, *The 1619 Project: A New Origin Story*, Random House, New York 2021.

N. L. Rosenberg, 'Personal Liberty Laws and Sectional Crisis: 1850–1861' (1971) 17 *Civil War History* 25.

N. Sublette and C. Sublette, *American Slave Coast: A History of the Slave-Breeding Industry*, Laurence Hill Books, Chicago 2016.

O. Patterson, 'Freedom in The Making of The Western Culture' (1991) 28:1 *Arethusa* 87.

O. Patterson, *Slavery and Social Death: A Comparative Study*, Harvard University Press, Cambridge 1982.

P. Brooks, 'Narrative in and of the Law' in J. Phelan & P. J. Rabinowitz (eds), *A Companion to Narrative Theory*, Blackwell, Oxford 2008, pp. 415–426.

P. Butler, *Let's Get Free: A Hip-Hop Theory of Justice*, New Press, New York 2009.

P. C. Christensen, I. Sarmiento-Barbieri and C. Timmins, 'Racial Discrimination and Housing Outcomes in the United States Rental Market' (2021) *Nat'l Bureau Econ. Rsch.*, Working Paper No. 29516.

P. D. Curtin, *The Atlantic Slave Trade: A Census*, University of Wisconsin Press, Madison 1972.

P. Finkelman, 'Slavery in the United States: Persons or Property' in J. Allain (ed), *The Legal Understanding of Slavery: From the Historical to the Contemporary*, Oxford University Press, Oxford 2012, pp. 105–134.

P. H. Franses and W. Van Den Heuvel, 'Aggregate statistics on trafficker-destination relations in the Atlantic slave trade' (2019) 31:3 *The International Journal of Maritime History* 624.

P. Iron, *White Men's Law: The Roots of Systemic Racism*, Oxford University Press, New York 2022.

P. Kline, E. K. Rose and C. R. Walters, 'Systemic Discrimination Among Large U.S. Employers,' (2022) 137 *Q.J. Econ.* 1963.

R. Olwell, 'Becoming Free: Manumission and the Genesis of a Free Black in South Carolina, 1740–90' (1996) 17:1 *Slavery and Abolition* 1.

R. A. Rutland and T. A. Mason, *The Papers of James Madison, vol. 14, 6 April 1791–16 March 1793*, University Press of Virginia, Charlottesville 1983.

R. Blackburn, *The Making of New World Slavery: From the Baroque to the Modern, 1492–1800*, Verso, London 2010.

R. D. G. Kelley, 'Kickin' Reality, Kickin' Ballistics: 'Gangsta Rap' and Postindustrial Los Angeles' in W.E. Perkins (ed) *Droppin' Science: Critical Essays on Rap Music and Hip Hop Culture*, Temple University Press, Philadelphia 1996, pp. 117–118.

R. L. Brooks, 'The Slave Redress Cases' (2005) 27 *N.C. Cent. L.J.* 130.

R. Krehbiel, *Tulsa 1921: Reporting a Massacre*, University of Oklahoma Press, Norman 2019.

S. A. Murphy, 'Securing Human Property: Slavery, Life Insurance, and Industrialization in the Upper South' (2005) 25:4 *The Journal of the Early Republic* 615.

S. E. Field, *Neighborhood Watch: Policing White Spaces in America*, Cambridge University Press, New York 2022.

S. Gikandi, *Slavery and the Culture of Taste*, Princeton University Press, Princeton 2011.

S. K. Kang, K. A. Decelles, A. Tilcsik, and S. Jun, 'Whitened Résumés: Race and Self-Presentation in the Labor Market,' (2016) 61 *Admin. Sci. Q.* 469.

S. Miers and I. Kopytoff (eds) *Slavery in Africa: Historical and Anthropological Perspectives*, University of Wisconsin Press, Madison 1977.

S. R. Ward, *Autobiography of a Fugitive Negro*, John Snow, London 1855.

S. J. Rombouts, 'The International Diffusion of Fundamental Labour Standards: Contemporary Content, Scope, Supervision and Proliferation of Core Workers' Rights under Public, Private, Binding, and Voluntary Regulatory Regimes' (2019) 50 *Colum. Human Rights L. Rev.* 78.

S. Sternberg Greene, 'Race, Class, and Access to Civil Justice,' (2016) 101 *Iowa L. Rev.* 1234.

T. Aiello, *The Routledge History of Police Brutality in America*, Routledge, New York 2023.

T. Chaimowicz, *Antiquity as the Source of Modernity: Freedom and Balance in the Thought of Montesquieu and Burke*, Routledge, New York 2018.

T. D. Morris, *Free Men All: The Personal Liberty Laws of the North, 1780–1861*, Johns Hopkins University Press, Baltimore 1974.

T. Foster, *Rethinking Rufus: Sexual Violations of Enslaved Men*, University of Georgia Press, Athens 2019.

T. R. Birckhead, 'The New Peonage' (2015) 72 *Wash. & Lee L. Rev.* 1595.

T. Y. Henderson and J. Jefferson-Jones, '#LivingWhileBlack: Blackness as Nuisance' (2020) 69 *AM. U. L. Rev.* 863.

W. H. Siebert and A. Bushnell, *The Underground Railroad: From Slavery to Freedom*, Russel and Russel, New York 1967.

APPENDIX 1

IACL Questionnaire: Contemporary Forms of Slavery, including Causes and Consequences

Adelle Blackett

Part 1 – The Presence of the Past: Slavery as a Global Institution and Its Legacies

1. Please provide a summary of your jurisdiction's relationship to the centuries-long, largely legal, and global institution of slavery, including the transatlantic and Indian ocean slave trades. In particular:
   a. Please explain the received narratives about the enslavement of Africans and people of African descent, and its legality in your jurisdiction, as well as initiatives to ensure its abolition in law and in practice.
   b. Please reference any specific declarations, constitutional or legislative enactments, key legal decisions or other decisive legal initiatives to abolish slavery and the slave trade.
   c. What are the different manifestations of the centuries long, global institution of slavery in your jurisdiction, whether or not it received significant slave populations. Areas might include the development of the shipping industry; the manufacturing of goods for use in the slave trade; the proceeds of slavery or reparations from slavery that fueled finance and industry; and of particular interest to this report, the development of concepts in various fields of law, including the law of contract, the law of (maritime) insurance, and the development of corporate governance principles.
   d. On or since the abolition of slavery, has your jurisdiction
      i. paid reparations to enslaved Africans;
      ii. paid reparations to enslavers;
      iii. Engaged in a restorative justice process or process of truth and reconciliation;
      iv. Engaged in a process of reconstruction?
2. In your learned opinion, what are the legacies of the global institution of slavery in your jurisdiction? In particular:
   a. Please include a brief discussion of your jurisdiction's historical relationship to the Slavery Convention, 1926 adopted by the League of

 DOI:10.1163/9789004723801_018

Nations, as amended by the Protocol of 1953, and the Supplementary Convention on the Abolition of Slavery, the Slave Trade, and Institutions and Practices Similar to Slavery, 1956, as well as the relevant ILO Forced Labour Convention, 1930 (No. 29) and the Abolition of Forced Labour Convention, 1957 (No. 105).

b. What legal measures – in particular criminal law and labour laws in your jurisdiction – are considered to have been introduced in light of your jurisdiction's historical relationship to slavery and the slave trade?
c. Is the constitutional or human rights protection against racial discrimination in your jurisdiction considered to be related to the legacy of slavery? In particular, is it interpreted by courts and other judicial or quasi-judicial mechanisms in this light?
d. Does your jurisdiction have constitutional or other legal exceptions permitting the use of slavery or forced labour under discrete circumstances (e.g. prison labour)? If so, how are they interpreted?

Part II – Understanding the Causes and Consequences of Contemporary Slavery

3. Is contemporary slavery considered to be a problem in your jurisdiction, or is it considered to be a problem in other jurisdictions that your jurisdiction shares responsibility for eradicating, or both? Please discuss and assess with examples.
4. What are the causes and consequences of contemporary slavery in your jurisdiction or in any jurisdictions with which your jurisdiction has concerned itself? In relation to these jurisdictions,
   a. please discuss the specific sectors of activity where this concern arises;
   b. please summarize the role of transnational enterprises, global value chains, and global care chains to the proliferation of contemporary slavery;
   c. please identify the forms of historical marginalization or vulnerability (including race, nationality and migration status, gender) that are associated with conditions of slavery and servitude in your jurisdiction;
   d. please explain and offer your critical reflection on whether the history and legacies of slavery as a global institution are seen as related to contemporary slavery, or distinct from it.

5. In your jurisdiction, how is slavery defined? Please offer your critical analysis on the definition and the following considerations:
   a. Please explain the legal nature of the definition, and identify the sources upon which it is derived.
   b. Please reference any treaties (including conventions and protocols) that your jurisdiction has ratified, and their legal effect in your jurisdiction.
   c. Is the notion of "ownership" central to the definition of slavery in your jurisdiction? If so, please explain the interpretation given to that notion. In particular, does the interpretation track private law notions of ownership otherwise operative within your jurisdiction's legal tradition(s)?
   d. Does your jurisdiction define the notion of "exploitation", or has it grappled with the concept in decisions?
   e. Does your jurisdiction define servitude, forced or compulsory labour, trafficking in persons and any other related concepts in a distinct manner, or are they/have they become subsumed in a more general definition of slavery? Are they all recognized to constitute peremptory norms at international law?
   f. Has your jurisdiction recognized a list of indicators of contemporary forms of slavery?
   g. Do your courts and other judicial or quasi-judicial decision-making bodies rely on the reports of treaty -based and other supervisory bodies of international organizations when it renders decisions? Does it reference the work of the United Nations Special Rapporteur on contemporary forms of slavery, including its causes and consequences? Does it rely on "persuasive authority" from other jurisdictions to render decisions in this field?
6. In your learned opinion, is the appellation 'contemporary slavery' helpful to understanding and addressing the underlying causes and consequences of the various forms of intense human suffering that it may cover?
   a. Are there any practices that are omitted from the definition of contemporary slavery that should garner greater attention?
   b. Do feel free to reflect on the role of human agency and resistance practices to this contemporary legal classification.
   c. In light of the global impacts of the Covid-19 pandemic – in which a range of service economy workers, including low-wage, often racialized and precarious workers, are labelled 'essential' and required to expose themselves and their families to extraordinary risk to life and

health – please consider any relevant insights about the causes and consequences of contemporary slavery, and whether the use of the language in this context illuminates or is counter-productive.

Part III – Redressing and Recalibrating Contemporary Slavery

7. Please discuss your jurisdiction's primary approaches to redressing contemporary slavery. In particular,
   a. What legal innovations have been undertaken in your jurisdictions to address contemporary slavery specifically, on a sectoral basis, or as part of a broader range of human rights measures?
   b. Is access to effective dispute resolution realistic for survivor of contemporary forms of slavery?
   c. What areas of legal activity are targeted by your jurisdiction? Is a criminal law approach prioritized, or have proactive, protective measures been preferred? Examples might include immigration measures, trade restrictions or remedies, and labour protections. Please discuss any unintended consequences of the approach adopted in your jurisdiction.
8. Please summarize and assess the significance and challenges of existing transnational, coordinated initiatives on contemporary slavery such as Alliance 8.7, including corporate social responsibility initiatives, to redressing contemporary slavery. In particular, please discuss the significance and limits of the United Nations Guiding Principles on Business and Human Rights, Implementing the United Nations "Protect, Respect and Remedy" Framework, on your jurisdiction's initiatives to redress contemporary slavery.
9. In your learned opinion, is the existing national legal architecture in your jurisdiction appropriate and sufficient for redressing forms of human exploitation included in the label of contemporary slavery? Please explain.
10. In your learned opinion, is the existing international legal architecture sufficient for redressing forms of human exploitation included in the label of contemporary slavery in or by your jurisdiction? Please explain.

Thank you

Index

www.ingramcontent.com/pod-product-compliance
Lightning Source LLC
LaVergne TN
LVHW020653300926
849161LV00004B/923